MESSIAH'S MISSION

by
James D. Bales

Cobb Publishing
2017

Edited by Bradley S. Cobb

Published by:

Cobb Publishing
(479) 747-8372

www.TheCobbSix.com
Bradley.Cobb2@gmail.com

Publisher's Preface

One person said that James Bales was the only person alive who wrote more books than he read. Of course, that is an exaggeration, but when you consider that Dr. Bales, during his life, wrote over 100 published books (not to mention his countless lectures, tracts, and his responsibility as a college professor), it is incredible that he had time to do anything else. When he died in 1995, he left behind an absolute treasure-trove of published material for Bible students to learn from.

What wasn't known until just recently, is that among the contents of Bales' library were some boxes of manuscripts. Some of these manuscripts were early versions of his published works, but some of them were manuscripts for books he had written, but which he hadn't yet published. Mark McWhorter, who was given the rights to all of Bales' material, has graciously permitted us to take some of these excellent manuscripts and make them available in print so that his work can continue to bless those who care about the Bible.

This book, *Messiah's Mission*, absolutely destroys the foundation of premillennialism, causing the whole structure to collapse. In it, he shows the truth about the purpose of Jesus' coming to earth, both from the Old Testament and the New Testament, and shows that the Premillennial doctrine of an earthly kingdom was *never* in God's plan for sending His Son.

Bales makes frequent references to other works, and the vast majority of them can be found in the Bibliography at the end of this book. However, there were some times when he quoted a writer, but neglected to include which work he was quoting from. When we came across those instances in the manuscript, we attempted to find the work under consideration (and succeeded most of the time), though there are a couple instances where we simply have to say "unspecified," and leave it at that.

We send this book out into the world with the hope that it will strengthen your faith in Jesus Christ and in the eternal importance of His church, and that it will be useful to combat the false doctrine of Premillennialism.

Bradley S. Cobb,
Publisher

CONTENTS

INTRODUCTION

The premillennialists teach that the kingdom which the prophets prophesied for the days of the Messiah is one in which Israel will be restored to the land of Palestine, exalted over the nations of the earth, and that the Gentiles will be blessed through and in subservience to restored Israel. Christ will rule on the throne of David. Jerusalem will be His capital, the temple will be rebuilt and the Levitical system restored—some say as a memorial. This kingdom was proclaimed as at hand by John and Jesus (Matt. 3:2; 4:17, 23; 10:7; Mark 1:14-15). Israel rejected Christ, the kingdom was postponed, but it will be established at the second coming for a thousand years on this earth.

Why is this an important question?

***First*, it involves a manner of interpreting the entire Bible which is not at all what one would expect from studying the New Testament**. John F. Walvoord is one of the preeminent premillennialists of today. He stated that:

> *There is a growing consciousness within the church that premillennialism is more than a dispute on the twentieth chapter of Revelation and that instead it involves a system of interpretation of the entire Scripture from Genesis to Revelation. The doctrine of a future millennium on earth affects the interpretation of the Abrahamic covenant with its promise to Israel of inheriting the land promised to Abraham their forefather. It Is by careful distinction of the promises made to Abraham, the promises made to Abraham's physical seed, and the promises made to Abraham's spiritual seed as contained in both the Old and New Testaments, that a full premillennial explanation is given of the Abrahamic covenant.*
>
> *To the Old Testament picture the New Testament adds its continuing revelation of future things. Of prime importance to the premillennial interpretation of Scripture is the distinction provided in the New Testament between God's present purpose for the church and His purpose for the nation Israel. Individuals who are descendants of Jacob in this present age have equal privilege with Gentiles in putting their trust in Christ and forming the body of Christ, the church. The New Testament as well as the Old, however, makes clear that the nation [of] Israel, as such, has its promises fulfilled ultimately in the future*

1

reign of Christ over them. At that time Israel will be His people and God will be their God. The New Testament makes plain according to the premillennial interpretation that God's present purpose is not the fulfillment of the prophecies of the Old Testament of the kingdom reign on earth, during which Satan will be bound and all the nations will come to worship at the feet of the King of Kings. The present age, according to premillennial interpretation, is the fulfillment of God's plan and purpose, revealed in the New Testament, to call out a people from Jew and Gentile alike to form a new body of saints. [1]

Second, **premillennialism is important because of its affirmations**. It affirms (1) that the kingdom was postponed, (2) that the present reign of Christ will end and be followed by another reign on earth, (3) that the kingdom will be church and state combined (a theocracy) wherein Christ will rule both by the sword of the Spirit and by the sword of carnal force, (4) that the distinction between Jew and Gentile will be restored, (5) that the Levitical system will be restored, and (6) that Israel will be central and supreme in the kingdom.

Third, **premillennialism is important because of its denials**. (1) It denies that the kingdom, which was "at hand" in Matthew 3:2, was established; (2) it denies that the church age was prophesied; (3) it denies that the present calling of the Gentiles was prophesied; (4) it denies that Christ is now reigning as King in fulfillment of Old Testament prophecy; and (5) it denies that the new covenant has been established in fulfilment of Jeremiah's prophecy, since literal Judah and Israel did not all accept it.

Fourth, **premillennialism is important because it gives aid and comfort to the Jewish delusions** concerning kingdom and God's purposes for the law, the temple, and the kingdom.

Fifth, **the premillennial position is important because it could be a factor in getting the United States into war over Jerusalem**, and further alienating and activating the entire Islamic world. One of the reasons why there are politicians in America who want to guarantee the existence Israel, by the force of U. S. arms and men if necessary, is because of Jewish influence in the United States. If there had been an equal amount of Vietnamese money, influence, and votes in the United States, would we have let North Vietnam conquer South

---

[1] John F. Walvoord, *The Millennial Kingdom*, pages vii-viii.

Vietnam? Another reason is that Israel was once the people of God. Some feel a kinship because of the relationship of Christianity to the Old Testament; however, they overlook the fact that most Jews do not believe in the inspiration of the Old Testament as did that generation which rejected Christ in the first century. This sympathy for Israel, and the position that the U. S. should go to war if necessary to guarantee the existence of Israel, is backed by the conviction of premillennialists.

Premillennialists maintain that: "The Jews who believe in the Messiah will also possess the land which is bordered on the east by the Euphrates River, and on the west by the Nile (Genesis 15:18-21). "[1] They believe that prophecies are now being fulfilled which will result in a state of Israel of this size. They think that Israel, even in her unbelief today, has laid the ground work for what will be the capitol of the world in the millennium, although *then* Israel will believe.

The same attitudes concerning an earthly Messiah and kingdom which led to Israel's rejection of Christ in the first century, are at the root of Israel's expansionism today. There are some changes in belief; for example, many Jews now believe that Israel is the Messiah who must establish herself firmly in the land in order to redeem the world. [2] The determination to have an earthly kingdom led to the rebellion against Rome and the destruction of Jerusalem in A. D. 70. The leaders in the rebellion thought it was the duty of every Jew in Palestine to fight for the city against Rome. However, Christ told His disciples to flee when they saw Jerusalem surrounded by armies (Matt. 24:15-20). This would certainly have aroused the hostility of those Jews who gathered in Jerusalem to fight against Rome. They must have felt, that in their hour of travail, Christians Jews had abandoned them. However, Christians were following God's instructions, and God was not on the side of Israel in that particular struggle. Christ wept for Jerusalem because of her transgressions and the judgment which would come upon her. We should weep for Jews, for Arabs, and also lament for Lebanon.

Sixth, premillennialists have said their doctrine is required for God to keep His promises:

> *To us the biggest issue is over the question, "Does God keep His promises?" For God unconditionally promised Abra-*

---

[1] Hal Lindsey, *The Late, Great Planet Earth*, page 176-177.
[2] Joseph Klausner, *The Messianic Idea in Israel*, pages 167-168, 530-531.

> *ham's descendants a literal world-wide kingdom over which*
> *they would rule through their Messiah who would reign upon*
> *King David's throne. The Jews who believe in the Messiah will*
> *also possess the land which is bordered on the east by the Eu-*
> *phrates River, and on the west by the Nile (Genesis 15:18-21).*
>
> *It is promised that Jerusalem will be the spiritual center of*
> *the entire world and that all people of the earth will come an-*
> *nually to worship Jesus who will rule there (Zechariah 14:16-*
> *21; Isaiah 2:3; Micah 4:1-3). The Jewish believing remnant*
> *will be the spiritual leaders of the world and teach all nations*
> *the ways of the Lord (Zechariah 8:20-23; Isaiah 66:23).* [1]

Lindsey agrees with the Jews, who came to John, that because they have Abraham as their father, the promises must be fulfilled to Abraham's *literal* seed as a nation. John the Baptist, at a time when the premillennialists say the kingdom predicted by the Old Testament prophets was at hand (Matt. 3:2), said God did not depend on Israel and that if they did not repent they would be chopped down. Instead of them, God if necessary would raise up children unto Abraham from stones (Matt. 3:2-10). He did not raise up children from stones, but children by faith whether of a Jewish or Gentile background (Gal. 3:26-29).

God does keep His promises, but the issue concerns the *duration* of certain promises and the *nature* of certain other promises. Did Christ fail to do what He said He would do when He did not raise up the physical temple in three days? No, because His promise concerns the temple of His body (John 2:19-22). Does God fail to keep His promises, because even the premillennialists do not believe that David will be resurrected and reign over united Israel in the place of Christ? However, their literal interpretation should lead them to say this is what God must do in order to fulfill Ezekiel 37:15-28.

In the light of all these considerations, it should be clear that discussions over premillennialism do not concern one or two passages of Scripture, and that these discussions involve some very important matters. In this book, I shall discuss the question of why Jesus came to earth, and whether He did what He came to do. What was the Messiah's Mission?

---

[1] Lindsey, *The Late, Great Planet Earth,* pages 176-177.

CHAPTER 1:
WHY CHRIST CAME TO EARTH

Why did the Word become flesh and dwell among us? He came to be the Messiah who redeems mankind. The word "Messiah" or "Christ" meant originally to *anoint*, as to anoint with oil. "In the Holy Scriptures kings, Israelite and foreign, and high priests are described by this word, for all of these were anointed with oil."It "gradually became a title of honor signifying 'chosen, ' because the act of anointing with oil was the sign of choice and elevation."Although Klausner argued that the idea of the Messianic age was not always connected with the idea of a *personal* Messiah, he agreed that the term did come to designate "the expected redeemer, the king of the future, the one chosen of God from birth. "[1] In The light of the full teaching, we know He was chosen before His birth and that He came into the world as the Messiah. He was God's chosen one, and His personal ministry had to do with the presentation of His credentials to Israel, the preparation for the kingdom, and the undergoing of those trials and temptations which would qualify Him, not to be prophet and king only, but also to be our high priest and Redeemer.

The theme of the book of John is the manifestation of the Word in the world in His incarnation. As the Son of God in the flesh, He presented Himself and His credentials to that generation. John's book shows us why on the one hand some received Him, and why, and on the other hand, the majority rejected Him and what the reasons were for their unbelief. That Jesus is the Christ was manifested to John at the baptism of Jesus (John 1:19-34). John recognized that Jesus came as the Lamb of God "that taketh away the sin of the world" (John 1:29). Among the credentials of Christ were His miracles (John 3:3), John's witness (John 5:33-36), His works (John 5:36), the Father (John 5:37-38), the Scriptures (John 5:39, 45-47), His fulfilment of prophecy (Luke 24:27, 44), and His resurrection (Acts 2:32). With great boldness and confidence the apostles proclaimed on Pentecost that Jesus of Nazareth, whom Israel had rejected, had been made by God both Lord and Christ (Acts 2:36).

Christ came to be the Messiah and His credentials prove that He was and is the Messiah. What are some of the reasons why the Messi-

---

[1] Joseph Klausner, *The Messianic Idea in Israel,* page 8.

ah came into the world? What purposes were and are involved in the Messiah's mission?

Christ came to earth to do many things, but all of these things harmonized with one another. Christ could not have come to do two things if they contradicted or excluded one another. He could not have come to go the way of a triumphant reception by Israel in a kingdom of earthly glory, and at the same time have come to go the way of rejection and death and then to enter a spiritual-kingdom reign. He could not have come to receive a crown without the cross and also have come to go the way of the cross to the crown. He could not have come to reign on earth on David's throne in Jerusalem, and have come expecting to be rejected by Israel and Jerusalem and reigning—after His rejection—on the throne at God's right hand in heaven. He could not have come to prepare for the establishment of the kingdom and at the same time have come to prepare for the establishment of the church if it is something different from the kingdom. He could not have come to proclaim the kingdom was at hand if instead the cross was at hand; that is, unless the nature of the kingdom harmonized with the fact of the cross.

To Reveal God

Man needs to know about God. Who or what is God like? This determines what I ought to be like. Philip expressed a universal longing and need when he said; "Lord, show us the Father, and it sufficeth us. Jesus saith unto him, Have I been so long time with you, and dost thou not know me, Philip? He that hath seen me hath seen the Father; how sayest thou, Show us the Father? Believe thou not that I am in the Father, and the Father in me? The words that I say unto you I speak not from myself: but the Father abiding in me doeth his works" (John 14:8-10). The fullest revelation of God to man on earth is found in God's Son, the Word who was in the beginning with God and was then manifested in the flesh (John 1:1-14; 1 Tim. 3:16).

Of no one who came before Him, or after Him, could it be said, *God is like that person*. Revelation flowered forth in its fullness in Jesus Christ and in no one else. He is the complete revelation to man on earth of the Divine, and in Him we find our completeness (Col. 2:9-10). The greatest thing is the full manifestation, in word and deed, that "God is love. Herein was the love of God manifested in us, that God hath sent his only begotten Son into the world that we might live through Him. Herein is love, not that we loved God, but that he loved us, and sent his Son to be the propitiation for our sins" (1 John 4:8-10). God so loved the world that while we were weak, ungodly sinners, and at enmity with God, that God commended His own love toward us in that Jesus Christ died for us (John 3:16; Rom. 5:6-11). *"As I have loved you"* becomes the standard of our love for one another (John 13:34-35).

To Israel came this revelation of God and His love in the person of Jesus, but the world knew Him not. "He came unto his own, and they that were his own received him not. But as many as received him, to them gave he the right to become children of God, even to them that believe on his name" (John 1:10-11). He knew this before He came, therefore He knew before He came that He would not be triumphantly received by Israel. It follows, as night follows the day, that He did not come expecting nor proclaiming as *at hand* a kingdom whose establishment depended on the national reception of Himself by Israel. Furthermore, since He is the supreme demonstration of God's love to us, and since that supreme demonstration is found in His death for our sins, it is obvious that the kingdom which was at hand had to harmonize in its nature with the fact that the cross was at hand also (Rom. 5:6-11). No matter how many things He came to do, they all in one way or another tie in with the fact that He came to go the way of the cross.

Do God's Will

"Jesus saith unto them, My meat is to do the will of him that sent me, and to accomplish his work."He then spoke of the fields being white unto harvest (John 4:34-38). Since Christ came to put away sin by the sacrifice of Himself, it is beyond controversy that it was the will of the Father that He die for the sins of the world (Matt. 20:28; John 6:38; Heb. 9:26). Why did He send the Son? "For God so loved the world, that he gave his only begotten Son, that whosoever believeth on him should not perish, but have eternal life. For God sent not the Son into the world to judge the world; but that the world should be saved through him" (John 3:16-17; Matt. 1:21). Though Jesus sweat as it were drops of blood in the Garden, His constant prayer was: "My Father, if it be possible, let this cup pass away from me: nevertheless, *not as I will, but as thou wilt"* (Matt. 26:39, 42, 44). "Thy will be done" (Matt. 6:42) was the determination which ruled His will. He could not have come to do what God willed for Him to do unless He drank of the cup, of which He had told His disciples He must drink (Matt. 20:22).

When Christ proclaimed that the kingdom was at hand, He was obviously doing the will of the Father (John 4:34; Matt. 4:17, 23). The Father did not will that He proclaim as "at hand" a kingdom which, if established, would have kept Him from going the way of the cross. The Father's will for the kingdom and for the cross did not conflict. He carried out the Father's will in both cases, for He first suffered (the cross) and then entered into His glory (the crown).

Since Christ's will was to do the will of the Father, He willed to give His life. "I lay down my life for the sheep... Therefore doth the Father love me, because I lay down my life, that I may take it again. No one taketh it away from me, but I lay it down of myself, I have power to lay it down, and I have power to take it again. This commandment received I from my Father." (John 10:15-18).

"And other sheep I have, which are not of this fold: them also I must bring, and they shall hear my voice; and they shall become one flock, one shepherd (John 10:16). This flock was made up of His disciples, those who had heard and followed Him (John 10:26-29). The other sheep were those who later on, whether of Jews or Gentiles, heard Christ's call through His gospel (Acts 2:38-42; 28:28). The sheep which were of "this fold" during the personal ministry was the little flock to whom He promised to give the kingdom. (Luke 12:32; Matt. 21:43; Acts 2:30-36; 1 Pet. 2:5, 9).

We must will to do God's will (John 7:17), and if this is our will above all else, we shall know both that Christ was sent of God and why God sent Him.

To Fulfill the Law and the Prophets

Christ summed up His purposes in coming to this earth by saying: "Think not that I came to destroy the law or the prophets: I came not to destroy, but to fulfill. For verily I say unto you, Till heaven and earth pass away, one jot or one tittle shall in no wise pass away from the law, till all things be accomplished" (Matt. 5:17-18). He did not come to perpetuate the law and the prophets. To perpetuate them would have destroyed them, for the promises, types, and prophecies which are never fulfilled are destroyed. In fulfillment of the Old Testament teaching concerning the Messiah's earthly ministry, and the beginning of the gospel dispensation, Christ fulfilled the law and the prophets.

"Behooved it not the Christ to suffer these things, and to enter into his glory? (Luke 24:26). "And he said unto them, These are my words which I spake unto you, while I was yet with you, that all things must needs be fulfilled, which are written in the law of Moses, and the prophets, and the psalms, concerning me. Then opened he their mind, that they might understand the scriptures; and he said unto them, *Thus it is written*, that the Christ should suffer, and rise again from the dead the third day; and that repentance and remission of sins should be preached in his name unto all the nations beginning from Jerusalem. Ye are witnesses of these things" (Luke 24:44-48). The gospel age was prophesied, for this is the age in which repentance and remission of sins are preached to all nations.

When Christ said that none of the law and the prophets would pass until all passed, He was not saying that the reign at God's right hand would have to end before the law and the prophets were fulfilled. He spoke of all things concerning Him, His personal ministry, and the beginning of His reign at God's right hand. For with the incoming of the new covenant, the old passed away (Rom. 7:1-7; Col. 2:14-17; Heb. 10:9-10). Since *none* was to pass until *all* passed, and since certainly the old covenant *has* passed, **all that Jesus had in mind passed**. The reference to heaven and earth (Matt. 5:18) did not mean that the law and the prophets would stand as long as heaven and earth stood. It had reference to the certainty of the fulfillment of the law and the prophets. "But it is easier for heaven and earth to pass away, than for one tittle of the law to fall" (Luke 16:17). The law and the prophets predicted the sufferings of Christ (the cross) and the coronation of Christ; therefore these two harmonize with one another. He went to the crown by way of the cross (Luke 24:24-27).

Christ's personal ministry was preparatory to the establishment of the kingdom as is indicated by the fact that He preached it was at hand. He came to fulfill those things prophesied for His first coming; and since He did not fail to do what He came to do, He was then received up into glory—into His kingdom (1 Tim. 3:16; Acts 2:30-36; Col. 1:13; Heb. 1:3, 13). /.

Did John Fail?

John the Baptist came to prepare the way for the Messiah. His work had been prophesied by Isaiah (Mark 1:2) and by Malachi who designated him as Elijah (Malachi 4:4-6; Matt. 11:14; 17:10-13; Luke

1:17). "Even as it is written in Isaiah the prophet, Behold, I send my messenger before thy face, who shall prepare thy way; the voice of one crying in the wilderness, make ye ready the way of the Lord, make his paths straight" (Mark 1:2-3). John called on people to "repent, for the kingdom of heaven was at hand" (Matt. 3:2), and he announced that the Messiah was to be manifested (Matt. 3:11-12). Jesus was revealed unto John as the Messiah when John baptized Him (Matt. 3:13-17), and John bore witness to the Messiah (John 1:19-34). Jesus drew His first disciples from the ranks of the disciples of John the Baptist (John 1:35-42). John did not fail in his work, although men may have thought that he failed, since he died a violent death (Matt. 14:1-12). Jesus clearly taught that John did not fail. John was a prophet, "and much more than a prophet," for he was the messenger who went before the Messiah to prepare the way for Him. "Verily I say unto you, Among them that are born of women there hath not arisen a greater than John the Baptist: yet he that is but little in the kingdom of heaven is greater than he" (Matt. 11:9-11).

However, if premillennialism is right, John was basically a failure. *First*, he announced that the kingdom was at hand (Matt. 3:2), and then he announced a contradictory thing which ruled out the kingdom, i.e., that the Messiah was the Lamb of God who taketh away the sin of the world (John 1:29, 36). It was contradictory if John had announced as at hand a kingdom of the type conceived of by the Jews and the premillennialists. *Second*, he was a failure because he did not prepare the way for the Messiah to be the type of king which both the Jews and the premillennialists agree was prophesied by the prophets. John did not prepare sufficient people (the nation as a whole) for the Messiah, the nation did not accept him, and the kingdom was postponed. *Third*, the kingdom which John said was at hand got out of hand, because John and Jesus were not able to persuade enough people to accept it, and it was postponed. John failed, for the way was not prepared sufficiently for the Messiah to enable Him to establish His kingdom, and the kingdom which he said was at hand did not come into existence. When one takes the Jewish and premillennialist view of the kingdom, the only verdict one can pronounce on John's ministry is that he failed, for the people were not prepared by John or by Jesus and the kingdom was not established.

We know that John's work did not fail, and one of the proofs of this is that his work diminished as disciples of John identified themselves with Jesus. John's work was successful, for he prepared people for Christ, and out of the ranks of John's disciples came many disciples of Jesus. John said he was but the friend of the bridegroom and not the bridegroom himself. "He must increase, but I must decrease" (John 3:26-30).

> *The friend of the bridegroom had, at the beginning of the relation, the principal part: it was he alone who appeared. But, in proportion as the relation develops itself, this part diminishes; he must disappear and leave the bridegroom to become the sole person. This is the position of John the Baptist; he accepts it, and desires no other. No one could have invented this admirable saying, a permanent motto of every true servant of Christ.[1]*

Christ continued His work and in His personal ministry soon baptized more disciples than John (John 4:1-2).

Christ Came to Preach the Kingdom Was at Hand

"I must preach *the good tidings of the kingdom of God* to the other cities also: *for therefore was I sent*" (Luke 4:43). "I came forth and am come from God; for neither have I come of myself, but he sent me" (John 8:42; 16:28). In preaching the good tidings of the kingdom, what did He preach? *First,* the time was fulfilled. The time had arrived, the events had taken place in the working of God's time schedule. What time? The time for the kingdom to be at hand (Mark 1:14-15). *Second,* He preached that it was at hand and that the people needed to repent. "From that time began Jesus to preach and to say, Repent ye; for the kingdom of heaven is at hand" (Matt. 4:17). This was the gospel, or good news, concerning the kingdom (Matt. 4:23; 9:35; 10:7). "At hand" meant that in point of time, the kingdom was nearby.

Christ was sent to preach the kingdom was at hand, and He did not fail to do so. However, He also taught that He would not always be with His disciples (Mark 2:19-20). He told His disciples that He would die, but death would not hold Him (Matt. 16:21).

The Kingdom in John

The Gospel of John deals with the same Christ, the same incarna-

---

[1] Frederich Godet, *Gospel of John*, Vol. 1, page 410.

tion, the same personal ministry, and the same basic message with which the other three Gospels deal. However, in John's Gospel Christ is presented as the Lamb of God (John 1:29, 36) before He is mentioned as king (John 1:49), and before the kingdom is specifically mentioned (John 3:3). The Christ of the cross is mentioned before the Christ of the kingdom. Furthermore, in the book of John there are very few references to the kingdom but many references to salvation and eternal life. There are no references in John or the other Gospels to a kingdom of earthly glory wherein Israel will be restored to the land, exalted over the nations of the earth, with the Gentiles being in subservience to Israel.

The rejection is clearly set forth in the first verses of John. The darkness existed, and the darkness would like to have apprehended or overcome the light but it was unable to do so (John 1:5). "The world "knew him not." This included Israel. "He came unto his own, and they that were his own received him not" (John 1:10-11), There were some who did receive Him and to them "gave he the right to become children of God" (John 1:12). Israel did not receive Him, but Israel did not frustrate the purposes of His coming. That He came to save men from their sins was stated by Matthew with reference to His name Jesus (Matt. 1:21) and by John in connection with Christ as the Lamb of God. "Behold, the Lamb of God, that taketh away the sin of the world!" (John 1:29). In fact, God gave Him, and therefore this is the basic purpose of His coming, "that whosoever believeth on him should not perish, but have eternal life" (John 3:16). This was an essential part of the work of the Messiah (John 1:41) who had been prophesied by Moses and the prophets (John 1:45). This was the one of whom Nathanael said, "Thou art the Son of God; thou art King of Israel" (John 1:49). As the Lamb of God, He knew that the temple of His body would be put to death but that He would be raised (John 2:19-21). Moses had foreseen this and foreshadowed it in the lifting up of "the serpent in the wilderness" (John 3:14).

Jesus stressed that the new birth is essential to entering into the kingdom, and thereby taught that the fleshly birth, even though Jewish, did not give one a place in the kingdom (John 3:3-5). Membership in the kingdom is for believers (John 3:16-18, 36). The stress in John, however, is not on the kingdom but on eternal life. These two things must be related in some way or another because John is dealing with the same Christ and His mission that the other Gospels dealt with.

Consider the stress in John on eternal life. "He that believeth on the Son hath eternal life (John 3:36), "a well of water springing up unto eternal life" (John 4:14), "gathereth fruit unto eternal life" (4:36), and He was recognized as "indeed the Savior of the world" (John 4:42). It should be observed, that the work of Jesus' disciples was to be that of harvesters who gather "fruit unto life eternal" (4:36). It was not that of rulers in an earthly kingdom. "He that heareth my word, and believeth him that sent me, hath eternal life, and cometh not into judgment, but hath passed out of death into life... they that hear shall live. For as the Father hath life in himself, even so gave he to the Son also to have life in himself" (John 5:24-26). Nothing about the glories of the premillennial type kingdom. Christ spoke "these things, that ye may be saved" (John 5:34). Life is in Him and men must come to Him (john 5:40). He fed the multitudes, but withdrew when they wanted to take him by force and "make him king" (John 6:15). "Work not for the food which perisheth, but for the food which abideth unto eternal life, which the Son of man shall give unto you" (John 6:27). He came down out of heaven "and giveth life unto the world" (John 6:33). He is "the bread of life" (John 6:35). He will raise up at the last day those given to Him (John 6:39), Those that "believeth on him, should have eternal life; and I will raise him up at the last day". (John 6:40, 44, 47-48, 54). He is the bread of life (John 5:48), of which a "man may eat thereof, and not die... if any man eat of this bread, he shall live forever; yea and the bread which I will give is my flesh, for the life of the world" (John 6:43, 50-51, 58). Peter knew there was no one else to whom they could go, "thou hast the words of eternal life" (John 6:68). The emphasis on life, on salvation, and on eternal life is evident through the entire book (John 8:51-52; 10:9, 11, 15, 17, 28; 11:52; 12:25, 32, 46-47, 50; 14:19; 17:2-3). In fact the book was written, the signs recorded "that ye may believe that Jesus is the Christ, the Son of God; and that believing ye may have life in his name" (John 20:30-31). God gave His Son that we might have eternal life (John 3:16), and Christ fulfilled His mission. That which is so important to the Jews and to the premillennialists (the kingdom as they envision it) finds no place at all in the writings of John. He mentions the kingdom but little, but what he does say about it harmonizes with the theme of his book which is salvation through Jesus Christ.

Although the little flock was soon to receive the kingdom (Luke

12:32; Mk 9:1), the ultimate object of the kingdom and of their hope was eternal life with Christ. They did not look forward to what the premillennialists call the hope of Israel, to be fulfilled in a kingdom of earthly glory; instead they looked forward to heavenly mansions in the father's house (John 14:1-6).

John does not specifically mention the church although some things which he records imply the church. Christ gave those who believe on Him the right to become children of God (John 1:12-13), and we are children of God by faith in Christ Jesus (Gal. 3:26-27). The new birth is into the kingdom (John 3:3-5), but those who are translated into the kingdom are in Christ's body, the church (Col. 1:13-14, 18; Titus 3:4-7).God gave His Son that believers may be saved (John 3:16), He is the Savior of the world (John 4:42), and in the church age He is preached as Savior (Acts 2:36-38; 3:25; 4:11-12; 5:31; Eph. 5:23). Christ went to prepare a place for them, and after His departure and before His second coming He established the church (Eph. 1:19-23). The church age started on earth with Christ sending the Holy Spirit after His ascension (John 14:26; 16:7-15; 17:8, 20-21; Acts 1:8; 2:1-4, 36-38). John teaches that Christ *was to die*, and that *He did die* (John 1:29; 3:14-16; 12:32-33). His death made possible the abolition of the law and the creation of the church (Eph. 2:13-16).

To Become King in the Kingdom of Truth

"Pilate therefore entered again into the Praetorium, and called Jesus, and said unto him, Art thou the King of the Jews? Jesus answered, Sayest thou this of thyself, or did others tell it thee concerning me? Pilate answered, Am I a Jew? Thine own nation and the chief priests delivered thee unto me: what hast thou done? Jesus answered, My kingdom is not of this world: if my kingdom were of this world, then would my servants fight, that I should not be delivered to the Jews: but now is my kingdom not hence. Pilate therefore said unto him, Art thou a king then? Jesus answered, Thou sayest that I am a king. *To this end have I been born, and to this end am I come into the world, that I should bear witness unto the truth.* Every one that is of the truth heareth my voice. Pilate saith unto him, What is truth?" (John 18:33-38). Is it not clear as crystal that Christ came to be king, and that He was not frustrated and defeated in this purpose by the rejection 'by the nation of Israel and His crucifixion by Rome? Consider carefully what is stated, or necessarily implied, in these statements.

First, consider Pilate's question: "Art thou the King of the Jews?" (John 18:33). Why did Pilate ask this question? (1) The Jewish leaders knew that Pilate would not put Jesus to death because they said He violated something in their religion. They knew that a political charge would have to be made. They wanted the death sentence, and in seeking it from Pilate they must have made a political charge concerning Christ as a king, who was therefore a threat to Caesar (John 18:31). This was exactly what they did, "And they began to accuse him, saying, We found this man perverting our nation, and forbidding to give tribute to Caesar, and saying that he himself is Christ, a king. And Pilate asked him, saying, Art thou the King of the Jews? And he answered him and said, Thou sayest" (Luke 23:2-3). As a result of his examination of Jesus, Pilate recognized Jesus was not a king in the sense that Jesus would be a threat to Caesar. "I find no fault in this man," (Luke 23:4). (2) Pilate may have heard what the multitude said a few days earlier when Christ triumphantly entered into Jerusalem. "Hosanna; Blessed is he that cometh in the name of the Lord, even the King of Israel" (John 12:13). A Roman ruler would undoubtedly be informed about such a public display and acclamation.

The *thou* or *you* "is in the emphatic position in the Greek sentence, expressing his amazement and his unbelief that someone like Jesus should be accused of being a king. It seemed simply incredible to him."[1] "The form of the sentence... suggests a feeling of surprise in the questioner: 'Art thou, poor, and bound, and wearied, the King of whom men have spoken?'"[2] Christ was born king of the Jews (Matt. 2:2), and Nathanael had recognized that: "Rabbi, thou art the Son of God; thou art King of Israel" (John 1:49). Westcott remarked that: "The theocratic title the king of Israel (1:49) stands in marked contrast with his civil title."[3]

Second, Jesus in effect asked Pilate for more information as to the nature of the charge, and what Pilate meant by "king of the Jews." "Jesus answered, Sayest thou this of thyself, or did others tell it thee concerning me?" (John 18:34).

*In the political sense of the term **king of the Jews**, the only*

---

[1] Frank Pack, *The Gospel According to John*, Vol. 2, page 123.
[2] Brooke Westcott, *The Gospel According to St. John*, page 259.
[3] *Ibid.*

one known to Pilate, Jesus might reject this title; but in the religious sense which every believing Jew gave to it and in which it was equivalent to the Messiah, Jesus must accept it, whatever the consequences of this avowal might be. Jesus must know, then, whether this title, with regard to which Pilate was interrogating Him, was put forward by Pilate himself, or had been put forward by the Jews in the conversation which he had just had with them.[1]

Of course, Jesus knew, but Pilate needed to have the matter brought clearly to a focus in his consciousness.

The Lord's question is suited to lead Pilate to reflect on the nature of the charge which he had to judge. In this sense it is an appeal to his conscience. If he admits the alleged assumption of the title to be a crime, he must ask himself whether the title has any meaning for him? whether he desires to learn what further it may signify? or whether he has simply adopted a vague accusation, an ambiguous phrase, at random? Pilate's reply affirms his utter indifference to matters which only concerned (as he assumes) a despised people. "Am I a Jew?" Is it then possible for me to care for these things?[2]

Then, abandoning the Jewish jargon which he had allowed his accusers to impose on him for the moment, he interrogates Him as a frank and simple Roman: "Now then, to the point! By what fault hast thou brought upon thyself all that which is taking place at this moment?"[3]

*Yet in the words which follow he implies that there is something strange in the case. The Jews were ready for the most part to favour any asserter of their national liberty. Now they had brought one called their King to be put to death. "Thine own nation," and no Roman informer, "and the chief priests," the natural leaders of the people, "delivered... **thee unto me: what hast thou done?** Or, more exactly, "**what didst thou do,**" that is, to turn those who would naturally favour such as thee*

---

[1] Godet, *Gospel of John*, Vol. 2, pages 368-369.

[2] Westcott, *The Gospel According to St. John*, page 260.

[3] Godet, *Gospel of John*, Vol. 2, page 369.

into relentless enemies?[1]

Third, Christ acknowledges that He is a king, as is evident from His reference to "my kingdom" (John 18:36). Since it is His kingdom, He is in some sense King of the Jews. Pilate had asked, "What hast thou done?" (John 18:35). Jesus gave an answer when He set forth the nature of the kingdom, and the purpose of His coming into the world. He was not guilty of the charges which had been made against Him, but He had done that for which He was sent into the world. Human will and force were not the source of His kingdom. Westcott pointed out:

> *Without directly replying to Pilate, the Lord indicates the real ground of the antagonism of the people and of the rulers to Himself, and at the same time explains how He is a King: "His kingdom was not of this world" ... He would not make any concessions to the false patriotism of zealots (6:15), and yet He did claim a sovereignty, a sovereignty of which the spring and source was not of earth but of heaven. In both respects He was opposed to those who profess from different sides to represent the nation ("the Jews"). But as a spiritual King He was open to no accusation of hostility to the empire. His willing surrender was a sufficient proof that he had never contemplated violence.*[2]

Fourth, the nature of the kingdom explains why His servants did not fight to keep Him from being delivered into the hands of His enemies. "If my kingdom were of this world, then would my servants fight, that I should not be delivered to the Jews" (John 18:36),

> *The original... describes a continuous effort, and not merely one definite conflict; "they would now be striving" (Luke 13:24)... and not "they would have fought" at the moment of my arrest.*[3]

Christ had forbidden Peter, for example, to fight with the sword (John 18:11; Matt. 25:52). If Christ wanted to set up His kingdom by

---

[1] Westcott, *The Gospel According to St. John,* page 260.
[2] *Ibid.*
[3] *Ibid.*

force, He would have requested "more than twelve legions of angels" (Matt. 26:53). Lewis S. Chafer, a prominent premillennialist, recognized that this taught something basic about Christ's kingdom in contrast with other types of kingdoms.

> *It is a noticeable fact that the governments of the world depend upon physical power and a display of armament to maintain their position and authority, and the superior law of love is not adapted to, or understood by, the elements that make up the Satanic order.*[1]

The premillennial kingdom is set up by an overwhelming display of force which conquers all of Christ's enemies at the beginning of His reign. How different the New Testament teaching! If Christ's kingdom had been of this world, force would have been involved in its establishment, spread, and rule. Jesus did not say that His disciples did not fight because He would do the fighting for them through superhuman force which would conquer His enemies and establish His kingdom. He said His servants did not fight because *His kingdom is not of this world*. This reason would keep not only His disciples from fighting, but it would also keep their Master, Christ the King, from fighting. Just as human will, flesh, and power did not bring one into the kingdom (John 1:11-13; 3:2-5), they were not involved in the *establishment* of Christ's kingdom.

Fifth, Jesus clearly told Pilate that He was a king when He said; "*My* kingdom... *my* kingdom... *my* kingdom..." (John 18:36). "Pilate therefore said unto him, Art thou a king then?" (John 18:37).

> *The particle... which occurs here only in the New Testament, gives a tinge of irony to the words, which are half interrogative in form and half an exclamation: "So then, after all, thou art a king?" This scornful tone is further accentuated by the personal pronoun at the end of the sentence: "thou, a helpless prisoner."*[2]

Westcott thought that Christ's reply "neither definitely accepts nor rejects the title." "Thou sayest that I am a king" (John 18:37). However, Westcott did go on to say that Christ in reality accepted the claim.

---

[1] Lewis S. Chager, *Satan: His Motive and Methods*, page 59.
[2] Westcott, *The Gospel According to St. John*, page 260.

> *He leaves the claim as Pilate had put it forward. Pilate had*
> *quoted the words of others, and the Lord had made clear in*
> *what general sense they must be interpreted. He now signifies*
> *further the foundation and character of His sovereignty, and*
> *the right which He has to the allegiance of men.* [1]

The margin translates it; "Thou sayest it, because I am a king." Godet
thought it meant: "Thou sayest (it) well, *that* I am a king." [2]

Sixth, Christ explained that His mission related to Him as king
over "my kingdom." "*To this end have I been born, and to this end am*
I come into the world, that I should bear witness unto the truth. Every
one that is of the truth heareth my voice. Pilate saith unto him, What is
truth (John 18:37-38). Clearly our Lord stated that His purpose in coming into the world had to do with the kingdom, for He is speaking of
the kingdom. However, He has made clear that His kingdom is not of
this world, and He makes clear that His kingdom is related to and
grounded in truth and not in force.

> **To this end... that** *(..., in order that). The first words (**To***
> ***this end**) affirm generally the fact of the sovereignty which*
> *Christ exercised: He was born for the very purpose that He*
> *should reign; and the last (**that I may**) the special application*
> *of it; His reign was directed to the execution of a divine pur-*
> *pose.*

The purpose of His birth ("*to this end* have I been born") and the
"sphere of the Lord's mission" ("*to this end* am I come into the
world"), are harmonious.

> *The emphatic pronoun at the head of the sentence... and the*
> *repeated clause **to this end**, fix attention upon the Speaker and*
> *His office. Christ not only affirms the fact of His kingship, but*
> *also bases the fact upon the essential law of His being... And*
> *He described His coming as permanent in its effects... and not*
> *simply as a past historic fact...* [3]

Christ's mission had to do with His kingdom, and this is affirmed

---

[1] *Ibid.,* pages 260-261.
[2] Godet, *Gospel of John*, Vol. 2, page 370.
[3] Westcott, *The Gospel According to St. John*, page 261.

in the shadow of the cross which was the culmination of Israel's rejection of Christ. The kingdom which Jesus had preached was at hand (Matt. 4:17; 10:7), was now very near, for His glorification in heaven at God's right hand, to reign until all enemies are conquered, was very near (Luke 24:25-27; Heb. 1:3, 13; Acts 2:34-35; 1 Cor. 15:24-28).

Seventh, after speaking of His kingdom, in stating why He came into the world Jesus spoke of truth "...*that I should bear witness unto the truth. Everyone that is of the truth heareth my voice*" (John 19:37). This makes it clear that Christ's kingdom is somehow vitally related to truth.

> *Truth, absolute reality, is the realm of Christ. He marks out its boundaries; and every one who has a vital connection with the Truth recognizes His sway. He does not only "bear witness concerning the truth" (... 1:7, 8, etc.), but "bears witness to, maintains, the truth" (...3:26), as John had done in his place, v. 33. Compare Acts 10:43... 3 John 12.*[1]

Since Christ is talking about His kingship and kingdom, is not Godet right when he wrote that:

> *Jesus means to explain by what follows the sense in which He is a **king**. He comes to conquer the world, and dor this end His only weapon is to bear witness to the truth; His people are recruited from all men who open themselves to the truth... It is His work as prophet which is the foundation of His kingly office. The truth, the revelation of God—this is the scepter with which He bears sway over the earth. This mode of conquest which Jesus here unveils to Pilate is the opposite of that by which the Roman power was formed, and Lange brings out with much reason that, as in 12:25 contained the judgment of the Greek genius, this declaration of Jesus to Pilate contains the judgment of the Roman genius by the gospel.*[2]

The truth to which He bore witness, in His person, in His teaching, and in His miraculous confirmation of the truth which He taught, centers in Him and is embodied in His teaching. It centers in Him who is the truth (John 14:6), and is the truth which He revealed to His disciples, plus the truth in all of its parts into which they were guided by the

---

[1] *Ibid.*
[2] Godet, *Gospel of John*, Vol. 2, page 370.

Spirit (John 16:12-15). This is the truth by which we are sanctified (John 17:17). This mission of Jesus to bear witness to the truth was stated early in the Gospel of John when he wrote: "For the law was given through Moses; grace and truth came through Jesus Christ" (John 1:17). Moses taught truth, not falsehood, but the revelation through Moses was not only incomplete, but much of it was in the form of the shadow of which the revelation in Christ is the substance (Heb. 10:1). Those who are of the truth are those who want the truth above all else, those whose will is to do God's will (John 7:17). They have "the moral disposition to receive the truth" and to put themselves "under its holy power when it presents itself in living form in the person of Jesus Christ."[1]

The kingdom is the kingdom of truth, for Christ is truth; it is the way (Acts 9:2) because Christ is the way to God; it is the life, for life is in Him who is the life (John 14:6; 1 John 5:11-12).

Christ did not fail to do what He came to do! His coming had to do with the kingdom, for to this end was He born. His coming had to do with truth and to bear witness unto the truth, and this He did. The kingdom and the truth are tied together. *He no more postponed the truth than He postponed the kingdom.* If Christ had failed with reference to His kingdom, He would have failed with reference to His mission. He came to proclaim the kingdom as at hand, and to make possible its establishment. He came to bear witness to the truth. These two purposes harmonize with each other for, in fulfillment of the promises of God, Christ ascended into heaven to reign at God's right hand, and the apostles began to proclaim the truth, concerning the kingdom of truth, on Pentecost (John 16:12-13; 17:8, 20-21; Acts 2:30-36).

One Jewish writing said: "When the great synagogue had been weeping, praying, and fasting, for a long time, a little roll fell from the firmament to them in which was written Truth. R[abbi] Chaniach saith, Hence learn that Truth is the seal of God."[2] Jesus is the Truth and truth is found in Jesus' teaching. Among other things, it is the substance of which the Old Testament was but the shadow

---

[1] *Ibid.*
[2] Sanh. Bab. F. 64.1, as found in Westcott, *The Gospel According to St. John,* page 261.

Nicodemus did not Know the Heavenly Things

The apostles and disciples of the Lord did not understand the prophecies concerning the Christ and His kingdom, and therefore did not understand His mission. Nicodemus, a Pharisee, ruler of the Jews, and "the teacher of Israel" did not understand either (John 3:1, 10). He knew Jesus was a teacher sent from God (John 3:2), but he did not know the nature of the kingdom (John 3:3-5) nor the mission of Christ (John 3:12-17). Nicodemus was a Pharisee and John calls attention to this fact. As a "man of the Pharisees," he shared their view of Israel, the Messiah, and the kingdom. This throws light on the conversation which he had with Jesus concerning the kingdom,

> *The most narrow and exalted national particularism had created for itself an organ in the Pharisaic party. According to the ideas of that sect, every Jew possessing the legal virtues and qualities had a right of entrance into the Messianic kingdom. **Universo Israeli est portio in mundo futuro,** [All Israelites have a portion in the future kingdom] said the Rabbis. The Messiah Himself was only the perfect and all-powerful Jew, who, raised by His miracles to the summit of glory, was to destroy the Gentile power and place Israel at the head of humanity. This Messianic programme, which the imagination of the Pharisaic doctors had drawn out of the prophecies, was that which brought with it Nicodemus to the presence of Jesus.[1]*

As a ruler of the Jews who associated with the chief priests (John 7:45-52), he knew of John's work, and likely the answer which John the Baptist gave when he denied he was the Messiah and said he was the voice of one crying in the wilderness, preparing the way for the Lord. The Pharisees were the ones who had John questioned (John 1:19-28). It is difficult to see how he could have avoided hearing that Jesus had cleansed the temple (John 2:13-18).

Nicodemus did not come to Jesus to ask what he must do to be saved, for as a Pharisee he would not have been in doubt concerning his own salvation. In fact, Jesus' reply to him indicated that Nicodemus had no idea that he needed to undergo a change in order to enter the kingdom. Jesus, who knew what is in man, knew both what Nicodemus wanted to talk about and what he needed whether he realized it

---

[1] Godet, *Gospel of John*, Vol. 2, page 374.

or not. He had come to learn from the teacher sent from God, and since both John and Jesus had preached the kingdom was at hand (Matt. 3:2; 4:17, 23), and since Jesus immediately dealt with the kingdom, it is fair to assume that Nicodemus wanted to talk about the Messiah and the kingdom. Regardless of what Nicodemus had in mind, Jesus' answer did deal with Nicodemus' need, and it revealed Nicodemus' misunderstanding of the nature of the kingdom. He addressed Jesus as a teacher sent from God, and in that capacity Jesus answered him with "verily, verily" and then the statement concerning the necessity of the new birth. As a pious Jew and Pharisee, Nicodemus shared with Jews the idea that being a child of Abraham would give him a place in the kingdom (Matt. 3:7-11).

> *Jesus reveals to him an altogether spiritual conception of that kingdom, and, consequently, of all other moral conditions for entrance into it: "It is not a glorified earthly life; it is not a matter of expelling the Roman legions and of going to conquer the Capitol! The true kingdom of God is a state of the soul, the submission of the heart to the Divine will; to enter it, there must be wrought within the man a work at once spiritual and individual, which has nothing in common with the great political drama which thou hast in view." It is, then, the false security in which Nicodemus is living with regard to his participation in the kingdom of the Messiah, that Jesus wishes to break up, by answering him in this way.[1]*

Jesus told Nicodemus, a man who trusted in his fleshly ancestry and thought that the door of flesh was for the Jew the entrance into the kingdom, that the door of flesh was *not* the door into the kingdom. A Jewish man, even though a Pharisee, could not enter the kingdom as a Jew—a once-born person. He had to be born again in order to enter the kingdom. The Pharisees had seen no reason to accept the baptism of John which was administered to the penitent (Luke 7:30), and the Pharisee Nicodemus denied that it was possible for a man to undergo a new birth (John 3:4), and then asked: "How can these things be?" (John 3:9) "Jesus answered and said unto him, Art thou the teacher of Israel, and understandest not these things? Verily, verily, I say unto

---

[1] *Ibid.,* page 376.

thee, We speak that which we know, and bear witness of that which we have seen; and ye receive not our witness. If I told you earthly things and ye believe not, how shall ye believe if I tell you heavenly things? (John 3:10-12). Nicodemus should have understood from the old covenant teaching itself that God could make a new man (Jer. 31:33; Ezek. 36:26-28; Psa. 143:10-11). "But the Pharisees set their hearts only on the *glory* of the kingdom, rather than on its *holiness*."[1]

Nicodemus, however, was possessed of a humility which did not characterize all the Pharisees. He accepts the rebuke of Jesus ("Art thou the teacher of Israel, and understandest not these things?") and listens in silence as Jesus "declares to him what he *is* (verses 11-13); what He comes to do (verse 14-17); and what will *result* for humanity from His coming (verses 18-21)." Instead of a violent political revolution bringing into existence the kingdom, one must come into the kingdom through such a radical individual change that it involves the new birth. Furthermore, Jesus shows Him that "the supreme revelator is present; redemption is about to be accomplished; the universal judgment is preparing. Such are the divine facts which are displayed before the eyes of Nicodemus in the second part of the conversation. The conduct of Jesus with this man is thus in complete contrast with that which had been mentioned in 2:24. He *trusts Himself to him*; for He has recognized" Nicodemus' sincerity and desire for truth (John 3:21).[2]

Jesus showed Nicodemus that redemption came not through the Son of man being elevated to a throne of earthly glory but of being lifted up on the cross. "And as Moses lifted up the serpent in the wilderness, even so must the Son of man be lifted up; that whosoever believeth may in him have eternal life" (John 3:14-15). The Pharisees thought the Messiah would be lifted up on a throne of earthly glory, but the true Messiah was first lifted up on the cross and then He entered into His glory (Luke 24:25-26). The way to the crown was through the cross.

The work of the Messiah was the work of redemption but redemption was through God's love which involved the sending of His Son, the Messiah, into the world to save the world (John 3:16-17). Faith, not flesh, was the way into the kingdom and its redemption,

---

[1] *Ibid.,* page 383.
[2] *Ibid.,* page 384.

"...whosoever believeth on him should not perish, but have eternal life" (John 3:16). How different it all was from what Nicodemus, a Pharisee, expected.

*We are now in a condition to give a judgment respecting this interview. It seems to me that its historical character follows from the perfect appositeness, which we have established, in all the words of Jesus and in their exact appropriateness to the given situation. The statement of ver. 1, "A man **of the Pharisees**" is found to be the key of the whole passage. Every word of Jesus is like a shot fired at close quarters with such an interlocutor. He begins by bringing home to this man who approaches Him, as well assured of his participation in the divine kingdom as of his very existence, a sense of all that which he lacks, and by saying, although in other terms: "**Unless thy righteousness surpasses that of the Scribes and Pharisees, thou shalt not enter the kingdom of heaven.**" After having thus made a void in this heart full of itself and its own righteousness, he endeavors to fill this void in the positive part of the conversation, in which He answers the questions which Nicodemus had proposed to present to Him. In this answer, He opposes, from the beginning to the end, programme to programme: first, Messiah to Messiah, then, salvation to salvation, finally, judgment to judgment, substituting with regard to each of these points the divine thought for the Pharisaic expectation. There is enough, as it seems to me, in this direct application, this constant fitness, and this unshaken steadiness of course in the conversation to guarantee its reality.*[1]

To Qualify as our High Priest

Christ came to qualify Himself to be our high priest. He could not be our high priest until He was tempted in all points like as we are, and until the law of Moses was abolished. Christ was always perfect, but perfect is used sometimes in the sense of *complete*, and until He qualified Himself through suffering, Christ had not *completed* His qualifications for being high priest. He is the leader or pioneer of our salvation, who has opened the way into heaven for us. "For it became him, for

---

[1] *Ibid.,* page 402.

whom are all things, and through whom are all things, in bringing many sons unto glory, to make the author of their salvation perfect through sufferings" (Heb. 2:10).

*Some understand the author to be saying simply that through death Jesus completed His earthly work and overcame all His earthly limitations. But the word **perfect**, which with its cognates is characteristic of the Epistle, demands more than this. Ordinarily it means to bring to completeness or wholeness; to do a thing fully; to put into effect; to finish, for example, a tower or a work of art. But here its meaning is determined by the Septuagint, which regularly uses the term in the Pentateuch to refer to the consecration of priest (Ex. 29:9, 29, 33, 35, etc.). As in the Old Testament the priests were perfected or consecrated by various rites, so Christ in the New was perfected or consecrated or qualified. The thought is that, apart from suffering, Christ could not have been made a thoroughly effective, perfect Leader of His people.[1]*

"Who in the days of his flesh, having offered up prayers and supplications with strong crying and tears unto him that was able to save him from death, and having been heard for his godly fear, though he was a Son, yet learned he obedience by the things which he suffered; and having been made perfect, he became unto all them that obey him the author of eternal salvation; named of God a high priest after the order of Melchizedek" (Heb. 5:7-10).

The fact that the cup was not removed qualifies Him all the more to sympathize with His people; when they are faced with the mystery and trial of unanswered prayer they know that their high priest was tested in the same way and did not seek a way of escape by supernatural means of a kind they do not have at their disposal. At no point can the objection be voiced that because He was the Son of God it was different, or easier, for Him. He who would not have recourse to miraculous means to relieve His hunger in the wilderness refused to summon angelic forces to rescue Him from his enemies... He set out from the start on the path of obedience to God, and learned by the

---

[1] Neil Lightfoot, *Jesus Christ Today: A Commentary on the Book of Hebrews*, page 76.

*sufferings which came His way in consequence just what obe-
dience to God involved in practice in the conditions of human
life on earth.*[1]

*It is not as though He had not known obedience before. But
being a Son, it was still necessary for Him, through the bitter-
est of all trials, to learn perfect obedience and so be perfectly
qualified as God's chosen high priest.*[2]

"Wherefore it behooved him in all things to be made like unto his
brethren, that he might become a merciful and faithful high priest in
things pertaining to God, to make propitiation for the sins of the people. For in that he himself hath suffered being tempted, he is able to
succor them that are tempted" (Heb. 2:17-18). We know He under-
stands. "For we have not a high priest that cannot be touched with the
feeling of our infirmities; but one that hath been in all points tempted
like as we are, yet without sin. Let us therefore draw near with boldness unto the throne of grace, that we may receive mercy, and may
find grace to help us in time of need" (Heb. 2:15-16).

Christ could not have come to establish a kingdom into which He
would enter without suffering. If He had not suffered He could not
have become our sympathetic high priest. No wonder He had to first
suffer and then enter into His glory, for in entering into His reign He is
not only king, but also high priest after the order of Melchizedek (Heb.
5:6; 7:1-2; 8:1-2; Luke 24:25-27), The kingdom in which He was to be
king could not be a kingdom in which He was not to be our high priest.
But to be our high priest He had to go the way of rejection and suffering. The kingdom into which He entered, after His ascension, is such a
kingdom. The kingdom as envisioned by the Jews and the premillennialists is not such a kingdom and could not have been at hand during an
earthly ministry in which He underwent suffering in preparation for
His priesthood.

A *second* significant thing which is revealed by the fact that He
came to prepare Himself to be our sympathetic high priest, is that His
kingdom which was at hand could not be one in which the law of Moses, with the Levitical priesthood and its temple, could be in force.

---

[1] F.F. Bruce, *The Epistle to the Hebrews*, pages 102-103.
[2] Lightfoot, *Jesus Christ Today*, page 110.

"Now if there was perfection through the Levitical priesthood (for under it hath the people received the law), what further need was there that another priest should arise after the order of Melchizedek, and not be reckoned after the order of Aaron? For the priesthood being changed, there is made of necessity a change also of the law. For he of whom these things are said belongeth to another tribe, from which no man hath given attendance at the altar. For it is evident that our Lord hath sprung out of Judah; as to which tribe Moses spake nothing concerning priests" (Heb. 7:11-14). As long as the law of Moses was in force—and it was in force during His personal ministry—Christ could not be a priest. This is the reason that while He was on earth he was not a priest, "Now if he were on earth, he would not be a priest at all, seeing there are those who offer the gifts according to the law; who serve that which is a copy and shadow of the heavenly things..." (Heb. 8:4-5). He had to die to remove the old law and to serve in heaven as our high priest (Eph. 2:13-16; Col. 2:14-17; Heb. 1:3, 13; 8:1-2; 10:9-10, 19-21).

Christ's coming to qualify Himself as our high priest, and to make possible through His death the abolition of the law, all tie in with the fact that He came to put away sin by the sacrifice of Himself. All this harmonizes with the kingdom which He actually established, and not with the kingdom envisioned by the Jews and the premillennialists.

Temptations

In coming to qualify Himself as oar high priest, Jesus Christ came to be tempted in all points like as we are (Heb. 2:17-18). He was made perfect or complete in His qualifications to be our high priest through the things which He suffered (Hebrews 5:7-9; 4:15). Therefore, *He came to undergo the testing, the temptations, which were involved in this preparation.* A very critical temptation came at the beginning of the public ministry when He was tempted by the devil (Matt. 4). However, there was temptation throughout His entire ministry. It may be called the time of temptations. He said: "But ye are they that have continued with *me in my temptations*" (Luke 22:28).

To be Our Example

Christ left us an example, and no one of us can believe that this is not what He intended to do. Therefore, it was involved in the purposes of His coming. He is the perfect example of doing the will of God, and no one else has given us the perfect example in all things. He is the example of humble service, for His entire life was a demonstration of the fact that He emptied Himself and became obedient even unto death (Phil. 2:4-9). In washing the feet of the disciples, He was giving a concrete example of humble service (John 13:1-17). Special attention is drawn by the scriptures to His example in suffering in carrying out the will of God and the manner in which He bore the suffering. In the following statement of Peter we see again how the purposes of Christ's coming tie in one way or another with the death of Christ. "For this is acceptable, if for conscience toward God a man endureth griefs, suffering wrongfully. For what glory is it, if, when ye sin, and are buffeted for it, ye shall take it patiently? But if, when ye do well, and suffer for it, ye shall take it patiently, this is acceptable with God. For hereunto were ye called: because Christ also suffered for you, leaving you an example, that ye should follow his steps: who did no sin, neither was guile found in his mouth: who, when he was reviled, reviled not again; when he suffered, threatened not; but committed himself to him that judgeth righteously: who his own self bare our sins in his body upon the tree, that we, having died unto sins, might live unto righteousness; by whose stripes ye were healed. For ye were going astray like sheep; but are now returned unto the Shepherd and Bishop of your souls" (1 Peter 2:19-25).

Christ Came to Serve

The emphasis of the Jews, and even of the disciples, was on the Messiah and the kingdom which stressed the rule over, and the subjection of, the nations as servants of the Messiah and of Israel. Christ's people do serve Him, but the emphasis of Christ was on the fact that "the Son of man came not to be ministered unto, but to minister." Of course, His greatest ministry or service was "to give his Life a ransom for many" (Matt. 20:28). "But I am in the midst of you as he that serveth" (Luke 22:27). He came as God's servant and in the service of humanity. *This emphasis on service is directly related to the nature of the kingdom.*

Christ had again told the disciples of His coming condemnation in Jerusalem, but evidently they did not yet understand. They still thought of the kingdom as one of earthly glory and power. Even in the shadow of the cross, they did not understand. Therefore, the mother of the sons of Zebedee asked Jesus: "Command that these my two sons may sit, one on thy right hand, and one on thy left hand, in thy kingdom" (Matt. 20:21). Christ a bit earlier had spoken of the twelve apostles being on thrones (Matt. 19:28). He told her that she did not know what she asked. There was a cup of suffering—the cross—which they still did not recognize. Further, He told her that God the Father made the decision as to who was to be on the right and the left hand (Matt. 20:22-23). The rest of the apostles were indignant at the request.

"But Jesus called them unto him, and said, Ye know that the rulers of the Gentiles lord it over them, and their great ones exercise authority over them. Not so shall it be among you: but whosoever would become great among you shall be your minister; and whosoever would be first among you shall be your servant: even as the Son of man came not to be ministered unto, but to minister, and to give his life a ransom for many" (Matt. 20:25-28). The Jews wanted the Gentile type of rulers and greatness. They would be great in the kingdom, for all the world would serve Israel. The rulership position, and the possession of many servants, were essential to the Jewish concept. The servantship concept is essential to Jesus' concept of the kingdom. *The two kingdom concepts are radically different.* A rabbinical statement said: "And all shall come and fall on their faces before Messiah and before Israel, and say, We will be servants to Him and to Israel. And every one in Israel shall have 2,800 servants, as it is written, Zech. 8:23." Edersheim said: "The number is thus reached: as there are *seventy* nations, and *ten* of each are to take hold of each of the *four* corners of a Jew's garment, we have $70 \times 10 \times 4 = 2,800$."[1]

The Lord did say that the apostles would be on twelve thrones judging the twelve tribes of Israel (Matt. 19:28; Luke 22:29-30), but the rulership was not to be similar to that in kingdoms of earthly glory. They were fools for Christ's sake and buffeted for Him and in order to reach people with the gospel (1 Cor. 4:6-13).

Abundant Life

"The thief cometh not, but that he may steal, and kill, and destroy: I came that they may have life, and may have it abundantly" (John 10:10). In order for people to have life, Christ had to lay down His life (John 10:16-18). Christ is the, "Word of Life" and He has been pro-

---

[1] Alfred Edersheim, *The Life and Times of Jesus the Messiah*, Vol. 1, page 293.

claimed that we may have life in Him (1 John 1:1-4). "And the witness is this, that God gave unto us eternal life, and this life is in his Son. He that hath the Son hath the life; he that hath not the Son of God hath not the life" (1 John 5; 11, 13). When our faith functions in obedience to the gospel we are translated out of darkness into light (Col. 1:13-14), and in Christ we are to love the brethren—this is one of the ways "we know that we have passed out of death into life" (1 John 3:14). We cannot have this life as long as we are walking in trespasses for he that walketh in sins is dead (Eph. 2:1-10).

Having the abundant life is the result of Christ putting away sin by the sacrifice of Himself. Unless He had laid down His life for us, we could not have the life which now is and the hope of life to come. Christ's mission of bringing abundant life is based on His mission of dying for the sins of mankind.

The Bread of Life

Christ came to be the bread of life for man. "For the bread of God is that which cometh down out of heaven, and giveth life unto the world. They said therefore unto him, Lord, evermore give us this bread. Jesus said unto them, I am the bread of life: he that cometh to me shall not hunger, and he that believeth on me shall never thirst. But I said unto you, that ye have seen me, and yet believe not" (John 6:33-36). "I am the bread of life. Your fathers ate the manna in the wilderness, and they died. This is the bread which cometh down out of heaven, that a man may eat thereof, and not die. I am the living bread which came down out of heaven: If any man eat of this bread, he shall live forever: yea and the bread which I will give is my flesh, for the life of the world" (John 6:48-51).

Christ is the bread of life for He died that we might live. We must partake of Him through faith by receiving and acting on His words which are spirit and life (John 6:63).

To Bring to Naught the Devil

"Since then the children are sharers in flesh and blood, he also himself in like manner partook of the same; that through death he might bring to naught him that had (margin: hath) the power of death, that is, the devil" (Heb. 2:14). "To this end was the Son of God manifested, that he might destroy the works of the devil (1 John 3:8).

Christ's manifestation in the flesh, with which the Gospels deal, was to die for the sins of the world and through His death to bring to naught the devil. He was born and He died a real death. When He died, the devil and death seemed to have conquered. Hopes of the disciples were shattered. As two said: "But we hoped that it was he who should redeem Israel" (Luke 24:21). Christ is the one who was stronger than the strong man (Luke 11:20-22). He died, but Jesus "God raised up, having loosed the pangs of death: because it was not possible that he should be holden of it" (Acts 2:24). Through His death for our sins, He broke the power of the devil and the dominion of sin over our lives. He put away sin by the sacrifice of Himself (Heb. 9:26). Through His resurrection He has abolished death and brought life and immortality to light through the gospel (2 Tim. 1:10). The complete destruction of death comes with the resurrection and the casting of death and hades (the unseen abode of disembodied spirits) into the lake of fire (Rev. 20:14; 1 Cor. 15:26; Acts 2:34-35). In this way Christ destroys, brings to naught, makes ineffective, and renders powerless, by putting out of use, the works of the devil.[1] The devil brought sin and death into the world and Christ was manifested to put away sin by the sacrifice of Himself and to destroy the work of the devil.

To Bring Many Sons to Glory

"But we behold him who hath been made a little lower than the angels, even Jesus, because of the suffering of death crowned with glory and honor, that by the grace of God he should taste of death for every man. For it became him, for whom are all things and through whom are all things, in bringing many sons unto glory, to make the author of their salvation perfect through suffering" (Heb. 2:9-10). The humiliation and sufferings of Christ came before His exaltation. He was not crowned with glory and honor in order that He might suffer, but crowned *because* He had suffered. God glorified His Son (John 17:1-2). He first suffered and then entered into His glory (Luke 24:26). In His incarnation, He laid aside the heavenly glory of being in the form of God, and "emptied himself, taking the form of a servant, being made in the likeness of men; and being found in fashion as a man, he humbled himself, becoming obedient even unto death, yea, the death of the cross. *Wherefore* also God highly exalted him, and gave unto

---

[1] Neil Lightfoot, *Jesus Christ Today*, page 78.

him the name which is above every name; that in the name of Jesus every knee should bow, of things in heaven and things on earth and things under the earth, and that every tongue should confess that Jesus Christ is Lord, to the glory of God the Father" (Phil. 2:7-11). As Bruce pointed out: throughout Hebrews

> *[T]he glory is consistently presented as the sequel to the passion (12:12). The phrase "because of the suffering of death" more naturally suggests that the crowning followed the suffering as its divinely appointed end than that the crowning took place **with a view to** the Suffering of death. As for the clause "that... he should taste death for every man," it does indeed express purpose—not, however, the purpose of the crowning by itself, but rather the purpose of the whole sequence of preceding events, the humiliation, passion and glory combined.[1]*

No wonder the ascended Christ was received up into glory and into His kingdom (1 Tim. 3:16; Acts 2:34-35; Heb. 1:3, 13).

As the one who tasted of death for every man, and because He has done so, He is the author of our salvation. He is enabled to bring "many sons unto glory" because He died to make their redemption possible, and they have accepted the redemption and are saved through Him.

Christ's mission to bring many sons unto glory was not frustrated by the cross. Instead, the cross was the means whereby He tasted death for every man, made redemption possible, and through His atoning blood He brings many sons to glory. Nor did His death frustrate or defer His enthronement. Instead it was "because of the suffering of death" that He was after His resurrection and ascension "crowned with glory and honor" (Heb. 2:9). It was "by the grace of God" that He did this. In fact, this is the manifestation in its ultimate sense of God's grace (John 3:16).

To Deliver Man from Bondage to Death

"... and might deliver all them who through fear of death were all their lifetime subject to bondage" (Heb. 3:15). The gloom of the tomb

---

[1] F.F. Bruce, *The Book of the Acts*, pages 38-39.

hangs over life, and if death has the last word, all life finally crumbles into dust. Death has not only the terror of the unknown but even the atheistic person cannot know that death ends all. If there is a spiritual law of sowing and reaping, there may be terrors beyond death. Christ died on our behalf, in our stead and for our sins in order to bring to naught the devil, who has the power of death. The sting of death is sin (1 Cor. 15:56). Christ not only died, but He was also raised. He is the Prince or Author of life (Acts 3:15). F. F. Bruce well said:

> *If death had had the last word with Him too, how would anyone have supposed that through death He had disabled the prince of death? The fear of death is a most potent fear. Through fear of death many men will consent to do things that nothing else could compel them to do. Some braver souls, it is true, will accept death sooner than dishonor; but for the majority the fear of death can be a tyrannous instrument of coercion. And death is indeed the king of terrors to those who recognize in it the penalty of sin. But by the death of their Sanctifier, the brethren of Christ are sanctified; His death has transformed the meaning of death for them. To them His death means not judgment, but blessing; not bondage, but liberation. And their own death, when it comes, takes its character from His death [not in that we die for the sins of the world, but in that death is not the final word, for He has been raised, JDB]. If, then, death itself cannot separate the people of Christ from God's love which has been revealed in Him, it can no longer be held over their heads by the devil or any other malign power as a means of intimidation.*[1]

He has brought life and immortality to light through the gospel (2 Tim. 1:10). "Now this I say, brethren, that flesh and blood cannot inherit the kingdom of God; neither doth corruption inherit incorruption. Behold, I tell you a mystery: We all shall not sleep, but we shall all be changed, in a moment, in the twinkling of an eye, at the last trump: for the trumpet shall sound, and the dead shall be raised incorruptible, and we shall be changed. For this corruptible must put on incorruption, and this mortal must put on immortality. But when this corruptible shall have put on incorruption, and this mortal shall have put on immortali-

---

[1] *Ibid.,* page 51.

ty, then shall come to pass the saying that is written, Death is swallowed up in victory. O death, where is thy victory? O death, where is thy sting? The sting of death is sin; and the power of sin is the law: but thanks be to God, who giveth us the victory through our Lord Jesus Christ. Wherefore, my beloved brethren, be ye steadfast, unmovable, always abounding in the work of the Lord, forasmuch as ye know that your labor is not vain in the Lord" (I Cor. 15:50-58).

Again we see that the purposes of His coming all harmonize with the fact that He came to go the way of the cross to the crown.

Christ Came to Separate

Christ wants to unite men to God and to one another. However, He knew that there is sin in the heart of man and that there would be those who would reject Him as well as those who would accept Him. He did not come expecting all of Israel to accept Him. In fact both John and Jesus said that Jesus came to do a work of separating the wheat from the chaff, "Whose fan is in his hand, and he will thoroughly cleanse his threshing-floor; and he will gather his wheat into the garner, but the chaff he will burn up with unquenchable fire" (Matt. 3:12). Before Jesus started His personal ministry (Matt. 3:13-4:17), John announced that Jesus was coming with this fan in His hand with which He would separate the good from the bad. John had just said that an axe was already at the root of the trees (Matt. 3:10).

Somewhat later Jesus said: "Think not that I came to send peace on the earth: I came not to send peace, but a sword. For I came to set a man at variance against his father, and the daughter against her mother, and the daughter in law against her mother in law: and a man's foes shall be they of his own household. He that loveth father or mother more than me is not worthy of me; and he that loveth son or daughter more than me is not worthy of me; And he that doth not take his cross and follow after me, is not worthy of me. He that findeth his life shall lose it; and he that loseth his life for my sake shall find it" (Matt. 10:34-39). Does this sound like the Messiah who came to proclaim as at hand a kingdom which national Israel would accept and in which she would be exalted, and Christ and His followers among the Israelites would reign over the Israelites and the Gentiles?

At this very time the apostles were being sent out by Jesus to preach "saying, The kingdom of heaven is at hand" (Matt. 10:7; 11:1).

He said clearly that: "Behold. I send you forth as sheep in the midst of wolves: be ye therefore wise as serpents, and harmless as doves. But beware of men: for they will deliver you up to councils, and in their synagogues they will scourge you; yea and before governors and kings shall ye be brought for my sake, for a testimony to them and to the Gentiles... And brother shall deliver up brother to death, and the father his child: and children shall rise up against parents, and cause them to be put to death. And ye shall be hated of all men for my name's sake: but he that endureth to the end, the same shall be saved. But when they persecute you in this city, flee into the next: for verily I say unto you, Ye shall not have gone through the cities of Israel, till the Son of man be come" (Matt. 10:16-23).

Jesus went on to say: "A disciple is not above his teacher, nor a servant above his lord. It is enough for the disciple that he be as his teacher, and the servant as his Lord. If they have called the master of the house Beelzebub, how much more them of his household! Fear them not therefore: for there is nothing covered, that shall not be revealed; and hid, that shall not be known. What I tell you in the darkness, speak ye in the light; and what ye hear in the ear, proclaim upon the house-tops. And be not afraid of them that kill the body, but are not able to kill the soul: but rather fear him who is able to destroy both soul and body in hell. Are not two sparrows sold for a penny? and not one of them shall fall on the ground without your Father: but the very hairs of your head are all numbered. Fear not therefore; ye are of more value than many sparrows. Every one therefore who shall confess me before men, him will I also confess before my Father who is in heaven. But whosoever shall deny me before men, him will I also deny before my Father who is in heaven" (Matt. 10:24-33). Then Jesus made the statement about not coming to send peace but a sword.

This certainly is contrary to the idea that Christ came to proclaim that a kingdom was at hand which would place Israel in triumph over the nations of the earth, with Christ reigning on earth over Israel and the world. Christ came to do this work of separation—and He did this work of separation (John 3:16-21). As a whole "his own" received Him not, but those who did receive Him were given the right to "become children of God" (John 1:10-13). It is obvious that those who did not receive Him did not have the right to become children of God even though they were born of Jewish flesh (John 1:12-13). All these things fit in with the kind of kingdom which was proclaimed as in existence on Pentecost (Acts 2:30-36), but not with the premillennial concept of the kingdom.

For Judgment

"And Jesus said, *For judgment came I into this world,* that they that see not may see; and that they that see may become blind. Those of the Pharisees who were with him heard these things, and said unto him, Are we also blind? Jesus said unto them, If ye were blind, ye would have no sin: but now ye say, We see: your sin remaineth" (John 9:39-41). Earlier Jesus said: "For God sent not the Son into the world to judge the world; but that the world should be saved through him. He that believeth on him is not judged: he that believeth not hath been judged already, because he hath not believed on the name of the only begotten Son of God. And this is the judgment, that the light is come into the world, and men loved the darkness rather than the light; for their works were evil. For every one that doeth evil hateth the light, and cometh not to the light, lest his works should be reproved. But he that doeth the truth cometh to the light, that his works may be made manifest, that they have been wrought in God" (John 3:17-21).

How do these statements harmonize, and what light do they throw on the purposes of Christ's coming? Christ came not to condemn the world. It was condemned already, for the Gentiles (Rom. 1:18-2:15) and the Jews (Rom. 2:1-3:20) had each sinned against the truth which each had. Jesus came to save men from condemnation (John 3:17; 4:32; 1 John 4:14; 2:1-2).

On the other hand, there is a process of judgment in Jesus' coming in that the presence of the light of the world is the occasion of the manifestation of the different attitude of people toward the light, toward good and evil. (John 3:19-21). Those Pharisees in John 9 were revealing, in their rejection of "the light of the world" (9:5), their attitude toward the light, while others such as the man whom Jesus had healed showed their love of the light by accepting Jesus (John 9:35-38). Christ came "not to execute judgment. But that judgment…might issue from His presence. The Son was not sent to judge (3:17), but judgment followed from His advent in the manifestation of faith and unbelief (3:18-19)."[1] "The coming of Jesus has for its end, strictly, to

---

[1] Westcott, *The Gospel According to St. John,* page 150.

enlighten the world; but as this end cannot be attained in all, because all are not willing to allow themselves to be enlightened, it has another secondary end: that those who reject the light should be blinded by it."[1] Therefore He came "that they that see not may see; and that they that see may become blind" (John 9:39). Those who wanted the light, who were determined to do God's will (John 7:17), even though they were ignorant of many things in the light, would see, for it was light which they sought. On the other hand, those who thought that they saw, and who prided themselves in their knowledge of the law, but who did not want the light above all, would be blinded and reject the light. They did not come to the light for their works were evil (John 3:17-21).

Certain Pharisees ask: "Are we also blind?" (John 9:40) "The form of the question in the Greek can better be stated in English, 'We are not blind, are we?' expecting a negative answer. Jesus answered them as expected by saying that if they were really blind they would not be guilty."[2] "Jesus said unto them. If ye were blind, ye would have no sin: but now ye say, We see: your sin remaineth" (John 9:41), They were students of the law, they had every opportunity to see, and they claimed that *they* knew, but that the *multitudes* were ignorant (John 7:49). They had the key of knowledge in the Scriptures, but failed to use it and turned others away from the kingdom (Luke 11:52). They claimed to see, and they had every opportunity to see, therefore they were guilty for not seeing. On the other hand, those who recognized they were ignorant, but wanted the light, were the little children (as it were) who understood the truth in that they accepted Jesus (such as the blind man, John 9:36-38); but the leaders, as a whole, were the so-called wise men who did not understand, (Matt. 11:25; Luke 10:21). It was not that light was not available to these leaders, but they were unwilling to see and walk in the light.

This work of separation, to salvation on the one hand and judgment on the other hand, was accomplished by Jesus. His own received Him not and rendered judgment on themselves (John 1:10-11), but those who received Him were given the right to become children of God. This sonship was not based on human will or ancestry, but on faith as John (1:13) and John the Baptist taught (Matt. 3:8-10). It is those who

---

[1] Godet, *Gospel of John*, Vol. 2, page 137.

[2] Frank Pack, *The Gospel According to John*, Vol. 1, page 165.

are sons by faith who are Abraham's seed and heirs according to promise (Gal. 3:26-29). He came with a fan in His hand and He separated the wheat from the chaff (Matt. 3:12). The obedient were gathered into the church and the disobedient were cut off by their unbelief (Acts 2:38, 41; 3:22-26; Rom. 11:5-24).

Christ came for judgment, and this purpose was accomplished. Christ came "that they that see not may see; and that they that see may become blind" (John 9:39), and He fulfilled His mission. It pleased God in His mission to reveal the truth to babes and to hide it from the wise and understanding—as they viewed themselves (Matt. 11:25; Luke 10:21). It had been foreseen and foretold that some would accept Him and some would not. Christ's mission of judgment and of salvation failed not in any respect.

Christ Came not to Judge but to Save the World

"For God so loved the world, that he gave his only begotten Son, that whosoever believeth in him should not perish, but have eternal life. For God sent not the Son into the world to judge the world; but that the world should be saved through him He that believeth on him is not judged: he that believeth not hath been judged already, because he hath not believed on the name of the only begotten Son of God. And this is the judgment, that the light is come into the world, and men loved the darkness rather than the light; for their works were evil. For every one that doeth evil hateth the light, and cometh not to the light, lest his works should be reproved. But he that doeth the truth cometh to the light, that his works may be made manifest, that they have been wrought in God" (John 3:16-21).

Jesus is continuing His discussion with Nicodemus, a leader of the Jews. This discussion has started with the necessity of the new birth in order to enter into the kingdom (John 3:3-5), and has gone on to speak of heavenly things, the chief of which was God's gift of His Son for our salvation; which gift was typified by the lifting up of the serpent in the wilderness (John 3:11-16). The Jewish expectation of the kingdom was that the Jews would be the ones supremely blessed, and blessings would go to the Gentiles through and in subservience to exalted Israel. Jesus clearly stated that God's supreme gift involved the entire world. "God so loved the world," and in verse 17 Jesus used "the world" three times to emphasize that God's purpose was as wide as humanity, and

God's gift concerned humanity—not just Israel. Not only was a Jew not to have a place in the kingdom because of his Jewish birth, but God's purpose involved the entire human race.

Since Christ's mission is the mission of love, His mission is to save the world and not to condemn the world. "The divine purpose is, like the divine love, without any limitation. The true title of the Son is 'the Saviour of the world' (4:42; 1 John 4:14; Comp. John 1:29, 1 John 2:2)."[1] Commenting on John 3:17, Godet wrote:

> *For: the purpose of the mission of the Son, as it is indicated in this verse, proves that this mission is indeed a work of Love (ver. 16). The word **world** is repeated three times with emphasis. Nicodemus must hear in such a way as no more to forget that the divine benevolence embraces all humanity. The Universalism of Paul, in its germ, is in these verses 16, 17. The first clause, by its negative form, is intended to exclude the Jewish idea, according to which, the immediate purpose of the coming of the Messiah was to execute judgment on the Gentile nations... His coming into the world has for its purpose not an act of judgment, but a work of salvation."*

A future judgment is taught in John 12:48 and elsewhere, but in John 3:17—

[the] idea which Jesus set aside in this saying, is only that the present corning of the Messiah has for its purpose a great external judicial act, like that which the Pharisee Nicodemus was expecting. If a judgment is to take place as a personal act of the Messiah, it does not appertain to this coming. However, although the purpose of His coming is to save, not to judge, a judgment, but an altogether different one from that of which the Jews were thinking, was about to be effected because of that coming: a judgment of a moral nature, in which it is not Jesus who will pronounce the sentence, but every man will himself decide his own salvation or perdition.[2]

Christ came to save, not to judge the world, but "he that believeth on him is *not judged*: he that believeth not hath been *judged already*, because he hath not believed on the name of the only begotten Son of God. And *this is the judgment*, that the light is come into the world, and men loved the darkness rather than the light; for their works were

---

[1] Westcott, *The Gospel According to St. John*, page 55.
[2] Godet, *Gospel of John*, Vol. 1, pages 396-397.

evil. For every one that doeth evil hateth the light, and cometh not to the light, lest his works should be reproved. But he thatthe light, that his works may be made manifest, that they (John 3:18-21). "But though judgment was not the object of Christ's mission, judgment is in fact the necessary result of it. This judgment is self-executed, and follows inevitably from the revealed presence of Christ."[1] The believer will not be judged, and the unbeliever is judged already; "consequently, the Son does not have to intervene personallt in order to judge."[2]

"Thus far, Jesus has proved that He does not judge, but He does this by contrasting with the outward judgment, which was expected, a moral judgment of which no one dreamed. This judgment it is which He now explains." In verse 19 He shows that in rejecting Him, "man judges himself. The strictest inquiry into his whole life would not *prove* his disposition, as opposed to what is good, better than does his unbelief. The final judicial act will have nothing more to do than to ratify this sentence which he pronounces on himself... In order to make the matter understood, the Lord here calls Himself *the light*, that is to say, the manifested good, the divine holiness realized before the human conscience. It follows from this, that the attitude which the man takes in relation to Him, reveals infallibly his inmost moral tendency."[3]

> *The alternatives were offered to men in their most absolute form; the contrast of "the light" and "the darkness" was complete; and so men made their choice... The tragic issue of Christ's coming, the judgment which followed it, was due to the action of a moral law. All that has affinity with the light comes to it; all that is alien from it shrinks from it. Men's works were evil, and therefore they sought to avoid conviction under the darkness.*[4]

On the other hand, those who wanted the light and truth came to the light. The unbelieving were those who continued in their unbelief because they did not want the light and the believing were those who wanted the light (John 3:36).

---

[1] Westcott, *The Gospel According to St. John*, page 56.

[2] Godet, *Gospel of John*, Vol. 1, page 397.

[3] *Ibid.,* page 398.

[4] Westcott, *The Gospel According to St. John*, page 56.

What a contrast there is between Christ's statement of the purpose of His coming (to save, not to judge), and the view of the Jews and the premillennialists!

The theme of John is that the incarnation took place in order that Jesus Christ might save men. Faith is necessary to salvation, and the work of John the Baptist was related to Christ's work of salvation, for John "came for witness, that he might bear witness of the light, that all might believe through him" (John 1:7). John knew Jesus was "the Lamb of God, that taketh away the sin of the world" (John 1:29). God gave His Son that men should not perish, "but have eternal life. For God sent not the Son into the world to judge the world; but that the world should be saved through him" (John 3:16-17). He is "indeed the Savior of the world" (John 4:42; 12:47, 50). He came to save His people from their sins (Matt. 1:21). "I bring you good tidings of great joy which shall be to all the peonle: for there is born to you this day, in the city of David, a Savior, who is Christ the Lord" (Luke 2:10-11).

Zacchaeus was a son of Abraham, and Christ came to save him because he was lost. "For the Son of man came to seek and to save that which was lost" (Luke 19:10). Can there be anything clearer than "faithful is the saying, and worthy of all acceptation, *that Christ Jesus came into the world to save sinners...*"? (1 Tim. 1:15). Nothing which He came to do is unrelated to this. All that He came to do harmonizes with this.

Premillennialists teach that when Christ comes to set up His kingdom at His second coming He will come "to judge the earth... The major portion of Matthew 24:29-25:46 bears out that Christ will judge both Jew and Gentile living in the world at the time of His second advent."[1] Among other passages, Walvoord cited 2 Thessalonians 1. The establishment of Christ's kingdom is accompanied by the judgment of the world.

This means that the kingdom could not be established without this judgment. The Bible teaches that both John and Jesus told people in the first century that the kingdom of heaven was then at hand (Matt. 3:2; 4:17; 10:7). Premillennialists as a general rule—perhaps there are some exceptions—maintain that this was the kingdom prophesied by the Old Testament, and that it was then and there offered to Israel. Since Christ proclaimed the kingdom was at hand, it is obvious that to

---

[1] John Walvoord, *The Millennial Kingdom*, page 271.

CHAPTER ONE: WHY CHRIST CAME |
43

do this was one of the purposes of His coming. However, if the kingdom was at hand, judgment also had to be at hand; if the premillennialists are right. However, Jesus said that He came not to judge the world. The world was already in sin, but Jesus came to *save* the world. Since Jesus did not come in His first coming to judge the world, He could not have come to proclaim as at hand a kingdom which necessitated a judgment of the world at the very beginning of the kingdom. Therefore, Jesus did not come to proclaim as at hand a kingdom which would involve such a judgment at its beginning. But Jesus did come to proclaim that the kingdom, prophesied by the prophets, was at hand. Therefore, the kingdom prophesied by the prophets was not one that was introduced by a judgment of all mankind. This means the premillennialists have misinterpreted the prophecies of the kingdom. Christ came to redeem men (Gal. 4:5).

To Go the Way of the Cross

Isaiah foresaw that Christ must go the way of the cross, and Jesus said that the Scriptures taught that the Christ must "suffer these things, and to enter into his glory" (Luke 24:26-27, 44-47). If the New Testament has any meaning at all, it teaches that Christ came in His first coming to die on the cross for the sins of the world, "... but now once at the end of the ages hath he been manifested to *put away sin by the sacrifice of himself*" (Heb. 9:26). Why was the Son of God manifested in the flesh? To put away sin by the sacrifice of Himself. This necessitated the death of Christ on the cross. Was this made clear from the very beginning of the advent of Christ? *It was announced before His birth.* "And she shall bring forth a son; and thou shalt call his name Jesus; *for it is he that shall save his people from their sins*" (Matt. 1:21).

The high priest entering into the holy of holies once each year with the sacrifice for sin typified Christ entering heaven with the sacrifice for sins. "It was necessary therefore that the copies of the things in the heavens should be cleansed with these; but the heavenly things themselves with better sacrifices than these, for Christ entered not into a holy place made with hands, like in pattern to the true; but into heaven itself, now to appear before the face of God for us" (Heb. 9:23-24). "When he had made purification of sins, sat down on the right hand of the Majesty on high" (Heb. 1:3, 13).

John the Baptist announced that Jesus the Christ would die for the sins of man. He did not use the word death, but it is included in his announcement "Behold, the Lamb of God, that taketh away (margin: beareth the sin) the sin of the world!" (John 1:29, 36). The Lamb of God had to die, and the offering in heaven be made (Heb. 1:3), before He could take away or bear the sin of the world. "Who his own self bare our sins in his body upon the tree, that we, having died unto sins, might live unto righteousness; by whose stripes ye were healed. For ye were going astray like sheep; but are now returned unto the Shepherd and Bishop of your souls" (1 Pet. 2:24-25).

Christ announced quite early in His ministry that Israel would put Him to death. "The Jews therefore answered and said unto him, What sign showest thou unto us, seeing that thou doest these things? Jesus answered and said unto them, Destroy this temple, and in three days I will raise it up. The Jews therefore said, Forty and six years was this temple in building, and wilt thou raise it up in three days? But he spake of the temple of his body. When therefore he was raised from the dead, his disciples remembered that he spake this; and they believed the scripture, and the word which Jesus had said" (John 2:18-22). Jesus had not quoted the scripture, in so far as the record goes, but in the light of His resurrection and what Jesus taught them about the scriptures (Luke 24:25-27, 44-45), they now understood and believed that the suffering and death of Christ had been prophesied. Hithertofore they had been foolish and slow of heart to believe all that the prophets had spoken (Luke 24:25). Whether the people to whom Jesus spoke understood about His death or not, it is still true that Jesus spoke of His coming death.

Soon after this Jesus said; "And as Moses lifted up the serpent in the wilderness, even so must the Son of man be lifted up; that whosoever believeth may in him have eternal life. For God so loved the world, that he gave his only begotten Son, that whosoever believeth on him should not perish, but have eternal life. For God sent not the Son into the world to judge the world; but that the world should be saved through him. He that believeth on him is not judged; he that believeth not hath been judged already, because he hath not believed on the name of the only begotten Son of God" (John 3:14-18). These verses contain clear announcements of Christ's mission. He came to be lifted up. He was sent of God into the world, that men might be saved through Him. The lifting up of the serpent by Moses typified Christ's being lifted up on the cross. Godet observed that:

> *The fact related in Numbers 21:9 is one of the most aston-ishing in sacred history. Three peculiarities distinguish this mode of deliverance from all the other analogous miracles; 1. It is **the plague itself** which, represented as overcome, be-comes, by its ignominious exposure, the means of its own de-feat; 2. This exposure takes place, not in a **real** serpent—the suspension in that case would have proclaimed only the defeat of the individual exposed—but in a typical copy, which repre-sents the entire species; 3. This expedient becomes efficacious through the intervention of a moral act, the look of faith on the earth of each injured person. If this is the type of salvation, it follows from this fact that this salvation will be wrought in the following ways; 1. Sin will be exposed publicly as vanquished, and for the future powerless; 2. It will not be in the person of a real sinner—which would proclaim only the particular defeat of **that** sinner—but in the person of a holy man, capable of rep-resenting, as a living image, the condemnation and defeat of sin, **as such**; 3, This exhibition of sin as one who is vanquished, will save each sinner only by means of an act on his part, the look of faith upon his spiritual enemy condemned and van-quished.[1]*

Christ who knew no sin, "his own self bare our sins in his body upon the tree, that we, having died unto sins, might live unto right-eousness; by whose stripes ye are healed" (1 Pet, 2; 24), "To the look of the dying Israelite, the faith of the sinner in the crucified one corre-sponds; to the life restored to the wounded one, the salvation granted to the believer."[2] The purpose of God sending His Son into the world was to die for the sins of the world, in order that men might be saved through Him. Christ came because the world was already condemned by sin, and He was sent that "the world should be saved through him." *The golden text of the Bible contains the theme of the Bible, and the mission of Christ, but it deals with salvation and not with earthly glory.* How can anyone who believes the New Testament interpret the

---

[1] Godet, *Gospel of John*, Vol. 1, page 392.
[2] *Ibid.,* page 393.

purpose of the first coming of Christ in terms other than those which harmonize with the crystal clear reason why God sent "the Son into the world" (John 3:17)? "For God so loved the world, that he gave his only begotten Son, that whosoever believeth on him should not perish, but have eternal life" (John 3:16).

Later to certain Greeks, in the presence of the multitude, Christ clearly set forth the fact that He must die, although they did not understand it (John 12:20, 34). "The hour is come, that the Son of man should be glorified. Verily, verily, I say unto you, Except a grain of wheat fall into the earth and die, it abideth by itself alone; but if it die, it beareth much fruit. He that loveth his life loseth it; and he that hateth his life in this world shall keep it unto life eternal. If any man serve me, let him follow me; and where I am, there shall also my servant be: if any man serve me, him will the Father honor. Now is my soul troubled; and what shall I say? Father, save me from this hour. *But for this cause came I unto this hour.* Father, glorify thy name. There came therefore a voice out of heaven. saying, I have both glorified it, and will glorify it again. The multitude therefore, that stood by, and heard it, said that it had thundered: others said, An angel hath spoken to him. Jesus answered and said, This voice hath not come for my sake, but for your sakes. Now is the judgment of this world: now shall the prince of this world be cast out. And I, if I be lifted up from the earth, will draw all men unto myself. But this he said, signifying by what manner of death he should die" (John 12:23-33).

Jesus spoke of the necessity of His death in order to bear fruit unto the salvation of men.

Before He can answer the need of salvation for the heathen world, the first symptom of which has just reached Him, something of serious moment must happen in Himself. So long as the grain of wheat remains in the granary, it is preserved, but without acquiring the power of reproducing itself; it is necessary that it should be cast into the earth, that its covering should be decomposed, that it should perish as a seed, in order that it may live again with a new existence, and may have a new birth in a multitude of beings like itself. We know the considerable part which is played by the grain of wheat in the Greek mysteries. The emphatic affirmation, **amen, amen**, refers to the contrast which Jesus knows to exist between this painful necessity of His death and His disciples' dreams of glory.[1]

Jesus then spoke of self-sacrifice, of losing one's life in the sense of self-renunciation in order to make the will of God supreme in one's life. Jesus applied this principle not only to His disciples, but also to Himself, and this was the reason that He would die; this was the reason that God had not only glorified His name, but would also glorify it again.

> *Lange has profoundly remarked that this saying contains in particular the judgment of Hellenism. What was Greek civilization? The effort to realize an ideal of human life consisting in enjoyment and escaping the law of sacrifice.*[2]

His disciples must follow Him in the way of sacrifice which leads to ultimate glorification.

The thought of His approaching death, which was near, brought its agony. "Now is my soul troubled; and what shall I say? Father, save me from this hour. But for this cause came I unto this hour. Father, glorify thy name" (John 12:27-28). Jesus did not pray a prayer for deliverance, for His deliverance from death would have meant that mankind could not be delivered from death eternally, i.e., eternal separation from God. Even when He agonized in the Garden, He prayed that the cup pass only if it be possible, but in all things He wanted the Father's will to be done (Matt. 26:39). "*But for this cause came I unto this hour.*" He came into the world to put away sin by the sacrifice of Himself (Heb. 9:28), and He was not going to turn back now. Therefore, He said: "Father, glorify thy name." "That is to say, 'Derive from me, Thy glorym by doing with me what Thou wilt. Nothing for me, everything for Thee!'"[3] Christ came unto this hour for the purpose of dying, and this means that the mission of His first coming had to do with His death. Therefore, it could not have had to do with any kind of kingdom which did not take into consideration the fact of His death. In fact, He could not have proclaimed as at hand a kingdom which was not to be built on the fact of His death. He could not be received up into the glory of His reign as King and Priest unless first He died (Luke 24:25-26; 1 Timothy 3:16).

---

[1] *Ibid.,* page 220.

[2] *Ibid.,* page 221.

[3] *Ibid.,* page 223.

God said He had glorified His name, and that He would do it again.

> *The past **I have glorified** refers to the ministry of the Lord in Israel, which is close upon its end; the future **I will glorify**, to the approaching action of Jesus on the whole world, when from the midst of His glory He will enlighten the heathen. Between these two great works which the Father accomplishes through the Son, is placed precisely the hour of suffering and death which is the necessary transition from the one to the other. There is no ground therefore to draw back before this hour. It is, moreover, well surrounded. Before—the name of God glorified in Israel; after—the name of God glorified in the whole world. Here indeed is the most consoling response for the filial heart of Jesus (John 17:1-2, 4-5).[1]*

Christ's troubled soul was strengthened because God would glorify His name, and this involved, through the cross, the judgment of the prince of the world and the drawing of people unto Himself through the message of the cross. "The hour of the call of the Greeks draws near; but, before it strikes, another hour is to strike!"[2] "The judgment of this world," the casting out of "the prince of this world," and then the drawing of men unto Himself (John 3:31-32). These things are accomplished through the cross (Col. 2:14-15; 2 Cor. 5:14-21).

Jesus clearly told, after a period of time, "his disciples, that he must go unto Jerusalem, and suffer many things of the elders and chief priests and scribes, and be killed, and the third day be raised up" (Matt. 16:21).

Although he did not know what he was doing, Caiaphas prophesied the death of Christ for the nation, and for all. "The chief priests therefore and the Pharisees gathered a council, and said, What do we? for this man doeth many signs. If we let him thus alone, all men will believe on him: and the Romans will come and take away both our place and our nation. But a certain one of them, Caiaphas, being high priest that year, said unto them, Ye know nothing at all, nor do ye take account that it is expedient for you that one man should die for the people, and that the whole nation perish not. Now this he said not of

---

[1] *Ibid., page 225.*

[2] *Ibid.,* page 228,

himself; but being high priest that year, he prophesied that Jesus should die for the nation; and not for the nation only, but that he might also gather together into one the children of God that are scattered abroad. So from that day forth they took counsel that they might put him to death" (John 11:47-53).

Mauro well said that:

> ...*our Lord's earliest teaching (given while John was yet baptizing in Jordan) had for its theme **the Kingdom of God**, and the one and only way of entering into it—by the new birth of water and the Spirit (John 3:3-16). This best known passage in the Bible links the Kingdom of God directly with the death of Christ upon the cross, whereby God's great love for the perishing world was to be revealed, and the ground of the salvation of men was eternally established. The passage shows clearly moreover, **what the term "Kingdom of God" meant in the days of John the Baptist** (vv. 23, 24). How then can anyone, viewing the subject of **the Kingdom** in the light of this great passage, suppose for a moment (except he be under the spell of a strong delusion) that our Lord and His forerunner were at that very time offering to the Jews, and by the preaching of **the Kingdom of God**, a kingdom of earthly pomp and grandeur, such as their false teachers—those "blind leaders of the blind"—had taught them to expect?*[1]

The nature of the kingdom had to be related to Christ's death for our sins.

Disciples Did Not Understand

More than once Christ had told them that He would die, but they understood it not. Peter said that it would not be (Matt. 16:21-23). Christ not only said it would take place, but said that in the lifetime of some that were there the Son of man would come in His kingdom (Matt. 16:28). Moses and Elijah talked with Jesus about His coming death (Luke 9:31; Matt.17:3-9). He again told them that He would die, but shortly they were concerned about places of supremacy in the kingdom (Matt. 20:17-28). Luke tells us that after Jesus spoke of His

---

[1] Philip Mauro, *The Gospel of the Kingdom*, pages 76-77.

death and resurrection, "they understood none of these things; and this saying was hid from them, and they perceived not the things that were said" (Luke 18:34). Jesus not only told them that He would die, but He said these things were prophesied. "And he took unto him the twelve, and said unto them, Behold, we go up to Jerusalem, and all the things that are written through the prophets shall be accomplished unto the Son of man" (Luke 18:31). These things were hidden from them because their view of the nature of the kingdom blinded them to the fact that He must first suffer and then enter into His glory, They were responsible for this failure to understand, for Jesus said of the two on the road to Emmaus that they were "foolish men, and slow of heart to believe in all that the prophets have spoken" (Luke 24:25).

These truths had not sunk into their consciousness, even though Jesus had before told them about these things, "But while all were marveling at all the things which he did, he said unto his disciples, Let these words sink into your ears: for the Son of man shall be delivered up into the hands of men. But they understood not this saying, and it was concealed from them, that they should not perceive it; and they were afraid to ask him about this saying" (Luke 9:43-45).

> *It was because the people were so constantly in an attitude of empty admiration and wonder at His miracles, that Jesus again tells the disciples of the real nature of His Messiahship. He is not going to reign as an earthly king, but to suffer as a criminal... "Do ye lay up in your ears," in contrast to the gaping crowd. It perhaps means "Store My words in your memories, even if you do not understand them." Or again, "Do not let men's admiration of My miracles make you forget or doubt My declarations. It is into men's hands that I must be delivered."[1]*

It was not until later that they understood—after the events. "These things (which included more than His death) understood not his disciples at the first: but when Jesus was glorified, then remembered they that these things were written of him, and that they had done these things unto him" (John 12:16; 2:22). Broadus well said:

> *It was utterly contrary to all their ideas of the Messiah and*

---

[1] Alfred Plummer, *A Critical and Exegetical Commentary on the Gospel According to St. Luke*, page 256.

his work... Hanna: "This only proves what a blinding power preconception and misconception have in hiding the simplest things told in the simplest language—a blinding power often exercised over us now as to the written, as it was then exercised over the apostles as to their Master's spoken, words... They had made up their minds, on the best of evidence, that he was the Messiah. But they had their own notions of the Messiahship. With these, such sufferings and such a death as actually lay before Jesus were utterly inconsistent."[1]

Are not the premillennialists blind who think that Christ could have proclaimed as *at hand* a kingdom which was in harmony with the basic expectations of the Jews and of the apostles of Christ during the personal ministry?

How can anyone who believes in Christ deny this basic and central purpose of His coming? Furthermore, how can anyone deny that this purpose must harmonize with the nature of the kingdom which was at hand and the nature of the kingdom must harmonize with the fact that Christ had to die on the cross as the ransom for our sins? It was in God's purpose. "And all that dwell on the earth shall worship him, every one whose name hath not been written from the foundation of the world in the book of life of the Lamb that hath been slain" (Rev. 13:8). How could names have been written in that book of life if it was not in God's purpose for the Lamb to be slain? It was not just in God's purpose, unrevealed to man, but was revealed through the prophets that He must suffer (Luke 24:25-27). All who want to know, "know *that he was manifested to take away (bear) sins*" (1 John 3:5).

Paul clearly stated the fact that God sent His Son in the first advent to go the way of the cross. "For what the law could not do, in that it was weak through the flesh, God, *sending his own Son in the likeness of sinful flesh and for sin*, condemned sin in the flesh: *that* the ordinance of the law might be fulfilled in us, who walk not after the flesh, but after the Spirit" (Rom. 8:3-4; 1 Pet. 2:24). The Incarnation did not have to do with a kingdom on this earth in which Christ would be triumphantly received by Israel, but to go the way of the cross to die for the sins of man. This was in order that what the law required but could

---

[1] John Broadus, *A Harmony of the Gospels in the Revised Version with New Helps for Historical Study*, page 416.

not bring (i.e., justification) might be fulfilled in us. The "us" is those who are in Christ, the church. It is not physical Israel as such for she did not accept the justification brought through the cross (Rom. 9:6-7; 9:30-10:4).

For This Cause

Jesus came to drink the cup of sorrow and pain which is but another way of saying that He came to go the way of the cross. If it was the Father's will, He wanted the cup to pass away from Him (Matt. 26:39, 42, 44), but it was not the Father's will. When Peter drew a sword to protect Him, "Jesus therefore said unto Peter, Put up the sword into the sheath: the cup which the Father hath given me, shall I not drink of it?" (John 18:11). "The cup was not taken away, but given, and the Lord now shows that He had received it willingly."[1] Further, Jesus showed that the cup was prophesied. He accepted neither Peter's defense with the sword, nor requested "more than twelve legions of angels" (Matt. 26:52-53). Why? "How then should the scriptures be fulfilled, *that thus it must be?"* (Matt. 26:54).

"Now is my soul troubled; and what shall I say? Father, save me from this hour. *For this cause came I unto this hour"* (John 12:27). He went on to speak of the manner of His death by being lifted up from the earth (John 12:32-33). Since He came for this cause, to go the way of the cross, He could not have proclaimed as at hand a kingdom which, if it had been established, would have eliminated the cross.

Israel wanted a Messiah who would save them from foreign dominion, but Christ came to save them from mankind's basic enemy—sin—which enslaves both Jews and Gentiles. To Jews who were Abraham's seed, Jesus said that truth was necessary to free them (John 8:31-59). They did not realize that the redemption, the salvation from enemies, which He brought was from slavery to Satan (Luke 1:67-79). Of course, as His message penetrates the hearts of men, other freedoms also come to men.

Christ's Rejection Foretold

The sin offerings had typified the death of Christ, the Lamb of God, for our sins. The prophet Isaiah prophesied that His rejection, sufferings, and death would come before His triumphs. Isaiah even

---

[1] Westcott, *The Gospel According to St. John*, page 254.

foresaw the complaint of the first preachers of the gospel, after Christ's ascension and the sending of the Spirit, that the message was not being readily received. We know Isaiah spoke both of Christ's sufferings, and of the fact that after the gospel was preached the majority did not hearken unto it. We know this for Paul said: "But they did not all hearken to the glad tidings. For Isaiah saith, Lord, who hath believed our report? So belief cometh of hearing, and hearing by the word of Christ, But I say, Did they not hear? Yea, verily, Their sound went out into all the earth, and their words unto the ends of the world. But I say, Did not Israel know? First Moses saith, I will provoke you to jealousy with that which is no nation, with a nation void of understanding will I anger you. And Isaiah is very bold, and saith, I was found of them that sought me not; I became manifest unto them that asked not of me. But as to Israel he saith, All the day long did I spread out my hands unto a disobedient and gainsaying people" (Rom. 10:16-21).

The complaint of the first teachers of the gospel, and the fact that His rejection and death took place before His triumphs, is clearly set forth in Isaiah fifty-three. "Who hath believed our message? and to whom hath the arm of Jehovah been revealed? For he grew up before him as a tender plant, and as a root out of a dry ground: he hath no form nor comeliness: and when we see him, there is no beauty that we should desire him. He was despised, and rejected of men; a man of sorrows, and acquainted with grief: and as one from whom men hide their face he was despised; and we esteemed him not. Surely he hath borne our griefs, and carried our sorrows; yet we did esteem him stricken, smitten of God, and afflicted. But he was wounded for our transgressions, he was bruised for our iniquities; the chastisement of our peace was upon him; and with his stripes we are healed. All we like sheep have gone astray; we have turned every one to his own way; and Jehovah hath laid on him the iniquity of us all. He was oppressed, yet when he was afflicted he opened not his mouth; as a lamb that is led to the slaughter, and as a sheep that before its shearers is dumb, so he opened not his mouth. By oppression and judgment he was taken away; and as for his generation, who among them considered that he was cut off out of the land of the living for the transgression of my people to whom the stroke was due? And they made his grave with the wicked, and with a rich man in his death; although he had done no violence, neither was any deceit in his mouth. Yet it pleased Jehovah to bruise him; he hath put him to grief: when thou shalt make his soul an offering for sin, he shall see his seed, he shall prolong his days, and the pleasure of Jehovah shall prosper in his hand. He shall see of the travail of his soul, and shall be satisfied: by the knowledge of himself shall my righteous servant justify many, and he shall bear their iniquities. Therefore will I divide him a portion with the great, and he shall divide the spoil with the strong because he poured out his soul unto death, and was numbered with the transgressors: yet he bare the sin of many, and made intercession for the transgressors" (Isaiah 53).

It was Impossible for a kingdom to have been at hand in the personal ministry which did not take into consideration the fact that He must suffer before His triumphs.

The Bridegroom would be Taken Away

"And John's disciples and the Pharisees were fasting: and they come and say unto him, Why do John's disciples and the disciples of the Pharisees fast, but thy disciples fast not? And Jesus said unto them, Can the sons of the bridechamber fast while the bridegroom is with them? as long as they have the bridegroom with them, they cannot fast. But the days will come, when *the bridegroom shall be taken away from them*, and then will they fast in that day" (Mark 2:18-20).

"The contrast between their Master in prison and Jesus at the feast could not fail to be felt. Perhaps the Pharisees had solicited them to make common cause with themselves in this matter. Their rigorous asceticism offered various points of contrast between them and the disciples of the Baptist." Christ's disciples were the friends of Christ the bridegroom. John had likened Jesus to the bridegroom. "Ye yourselves bear me witness, that I said, I am not the Christ, but, that I am sent before him. He that hath the bride is the bridegroom: but the friend of the bridegroom, that standeth and heareth him, rejoiceth greatly because of the bridegroom's voice: this my joy therefore is made full. He must increase, but I must decrease" (John 3:28-30).

Jesus said that the friends of the bridegroom rejoiced, and did not fast, when the bridegroom was with them. They would mourn or fast when they were separated from the bridegroom. *Jesus here teaches that He was not to be with the disciples on earth forever.* The Jews thought that the law taught that the Christ would abide on earth forever. When Jesus spoke of the manner of His death, they said: "We have heard out of the law that the Christ abideth for ever: and how sayest thou, The Son of man must be lifted up? who is this Son of man? Jesus therefore said unto them, Yet a little while is the light among you." He was the light who soon was to leave (John 12:32-36). He was not going to abide on earth forever. *They were mistaken in their interpretation of the law.* The bridegroom was to leave, as Jesus said (Mark 2:20). "The thought of death accompanies our Lord even to the social meal (Mark 2:15), and in the now undisguised hatred of His opponents, He sees a token of what must hereafter come to pass. A dim hint of the same kind He had already given in His saying to the Jewish rulers" concerning the destruction of His body and the statement to Nicodemus of His being lifted up as was the serpent (John 2:19; 3:14).

The expression *taken away* "implies a violent termination of His life. The words occur nowhere else in the New Testament. This is the first open allusion recorded by Mark, though probably little understood at the time, to the death, which was so soon to separate Him from His disciples."[1]

To Train Disciples to Carry on His Work

Christ is the supreme fisher of men. He called disciples to make them fishers of men (Mark 1:17). "For the Son of man came to seek and to save that which was lost" (Luke 19:10; 1 Tim. 1:15). This involved more than instructing them, though it did involve instruction. However, the Spirit could instruct without the personal presence of Jesus. The training of the disciples to carry forward His work involved, with special reference to the twelve, the selection of certain people to be *with Him* (Matt. 4:18; Luke 6:13). They came to know Him in so many ways through their constant association with Him, although they did not come to know Him during His personal ministry as they *ought* to have known Him. They were to bear witness of Him "because ye have seen with me from the beginning" (John 15:27). He would send them forth as He had been sent (John 13:20). They were to bear fruit which would abide (John 15:16). After the coming of the Spirit they were taught by Christ from heaven. What He had told them in the personal ministry was brought to their remembrance (John 14:26), and they were guided into additional truths which resulted in

---

[1] George Frederick Maclear, *A Class-Book of New Testament History*, page 42.

their reception of the truth in all of its parts (John 14:26; 16:12-15). They were His special group of witnesses (Acts 1:2-3, 8, 21-26; 2:32; 1 John 1:1-4). Christ did not fail in this aspect of His ministry, and after His ascension and the sending of the Spirit they began their world-wide work whose fruit continues until this day (Acts 1:8).

The Apostles and Disciples did not Understand His Mission

The apostles and other disciples did not understand the purpose of Christ's coming into the world to put away sin by the sacrifice of Himself (Heb. 9:28). Since the apostles did not understand it, and they were the disciples nearest Christ, and those whom He chose to be with Him (John 15:27), it is obvious that disciples who were not so close to Jesus did not understand His mission either. After the apostles had recognized that Jesus is "the Christ, the Son of the living God" (Matt. 16:16), "from that time began Jesus to show unto his disciples, that he must go unto Jerusalem, and suffer many things of the elders and chief priests and scribes, and be killed, and the third day be raised up. And Peter took him, and began to rebuke him, saying, Be it far from thee, Lord: this shall never be unto thee. But he turned, and said unto Peter, Get thee behind me, Satan: thou art a stumbling-block unto me; for thou mindest not the things of God, but the things of men" (Matt. 16:21-23).

Mark tells us that "he spake the saying openly" (Mark 8:32). This meant *plainly*, not publicly to the multitudes. Christ had already indicated, as had John the Baptist, that He was to die. John had said that He was the Lamb of God who taketh away the sin of the world (John 1:29, 36). Christ had spoken of the temple of His body being destroyed and rebuilt (John 2:19). Nicodemus had been told the Son of man must be lifted up as was the serpent (John 3:12-16). When the disciples of John asked why Christ's disciples did not fast, "Jesus said unto them, Can the sons of the bride-chamber *mourn*, as long as the bridegroom is with them? but the days will come, when the bridegroom shall be taken away from them, and *then will they fast*" (Matt. 9:14-15). He was not to be with them forever, He would leave them. Then they could mourn, and they would fast because they had an excellent reason to refrain from food. In Capernaum, Christ had said that "the bread which I will give is my flesh, for the life of the world" (John 6:51). He had to die in order to be the Bread of Life which could sustain men unto eternal life (John 6:47-48).

These statements of Jesus were not as plain as those which He now spoke to the disciples, concerning His death. Jesus said that "he must go unto Jerusalem… suffer… be killed… be raised up." Peter's concept of the Messiah and the kingdom was such that he rebuked Christ, and said *"this shall never be unto thee."* "The idea of a suffering Messiah was abhorrent to him and to all the Twelve." Christ looked on His disciples (Mark 8:33), "and said unto Peter, Get thee behind me, Satan: thou art a stumbling-block unto me: for thou mindest not the things of God, but the things of men" (Matt. 16:23). Christ used similar words, "get thee hence," or "get thee behind me," to Satan when He tried to turn Jesus from His spiritual mission to a mission of a carnal kingdom of the world (Mark 8:33; Matt. 4:10; 16:23). *Peter was minding the things of men* for he had in mind an earthly triumph and exaltation of the Messiah in a kingdom of earthly glory. This kind of kingdom they wanted Him to establish on earth, but in so doing they had no room for the cross. Peter was *not minding the things of God.* Those who understand and mind the things of God know that He came to put away sin by the sacrifice of Himself and that a kingdom which did not harmonize with this could not have been proclaimed by Him as at hand, (Matt. 4:17, 23). Christ went on to show them that following Him involved one taking up his own cross; a life of self-denial which would result in losing one's life for His sake but also in finding it (Matt. 16:24). Finally He spoke of His kingdom coming in the lifetime of those who stood there, and this was the very kingdom, the keys of which Jesus had already mentioned (Matt. 16:19, 28).

Foolish and Slow of Heart to Believe

Although Christ had spoken more than once of His resurrection, the apostles did not believe it when the women told them about it (Luke 24:1-12). Two disciples on the road to Emmaus were joined by Jesus but "their eyes were holden that they should not know him" (Luke 24:16). They spoke of Jesus the prophet who had been crucified. "But we hoped that it was he who should redeem Israel" (Luke 24:21). This indicated that their hope had waned. Although they had heard that He had been raised, they were not even then hoping that He would redeem Israel. "'But *we* were hoping,' until His death put an end to our expectation, 'that precisely He,' and no other, 'was the one who should redeem Israel.'"[1]

Did Jesus say that the prophecies were so cloudy that one could not be held responsible for not perceiving the fact of His suffering and death? "And he said unto them, O foolish men, and slow of heart to believe in *all that the prophets have spoken!* Behooved it not the Christ to suffer these things, and to enter into his glory?" (Luke 24:25-26) "Like most Jews, they remembered only the promises of the glories of the Messiah, and ignored the predictions of His sufferings."[2] They were *foolish* not to understand that the sufferings came before the exaltation, the cross before the crown. They were *sluggish of heart to believe all* that the prophets predicted concerning the Messiah. He who believes all that the prophets spoke concerning the Messiah recognize that there could have been no kingdom which was at hand (Matt. 3:2) which did not take into consideration the fact that the cross was at hand (Heb. 9:28). With just the light of the Old Testament they were foolish, and slow to believe all. How much more foolish, and slow of heart to believe all that the Old Testament and the New Testament teach *if one does not realize that Christ never offered in His personal ministry a kingdom to Israel which could have been realized without the cross first taking place.* The glory into which He entered, and which the prophets had predicted, came *after* His cross and was the glory of the kingdom rule as King and Priest (1 Tim. 3:16; Heb. 1:3, 13; 8:1-4). These two disciples had allowed the sufferings of Christ to dim their hope that Christ would redeem Israel, but in reality the fact that He must first suffer before He entered into His glory should have confirmed their belief that He would redeem Israel as well as others from sin (Matt. 1:21).

"And beginning from Moses and from all the prophets, he interpreted to them in all the scriptures the things concerning himself" (Luke 24:27). On this Farrar wrote:

> *The promise to Eve (Gen. 3:15); the promise to Abraham (Gen. 22:18); the Pascal lamb (Ex. 12); the scapegoat (Lev. 16:1-34); the brazen serpent (Numb. 21:9); the greater Prophet (Deut. 18:15); and the star and sceptre (Numb. 24:17); the smitten rock (Numb. 20:11; 1 Cor. 10:4), etc.* **and all the prophets***... (Is. 7:14, 9:6-7, 40:10-11, 50:6, 53:4-5; Jer. 23:5,*

---

[1] Plummer, *Commentary on St. Luke*, page 553.
[2] *Ibid.,* page 555.

33:14-15; Ezek. 34:23; Mic. 5:2; Zech. 6:12, 9:9, 12:10, 13:7; Mal. 3:1, 4:2; and many other passages)."[1]

"He opened to us the scriptures" (Luke 24:32), concerning which they had once been foolish and slow of heart to believe in all the scriptures which predicted things concerning the Messiah.

Mission Misunderstood by the Multitude

One of the devil's temptations was designed to induce Jesus to use His miraculous power for His own personal benefit, and to turn the stones into bread (Matt. 4:3-4). Jesus had the power to become the Bread King to whom the multitudes would flock. They wanted a kingdom which made the physical power and glory and satisfactions central. Later on when He multiplied the loaves and fishes, and fed thousands, they wanted to make Him king. "When therefore the people saw the sign which he did, they said, This is of a truth the prophet that cometh into the world. Jesus therefore perceiving that they were about to come and take him by force, to make him king, withdrew again into the mountains himself alone" (John 6:14-15). Instead of seeing in the bread the sign, they saw in the sign the bread, the physical, and not a sign that they should listen to the teaching of this Teacher sent from God and certified by miracles (John 3:2; 6:14). One who could do these things, they reasoned, was the promised prophet (Deut. 18:16-18). He was, but not the kind they imagined. They reasoned that this powerful prophet, who could multiply the loaves and fishes could rule. So they wanted to force Him to be king. And they would have backed up His kingship by fighting for Him if necessary. Godet pointed out that this was a crisis:

[a] selection among the adherents of Jesus becomes necessary to purify His work from all political alloy. Jesus had received this multitude with open arms; He had made a feast for them. It was an emblem of the feast which He was procuring for them in a higher realm. By thus giving His bread, He had symbolized that gift of Himself which He had just made to mankind. But instead of rising to the hope and desire of such a spiritual banquet, the Galileans occupy their thoughts only

---

[1] Frederic W. Farrar, *The Gospel According to St. Luke*, page 261.

with the material miracle, and in their exalted state see in it already the inauguration of a Messianic Kingdom such as they picture to themselves.[1]

Christ sent away His disciples and then withdrew from the multitude into the mountain (Mark 6:45; John 6:15). They did not discern the true Bread of Life, Christ Himself, who must be partaken of by faith (John 6:33-35, 63, 68). Since the inner group of disciples did not yet understand the mission of the Messiah, should we be surprised that the multitudes did not understand it?

Jesus Did what He Came to Do

"I glorified thee on the earth, having accomplished the work which thou hast given me to do" (John 17:4). "The historical mission of Christ is now regarded as ended; the earthly work as accomplished. By a life of absolute obedience and love Christ had revealed—and therefore glorified—the Father." Earlier Jesus had spoken of "the works which the Father hath given me to accomplish, the very works that I do bear witness of me, that the Father hath sent me" (John 5:36). In John 5:36, His work is viewed "in its manifold parts, as still to be done," but in John 17:4, "the work is contemplated in its unity, as accomplished."[2] He had not omitted, He had not failed to do, anything which the Father sent Him to do. He had failed in nothing.

On the cross "Jesus, knowing that all things are now finished, that the scripture might be accomplished, said, I thirst... he said, It is finished: and he bowed his head, and gave up his spirit" (John 19:28, 30).

Christ came to proclaim the nearness of the kingdom, not to proclaim and then to postpone. If He had come to proclaim the kingdom was nearby in point of time, and then it was postponed so that it was no longer nearby in point of time, one of the purposes for which He came failed. He did not, in His personal ministry, make possible the establishment of the kingdom when the time was fulfilled for its nearness and then its establishment. Premillennialism teaches that Christ failed to bring into being the kingdom in the first century. He did not establish His kingdom on earth in His personal ministry, for the prophecies showed that He would reign in heaven at God's right hand. But the kingdom was nearby during His personal ministry, and after His

---

[1] Godet, *Gospel of John*, Vol. 2, page 10.
[2] Westcott, *The Gospel According to St. John*, page 240.

suffering, He entered into His glory which included His reign as king and priest (Luke 24:25-27; Acts 2:30-36; 1 Tim. 3:16; Heb. 7:1-8:2).

Nothing He came to do failed, therefore the preparation for the kingdom did not fail due to a postponement of the kingdom. It was successful, for in spite of Israel's rejection God enthroned Christ on the holy hill of Zion (Psa. 2; Acts 2:3036; Heb. 12:22-23; Acts 4:24-28).

CHAPTER 2:
THE KINGDOM WAS AT HAND
DURING THE PERSONAL MINISTRY

John the Baptist was sent to prepare the way for the Lord (Luke 3:2-6). He came preaching: "Repent ye; for the kingdom of heaven is at hand" (Matt. 3:2). He warned the people not to depend on their physical relationship to Abraham, for God was able to raise up children to Abraham from other than Abraham's physical seed (Matt. 3:9). The impenitent would be eliminated from God's purposes, and soon. *"And even now the axe lieth at the root of the trees*: every tree therefore that bringeth not forth good fruit is hewn down, and cast into the fire" (Matt. 3:10). Christ preached the kingdom was at hand, as did also the apostles (Matt. 4:17, 23; 9:35; 10:7). "But he said unto them, I must preach the good tidings of the kingdom of God to the other cities also: *for therefore was I sent*" (Luke 12:43). God sent Jesus into the world to preach that the kingdom was at hand—and Jesus Christ did not preach a falsehood.

What Did "At Hand" Mean?

The word translated "at hand" is used around forty-two times in the New Testament. Around fourteen times it is used in the perfect tense and in the third person singular as it is found in Matthew 3:2. Arndt-Gingrich defined it as "approach", or "come near."[1] "The kingdom of heaven is at hand" (Matt. 3:2; 4:17; 10:7), "the kingdom of God is at hand" (Mark 1:15), "the kingdom of God is come nigh" (Luke 10:9, 11), "the hour is at hand" (Matt. 26:45), " behold, he is at hand that betrayeth me" (26:46; Mark 14:42), "the time is at hand: go ye not after them" (Luke 21:8), "when ye see Jerusalem compassed with armies, then know that her desolation is at hand" (21:20), "the night is far spent, and the day is at hand" (Rom. 13:12), "the coming (presence) of the Lord is at hand" (Jas. 5:8), and "the end of all things is at hand" (1 Pet. 4:7).

At hand meant *nearby in point of time or place*, as the case may be. When Christ and the apostles preached that the kingdom was at hand, they meant it was nearby in point of time. The only problem with any

---

[1] William F. Arndt and F. Wilbur Gingich, *A Greek-English Lexicon of the New Testament and Other Early Christian Literature*, page 212.

of the above passages is the meaning of the coming of the Lord in
James 5:8 and the end of all things in 1 Peter. 4:7. Since "at hand"
means nearby in point of time, or place as the case may be, the coming
of the Lord in James 5:8 does not refer to the second coming, which
was not then nearby in point of time. Christ did shortly come in a day
of vengeance and destruction on Jerusalem and Israel. The end of literally everything was not nearby in 1 Peter 4:7, therefore it must refer to
something other than the end of the world. The *"all things* which are
written may be fulfilled" did not mean everything the Old Testament
predicted, including the conquest of the last enemy (Psa. 110:1-4), but
of all things predicted about the destruction of Jerusalem and the temple (Luke 21:22). The only "all things" which was shortly to end when
Peter wrote was the destruction of *the outward aspects* of the old covenant, when Jerusalem was destroyed. It was nigh unto vanishing,
close to vanishing, near to vanishing, when Hebrews was written (Heb.
8:13), and did vanish shortly thereafter. In fact, God had already abolished the Old Covenant that He might establish the New (Heb. 1:3, 13;
Acts 2:34-36; Heb. 10:9-10; Col. 2:14-17; Eph. 2:11-20). Israel continued to cling to the lifeless forms of Judaism, which God had abolished. In AD 70 even these lifeless forms were destroyed and vanished.

The Time is Fulfilled

Jews wondered when the Messianic kingdom would come, and
what was holding it up. Could man hasten its coming? Some thought
they could, but others thought that they could not. To those who took
this position, "the time was said to be fixed, and the end could not
come until this time had been completed (or 'fulfilled'), or until the
measure of evil was 'full,' or the number of the elect. The time is
wholly in God's hands (Acts 1:8); he alone determines it, he alone
knows what it is. And though 'for the elect's sake' he may 'shorten the
days'... or in the interest of repentance may extend the interval of
grace, still it is he alone who does this—and no human being can alter
or modify his decree."[1] Great tribulation would come before and cul-
minate in this day of the Lord which would be followed by peace. The
old age would end, and the messianic age would be ushered in. Some

---

[1] P.W. Grant, *The Revelation of John*, pages 68-69.

thought of a personal Messiah and some of a messianic age with God as the Redeemer and King.[1]

Of course, if the kingdom could either be *hastened* or *postponed* by the repentance or lack of it by man, the time in reality would be set by man and not by God. The premillennial view is that the Messianic age would have been brought into existence if Israel had repented, and that her failure to accept Christ led to the postponement of the kingdom. Whether he realized it or not, Boll affirms that it is man's action which determines the time. "The only thing that ever stood between Israel and her glorious promises, kingdom and all, was her sinful condition. That removed, every other promise must necessarily be fulfilled to them, and that speedily."[2]

There is nothing of this in the message of John the Baptist (Matt. 3:2), or of Jesus Christ (Matt. 4:17, 23). "Now after John was delivered up, Jesus came into Galilee, preaching the gospel of God, and saying, *The time is fulfilled*, and the kingdom of God is at hand: repent ye, and believe in the gospel" (Mark 1:14-15). Gospel means good news. Good news was preached to Israel when she came out of Egypt and headed for the promised land, but she failed to enter into that promised land because "the word of hearing did not profit them, because it was not united by faith with them that heard" (Heb. 4:2). Today, because the good news of Christ's death for our sins, His burial, and His resurrection so overshadows all other good news, the word "gospel" to us means *this* good news (1 Cor. 15:1-4). However, it was good news in the first century that the kingdom which had so long been promised and prophesied was now at hand. The Messiah, the Son of God, who knew His own mission and the nature of the kingdom, said clearly "*the time is fulfilled, and the kingdom of God is at hand.*" This was the reason he called on them to "repent... and believe in the gospel." Whatever time had to run its course before the kingdom could be at hand, had run its course, or Jesus could not have announced the kingdom was at hand. *The time was fulfilled in connection with His first coming*, not in connection with His second coming which has not yet taken place. Jesus knew it was time for the nearness of the kingdom, even though Israel had not yet repented, and even if Israel did not repent. If the prophetic timetable has not even yet been accom-

---

[1] *Ibid.*, pages 70-71.
[2] R.H. Boll, *The Kingdom of God*, page 86.

plished so that the kingdom has been established, how could Jesus have said in the first century, and before the establishment of the church, that the time was fulfilled? Was not what God designed to take place (i.e., for the kingdom to be at hand and then to be established) accomplished in the time which God set for it? It was time then and there for the kingdom of the Messiah, prophesied by the prophets, to be at hand, and it was at hand. The statement of John, concerning God raising up children unto Abraham out of these stones, is one of the clear proofs that nothing that Israel did or did not do would result in the kingdom getting out of hand so that for centuries it was no longer at hand. That which was at hand either got to be in hand or the time was not fulfilled, or if fulfilled it was defeated by Israel's failure to repent.

John the Baptist did not say: "Repent and the kingdom will be at hand." If he had said this, he would have Implied that the coming of the kingdom was contingent on their repentance. John said: "Repent ye; for the kingdom of heaven is at hand (Matt. 3:2). The repentance was not necessary in order for the kingdom to be at hand. Its nearness in point of time was preached as motivation to repentance, and as proof of the need for repentance.

The postponement theory was held in essence by the Pharisees for they held that the coming of the kingdom was contingent on the repentance of Israel. There were Jews who maintained that if Israel kept one Sabbath strictly, or was truly penitent for one day, the Messiah would come.[1] "Abrahams admits that there was a difference between the Pharisaic formula, 'Repent *and* the kingdom is at hand,' and the Johannine, 'Repent *for* the kingdom is at hand.' In the message of John the attitude of his hearers had no effect on the coming of the Kingdom, but only on their relationship to it."[2] Because Israel did not repent, the premillennialists believe the kingdom did not come. It was postponed. John said that it was at hand whether they repented or not, and it came in spite of their rebellion (Psa. 2; Acts 4:25-27).

Premillennialists agree that the one which was at hand was the kingdom prophesied by the prophets. Since it was not postponed (not being contingent on the repentance of the Jews), the kingdom prophe-

---

[1] Roy A. Stewart, *Rabinic Theology*, page 48.
[2] H.G. Marsh, *The Origin and Significance of the New Testament Baptism*, page 40.

sied by the prophets was established. The one which was established was the kingdom of Christ (Acts 2:30-36; Col. 1:13). Therefore, the present, spiritual kingdom of Christ was the one which was prophesied by the prophets.

If the time had not been fulfilled, the kingdom of heaven could not have been at hand. If it had not been at hand, Jesus would never have said that it was at hand. Could the kingdom have been established in the days of Daniel? No, Why? Because it was not time for it. Could it have been established in the days of the Medes and Persians? or the Grecian empire? (Dan. 5:28; 8:20-21) No, and for the same reason. The dream of Nebuchadnezzar, which Daniel interpreted, showed that the kingdom of heaven would not be established until the time of the fourth empire—the Roman. Boll said: "We trust, however, that the reader would even without this discussion have perceived that the kingdom announced by John (and afterward by the Lord Jesus Himself, Matthew 4:17; Mark 1:14, 15) could have been none other than that of Old Testament prophecy and of Jewish expectation in so far as that expectation accorded with the prophecies."[1] "Since the kingdom-promise was national, the preparatory repentance must of course also be national..."[2] "Jerusalem had missed her chance. What would have happened had she understood and seized upon her opportunity? Who would doubt *what?* He certainly would have gathered them 'as a hen doth gather her brood under her wings' (Matthew 23:37) and bestowed on them all the riches of His grace and His salvation. And nothing could then have hindered the fulfillment of the promises God had made to their fathers... Undoubtedly she *might have* realized her ancient promises then; but God knowing that she would in no wise hear, had laid His plans accordingly from of old; yet not presuming upon His foreknowledge, but all along and earnestly, lovingly, giving them the full opportunity to make their own choice and to decide their own destiny."[3] But Israel rejected Christ and in place of the kingdom the church was established.[4]

This clearly affirms that the time was ready for the establishment of the kingdom when Jesus preached it was at hand. This means that whatever time had to lapse before the kingdom, foretold by Daniel,

---

[1] R.H. Boll, *The Kingdom of God*, page 62.
[2] *Ibid.,* page 63.
[3] *Ibid.,* pages 80-81.
[4] *Ibid.,* page 85.

could be established had already lapsed. However, if the premillennialists are right, *the Roman Empire in the first century had not reached the stage of development which it must reach in order for the kingdom to be established.* "Four world-powers—then the Kingdom of God. There were not to be five world-powers."[1] "The difficulty ought, however, to be faced. It consists in the fact that Rome, the fourth world-power, *is gone.* There are not to be five world-powers."[2] The solution is that the Roman Empire will be restored. "The Roman world-power then, though now it does not exist, as such, is to return. When it returns, the Roman power will be in the form of a ten-kingdom confederacy under one dominant head; which fact is indicated by *the toes* of the Image; more fully set forth in the ten horns of the fourth beast (Daniel 7); and clearly revealed to John in Revelation" 17:12-13 and 19:11-21.[3] Before the kingdom can be established, Rome must reach such a state or stage of development. "But she has never as yet, nor at any time in the past, taken on its final shape as the ten-kingdom world-power which Daniel and John beheld (Daniel 2 and7, and Revelation 13)."[4]

If this is true, the time was *not* fulfilled when Jesus preached that the time *was* fulfilled. The kingdom could *not* have been at hand, for Rome had not reached the stage of development necessary before the kingdom could be established. It should not be hard to make a decision as to who is right. Jesus said the time was fulfilled and the kingdom was at hand, and premillennialism says the time has not yet been fulfilled for the prophetic chart of Daniel had not run its course in the first century, the ten-kingdom stage of Rome had not yet developed; the kingdom, therefore, could not have been at hand. It is not my responsibility that the premillennialists contradict the Lord, but it is my duty to point out the contradiction.

Law and Prophets until John

Jesus spoke of John's work, and then said: "Among them that are born of women, there hath not arisen a greater than John the Baptist: yet he that is but little in the kingdom of heaven is greater than he. And

---

[1] *Ibid.,* page 31.
[2] *Ibid.,* page 29.
[3] *Ibid.,* page 32.
[4] *Ibid.,* page 30.

from the days of John the Baptist until now the kingdom of heaven suffereth violence, and men of violence take it by force. For all the prophets and the law prophesied until John. And if you are willing to receive it, this is Elijah, that is to come. He that hath ears to hear, let him hear" (Matt. 11:11-15).

This passage also shows that the first century was the time for the establishment of the kingdom. *The kingdom was to come in connection with the first coming of Christ, not in connection with His second coming.* The law and the prophets had long held sway, but they had pointed to the time of John the Baptist and Christ and that John would announce the presence of the Messiah. John's work would form the transition time between the time of the law and the prophets and the coming of the kingdom. The kingdom did not come at the moment of John's preaching, nor at his death, for the teaching of repentance in preparation for the coming of the kingdom continued after John died. We know the kingdom was not established by John.

First, John was not in the kingdom, for he that is least in the kingdom is greater than John. If John had been in the kingdom, he would have been greater than himself.

Second, Jesus did not say: "For all the prophets and the Law prophesied until John" (Matt. 11:13). And then the kingdom was established. He said: "The law and the prophets were until John: from that time the gospel of the kingdom of God is preached, and every man entereth violently into it" (Luke 16:16). How was the kingdom preached? In hand? No. *At* hand (Matt. 3:2, 4:17, 23; 10:7; Mark 1:14-15). I shall return to the expression about the kingdom being pressed into violently. The long period of prophecy of the coming kingdom was now at an end. John was a "predictor of the kingdom of heaven, and the first preacher" to say that the people needed to repent for the kingdom was at hand.

If the time had not been fulfilled, Jesus would not have said that the law and the prophets were until John, and that since then the kingdom was preached, and we know it was preached as being *at hand.* If the premillennialists are right, the passage should read: "The law and the prophets were until John, then John and Jesus both preached the kingdom of heaven was at hand, then the kingdom got out of hand, and the church age was established. The law, the prophets, John, and the church age are until the second coming, and *then* the kingdom will be established." This is not the time schedule of which Jesus spoke. The

law, the prophets, John, and the preaching of the nearness of the kingdom is the time schedule of which Jesus spoke. What would follow
this? The very establishment of the kingdom which John said was
near! If someone said that Elijah must come before the Messiah came
and the kingdom be at hand, Jesus said: "And if ye are willing to receive it, this is Elijah, that is to come" (Matt. 11:14). Of course,
whether they received it or not it *was* Elijah. "But I say unto you, that
Elijah is come already, and *they knew him not*, but did unto him whatsoever they would" (Matt. 17:12). The rejection of Elijah in the person
of John did not mean that John was not the Elijah prophesied by Malachi. It meant that those who rejected him and his baptism rejected the
counsel of God against themselves (Luke 7:29-30). The fact that "even
so shall the Son of man also suffer of them," did not mean Jesus was
not the Messiah, just because they rejected Him (Matt. 17:12).

Jesus made it clear that things were following their God-ordained
course. (1) The law and the prophets. (2) John and the preaching of the
gospel of the kingdom, i.e., the good news that the kingdom was at
hand (Luke 16:16; Matt. 3:2; 4:17, 24; 10:7; Mark 1:14-15). (3) Although He did not say it in this place, what followed the preaching that
the kingdom was at hand? His suffering, and then entering into His
glory or kingdom (Luke 24:25-27; 1 Tim. 3:16; Matt. 20:21; Mark
10:37; Acts 2:34-35). Israel's rejection of the Elijah who was to come
did not postpone the establishment of the kingdom, any more than
their rejection of Jesus did. Christ did not fail to do what He came to
do in connection with His first coming. In fact, after the statement
about the law, the prophets, and John, Jesus said: "But it is easier for
heaven and earth to pass away than for one tittle of the law to fall"
(Luke 16:17). Jesus did not fail to accomplish that which He came to
do in the fulfillment of the law and the prophets (Matt. 5:17-18).

What was meant by the kingdom "suffereth violence, and men of
violence take it by force" (Matt. 11:12), or "every man entereth violently into it" (Luke 16:16)? Whatever it meant, it took place in the "at
hand" stage, for neither John nor Jesus established the kingdom in
their personal ministry. We know that Jews had a misconception of the
kingdom, and that multitudes were flocking to Him (Luke 15:1; John
12:19). They wanted an earthly kingdom of glory for themselves as a
part of Israel. In fact, some were so zealous they wanted to make Jesus
king by force (John 6:15). Concerning Matthew 11:12, Milton Terry

wrote:

> *We believe the true view will be attained only by giving each word its natural meaning, and keeping attention strictly to the context. The common meaning of **Biadzetal is to take something by force, to carry by storm**, as a besieged city or fortress; and it here refers most naturally to the violent and hasty efforts to seize upon the kingdom of God which had been conspicuous since the beginning of the ministry of John. For this view seems to be demanded by the context. John had heard, in his prison, about the works of Christ, and, anxious and impatient for the glorious manifestation of the Messiah, sent two of his disciples to put the dubious question, "Art thou he that is coming, or look we for another?" (Matt. 11:2-3). Jesus' answer (verses 4-6) was merely a statement of his mighty works, and of the preaching of the Gospel to the poor—Old Testament prophetic evidence that the days of the Messiah were at hand—and the tacit, rebuke: "Blessed is he whosoever shall not be offended (**find occasion of stumbling**) in me," was evidently meant for John's impatience. When John's disciples went away Jesus at once proceeded to speak of John's character and standing before the multitudes: "When ye all flocked to the wilderness to hear John preach, did ye expect to find a wavering reed, or a finely dressed courtier? Or did ye expect, rather, to see a prophet? Yes," he explained, "much more than a prophet. For he was the Messiah's messenger, himself prophesied of in the Scriptures" (Mal. 3:1). He was greater than all the prophets who were before him, for he stood upon the very verge of the Messianic era and introduced the Christ. But, with all his greatness, he misunderstands the kingdom of heaven; and from his days until now the kingdom of heaven suffers from many who, like him, think it may be forced into manifestation. That kingdom comes according to an ordered progress. First, the prophets and the law until John—the Elijah foretold in Mai. 4:5. John was but the forerunner of Christ, preparing his way, and Christ's manifestation in the flesh was not his coming in his kingdom. Herein, we think, expositors have generally misapprehended our Lord's doctrine. Thus Hash: "The Lord speaks of the absolutely certain and momentous fact that the kingdom of heaven has come, proclaims its presence, and*

*sends forth its invitations in tones not to be misunderstood
(verse 15)." We believe, on the contrary, that this is a grave
misunderstanding of our Lord's words. He neither says, nor
necessarily implies, that his kingdom **has come**. John's preaching and Christ's preaching alike declared the kingdom to be at
hand, and not fully come. Compare Matt. 3:2 and 4:17. But
from the beginning of this gospel men had been over anxious to
have the kingdom itself appear, and in this sense it was suffering violence, both by an inward impatience and zeal, such as
John himself had just now exhibited, and by an open and outward clamor, such as was exhibited by those who would fain
have taken Jesus by force and made him king (John 6:15). This
same kind of violence is to be understood in the parallel passage in Luke 16:16. The preaching of "the gospel of the kingdom" was the occasion of a violence of attitude regarding it.
Every man would fain enter violently into it.*

*The word **biadzetai**, accordingly, denotes not altogether a
hostile violence, nor yet, on the other hand, a commendable
zeal; but it may combine in a measure both of these concep-
tions. Stier finely says: "In a case where exegesis perseveringly
disputes which of the two views of a passage capable of two
senses is correct, it is generally found that both are one in a
third deeper meaning, and that the disputants in both cases
have both right and wrong in their argument." The word in
question may combine both the good and the bad senses of violence: not, however, in the manner in which Stier explains, as
above, but as depicting the violent zeal of those who would
hurry the kingdom of God into a premature manifestation. Such
a zeal might be laudable in its general aim, but very mistaken
in its spirit and plan and therefore deserving of rebuke."[1]*

The men of violence denotes "persons who engage in anything im-
petuously and eagerly." Reference is made to the same persons "in the
parallel passage of Luke 16:16 (which has been too little attended
to)."[2]

---

[1] Milton S. Terry, *Biblical Hermeneutics*, pages 217-218.
[2] S.T. Bloomfield, *The Greek Testament with English Notes*, Vol. 1, page 54.

*I find in it two thoughts: one expressed, the other implied.
(1) There has been a powerful movement since John's time to-
wards the Kingdom of God. (2) The movement derived its ini-
tial impetus from John.*[1]

John did not take the law away (contrast Col. 2:14), so the passage
does not mean that the law ceased when John began his work. But until the time of John, all that the people had was the law and the prophets; but beginning with John they had the preaching of the kingdom of
God as being at hand. Things were now in a preparatory stage for the
establishment of the kingdom. The prophets had prophesied of the
Christ to come, but John announced the Messiah. A new revelation
was given with John, the revelation that the kingdom was *at hand*
(Matt. 3:2; 4:17-23).

John the Forerunner, Then Jesus

God's time schedule continued to operate when Jesus was manifested to John and entered into His ministry. The law and the prophets
were until John, and then the preaching that the kingdom of heaven
was at hand. (Luke 16:16; Matt. 3:2; 4:17, 23). John first started
preaching the kingdom was at hand, but he made it clear that his work
was preparatory. "And he preached, saying, There cometh after me he
that is mightier than I, the lachet of whose shoes I am not worthy to
stoop down and unloose" (Mark 1:17). Things were on schedule: The
law, the prophets, John, and then the personal ministry of Jesus. If the
premillennialists are right, during the personal ministry of Jesus, things
got off-schedule. The kingdom which was at hand ("The time is fulfilled, and the kingdom of heaven is at hand," Mark 1:14) got out of
hand because the people did not receive Christ. It was postponed and
has not been established yet.

Fishers of Men

Christ proclaimed that the time was fulfilled, the kingdom was at
hand, and men needed to repent. It was not long after this that he
called certain ones saying *"Come ye after me, and I will make you
fishers of men"* (Matt. 4:17-19; Mark 1:14-15, 17). Luke tells us that
Jesus said to certain ones "thou shalt catch men." The margin says
"take alive" (Luke 5:10). "Both substantive and verb have special

---

[1] *Expositor's Greek Testament*, Vol. 1, page 173.

point (*men* instead of fish; *for life* instead of for death)."[1]
fPluEjmer^—14£). This is a description of the work which Jesus was
doing and to which He called them. He was fishing for men through
preaching the good news that the kingdom was at hand (Matt. 4:17,
23), and He was inviting them to do the same work. They did this in
the personal ministry through preaching the good news that the kingdom was at hand (Matt. 9:35; 10:7), and after His ascension by preaching the gospel of His death for our sins, His burial, and His resurrection (1 Cor. 15:1-4). Is there no relationship between the work to
which He called them and the kingdom which was at hand? He did not
call them to be *conquerors of men* in violent conflict between the Messiah and His enemies. He did not call them to be *rulers of men* who
would have positions of earthly power and glory in His kingdom. They
were under the misapprehension that greatness in His kingdom would
be like greatness in other kingdoms, but He said that the great in His
kingdom must achieve greatness through service (Matt. 20:20-28). The
kingdom necessitates fishers of men who persuade men to accept
Christ and His rule in their lives. Of course, the apostles did become
spiritual rulers in that through them Christ, after being crowned king,
ruled through the message sent to, and revealed and confirmed
through, them. (Matt. 19:28).

The Twelve Preached the Kingdom was at Hand

Christ gave twelve disciples authority over unclean spirits, and
designated them as apostles (Matt. 10:1-4). "These twelve Jesus sent
forth, and charged them, saying, Go not into any way of the Gentiles,
and enter not into any city of the Samaritans: but go rather to the lost
sheep *of the house of Israel*. And as ye go, preach, saying, The kingdom of heaven *is at hand*" (Matt. 10:7). In instructing them *before
they went* Jesus spoke of the type of reception which they would receive. There would be cities and houses which would reject them
(Matt. 10:12-15). They were sent "forth as sheep in the midst of
wolves" (Matt. 10:16). These wolves included Israelitish wolves, for
they were preaching to Israelites (Matt. 10:6, 23). They would be involved in legal opposition by rulers and brought before councils, governors and kings. This would be "for my sake" (Matt. 10:17-18). Peo-

---

[1] Plummer, *Commentary on the Gospel According to St. Luke*, page 146.

ple would be put to death, and they would be hated and persecuted (Matt. 10:21-23). Instead of Israel as a whole receiving the Messiah, Jesus said they called Him, "the master of the house," "Beelzebub," and his disciples could not expect better treatment (Matt. 10:24-25). God took notice of them, they were not to fear, and if they confessed Him before men, or if anyone else did, God would hear them confessed by Jesus; or if they denied Him, Jesus would deny them before the Father in heaven (Matt. 10:28-33). Christ made it clear that He came to bring not peace but a sword, that people would become enemies of one another because of His teaching, families would be divided, and He must be the one to whom they were supremely loyal (Matt. 10:34-37). Following Him involved cross bearing and finding one's life through losing it for His sake (Matt. 10:38-39). He then spoke of those who received them as receiving Him, "and it came to pass when Jesus had finished commanding his twelve disciples, he departed thence to teach and preach in their cities" (Matt. 11:1).

All these things which Jesus told them, before they went forth as His apostles to preach the kingdom, were in harmony with the type of kingdom which was established after His ascension (Heb. 1:3, 13; Acts 2:30-36), but it is not in harmony with the kind of kingdom envisioned by the premillennialists. Christ could not have sent them out, in the context in which He sent them, to preach as at hand the earthly-type of conquering kingdom.

Time Interval between Advents?

Walvoord wrote: "Nothing should be plainer to one reading the Old Testament than that the foreview therein provided did not predict a period of time between the two advents. This very fact confused even the prophets (cf. 1 Pet. 1:10-12). At best such a time interval was only implied. In the very passage involved, Daniel 9:24-27, it is indicated that there would be a time interval."[1]

First, the prophets were puzzled about the time, but they definitely prophesied the grace which is preached to us in this gospel age. Furthermore, they definitely prophesied that the sufferings came before the glories— "when it testified beforehand the sufferings of Christ, and the glories that should follow them" (1 Pet. 1:10-12). *Second*, it would be absolutely impossible for two comings to have been prophe-

---

[1] John Walvoord, *The Millennial Kingdom*, page 228.

sied without there being a time interval between them. How could the
first and second advent been prophesied for the same time? They could
not have been, so whatever the Old Testament said about the first and
about the second coming, in the very nature of the case there had to be
a time interval. *Third*, the Old Testament clearly distinguished between His reign at God's right hand and His second coming. Psalm
110 prophesied His reign as king and priest at God's right hand. This
is a prophecy of His reign that began on Pentecost (Acts 2:34-36). He
reigns until the last enemy, death, is conquered, and this takes place at
the last day, the last time, and the last trump (1 Cor. 15:24-28; 1 Pet.
1:5; Rev. 20:11-15).

Church Came at the Wrong Time?

The kingdom prophesied by the prophets was at hand (Mark 1:14-
15). Israel rejected Christ *and His kingdom message* and the kingdom
was postponed. The church age was not prophesied by the prophets,
and it could not be at hand as long as the kingdom was at hand. The
kingdom which was in hand *got out of hand*, or rather we should say
was *knocked out of hand by Israel* because she failed to accept Christ,
and the church or kingdom of God's Son which was not at hand, very
quickly was at hand and was established on Pentecost. The *at* hand got
out of hand and the *not at* hand came *in* hand. Some mix-up, but the
mix-up is in premillennialism and not in the Bible.

Those who teach that the kingdom was postponed until the second
coming overlook many passages of scripture, but one is sufficient to
overthrow their position. "Why do the nations rage, and the peoples
meditate a vain thing? The kings of the earth set themselves, and the
rulers take counsel together, against Jehovah, and against his anointed,
saying, Let us break their bonds asunder, and cast away their cords
from us" (Psa. 2:1-3). Who are these who are in rebellion to God and
His Son, the Messiah or "his anointed"? They are the Jews and Gentiles of Jesus' day. "Who by the Holy Spirit, by the mouth of our father
David thy servant, didst say, Why did the Gentiles rage, and the peoples imagine vain things? The kings of the earth set themselves in array, and the rulers were gathered together against the Lord, and against
his Anointed: for of a truth in this city against thy holy Servant Jesus,
whom thou didst anoint, both Herod and Pontius Pilate, with the Gentiles and the peoples of Israel, were gathered together, to do whatsoev-

er thy hand and thy counsel foreordained to come to pass" (Acts 4:25-28).

Were they successful in their rebellion? Their efforts were so futile that: "He that sitteth in the heavens will laugh: the Lord will have them in derision. Then will he speak unto them in his wrath, and vex them in his displeasure: Yet I have set my king upon my holy hill of Zion" (Psa. 2:4-6). In spite of their opposition God enthroned His Son. The postponement theory says that Israel's rebellion was so successful that God postponed the kingdom, but the Psalmist foresaw that it would be such a failure that God would hold their efforts in contempt. "...the God of our fathers, hath glorified his Servant Jesus; whom ye delivered up, and denied before the face of Pilate, when he had determined to release him" (Acts 3:13-15; 4:8-12). "The God of our fathers raised up Jesus, whom ye slew, hanging him on a tree. Him did God exalt with his right hand to be a Prince and a Savior, to give repentance to Israel, and remission of sins" (Acts 5:30-31). He was glorified after His rejection, as the prophets prophesied (Luke 24:25-27). He was received up into glory to reign at God's right hand in the heavenly Jerusalem (1 Tim. 3:16; Heb. 12:22). The kingdom was not postponed, but Israel as a nation was rejected and eliminated from the kingdom, which was given to Jews and Gentiles who accepted Christ (Matt. 21:43; Heb. 12:28).

The Right Time for His Death

Christ died at the right time, i e., at the time selected by the Father. "For while we were yet weak, *in due season* Christ died for the ungodly" (Rom, 5:6). Did Christ die at the right time? Who can deny it if they believe that His death was involved in the unfolding of God's plan of salvation for the world? "'At the set time'—*kata kairon*, at the exact time fixed by the Father, and therefore precisely when it would do the world the largest measure of good."[1] Sadler thought that: "This may mean either at the time appointed, or when iniquity was at its heights, and the long-suffering of God well nigh exhausted."[2] However, in either case it was the right time for His death. Sanday said: "Paul is strongly impressed with the fitness of the moment in the world's history which Christ chose for His intervention in it. This idea is a striking link of connexion between the (practically) acknowledged and the

---

[1] Moses E. Lard, *Commentary on Paul's Letter to the Romans*, page 157.

[2] M.F. Sadler, *The Epistle to the Romans*, page 96.

disputed Epistles; compare on the one hand Gal. 4:4; 2 Cor. 6:2; Rom. 3:26; and on the other hand Eph. 1:10; 1 Tim. 2:6; 6:15; Tit. 1:3."[1] "The *opportuneness* of Christ's death is expressed by *kata kairon*. He died when the hour of man's necessity had struck. The Divine *anoka* (3:26) had been worn out by the accumulated sins of men. This was the *plaroma ton kairon* Eph. 1:10; Gal. 4:4. Cf. *kairois idiois* 1 Tim. 2:26; 6:15."[2]

Even those who may deny that "in due season" means that Christ died at the time selected by the Father, will not deny that Christ did die at the place and time appointed by the Father. "Now" could not be "the acceptable time," and "now" could not be "the day of salvation" (2 Cor. 6:2), unless Christ had died for us. Since God purposed that "now" be the acceptable time, the day of salvation, it cannot be that Christ died at the *wrong* time in order to make salvation possible at the *right* time.

Paul preached this message of salvation, and the fact that this was the time of salvation. He was an ambassador of Christ entreating men to be reconciled to God (2 Cor. 5:11-21). "And working together with him we entreat also that ye receive not the grace of God in vain" (2 Cor. 6:1). Paul did all this at the right time, the time purposed by God. "...eternal life, which God, who cannot lie, promised before times eternal; but *in his own seasons manifested his word in the message*, wherewith I was entrusted according to the commandment of God our Savior" (Titus 1:2-3).

How can one deny that God brought about the gospel dispensation, the time when the message entrusted to Paul and others was preached, at the time prepared for in His divine plan? Furthermore, as the evidence makes clear, this time was spoken of by the prophets, i.e., the time when the gospel would be preached to men, and therefore the gospel dispensation was not only purposed but promised by the prophets. "Concerning which salvation the prophets sought and searched diligently, who prophesied of the grace that should come unto you: searching what time or what manner of time the Spirit of Christ which was in them did point unto, when it testified beforehand the sufferings of Christ, and the glories that should follow them. To whom it was re-

---

[1] William Sanday, *The Epistle to the Romans*, page 127.

[2] Henry Liddon, *Explanatory Analysis of Paul's Epistle to the Romans*, page 99.

vealed, that not unto themselves, but unto you, did they minister these things, which now have been announced unto you through them that preached the gospel unto you by the Holy Spirit sent forth from heaven; which things angels desire to look into" (1 Peter 1:10-12).

Testimony concerning the gospel is borne in its proper time, which is now, i.e., the gospel age. "This is good and acceptable in the sight of God our Savior; who would have all men to be saved, and come to the knowledge of the truth. For there is one God, one mediator also between God and men, himself man, Christ Jesus, who gave himself a ransom for all; *the testimony to be borne in its own times whereunto I was appointed a preacher and an apostle* (I speak the truth, I lie not), a *teacher of the Gentiles* in faith and truth" (I Tim. 2:3-7).

"To be testified in due time, or, the testimony (appointed) for its own times. This is in apposition to the whole preceding statement in the verse. That God is the God of all men, Gentiles as well as Jews, and that Christ is the one Mediator between God and all mankind, having offered himself a ransom for all—is the testimony to be borne in the Christian ages. This forms the grand massage of the Christian ministry; they are to proclaim the fullness and freeness of salvation in the gospel, as sufficient for, and offered to, all men, of every race and clime and tongue under heaven."[1]

"At the time appointed by his heavenly Father, Jesus bore witness to God's will that all should be saved, and in his turn St. Paul, fully conscious of his special mission to proclaim the universality of the Gospel, recalls his commission as the Apostle of the Gentiles."[2] If the first century was not the time for the kingdom, it could not have been at hand. The time could not have been fulfilled unless the kingdom was actually at hand. But the first century was also the time for the gospel to be proclaimed to all men, and for Paul to do his work as the apostle to the Gentiles. However, Paul's work was as a member of the church, with a special position (apostle) and mission (to the Gentiles); it was in connection with the present kingdom of God's dear Son (Col. 1:13) and not an entirely different kind of kingdom. Since the first century was the time for the gospel, and therefore for the beginning of the gospel age, it must be that the kingdom which was also at hand in Jesus' personal ministry was the one which was actually established.

---

[1] Harvey, page 32.
[2] Bernard Orchard, *A Catholic Commentary on the Book of Hebrews,* page 1146.

Who can deny that the testimony, which was borne "in its own time" was borne at the right time? Since this gospel we now enjoy was prophesied, this gospel age was prophesied— (1 Pet. 1:10-12).

Time Appointed by the Father

"But I say that so long as the heir is a child, he differeth nothing from a bondservant though he is lord of all; but is under guardians and stewards *until the day appointed by the father*. So we also, when we were children, *were* held in bondage under the rudiments of the world: but *when the fullness of the time came*, God sent forth his Son, born of a woman, born under the law, that he might redeem them that were under the law, that we might receive the adoption of sons... So that thou art no longer a bondservant, but a son; and if a son, then *an heir* through God" (Gal. 4:1-6).

"But before faith came, we were kept in ward under the law, shut up unto the faith which should afterwards be revealed. So that the law is become our tutor to bring us unto Christ, that we might be justified by faith. But now that faith is come, we are no longer under a tutor. For ye are all sons of God, through faith, in Christ Jesus. For as many of you as were baptized into Christ did put on Christ. There can be neither Jew nor Greek, there can be neither bond nor free, there can be no male and female; for ye all are one man in Christ Jesus. And if ye are Christ's then are ye Abraham's seed, heirs according to promise" (Gal. 3:23-29).

The law fulfilled the purpose of a tutor, guardian, and steward *until the day appointed by the Father*. When the day appointed by the Father came, they were no longer under a tutor but in Christ are sons of God. As sons, they are heirs through God (Gal. 4:4), but they must be in Christ to be sons and to be "Abraham's seed, heirs according to promise" (Gal. 3:29). When the time had matured, when the time which the Father appointed was at hand for the gospel age, the age of the faith, "God sent forth his Son, born of a woman, *born under the law"* (Gal. 4:4). The law was in force when Christ was born. Men did not cease to be under the tutor at His birth. The law did not pass away at the moment of His birth. During His personal ministry He sent people to go through a purification ceremony required by the law (Matt. 8:4). He told His disciples that the scribes and Pharisees were in Moses' seat (i.e., when they expounded the law of Moses, not their traditions which made void the law, Matt. 15), and that His disciples were to hearken to them (Matt. 23:1-3). It was His cross which made possible the abolition of the law (Col. 2:14-17; Eph. 2:13-16). The law did not pass away at the moment of His death, but by virtue of His death, for after He died on the cross as the Lamb of God, He had to appear in the holy of holies (heaven), make purification for our sins and then He sat down at the right hand of God to reign as king and priest (Heb. 1:3, 13; 8:1-4). The world was informed of this on the first Pentecost after His resurrection and ascension (Acts 2:34-35). Then the gospel began to go forth from Jerusalem unto all the world (Luke 24:44-47; Acts 1:8; 2:39).

When did Christ come? At the time appointed by the Father (Gal. 4:4). He came at the right time, "the fullness of the time." Why did He come? "That he might redeem them that were under the law, that we might receive the adoption of sons" (Gal. 4:5). What was necessary in order for us to be redeemed? He had to die (Acts 20:28; 1 Pet. 2:23-25). Did the law and the prophets point to the redemption which is in Christ? "But now apart from the law a righteousness of God hath been manifested, being witnessed by the law and the prophets; even the righteousness of God through faith in Jesus Christ unto all them that believe; for there is no distinction" (Rom. 3:21-26). Therefore, Jesus Christ came in the fullness of time, the time set by the Father, to die for the sins of the world that in Christ, in His body the church, we may be children of God and heirs according to promise (Acts 20:28; Rom. 3:22-26; Gal. 3:25-29; 4:1-7). It all happened at the right time, with the right purposes, and with the right results. Therefore, it could not have been the time, when Jesus came, for a kingdom to have been at hand like the one the Jews wanted and which the premillennialists believe was at hand in the first century when John and Jesus preached (Matt. 3:2; 4:17, 23; 10:7). It was the right time for the age of the justification by faith in Jesus Christ, the time to be sons of God in Christ, the time to be Abraham's seed, the time to be heirs according to promise, the time for the law to pass and the gospel age to come in.

God's Eternal Purpose Found in Christ

"Blessed be the God and Father of our Lord Jesus Christ, who hath blessed us with every spiritual blessing in the heavenly places in Christ: even as he chose us in him before the foundation of the world, that we should be holy and without blemish before him in love: having

foreordained us unto adoption as sons through Jesus Christ unto himself, according to the good pleasure of his will, to the praise of the glory of his grace, which he freely bestowed on us in the Beloved: in
whom we have our redemption through his blood, the forgiveness of
our trespasses, according to the riches of his grace, which he made to
abound toward us in all wisdom and prudence, making known unto us
the mystery of his will, according to his good pleasure which he purposed in him unto a dispensation of the fullness of the times, to sum up
all things in Christ, the things in the heavens, and the things upon the
earth; in him, I say, in whom also we are made a heritage, having been
foreordained according to the purpose of him who worketh all things
after the counsel of his will; to the end that we should be unto the
praise of his glory, we who had before hoped in Christ: in whom ye
also, having heard the word of the truth, the gospel of your salvation,
—in whom, having also believed, ye were sealed with the Holy Spirit
of promise, which is an earnest of our inheritance, unto the redemption
of God's own possession, unto the praise of his glory" (Eph. 1:3-14).

First, it was God's purpose, before the foundation of the world, to
choose people in Christ, to adopt as sons those who believe in Christ
and come into Him (Eph. 1:4). Redemption through the blood of
Christ "who was *foreknown* indeed before the foundation of the world,
but *was manifested at the end of the times for your sake*, who through
him are believers in God, that raised him from the dead, and gave him
glory; so that your faith and hope might be in God" (1 Pet. 1:20-21).
Although the plan of redemption through Christ was foreknown, Christ
was manifested at the time set by the Father (Gal. 4:2) in the fullness
of time (Gal. 4:4). His manifestation "at the end of the times" was in
fulfillment, therefore, of God's purpose. The manifestation which resulted in the establishment of the church, and our being in Christ
where are all spiritual blessings (Eph. 1:3, 7), is the result of God's
eternal purpose. It was His eternal purpose that those who are in Christ
be sons of God and heirs according to promise (Gal. 3:26-29). Redemption in Christ is not a minor thing in the purpose and plan of God,
but is at their heart.

Second, the "mystery of his will" has been made known and it
concerned what God had purposed in Christ "unto a dispensation of
the fullness of the times, to sum up all things in Christ" (Eph. 1:9-10).

Mystery *here refers to God's plan to unite all things in*

*Christ (cf. [Eph.] 3:3-4; 5:32; 6:19). God's purposes of recon-
ciliation, revealed to Paul by special revelation (3:3), are
made known to all Christians through the preached message.
More precisely, what God has **set forth in Christ** is his plan for
the redemption of the universe, a plan now unfolding in history.
Fullness is a difficult word, which here probably refers to the
completion (cf. the use of **pleromatos** in Gal. 4:4) of the suc-
cessive stages or periods of redemptive history (cf. 1 Peter
1:20). The scope of God's plan is all-embracing, being nothing
less than the ultimate conclusion of all things in subjection to
Christ.[1]*

*Having mentioned the secret (9a), the Apostle describes its
unfolding. First, it is centered in Christ (**in him,** 9c). Secondly
(10), it is executed and revealed in the fullness of times (10a),
i.e., in the Messianic age. Before the Incarnation there was a
succession of periods; but they were incomplete, without harmony, unless they were seen as preparing the way for a period
which would make them an harmonious whole (cf. Gal. 4:4).
Hence the Divine secret was a 'dispensation' (10a), i.e., a sys-
tematic arrangement.[2]*

A mystery can refer to something which cannot be discerned by
man's reason, but must be revealed by God. It can refer to something
which is not known to someone, regardless of why they have not
known it, i.e., because it was unrevealed or because they did not see
and understand what was revealed. It can refer to some *aspect* of a revealed plan which was either not revealed, or only dimly revealed.
Does Paul mean that the gospel age, the age of redemption in Jesus
Christ, the present church age, was a mystery which was not at all
prophesied by the prophets? He did not mean this, for this would have
contradicted other passages of Scripture. How could Christ have come
to fulfill the law and the prophets if they did not prophecy His work
which He actually did while on earth (Matt. 5:17-18)? How could He
have said time and time again, and how could the Gospels have repeatedly stated, that thus and so fulfilled the Scriptures? How could
the scriptures have foretold that He must first suffer and then enter into

---

[1] Michael R. Weed, *Ephesians* (The Living Word Commentary), pages 126-127.
[2] Orchard, *Catholic Commentary*, page 1121.

His glory (Luke 24:25-27)? How could the scriptures have foretold His suffering, death, resurrection, and the proclamation of His message if these things were not prophesied (Luke 24:44-47; Isa. 53)? How could His present reign as king and priest be predicted and yet not predicted (Psa. 110:1-4; Acts 2:34-36; Heb. 8:1-4)?

Paul made clear that the gospel which he preached was promised and prophesied. "...the gospel of God, which *he promised afore through his prophets in the holy scriptures*, concerning his Son, who was born of the seed of David according to the flesh, who was declared to be the Son of God with power, according to the spirit of holiness, by the resurrection from the dead; even Jesus Christ our Lord" (Rom. 1:1-4). "But now apart from the law a righteousness of God hath been manifested, *being witnessed by the law and the prophets*; even the righteousness of God through faith in Jesus Christ unto all them that believe" (Rom. 3:21-22). If the gospel and the time when men are justified by faith in Jesus Christ were not prophesied, the prophets could not have borne witness to them. Even in speaking of the revelation of the mystery, Paul showed it had been prophesied. "Now to him that is able to establish you according to my gospel and the preaching of Jesus Christ, according to the revelation of the mystery which hath been kept in silence through times eternal, but now is manifested, *and by the scriptures of the prophets*, according to the commandment of the eternal God, is made known unto all the nations unto obedience of faith" (Rom. 16:25-26). It is obvious that Paul is not saying that nothing was known of the mystery in the days of the Old Testament prophets. The revealed relationship between Christ and the church is called a great mystery (Eph. 5:32). The salvation which we find now in Christ was prophesied by the prophets (1 Pet. 1:10-12). This makes clear that the mystery of God's will (Eph. 1:9) did not mean that nothing was known about the gospel and the gospel age, the church age, before the first century. The mystery of God's will in redemption began very early in the Old Testament to be revealed, although revelation flowered forth in its fullness in Jesus Christ and His new covenant, which covenant was prophesied (Jer. 31:31-34; Heb. 8:5-13; 12:24; 13:20).

What did Paul mean by the mystery concerning the Gentiles? "For this cause I Paul, the prisoner of Christ Jesus in behalf of you Gentiles, —if so be that ye have heard of the dispensation of that grace of God which was given me to you-ward; how that by revelation was made known unto me the mystery, as I wrote before in few words, whereby, when ye read, ye can perceive my understanding in the mystery of Christ; which in other generations was not made known unto the sons of men, as it hath now been revealed unto his holy apostles and prophets in the Spirit; to wit, that the Gentiles are fellow-heirs, and fellow-members of the body, and fellow-partakers of the promise in Christ Jesus through the gospel" (Eph. 3:1-6).The mystery of which Paul spoke in Ephesians 1:10, in so far as it pertains to men on earth, is identified by Paul. For the very mystery concerning which he had written "before in few words" (Eph. 3:3), is spelled out by saying that it referred to the complete equality of Jew and Gentile in Christ, "fellow-heirs, and fellow-members of the body, and fellow-partakers of the promise in Christ Jesus through the gospel" (Eph. 3:6). Furthermore, Paul did not say that nothing was known of this before, but that it was not in other generations "made known unto the sons of men, *as it hath now been revealed* unto his holy apostles and prophets in the Spirit" (Eph. 3:5). There is a fullness of revelation in the new covenant, about this matter, which goes beyond the revelation in the Old Testament. It was known that the Messiah would also bless the Gentiles. The seed of Abraham was to bless all nations (Gen. 22:17-18). "And now saith Jehovah that formed me from the womb to be his servant, to bring Jacob again to him, and that Israel be gathered unto him (for I am honorable in the eyes of Jehovah, and my God is become my strength); yea, he said, It is too light a thing that thou shouldest be my servant to raise up the tribes of Jacob, and to restore the preserved of Israel: I will also give thee for a light to the Gentiles, that thou mayest be my salvation unto the end of the earth." (Isa. 49:4-6). This servant was not Israel, but was to do a work for Israel and for the Gentiles. Furthermore, the fact that God would make a new covenant (Jer. 31:31-34), and that a new priesthood was to come into existence (Psa. 110:4; Heb. 7:1-17), show that the old law which was the middle wall of partition (Eph. 3:13-16) between Jew and Gentile was to be abolished. In fact, Isaiah's prophecy was a command for gospel preachers to preach to the Gentiles (Acts 13:46-48). Something was known about the Gentiles and the gospel, but the fullness of the revelation concerning their *complete equality* in Christ with the Jews had not been revealed in the past *as it is now revealed.*

The Kingdom Prophesied for the Second Coming?

There are premillennialists who maintain that the Old Testament predicted that the kingdom would be set up at the second coming of Christ.

> *As far as the Old Testament foreview is concerned, Israel's hope of glory was the glorious return of Christ in His second advent. They were promised a share in His glorious govern-ment of the earth during the kingdom.*[1]
>
> *The viewpoint of Old Testament prophecies is that saints on earth at the time of the second advent will enter the millennial kingdom **in the flesh**...*[2]

Israel's hope of glory is her exalted position in the millennial kingdom. Walvoord makes clear that he believes the Old Testament predicted that the kingdom would be established in connection with the second coming of Christ.

> *...the second coming is determinative in tracing the future course of Gentiles and Israel in the world, the resurrection of the righteous, and the fulfillment of prophecies concerning the kingdom of God on earth.*[3]

He cited the following as examples of prophecies of the second coming and the establishment of the kingdom: Deut. 30:3-9; Psa. 2:24; 50; 72; 96; 110:2; Isa. 11:1-12:6; Daniel 7:13-14; 2:44; Zechariah 2:10-11; 14:3-11.[4]

Prophecies which teach that Christ would establish His kingdom after the second advent cannot also teach that He would or could establish His kingdom in connection with the first coming. *Christ could not come in His first coming to establish a kingdom which was predicted for His second coming.* Therefore, the prophesied kingdom could not have been at hand when John, Jesus, and the apostles preached that the kingdom was at hand, i.e., nearby in point of time (Matt. 3:2; 4:17, 23; 9:35; 10:7). Since the time was not in connection with the first coming, the time for the kingdom to be at hand was not fulfilled when Jesus

---

[1] Walvoord, *The Millennial Kingdom*, page 239.
[2] *Ibid.,* page 242.
[3] *Ibid.,* page 264.
[4] *Ibid.,* pages 265-267.

preached: *"The time is fulfilled, and the kingdom of God is at hand;*
repent ye, and believe in the gospel"* (Mark 1:15). One has to have a
veil over his heart when he reads the New Testament to fail to realize
that the kingdom of Old Testament prophecy was then and there nearby in point of time (Compare 2 Cor. 3:12-16). Take off Israel's veil of
blindness and read the Old Testament in the light of the revelation
which Christ made in the New Testament.

A Prophesied Age Which Premillennialists Overlook

The premillennialists insist that they interpret prophecy literally
and that those who oppose them try to escape contradictions and prob-
lems in their position by spiritualizing prophecy. As far as I know,
they maintain that but one kingdom age for the future was prophesied
by the Old Testament prophets. As a matter of fact, the literal interpretation of all kingdom prophecies leads to the position that *four* different kingdoms were prophesied by the prophets!

First, the rule of Christ on the throne of David. In commenting on
2 Samuel 7:12-16, Walvoord wrote:

> *By the term "kingdom" there is reference to David's politi-
> cal kingdom over Israel. By the expression "for ever" it is sig-
> nified that the Davidic authority and Davidic kingdom or rule
> over Israel shall never be taken from David's posterity. The
> right to rule will never be transferred to another family, and its
> arrangement is designed for eternal perpetuity. Whatever its
> changing form, temporary interruptions, or chastisements, the
> line of David will always have the right to rule over Israel and
> will, in fact, exercise this privilege. This then, in brief, is the
> covenant of God with David.*[1]

Christ was to rule on David's throne (Isa. 9:7).

Second, the Old Testament prophesied that Christ would reign as
king and priest at the right hand of God (Psa. 110:1-4). If this prophe-
sies His present reign, then the gospel age with Christ as king and
priest was prophesied and premillennialism is wrong. If it does not refer to the gospel age, it must refer to a future reign. It will not be the
millennial reign, and there seems to be no place to put it. If the kingdom which was at hand in the first century (Matt. 3:2) was postponed,
perhaps the reign on the throne at God's right hand was totally can-

---

[1] *Ibid.,* page 196.

celled. Walvoord splits up the Psalm 110:1 reign and the 110:2 reign; the *first* being the reign in heaven and the *second* the reign on earth after the second coming. This contradicts his position that the church age was not prophesied.

Third, although the Old Testament did not prophesy it, according to premillennialism it was in God's eternal purpose to have a church age (the kingdom of God's son, Col. 1:13) before He established the kingdom prophesied by the prophets. The unprophesied one came before the prophesied one. But Walvoord said the church reign was prophesied in Psalm 110:1.

Fourth, if one gives a literal interpretation to all the kingdom prophecies, somewhere in the future David must reign over Israel again, and this time forever. Ezekiel foretold the coming reign of David, and unless the premillennialist "stoops," to spiritualizing and makes this *spiritual* David (Christ), he must believe that though Christ will reign on David's throne for a thousand years (according to their theory), David will take over and rule forever over Israel. Although the New Testament spoke of Christ being on this throne forever (Luke 1:32-33), if premillennialism is right, Christ must give place to David. "The word of Jehovah came again unto me, saying, And thou, son of man, take thee one stick, and write upon it, For Judah, and for the children of Israel his companions: then take another stick, and write upon it, For Joseph, the stick of Ephraim, and for all the house of Israel his companions: and join them for thee one to another into one stick, that they may become one in thy hand. And when the children of thy people shall speak unto thee, saying, Wilt thou not show us what thou meanest by these? say unto them, Thus saith the Lord Jehovah: Behold, I will take the stick of Joseph, which is in the hand of Ephraim, and the tribes of Israel his companions; and I will put them with it, even with the stick of Judah, and make them one stick, and they shall be one in my hand. And the sticks whereon thou writest shall be in thy hand before their eyes. And say unto them, Thus saith the Lord Jehovah: Behold, I will take the children of Israel from among the nations, whither they are gone, and will gather them on every side, and bring them into their own land: and I will make them one nation in the land, upon the mountains of Israel, and one king shall be king to them all; and they shall be no more two nations, neither shall they be divided into two kingdoms any more at all; neither shall they defile themselves any more with their idols, nor with their detestable things, nor with any of their transgressions; but I will save them out of all their dwelling-places, wherein they have sinned, and will cleanse them: so shall they be my people, and I will be their God. And my servant David shall be king over them, and they all shall have one shepherd: they shall also walk in mine ordinances, and observe my statutes, and do them. And they shall dwell in the land that I have given unto Jacob my servant, wherein your fathers dwelt; and they shall dwell therein, they, and their children, and their children's children, forever: and David my servant shall be their prince forever. Moreover I will make a covenant of peace with them; it shall be an everlasting covenant with them; and I will place them, and multiply them, and will set my sanctuary in the midst of them forevermore. My tabernacle also shall be with them; and I will be their God, and they shall be my people. And the nations shall know that I am Jehovah that sanctifieth Israel, when my sanctuary shall be in the midst of them for evermore" (Ezekiel 37:15-28).

If one interprets this passage to mean spiritual David (Christ), what is wrong with interpreting the people of God (Israel) as spiritual Israel? Walvoord gives it a literal interpretation without realizing that this interpretation contradicts the promise that it would be Christ who ruled on this throne over Israel.

> *According to Ezekiel 37:24, after Israel is regathered to their ancient land, David is going to be raised from the dead to be king over Israel, and God will make a covenant of peace with His people (Ezek. 37:26). To be fulfilled also is the prediction of the angel to Mary in Luke 1:31-33 in regard to Jesus: "He shall be great, and shall be called the Son of the Most High; and the Lord shall give unto him the throne of his father David: and he shall reign over the house of Jacob forever; and of his kingdom there shall be no end.*[1]

With both Christ and David on the throne of David ruling over Israel, the throne is certainly going to be crowded!!!

First, there cannot be two thrones for Ezekiel said there would be "one nation in the land," and "one king shall be king to them all; and they shall be no more two nations, neither shall they be divided into two kingdoms any more at all" (Ezek. 37:22).

---

[1] *Ibid.,* page 274.

Second, God said it again: "And my servant David shall be king over them; and they all shall have one shepherd... and David my servant shall be their prince forever" (Ezek. 37:24-25). Is it not clear that David also is the shepherd, or will David be king and Christ be the shepherd?

Third, an "everlasting covenant" of peace will be made with them, and God's tabernacle and sanctuary will be in their midst for evermore (Ezek. 37:26-28). Just when will this reign be? Since the millennial kingdom is but a thousand years, perhaps David will reign in eternity over Israel and be their only king and shepherd. The fact that the New Testament says nothing about it should not bother the premillennialists since he does not allow the New Testament to shape his interpretation of Old Testament prophecies anyway!

Walvoord said the reign would be in the millennium, but how can this be since it is Christ who is to rule over Israel from David's throne?

The Old Testament prophesied but one reign of the Christ. It prophesied it as the reign on David's throne, the reign at God's right hand, as David (the type) reigning over God's people, as mediator of the new covenant (Jer. 31:31-34; Heb. 8:5-13; 9:15; 12:24), and as the everlasting kingdom which would not be shaken and taken out of the way (Dan. 2:44; Heb. 12:26-28). Since the new covenant is in operation today, and since Christ reigns at God's right hand until all His enemies are conquered, it is obvious that the kingdom prophecies are fulfilled in Christ's present reign. This was the reign which John (Matt. 3:2) and Jesus preached was at hand (Matt. 3:2; 4:17, 24; 10:7).

CHAPTER 3:
THE NEW TESTAMENT
ON THE NATURE OF THE KINGDOM

What the New Testament teaches about the nature of the kingdom must be decisive for the Christian. It would be an arrogant Christian, whose arrogance would disqualify him from being a disciple of Christ, who would consciously say that his own uninspired interpretations of the Old Testament prophecies of the kingdom must be the standard in the light of which the New Testament teaching on the kingdom must be understood. What one would not do consciously, he must exercise care lest he act as if such an attitude is right.

First, the Holy Spirit, who through the Old Testament prophecies made the predictions concerning Christ and His mission, is the same Holy Spirit who revealed the New Testament and gives us the meaning of any prophecies which are interpreted by Him in the New Testament. Furthermore, we must not interpret any prophecies so as to contradict anything which the Spirit teaches in the New Testament (1 Pet. 1:10-12).

Second, as disciples of Christ we must accept what He says about Old Testament prophecy and about the kingdom of heaven. We must learn from Him, and not assume that we can teach Him.

What does the New Testament teach concerning the kingdom of God? Surely if we consider all the passages in the New Testament we shall be able to learn the meaning of the kingdom promises of the Old Testament. Surely the greater light which came through Jesus Christ will enlighten us. In this chapter we shall try to mention briefly some of the passages on the kingdom in the New Testament. Some of them will be discussed in detail in other places in this book.

King of the Jews

The angel Gabriel, in announcing to Mary the conception of Jesus, said that "the Lord God shall give unto him the throne of his father David: and he shall reign over the house of Jacob forever; and of his kingdom there shall be no end" (Luke 1:32-33). The throne was not given to Him at that moment, nor at the moment of His birth, although the wise men asked: "Where is he that is born King of the Jews?" (Matt. 2:2). He was born under the law (Gal. 4:4), but He did not at that moment ascend to His throne. He had the right to the throne, and was promised the throne. However, when He entered into His personal ministry He preached that the kingdom was *at hand, not in hand* (Matt. 4:17). Early in His ministry, Nathanael said: "Rabbi, thou art the Son of God; thou art King of Israel" (John 1:49). However, even after this the apostles preached that the kingdom was *at hand* (Matt. 10:7).

John the Baptist and the Kingdom

John the Baptist preached "saying, Repent ye; for the kingdom of heaven is at hand" (Matt. 3:2). What kingdom was at hand? The pre-millennialists agree that the kingdom prophesied by the prophets was the one which John announced as at hand. They are right about this, but they are wrong in that they have a misconception of the kingdom. R.H. Boll said the Jews to whom John preached rightly understood the nature of the kingdom.

> *John took it for granted that it was understood; never a word of explanation was given, so far as the record shows; and never a question or dispute arose between John and his countrymen as to the nature of the Kingdom. To the Jews that announcement meant but one thing. The promise of the Messianic Kingdom, with all it involved—the appearance of the Great King of David's line, the destruction of the Gentile world power; the deliverance and national restoration of Israel, and her exaltation to earthly sovereignty; the promises God made to the fathers, and the prophets' visions of the future glory of the People, the Land, the City, and the Kingdom "in that day" — had imbedded itself in the very hearts of the people. They did not indeed understand **everything** the Scriptures had foretold concerning the Kingdom; and it will be seen that in certain particulars they had erred in their conception. But they were not ignorant of the nature of the Kingdom promises.[1]*
>
> *All this we mention merely to show what expectation was existing in Israel at the time of John's announcement, and how the very words John used had their common and current meaning among the people. The burden of proof would certainly lie wholly and heavily with any man who would maintain that this kingdom of John's announcement was a thing entirely different*

---

[1] R.H. Boll, *The Kingdom of God*, page 60.

from that which Israel was expecting. The very suggestion that God would so trifle with the hope of the people, and by adopting their own language without explanation would leave them under so fundamental a mistake; yea, and would base His call to repentance upon this mistake, and would so confirm them in it, is quite repugnant and unworthy of God, the more so when it is remembered that their kingdom expectations were legitimately derived from the language of their scriptures. But if the Jewish expectations had been utterly wrong (which, as we have seen in our former articles, was not the case), even then a sense of justice would suggest that God would not have left the people under such a misapprehension without a clear protest and correction.[1]

God was not using Israel's "own language" when He announced the kingdom was at hand. He was using language which *He* had used in the Old Testament when *He* prophesied that the kingdom would be established. That which He had long promised was now at hand. Furthermore, John did make clear that they had a fundamental misconception of the kingdom and that Israel as a nation was not guaranteed a place in it. Therefore, Israel's view that Israel must have the place of pre-eminence in the kingdom was false. The Gospels are filled with instances where the Jewish misconceptions of the Messiah and the kingdom are corrected, and one can easily find them unless he wears a veil over his heart when he reads the Old and the New Testaments. Does anyone think that the Jews, who have a veil on their hearts when they read the Old Testament, understand the nature of the kingdom (2 Cor. 3:12-16)? In fact, the Jewish misconception of the kingdom and Israel's position in it were essential parts of this veil.

John corrects several misconceptions which some Jews had of the kingdom.

First, John said; "Repent ye; *for* the kingdom of heaven is at hand" (Matt. 3:2). The idea of some of the Jews was quite different. John said for them to repent *because* of the nearness of the kingdom, but he did not say that if they repented it would *bring* the kingdom. The idea of some of the Jews was: "if Israel repented but one day, the Son of David would immediately come."[2] Klausner said; "There is a common

---

[1] *Ibid.,* pages 61-62.
[2] Quoted by Edersheim, *The Life and Times of Jesus the Messiah*, page 272.

idea in the *Talmud* that King-Messiah's kingdom would come, or be hastened, as a result of repentance: 'If Israel were to repent, they would straightway be redeemed,' and 'Great is repentance which hastens the redemption.'"[1] Rabbis said: "If Israel would repent only one day, the Son of David would come forthwith... If Israel would observe only one sabbath according to the ordinance, forthwith would the Son of David come... All the states are passed, and all depends solely on repentance and good works."[2]

This position of the Jews was false. Their repentance had nothing to do with the coming of the kingdom, although their being a part of it when it did come did depend on their repentance. If they did not repent, they would be eliminated. God did not depend on them to establish the kingdom. The kingdom was at hand whether they believed or not. This was the reason for their being called to repentance, but their repentance was not the cause or the condition of the coming of the kingdom. The premillennialists share this false idea of the Jews. They think that because Israel did not repent, the kingdom was postponed. If Israel will repent, the kingdom will come speedily. As Boll put it:

> The only thing that ever stood between Israel and her glorious promises, kingdom and all, was her sinful condition. That removed, every other promise must necessarily be fulfilled to them, and that speedily. Whether there had been any formal **offer of the kingdom** made to them, and, upon their rejection of it the same was withdrawn and postponed, is no essential matter. But if **salvation** was offered to the nation by Jesus, all else was implied therein as a matter of course; and if **that** was nationally rejected, the fulfillment of all their prophetic hopes was thereby made impossible, and automatically deferred until the time when the nation would turn to acknowledge Jesus Christ and be forgiven.[3]

Israel's rebellion did not lead to the postponement of the kingdom, but to Israel's rejection (Psa. 2; Acts 4:25-29). John corrected their mistake that it was necessary for them to repent in order for the kingdom to come. The coming of the kingdom did not depend on Israel's

---

[1] Joseph Klausner, *Jesus of Nazareth: His Life, Times, and Teaching*, page 246.
[2] Plummer, *Commentary on the Gospel According to St. Luke*, page 89.
[3] Boll, *The Kingdom of God*, page 86.

repentance.

Boll wrote:

> *Since the kingdom-promise was national, the preparatory repentance must of course also be national... The announcement of the kingdom thus became the basis of the call to repentance. In it also is found the first covered intimation that God would reject the fleshly seed of Abraham if they failed to repent and would raise Him up another people (Matthew 3:9).*[1]

How could John have made clearer that the kingdom promise did not depend on national Israel for its fulfillment? Boll understood, although he did not draw the right conclusion from it, that the *basis* for the call to repentance was the fact the kingdom was at hand. There was no intimation that the basis for the coming of the kingdom was the national repentance of Israel. Furthermore, since Boll recognized that God would reject Abraham's fleshly seed, if they did not repent, and raise up another people, why cannot he understand that the kingdom promise was fulfilled? That which was then *at* hand, before too many years was not *at* hand but *in* hand and Christ reigned at God's right hand (Acts 2:34-35). His reign started over thousands of literal Israelites, although they had to become *spiritual* Israel through the new birth in order to be in His kingdom. Repentance was involved in their *coming into* the kingdom (Acts 2:38).

Second, John corrected in three clear and emphatic ways their misconception that in the very nature of the case physical Israel must have not only a place, but the place of prominence in the kingdom. John said that unless they repented they would not even be in the kingdom. One has to read what John said with a veil over his heart not to understand it.

(1) To those who prided themselves on being sons of Abraham, but were not penitent, John said: "Ye offspring of vipers, who warned you to flee from the wrath to come? Bring forth therefore fruit worthy of repentance: and think not to say within yourselves, We have Abraham to our father: for I say unto you, that God is able of these stones to raise up children unto Abraham" (Matt. 3:7-9).

> *The very presence of his hearers at this call to, and baptism of, repentance, gave point to his words. Did they who, notwith-*

---

[1] *Ibid.*, page 63.

standing their sins, lived in such security of carelessness and self-righteousness, really understand and fear the final conse-quences of resistance to the coming Kingdom? If so, theirs must be a repentance not only in profession, but of heart and mind, such as would yield fruit, both good and visible. Or else did they imagine that, according to the common notion of the time, the vials of wrath were to be poured out only on the Gen-tiles, while they, as Abraham's children, were sure of escape— in the words of the Talmud, that "the night" (Is. 21:12) was "only to the nations of the world, but the morning to Israel"?

For, no principle was more fully established in the popular conviction, than that all Israel had part in the world to come (Sanh. 10.1), and this, specifically, because of their connection with Abraham. This appears not only from the New Testament, from Philo, and Josephus, but from many Rabbinic passages. "The merits of the Fathers," is one of the commonest phrases in the mouth of the Rabbis. Abraham was represented as sitting at the gate of Gehenna, to deliver any Israelite who otherwise might have been consigned to its terrors. In fact, by their de-scent from Abraham, all the children of Israel were nobles, in-finitely higher than any proselytes. "What," exclaims the Tal-mud, "shall the born Israelite stand upon the earth, and prose-lyte be in heaven?" In fact, the ships on the sea were preserved through the merit of Abraham; the rain descended on account of it. For his sake alone had Moses been allowed to ascend into heaven, and to receive the Law; for his sake the sin of the gold-en calf had been forgiven; his righteousness had on many oc-casions been the support of Israel's cause; Daniel had been heard for the sake of Abraham; nay, his merit availed even for the wicked. In its extravagance the Midrash thus apostrophizes Abraham: "If they thy children were even (morally) dead bod-ies, without bloodvessels or bones, thy merit would avail for them!"[1]

But some said: "If Israel repent, they will be redeemed; if not, they will not be redeemed."[2] "If Israel will not repent they will not be de-

---

[1] Edersheim, *Life and Times of Jesus the Messiah*, pages 270-272.
[2] bSanhedrin, 97b.

livered, Israel only repents because of distress, oppression, exile, and lack of sustenance. Israel does not repent quite sincerely until Elijah of blessed memory comes."[1] But Elijah came, and most of Israel did not repent.

Did not John correct their misconception and make it crystal clear that God does not depend on Abraham's literal seed to fulfill His promises concerning the kingdom? The kingdom was going to come whether they repented or not, and the kingdom did not have to be made up of literal Jews. God did not raise up children unto Abraham from the literal stones, but this statement of John is positive proof that God did not depend on literal Israel. God gave the kingdom to a nation bringing forth the fruits thereof, and crushed the rejecters (Matt. 21:41-45).

(2) John also made clear that they had to repent to be a part of the kingdom, and that their rejection of the kingdom would result in their rejection and not in the postponement of the kingdom. The kingdom was at hand no matter what they did or did not do. What if they did not repent? Did John suggest that the kingdom would be postponed? No. The nearness of the kingdom was the reason they needed to repent, but the nearness of the kingdom did not *depend* on their repentance (Matt. 3:2). What would happen? They would be eliminated. "And even now the axe lieth at the root of the trees: every tree therefore that bringeth not forth good fruit is hewn down, and cast into the fire" (Matt. 3:10). Repent or perish. Turn or burn. Bring forth fruit or be chopped down. The idea that the axe was laid or lies at the root of the trees indicated the nearness of the judgment on the impenitent. "The notion is that of a woodman touching a tree with the edge of his axe to measure his blow before he lifts his arm for the sweep which fells it."[2] Israel at times had been likened unto a fig tree (Jer. 24:3-10; Hosea 9:10). The barren fig tree which Christ withered was a symbol of unfruitful Israelites (Matt. 21:19). After warning some that unless "ye repent, ye shall all likewise perish"—and the context indicated that it included a physical perishing (Luke 13:1-5), Jesus "spake this parable; A certain man had a fig tree planted in his vineyard; and he came seeking fruit thereon, and found none. And he said unto the vinedresser, Behold, these three years I come seeking fruit on this fig tree, and find none: cut it down; why

---

[1] Pirke de R. Eliezer, ch. 43, end, quoted by Jack. P. Lewis, *The Gospel According to Matthew* (Living Word Commentary), Vol. 1, pages 54-55.

[2] F.W. Farrar, *Luke*, page 85.

doth it also cumber the ground? And he answering saith unto him, Lord, let it alone this year also, till I shall dig about it, and dung it: and if it bear fruit thenceforth, well; but if not, thou shalt cut it down" (Luke 13:6-9). Our Lord in His personal ministry had time after time looked for fruit from Israel, but found it not. Instead of chopping it down at the end of His personal ministry, the gospel was preached to Israel for about forty years after His death, ascension, and coronation. God did not want Israel as a shade tree but as a fruit tree. It was not preserved for ornamental value if it did not bear fruit. Later on they were reminded, after the enthronement of Christ (Acts 2:34-36), that unless they accepted the prophet like unto Moses they would be destroyed from among the people (Acts 3:22-23). They were cut off from covenant relationship because of their unbelief, and to be grafted in they must believe in the same Christ and the same gospel their ancestors rejected in the first century (Rom. 11:20-23).

(3) The illustration of the unfruitful tree made clear that there would be a separation and judgment brought about by Christ with reference even to Israel—John was specifically talking to Jews. The good tree is kept; the unfruitful tree is cut down and burned (Matt. 3:10). John said the same thing in using the illustration of the wheat and the chaff. "Whose fan is in his hand, and he will thoroughly cleanse his threshing-floor; and he will gather his wheat into the garner, but the chaff he will burn up with unquenchable fire" (Matt. 3:12), The Messiah comes with a fan in His hand which will separate Israelites with some being saved and some being lost. Christ was not to indiscriminately put all Israelites into His garner. Only the penitent would go into it. The Jewish view of the kingdom was that all Israel would be gathered by the Messiah into His kingdom or garner. But Jesus came to do a work of discrimination in which He would discriminate between the wheat and the chaff. The wheat he would accept and the chaff He would reject. He would "thoroughly cleanse his threshing-floor" (Matt. 3:12). "The examination and the discrimination will be complete."[1] The nation, as a nation, would not enter in. Only the wheat would be gathered into His garner. Only the penitent would enter the kingdom (Matt. 3:2). And this was stressed after the church was established, for repentance and remission of sins in Jesus' name began first

---

[1] John Broadus, *A Harmony of the Gospels*, page 52.

to be preached in Jerusalem (Luke 24:47; Acts 2:38). The work of separation, of some unto salvation and some unto judgment, was also proclaimed on Pentecost and thereafter. He reigned in the midst of His enemies, but would reign until all were conquered (Psa. 110:1-4; Acts 2:34-36). There was salvation for those who accepted Christ and judgment for those who did not (Acts 2:21, 35, 38). "Moses indeed said, A prophet shall the Lord God raise up unto you from among your brethren, like unto me; to him shall ye hearken in all things whatsoever he shall speak unto you. And it shall be, that every soul that shall not hearken to that prophet, shall be utterly destroyed from among the people. Yea and all the prophets from Samuel and them that followed after, as many as have spoken, they also told of these days. Ye are the sons of the prophets, and of the covenant which God made with your fathers, saying unto Abraham, And in thy seed shall all the families of the earth be blessed. Onto you first God, having raised up his Servant, sent him to bless you, in turning away every one of you from your iniquities" (Acts 3:22-26). Those who hearkened to Christ became a part of His covenant, and those of Israel who did not hearken were cut off because of their unbelief. If they are grafted in, it must be through accepting the gospel which those who are cut off rejected (Rom. 11:20-24).

How could John have made it clearer that Israel was not to be given a place in the kingdom on the basis of her fleshly relationship to Abraham?

They may not have liked what John said, but it is difficult to see how they could have misunderstood what he said. And it is difficult to see how premillennialists today can misunderstand the bearing of these statements of John on the nature of the kingdom which was at hand. Since the kingdom which was at hand was throne prophesied by the prophets, it is clear from John's statements that in order for that kingdom to be established Israel did not even have to be in it. Further, she would not be in it unless she repented.

Klausner understood that John made it clear that God did not depend on the nation of Israel to establish His kingdom. With reference to John's statement about God being able to raise up children unto Abraham from these stones, he said:

> *This is an anti-nationalist touch omitted by Mark, yet it is none the less genuine: had not the movement from the very beginning been impregnated with some seed, no matter how mi-*

*nute, of anti-Jewish nationalism, there never could have arisen
the religion which so definitely tears away national barriers.
Ex nihilo nihil fit.[1]*

Klausner recognized that John did not teach that a nationalistic
kingdom was at hand in which Israel must of necessity occupy the exalted position. John taught that a kingdom was at hand which in no
way depended on physical Israel for its establishment and existence. It
could exist as the Messiah's kingdom whether any literal Israelites
were in it or not. That John and Jesus did not fulfill Israel's nationalistic hopes is clear from the New Testament. Unbelieving Jews understand it, why cannot believing premillennialists understand it?

Third, John taught that Jesus would baptize in the Holy Spirit
(Matt. 3:11). Walvoord said: "The baptism of the Spirit which is the
subject of predictive prophecy in the Gospels and in Acts 1 finds its
first fulfillment in Acts 2... it becomes apparent that a new thing has
been formed—the body of Christ. It did not exist before Pentecost, as
there was no work of the baptism of the Spirit to form it."[2] Walvoord
is saying, although he may not recognize that it is involved in his
statements, that the baptism predicted by John in Matthew 3:11 began
to be fulfilled on Pentecost and it resulted in the creation of the church.
In effect, therefore, John was predicting the establishment of the
church for he predicted what happened on Pentecost and that then the
church was formed in connection with the baptism of the Spirit. The
formation or creation of the body of Christ on earth did take place on
Pentecost. The Spirit was involved in the creation of the body of Christ
on earth, for I believe that the apostles and around one hundred and
twenty (Acts 1:15) were miraculously set in the church by the Spirit,
by Christ, or by Christ through the Spirit. I do not think that any except
the apostles, however, were baptized in the Spirit on Pentecost. I have
discussed this in *The Hub of the Bible*, *Pat Boone and the Gift of
Tongues*, and *The Holy Spirit and the Christian*. John by predicting
what happened on Pentecost, and by Walvoord saying that the Spirit
then formed the church, one must conclude that Walvoord should
agree that John was in effect predicting the establishment of the

---

[1] Klausner, *Jesus of Nazareth*, page 246. The Latin phrase at the end means "Out
of nothing, nothing comes."

[2] Walvoord, *The Millennial Kingdom*, page 226.

church. However, John said the kingdom was at hand. In promising that Christ would baptize in the Spirit, and since that work started in around three years after the events in Matthew 3, John was saying that the establishment of the church was at hand. But John could not have announced as at hand the church and the kingdom if they were two different reigns of God and Christ. The kingdom was at hand, the time was at hand when children would be raised up as Abraham's seed, when the unfruitful trees were cut down, when the baptism of the Spirit would come, and when the wheat would begin to be garnered and the chaff rejected. All these things harmonize with one another. They harmonize with the kingdom established on Pentecost, but not with the kingdom envisioned by the premillennialists Therefore, the premillennialists are wrong.

Fourth, what John preached concerning the nature of the kingdom harmonizes with what John taught concerning the nature of the Messiah's mission. This mission involved Christ's being the Lamb of God "that taketh away the sin of the world" (John 1:29). The Messiah's mission involved not merely the proclamation of the nearness of the kingdom but also the nearness of the cross. Christ went to the crown by way of the cross. He first suffered, and then entered into His glory as was prophesied (Luke 24:25-27).

John's teaching is not only a proclamation of the nearness of the kingdom but it also included powerful protests against the Jewish misconception of the nature of the kingdom.

Fifth, Jesus said: "The law and the prophets were until John: from that time the gospel of the kingdom of God is preached, and every man entereth violently into it" (Luke 16:16). How was it preached? It was preached as "at hand" by John (Matt. 3:2), by Jesus (Matt. 4:17), and by the apostles (Matt. 10:7). To "publish abroad the kingdom of God" was to teach that it is "come nigh unto you" (Luke 9:60, 10:9, 11). There is not the remotest suggestion that the kingdom which was at hand was different from the one which had been promised to Jesus as the Son of God and the son of David (Luke 1:32-33; Matt. 2:2).

Sixth, John was dealing with a people whose expectations of the Messiah's advent were high. "And as the people were in expectation, and all men reasoned in their hearts concerning John, whether haply he were the Christ" (Luke 3:15). It is obvious that they had expectations concerning the Messiah and the kingdom, because John had preached the kingdom was at hand (Matt. 3:2; Luke 3:3, 18), and he denied that he was the Messiah (Luke 3:16-17). What did he tell people who were in expectation? He told all of them to repent. (a) He warned some not to trust in their relationship to Abraham, and that the axe was at the root of the trees (Luke 3:7-9). (b) To the multitudes he said to share with those in need (Luke 3:10-11). (c) To the publicans—the collectors of Roman taxes, he said: "Extort no more than that which is appointed you" (Luke 3:13). (d) "And soldiers (margin: soldiers on service) also asked him, saying, And we, what must we do? And he said unto them, Extort from no man by violence, neither accuse any one wrongfully; and be content with your wages" (Luke 3:14). None of this hinted of any violent revolution, or carnal kingdom being at hand, though all of it spoke of a revolution, a drastic change, in the attitude and actions of people in moral and spiritual ways.

Nothing in John's preaching harmonizes with the premillennial view of the kingdom but is in harmony with the spiritual kingdom which Christ actually established when He ascended to the throne at God's right hand (Acts 2:34-36).

The Temptation and the Nature of the Kingdom

There was a Rabbinical saying that: "The Holy One, blessed be His Name, does not elevate a man to dignity till He has first tried and searched him; and if he stands in temptation, then He raises him to dignity." However, they did not think of the Messiah as being assaulted or tempted by Satan, but of Satan being overwhelmed and defeated at the sight of the Messiah. Instead of being tempted by Satan on the pinnacle of the temple, a tradition said: "In the hour when King Messiah cometh, He standeth upon the roof of the Sanctuary, and proclaims to Israel, saying, Ye poor (suffering), the time of your redemption draweth nigh." The Gentiles come and submit themselves to the Messiah *and to Israel*. In fact, "every one in Israel shall have 2,800 servants."[1] Christ came to rescue men from sin, from bondage to Satan and the kingdom of darkness, and Satan endeavored in the temptation to change the nature of the mission of the Messiah. If the Messiah was successful in His coming, Satan would suffer irreparable loss. If Satan could change the nature of Christ's mission and work, He would defeat the Messiah. Satan had a kingdom (Matt. 12:26; 2 Cor. 4:4), and Christ

---

[1] Edersheim, *Life and Times of Jesus the Messiah*, Vol. 1, pages 292-293.

came to defeat Satan (Heb. 2:14-15). However, Satan would defeat Christ if Christ gave way to Satan's temptations. *It would be absurd to conclude that Satan's temptations had absolutely no relationship to the Messiah and His mission and therefore to the kingdom which He came to proclaim as at hand.* The devil wanted to change Christ's methods, mission, and kingdom, and to do it under the disguise of the world being won to Christ, and He being its king. Christ had been baptized by John, and the devil knew that shortly Christ would also proclaim that the kingdom was at hand (Matt. 4:17). What a victory for Satan if he could persuade Christ to take the wrong means to realize His goal! By perverting the means Satan could pervert the outcome, and the kingdom would not be of *heaven* but of the evil one. To bring in the kingdom of God Christ had to be in absolute submission to the will of God both as to the means to be utilized as well as the ends to be achieved. And submission to the will of God meant that He must go the way of the cross (Heb. 9:28). He must first suffer and then enter into His glory (Luke 24:25-27). The devil is hostile to the mission of the Messiah, therefore the temptations are an effort to defeat that mission. *The devil knew what Christ's mission was.*

In what ways are the temptations efforts of the devil to pervert, and thereby to destroy, the mission of Christ as He enters on His public ministry to proclaim the nearness of the kingdom and to make possible its establishment?

First, "And when he had fasted forty days and forty nights, he afterward hungered. And the tempter came and said unto him, If thou art the Son of God, command that these stones become bread. But he answered and said, It is written, Man shall not live by bread alone, but by every word that proceedeth out of the mouth of God" (Matt. 4:2-4). Christ was hungry. Why not use His miraculous power both to prove that He was God's Son, and to satisfy legitimate physical hunger? Later Christ multiplied the loaves and the fishes to feed the multitude. However, Christ left everything in the hand of God. If it was not God's time for His hunger to be fed, He was not going to use His miraculous power to feed Himself. He was not going to become impatient and despair because of His hunger. He had power to do it, but He would not exercise His power apart from the will of God. He could change the situation in a moment, and have bread, but He was not impatient, nor in despair; that He thought He had to take things in His own hands. He did not manifest "impatience under the suffering of hunger, which he was to sustain until God sent him supplies, which was therefore done at the best time by the ministry of angels. Our Lord would not shorten the assigned duration of his trial by taking his cause out of the hands of God."[1] ("His Spirit had driven Him into that wilderness. His circumstances were God-appointed; and where He so appoints them, He will support us in them, even as, in the failure of bread, He supported Israel by the manna (Deut. 8). And Jesus absolutely submitted to that Will of God by continuing in His present circumstances. To have set Himself free from what they implied, would have been *despair* of God, and rebellion."[2]

Does not this temptation relate not only to whether He is willing to wait on things to be accomplished in God's good time, but also to the nature of His mission? If He fell back on His miraculous power to supply His own needs, and to hasten the time when His hunger could be satisfied, would it not have been right to have used His miraculous power to feed people continually and to have extended His influence over them in order that He might not only establish, but especially enlarge very quickly His kingdom? Why not become the Bread King? It is a fact that God has created man with the need for physical bread to sustain physical life. Feeding the hungry is a part of a Christian's duty (Matt. 25:44-45). The Jews, as well as others, would have welcomed the Bread King. It was after He had fed the multitude with a few loaves and fishes that they wanted to take Him and by force make Him king (John 6:1-15). This would have been a short-cut to the kingdom indeed, but what sort of kingdom would it have been? It would not have been a kingdom composed of twice-born men but of an earthly kingdom in which the satisfaction of the physical appetite for bread was primary.

Second, "Then the devil taketh him into the holy city; and he set him on the pinnacle of the temple, and saith unto him, If thou art the Son of God, cast thyself down: for it is written, He shall give his angels charge concerning thee: and, on their hands shall bear thee up, lest haply thou dash thy foot against a stone. Jesus said unto him, Again it is written, Thou shalt not make trial of the Lord thy God" (Matt. 4:5-7). Christ had quoted Scripture and the devil now quoted Scripture.

---

[1] Watson, (book not specified), page 59.
[2] Edersheim, *Life and Times of Jesus the Messiah*, Vol. 1, page 303.

> *The choice of the distant temple for the scene of the second temptation evidently has point: it suggests the achievement of the popular Messianic acclaim by means of a public prodigy worked in the sacred precincts. In each case our Lord is called upon for an unwarranted provocation of God's power. The instinct of the tempter is sound: he probes for the defects which normally accompany human qualities, assuming that where he finds great trust in God he will find presumption.*[1]

Without divine warrant the devil tempted Him to dazzle the people by a spectacular display which would grab the attention and devotion of the masses. What a glorious display of Messianic power, what a mighty appeal to the popular imagination, and with what a shock to the Roman rulers in Jerusalem. What a marvelous way for Christ's trust in God to be vindicated, and for God to accredit His Messiah in a public way at the very center of the Jewish system of worship—the temple.

> *Jesus had overcome in the first temptation by simple, absolute trust. This was the time, and this the place to act upon this trust, even as the very Scriptures to which Jesus had appealed warranted. But so to have done would have been not trust—far less the heroism of faith—but **presumption**.*[2]

It was not God's will that Christ presumptuously wield or appeal to divine power in the work which He came to do. All must be done in harmony with God's will.

Third, "Again, the devil taketh him unto an exceeding high mountain, and showeth him all the kingdoms of the world, and the glory of them; and he said unto him, All these things will I give thee, if thou wilt fall down and worship me. Then saith Jesus unto him, Get thee hence, Satan; for it is written, Thou shalt worship the Lord thy God, and him only shalt thou serve" (Matt. 4:8-10). In some sense, the Devil had the kingdoms of the world to offer Christ (Luke 4:6; Matt. 1:26; John 14:30; 2 Cor. 4:4). Christ has manifested trust in God, and this kept Him from succumbing to the devil's temptations. The devil makes a frontal assault on His trust in God and urges Christ to depart from God and accept the sovereignty of Satan who will then give Him, and it would be as Satan's subordinate, the kingdoms of the world. He

---

[1] Orchard, *Catholic Commentary*, page 859.
[2] Edersheim, *Life and Times of Jesus the Messiah,* Vol. 1, page 304.

asks Christ to be a defector from the plan and purposes of God. Instead of establishing and spreading His kingdom in God's way, the devil asks Him to do it in the devil's way. Christ came to make possible a kingdom, but not in Satan's way. Countless human beings during the centuries have accepted Satan's offer to achieve an earthly kingdom through Satan's means. If Christ had accepted Satan's offer He would have had to take the way of the world, but the way of the world would not have established a kingdom which is not of this world (John 18:36). Christ did not come to establish the kingdom of Satan nor to advance it, but to establish the kingdom of God. And this could be done only in God's way.

The heart of each temptation is the devil's effort to get Christ to abandon God's way. God's way was that the cross came before the crown. The devil wanted to defeat God's purposes by trying to get Christ to use His will and power to establish and spread the kingdom without the cross. Griffith suggested that:

> The successive temptations may be ranked as temptations to under-confidence, over-confidence, and other confidence. The first, to take things impatiently into our hands; the second, to throw things presumptuously on God's hands; the third, to transfer things disloyally into other hands than God's.[1]

Christ refused on all counts. He went through with God's plan which was for Him to go the way of the cross to the crown.

By being the bread king, by the presumptuous use of His power and God's power to dazzle and sway the multitudes, by using the devil's way to the kingdom, Christ could have easily established a kingdom which Israel would have welcomed and which the entire world would have welcomed. Instead of men needing to be born again to enter such a kingdom, they could have entered it as carnal human beings fed by the bread king, led by the king who used His power primarily to dazzle and control people, and as one who appealed to the carnal in man in both the means and ends which he set before them. Cannot the premillennialists see in all this at least some aspects of the type of kingdom which they said Christ came to establish? It would be a kingdom of great physical prosperity, a kingdom which would be estab-

---

[1] Quoted by Broadus, *Harmony of the Gospels*, page 70.

lished by an overwhelming display of power of the Messiah which would bring immediately all the world into subjection, and a kingdom which would be of this world for it would have in it places of earthly power and rulership? Israel would have welcomed such a kingdom in which she would be exalted over the nations of the world, and the world would be blessed through and in subservience to restored Israel.

Does not Israel still seek for some sort of Messiah, whether personal, collective, or as a symbol, which will do in essence the very type of things which our Lord refused to do when tempted by the devil? Was it not fitting, at the beginning of His public ministry, that the issues of the mission of Christ and the coming kingdom be clearly defined,

> ... that the Divine method by which that Kingdom should be established, should have been clearly brought out, and its reality tested; and that the King, as Representative and Founder of the Kingdom, should have encountered and defeated the representative, founder, and the holder of the opposite power, "the prince of this world"—these are thoughts which must arise in everyone who believes in any Mission of the Christ. Yet this only as, after the events, we have learned to know the character of that Mission, not as we might have preconceived it. We can understand, how a Life and Work such as that of Jesus, would commence with "the Temptation," but none other than His. Judaism never conceived such an idea; because it never conceived a Messiah like Jesus.[1]

Edersheim in this statement distinguishes between the Judaism of Jesus' day and the actual teachings of the Old Testament prophets.

Israel wanted a Messiah who would bring Israel earthly prosperity, and the Bread King could easily have done this. Israel would have welcomed a Messiah who would have come to Israel from the temple in an overwhelming display of power. She sought a kingdom of this world, where nations would serve Israel rather than a kingdom in which he is great who serves (Matt. 20:20-28). As Edersheim put it:

> [These things] were regarded as the rightful manifestation of Messiah's dignity; whereas in the Evangelic record they are presented as the suggestions of Satan, and the Temptation of

---

[1] Edersheim, *Life and Times of Jesus the Messiah*, Vol. 1, pages 291-292.

*Christ. Thus **the Messiah of Judaism is the Anti-Christ of the Gospels.**[1]*

As Daniel-Rops put it:

> *The inclusion of this episode at the very beginning of the Gospel conveys an important message. It explains Jesus' own conception of his role as Messiah. The Kingdom of God was not to be established by the means appropriate to earthly powers. The Messiah was not to be the conquering King awaited by almost the whole of Israel. In exposing the wiles of the tempter, in refusing the kingdoms of the world, in denying the facile manifestation of a dramatic sign, Jesus had said "no" to all this. In refusing to change the stones to bread, he displays the characteristic that we shall always notice, that he, who was to work so many miracles for the benefit of mankind, would work none to his own advantage any more than he would deliver himself from the cross.[2]*

The Kingdom Not a Jewish Kingdom

When Jesus told a Jewish leader that he must be born again in order to enter the kingdom, He was implicitly teaching that the kingdom would not be a Jewish, nationalistic kingdom (John 3:3-5). The kingdom would not be made up of those whose birth was dependent on human will or human flesh, but on God's will (John 1:11-13). This is in line with the truth stated by John the Baptist that they were not to depend on their Jewishness but on repentance (Matt. 3:8-10). In speaking of God being able to raise up children unto Abraham from stones, "there is a play upon words between 'children' (*banim*) and 'stones' (*abanim*). It was God who made Abraham to be the rock whence the Jews were hewn (Is. 51:1-2)." The verses say: "Hearken to me, ye that follow after righteousness, ye that seek Jehovah: look to the rock whence ye were hewn, and to the hole of the pit whence ye were digged. Look unto Abraham your father, and unto Sarah that bare you: for when he was but one I called him, and I blessed him, and made him many." As Plummer went on to say, "out of the most unpromising material He can make genuine children of Abraham (Rom. 4; 9:6-7;

---

[1] *Ibid.,* page 293.
[2] Daniel-Rops (Henry Petiot), *Jesus and His Times*, page 191.

11:13-24; Gal. 4:21-31)."[1]

One's fleshly relationship did not determine one's kingdom relationship to Jesus, even if they were His mother and His brethren. "And there came to him his mother and brethren, and they could not come at him for the crowd. And it was told him, Thy mother and thy brethren stand without, desiring to see thee. But he answered and said unto them, My mother and my brethren are these that hear the word of God, and do it" (Luke 8:19-21; 11:28; Matt. 12:46-50). Alfred Plummer well said:

> *Family ties at the best are temporal; spiritual ties are eternal. Moroever, the closest blood-relationship to the Messiah constitutes no claim to admission into the Kingdom of God. No one becomes a child of God in virtue of human parentage (Jn. 1:13).*[2]

A woman said "unto him, Blessed is the womb that bare thee, and the breasts which thou didst suck. But he said, Yea rather, blessed are they that hear the word of God, and keep it" (Luke 11:27-28). Again Plummer said:

> *Here Jesus does not deny the woman's statement, but He points out how inadequate it is. She has missed the main point. To be the Mother of Jesus implies no more than a share in His humanity. To hear and keep the word of God implies communion with what is divine... The relationship with Christ which brings blessedness is the spiritual one.*[3]

Humility Essential to Enter Kingdom

The apostles knew that Jesus was the Christ, and that the keys of the kingdom had been promised (Matt. 16:16-19), but they still did not understand the nature of the Messiah's kingdom. "In that hour came the disciples unto Jesus, saying, Who then is greatest in the kingdom of heaven? And he called to him a little child, and set him in the midst of them, and said, Verily I say unto you, Except ye turn, and become as little children, ye shall in no wise enter into the kingdom of heaven. Whosoever therefore shall humble himself as this little child, the same

---

[1] Plummer, *Commentary on St. Luke*, page 90.
[2] *Ibid.*
[3] *Ibid,*

is the greatest in the kingdom of heaven" (Matt. 18:1-5).

The spirit of the disciples, concerning places of greatness, is the spirit of kingdoms of this earth. Jews thought of the Messianic kingdom as one in which the place of pre-eminence would be given to Israel; she would be exalted over all the nations of the earth, and they would be in subservience to Israel. The disciples wanted to know what individual, or individuals, would be greatest or greater in the kingdom. Israel would be supreme but who amongst the Jews would be in the place or places of honor? Jesus said that their concern should be whether they got *into* the kingdom. He said to enter, it was essential to become as a little child, and humility was the characteristic of the little child which He had in mind. (Matt. 18:3-4; Mark 10:14-15). *The spirit of humility which was essential to enter the kingdom was the spirit which would keep people in the kingdom from striving about who was greatest.* This teaching concerning the kingdom was not new. It was proclaimed in the beatitudes when Jesus said: "Blessed are the poor in spirit: for theirs is the kingdom of heaven" (Matt. 5:3). Poverty of spirit is the opposite of pride of spirit. Poverty of spirit means that one is humble. Since the kingdom is composed of redeemed sinners, one who is too proud to admit he is a sinner cannot enter the kingdom. Since we are translated out of darkness into the kingdom (Col. 1:12-14), one who refuses to admit that he has been in darkness will not seek to enter into the kingdom of light. The person who is proud of his race, position, power, of so-called goodness, will not be humble enough to admit that he needs to be born again, and without the new birth he cannot enter the kingdom (John 3:3-5). Jesus did not change the kingdom and kingdom message with the parables. He is still speaking of the same kingdom and humility. To enter the kingdom, humility is essential, and the humility when continued in makes the humble "the greatest in the kingdom of heaven" (Matt. 18:4).

The kingdom was not one wherein one would rejoice over his position of power and rulership. Christ gave the seventy power over demons "and over all the power of the enemy," but He said: Nevertheless, in this rejoice not, that the spirits are subject unto you: but rejoice *that your names are written in heaven*" (Luke 10:17-20; Phil. 4:3; Heb. 12:23; Rev. 13:8; 20:12; 21:27).

To Such Belongeth the Kingdom

"Then were there brought unto him little children, that he should lay his hands on them, and pray: and the disciples rebuked them. But Jesus said, Suffer the little children, and forbid them not to come unto me: for to such belongeth the kingdom of heaven. And he laid his hands on them, and departed thence" (Matt. 19:13-15). Jesus did not say that to *these* belongeth the kingdom but "to such" "of such is." We know that he is speaking of childlike persons. *First,* Christ had taught the same basic lessons in 18:3. *Second,* parallel passages state: "Verily I say unto you, Whosoever shall not receive the kingdom of God as a little child, he shall in no wise enter therein" (Mark 10:15; Luke 18:17). These statements do not describe the type of kingdom which the premillennialists and the Jews believe was prophesied by the Old Testament.

The Kingdom of the Merciful

In speaking to Peter's question, whether one should forgive "until seven times," Christ not only said "until seventy times seven," but He went on to deliver the parable of the merciful ruler and the unforgiving servant. "Therefore is the kingdom of heaven likened unto a certain king, who would make a reckoning with his servants" (Matt. 18:21 - 23). The kingdom is the result of God's mercy toward mankind. Those who have been shown mercy are to show mercy. If we do not forgive, if we do not show mercy, we shall not be forgiven (Matt. 18:33-35). This is not new teaching concerning the kingdom. The beatitudes do not concern eight different people, with one having the kingdom, another being comforted, a different person being filled, and another one obtaining mercy. The same person is to have all the beatitudes, and he has all the blessings, some of which are but different ways of stating the same blessing. "Blessed are the merciful: for they shall obtain mercy" (Matt. 5:7). In the prayer the Lord taught His disciples, forgiving others was essential to forgiveness of one's self by God (6:12-15). James repeated the same truth long after the kingdom was established (James 2:13).

The Rich and the Kingdom

"It is hard for a rich man to enter into the kingdom of heaven... It is easier for a camel to go through a needle's eye, than for a rich man to enter into the kingdom of God" (Matt. 19:23-24). *First,* Jesus said it was hard, He did not say it was impossible. In fact, He said, "with men this is impossible; but with God all things are possible" (Matt. 19:26). *Second*, Mark's account says: "Children, how hard it is for them *that trust in riches* to enter into the kingdom of God!" (Mark 10:24). *Third*, Abraham was wealthy, as were Isaac, Jacob, David, and others. There were Christians who were rich and they were admonished to use rightly their riches (1 Tim. 6:17-19). *Fourth*, Jesus is not saying that all poor people will be saved. He has shown that not material possessions, or lack of them, but certain *spiritual* possessions determine whether one will enter the kingdom (Matt. 18:3; 5:1-10; John 3:3-5). There are rich people who do not trust in riches and there are poor people who trust in them in that they seek them as the goal of life. There are poor people who have the wrong attitude toward wealth, and there are rich people who have the right attitude. However, Jesus shows that there are temptations of wealth, as in some other places He shows there are other stations in life in which there are temptations (Luke 8:14).

Eunuchs for the Kingdom of Heaven's Sake

Jesus contrasted the marriage law which would be in force in His kingdom, which at the moment had not been established, with that of Moses' which held sway during the period of the old covenant. In this connection He spoke of some "that made themselves eunuchs for the kingdom of heaven's sake. He that is able to receive it, let him receive it" (Matt. 19:12). There were some who were able to marry who would not marry in order that they might devote themselves single-mindedly to the work of the kingdom. This refers to the kingdom of heaven on earth, which came with power after Christ's ascension (Mark 9:1; Acts 2:30-36; Col. 1:12-13). It does not refer to a kingdom after Christ's second coming. In the resurrection, which takes place when Christ comes, and the eternal kingdom in heaven there is neither marriage nor giving in marriage (Matt. 22:30). It cannot refer to heaven, for the eunuchs for the sake of the kingdom are contrasted with those who married (Matt. 19:10-11). If the premillennialists are right, the church will rule with Christ in the millennium but the church will be in the glorified state. Therefore, there would be no marriage, for spirit beings in the glorified state do not marry.

Into the Kingdom before You

Christ told the chief priests and elders of the two sons, one of whom said he would not go and work as his father ordered, but afterward changed his mind and went, and one who said he would go, "and went not. Which of the two did the will of his father? They say, The first. Jesus said unto them, Verily I say unto you, that the publicans and the harlots go into the kingdom of God before you. For John came unto you in the way of righteousness, and ye believed him not; but the publicans and the harlots believed him: and ye, when ye saw it, did not even repent yourselves afterward, that ye might believe in him" (Matt. 21:29-32). "And all the people when they heard, and the publicans, justified God, being baptized with the baptism of John. But the Pharisees and the lawyers rejected for themselves the counsel of God, being not baptized of him" (Luke 7:29-30).

The publicans were sinners and were looked down on as were also the harlots. These religious leaders (Matt. 21:23) must have been shocked to hear that those whom they view as the moral scum of society were nearer to the kingdom than were they. They were the people who had refused to obey God, but now had repented. The leaders were the ones who said they would do God's will but failed to do so. These people recognized they were sinners, and then repented. The religious people, trusting in themselves that they were righteous, did not recognize themselves as sinners and therefore saw no need for repentance (Luke 18:9-14). John taught the way of righteousness, but they refused his call to repentance (Matt. 3:2). The publicans and the harlots believed John, and therefore evidently repented. When the religious leaders saw the impact of John's message on those whom they recognized as sinners, they did not reconsider and believe John's message and repent. "You not only do not lead them forward, as you ought to do, but will not even follow their lead."[1] Since the penitent had repented at John's preaching, and John preached that the kingdom was at hand (not "in hand"), it is obvious that they entered only the preparatory stages of the kingdom; but those who did this and continued in the penitent state would accept the Kingdom when it was established.

The Kingdom of the Meek

Christ entered Jerusalem riding on a colt (Mark 11:1-9). "Now this

---

[1] Broadus, *Harmony of the Gospels*, page 437.

is come to pass, that it might be fulfilled which was spoken through the prophet, saying, Tell ye the daughter of Zion, Behold, thy King cometh unto thee, meek, and riding upon an ass, and upon a colt the foal of an ass" (Matt. 21:4-5). They spoke of the kingdom of David (Mark 11:10).

> *In the East the ass is in high esteem. Statelier, livelier, swifter than with us, it vies with the horse in favor. Among the Jews it was equally valued as a beast of burden, for work in the field or at the mill, and for riding. In contrast to the horse, which had been introduced by Solomon from Egypt, and was used especially for war, it was the symbol of peace. To the Jew It was peculiarly national, for had not Moses led his wife, seated on an ass, to Egypt; had not the Judges ridden on white asses; and was not the ass of Abraham, the friend of God, noted in Scripture? Every Jew, moreover, expected, from the words of one of the prophets (Zech. 9:9), that the Messiah would enter Jerusalem riding on an ass. No act could be more perfectly in keeping with the conception of a king of Israel, and no word could express more plainly that the king proclaimed Himself the Messiah.* [1]

Christ is the Meek King ruling over the kingdom of the meek. He is not a military Messiah such as Israel want to overthrow Roman rule. He was born king of the Jews and was promised the throne of David (Matt. 2:2; Luke 1:32-33). The kingdom was at hand, and He began His reign after His ascension (Matt. 3:2; 4:17; 10:7; Acts 2:30-36). We should not be surprised that the King is meek, for the King Himself said: "Blessed are the meek: for they shall inherit the earth" (Matt. 5:5). Those to whom the kingdom belongs have among other qualities that of meekness (Matt. 5:3, 5, 10). The meek King made no change in the nature of the kingdom message from the time when He spoke the beatitudes until the time He rode into Jerusalem; nor thereafter, except the message was changed from *at* hand to *in* hand, in that it was finally established (Acts 2:30-36; Col. 1:13). The Multitudes did not recognize the nature of the kingdom, but they did realize that prophecy was

---

[1] Cunningham Geikie, *Hours with the Bible*, Vol. 2, page 395; George Frederick Maclear, *A Class-Book of New Testament History*, page 120.

being fulfilled, for they said: "Blessed is the King that cometh in the name of the Lord: peace in heaven, and glory in the highest" (Luke 19:38). "John points out that the Messianic enthusiasm had been mainly kindled by the raising of Lazarus."[1]

Not with Observation

"And being asked by the Pharisees, when the kingdom of God cometh, he answered them and said, The kingdom of God cometh not with observation: neither shall they say, Lo, here! or, There! For lo, the kingdom of God is within you (margin: in the midst of you)" (Luke 17:20-21). Christ had preached the kingdom was at hand (Matt. 4:17), and the Pharisees asked when it would come. If Jesus set a date, it would come on that date, but they would deny that it had come because they had misconceptions concerning the nature of the kingdom. They thought that it would arrive with an overwhelming display of power which would destroy or conquer the Messiah's enemies. It would have all the trappings of a glorious kingdom of this world. Jesus showed that:

> There will be no such signs as would enable a watcher to date the arrival. A spiritual Kingdom is slow in producing conspicuous material effects; and it begins in ways that cannot be dated.[2]

Since the disciples had to know when the kingdom had started in order that they could invite people into it by being born of water and Spirit (John 3-3-5), they had to know when it started in so far as earth is concerned. But they would know because the Lord informed them, and not because that by careful watching, by close observation, they would be able to detect its presence. They knew it would come with power in their lifetime, for Jesus said so (Mark 9:1). They knew that they would receive power when the Spirit came, for Jesus said so (Acts 1:8). As they waited on Pentecost they could not know when Christ in heaven had made purification for our sins, and had sat down at God's right hand to reign (Heb. 1:3, 13). When the Spirit came on Pentecost with miraculous manifestations there was nothing in anything that was done which one could point to and say that this event or thing proves that the kingdom has arrived. The only way that they

---

[1] F.W. Farrar, *Luke*, page 218. See also John 12:9-19.
[2] Plummer, *Commentary on St. Luke*, page 405.

knew that the kingdom had arrived, that Christ was now ruling at God's right hand, was that Jesus Christ through the Spirit said so (Acts 2:30-36). Not what people saw, but by what they heard (although what they heard was confirmed by what they saw in that the miraculous was a proof of the inspiration of the speakers) they knew that Christ is king and the kingdom was now there, and that it had come with power.

What is meant by "the kingdom of God is within you"? Some think that it means that the kingdom of God is inward, spiritual, and therefore is not detected in the same way that kingdoms of this earth are discerned. It is true that the kingdom is spiritual, and is entered by the new birth and not by the physical birth. "If 'within you' be adopted, the meaning will be, 'Instead of being something externally visible, the Kingdom is essential spiritual; it is in your hearts, *if you possess it at all.*"[1] However, Jesus is talking to the Pharisees, and they did not have their hearts prepared for the kingdom. Just after this He addressed Himself to His disciples (Luke 17:22). Unless Jesus meant it simply as a general statement about the nature of the kingdom, that it was within man's hearts though obviously not in the hearts of all men, the marginal translation "in the midst of you" is preferable. It was in their midst in the person of Christ and of His disciples, for Christ was even born king of the Jews (Matt. 2:2). In actuality the kingdom had not been established, for the giving of it to the little flock had not yet taken place (Luke 12:32).

> *Godet thus combines the two: "Humanity must be prepared for the new external and divine state of things by a spiritual work wrought in the depths of the heart; and it is this internal advent which Jesus thinks good to put first in relief before such interlocutors."[2]*

Christ then spoke to His disciples of an implied absence when He said: "The days will come, when ye shall desire to see one of the days of the Son of man, and ye shall not see it" (Luke 17:22). They would long for His presence, but He would not be there. He again showed that "first must he suffer many things and be rejected of this generation" (Luke 17:25). Then He went on to speak of His second coming,

---

[1] *Ibid.,* page 406.
[2] H.M. Riggle, *Christ's Kingdom and Reign,* page 461.

in my judgment (Luke 18:26-3 7). His statements seem to indicate that there would be such a clear manifestation of the fact of His coming that everyone would know about it. This does not contradict verse twenty-one for it refers to the coming of the kingdom, and Luke 17:22-24, 26-37 refer to the second coming at the end of the world. Verse, twenty-eight "covers all premature announcements of the approach of the Last Day. *All prediction of exact dates, and all statements as to local appearance are to be mistrusted.*"[1]

The Appointed Kingdom

"And there arose also a contention among them, which of them was accounted to be greatest. And he said unto them, The kings of the Gentiles have lordship over them; and they that have authority over them are called Benefactors. But ye shall not be so: for he that is the greater among you, let him become as the younger; and he that is chief, as he that doth serve. For which is greater, he that sitteth at meat, or he that serveth? is not he that sitteth at meat? but I am in the midst of you as he that serveth. But ye are they that have continued with me in my temptations and I appoint unto you a kingdom, even as my Father appointed unto me, that ye may eat and drink at my table in my kingdom and ye shall sit on thrones judging the twelve tribes of Israel" (Luke 22:24-30).

First, even in the shadow of the cross the apostles are contentious as to who was greatest. They have a misconception of the kingdom and therefore of what Christ came to do. Jesus in His reference to the Gentiles shows that they partake of the spirit of the world, of the pagans, and not of the spirit which He inculcates and demonstrates. Christ reverses the spirit of the world, and shows that he who serves is great. He illustrated this by the fact that "I am in the midst of you as he that serveth." Some think that at this point Christ washed the disciples' feet (John 13:16). "Having rebuked them for raising the question of precedence among themselves, Jesus shows them wherein the privileges which they *all* enjoy consist, viz. in their standing by Him in His service to others. He gives preference to none."[2] Greatness is not a gift, it comes through service. The kingdom of Christ is not the kind the Jews wanted nor the premillennialists envision.

Second, the apostles were to be rewarded for their loyalty to

---

[1] Plummer, *Commentary on St. Luke*, page 407.
[2] *Ibid.,* page 502.

Christ. They were those who had "continued with me in my temptations" (Lk, 22:28). They were to be rewarded by Christ, to whom God had appointed a kingdom and now to whom He appoints positions of pre-eminence in His kingdom. "In my temptations" was during the personal ministry. Christ was speaking not of a reward to be given to them over two thousand years later in some so-called millennial kingdom, but of a reward He would give them in His kingdom which soon He received. (Mark 9:1; Acts 1:8; 2:30-36; Col. 1:13). *Jesus spoke of their reward for faithfulness to Him in His personal ministry, and not a reward for their faithfulness to Him in the church age after His ascension.* "The meaning of the promise is parallel to what precedes. As they have shared the trials, so they shall share the joy; and as they have proclaimed the Kingdom to Israel, so they shall exercise royal power over Israel, judging them according as they have accepted or rejected what was proclaimed." It was not long after this that the kingdom was given to the little flock (Luke 12:32). The apostles laid down the conditions, as inspired by the Spirit, which all the house of Israel had to meet to enter the kingdom (Acts 2:30-38), and those who entered the kingdom "continued steadfastly in the apostles' doctrine" (Acts 2:42; 1 Cor. 14:37).

If this referred to the so-called millennial kingdom, the premillennialists are confronted with the fact that it destroys their picture of that kingdom; for instead of Israel being supreme, the apostles, who were set in the church (1 Cor. 12:28), rule over Israel and the saints. The church, the premillennialists say, will judge the world at the second coming (1 Cor. 6:2). This is true, but the second coming will bring the judgment and the eternal destiny—not a reign on earth. But if the premillennialists are right in the chain of command of the millernial kingdom it will not be the Messiah, Israel, and the Gentiles, but the Messiah, the church, Israel, and the Gentiles.

Third, Jews viewed the Messianic reign as a banquet, and Jesus showed that the apostles would "eat and drink at my table in my kingdom" (Luke 22:30). They did it (1 Cor. 12:23-33).

Fourth, Christ spoke of the new covenant just before this (Luke 22:20). The new covenant and the new kingdom are but different ways of expressing Christ's relationship to His people. The new covenant is

---

[1] *Ibid.,* pages 502-503.

everlasting, for Christ's blood is the blood of the everlasting covenant (Heb. 13:20), and the kingdom they were receiving in the first century was and is the unshakeable kingdom (Heb. 12:28).

The Kingdom Taken Away and Given

Jesus told the religious leaders the parable of the householder who had a vineyard let out to husbandmen while he was in a far country. At the season of the fruits he sent servants to receive his fruits. This he did twice, and each time they "beat one, and killed another, and stoned another" (Matt. 21:33-36). He sent his son, and they said: "This is the heir; come, let us kill him, and take his inheritance... they...killed him. When therefore the lord of the vineyard shall come, what will he do unto those husbandmen? They say unto him, He will miserably destroy those miserable men, and will let out the vineyard unto other hus-bandmen, who shall render him the fruits in their seasons. Jesus saith unto them, Did ye never read in the scriptures, The stone which the builders rejected, the same was made the head of the corner; this was from the Lord, and it is marvelous in our eyes? Therefore say I unto you, The kingdom of God shall be taken away from you, and shall be given to a nation bringing forth the fruits thereof. And he that falleth on this stone shall be broken to pieces: but on whomsoever it shall fall, it will scatter him as dust. And when the chief priests and the Pharisees heard his parables, they perceived that he spake of them. And when they sought to lay hold on him, they feared the multitudes, because they took him for a prophet" (Matt. 21:38-46).

First, it is obvious that the householder is God and the vineyard is the kingdom of God, for in the application of the parable it is the king-dom which is taken from one group and given to another. The king-dom is God's kingdom (Matt. 21:43).

Second, it is obvious that Israel makes up the group of husband-men to whom the vineyard was first let out, i.e., to whom the kingdom of God was previously given. God's rule or kingdom had been with Israel. They were the ones with whom the old covenant had been made. The servants whom He sent represented the prophets, and the Son represented Jesus Christ. Stephen was saying the same thing when he said: "Ye stiff-necked and uncircumcised in heart and ears, ye do always resist the Holy Spirit: as your fathers did, so do ye. Which of the prophets did not your fathers persecute? and they killed them that showed before of the coming of the Righteous One; of whom ye have now become betrayers and murderers; ye who received the law as it was ordained by angels, and kept it not" (Acts 7:51-53). We know that Israel was represented in the parable, for the kingdom was to be "taken away from you... they perceived that he spake of them" (Matt. 21 43, 45). Instead of their receiving the kingdom they would be judged, for the stone would fall on them (Matt. 21:44).

Third, the "kingdom of God... shall be given to a nation bringing forth the fruits thereof" (Matt. 21:43). This nation was not made up of Gentiles as such, or of Jews as such, but of converts from both backgrounds who accepted Christ. The kingdom was first given to the faithful little flock who had followed Jesus in His personal ministry (Luke 12:32), and then others were invited and urged to come into Christ (Acts 2:30-42). The old covenant was abolished and the new covenant was established. God's rule had been with His people Israel through the old covenant, but now God's rule, reign, or kingdom was with His spiritual people through the new covenant. Spiritual qualifications, not national, were necessary to receive the kingdom—the kingdom which people began receiving after Christ ascended and sent the Spirit (Acts 2:30-36; Heb. 12:23). The new nation is the church, the kingdom of God's Son (Col. 1:13-14). The privileges and responsibilities of the kingdom of God now belonged to the spiritual nation, those who were born of water and Spirit into the kingdom (John 3:3-5). This is the church, God's holy nation.

Peter makes this crystal clear. "Unto whom coming, a living stone, rejected indeed of men, but with God elect, precious, ye also, as living stones, are built up a spiritual house, to be a holy priesthood, to offer up spiritual sacrifices, acceptable to God through Jesus Christ. Because it is contained in scripture. Behold, I lay in Zion a chief corner stone, elect, precious: and he that believeth on him shall not be put to shame. For you therefore that believe is the preciousness: but for such as disbelieve, the stone which the builders rejected, the same was made the head of the corner; and, A stone of stumbling, and a rock of offence; for they stumble at the word, being disobedient: whereunto also they were appointed. But ye are an elect race, a royal priesthood, *a holy nation*, a people for God's own possession, that ye may show forth the excellencies of him who called you out of darkness into his marvelous light: who in time past were no people, but now are the people of God: who had not obtained mercy, but now have obtained mercy" (1 Pet. 2:4-10). These were indeed "the elect who are sojourn-ers of the Dispersion" (1 Pet. 1:1).

Fourth, the warning of Jesus was in essence nothing new. It is similar to John's statement that they had to repent, that they must not depend on their physical relationship to Abraham, and that God was able of these stones to raise up children to Abraham (Matt. 3:1-10). It is the heart of what the apostle said, after the church was established, when he cited the statement about the chief corner stone, which had been rejected of those who were supposed to be the builders, but whom God had made the head of the corner, (Acts 4:11-12). In other words, from the days of John until the establishment of the church, or kingdom, there was no basic change in the message. The change was that the kingdom which had been *at* hand was *in* hand from Pentecost on, (Acts 2:30-36; 1 Cor. 15:24-28).

Can anything be clearer? God's reign, God's kingdom, was taken from Israel and given to the spiritual nation which has been born of water and the Spirit. Premillennialism teaches that the nature of God's old covenant prophecies and promises make it impossible for God to take the kingdom from Israel. It must be given to Israel—it will be given to Israel. *They are wrong.* It was taken from Israel and it will never be given again to Israel as a nation, as a people. Any Israelite can come into the kingdom of God but it will have to be through the new birth and not through the fleshly birth. Premillennialists say that God postponed the kingdom and will give it to Israel at the second coming. Christ said that the kingdom was taken away from Israel and was given "to a nation bringing forth the fruits thereof." Christ is right, the Jews and the premillennialists are wrong in their interpretation of the kingdom promises and prophecies. If premillennialists will take the veil off their heart when they read both the Old and the New Testa-ments they shall be able to see the significance and outcome of this tremendous truth about the kingdom of God and to whom it was given.

Israel Cast Out and Gentiles Brought In

The kingdom of the Messiah was sometimes thought of as a ban-quet (Luke 14:15). Jesus said: "I appoint unto you a kingdom, even as my Father appointed unto me, that ye may eat and drink at my table in my kingdom; and ye shall sit on thrones judging the twelve tribes of Israel" (Luke 22:29). This was in contrast with their situation when they had been with Him "in my temptations" (Luke 22:28). Christ had likened the kingdom to a grain of mustard seed and to leaven (Luke 13:18-21). Sometime afterwards "one said unto him, Lord, are they few that are saved? And he said unto them, Strive to enter in by the narrow door; for many, I say unto you, shall seek to enter in, and shall not be able. When once the master of the house is risen up, and hath shut to the door, and ye begin to stand without, and to knock at the door, saying, Lord, open to us: and he shall answer and say to you, I know you not whence ye are; then shall ye begin to say, We did eat and drink in thy presence, and thou didst teach in our streets and he shall say, I tell you, I know not whence ye are; depart from me, all ye workers of iniquity. There shall be the weeping and the gnashing of teeth, when ye shall see Abraham, and Isaac, and Jacob, and all the prophets, in the kingdom of God, and yourselves cast forth without. And they shall come from the east and west, and from the north and south, and shall sit down in the kingdom of God. And behold, there are last who shall be first, and there are first who shall be last" (Luke 13:23-30). Matthew tells us that "the sons of the kingdom shall be cast forth Into the outer darkness" (Matt. 8:12). The sons of the kingdom were Jews whom God wanted to be heirs of the kingdom, but who disqualified themselves by their rejection of Jesus Christ.

Consider some of the things which Jesus taught in these statements. *First*, there are many (Matt. 8:11) who will be saved but how many this will be in comparison with the total number of people we do not know. Jesus did not directly answer the question of whether many would be saved. His answer was personal while that of the questioner was more theoretical. Jesus told him that what he should give attention to was to "strive to enter." "Keep on striving to enter," or, "Strain every nerve."[1] Jesus went on to say that when It was too late, after the master had "shut to the door," that some would try to enter but would not be able to do so. "The futures are most important... Jesus does not say that there *are* many who *strive* in vain to enter, but that there *will* be many who *will seek* in vain to enter, *after the time of salvation is past.*"[2] They will be unable to either force the door or to talk their way into the kingdom after the door is shut. The fact that they had eaten in His presence, and He had taught in their streets, did not change the sit-

---

[1] *Ibid.,* page 346.
[2] *Ibid.*

uation. Physical contact and closeness to the Messiah is not sufficient to bring one into the kingdom, any more than one's fleshly birth as a Jew brought one into the kingdom (Matt. 3:8-10; John 1:10-13; 3:3-5).

Second, there would be Jews who were excluded because they had not striven to enter in the time of salvation, and there would be Gentiles who would be included because they had entered in the time of salvation. The statement concerning the gathering of Gentiles from the various points of the compass may contain a reference to Isaiah 49:12. But at any rate, it makes clear that many Gentiles would come in and share the blessings of the Messianic kingdom with the patriarchs. "In Matt. 8:11-12 the exclusion of the Jews and admission of the Gentiles is still more clearly expressed. This was the exact opposite of Jewish expectations... [they expected] the Gentiles were to be put to shame at the sight of the Jews in bliss. Here it is the Jews who gnash their teeth, while the Gentiles are in bliss."[1]

Christ clearly warned Israel that she could be shut out of the kingdom by her disobedience. He clearly stated that Gentiles would be in the kingdom if they were obedient, as other passages show. Israel was not going to have a place in the kingdom just because of the relationship of Israel to the patriarchs. Regardless of how many promises were made to the patriarchs, Israel would not partake of them if she was not obedient. On the other hand, Gentiles who were of the faith of Abraham, in that they accepted God's revelation of Himself to them, would be in the kingdom. They were not shut out, nor were they in an inferior position, because they were Gentiles. They would be with Abraham, Isaac, Jacob, and the prophets.

How could Christ have made it clearer that Israel, the sons of the kingdom, could shut themselves out of the kingdom? And this they did, and tried to keep others from entering (Matt. 23:13-14).

It took more than one's physical relationship to Abraham, and an invitation to the banquet, in order to enter into the kingdom. "And when one of them that sat at meat with him heard these things, he said unto him, Blessed is he that shall eat bread in the kingdom of God. But he said unto him, A certain man made a great supper; and he bade many; and he sent forth his servant at supper time to say to them that were bidden, Come; for all things are now ready. And they all with one consent began to make excuse... And the servant came, and told

---

[1] *Ibid.*, pages 347-348.

his lord these things. Then the master of the house being angry said to his servant, Go out quickly into the streets and lanes of the city, and bring in hither the poor and maimed and blind and lame. And the servant said, Lord, what thou didst command is done, and yet there is room. And the Lord said unto the servant, Go out into the highways and hedges, and constrain them to come in, that my house may be filled. For I say unto you, that none of those men that were bidden shall taste of my supper" (Luke 14:15-24).

The statement, "Blessed is he that shall eat bread in the kingdom of God" brings up "the Jewish idea that the Messianic age will be inaugurated by a banquet and will be a prolonged festival (Isa. 25:6)."[1] The banquet was ready, and the people were invited first and then they were told "Come; for all things are now ready" (Luke 14:17). When the summons to the banquet was turned down, did the man call off the banquet? No. He did not even postpone it. "Not because his anger makes him impatient; but because he has no intention of putting off anything to please the discourteous persons who have insulted him. He goes on with his arrangements at once."[2] There are others who are invited, and the banquet is held. What happened to those who refused? "For I say unto you, that none of those men that were bidden shall taste of my supper" (Luke 14:24). He did not postpone it and invite them to the banquet at a later time.

The parable which the Lord used was His comment on the man's statement that, "Blessed is he that shall eat bread in the kingdom of God" (Luke 14:15). The kingdom was at hand, just as the banquet was ready for the guests to be summoned. "Come; for all things are now ready" (Luke 14:17). The time is fulfilled, repent ye, for the kingdom of heaven is at hand (Matt. 3:2; 4:17; 10; 7; Mark 1:15). Israel was bidden to come, but as a whole she refused. The leaders refused, and were filled with murmuring because Jesus "receiveth sinners, and eateth with them" (Luke 15:2). He and the message of His disciples had been rejected in many places (Luke 4:29; 10:13). The publicans and harlots were going into the kingdom of heaven before the religious leaders (Matt. 21:23-32), and it would not be long before the gospel would go forth to all the world—including the Gentiles (Matt. 28:19;

---

[1] *Ibid.,* page 360.
[2] *Ibid.,* page 362.

Luke 24:45-49; Acts 1:8; 13:46).

These are clear warnings of Jesus that no Jew would be in the kingdom just because he was a Jew, and that instead of the kingdom being postponed, these "sons of the kingdom" would be eliminated by their unbelief.

Kingdom Given to the Little Flock

They were seeking first the kingdom of God (Matt. 6:33; Luke 12:31). Jesus said: "Fear not, little flock; for it is your Father's good pleasure to give you the kingdom" (Luke 12:33). They had been preaching that it was at hand, and it was to come in their lifetime (Matt. 3:2; 4:17; 10:7; Mark 9:1). It was given to the little flock on Pentecost (Mark 9:1; Acts 1:8; 2:30-36). Observe: *First*, it was given to the little flock, and not to a great multitude at the second coming. The little flock received it first, and then as the gospel was preached, beginning on Pentecost, those who accepted it and obeyed the King received the kingdom for they were translated into the kingdom (Heb. 12:28; Col. 1:13). *Second*, it was the little flock, and not physical Israel, to whom Christ promised the kingdom. Although the little flock was made up of Jews, it was made up only of those who believed in Jesus Christ. After the little flock received the kingdom, there is not the remotest suggestion that the nation of Israel was to be given the kingdom. Instead, it was given to a nation bringing forth the fruits thereof (Matt. 21:43). Those who were bidden to "eat bread in the kingdom of God" and refused the invitation will not get to do so (Luke 14:15-24).

The Places of Pre-Eminence

"She saith unto him, Command that these my two sons may sit, one on thy right hand and one on thy Left hand, in thy kingdom. But Jesus answered and said, Ye know not what ye ask. Are ye able to drink the cup that I am about to drink? They say unto him, We are able. He saith unto them, My cup indeed ye shall drink: but to sit on my right hand, and on my left hand, is not mine to give; it is for them for whom it hath been prepared of my Father. And when the ten heard it, they were moved with indignation concerning the two brethren. But Jesus called them unto him, and said, Ye know that the rulers of the Gentiles lord it over them, and their great ones exercise authority over them. Not so shall it be among you; but whosoever would be great among you shall be your minister; and whosoever would be first among you shall be your servant: even as the Son of man came not to be ministered unto, but to minister, and to give his life a ransom for many" (Matt. 20:20-28).

First, neither she, her two sons, nor the other ten apostles, understood the nature of the kingdom. Christ was on His way to Jerusalem, and had just told them that there He would suffer, die, and be raised up (Matt. 20:17-19). "Nothing could have been more ill-timed than this selfish petition when He was going forth to His death."[1] Christ had promised each apostle a throne (Matt. 19:28), but these two wanted the places which were next to the king himself. Their ignorance of the nature of the kingdom is indicated in Jesus' answer: "Ye know not what ye ask. Are ye able to drink the cup that I am about to drink?" They said they were able, Jesus said they would drink of it. They did not realize that cup of which Jesus would drink. They did not realize that the cross came before the crown (Luke 24:25-27). It is likely they were willing to fight for Jesus and His kingdom, but they did not understand that the suffering to be endured was that which would come upon them because of the spiritual weapons they were to wield on the behalf of the kingdom.

Second, Christ said the two positions which they were requested were not His to give. "He thus lifts their minds away from the idea of a human sovereign bestowing earthly honors to that of divine gifts He speaks of himself (comp. John 14:28) as officially subordinate to the Father in His office as the God-man, the Mediator, in which he has derived all his authority and power from the Father (Matt. 28:18), and will at length return it to him (1 Cor. 15:28)... All the arrangements of the Messianic kingdom have been already made by the Father, indeed made 'from the foundation of the world,' (Matt. 25:34)."[2] Is it not sad? "So near the end, and they are still thinking of a worldly kingdom, and full of selfish scheming and unkindness."[3]

Third, Christ's kingdom differed from the kingdoms of the world, for "the rulers of the Gentiles lord it over them, and their great ones exercise authority over them. Not so shall it be among you" (Matt 20:25-26). "The word [exercise lordship] is used in an unfavorable

---

[1] Maclear, *Class-Book of New Testament History*, page 115.
[2] Broadus, *Harmony of the Gospels*, page 417.
[3] *Ibid.,* page 418.

sense. It is applied in Acts 19:16 to the man possessed with an evil spirit, *prevailing against and overcoming* the seven sons of Sceva. Peter himself uses it in his first Epistle (5:3), recalling possibly this very incident, where he warns the elders of the Church 'not to be *lords over* God's heritage,' or as it is in the margin, 'to *overrule.*' The preposition in the original is emphatic, and gives the force of oppressive, tyrannical rule, where the ruler uses his rights for the diminution of the ruled and the exaltation of himself. The same unfavorable sense attaches to the word rendered '*exercise authority,*' which only occurs here and in the parallel in Matt. 20:25."[1]

Fourth. Christ said that the principle of service, not of rulership, is the principle of greatness in His kingdom (Matt. 20:27). It is one of sacrificial service, for He said: "But whosoever would become great among you shall be your minister; and whosoever would be first among you shall be your servant: even as the Son of man came not to be ministered unto, but to minister, and to give his life a ransom for many (Matt. 20:27-28). The supreme principle of service through self-sacrifice is found in what Christ did. The principle of greatness in Christ's kingdom is contrary to the premillennial conception that in the kingdom the house of Israel will be exalted over the nations of the earth and that these nations, in effect, will be servants of Israel, for Israel will rule. If it were such a kingdom, the principle of Matthew 20:27-28 would mean that the Gentile nations will be greater in the kingdom than Israel for they will be in the position of servants with Israel in the position of ruler over them.

Fifth, Christ's statement concerning the giving of His "life a ransom for many" (Matt. 20:28), sums up His mission, i.e,, why He came to earth. It was His death which made possible the creation of the church (Eph. 2:13-16), which is His kingdom (Col. 1:13-14). He went to the crown by way of the cross (Luke 24:25-27; 1 Tim. 3:16; Heb. 1:3, 13; Acts 2:30-36). Is it surprising that the kingdom which was created by the self-sacrifice of Christ (in a way in which we cannot sacrifice ourselves, for we cannot give our lives as a ransom for others), should have, as its principle of greatness, greatness through service? What a flood of light all these things throw on the nature of the kingdom of heaven. However, it is not new teaching concerning the nature of Christ's mission, and therefore of the kingdom, for the angel

---

[1] Maclear, *Class-Book of New Testament History*, page 117.

announced that His name would be called Jesus because He would save His people from their sins, and Hebrews tells us that He came to put away sin by the sacrifice of Himself (Matt. 1:21; Heb. 9:26, 28). There was no change in the kingdom which was offered, as Boll had to imagine in order to save his theory of the nature of the kingdom, and the one which was established.

Apostles on Twelve Thrones

"Then answered Peter and said unto him, Lo, we have left all, and followed thee; what then shall we have? And Jesus said unto them, Verily I say unto you, that ye who have followed me, in the regeneration when the Son of man shall sit on the throne of his glory, ye also shall sit upon twelve thrones, judging the twelve tribes of Israel. And every one that hath left houses, or brethren, or sisters, or father, or mother, or children, or lands, for my name's sake, shall receive a hundredfold, and shall inherit eternal life" (Matt. 19:27-30). Mark (10:31) and Luke (18:30) are more specific and said "in the world to come, eternal life." Of course, it is in heaven that we inherit eternal Life. Or, to put it another way, to enter heaven is to enter eternal life; although in one sense we now have it in that we have Christ (1 John 5:11-13).

First, Christ said that the apostles would be rewarded by being on thrones judging Israel. When? "In the regeneration when the Son of man shall sit on the throne of his glory." When is the regeneration? It is the time when regeneration is going on, and it is going on in the gospel age for we are now saved by His mercy, "through the washing of regeneration and renewing of the Holy Spirit" (Titus 3:5). The regeneration is the time when people are being born of water and Spirit into the kingdom of God (John 3:3-5). The regeneration is the time when we are made new creatures in Christ (2 Cor. 5:17; Gal. 6:15; Eph. 2:15; 4:24). The regeneration is the gospel age, and the apostles rule by virtue of the fact that through them the word of Christ was revealed and confirmed (Matt. 16:18-19; 28:20; Acts 2:36-42; 1 Cor. 14:37).

If someone says that the regeneration is a time when there will be no sin, we point out that premillennialists believe there will be some sin in the millennium.[1] If there were none, how could there be a terrible uprising of the nations at the end of it (Rev. 20:7-9)?

Furthermore, after speaking of the reward of the apostles, who had followed Him in His personal ministry, Christ then spoke of anyone else who followed Him and sacrificed for Him: they would receive rewards now in time and in the world to come eternal life. "...manifold more in this time, and in the world to come eternal life" (Luke 18:29-30; Matt. 19:29-30). "In this time" refers to this present life, for Mark said concerning the rewards in this time that these would be also "with persecutions" (Mark 10:30). The kingdom of Christ is one in which He reigns in the midst of His enemies (Psa. 110:1-4; Acts 2:30-34). There are enemies who persecute members of His kingdom. This is not a new teaching concerning the kingdom, for in the sermon on the mount Jesus said: "Blessed are they that have been persecuted for righteousness' sake: for theirs is the kingdom of heaven" (Matt. 5:10). And just as Jesus taught that their ultimate reward would be eternal life in heaven (Mk, 10:30), so in the sermon on the mount He said concerning the persecuted: "great is your reward in heaven: for so persecuted they the prophets that were before you." (Matt. 5:12).

Second, Christ is now on the throne of glory, for He was received up into glory and into His kingdom (Luke 24:25-27; Matt. 20:21; Mark 10:37; 1 Tim. 3:16; Heb. 1:3, 13; 7:1-8:4; 10:12-13; Acts 2:34-36). This reign lasts until the last enemy (death) is conquered and this is followed by the eternal state, and not by a reign on earth (1 Cor. 15:24-28; Rev. 20:11-21:5). Since Christ is now on the throne of His glory, the apostles are now on thrones ruling over Israel. They laid down the law to Israel, and those who did not accept the gospel were cut off from covenant relationship to God by their unbelief (Acts 2:36-42; 3:22-23; Rom. 11:1-25). They bind and loose (Matt. 16:18-19).

Third, the second coming of Christ is apart from sin and sin-offerings and is unto salvation (Heb. 9:28), eternal salvation (1 Pet. 1:3-6). Christ will come as Judge of the wicked and to deliver the righteous from the very presence of evil (2 Thess. 1:5-12). The regeneration will not go on after His coming, but will be consummated. People are born again on this earth, not in heaven after the judgment.

Fourth, not only the apostles, but the saints shall judge the world in some sense in the future (1 Cor. 6:1-4). The judgment will not be

---

[1] Boll, *The Kingdom of God*, pages 162-163.

the time of the unique rule of the apostles over the twelve tribes of Israel. If Matt. 19:28 refers to a millennial reign as envisioned by premillennialists, it follows that the apostles and the saints of the gospel age will judge mankind. Therefore, the bride of Christ, not Israel, will be the most exalted body of people in the millennium. This destroys the premillennial picture of the kingdom as composed of the Messiah, then Israel, and then the Gentile nations. It would be the Messiah, the church (the bride of Christ) over Israel and the nations, then Israel, and then the nations.

Fifth, does Matthew 19:28 refer to Matthew 25:31? No. *First*, the reward which comes after the reign for both apostles and others is eternal life in the world to come (Mark 10:30). It is the eternal life which is entered when Christ comes and judges the world (Matt. 25:46). *Second*, entering into eternal life is not entering into a thousand year reign in which there is sin, and which is followed by the end of the thousand-year kingdom, and the ushering in of a little season of rebellion. It is not until after whatever these represent that saints enter into eternal life (Rev. 21). The judgment scene of Matt. 25:31-46 is the consummation, through the final judgment of the present age, of the regeneration which is now going on and in which the apostles are ruling, with Christ being on His throne of glory.

The Son of Man Coming in His Kingdom

Jesus told His disciples of His coming death at the hands of the religious leaders in Jerusalem. Peter rebuked Him and said it would not happen. Christ "said unto Peter, Get thee behind me, Satan: thou art a stumbling-block unto me: for thou mindest not the things of God, but the things of men. Then said Jesus unto his disciples, If any man would come after me, let him deny himself, and take up his cross, and follow me. For whosoever would save his life shall lose it: and whosoever shall lose his life for my sake shall find it. For what shall a man be profited, if he shall gain the whole world, and forfeit his life? or what shall a man give in exchange for his life? For the Son of man shall come in the glory of his Father with his angels; and then shall he render unto every man according to his deeds. Verily I say unto you, There are some of them that stand here, who shall in no wise taste of death, till they see the Son of man coming in His kingdom" (Matt. 16:23-28).

First, Christ spoke of His death. The apostles did not understand that He would die. It is evident that they shared the view of others of their day that the Christ would abide forever on earth, and therefore would not die (John 12:31-35). As a matter of fact, the suffering was necessary before He could enter into His glory, which involved entering into His kingdom (Luke 24:25-27; 1 Tim. 3:16; Acts 2:30-36).

Second, after speaking of the necessity of His death, and being rebuked by Peter, Jesus said that Peter "mindest not the things of God, but the things of men" (Matt. 16:23). Any interpretation of prophecies of the kingdom which did not take into consideration that Christ came in His first coming to go the way of the cross, as well as to proclaim that the kingdom was at hand (Mark 1:14-15), is not scriptural. *It is the minding og the things of men rather than the things of God.* Premillennialism says that Christ proclaimed as at hand the type of kingdom which they believe the Old Testament predicted. The apostles evidently had this type of kingdom in mind. Therefore, they could not accept the idea of His death. The sooner the premillennialists face it the better: The view of Peter, the Jews of his day, and of the premillennialists is the result of minding things of men and not the things of God.

Third, having spoken of His coming death, and having rebuked Peter, Christ went on to speak of the cost of discipleship. It involved self-denial, the cross, following Christ, and finding one's life through losing it (Matt. 16:24 -25). This certainly does not refer to discipleship in a millennial kingdom which will begin with the supernatural overthrow of all of Christ's enemies, and the enthronement of the apostles with other disciples of the church age being in places of rulership in various cities if they have been faithful. The premillennialists believe that these passages concerning rulership refer to the millennial kingdom (Matt. 19:28; 25:21, 23; Luke 19:17, 19).

Fourth, a very natural thing to follow the discussion of the cost of discipleship was the statement which emphasized that being His follower is worth anything it costs. "For what shall a man be profited, if he shall gain the whole world, and forfeit his life? or what shall a man give in exchange for his life? For the Son of man shall come in the glory of his Father with his angels; and then shall he render unto every man according to his deeds" (Matt. 16:26-27). Of course, the apostles were disciples of Christ in the personal ministry, as were some others, but Christ's statement concerning the cost of discipleship also embraces the gospel age. It is during the gospel age that we are finding or losing our life for Christ's sake.

What happens at the end of the gospel age? The judgment when, coming in the glory of His Father with the angels, men are dealt with according to their deeds Matt. 25:31-46). It is when the wicked receive tribulation, and the righteous receive rest. This is when He is revealed "from heaven with the angels of his power in flaming fire, rendering vengeance to them that know not God, and to them that obey not the gospel of our Lord" (2 Thess. 1:5-12; 1 Thess. 4:16).

Fifth, then Christ spoke of His coming in His kingdom in their Lifetime—the very kingdom to which He went by way of the cross; (Luke 24:25-27; Matt. 19:28). "Verily I say unto you, There are some of them that stand here, who shall in no wise taste of death, till they see the Son of man coming in his kingdom" (Matt. 16:28). We know that at least one person was dead before the kingdom was established on Pentecost—Judas (Acts 1:17-20). Mark gives us some additional information. "There are some here of them that stand by, who shall in no wise taste of death, till they see the kingdom of God come with power" (Mark 9:1). Luke records: "But I tell you of a truth, There are some of them that stand here, who shall in no wise taste of death, till they see the kingdom of God" (Luke 9:27). Consider the following observations.

(1) The kingdom was to come in the lifetime of some who stood there. Did this take place? Christ first suffered and then was glorified (Luke 24:25-27; 1 Tim. 3:16). He ascended, made purification for our sins, sat down at the right hand of God, sent the Holy Spirit, and the Spirit through the apostles proclaimed to men that Christ is reigning at God's right hand (Acts 2:34-35) as king and priest (Psa. 110:1-4; Heb. 7:1-8:4). All the house of Israel could know assuredly that God hath made Jesus both Lord and Christ. Did power come on Pentecost? The kingdom was to come with power, and later Jesus said they would receive power when the Spirit was come upon them. With miraculous manifestations on Pentecost the message that Christ is ruling, in fulfilment of the promise *to* David (and the prophecy came *through* David), at God's right hand. Paul spoke of the existence of the kingdom, so it must have come (Col. 1:13-14; 1 Thess. 2:12; Heb. 12:28; Rev. 1:9).

(2) It is implied that at some time after the coming of the kingdom they *would* taste of death. They would not taste of it till the kingdom

came. Broadus pointed point out:

> *[this] naturally, though not necessarily, implies that after the coming in question they will taste of death; and is so far an argument against understanding our Lord's **final** coming to be meant.*[1]

In commenting on "and knew her not till she had brought forth a son" (Matt. 1:25), he said: "The word till inevitably suggests that afterwards it was otherwise, unless there be something in the connection or the nature of the case to forbid such a conclusion.[2]

(3) Some object that Christ would not have spoken in Matthew 16:27 of the final judgment, and of the establishment of the church in the next verse? Why not, when the context makes clear that verse 27 does refer to the judgment, and that verse 28 cannot refer to something which was to happen long after the death of everyone who heard Jesus say these words? In Acts 3:20, Peter speaks of a sending of the Lord at the end of time, and in Acts 3:26, he speaks of Christ being sent then through the preaching of the gospel.

(4) Some have claimed that the transfiguration which took place about a week later was the fulfilment of Matthew 16:28. At that time the apostles were "eyewitnesses of his majesty" (2 Pet. 1:16-18; Matt. 17:1-8). However, this was not a coming of Christ, for He had not departed, and it was not a coming of the kingdom with power. The kingdom no more existed in any sense the day *after* the transfiguration than it did on the day *of* the transfiguration or the day *before* it. Why overlook the time when the kingdom *did* come (Acts 2:30-36) and settle on a time when it did *not* come?

(5) Boll said that he had no difficulty in accepting the idea that it referred to the establishment of the church, for "the church is God's kingdom on earth today."[3] However, he argued that the kingdom of Matthew 11:11 is the kingdom promised to Israel.[4] He thinks the kingdom message was changed to the church-age message in the parables but, as shown in commenting on Matt. 13:11, Jesus is speaking of the same kingdom of which He spoke earlier, although He dealt with some of its mysteries. He did not say the kingdom itself was a mystery un-

---

[1] Broadus, *Harmony of the Gospels*, page 368.
[2] *Ibid.*, page 13.
[3] Boll, *The Kingdom of God,* page 75.
[4] *Ibid.*, page 66.

known to prophecy.

(6) There are some who say that it could not have been fulfilled on Pentecost, because Jesus did not come in person at that time. However, if it was not fulfilled on Pentecost, there must have been sometime within their lifetime that it was fulfilled; otherwise Jesus' promise failed. If not Pentecost, then when did Christ come in person with His kingdom? Since Jesus' promise did not fail, let us consider whether the coming *of* His kingdom can be said to be His coming *in* His kingdom. God may be said to come when He visits the earth with a judgment or a blessing. In speaking of the destruction of Babylon, Isaiah said: "They come from a far country, from the uttermost part of heaven, *even Jehovah, and the weapons of his indignation*, to destroy the whole land" (Isa. 13:5). There was no personal coming of God in that judgment on Babylon. Christ may be said to come in a visitation of His mercy, for example, on people. In speaking of the *resurrected* Christ, Peter said to his audience of Jews: "Unto you first God, having raised up his Servant, sent him to bless you, in turning away every one of you from your iniquities" (Acts 3:26).

The proclamation of salvation through the risen and reigning Savior (Acts 2:30-36) was the sending of Jesus to Israel to bless them in turning them from their iniquities. Why cannot the coming of His kingdom, and His being proclaimed as king, be His coming in His kingdom—especially since there is no other place and time when before the death of the apostles the kingdom came with power. Christ was said *to have come to the Gentiles and preached peace to them after His creation of the church.* He died to create the one new man (Eph. 2:13-16), "and *he came and preached* peace to you that were far off [Gentiles, see 2:11-12], and "peace to them that were nigh" (Eph. 2:17). He came in that *He* is said to do that which He did *through others*, i.e., those sent to preach the gospel. He came on Pentecost in that His kingdom then came with power in the lifetime of some who heard Him say these words.

Boll said concerning the time of the fulfillment of Matthew 16:28 that the "question has no essential bearing on our present study."[1] It does, for since the kingdom came with power in the lifetime of the apostles, we do not look for its establishment on earth at the second

---

[1] *Ibid.,* page 76.

coming.

The Throne of Glory and the Judgment

"But when the Son of man shall come in his glory, and all the angels with him, then shall he sit on the throne of his glory; and before him shall be gathered all the nations: and he shall separate them one from another, as the shepherd separateth the sheep from the goats; and he shall set the sheep on his right hand, but the goats on the left. Then shall the King say unto them on his right hand, Come, ye blessed of my Father, *inherit the kingdom* prepared for you from the foundation of the world... the King shall answer and say unto them, Verily I say unto you, Inasmuch as ye did it unto one of these my brethren, even these least, ye did it unto me... Then shall he say also unto them on the left hand, Depart from me, ye cursed, into the eternal fire which is prepared for the devil and his angels... And these shall go away into eternal punishment: but the righteous into *eternal life*" (Matt. 25:31-46).

Boll taught that this takes place at the second coming, but that it is not the final judgment, or general judgment, which comes at the end of the world.[1] What are his arguments?

First, it "is nowhere called the 'general judgment.'"[2] If the judgment of the nations living when Christ comes takes place then, and they go either into eternal life or eternal condemnation, they would not be there at the final judgment of others; therefore the coming judgment at the end of the world could not be a "general judgment." Boll rightly sees that there will be a judgment in Revelation 20:11-15,[3] but it is not called the "general judgment." John 5:28 is not called the general judgment. In fact, so far as I recall *no judgment is called the general judgment*. The fact that it is not *called* the "general judgment" does not mean that it is not the final judgment for all mankind.

Second, "There is not one word said about any resurrected dead being in it, but simply the 'nations.'"[4] This no more proves that the resurrected dead are not there, than the fact that nothing is said about the gospel, but only about good works, means that people will be saved solely on the basis of how they treated Christ's brethren (Matt. 25:46). Not one word is said about what they believed or did not be-

---

[1] *Ibid.,* pages 83, 163.
[2] *Ibid.,* page 163.
[3] *Ibid.,* pages 148-149.
[4] *Ibid.,* page 163.

lieve. Will people enter into "eternal life" and "inherit the kingdom prepared for you from the foundation of the world" through benevolent works even though they have not been born again (John 3:3-7)? Boll said; "The point they are judged on is their treatment of Christ's brethren, by which is not meant any and everybody, but those who are Christ's own. Such a standard of judgment, moreover, would not be applicable to the vast number of nations in former ages and heathen lands."[1] If this is the total picture of this judgment, men are saved on the basis of their good works without one reference to the grace of God, to their faith, or to the new birth. Yet on the previous page, Boll wrote: "There can never be any salvation for anyone, anywhere, any time, except by faith in the Lord Jesus Christ, and obedience to the gospel. Whatever changes that new era may bring, there can never be any altering of this fundamental and essential truth."[2] However, if Boll leaves out Israel, and the resurrected dead from Matthew 25:31-46, he must also leave out faith in Christ, obedience to the gospel, and the new birth. The truth of the matter is that this is but one place, among several others, in the Bible where the final judgment is dealt with. Not everything about the final judgment is found in one passage. Shall we rule out the resurrection of the unjust because there is no reference to their resurrection at the time the righteous are raised (1 Thess. 4:13-18)? There are scriptures which show that the just and the unjust will be raised the same hour, i.e., period of time (John 5:28-29; Acts 24:15). In John 12:48, Jesus spoke of people being judged by whether they reject Him and receive not His word (John 12:48). If this were the only passage on judgment it would mean that people who have never heard of Christ under this age, or who lived in the ages before Christ, will not be judged at all because they did not actually reject Jesus, for they never heard of Him.

Third, "Furthermore, in this judgment *Christians* are not among those who are being judged, for they are already with their Lord, past all judgment (Colossians 3:4) and are themselves associated with the Lord in His judging (1 Corinthians 6:2)."[3] If Boll is right, it means that Christians will be in no judgment at any time for they are "associated with the Lord in His judging." If this is the judgment of people on the

---

[1] *Ibid.*

[2] *Ibid.,* page 162.

[3] *Ibid.,* page 163.

basis of how they have treated Christians (Christ's own brethren), why are not Christians involved in the very judgment which concerned how others treated them? Furthermore, as already mentioned, Boll's comment here means that non-Christians (since no Christians are in this judgment) are saved or lost on the basis of how they treated Christians. In other words, according to Boll, *there was in operation at the same time two different plans of salvation.* (1) The gospel plan which saved people and the saved became Christians in the process of salvation. (2) Since Christians had to be on earth to be treated or mistreated by the nations, it follows that those who were kind to Christians were saved by their deeds of kindness. Boll is saying that at this very time the Christians "are associated with the Lord in His judging (1 Corinthians 6:2)." How can he say this, when there is no reference in the passage to Christians at all if Boll is right? Christians are not mentioned as being on the throne, or on thrones, with Christ in this judgment scene. If they are not among the people who make up the nations, where can they be? Boll says the resurrected dead are not there, because they are not mentioned, and Israel is not there, because she is not mentioned by name. Therefore, he should argue that Christians are not there associated with the Lord in His judging, for they are not mentioned by name. Paul spoke of Christians going to judge the world and angels (1 Cor. 6:1-6), and here the world is being judged and Christians are not even mentioned. If they can be there without being expressly mentioned in this specific passage (Matthew 25:31-46), there are others who can be there without being specially mentioned.

Fourth, "Moreover *Israel* is not in this judgment; for it is 'the nations' that are here judged before the King; which term is elsewhere translated 'Gentiles,' and always means the nations as distinguished from Israel, who are 'not reckoned among the nations' (Numbers 23:11)."[1] (1) When, then, is Israel judged? Is there any passage in the New Testament which specifically states Israel will be judged at the beginning of the millennium? Or at the end of time? Will unredeemed and unjudged Israel enter into the millennial kingdom? (2) The nation of Israel and its leaders were the first to persecute Christians and did persecute them for decades (1 Thess. 2:14-16). Why are not they among those judged for their treatment of Christ's brethren? (3) The Jews were a part of the world which Christ said would persecute His

---

[1] *Ibid.*

disciples (John 15:18-26; 16:1-4). Why can she not be classified among the nations, even though this was not the Old Testament designation for Israel? We are not now in old covenant days. Israel was one of the nations which sprang from Abraham (Gen 17:16; 17:5; Rom. 4:17). Further, the gospel was to be preached to all *nations* beginning at Jerusalem (Luke 24:47). Discipling the *nations* began with discipling the *Jews* (Matt 28:19; Acts 2:36). (4) Israel does not have to be specifically mentioned in this judgment scene in order to be there. (5) When the kingdom was taken from Israel (Matt. 21:43) and given to the spiritual nation, the church (1 Pet. 2:5, 9), Israel ceased to be God's Israel and became a Gentile nation, i.e., a nation which is outside of God's covenant. Israel is no longer God's true vine (John 15). The New Testament views those outside of the new covenant as Gentiles, and all Jews who have not obeyed the gospel are outside the covenant (Matt. 5:47; 18:17; 1 Cor. 5:1; 10:20; 12:2; 2:11-19; Eph. 4-17-18; 1 Pet. 1:1; 3:15, 21; 2:11-12; 4:3; 1 Thess. 4:5; 3 John 7). The Israel after the flesh is the descendant of Hagar and not of Sarah (1 Cor. 10:1; Gal 4:21-31). The sons of the slave woman do not inherit with the seed of Abraham (Gal. 3:26-29; 4:21-31). In speaking of those Jews who had become a synagogue of Satan, the Spirit said: "Behold, of them that say they are Jews, and they are not, but do lie; behold, I will make them to come and worship before thy feet, and to know that I have loved thee" (Rev. 3:9). Gentiles were represented as bending before Israel (Isa. 60:14), but some Israelites after the flesh are represented as bowing before the church, i.e., they acknowledge the church as the true Israel of God, and they (Israel after the flesh) take the role of the Gentiles in bowing before spiritual Israel.

Fifth, Walvoord thought that the brethren of Christ who were well treated by the nations were "specifically the Jews of the tribulation time who were the objects of fearful persecution."[1] This is indeed an unscriptural conclusion. (1) Christ showed that family and national distinctions did not hold when it came to one's relationship to Him. It must be on the basis of a spiritual relationship (John 3:3-5; Matt. 12:46-50; Gal. 3:26-29). (2) The Biblical teaching concerning the unbelieving Jews proves they are not brethren of Christ in any sense which counts (John 8:37-45; 15:17-20; Rom. 11:1-23). (3) Since Wal-

---

[1] Walvoord, *The Millennial Kingdom*, page 288.

voord believes that the church was translated before the tribulation, there were no Christians *during* the tribulation; therefore all, both Jews and Gentiles were unbelievers. However, if people are converted during the tribulation, the Jews who were converted would have to be converted by the gospel, and this would make them a part of the new man in Christ (Eph. 3:13-16).

Sixth, when is Christ on the throne of glory mentioned in Matthew 25:31? "The Jews, including the Twelve, expected the Messiah to sit on a throne of temporal dominion. Our Lord here shows the disciples that at his second coming he will sit on a throne of judgment, making awards for eternity. He sits now already on the throne of mediatorial authority (28:18), spiritually conquering and ruling (1 Cor. 15:25; Heb. 12:2)."[1]

(1) The evidence shows that the throne of His glory is not a different throne from the one He now occupies, for the one which He now occupies is the one on which He reigns until all enemies are conquered. The last enemy is death (Acts 2:30-36; 1 Cor. 15:24-28; Rev. 20:11-15).

(2) In speaking of His coming to "render unto every man according to his deeds, Jesus said that "the Son of man shall come in the glory of his Father with his angels" (Matt. 16:27). Christ is now ruling in glory, for He was received up into glory (1 Tim. 3:16). He was received up into the reign at God's right hand (Heb. 1:3, 13; Acts 2:34-36). "We have such a high priest, who sat down at the right hand of the throne of the Majesty in the heavens" (Heb. 8:1). What more exalted position can there be than one wherein He has all power, and everyone except the Father is subject to Him (Matt. 28:18; 1 Cor. 15:24-28)? The judgment scene in Matthew 25:31-46 does not place Him on a different throne, but on the very throne on which He now reigns! He will exercise His power at that time to call men to the final judgment instead of calling them through the gospel to everlasting Life (Jude 14). "For we must all be made manifest before the judgment-seat of Christ; that each one may receive the things done in the body, according to what he hath done, whether it be good or bad" (2 Cor. 5:10; Rom. 2:1-11). Matthew several times spoke of the separation of the good and of the bad (3:12; 7:13-14; 7:24-27; 13:24-30; 13:41-43, 47-50; 21:28-32; 22:10-14; 25:10-13, 46).

---

[1] Broadus, *Harmony of the Gospels*, page 508.

(3) Christ's second coming brings salvation to the saints in a sense different from the salvation which they now experience. "So Christ also, having been once offered to bear the sins of many, shall appear *a second time*, apart from sin, to them that wait for him, unto salvation" (Heb. 9:28). The first coming had to do with sin in that He was "manifested to put away sin by the sacrifice of himself" (Heb. 9:26). We are now saved by His blood (Rom. 5:1-11; Eph. 2:5; Rom. 1:16). However, the salvation which He brings to those who wait for Him at His second coming is the consummation of our *present* salvation in *eternal* salvation in heaven. This is the rest which the saints received when the wicked received tribulation (2 Thess. 1:6-12). It is the eternal life which the righteous receive when the wicked enter into eternal punishment after the judgment (Matt. 25:31, 46). It would not be salvation in a sense which differs from the salvation we now enjoy, if at the second coming we go into a kingdom for a thousand years; and in this kingdom there is some sin, and which is followed by a tremendous rebellion against Christ and His people (Rev. 20:1-10).

(4) To enter "*into eternal life*" is to "*inherit the kingdom* prepared for you from the foundation of the world (Matt. 25:46, 34). If premillennialism is right, the kingdom which the saints will inherit after this judgment scene is one which will last but a thousand years, then it will end. It will end for the simple reason that the millennial reign is but for "a thousand years" (Rev. 20:4). It will not be a year longer, regardless of whether it is a literal thousand years or whether it is a symbol for a definite period of time. The reign will end, for "when the thousand years are finished, Satan shall be loosed out of his prison, and shall come forth to deceive the nations which are in the four corners of the earth. Gog and Magog, to gather them together to the war: the number of whom is as the sand of the sea. And they went up over the breadth of the earth, and compassed the camp of the saints about, and the beloved city: and fire came down out of heaven, and devoured them. And the devil that deceived them was cast into the lake of fire and brimstone, where are also the beast and the false prophet; and they shall be tormented day and night for ever and ever" (Rev. 20:7-10). Then follows the judgment of humanity (Rev. 20:11-15). The thousand-year reign lasts as long as Satan is bound, and he is loosed after the thousand years (Rev. 20:2-3, 7). The little season of rebellion and warfare against the saints could easily be one hundred or more years for one or

two or three hundred years would be a little season in contrast with the thousand years. If the premillennialists are right, the judgment scene of Matthew 25:31 is followed by an inheriting of the kingdom for one thousand years, and then it ends. If it ends then, why does not the punishment of the wicked end then, since everlasting is used to describe both the punishment and the life? Inheriting the kingdom is to enter the prepared mansions (John 14:1-3). It is to be forever with the Lord (1 Thess. 4; 17).

The premillennial interpretation of Matthew 25:31-46 contradicts the New Testament and it introduces contradictory elements into their own picture of the kingdom, for if the saints judge the world with Christ and rule with Him in the millennium, the church—not Israel—will be supreme in the millennial kingdom.

Fulfilled in the Kingdom of God

"And he said unto them, With desire I have desired to eat this Passover with you before I suffer: for I say unto you, I shall not eat it, until it be fulfilled in the kingdom of God... I shall not drink from henceforth of the fruit of the vine, until the kingdom of God shall come" (Luke 22:15-18). Again Christ mentioned His suffering, which indeed the Lord's supper would commemorate, and showed that He must die before the kingdom is established (Luke 24:25-27). The Passover signified deliverance. Some think that Jesus meant He would not partake with them again until He came again, and in the eternal kingdom in the new heavens and the new earth we participate in the Messianic banquet. This is a spiritual banquet.

However, Jesus indicated that after its fulfilment in the kingdom He would eat the Passover with them. Christ is our Passover (1 Cor. 5:7). The type of the Old Testament Passover lamb is fulfilled in Jesus Christ, the Lamb of God who taketh away the sin of the world (John 1:29). The feast which we keep is the Christian life (1 Cor. 5:6-3). However, the Lord's supper is a memorial of the death of our Passover Lamb. *The kingdom of God is based on His sacrifice, and the Lord's supper is the memorial to this sacrifice.* Does not Christ partake of it with us in some sense as we commune with His blood and body (1 Cor. 10:16-17)? Does He not in some sense partake with us of the fruit of the vine now that the kingdom is come (Luke 22:18; Acts 2:30-36)?

He eats the paschal food, and then says that it is the last time under these conditions; and He drinks of the paschal cup, and then says that it is for the last time under these conditions.[1]

"When ye see...know...the Kingdom of God is nigh."

"Even so ye also, when ye see these things coming to pass, know ye that the kingdom of God is nigh. Verily I say unto you, This generation shall not pass away, till all things be accomplished" (Luke 21:31-32). Jesus had been speaking of Jerusalem at least up until Luke 21:25. If Luke 21:27 refers to the second coming of Christ, the redemption in verse twenty-eight refers to eternal redemption. If the reference is not to the second coming, but to the destruction of Jerusalem, the redemption was the release or deliverance from Jewish persecution which came with the destruction of Jerusalem. If Luke 21:31 refers to the second coming, the kingdom of God has reference to the eternal kingdom when Christ delivers the kingdom to the Father (Acts 2:34-35; 1 Cor. 15:24-28). If it refers to the kingdom, which during the personal ministry was at hand, it must refer either to its establishment on Pentecost or Christ the king coming in judgment on Israel and Judaism. The destruction of Jerusalem swept away the external remains of the old covenant system, made impossible even the external keeping of the old covenant. Christ had abolished the old covenant when he took it out of the way to establish the new (Heb. 10:9-10; Col. 2:14-17). At the time Hebrews was written, the old was nigh unto vanishing away (Heb. 8:13). Of this event, Jesus said: "Verily I say unto you, This generation shall not pass away, till all things be accomplished. Heaven and earth shall pass away: but my words shall not pass away." (Luke 21:32-33). "This cannot well mean anything but *the generation living when these words were spoken*: [Luke] 7:31, 11:29-32, 50-51 17:25; Matt. 11:16, etc. The reference, therefore, is to *the destruction of Jerusalem* regarded as the *type of the end of the world...* [To make it mean] the Jewish race, or the generation contemporaneous with the beginning of the signs, is not satisfactory."[2] Christ had already taken the kingdom from Israel and given it to the spiritual nation which was then receiving it (Matt. 21:43; Heb. 12:28). With the destruction of Jerusalem, God made clear by demonstration that He had already rejected Israel as His nation, and that His time of longsuffering with that generation was at an end.

---

[1] Plummer, *Commentary on the Gospel According to St. Luke*, page 496.
[2] *Ibid.*, page 485.

Remember Me

One robber knew that Jesus was innocent, and said, "Jesus, remember me when thou comest in thy kingdom. And he said unto him, Verily I say unto thee, Today shalt thou be with me in Paradise" (Luke 23:42-43). "The robber knew that he had only a few hours to live, and therefore this prayer implies a belief in a future state in which Jesus is to receive him in His Kingdom. Possibly he believed that Christ would raise him from the dead. In any case his faith in one who is crucified with him is very remarkable. Some saw Jesus raised from the dead, and did not believe. The robber sees Him being put to death, and yet believes... He believes that Jesus is the Messiah, and he knows that the Messiah is to have a kingdom."[1] Doubtless he had misconceptions of the nature of the kingdom as did the apostles, but he had faith in the Messiah, the King.

Kingdom in Eternity

The kingdom of God is to be consummated in eternity. God's kingdom continues into eternity. Therefore, Jesus sometimes speaks of the kingdom in eternity, and it is delivered to God for eternity when the last enemy is conquered (1 Cor. 15:24-28). Jesus taught that one must do the will of God in order to enter the kingdom in eternity, and certainly one must do His will to enter the kingdom in time. "Not everyone that saith unto me, Lord, Lord, shall enter into the kingdom of heaven; but he that doeth the will of my Father who is in heaven. Many will say to me in that day, Lord, Lord, did we not prophesy by thy name, and by thy name cast out demons, and by thy name do many mighty works? And then will I profess unto them, I never knew you: depart from me, ye that work iniquity" (Matt. 7:21-23). "That day" refers to the day of judgment. *First,* Jesus indicates that these people had claimed to serve Him, evidently while on earth. *Second,* the wicked are ordered to depart from Him, and we know that this happens on the day of judgment when they depart into the place prepared for the devil and his angels (Matt. 25:41, 46). One could claim to prophesy, to work miracles, and do many mighty works in Christ's name without actually doing God's will. We must hear and do (Matt. 7:24-27; Luke 6:46).

Christ also spoke of the kingdom in eternity when He said, after

---

[1] *Ibid.,* page 535.

stating that "I have not found so great faith, no, *not in Israel,*" that "many shall come from the east and the west, and shall sit down with Abraham, and Isaac, and Jacob, in the kingdom of heaven: but the sons of the kingdom shall be cast forth into the outer darkness: there shall be weeping and gnashing of teeth" (Matt. 8:10-12). The scene is evidently in heaven because Abraham, Isaac, and Jacob are there, and the rejected ones are "cast forth into the outer darkness." This was the eternal fate of the wicked (Matt. 22:13; 25:30; 8:12; 13:42, 50; 24:51; Luke 13:28). There would be Gentiles there whom the Jews did not expect to be in such a place of prominence with the patriarchs, and many Jews who expected to be there would not be there (Luke 13:28-29).

What is the Kingdom?

When the premillennialists describe the kingdom, the emphasis is on Israel's restoration to the land, her exaltation over the nations of the earth, her earthly glory, and the physical peace and prosperity of Israel and the Gentiles. It is true that Walvoord in describing the "spiritual life in the millennium," does stress righteousness, peace, and joy.[1] However, when Paul stressed what is the nature of the kingdom, he mentioned none of the earthly glories which premillennialists view as essential aspects of the kingdom, in so far as Israel is concerned. Paul said: "For *the kingdom of God* is not eating and drinking, but righteousness and peace and joy in the Holy Spirit. For he that *herein serveth Christ* is well-pleasing to God, and approved of men" (Rom. 14:17-18). Consider the following:

First, those who live in harmony with these qualities of the kingdom of God are not only in the kingdom, but they are serving Christ. They are serving Christ because it is not only the kingdom of God, but also the kingdom of Christ (Col. 1:13; Eph. 5:5). Christ's servants are in His kingdom (Col. 1:13). They are in Him, in His body (Eph. 1:14; Gal. 3:26-27).

Second, the kingdom is *not* meat and drink. The old covenant required that one abstain from certain foods. The new covenant teaches that such food regulations are not binding (1 Tim. 4:3-5). One would abstain from meats only if the eating of meat led a brother to sin and

---

[1] Walvoord, *The Millennial Kingdom*, page 308.

be lost (1 Cor. 10:23-11:1; Rom.14:14-21). The kingdom of David was in a literal land, made up of a physical nation (Israel), and one in which there was eating and drinking (1 Chron. 12:39-40; 16:3).

Third, what is the kingdom of God? It is *righteousness.* No wonder Jesus, in the Sermon on the Mount, said that instead of seeking what they would eat, drink, or wear (although we have need of them), we are to "seek ye first his kingdom, and *his righteousness*; and all these things shall be added unto you" (Matt. 6:31-33). The Gentiles sought these things (Matt. 6:32) in that they placed them first, but it is not to be so among His disciples. The righteousness which we seek is the righteousness of God which was prophesied by the prophets, and is found in Christ, in that we are justified by faith in Jesus Christ (Rom. 3:21-26; 5:1; 9:30-10:4). The justified are called on to live righteous lives, although no one perfectly does all the will of God.

Fourth, the kingdom of God is peace (Rom. 14:17). It is not basically peace within, or peace with others, but peace with God. "Being therefore justified by faith, we have peace with God through our Lord Jesus Christ" (Rom. 5:1). We have peace because we are reconciled to God through the cross, and this message is proclaimed in the gospel of reconciliation (Col. 1:19-23; 2 Cor. 5:11-6:2). Christ came to bring peace in every spiritual sense (Luke 2:14).

Fifth, the kingdom of God is joy (Rom. 14:17). The angel brought to the shepherds "good tidings of great joy which shall be to all the people: for there is born to you this day in the city of David a Savior, who is Christ the Lord" (Luke 2:10). He was not a Savior from Roman rule but from sin (Matt. 1:21).

Paul had summed up these three qualities of the kingdom, when he said: "Being therefore *justified* by faith, we have *peace* with God through our Lord Jesus Christ; through whom also we have had our access by faith into this grace wherein we stand; and we *rejoice* in the hope of the glory of God, And not only so, but we also *rejoice* in our tribulations: knowing that tribulation worketh steadfastness; and steadfastness, approvedness; and approvedness, hope: and hope putteth not to shame; because the love of God hath been shed abroad in our hearts through the Holy Spirit which was given unto us" (Rom. 5:1-5).

The blessings of the Kingdom of God are not the fruits of the land of Canaan, but the fruits of the Holy Spirit; and the "joy" that was in Israel because of the good things to eat and drink, is replaced by "joy in the Holy Ghost."[1]

Sixth, all of these things, are "in the Holy Spirit" (Rom. 14:17). The prophets in the Old Testament spoke by the Holy Spirit (Neh. 9:30), as do the New Testament prophets (John 14:26; 16:12-15; 1 Cor. 2:10-14). However, there is much more about the Spirit in the new covenant than in the old. Christ baptized certain people in the Spirit, as John predicted, in the inauguration, revelation, and confirmation of the new covenant (Matt. 3:11; Acts 1:5, 8; 2:1-4, 33). Joel prophesied that the Spirit would be poured out in the last days (Acts 2:16-ff). The Spirit was not given in the personal ministry in the sense in which He was given on Pentecost—first in a miraculous way (Acts 2:4, 6, 8, 11), and then in that each baptized believer is in some sense a temple of the Spirit (John 7:37-39; Acts 2:38; 1 Cor. 6:18-20). The new birth is of water and the Spirit (John 3:3-5). The very qualities in our lives of love, joy, peace, longsuffering, kindness, goodness, faithfulness, meekness, and self-control are said to be "the fruit of the Spirit" (Gal. 5:22). The Spirit through the apostles declared the conditions of remission of sins (John 20:22-23). Without this, we could not have righteousness, peace, and joy: in the Spirit. Romans 14:17 is one of the few places in the New Testament where the kingdom is defined, "The kingdom of God is..." Neither here nor elsewhere in the New Testament is it defined as a kingdom in which Israel is restored to sovereignty in the land of Palestine, exalted above the nations of the earth, with the Gentiles blessed through and in subservience to restored Israel. This is the definition of the kingdom given by Boll and many others.

---

[1] Philip Mauro, *The Gospel and the Kingdom*, page 96.

CHAPTER 4:
THE ESTABLISHMENT OF THE KINGDOM

Jesus was born "King of the Jews" (Matt. 2:2). The throne was His by divine and human right, although He was not crowned king at the moment of His birth (Luke 1:32-33). One might say that the kingdom which once had existed in prophecy, in the personal ministry existed in preparation. "But if I by the Spirit of God cast out demons, then is the kingdom of God come upon you" (Matt. 12:28). He did cast out demons by the Holy Spirit. In what sense had the kingdom come upon them? Certainly there was not the remotest hint of the type of kingdom envisioned by the premillennialists. Jack Lewis mentioned that "has come... is a difficult phrase.... The meaning seems to be 'has come before you expected it. The kingdom was advancing through Jesus' works."[1] Philip Schaff said: "The kingdom you profess to be waiting for, has come upon you suddenly, before you expected it, in spite of your opposition to me."[2] Myer wrote that "where the Messiah [who was born king of the Jews] is present and working, there, too is the *kingdom*; not yet, of course, as completely established, but preparing to become so through its preliminary development in the world."[3] "Besides, in casting out demons, he was to that extent destroying the kingdom of Satan (v. 26), and in so far establishing the correlative kingdom of God (Comp. v. 29)."[4] The kingdom was in its preparatory stage, and the power which Jesus utilized against the devil, the power by the Holy Spirit, showed that He was telling the truth when He preached the kingdom was at hand (Matt. 4:17).

Christ not only announced that the kingdom was at hand, but He clearly taught that it would come in their lifetime (Matt. 4:17; Mark 1:14-15; 9:1). Christ acknowledged before Pilate that He was King (Matt. 27:11; John 18:33-38). He was mockingly called "King of the Jews" (Matt. 27:29, 37). Religious leaders mocked saying: "He saved others; himself he cannot save. He is the King of Israel; let him now come down from the cross, and we will believe on him" (Matt. 27:41-42). They did not realize that in order to save others He could not save

---

[1] Jack P. Lewis, *The Gospel According to Matthew* (Living Word Commentary), Vol. 1, pages 175-176.

[2] Schaff, page 114 (note: book not specified in Bales' manuscript).

[3] Myer, page 241 (note: book not specified in Bales' manuscript).

[4] Broadus, *Harmony of the Gospels*, page 270.

Himself from the cross, and that He must first suffer and then enter into His glory, which involved entering into His kingdom (Luke 24:25-27; 1 Tim. 3:16 Acts 2:30-36). He now has all authority and power (Matt. 28:18), and they were cut off because of their unbelief (Acts 3:22-23; Rom. 11:1-24).

The kingdom was at hand in His personal ministry (Matt. 3:2; 4:17; 10:7), and the disciples prayed for its coming (Matt. 6:10). John the Baptist was not in it, for "he that is but little in the kingdom of heaven is greater than [John]" (Matt. 11:11). If John had been in it, and been the least, this would have made him greater than himself! Then when did the kingdom come?

Kingdom Came on Pentecost

There are several lines of argument which show that the kingdom came to earth on the first Pentecost after Christ's resurrection, ascension, and coronation in heaven.

First, Christ was crowned king after His suffering and rejection. He told His disciples that they were foolish not to realize that He must first suffer and *then* enter into glory (Luke 24:25-27). He was received up into glory (1 Tim. 3:16). Was He received up into His kingdom? Sometimes the expression "in thy kingdom" (Matt. 20:21) and "in thy glory" express the same truth (Mark 10:37). After Christ had ascended, and made purification for our sins, He sat down at the right hand of God to reign until all of His enemies are conquered (Heb. 1:3, 13). This fact was first proclaimed, as an existing reality, to the world on Pentecost (Acts 2:30-36).

Second, in speaking of Himself as the rejected stone, which God made the head of the corner, Jesus said: "Therefore say I unto you, The kingdom of God shall be taken away from you, and shall be given to a nation bringing forth the fruits thereof (Matt. 21:43). God's reign had been with the nation of Israel, but in the parable which preceded this statement Jesus said God would take it from Israel (Matt. 21:41, 45), and "will let out the vineyard unto other husbandmen, who shall render him the fruits in their seasons" (Matt. 21:41). God gave the kingdom to the little flock (Luke 12:32). The Christians were the nation (1 Pet. 2:9) who, in receiving the stone rejected by men (1 Pet. 2:4), were receiving the kingdom (Heb. 12:28).

Third, "Verily I say unto you, There are some here of them that stand by, who shall in no wise taste of death, till they see the kingdom of God come with power" (Mark 9:1). Jesus was not saying they would see a preview of the kingdom on the mount of transfiguration, but that they would "see the *kingdom* of God *come with power*." Not everyone who stood there lived until the kingdom came, for Judas died before its coming (Acts 1:18). Shortly before His ascension Jesus said to the apostles: "But ye shall receive power, when the Holy Spirit is come upon you: and ye shall be my witnesses both in Jerusalem, and in all Judaea and Samaria, and unto the uttermost part of the earth" (Acts 1:8). The Spirit came on Pentecost and therefore power came on Pentecost. This is what Jesus promised, and the Spirit inspired them to speak the truth and furnished them with miraculous power to confirm the truth (Acts 2:1-4, 6, 8, 11, 43; Heb. 2:3-4). Did the kingdom come with power when the Spirit came with power? Yes, for Jesus was preached as ruling at God's right hand as Lord (Acts 2:30-36).

Fourth, Christ was not a priest while on earth for He was of the tribe of Judah, and the law of Moses, which was in force, said that priests were to come from the tribe of Levi (Heb. 7:11-25; 8:1-4; Psa. 110:1, 4). He became high priest and king after His ascension, and the earth was informed of this on Pentecost (Acts 2:30-36).

Fifth, at the same time Christ was crowned king at God's right hand, He was placed over all things to the church (Eph. 1:19-22). The church is the kingdom of God's Son (Col. 1:13-14, 18). People who were baptized on Pentecost were born of water and Spirit into the kingdom of God (John 3:3-5; Acts 2:38, 41; Titus 3:3).

Sixth, although Christ has all authority in heaven and on earth (Matt. 28:18), only the church is the kingdom of God's Son into which we are translated through obedience to the gospel (Col. 1:13-14). The suffering of Christ was essential to the establishment of the kingdom (Luke 24:25-27), and the suffering (the cross) of Christ was essential to the establishment of the church (Eph. 2:11-17; Col. 2:14-17). In most references to the kingdom in the New Testament reference is made to the same reign of Christ which is presented in the figure of the church and Christ as head over the church. Head of the church is the position of authority over the body, which is equal to the king over the kingdom.

Seventh, Christ was not the chief cornerstone until after His rejection. Jesus spoke of the prophecy of the rejected stone in connection with the kingdom being taken away from Israel (Matt. 21:41-43). After

Pentecost, Peter said: "He is the stone which was set at naught of you the builders, which was made the head of the corner. And in none other is there salvation: for neither is there any other name under heaven, that is given among men, wherein we must be saved" (Acts 4:11-12). The rejected stone has been made the head of the corner of the foundation of the church, in Eph. 2:20-21, where the church is likened unto a growing temple. "Being built upon the foundation of the apostles and prophets, Christ Jesus himself being the chief cornerstone." We are come unto Christ, "a living stone, rejected indeed of men, but with God elect, precious, ye also, as living stones, are built up a spiritual house, to be a holy priesthood, to offer up spiritual sacrifices, acceptable to God through Jesus Christ. Because it is contained in scripture, Behold, I lay in Zion a chief corner stone, elected, precious: and he that believeth on him shall not be put to shame. For you therefore that believe in the preciousness: but for such as disbelieve, The stone which the builders rejected, the same was made the head of the corner; and, A stone of stumbling, and a rock of offence; for they stumble at the word, being disobedient: whereunto also they were appointed. But ye are an elect race, a royal priesthood, a holy nation, a people for God's own possession, that ye may show forth the excellencies of him who called you out of darkness into his marvelous light: who in time past were no people, but now are the people of God: who had not obtained mercy, but now have obtained mercy" (1 Pet. 2:4-10).

Eighth, the church of the new covenant was established when the new covenant became in force. The two covenants could not be in force at the same time, for He had to take away the first that He might establish the second (Heb. 10:9). To be under both covenants at the same time would have involved one in spiritual adultery (Rom. 7:1-7). The old covenant was in force during the personal ministry of Christ (Matt. 8:4; 23:1-3). The death of Christ made possible the abolition of the law (Col. 2:14-16). Christ's death had to take place before the new covenant could become operative (Heb. 9:15-17). The new covenant did not become operative at the moment of His death, but by virtue of His death, for He had to make the offering in heaven and sit down at God's right hand (Heb. 1:3, 13)

The Church and the Keys of the Kingdom

"And I also say unto thee, that thou art Peter, and upon this rock I will build my church; and the gates of Hades shall not prevail against it. I will give unto thee the keys of the kingdom of heaven: and whatsoever thou shalt bind on earth shall be bound in heaven; and whatsoever thou shalt loose on earth shall be loosed in heaven" (Matt. 16:18-19). If the kingdom of heaven and the church are not different ways of speaking of the same thing, how can we explain the following:

First, the coming of the kingdom and the building of the church were both future, "I will build my church" (Matt. 16:18), and: "Verily I say unto you, There are some of them that stand here, who shall in no wise taste of death, till they see the Son of man coming in his kingdom" (Matt. 16:28). How could Christ build His church on the rock, in the near future, and say that the kingdom would come in the lifetime of some who were there, if He was not speaking of the same reality? The premillennialists admit that the church was at hand, nearby in point of time, when Jesus spoke the words in Matthew 16:18, and both John and Jesus had said the kingdom was nearby (Matt. 3:2; 4:17; 10:9), and Jesus reaffirmed its nearness at this very time (Matt. 16:28).

Second, in this context Jesus spoke of His coming death and resurrection (Matt. 16:21). These two events, plus the ascension, had to take place before the kingdom would be established or the church built. He could not create the church, the body, unless He died on the cross, for it was through the cross that He made of the twain (Jew and Gentile) one new man (Eph. 2:13-16). He had to die before He entered His kingdom. He must die, and then make the offering in heaven for our sins, before He could sit down at the right hand of God to reign as king and priest (Heb. 1:3, 13; 8:1-2; Acts 2:30-36). The prophets taught that He must first suffer and then enter into His glory (Luke 24:25-27). He was received up into glory (1 Tim. 3:16). In some cases, at least, entering into His glory and entering into His kingdom are different ways of speaking of the same thing. Where Matthew said "in thy kingdom" (Matt. 20:21), Mark said "in thy glory" (Mark 10:37). They were both speaking of the same thing, i.e., the positions on the right and left hand of Christ in His kingdom. When Christ was received up into glory, was He received up into His kingdom? Yes (Acts 2:34-36; Heb. 1:3, 13; 8:1-2).

Third, keys are used to let someone into a building. If the keys did not pertain to the church, which the Lord said He would build on the rock, why were they mentioned in connection with the church? The one who has the keys can decide who and on what conditions the building is entered. If Peter being the doorkeeper with keys does not pertain to the church, why mention his position when talking about the church? The other apostles also had authority to proclaim the gospel.

Fourth, if the keys do not pertain to the present dispensation, the church age, Peter has been carrying around the keys for almost two thousand years and he has not used them yet. This is not the case, for the kingdom came in his lifetime when the power came, and the power came when the Spirit came on Pentecost (Matt. 16:28; Mk, 9:1; Acts 1:8; 2:1, 30-36).

Fifth, keys symbolize authority. What is symbolized by the keys is clearly stated in other words when Christ said, after the reference to keys, "*and* whatsoever thou shalt bind on earth shall be bound in heaven; and whatsoever thou shalt loose on earth shall be loosed in heaven" (Matt. 16:19). This had to do with declaring the conditions of the remission of sins and how to live after one was baptized into Christ (John 20:20-23; Matt. 28:20). "Jesus therefore said to them again, Peace be unto you: as the Father hath sent me, even so send I you. And when he had said this, he breathed on them, and saith unto them, Receive ye the Holy Spirit: whose soever sins ye forgive, they are forgiven unto them; whose soever sins ye retain, they are retained." (John 20:21-23). He was to send them forth under the great commission (John 13:20; Matt. 28:18-19; Acts 1:8). They were to start this work when the Spirit came and they were to proclaim repentance and remission of sins in Jesus' name to all nations beginning at Jerusalem (Luke 24:45-49; Acts 1:8; Acts 2:38).

Sixth, on Pentecost the church on earth was formed.[1] Did Peter make an authorized use of the keys when he declared what Jews must do in order to enter the kingdom, and also those who were afar off (Acts 2:38-40)? Was he not using the authority to bind and to loose when he told them what to do to be saved; and when the apostles set forth the doctrine in which the people continued, were they not exercising such authority (Acts 2:38-42)? Was not Peter using the authority of keys when as a result of God's choice he preached the gospel to the Gentiles in order that they might believe and be purified by faith and saved by grace (Acts 15:7-11)? Was not authority used on Pentecost and at the household of Cornelius—the authority of keys, the authority

---

[1] Walvoord, *The Millennial Kingdom*, page 226.

to let people enter through the door, the authority to bind and to loose, the authority to declare the conditions on which sins are remitted?

Seventh, were the keys of the kingdom used on Pentecost? Were people told what to do to enter the kingdom? Jesus said one must be born of water and Spirit *to enter* the kingdom (John 3:2-5). Premillennialists know that one must be born again today in order to be a Christian. Regardless of what understanding or misunderstanding they may have of the new birth they realize that one must be born again. If we are not born again *into the kingdom*, into what are we born today? On Pentecost, when people wanted to know what to do to be saved, Peter told them what to do, exhorted them to do it, and they that received the word in the proper spirit did it (Acts 2:37-42). Was anything said about the kingdom at that time? The kingdom of Christ or of God is the reign of Christ and of God. Christ was proclaimed as reigning at God's right hand (Acts 2:34-35). At God's right hand, Christ reigns as king and priest (Heb. 1:3, 13; 7:1-4; 8:1-2). Peter also proclaimed that Jesus is Lord and Christ (Acts 2:36). Lord means ruler, and He rules at God's right hand. The Messiah, having entered into His glory, is prophet, priest, and king (Acts 2:34-35; 3:22-23; Heb. 8:1-2). Furthermore, Peter showed that Christ was reigning on David's throne, which is but another way of designating the throne at God's right hand. Peter referred to God's promise to place the Christ on David's throne; he then gave the meaning of the promise (Acts 2:30-32), and then he mentioned the fulfilment of the promise. *"Being therefore* by the right hand of God exalted, and having received of the Father the promise of the Holy Spirit, he hath poured forth this, which ye see and hear, For David ascended not into the heavens: but he saith himself, The Lord said unto my Lord, Sit thou on my right hand, till I make thine enemies the footstool of thy feet. Let all the house of Israel *therefore* know assuredly, that God hath made him both Lord and Christ, this Jesus whom ye crucified" (Acts 2:33-36). God promised through David to enthrone Christ on David's throne. He promised through David that it would be at God's right hand, and in fulfillment of that promise Christ is reigning as king, as Lord, as Christ, over His people on earth. If Peter was not using the keys of the kingdom, what keys was he using when he told people what they must do in order to voluntarily come under the reign of Christ? Of course, David on his throne was a type of Christ on His throne. Christ's throne is superior to David's for Christ is superior. The church was established, the kingdom was established, the keys were used, and people were exhorted to enter the kingdom (Acts 2:36-41). Later Paul wrote "Who delivered us out of the power of darkness, and translated us into the kingdom of the Son of his love; in whom we have our redemption, the forgiveness of our sins" (Col. 1:13-14). They were in the kingdom. But they were also in Christ ("in whom"). Therefore, those who are in Christ are in the kingdom and those who are in the kingdom are in Christ. We are children of God in Christ (Gal. 3:26-27). The people on Pentecost came into Christ (Acts 2:38, 41; Gal. 3:26-27), therefore they were translated into the kingdom.

Eighth, if the kingdom has not yet been established, Peter and the apostles will use the "keys of the kingdom" and exercise their power to bind and loose in the millennial kingdom. They will do this not as Jews, but as Christians who are apostles in the church (1 Cor. 12:28) in which there is no distinction between Jew and Gentile, but all are one man in Christ (Eph. 2:13-16; 3:3-6; Gal. 3:26-29). Israel was not be next to Christ in rulership in the kingdom. Instead Christ will rule on His throne, the apostles on their twelve thrones over Israel (Matt. 19:28), declaring what is binding and what is not binding; what is lawful and what is not. The placing of the apostles as members of the bride of Christ over Israel destroys the premillennial picture of what the Old Testament prophecies teach about the kingdom.

Kingdom Preached in Acts

Before the coming of the Spirit, the apostles asked if the Lord would at this time restore the kingdom to Israel (Acts 1:6). Christ had been "speaking the things concerning the kingdom of God" (Acts 1:3). Christ did not give a direct answer to their question. It is not for you to know times or seasons, which the Father hath set within his own authority. But ye shall receive power, when the Holy Spirit is come upon you: and ye shall be my witnesses..." (Acts 1:7-8).

> *The kingdom of God which they were commissioned to proclaim was the good news of God's grace in Christ. The question in v. 6 appears to have been the last flicker of their former burning expectation of an imminent political theocracy with themselves as its chief executives. From this time forth they devoted themselves to the proclamation and service of God's spiritual kingdom, which men enter by repentance and faith.*

and in which chief honor belongs to those who most faithfully
follow the King Himself in the path of obedience and suffering.

Instead of the political power which had formerly been the object of their ambitions, a power far greater and nobler would be theirs. When the Holy Spirit came upon them, Jesus assured them, they would be clothed with heavenly power—that power by which, in the event, their mighty works were accomplished and their preaching made effective. As Jesus Himself had been anointed at His baptism with the Holy Spirit and power, so His followers were now to be similarly anointed and enabled to carry on His work. This work would be a work of witness-bearing—a theme which is prominent in the apostolic preaching throughout Acts (cf. 2:32; 3:15; 5:32; 10:39; 13:31; 22:15, etc.). An OT prophet had called Israel to be God's witnesses in the world (Isa. 43:10; 44:8); the task which Israel as a nation had not fulfilled was taken up by Jesus, as the perfect Servant of the Lord, and passed on by Him to His disciples. The close relation between God's call to Israel in those Isaianic passages, "Ye are my witnesses," and Christ's words to His apostles, "ye shall be my witnesses," will be appreciated the more if we consider the implications of Paul's quotation of Isa. 49:6 in Acts 13:47 (see p. 283). There the heralds of the gospel are described as being a light to the Gentiles, bearing God's salvation "unto the uttermost part of the earth"; here "the uttermost part of the earth" and nothing short of that is to be the limit of the apostolic witness.[1]

Instead of the kingdom being restored to physical Israel, *it was shortly to be taken away from her with the abolition of the old covenant and the institution of the new.* Jesus had made this clear in talking with the Pharisees (Matt. 21:41-43). It should be noticed that after Pentecost the apostles never asked whether God would restore the kingdom to Israel. Instead, beginning on Pentecost they preached that God had raised Jesus to His own right hand to reign on the throne of David which is now the throne at God's right hand (Acts 2:30-36). "*Let all the house of Israel* therefore, now assuredly, that God hath made him both Lord and Christ, this Jesus whom ye- crucified" (Acts 2:36). The kingdom was given to the little flock (Luke 12:32) and to around 3000 of literal Israel who accepted the gospel and became a part of spiritual Israel. The apostles now knew that there would be no

---

[1] F.F. Bruce, *The Book of Acts*, pages 38-39.

restoration of the kingdom to physical Israel for they now realized that all those who rejected Christ "shall be utterly destroyed from among the people" (Acts 3:23), as was prophesied by Moses (Deut. 18:15-18; Acts 3:22). Peter preached the very truth that Christ had preached in connection with the promise that the kingdom would be taken from Israel and given to a nation bringing forth the fruits thereof. He is the stone which was set at naught of you the builders, which was made the head of the corner" (Acts 4:11; Matt. 21:41, 43). Peter also knew that God had given His kingdom to the new nation, the believers, in the stone who had been rejected of men (1 Pet. 2:4-5, 9). Peter also stressed that Israel's rejection of Jesus did not lead to the postponement of the kingdom, but that God in fulfillment of prophecy had enthroned His Son as king on the holy hill of Zion in spite of their opposition (Acts 4:25-28).

Although the Invitation is still extended for physical Israel to become a part of spiritual Israel, Peter realized that there was no time in the future when a kingdom of a different nature could be given to Israel. This is the case because the present reign of Christ lasts until the end of time and the deliverance of the kingdom to the Father in eternity (Psa. 110:1-2; Acts 2:30-36; 1 Cor. 15:24-28; Rev. 20:11-21:5).

Philip preached the kingdom and the name of Jesus Christ in connection with one another. "But when they believed Philip preaching good tidings concerning the kingdom of God and the name of Jesus Christ, they were baptized both men and women" (Acts 8:12). Philip preached the same truth Christ preached, i.e., that Christ must first suffer and then enter into His glory—His reign in His kingdom (Acts 8:31-35; Luke 24:25-27). The book of Acts closes with the statement that Paul "abode two whole years in his own hired dwelling, and received all that went in unto him, preaching the kingdom of God, and teaching the things concerning the Lord Jesus Christ with all boldness, none forbidding him" (Acts 28:30-31). We know that Paul preached that Christ is exalted to the right hand of God to reign until all enemies are conquered (Eph. 1:20-23; Col. 3:1; 1 Cor. 15:24-28).

CHAPTER 5:
THE EVERLASTING KINGDOM (Daniel 2:44)[1]

How shall we interpret prophecies, which clearly pertain to the reign of the Christ, but which are not quoted and interpreted in the New Testament? They should be interpreted so as to harmonize with the New Testament. This will also harmonize them with other Old Testament prophecies. In this chapter we shall deal with the kingdom prophesied by Daniel. Here we also have common ground with the premillennialists for they agree that this refers to the kingdom which Jesus and John said was at hand (Matt. 3:2; 4:17, 23).[2] Their view of its nature has been set forth in previous chapters.

The Dream and the Interpretation

"Thou, O king, sawest, and behold, a great image. This image, which was mighty, and whose brightness was excellent, stood before thee; and the aspect thereof was terrible. As for this image, its head was of fine gold, its breast and its arms of silver, its belly and its thighs of brass, its legs of iron, its feet part of iron, and part of clay. Thou sawest till that a stone was cut out without hands, which smote the image upon its feet that were of iron and clay, and brake them in pieces. Then was the iron, the clay, the brass, the silver, and the gold, broken in pieces together, and became like the chaff of the summer threshing-floors; and the wind carried them away, so that no place was found for them: and the stone that smote the image became a great mountain, and filled the whole earth.

"This is the dream; and we will tell the interpretation thereof before the king. Thou, O king, art king of kings, unto whom the God of heaven hath given the kingdom, the power, and the strength, and the glory; and wheresoever the children of men dwell, the beasts of the field and the birds of the heavens hath he given into thy hand, and hath made thee to rule over them all: thou art the head of gold. And after thee shall arise another kingdom inferior to thee; and another third kingdom of brass, which shall bear rule over all the earth. And the fourth kingdom shall be strong as iron, forasmuch as iron breaketh in pieces and subdueth all things; and as iron that crusheth all these, shall

---

[1] This chapter originally appeared in Bales' book, *Prophecy and Premillennialism*, but he included it as part of the manuscript for this work as well.

[2] R.H. Boll, *The Kingdom of God*, page 60.

it break in pieces and crush. And whereas thou sawest the feet and toes, part of potters' clay, and part of iron, it shall be a divided kingdom: but there shall be in it of the strength of the iron, forasmuch as thou sawest the iron mixed with miry clay. And as the toes of the feet were part of iron, and part of clay, so the kingdom shall be partly strong, and partly broken. And whereas thou sawest the iron mixed with miry clay they shall mingle themselves with the seed of men; but they shall not cleave one to another, even as iron doth not mingle with clay. And in the days of those kings shall the God of heaven set up a kingdom which shall never be destroyed, nor shall the sovereignty thereof be left to another people; but it shall break in pieces and consume all these kingdoms, and it shall stand for ever. Forasmuch as thou sawest that a stone was cut out of the mountain without hands, and that it brake in pieces the iron, the brass, the clay, the silver, and the gold; the great God hath made known to the king what shall come to pass hereafter: and the dream is certain, and the interpretation thereof sure" (Daniel 2:31-45).

Only Four Earthly Kingdoms Mentioned

Daniel did not outline the entire history of the world from his day until the end of time. He is dealing with the kingdoms which would exist before the time God established His kingdom and then with the establishment and duration of Christ's kingdom. It is important to notice several things as we begin our study of this prophecy.

First, only four earthly kingdoms are mentioned, (a) The kingdom of Nebuchadnezzar, which was represented by the head of gold. "...the God of heaven hath given thee the kingdom...thou art the head of gold" (Dan. 2:37-38).

(b) "And after thee shall arise *another* kingdom inferior to thee" (Daniel 2:39). At a feast of Belshazzar Daniel said that God gave "Nebuchadnezzar thy father the kingdom..." (Daniel 5:18). He interpreted the handwriting on the wall. "And this is the writing that was inscribed; MENE, MENE, TEKEL, UPHARSIN. This is the interpretation of the thing: MENE: God hath numbered thy kingdom, and brought it to an end. TEKEL: thou art weighed in the balances, and art found wanting. PERES: thy kingdom is divided, and given to the Medes and Persians" (Dan. 5:25-28).

(c) "...and another *third* kingdom of brass, which shall bear rule over all the earth" (Dan. 2:39). What kingdom was this? It was the third; therefore, it was the one which succeeded the second, which was the Medo-Persian kingdom. Daniel makes clear that this third kingdom was the Grecian kingdom. In a vision Daniel saw a he-goat who overcame a ram (Dan. 8:5-8). What kingdom did these represent? "The ram which thou sawest, that had the two horns, they are the kings of Media and Persia. And the rough he-goat is the king of Greece; and the great horn that is between his eyes is the first king" (Dan. 8:20-21).

(d) "And the *fourth* kingdom shall be strong as iron, forasmuch as iron breaketh in pieces and subdueth all things; and as iron that crusheth all these, shall it break in pieces and crush. And whereas thou sawest the feet and toes, part of potters' clay, and part of iron, it shall be a divided kingdom: but there shall be in it of the strength of the iron, forasmuch as thou sawest the iron mixed with miry clay. And as the toes of the feet were part of iron, and part of clay, so the kingdom shall be partly strong, and partly broken. And whereas thou sawest the iron mixed with miry clay, they shall mingle themselves with the seed of men; but they shall not cleave one to another, even as iron doth not mingle with clay. And in the days of those kings shall the God of heaven set up a kingdom which shall never be destroyed, nor shall the sovereignty thereof be left to another people; but it shall break in pieces and consume all these kingdoms, and it shall stand for ever. Forasmuch as thou sawest that a stone was cut out of the mountain without hands, and that it brake in pieces the iron, the brass, the clay, the silver, and the gold; the great God hath made known to the king what shall come to pass hereafter: and the dream is certain, and the interpretation thereof sure" (Dan. 2:40-45).

Daniel did not name the fourth kingdom, but we know it was the Roman Empire, for it followed in point of time the third (the Grecian) kingdom. It is well described in the interpretation both as to its strength and as to its weaknesses. Although strong, it was unable through even colonization and armies to weld the kingdom together so that it held together of its own accord. In its latter days it was as iron and clay which did not mix, as represented by the feet, for they did not cleave one to another. The premillennialists agree that the fourth kingdom was the Roman kingdom.[1]

Second, God was to set up a kingdom during the days of the Ro-

---

[1] *Ibid.,*, pages 22, 26-27.

man empire. Did He do so? Jesus said the time was fulfilled (Mark 1:14-15). God did set up in the first century a kingdom without human agency or power, which was unlike the kingdoms of this world. It was small in its beginning, growing in its nature, universal in its ultimate spread, and everlasting in its duration (Acts 2:30-36; Eph. 5:5; Col. 1:13; Heb. 12:28; 13:20). Is this the kingdom prophesied by Daniel, or did Daniel skip Christ's present kingdom and speak of one which is yet to come?

And in the Days of "Those Kings"

Daniel said: "And in the days of those kings shall the God of heaven set up a kingdom which shall never be destroyed, nor shall the sovereignty thereof be left to another people; but it shall break in pieces and consume all these kingdoms, and it shall stand for ever. Forasmuch as thou sawest that a stone was cut out of the mountain without hands, and that it brake in pieces the iron, the brass, the clay, the silver, and the gold; the great God hath made known to the king what shall come to pass hereafter: and the dream is certain, and the interpretation thereof sure" (Daniel 2:44-45).

Who are "those kings" in whose days God would establish His kingdom? At least four answers have been given.

First, they represent the succession of kings within the Roman Empire.

Second, they represent the Emperor and the kings who ruled under him in Jesus' day.[1]

Third, the toes represent a ten kingdom division of Rome. This stage had not been reached in Jesus' day; nor has it yet been reached. "The Roman world-power then, though now it does not exist, as such, is to return. When it returns, the Roman power will be in the form of a ten-kingdom confederacy under one dominant head; which fact is indicated by the toes of the image; more fully set forth in *the ten horns* of the fourth beast (Dan. 7); and clearly revealed in John in Revelation."[2]

This interpretation is false. (a) If Rome had not reached the necessary stage of development in the first century, how could Jesus have said that *the time was fulfilled* and that the kingdom was at hand?

---

[1] H.C. Leupold, *Exposition of Daniel*, page 123.
[2] R.H. Boll, *The Kingdom of God*, page 32.

(Matt. 4:17, 23; Mark 1:14-15). Whatever stage Rome had to reach for the kingdom to be nearby in point of time, it had reached when John and Jesus preached. (b) Their interpretation cannot be proved from Daniel 7, because there an *eleventh* king arose and put down three kings. This would mean an eleventh toe eliminated three toes (Dan. 7:24, 7-8, 28). (c) The image was smitten on the feet while standing, yet Boll agrees that Rome has passed away.[1] (d) Boll's interpretation disconnects the toes from the image; and separates them by almost two thousand years so far. If Rome arose again, it would have no historical continuity with the Rome of the first century. It would not be a part of that Rome. But the Rome of which Daniel spoke had to be a part of the series of empires which started in Nebuchadnezzar's day; for these followed one another in point of time, and there were only four of them. On Boll's interpretation, God set up the kingdom of *Christ* (which is apparently ignored by Daniel), Rome later fell, then Rome will be revived as a *fifth* kingdom; and then God will set up the *everlasting* kingdom which was supposed to have been set up in the days of the fourth empire. Since Boll agrees that the first century was time for the kingdom of heaven, and since he agrees that Rome has vanished, how can he maintain that Rome and the kingdom which was to be established in Rome's day are both yet to come?

Fourth, the fourth interpretation of "those kings" is that it represents the kings or kingdoms set forth in the dream and the interpretation. The context makes it clear that this explanation is correct. Daniel sometimes identifies the *king with the kingdom* and calls the king the kingdom; even though more than one king was to reign in the kingdom. After speaking of Nebuchadnezzar's kingdom (Dan. 2:37), he called the king the kingdom. "*Thou art* the head of gold." Then he said, "And after *thee* shall arise *another kingdom* inferior to thee..." (Dan. 2:38-39). The head of gold represented the first kingdom, but the king could also represent the first kingdom; even though later Belshazzar ruled in the same kingdom. Furthermore, in a repetition of the same series of kingdoms, under the form of four beasts, Daniel called the beasts, or kingdoms, *kings.* "These great beasts, which are four, *are four kings* that shall arise out of the earth" (Dan. 7:17). "Thus he said the *fourth beast* shall be a *fourth kingdom* upon earth..." (Dan. 7:23).

Therefore, "those kings," during whose days God set up a king-

---

[1] *Ibid.,* page 22.

dom, represented the four kingdoms which made up the image which the king saw and the meaning of which Daniel interpreted to him. Before this series of kingdoms had vanished, God would establish a kingdom.[1] As Patrick Fairbairn put it: "...the only reference to which the days of the kings can legitimately apply, is the collective periods of the kings or kingdoms symbolized by the image."[2]

It should be observed that although these kingdoms were not contemporary, for one fell and another took its place, in the dream and the image they are all represented as one image which continued to stand as long as any one of the kingdoms stood. Furthermore, although Nebuchadnezzar had passed away long before Rome rose, the impact of the kingdom of heaven is represented as affecting the image, including the head of gold (Dan. 2:44). Why it is so represented, we are not told. It may be because they embodied the same type of spirit and covered more or less the same territory. But we do not have to know why, in order to know that it is so represented.

Before the fourth Empire was to pass, God was to establish His kingdom.

Expectation in the First Century

The New Testament, and documents outside the New Testament, reveal that in the first century there was an expectation of the coming of some great kingdom. *First*, John and Jesus said that the kingdom was at hand (Matt. 3:2; Mark 1:14-15).

Second, Josephus, a Jewish historian of the first century, said that Daniel had foretold what Israel would suffer under Antiochus Epiphanes. "In the very same manner Daniel also wrote concerning the Roman government, and that our country should be made desolate by them."[3] He mentioned the Babylonian Empire, the Medo-Persian, and the Grecian or Macedonian. So he thought that all four of these empires were mentioned by Daniel. "Daniel did also declare the meaning of the stone to the king; but I do not think proper to relate it, since I have only undertaken to describe things past or things present, but not things that are future; yet if anyone be so very desirous of knowing truth, as not to wave such points of curiosity, and cannot curb his in-

---

[1] Albert Barnes, *Commentary on Daniel*, Vol. 1, page 173.
[2] Patrick Fairbairn, *Prophecy,* page 295.
[3] Josephus, *Antiquities of the Jews* (William Whiston, translator), 10.2.

clination for understanding the uncertainties of futurity, and whether they will happen or not, let him be diligent in reading the book of Daniel, which he will find among the sacred writings."[1] Josephus thought that Rome was there in fulfillment of prophecy, and he knew that during the fourth empire the "little stone" kingdom would be established. Whether he did not want to antagonize the Romans, or whatever may have been his reason, he did not talk about the stone smiting the image—Rome. But he indicates that since the rest was past, the future will bring the kingdom. Since Rome was present, it was the period of time for the kingdom.

Third, The Roman historian Suetonius wrote that: "A firm persuasion had long prevailed through all the East, that it was fated for the empire of the world, at that time, to devolve on some who should go forth from Judaea. This prediction referred to a Roman emperor, as the event shewed; but the Jews, applying it to themselves, broke out into rebellion..."[2]

Tacitus, another historian of the first century, said that most of the Jews "firmly believed that their ancient priestly writings contained the prophecy that this was the very time when the East should grow strong and that men starting from Judea should possess the world. This mysterious prophecy had in reality pointed to Vespasian and Titus, but the common people, as is the way of human ambition, interpreted these great destinies in their own favor, and could not be turned to the truth even by adversity."[3]

Fourth, the premillennialists agree that the kingdom was at hand in the first century. The New Testament makes it clear that the kingdom was at hand, the Jews were expecting some great kingdom, and Romans thought that these things applied to certain of their Emperors.

Fifth, not only was there an expectation of a kingdom in the first century, but in the first century God did establish the kingdom of His Son (Acts 2:34-36; Col. 1:13). Did Daniel prophesy this kingdom?

Daniel Prophesied Christ's Present Reign

Consider how Daniel's prophecy is fulfilled in Christ's present reign.

First, the kingdom was at hand in Jesus' personal ministry, and the

---

[1] *Ibid.,* 20.4.
[2] Seutonius, *Lives of the Twelve Caesars,* Vespasian, c. 4.
[3] Clifford H. Moore (translator), *Tacitus: The Histories,* page 199.

time was fulfilled (Matt. 3:2; Mark 1:14-15). Christ's kingdom was set up at the right time (Mark 9:1; Acts 1:6; 2:34-36). Rome has ceased to exist, and this is acknowledged by the premillennialists.[1] A kingdom to be set up at the second coming, in another Roman Empire does not fit the time schedule announced by Daniel.

Second, the kingdom was to be established before Rome fell. Christ's kingdom was established before the fall of Rome.

Third, the kingdom was to be small in its beginning—a little stone (Dan. 2:34-35). Jesus-showed that His kingdom was to be small in its beginning, like the mustard seed (Matt. 13:31). Although thousands of Jews obeyed the gospel and became members of Christ's kingdom, it was but a remnant that did so in comparison with the entire nation (Rom. 11:4-5). The kingdom of Christ was the right size—small—in its beginning. According to premillennialism, when the kingdom is established it will, in a catastrophic blow, overthrow all Gentile world power and all Israel will accept it. It will not exist in a small state in its beginning, but will be world-wide.

Fourth, the kingdom Daniel prophesied was to be a growing kingdom. Beginning as a small stone it was to grow (Dan. 2:35, 44). Jesus' kingdom is a growing kingdom. The mustard seed did not remain just a seed, but it grew (Matt. 13:31-32; Acts 5:14; 6:1, etc.).

Fifth, the kingdom Daniel foresaw was to have a universal spread. From a small stone it became a world-filling mountain. This did not mean that everyone would be converted, any more than Dan. 2:38 meant that Nebuchadnezzar ruled over every individual in the world. The prophets showed that Christ would rule in the midst of His enemies, but that He would rule until all of them are conquered (Psa. 110:1-4). Christ now has all authority, and the scope of His kingdom is world-wide (Matt. 28:18-20; 25:30-46; 13:24-30, 36-43; Heb. 1:3, 8, 13; Acts 2:34-36; 1 Cor. 15:24-28; Eph. 1:20-23; Acts 1:8). Each Christian should have a part in its world-wide spread by backing with his money, time, influence, and prayers the evangelization of the world.

Sixth, the kingdom was to be set up without hands (Dan. 2:34, 44-45). Hands are a symbol of human power. Worldly kingdoms have been set up by man's wisdom, knowledge, might and hands. The king-

---

[1] Boll, *The Kingdom of God*, pages 20-22.

dom of heaven is divine in its origin, and was established by God
"without human power or assistance."[1] In fact, man did everything he
could to prevent its establishment. Man crucified Christ, but as the
prophet David had foreseen the efforts of man would be unavailing
against God's enthronement of His Son. They killed the Prince of Life,
but God raised and exalted Him (Psa. 2; Luke 24:25-27; Acts 2:23-36;
3:14-15; 4:25-28). The apostles did not enthrone Christ or even assist
in His enthronement. They were used by the Lord to announce that He
was now reigning. "Let all the house of Israel therefore know assuredly, *that God hath made him both Lord and Christ, this Jesus whom ye
crucified*" (Acts 2:36). Without hands, without human power or assistance, God established the kingdom.

The fact that the kingdom was not established by human hands indicates that its nature differs from the kingdoms of the world; as Jesus
clearly taught (John 18:36).

Seventh, the smiting of the image by the little stone. A major objection of the premillennialists to the position that the kingdom has
already been established, is based on the fact that the church did not
literally smite Rome. As Boll put it:

> *The church was established in the days of Rome. But Rome
> felt no shock nor tremor. Neither was she broken up, neither
> did she **begin** to be broken up, or to decline. On the contrary
> she went on prosperously, conquering and to conquer. Much of
> her territory was added to her after Pentecost—Egypt, Dacia,
> Great Britain, went to swell her boundaries. She arrived at her
> greatest territorial extent about 180 A.D. —a century and a
> half after Pentecost. During this time she came nearer destroy-
> ing the church than vice versa. Rome's real decline dates from
> the days of Constantine—but, alas, the church's decline began
> at the same time.*
>
> *Some would meet the difficulty by the claim that the influ-
> ence of the stone is permeating the kingdoms of the world so as
> to bring about their final disintegration and overthrow. With
> other words, that the stone's smiting represents a moral, or
> spiritual effect, and that the prophecy of Daniel 2:44 is not as
> yet fulfilled, but is really as yet in process of fulfillment. But the
> prophecy fairly taken represents, not a gradual process, but a*

---

[1] Edward J. Young, *The Prophecy of Daniel,* page 72.

catastrophic event—a complete and radical demolition of the world kingdom by supernatural agency. The stone's effect upon the Image is due to violent impact, not to "peaceful penetration." The stone falls for judgment and destruction upon the world-power—not for the conversion and salvation of individuals. The Image is suddenly broken up—pulverized—by an act of God. It is not stated that the Image is to be transformed into the likeness and image of Christ, but that it is to be destroyed. Neither does it say that the stone lies in peaceful contact with the Image's feet. The stone and the Image do not co-exist peacefully at all: when the one comes the other goes. Nor is it true that the stone by its growing gradually displaces the Image. The stone is not represented as growing at all until the Image has been reduced to chaff and the winds have swept away its fragments into the nowhere.[1]

What shall we say to this contention? (1) If Boll's explanation is right, when the kingdom is established it must engage in violent, carnal warfare with Rome. Daniel said that the little stone smote the image and ground it to powder. Boll spoke of the "stone's effect upon the image is due to violent impact, not to 'peaceful penetration.'"[2] To be consistent, he must contend that the kingdom will engage in carnal warfare with the kingdoms of the world and overthrow them. If he says that it is done by judgment of God, and not by the members of the little-stone kingdom itself, he has abandoned his position that the stone does it; as well as Daniel's representation in Dan. 2:44-45. Furthermore, if Rome's overthrow comes as a result of a judgment of God, and not through the direct impact of the kingdom of Christ itself, Boll cannot object to the establishment of the church on the ground that Rome felt no tremor when the church was established. What Daniel briefly represented in prophecy could take a long period of time to accomplish in actuality. Rome did fall after the establishment of the church, as Daniel foretold. It was a judgment of God on Rome.

(2) In one place Boll says that the little stone may already be in existence as the church age. This is the little stone phase of the king-

---

[1] Boll, *The Kingdom of God*, pages 20-21.
[2] *Ibid.*, page 21.

dom.[1] If this is true, then Rome has been smitten for it was to be smitten by the kingdom in the little stone stage. However, Boll does not believe that the image has been smitten.[2]

(3) Since everything else fits—including the final point which we plan to make later on the everlasting nature of the kingdom, and since to take the premillennial position involves one in the unscriptural postponement theory, one must explain the smiting in such a way as to harmonize with the fact that the New Testament shows that the present dispensation is the final dispensation or rule of God on this earth (Acts 2:34-36; 1 Cor. 15:24-28; Rev. 20:11-21:5; Heb. 12:28; 13:20).

What shall we say about the smiting? (a) We are not confined to one manner of interpreting all prophecy (Heb. 1:1-2). Therefore, if one part of a prophecy when interpreted literally leads to unscriptural conclusions, we must give an interpretation to that prophecy which harmonizes with the rest of the Bible. We know that in a series of prophecies there may be figurative descriptions as well as literal ones. For example, everything that Isaiah said about Babylon's fall was not literal, although some things were. Heavenly bodies did not literally fall; but kings and kingdoms were sometimes represented as heavenly bodies and their fall could be symbolized by the fall of heavenly bodies (Isa. 13:10, 13).

(b) The fact that the kingdom of heaven is different in its nature from the kingdoms of the world, and was therefore cut out of the mountain without hands, indicates that it would not be a kingdom which would use the human hands of members of the kingdom to overthrow Rome and to establish the kingdom of God.

(c) Daniel 7 presents some of the same facts presented in Daniel 2. He deals with the same kingdoms and with the establishment of the everlasting kingdom. However, in Daniel 7 there is no reference made to a smiting by the kingdom of the kingdoms of the earth. A judgment scene was set forth, and the four beasts or kingdoms destroyed, but no reference is made to the saints executing the judgment (Dan. 7:9-11, 13-14, 26-27).

(d) God in His providence brought an end to Rome. Boll agrees that it "has vanished."[3] But, he thinks it will be revived in the future. However, it was not to vanish until it was smitten. It has vanished,

---

[1] *Ibid.*, page 34.
[2] *Ibid.*
[3] *Ibid.*, page 27.

therefore it has been smitten.

The fall of Rome did not have to be immediate in order to fulfill the prophecy. The image of Dan. 2 is represented as all standing there at one time, yet as a matter of fact it took hundreds of years to fulfill what it symbolized. Why, then, must the fall of Rome be immediate instead of gradual?

(e) In order to emphasize that the smiting did not have to be done by the kingdom itself, nor Rome's fall to be immediate, consider some equally strong statements in the Bible which were not fulfilled literally. First, John the Baptist did not have to be a literal earth mover in order to fulfill the prophecy about his work (Luke 3:4-6). Haggai referred to a shaking of the heavens, and the earth; the sea and the dry land (Haggai 2:6-7). Did He refer to a literal shaking? No, for the New Testament makes it clear that he referred to the abolition of the law and the bringing in of the New Covenant kingdom. This was a far greater change than when God literally shook the earth at the giving of the law, but it was not a physical shaking (Heb. 12:18-28).

Eighth, Christ said that He was the stone which would fall on the Pharisees and grind them to powder, and those who fell on Him would be broken. "Therefore say I unto you, The Kingdom of God shall be taken away from you, and shall be given to a nation bringing forth the fruits thereof. And he that falleth on this stone shall be broken to pieces: but on whomsoever it shall fall, it will scatter him as dust. And when the chief priests and Pharisees heard his parables, they perceived that he spake of them" (Matt. 21:43-45). This is as strong language as Daniel used about the kingdom—the little stone—smiting the image. Did Christ personally fall on them, and they on Him? Did He personally grind them to powder? Christ is the stone (Matt. 21:43-45; Acts 4:11; Eph. 2:20), but He did not personally fall on them. In His overruling providence, He brought a judgment on that generation in the destruction of Jerusalem, and the final falling on them will take place on judgment day. Although it is true that Christ fulfilled and will fulfill His threat, the fulfillment does not have to be literally described by Christ in order to be actually fulfilled.

We must accept these things as figurative descriptions in order to harmonize them with the rest of the Bible. The same thing is true of Daniel's statement concerning the image being smitten by the little stone.

Ninth, Daniel said that the kingdom would be everlasting. It would not be destroyed (Dan. 2:44). Is Christ's kingdom everlasting, or is it to be replaced by another kingdom or rule on this earth? Christ's kingdom exists today (Acts 2:36; Col. 1:13). It is the everlasting kingdom.

(a) His present rule continues until all enemies are conquered, the last enemy is death. This takes place after whatever the thousand years in Rev. 20 represents, and this present rule is followed by the deliverance of the kingdom to the Father (Acts 2:34-36; 1 Cor. 15:24-28; Rev. 20:11-21:5).

(b) Christ's present covenant is sanctified by His blood. It became operative because of His death and not before His death (Heb. 9:15-17, 18-20). His covenant is the everlasting covenant; therefore it is not to give way to another covenant (Heb. 13:20). To speak of His covenant people is but another way of speaking of His kingdom people. The Old Testament promised but one reign of the Messiah, and in one place it promised it as a kingdom (Dan. 2:44), and in another it promised it as a covenant (Jer. 31:31-34). Christ is now the mediator of the new and everlasting covenant, and no covenant is to take its place (Heb. 8:6; 9:15; 12:24; 13:20).

(c) Hebrews shows that we are not to come to the Old Covenant but to Christ and the New Covenant (Heb. 12:18-24). The writer then shows that God through Haggai had promised that, in the future from Haggai's day, He would make one more great change. It would be a greater one than that which took place at the giving of the law. We are warned: "See that ye refuse not him that speaketh. For if they escaped not when they refused him that warned them on earth, much more shall not we escape who turn away from him that warneth from heaven: whose voice then shook the earth: but now he hath promised, saying. Yet once more will I make to tremble not the earth only, but also the heaven. And this word, Yet once more, signifieth the removing of those things that are shaken, as of things that have been made, that those things which are not shaken may remain. Wherefore, receiving a kingdom that cannot be shaken, let us have grace, whereby we may offer service well-pleasing to God with reverence and awe: for our God is a consuming fire" (Heb. 12:25-29). Haggai symbolized the removal of the Old Law, and perhaps also the blow to paganism that the church represents, by speaking of a shaking of the heavens and the earth. But God said He would make this one more great change, but not another, on this earth. The writer of Hebrews dropped the symbolism and plainly told us what abides and cannot be shaken. "And this word, yet once more [speaking from the time of Haggai, J.D.B.], signifieth the removing of those things that are shaken, as of things that have been made, that those things which are not shaken may remain." What does this mean? He immediately said: *"Wherefore, receiving a kingdom that cannot be shaken..."* (12:27-29). Haggai had promised one more great change. That great change was taking place in the reception in the first century of the kingdom. The kingdom they were then receiving would not be shaken and taken out of the way as had been the Old Covenant. Therefore, the present kingdom is the everlasting kingdom prophesied by Daniel, for no other kingdom is to take its place. The premillennial theory contradicts this for it says that the kingdom of Christ which they were receiving in the first century will be shaken and taken out of the way. The reign of Christ at God's right hand will come to an end, and the present kingdom will be replaced by the rule on the throne of David. But the present kingdom cannot be shaken. It will continue in eternity for Christ will deliver the kingdom to the Father.

Our conclusion is that in order to harmonize Daniel 2:44 with the New Testament, as well as with the Old Testament, we must interpret the prophecy in such a manner as to see that it is a prophecy of Christ's present rule. This rule, of course, is not yet over for it continues until the conquest of all of His enemies.

If we have been born again, we are in this kingdom (John 3:1-5). How wonderful it is to be identified with the kingdom which will never be destroyed. We want to be identified with something permanent. Everything of this earth is transient, but through being in Christ, and building on His word, we are identified with the permanent kingdom and the everlasting word (Dan. 2:44; Heb. 12:28, 13:20; Matt. 7:24-27; 1 Pet. 1:24-25).

A Process of Growth

"And he said, So is the kingdom of God, as if a man should cast seed upon the earth; and should sleep and rise night and day, and the seed should spring up and grow he knoweth not how. The earth beareth fruit of herself; first the blade, then the ear, then the full grain in the ear. But when the fruit is ripe, straightway he putteth forth the sickle, because the harvest is come" (Mark 4:26-29). The parable of the sower illustrated different types of hearts into which the seed fell, and this parable shows something of the nature of the successful growth of the kingdom. It teaches truth about the kingdom, but as is true of any one passage, it does not teach the total truth about the kingdom.

> *The kingdom of Christ is set forth in its relation, not to the forces of nature or the natural receptivity of man, but to the general operation of God in the world. As the farmer submits his seed to the operation of the powers of nature, so does the Messiah, whether sowing in person or through the agency of his followers, submit his truth and kingdom to that general operation of God in human history wherein God works in accordance with the nature that he has given to man. Not to nature or to man, but **to the world as ruled by God**, he commits his gospel. It takes its place among other powers in the world, and among them it does its work. He knoweth not how does not mean that the Messiah knows now how the true seed grows; it is a part of the picture of spontaneous growth in nature. The earth bringeth forth fruit of herself does not mean that the true seed bears its fruit without divine influences; for even in the parable, as Bengel remarks, the culture of the soil is not excluded, neither are the influences of sun and rain. But the gospel is cast into the world as an element in human life, and it does its work, not by startling divine interpositions, but as grain matures and seeds grow under the fostering influence of Divine Providence. This is the teaching of the parable, and the best commentary on it is found in the history of Christian truth among men. In exactly this way—silently, as seeds grow—has God's kingdom come thus far, and it is coming still. This is a parable of hope, for in the world in which Christ places his seed there are powers at work that render the harvest certain.*[1]

The kingdom was small in its beginning. There was the seed, then the blade, then the ear, then the full grain in the ear. It did not start, as does the premillennial kingdom, with an overwhelming display of divine power which crushes all opposition and immediately establishes the world-wide sway of the kingdom. It is a process of growth through

---

[1] W.N. Clarke, *Commentary on the Gospel of Mark*, pages 64-65.

the inherent nature of the seed as it produces its blade, ear, and ripe fruit in God's world. This kingdom continues until the harvest, and the harvest is at the end of the world (Matt. 13:39-43), when Christ delivers the kingdom to the Father (1 Cor. 15:24-28).

We must not only exercise patience, recognizing that it takes time to grow, but we should also recognize that the growth must be directed by God's spiritual laws and not by human wisdom and power.

CHAPTER 6:
COMMON GROUND AND
THE POSTPONEMENT THEORY

Two people are said to occupy common ground when they are in agreement on a particular point. To reason with anyone, there must be some common ground; something which both accept and from which they proceed to discuss their differences. If one had absolutely no common ground with another person, fruitful discussion would be impossible. One cannot reason with an insane person because there is no common ground. When we reason with an atheist, we are both proceeding on the common ground that the human mind can arrive at truth. If it cannot, it would be ridiculous to talk about the truth or falsity of any position. There are those who maintain that the mind cannot arrive at truth, but they contradict themselves. They maintain that their mind has learned so much that it knows that the attainment of truth is impossible. They have used their mind to arrive at the truth that there is no truth. While they may assail reason, they usually end up trying to give reasons against reason. Thereby they imply that there is power in reasoning and that valid reasons for a position exist.

In the discussion with the premillennialists we start on the common ground that the Bible is the word of God. However, the particular common ground to which we devote this chapter is the acknowledgment by the premillennialists that the kingdom which John and Jesus announced as at hand was the kingdom prophesied by the prophets.[1] Although we differ as to the nature of the kingdom, we agree that the prophesied *kingdom was then at hand.*

Starting with this common ground, we argue that the kingdom which was at hand was the kingdom of Christ which was proclaimed as in existence on the first Pentecost after Christ's resurrection (Acts 2:34-36; Col. 1:13). The one which was at hand was the one which was established. But, the one which was at hand was the one prophesied by the prophets. Therefore, the one which was established was prophesied by the prophets, and the prophecies concerning the kingdom are fulfilled, or are being fulfilled, in the present reign of Christ. Being wrong in their concept of the nature of the kingdom, the premillennialists are wrong in their manner of interpreting kingdom prophe-

---

[1] Boll, *The Kingdom of God*, pages 59-63.

cies.

How do premillennialists explain their position that the kingdom which was "at hand" got out of hand, so to speak, and in its place the church was established? They maintain that Israel refused to repent and accept Christ; so the kingdom was postponed until the second coming.

The Postponement Theory

As stated by R. H. Boll;

> *The dispute whether or not the kingdom of Old Testament prophecy (the restoration and sovereignty of The Nation of Israel) was "offered" to Israel by John the Baptist and by Christ in His earthly ministry is but a war of words, irrelevant and unnecessary. The only thing that ever stood between Israel and her glorious promises, kingdom and all, was her sinful condition. That removed, every other promise must necessarily be fulfilled to them, and that speedily. Whether there had been any formal **offer of the kingdom** made to them, and, upon their rejection of it the same was withdrawn and postponed is no essential matter. But if salvation was offered to the nation by Jesus, all else was implied therein as a matter of course; and if that was nationally rejected, the fulfillment of all their prophetic hopes was thereby made impossible, and automatically deferred until the time when the nation would turn to acknowledge Jesus Christ and be forgiven."[1]*

The kingdom is held in abeyance, but the promises have not been made void.[2]

When Did Jesus Indicate Postponement?

R.H. Boll said that after Matt. 12:43-45, and in the parables, "the Lord Jesus begins to teach *new truth and* in a *new an unusual* fashion."[3] "But one thing must have dawned upon us: the correspondence of these secrets [in the parables, J.D.B.] with the present conditions in this church-age! These parables are really an announcement *of the new and unexpected aspect the kingdom* would assume during an *anticipat-*

---

[1] *Ibid.,* page 86. Cf. Walvoord, *The Millennial Kingdom*, pages 206-207.
[2] *Ibid.,* pages 56-57.
[3] *Ibid.,* page 68.

ed age of the king's rejection and absence from the world. We have here the Savior's prediction of the circumstances as we find them unto this day."[1] Boll is inconsistent here on at least two counts.

First, he believes the rejection and the cross of Christ were predicted.[2] How could the church age be new and unexpected? **Second**, if the church and the kingdom are not the same, the church age cannot be an aspect of the prophesied kingdom. How could an entirely different rule (at God's right hand), and kingdom (the spiritual body of Christ), be an aspect of a different rule (on David's throne on earth) in a different type of kingdom (the combination of church and state)?

The Postponement Theory Evaluated

It is true that some prophecies were conditional. For example, Jonah announced the destruction of Nineveh in forty days, but Nineveh repented and she was spared. Is this true concerning the kingdom which Jesus announced as at hand?

First, if it is, how do the premillennialists know that Israel will accept Christ at His second coming?

Second, the Jews wanted the type of kingdom in which the premillennialists believe. They wanted to make Jesus king by force (John 6:15). Within a few years after His crucifixion, Israel engaged in a series of rebellions to establish her national sovereignty and was defeated and scattered by Rome.

Third, Jonah's prophecy involved a time element. Nineveh was *never* destroyed in fulfillment of his prophecy. His prophecy was *set aside* when she repented. The kingdom promise involved a time element, and Jesus said the time was fulfilled and the kingdom was at hand (Mark 1:14-15). Boll realizes that a time element was involved, and Rome was the fourth empire.[3] If Israel's failure to repent kept the kingdom from being established, the kingdom prophecies were *cancelled*, just as was Jonah's prophecy. If it was time in the first century for the kingdom, the prophets did not refer to a kingdom to be established in connection with the second coming. Of course, if Christ said that the kingdom was *postponed*, and that the prophecies which applied to the first coming were now to be applied to the second, we would accept it. However, this is not taught in the New Testament.

---

[1] *Ibid.,* page 70.
[2] *Ibid.,* page 56.
[3] *Ibid.,* page 29.

Where are the prophecies which show that the kingdom which was at hand in the first century is now prophesied to be established at His second coming?

Daniel's prophecy involved a time element. The kingdom was to be established in the days of the fourth, the Roman Empire. Boll agrees that Rome was the fourth empire, and that it has long since disappeared.[1] He thinks it will be revived in the future. However, Boll thinks that when it is revived. it will exist in a ten-fold division—represented he says by the toes—in which it did not exist in the first century.[2] However, if Rome had not reached the necessary stage of development in the first century, how could the time have been fulfilled and the kingdom have been at hand (Mark 1:14-15)?

Fourth, if the throne of David's rule was at hand, the rule at God's right hand could not have been prophesied for the first century. If the kingdom had been established, the church would not have been established; even though Boll realizes that the church "now fulfills a higher, spiritual mission in the world."[3]

Fifth, David's prophecy of Christ's rule clearly shows that the kingdom would not be postponed because of Israel's rebellion. David said:

> *Why do the nations rage, and the peoples meditate a vain thing? The kings of the earth set themselves, and the rulers take counsel together, against Jehovah, and against his anointed, saying, Let us break their bonds asunder, and cast away their cords from us. He that sitteth in the heavens will laugh: the Lord will have them in derision. Then will he speak unto them in his wrath, and vex them in his sore displeasure: yet I have set my king upon my holy hill of Zion.*
>
> *I will tell of the decree; Jehovah said unto me, Thou art my son; this day have I begotten thee. Ask of me, and I will give thee the nations for thine inheritance, and the uttermost parts of the earth for thy possession. Thou shalt break them with a rod of iron; thou shalt dash them in pieces like a potter's vessel.*
>
> *Now therefore be wise, O ye kings: be instructed, ye judges*

---

[1] *Ibid.*, pages 20, 22, 27.
[2] *Ibid.*, pages 27-30. Cf. R.H. Boll, *Lessons on Daniel*, page 12.
[3] Boll, *The Kingdom of God*, page 57.

*of the earth. Serve Jehovah with fear, and rejoice with trem-
bling. Kiss the son, lest he be angry, and ye perish in the way,
for his wrath will soon be kindled. Blessed are all they that
take refuge in him* (Psalm 2).

We shall briefly examine this prophecy. (a) Who were the raging
nations and people imagining vain or empty things? The New Testament teaches that they were the Jews and Gentiles of Jesus' day. "And
they, when they heard it, lifted up their voice to God with one accord,
and said, O Lord, thou that didst make the heaven and the earth and the
sea, and all that in them is: who by the Holy Spirit, by the mouth of
our father David thy servant, didst say, Why did the Gentiles rage, and
the peoples imagine vain things? The kings of the earth set themselves
in array, and the rulers were gathered together against the Lord, and
against his Anointed: for of a truth in this city against thy holy Servant
Jesus; whom thou didst anoint, both Herod and Pontius Pilate, with the
Gentiles and the peoples of Israel, were gathered together" (Acts 4:24-
27).

(b) Against whom were they in rebellion? Against God and His
anointed one, or Messiah, who was also His Son (Psa. 2:2, 12; Acts
4:27).

(c) What did they think they could do? They thought that they
could defy the authority of God and His Son, break their bonds, and
cast away their cords (Psa. 2:3). (d) How did God view their rebellion?
Did He postpone the kingdom? They were imagining a vain thing (Psa.
2:1), and God held their efforts in contempt. "He that sitteth in the
heavens will laugh: the lord will have them in derision" (Psa. 2:4).
Their efforts were puny and unavailing.

(d) Will they keep the Messiah, the Son, from being enthroned?
"Then will he speak unto them in his wrath, and vex them in his sore
displeasure: *Yet I have set my king upon my holy hill of Zion"* (Psa.
2:5-6). In spite of their opposition. He enthroned His Son. They did
not lead God to postpone the establishment of the kingdom. Their rebellion was not so successful that, instead of the kingdom being established in connection with the first coming, God postponed it until the
second coming. In spite of their opposition, Christ went the way of the
cross to the crown (Luke 24:25-27). Death could not hold Him, and
God exalted Him to His own right hand (Acts 2:22-36). He is on
Mount Zion, for we have come to Mount Zion in coming to Jesus the
Mediator of the New Covenant (Heb. 12:22, 24).

(e) The Messiah's rule is universal in its nature (Psa. 2:7-8; Matt. 28:18-20).

(f) Men are called on to submit to the Son or suffer the consequences (Psa. 2:9-12). Israel's rebellion was punished by the destruction of Jerusalem, and the coming judgment will also be a judgment on them. Christ will rule until every enemy is conquered (Acts 2:34-36).

(g) Those who take refuge in Him are blessed (Psa. 2:12). Think of the blessings which we have in Christ, both in time and for eternity (Eph. 1; 1 Pet. 1:3-9).

The fulfillment of this psalm shatters the postponement theory.

Sixth, some Pharisees taught that if Israel repented, the Messiah and His kingdom would come. Some even said that if Israel kept just one Sabbath perfectly, the Messiah would come. The premillennial position is that if Israel had repented in the first century, the kingdom would have been established. She did not repent; so it was not established. Boll said: "The only thing that ever stood between Israel and her glorious promises, kingdom and all, was her sinful condition. That removed, every other promise must necessarily be fulfilled to them, and that speedily."[1] In other words, the message which the Pharisees and Boll would have preached to the people was: Repent *and then* the kingdom of heaven is at hand. If they did not repent it would not be at hand, it would be postponed.

What did John the Baptist preach? He said: "Repent ye *for* the kingdom of heaven is at hand" (Matt. 3:2). There is a vast difference between these two messages. The first says the kingdom will be at hand, if you repent, and then it will be established. The second says that the kingdom is coming, it is at hand, and the nearness of the kingdom is a reason for repentance, but not a condition for the establishment of the kingdom. If some college boys were told: Clean up your rooms and then the girls will inspect them, the girls would never inspect some of them, for they would not meet the condition of cleaning up their rooms. However, if you say: Clean up the rooms for the girls are coming for an inspection, this means that regardless of whether you clean them up or not, they are coming. If you do not clean them up, they will find them disorderly when they inspect them. John the Baptist gave the nearness of the kingdom as a motivation to repentance, but he did not say that their repentance was a condition of the

---

[1] *Ibid.*, page 86.

coming of the kingdom.

What did John say would happen if they did not repent? Instead of saying that the kingdom would be postponed, he said that the impenitent would be cut off. "Even now the axe lieth at the root of the trees: every tree therefore that bringeth not forth good fruit is hewn down, and cast into the fire" (Matt. 3:10). They were not to think that God depended on physical Israel to accomplish His purpose concerning the kingdom. "Bring forth therefore fruit worthy of repentance: and think not to say within yourselves, We have Abraham to our father: for I say unto you that God is able of these stones to raise up children unto Abraham" (Matt. 3:8-9; Rom. 9:6; 11:4-6, 20-23).

Jesus also said that they were to repent because the kingdom was at hand.(Matt. 4:17). He too warned them: "And I say unto you, that many shall come from the east and the west, and shall sit down with Abraham, and Isaac, and Jacob, in the kingdom of heaven: but the sons of the kingdom shall be cast forth into the outer darkness: there shall be the weeping and the gnashing of teeth" (Matt. 8:11-12). Finally he said to the rebellious: "Did ye never read in the scriptures, The stone which the builders rejected, the same was made the head of the corner, this was from the Lord, and it is marvelous in our eyes? Therefore say I unto you, The kingdom of God shall be taken away from you, and shall be given to a nation bringing forth the fruits thereof. And he that falleth on this stone shall be broken to pieces: but on whomsoever it shall fall, it will scatter him as dust. And when the chief priests and the Pharisees heard his parables, they perceived that he spake of them" (Matt. 21:42-45):

How different from the message: Repent and then the kingdom is at hand, but if you do not repent the kingdom will be postponed until you do repent.

Seventh, if Israel's failure to repent kept the kingdom from being established in the first century, how do they know that it will be established at the second coming? Why do they think that Christ shall in some way cause them to repent at the second coming, when He did not do it in the first coming when He said that it was time for the kingdom?

The Kingdom Message Before the Parables

Although we believe that the above arguments show that the postponement theory is false, let us evaluate it by seeing that the nature of the kingdom is the same before, in, and after the parables.

What were the characteristics of the kingdom as preached *before* the parables? (1) It took into consideration that Christ came to die as the Lamb of God for the sins of the world (Matt. 1:21; John 1:29; Heb. 9:24-28). In other words, He had first to suffer and then to enter into His glory (Luke 24:25-27).

(2) It was at hand whether Israel repented or not, and its nearness was a reason that they should repent. (Matt. 3:2).

(3) God did not depend on physical Israel to establish the kingdom. If they did not accept the message, they would be cast out (Matt. 3:9-10; 8:11-12; 21:42-45). Abraham's seed is raised up not from stones, however, but through faith (Gal. 3:26-29).

(4) It was to be a spiritual kingdom into which one entered by the new birth. One did not have a place in it because of his physical birth, even if he were a Jew (John 3:3-5).

(5) Its spiritual nature is emphasized in the beatitudes; in fact, in the entire sermon on the mount (Matt. 5:1-10).

(6) It was to be a kingdom, in contrast with the Old Testament (Deut. 12:5, 11; 1 Kings 9:3), in which Jerusalem would no longer have the significance it once had. The temple would not be a part of the New Covenant, but worship would be in spirit and in truth (John 1:17; 4:20-23).

(7) His reign was to be during a time when enemies still existed and would persecute His disciples, although He will reign until all enemies are conquered (Matt. 5:11-12; Psa. 110:1-4; 1 Cor. 15:24; Heb. 1:3, 13; Rev. 20:11- 21:5).

(8) It would be a kingdom in which Christ's disciples would suffer at the hands of enemies, but the church or kingdom would not be the instrument God used to prosecute these enemies. Matt. 5:1-12; 43-48 makes this clear.

(9) The kingdom set forth in the sermon on the mount was to replace the Old Law, as Jesus repeatedly showed by saying: "Ye have heard that it was said by them of old time... But I say unto you" (Matt. 5:21, 27, 28, 31, 32, 33, 34, 38, 39). Christ came to fulfill the law and the prophets, not to perpetuate them (Matt. 5:17-18). The sermon on the mount does use the expression "kingdom of heaven" at least once with reference to the entrance into heaven (Matt. 7:21-23; 25:41-46; 2 Pet. 1:8-11).

These passages show that the nature of the kingdom which was at hand before the parables is the nature of the one established on Pentecost. They are the same kingdom.

The Kingdom Message In the Parables

What kingdom is presented *in* the parables? Does Christ change the message from the kingdom to the church, from one rule to an entirely different rule, as Boll maintains?[1]

(1) Christ's speaking in parables was prophesied, so how could the church age which is dealt with in the parables, be unforeseen and unprophesied (Matt. 13:34-35)?

(2) If the church age and the kingdom age differ, how can Boll maintain that the parables which speak of the church age are speaking of a phase of the kingdom age?[2] In commenting on Matt. 16:13-19, he said: "Of the church they knew as yet nothing."[3] They may not have known that the kingdom would also be called the church, but if the parables speak of the church age they knew something about it, on Boll's own admission, from the parables.

(3) Jesus is still speaking about the kingdom of heaven in the parables. He had preached that it was at hand (Matt. 4:17), that it belongs to the poor in spirit (Matt. 5:3), that the kingdom belongs to those who are persecuted for righteousness (Matt.5:10), that they are to seek first the kingdom (Matt. 6:33), the apostles preached it as at hand (Matt. 10:7), in some sense it had come unto them (Matt. 12:28), and in Matt. 13:11 he speaks of the mysteries of the *kingdom of heaven.* Time and time again in the parables, He reminds us that He is speaking of the kingdom, for He continually said "the kingdom of heaven is like..." (Matt. 13:24, 31, 33, 45, 47). There is no hint that Jesus is speaking of a different kingdom in Matt. 10:7 and Matt. 13:11, 24, etc. Where is the passage which says that Jesus has ceased talking about one kingdom and is now talking about another?

(4) The kingdom of which Jesus spoke was not unknown to the prophets, although they did not get to hear the details of it which five apostles heard. "For verily I say unto you, that many prophets and righteous men desired to see the things which ye see, and saw them not; and to hear the things which ye hear, and heard them not" (Matt. 13:17).

---

[1] *Ibid.,* pages 69-70.
[2] *Ibid.,* pages 66, 69-71.
[3] *Ibid.,* page 73.

(5) The kingdom mentioned in the parables is the everlasting kingdom of Daniel 2:44 and Psa. 110:1-4, because in several parables Jesus shows that this kingdom will last until the end of time, and the judgment wherein the good are separated from the evil and then, in heaven of course, the righteous shall shine forth in the kingdom undimmed by the presence of evil (Matt. 13:40-43).

(6) The kingdom spoken of in the parables will last until the judgment and the separation of the good from the evil, and not until a millennial kingdom in which, Boll admits, there will be sin and which will be followed by a tremendous rebellion against God and His people; for after the thousand years reign there will be a little season of rebellion. Boll said that there will be some sin in the millennium, according to prophecies which he applied to the millennium (Isa. 26:10; 65:20; Malachi 3:5); but he said it would be dealt with quickly. He also said: "The quick success of Satan's work at the end of the millennium, indicates the inward condition of many hearts (Revelation 20:7-10).[1] How, then, in such a kingdom could all evil be eliminated and the righteous shine forth as "the sun in the kingdom of their Father" (Matt. 13:41-43). However, the kingdom mentioned in the parables lasts until all sin is taken out, and we enter into the eternal state (Matt. 13:41-43, 49-50; see also Heb. 9:28; 1 Pet. 1:5; John 12:48; 1 Cor. 15:24-28; Acts 2:34-35).

The reference to the kingdom of the Father would mean, according to the logic of the premillennialists, that this age cannot be the millennial age, for the millennial age is the age of the kingdom of the Son! Of course, the present kingdom is Christ's (Col. 1:13), but it is also the Father's for Christ rules at God's right hand, and will rule until He delivers the kingdom to the Father (1 Cor. 15:24-28). "The kingdom of their Father" refers to the eternal state in Matt. 13:41-43.

(7) In his prefatory remarks about the parable of the sower, Jesus showed that Isaiah had prophesied the hardened condition of the people of Israel (Matt. 13:10-16).

(8) Boll argued that in speaking of the mysteries of the kingdom Jesus is speaking of a different kingdom (Matt. 13:11) He lists what he believes to be some of the mysteries.[2] However, regardless of what these mysteries are, they are mysteries of the very kingdom Jesus has

---

[1] *Ibid.*, pages 162-163
[2] *Ibid.*, pages 69-70.

talked about throughout His personal ministry. He is not dealing with a mysterious kingdom, unknown to the prophets, but some mysteries of the kingdom *which had been prophesied.* These mysteries Boll says were:

(a) The world-wide proclamation of the word of the kingdom, the good tidings. However, Daniel's prophecy shows it was to be a world-wide kingdom, and John said Jesus would die for the sins of the world (Dan. 2:38-44; John 1:29).

(b) Its limited success. Daniel, too, prophesied a small beginning for the kingdom, just as Jesus did in the parable of the mustard seed. Psa. 110:1-2 showed that His reign would begin in the midst of His enemies, and the beatitudes showed that His disciples would be persecuted (Matt. 5:10-12).

(c) The intermingling of good and evil until the harvest time. However, this was indicated by the fact that Christ was to rule in the midst of His enemies, but was to rule until they were all conquered—the last one being death, at the time of the judgment.

(d) The insignificant beginning of the kingdom and its vast issues. However, this was taught in Daniel where the little stone became a great mountain, and in the parable of the mustard seed which became a mighty tree (Matt. 13:31-32).

(e) The working of a secret, hidden influence, for the kingdom is likened unto leaven. The prophets may not have made this clear, but we know that Christ's teaching does work as such an influence.

(f) The kingdom, Boll said, was concealed and hidden in the world. The prophets however, knew that it would not be like the kingdoms of the world, for it was not to be set up by men's hands and Christ was to rule from heaven.

(g) The sorting out of the good from the evil at the end of the age. But the end of the age indicated in the parables is the final judgment, not a judgment to be followed by another reign of Christ on this earth, but this time in person.

(h) The "exceeding preciousness to the Lord" of the kingdom. This is clear, however, from prophecy since Christ died to make it possible—as Isaiah 53 had foretold.

Mysteries may be things which are revealed, but unknown to people because of their blindness, or they may be things which are not fully revealed. There is additional information in the parables concerning the kingdom, but not everything of which they spoke was unknown to prophecy (Compare Rom. 16:25-27). Most of them in one way or another were foretold or foreshadowed. However, even if nothing was known about these particular characteristics of the kingdom, Jesus was dealing with the kingdom of heaven and not some different kingdom. Some of these truths may have been veiled in types and symbols, but they all dealt with the prophesied kingdom.

The Kingdom Message After the Parables

Although Boll thinks that the parables in Matthew 13 announce the change to the church age instead of the kingdom age, Jesus continues to speak of the same kingdom after the parables that He spoke of before and in the parables. "And I also say unto thee, that thou art Peter and upon this rock I will build my church; and the gates of Hades shall not prevail against it. I will give unto thee the keys of the kingdom of heaven: and whatsoever thou Shalt bind on earth shall be bound in heaven; and whatsoever thou shalt loose on earth shall be loosed in heaven" (Matt. 16:18-19).

Boll said: "Of the church they knew as yet nothing."[1] As we have already mentioned, they did not have to know that the kingdom could also be called the church in order for it to be the same kingdom. Christ's exaltation to His throne was also His exaltation to headship over the church (Eph. 1:19-21). These are but different ways of expressing His relationship of authority over His people.

Several passages show that the kingdom message is the same *after* the parables. (1) As we have pointed out elsewhere in this book, why was Peter given keys to the kingdom, in an illustration concerning the church as a building, if he was not to be a doorkeeper of the church or kingdom with the authority to declare the conditions of admission? He was prominent in opening the door of faith to the Jew on Pentecost and to the Gentiles at the household of Cornelius (Acts 2:14, 22, 37, 38-41; Acts 10; 11; 15:7-11). If premillennialism is right, Christ gave Peter keys which he has not used yet. If they say he has used them, they must admit that the kingdom has been established, for how could the keys of the kingdom be used if the kingdom did not exist?

(2) From the time that Jesus spoke of building the church on the rock, He began "to show unto his disciples that he must go into Jerusalem, and suffer many things of the elders and chief priests and scribes,

---

[1] *Ibid.,* page 73.

and be killed and the third day be raised up. And Peter took him, and began to rebuke him, saying, Be it far from thee, Lord: this shall never be unto thee. But he turned, and said unto Peter, Get thee behind me, Satan: thou art a stumbling-block unto me: for thou mindest not the things of God, but the things of men" (Matt. 16:21-23). This is an announcement that He must go the way of the cross, but it does not differ in essence from the announcement of the angel that Jesus would be the Savior of His people from their sins (Matt. 1:21), or John's announcement that Jesus was the Lamb of God who would take away the sin of the world (John 1:29). The message both before and after the parables dealt with a kingdom which took into consideration that the cross came before the crown.

Peter disputed Jesus' words and said that His death would not take place. How could it take place if He was to establish the kind of kingdom that the Jews and the disciples of the Lord wanted? Jesus showed that Peter was not minding the things of God but of man. His view was based on man's view and not on God's plan and prophecies.

(3) After the parables of Matt. 13, Jesus was more definite about the time of the kingdom's establishment. "But I tell you of a truth, there are some of them that stand here, who shall in no wise taste of death, till they see the kingdom of God" (Luke 9:27). As He said elsewhere: "Verily I say unto you, There are some of them that stand here, who shall in no wise taste of death, till they see the Son of man coming in his kingdom" (Matt. 16:28). The same truth is recorded by Mark: "And he said unto them, Verily I say unto you, There are some here of them that stand by, who shall in no wise taste of death, till they see the kingdom of God come with power" (Mark 9:1). Before the parables, He had said it was at hand (Matt. 4:17, 23; 10:7). Now, in speaking of the kingdom, He shows that its nearness is such that it will come in their lifetime.

There are those who maintain that these promises were fulfilled when Christ was transfigured on the mount and when they had a preview of His glory. They quote Peter who said: "For we did not follow cunningly devised fables, when we made known unto you the power and coming of our Lord Jesus Christ, but we were eyewitnesses of his majesty. For he received from God the Father honor and glory, when there was borne such a voice to him by the Majestic Glory, This is my beloved Son, in whom t am well pleased: and this voice we ourselves heard borne out of heaven, when we were with him in the holy mount"

(2 Pet. 1:16-18). But a preview of the Christ in glory would not be a coming of the kingdom. The kingdom was present in Matt. 17 in the same sense that it was present before Matthew 17 and just after Matthew 17—not at all.

As a matter of fact that kingdom did come with power during the lifetime of some who stood before Jesus in Mark 9:1. (a) At least one person, Judas, had tasted of death before it came. Jesus said some would not die, but He did not say that *no one* would taste of death until the kingdom came (Acts 1:5-8). (b) Jesus said they would receive power when the Spirit came and this took place on Pentecost (Acts 1:6; 2:1-11). Did the kingdom come at that time? Yes, for Christ was proclaimed as reigning as Lord and Christ at the right hand of God (Acts 2:34-36). (c) This makes it clear the kingdom came with power during the lifetime of some to whom Jesus spoke in Mark 9:1.

(4) After Jesus had promised the kingdom within their lifetime (Luke 9:27), He went into the mount and was transfigured (Matt. 17:1-8). On the mount, Elijah and Moses talked about Christ's coming death in Jerusalem (Luke 9:31). This shows that the cross came before the crown, as was shown in passages before the parables. The disciples still did not understand it (Luke 9:44-45).

(5) After they came down from the mount of transfiguration (Luke 9:28-36), Christ sent out "other seventy also" and they were told: "say unto them, The kingdom of God is come nigh unto you" (Luke 10:9). As J. Early Arceneaux wrote:

> "Come nigh" in this passage is a translation of the same word translated "at hand" in Matthew, in all these passages; and in Mark also. "At hand," and "come nigh" are translations of the very same word: **that postponement theory then is completely exploded by the fact that the seventy said "the kingdom of God is at hand" long after these theorists say nobody said that any more.** One fact then explodes the whole theory of postponement. And one other thing. A negative fact. I have never yet seen a man, nor read anything from anybody who put down one single scriptural reference that he thought meant God decided to postpone the kingdom. Usually men find something they quote, but I've never seen a verse referred to that men thought conveyed the idea that God postponed the es-

tablishment of the kingdom.[1]

(6) Before the parables, John taught that Jews who did not accept Christ would be cut off (Matt. 3:8-10), and Jesus taught that there would be "children of the kingdom"—Jews—who would be lost (Matt. 8:12). They were "children of the kingdom" in that the kingdom had been promised to Israel, as well as to Gentiles. Their being in it, however, was conditional. They had to repent. They had to undergo the new birth (Matt. 3:2; John 3:1-5). *The establishment of the kingdom was not conditional, but their being in it was conditional.* As Ellicott wrote:

> *The form of the phrase is a Hebraism, indicating as in "the children of the bride-chamber," those who belonged to the kingdom, i.e., in this case, the Israelites, to whom the kingdom of heaven had, in the first instance, been promised, the natural heirs who had forfeited their inheritance.*[2]

After the parables, Jesus taught the same truth, "Therefore say I unto you, The kingdom of God shall be taken away from you, and shall be given to a nation bringing forth the fruits thereof. And he that falleth on this stone shall be broken to pieces: but on whomsoever it shall fail, it will scatter him as dust. And when the chief priests and the Pharisees heard his parables, they perceived that he spake of them" (Matt. 21:43-45). The kingdom would not be postponed, but would be taken from them and given to a nation bearing the fruit thereof. In other words, it would be to the spiritual nation composed of Jews and Gentiles who were born again and were the true seed of Abraham (Gal. 3:26-29).

Jesus did not mean that the Old Testament kingdom would be taken from them and the Old Testament kingdom given to another people. The Old Testament rule was to come to an end, and the Messiah was to rule. But God's rule would be taken from them, and God's rule would be through Christ over Christ's kingdom (Col. 1:13). The kingdom which John and Jesus offered Israel was rejected by Israel, and Israel was rejected, but the kingdom which was at hand was given to those who had receptive hearts. This is in harmony with the parable of

---

[1] J. Early Arceneaux, *The Bible Banner,* March 1947, pages 5-6.

[2] Charles Ellicott, *A New Testament Commentary for English Readers*, Vol. 1, page 46.

the sower which shows that the word of God is the seed of His kingdom, but that not all hearts receive it (Luke 8:11-15).

(7) The two on the road to Emmaus had hoped that Jesus would establish the kingdom, but He disappointed them and destroyed their hopes (Luke 24:21). But Jesus told them the cross had to come before the crown (Luke 24:25-27). This shows he was speaking of the same kingdom of which He spoke before the parables.

(8) Before the coming of the Spirit, the disciples wanted to know if Christ would restore the kingdom to Israel (Acts 1:6). Christ told them it was not theirs to know times and seasons (Acts 1:7). He promised the Spirit and power. On Pentecost they preached Christ as reigning at God's right hand (Acts 2:30-36). Thousands of Israelites accepted the rulership of Christ. After this the disciples no longer asked whether the kingdom will be restored, but preached the kingdom as a present reality (Acts 2:34-36; Col. 1:13).

The Conclusion

What is the conclusion which we draw from the fact that the kingdom spoken of before, in, and after the parables is the same kingdom? The premillennialists agree with us that the kingdom which was at hand in Matt. 3:2 was the one prophesied by the prophets. Since the one that was at hand was not postponed, but was established, it is evident that Christ's spiritual kingdom is the one prophesied by the prophets. Therefore, the premillennialists have misinterpreted prophecy and have misunderstood the nature of the kingdom.

However, if may be said that Boll maintained that the church is a phase of the kingdom.[1]

The Church a Phase of the Kingdom?

The position that the church is a phase of the kingdom does not do away with the unscriptural postponement theory, nor does it harmonize with his position that the church and the kingdom are different rules of Christ. *First*, Boll does not believe the church phase was at hand in Matt. 3:2, therefore that phase of the kingdom which was at hand was postponed and the new phase began to be taught in Matt. 13.[2]

Second, if, as Boll maintains, "these kings" of Dan. 2:44 did not exist in the first century, no phase of the kingdom could have been at

---

[1] Boll, *The Kingdom of God*, page 34.
[2] *Ibid.*, pages 68-70.

hand.[1] It was not true in such a case, but Jesus said the time was fulfilled (Mark 1:14-15).

Third, Boll denies that the establishment of the church was the fulfillment of Daniel 2:44.[2]

Fourth, it has been suggested that the church is the little stone
phase of the kingdom. If so, it is the phase predicted for the first century, for the kingdom started as a little stone cut out of the mountain
without hands. If any phase of the kingdom has been established, the
kingdom has been established. Then, too, a major objection of the
premillennialists to the position that the church and the kingdom are
the same is that Rome was not destroyed in a catastrophic blow when
the church was established. Rome did not even feel a tremor.[3] However, the image was to be smitten in the little stone stage, so if the little
stone phase has been established, Rome was smitten. The smiting connected, in point of time, with the establishment of the kingdom (Dan.
2:34, 44-45).

Fifth, Rome was not to vanish before it was smitten. It has vanished, therefore, it has been smitten in the sense meant in the prophecy. The kingdom had to be established before Rome vanished, and
Rome existed in the first century and for some time thereafter. But the
first century was the time for the establishment of the kingdom (Mark
1:14-15).

Sixth, if the church is one phase of the kingdom—the little stone
phase—mentioned in Dan. 2:44, it cannot be an unexpected aspect as
Boll maintains.[4] It was clearly prophesied in Daniel's reference to the
little stone.

Seventh, the premillennial theory cannot be consistent and maintain that the church is one phase of the kingdom. Why? (1) They believe that the rule at God's right hand and the rule on the throne of David are two different rules. How can the rule of the invisible king from
heaven, at God's right hand, in the kingdom of God's son, be a phase
of a rule on earth on the throne of David when He will be visible? (2)
They cannot be phases of the same kingdom, for Christ's kingdom has
no distinction between Jew and Gentile, but the Jews will reign over

---

[1] Boll, *Lessons on Daniel,* page 11.

[2] *Ibid.,* page 10.

[3] Boll, *The Kingdom of God*, pages 19-22.

[4] *Ibid.,* page 70.

the Gentiles in the coming kingdom (Eph. 3:3-6; Gal. 3:26-29).[1] (3) The New Testament church was established in grace, but the coming kingdom, they say, will be established in a crushing judgment on the world in an open clash of the kingdom with the world.[2] (4) They cannot be phases of the same kingdom, for Christ's kingdom does not have governmental authority, but the millennial kingdom will combine both church and state. It will not only preach the gospel, but it will exercise governmental rulership and execute vengeance.[3]

Just as these two kingdoms cannot be phases one of another, just so the kingdom prophesied by the prophets could not be both postponed and established! The postponement theory is false, and it is not helped by the idea of the church as a phase of the kingdom. Therefore, we conclude again that the prophesied kingdom, which they agree was at hand in Matt. 3:2, was established. The kingdom of God's dear Son is the kingdom of Dan. 2:44 (Acts 2:34-36; 1 Cor. 15:24-28; Col. 1:13; Heb. 13:20; Heb. 12:28). Starting with common ground, we have shown in this chapter that the premillennial view of the kingdom, and their interpretation of the kingdom prophecies, are false.

---

[1] *Ibid.,* page 120.
[2] *Boles-Boll Debate*, page 99. Boll, *The Kingdom of God*, page 21.
[3] Boll, *The Kingdom of God*, pages 79, 155, 162, 31.

CHAPTER 7:
CHURCH AGE FORETOLD BY THE PROPHETS

Under the heading of "The Church Age As A Parenthesis," Walvoord discussed the question "whether the present age is predicted in the Old Testament." It is a very important question. He recognizes that if the church age was predicted, premillennialism is false, and that they have "not always given a clear answer" to this question. "... some [premillennialists] have tended to strike a compromise interpretation, in which part of the Old Testament predictions are fulfilled now and part in the future. In some cases they have conceded so much...that for all practical purposes they have surrendered premillennialism as well."[1] Walvoord argued there is Scriptural support for the idea of a parenthesis and that it is reasonable.

By parenthesis, the premillennialists mean an unrecorded, an unpredicted, an unmentioned time span when the prophets spoke of the future. They did not speak of the church age. I do not believe that the word parenthesis is a good word to describe what they are talking about. *First*, every parenthesis which I have ever seen occupies space in the sentence and the reader sees it. *Second*, every parenthesis has something in it which the reader can read. The parenthesis, according to them, is the church age which was not predicted by the prophets. In so far as the Old Testament is concerned the church age is unrevealed. There are not even any parenthesis marks in the Old Testament to indicate that the church age was not predicted.

Walvoord thought that: "Nothing should be plainer to one reading the Old Testament than that the foreview therein provided did not predict a period of time between the two advents. This very fact confused even the prophets (cf. 1 Pet. 1:10-12). At best such a time interval was only implied." He thought Daniel 9:24-27 implied a time interval between the first and second coming.[2] Of course, if it was implied in prophecy, *it was predicted* to the extent it was implied.

Concerning 1 Peter 1:10-12, the prophets did not know all they wanted to know about the definite time or all the conditions and circumstances of the time of the gospel. "They earnestly sought to know both the exact time and the nature of the time. These two points in-

---

[1] Walvoord, *The Millennial Kingdom*, page 227.
[2] *Ibid.*, page 228.

volved desire to know more of him who was to suffer. They wanted to know more than they wrote, and to understand better what they did write."[1] However, this very passage shows the gospel age was prophesied.

First, they "prophesied of the grace that should come unto you" (1 Pet. 1:10). Since the grace was prophesied, the age in which this grace was to appear was prophesied.

Second, the Spirit "testified beforehand the sufferings of Christ, and the glories that should follow them" (1 Pet. 1:11). These sufferings were in connection with His first coming, therefore the first coming and His rejection by Israel were both prophesied.

Third, furthermore they prophesied that His glories would come after His sufferings. This is exactly what Jesus said that the disciples were foolish and slow of heart to believe, i.e., that He must first suffer and then enter into His glory. They prophesied the glory into which He would enter after His rejection, therefore they prophesied that He was received up into glory; even the glory of His reign as king and priest (Luke 24:25-27; 1 Tim. 3:16; Acts 2:34-36; Heb. 8:1-2).

Fourth, these things which they revealed were for our good, and these things are the very things "which now have been announced unto you through them that preached the gospel unto you by the Holy Spirit sent forth from heaven; which things angels desire to look Into" (1 Pet. 1:12). These things they prophesied are the things angels desire to look into and are the very things preached by the gospel preachers in the first century. But these things concerning our salvation in Christ are in this age of grace. Therefore, salvation in Christ in this age of grace was prophesied.

If the church age was not prophesied, the gospel was not prophesied, for the church age is the gospel age. Christ purchased the church with His blood (Acts 20:28). If redemption was prophesied, of necessity the redeemed group was prophesied (Isaiah 53).

Walvoord cited several scriptures on which he made arguments to try to prove that there were many parentheses in the Old Testament. For example, he wrote:

> *Psalm 22 predicts the sufferings of Christ (Ps. 22:1-21), anticipates the resurrection of Christ (Ps. 22:22), and then in*

---

[1] Nathaniel M. Williams, *Commentary on the Epistles of Peter,* page 17.

*the remainder of the psalm deals with millennial conditions
without a reference to the present age.*[1]

But if the sufferings were prophesied in connection with the first
coming, it was prophesied that He would not be triumphantly received
by Israel in His first coming. The sufferings were prophesied, and the
glories that should follow His sufferings were prophesied (1 Pet. 1:11).
Therefore, the present glories of Christ as well as His sufferings were
prophesied (1 Tim. 3:16).

If the prophets spoke of both the first coming and the second coming of Christ, and Walvoord indicated that they did predict both, it
must follow that they did predict a time interval between the two comings. Unless there was a time interval between the two comings, *two*
comings could not have been predicted. If no time interval was predicted or clearly implied between the two comings, His first and second coming would be at the same time which is ridiculous.

However, it is unnecessary to hunt for any proof for a parenthesis
in which an unpredicted church age can be placed in order to fit in the
church age with Old Testament predictions. It is unnecessary, and impossible to find such, for the simple reason that it is as clear as crystal,
that the church age, the present age, was prophesied. Walvoord and the
premillennialists are wrong in affirming that "the prophecies of the
Old Testament" predict "the millennium rather than the present age."[2]

What proof is there that the church age was prophesied? We are
not consistent disciples of Christ if we refuse to accept the New Testament teaching, that the present age was prophesied, just because it
contradicts our ideas and the ideas of those who taught us what they
viewed as the true meaning of prophecy.

There may be a long time between two events mentioned in one
passage of scripture. The existence of a time interval would have to be
proved by other scriptures, or by events themselves which the Scriptures justify us in concluding to be the fulfillment of the two events.
John said Jesus would baptize in the Holy Spirit and in fire. Baptism in
the Holy Spirit took place on Pentecost and at the household of Cornelius, but the baptism in fire takes place at the end of time when the
wicked are consigned to hell (Rev. 20:12-15).

---

[1] Walvoord, *The Millennial Kingdom*, page 228.
[2] *Ibid.*, page 230.

Time Schedule Eliminates Parenthesis

The idea that the church is a parenthesis, unprophesied, between the first and second coming. is destroyed by the fact that it does not fit the time schedule of prophecy, as I have shown elsewhere in this book. *First,* if the parenthesis was in God's mind, and it was time for it in the first century, the Spirit would not have inspired John (Matt. 3:2) and Jesus (Matt. 4:17) to announce that the kingdom was at hand. The parenthesis, the church age, was at hand. If it is not the kingdom, the kingdom could not have been at hand.

Second, premillennialism believes that the second coming brings the kingdom, therefore the first coming could not have been a preparatory period for the establishment of the kingdom. However, it was such a preparatory period.

Third, Jesus said; "The time is fulfilled, and the kingdom of God is at hand: repent ye, and believe in the gospel" (Mark 1:15). How could the time have been fulfilled, the time which was necessary to arrive for the kingdom to be at hand if it was not at hand but the church age was at hand?

Fourth, John and Jesus would not have used the nearness of the kingdom as a motivation for repentance if the church age instead was at hand and the establishment of the kingdom was a remote event.

Isaiah 53

Isaiah 53 prophesied that the message concerning Christ would not be received readily (53:1), His unfavorable conditions and that He was not what they wanted (53:2), that He would be despised (53:3), that He would bear our sorrows and transgressions and bring healing to us, but the people would think that He was smitten for transgressions of His own (53:4-8). God's way of correcting man's strayings was through placing on Him our iniquity (53:6). He died (53:8-9), He died for our sins (53:10, 15), He was raised (53:10), and was triumphant (53:10-12). *This is a brief outline of the Gospels and the rest of the New Testament.* How could the gospel age be unpredicted when this is a prediction of the gospel and Christ's triumphs? Christ's triumphs are the result of His gospel and all that it means.

Jesus could have cited Isaiah 53 to prove His statements that the prophets had taught that He must first suffer and then enter into His glory (Luke 24:25-27). In speaking of Israel's rejection of Christ, which premillennialists maintain resulted in the postponement of the kingdom and the establishment of the church, Peter said: "But the things which God foreshowed by the mouth of all the prophets, that His Christ should suffer, he thus fulfilled" (Acts 3:18). But the premillennialists tell us that the church, which was created by His suffering and death (Eph. 3:13-16), was not prophesied. Philip preached Jesus unto the eunuch beginning with Isaiah 53. As a result the eunuch accepted Christ (Acts 8:32-39). The gospel age is the age in which the prophets prophesied that Christ would be glorified after His suffering. They prophesied of the salvation which has come to the people in the church age (1 Pet. 1:10-12). Did they not prophecy of the church age? To whom were they prophesying that the message of salvation would come?

In speaking of the fact that many had not accepted the message of salvation which Paul preached, Paul cited many Old Testament references. Among other things he said concerning the present preaching of the gospel, and the present rejection of it by many; "But they did not all hearken to the glad tidings. For Isaiah saith, Lord, who hath believed our report?" (Rom. 10:16; Isa. 53:1). Isaiah also foretold the *present reception* of the gospel by the Gentiles (Rom. 10:20; 9:30-33). What about Israel's disobedience at the very time Paul wrote Romans, disobedience which is taking place in this gospel age? Was it foreseen and prophesied? "But as to Israel he saith, All the day long did I spread out my hands unto a disobedient and gain-saying people" (Rom. 10:21; Isa. 65:2).

How could the church age be unprophesied when Isaiah saw and foretold the rejection of Christ, the disobedience of Israel, and the present proclamation of the gospel?

The Church the Bride of Christ

Walvoord thinks that one thing which shows the church age was not prophesied is that the New Testament, not the Old, reveals the doctrine that the church is the bride of Christ. Ephesians 5:22-33 shows that the bride of Christ is made up of "the believers of this age."[1] These believers are those who, whether Jew or Gentile are on an equal standing in Christ (Eph. 3:3-6; 2 Cor. 11:2). The fact that the Old Testament prophesied the death of Christ, and the fact that Christ gave

---

[1] *Ibid.,* page 245.

Himself up for the church (Eph. 5:25) proves that the church (the creation of which was the object of His death (Eph. 2:13-16), was not unknown to prophecy. How could it be that His death was known but not
the outcome of His death (Acts 20:28)?

The fact that the church is the bride of Christ is one of the mysteries which relates "to the church as a distinct entity in the present age.
They mark out the church as a separate purpose of God to be consummated before the resumption of the divine program for Israel."[1] Walvoord said that Christ would come for His saints, without coming to
earth itself, and receive the church unto Himself (Thess. 4:13-18).[2]
This is before the second coming.[3] The marriage of the Lamb takes
place. "The church in heaven returning with Christ is one wife, not two
(Rev. 19:7-9)."[4] The "rapture of the church occurs before the entire
seven-year period of Daniel's seventieth week."[5] The church "is delivered from the tribulation."[6] "At the rapture the church will meet Christ
in the air, living saints will be translated and will return with Christ to
heaven."[7] The church "in heaven will become the wife of Christ when
she is presented a glorious church (Eph. 5:27)."[8] Christ will return to
earth with His bride, at some time after the marriage feast.[9]

What a strange situation it will be in the millennium. If Christ does
not bring the church with Him from heaven for the thousand year
reign, He will leave the bride shortly after the marriage. He will be absent from heaven for a thousand years. On the other hand, if Christ
brings the bride with Him, consider how it mixes up things in the millennium.

First, Israel "the nation will again be related to Jehovah by marriage (Isa. 54:1-17; 63:2-5; Hos. 2:14-23)."[10] Israel could not be married to Christ regardless of whether He brings His bride with Him or
leaves her in heaven.

---

[1] *Ibid.*, page 247.
[2] *Ibid.*, page 243.
[3] *Ibid.*, page 244.
[4] *Ibid.*, page 246.
[5] *Ibid.*, page 251.
[6] *Ibid.*, page 252.
[7] *Ibid.*, page 253.
[8] *Ibid.*, page 245.
[9] *Ibid.*, page 270.
[10] *Ibid.*, page 303.

Second, in the millennium Jehovah will be married to Israel and Christ will be married to the church.

Third, in the millennium there will be Jews and Gentiles in the flesh who have families. The church, the bride of Christ, will be there but all of these will be in the heavenly, not fleshly body.

Fourth, the church, married to Christ, is composed of both Jews and Gentiles, and there is no distinction between them. However, in the millennium Israel will be exalted over the Gentile nations.[1] "The lesser role of Gentiles in the millennium is the subject of many Old Testament Scriptures... They will, however, occupy a subordinate role to Israel (Isa. 14:1-2; 49:22-23; 61:5-9)."[2]

Fifth, "Any literal interpretation of the Old Testament will make plain that the purpose of God revealed for Israel in the millennial kingdom is quite different from the purpose of God in the present age in relation to the church as the body of Christ."[3] The kingdom prophesied by the Old Testament was the millennial kingdom, not the church. "The Old Testament strictly maintains the distinction between Jew and Gentile, distinguishes their hope, their promises, and God's dealing with them. That is the main point of the Old Testament. The idea that Jews and Gentiles might be united in one entity without any distinction whatever, with equal privileges, rights, and fellowship is foreign to the Old Testaments."[4]

Sixth, since the Levitical system, under which the people received the law (Heb. 7:11), will be restored in the millennium,[5] the law must be restored. The distinction between Jew and Gentile will be restored. *What is the church to do in this millennial reign?* There are premillennialists who maintain that the church will reign with Christ in the millennium. Walvoord viewed the apostles as rulers at that time since he cited Matthew 19:28 as one of the proofs there would be other rulers than Christ in the millennium, although they will be under Christ. "Verily I say unto you, that ye who have followed me, in the regeneration when the Son of man shall sit on the throne of his glory, ye shall sit upon twelve thrones, judging the twelve tribes of Israel" (Matt. 19:28). The apostles and other members of the church, the church in

---

[1] *Ibid.*

[2] *Ibid.*, pages 303-304.

[3] *Ibid.*, page 236.

[4] *Ibid.*, page 237.

[5] *Ibid.*, pages 309-315.

which there is no distinction between Jew and Gentile, will rule with
Christ in the very kingdom in which the Jews as a nation are exalted
and the Gentiles in a subordinate position. The church is made up of
Jews and Gentiles, with the Gentiles predominating. How can Gentile
Christians as a part of the bride of Christ function in a kingdom in
which the distinction between Jew and Gentile is restored and the Gentiles subordinated to Israel? The premillennialists have created such a
view of the future by their theory, but they cannot straighten it out
without abandoning their theory.

Seventh, Jews and Gentiles in the church on earth are one new
man, and were to keep the unity of the Spirit in the bond of peace
(Eph. 2:13-16; 4:3). With the distinction between Jew and Gentile restored, unless the bride of Christ is exempt, the bride of Christ will be
split into the exalted Jewish part and the subordinate Gentile part.
Walvoord said Christ would return from heaven with his bride and that
the church "is one wife, not two (Rev. 19:7-9)." However, when the
bride reaches earth and the millennial reign starts, with the distinction
between Jew and Gentile, the wife of Christ will suffer with a split
personality for a thousand years!! The bride is composed of Jews and
Gentiles, and at the marriage they were one, but on earth in the millennium reign the bride is split and the Jewish part rules over the Gentile
part. What a sad situation!

Premillennialists may say that the church, in the millennium, will
be composed of resurrected and translated saints with heavenly bodies.
These have no nationality. It will still be a contradictory situation for
the bride, made up of redeemed from Jewish and Gentile backgrounds,
to live in a kingdom, in which the Israelites dominate the nations of the
earth. Literal Israel in physical, mortal bodies, will rule over Gentile
Christians who are part of the immortal brode of Christ, who suppos-
edly rule with Christ in the millennium.

Eighth, Israel will not be exalted above all the nations if the pre-
millennialists are right. The spiritual nation, the church, will rule over
Israel (Matt. 21:43). This is clear when we realize that Walvoord cited
Luke 19:12-17 as one of the proofs that there would be "other rulers"
than Christ in the millennium although they would be under Christ.[1]
The ten servants in the parable represent Christians who work while

---

[1] *Ibid.,* page 301.

waiting for the king to return. Only three of them are specifically mentioned in the parable of the pounds, one of them was placed over ten cities (Luke 19:17), and another over five (Luke 19:19). The servant who made nothing had his pound taken from him. It was given to the one who had ten pounds (Luke 19:24-26). This would place him over eleven cities.

At the beginning of the millennium there will not be a large nation of Israel. We say this because there are now only a few million Jews throughout the entire earth. There are around four million in Israel. Literal Israel, according to Walvoord, will pass through the great tribulation which will "be unprecedented in its character and severity. It is predicted that Israel's trials will bring spiritual revival to a portion of the nation and a godly remnant will emerge." Christ will return, Israel "will then be regathered from all over the earth, restored as a nation, and given a place of honor, safety, and prominence in the millennial kingdom."[1] Even if Israel, which is exalted, is composed of Jews other than the godly remnant, they will be few in number compared with the redeemed who were redeemed during the church age.

> *Walvoord quoted with approval from Nathaniel West that in the millennium Christ will stand "between God and mankind... Identified with Him, individually, and called by His name, stands Israel collectively, in His whole Messianic work and kingdom. Neither acts without the other...* **Old Testament prophecy knows of no other subjects of discourse than these, Israel, Messiah, and the nations.** *As to the kingdom, Israel had it, under the Old Testament, in its outward form; the Gentiles have it under the New Testament in its inward form; in the age to come, Jews and Gentiles together, shall have it, both forms in one, one kingdom of Messiah, spiritual, visible and glorious, with Israel still the central people, the prelude of the New Jerusalem and the nations walking in its light forever."[2]*

Consider carefully that the Old Testament prophesied nothing about the church.[3] The prophecies of the kingdom, which will be in existence in the millennium, are concerned with, as they are aware, "*no other subjects of discourse than these: Israel, Messiah, and the*

---

[1] *Ibid.*, page 257.
[2] *Ibid.*, pages 263-264.
[3] *Ibid.*

nations."[1]

Israel is going to be sorely disappointed, and the prophets are going to know that the church, of which they had known and predicted nothing, is going to be superior to Israel in the millennial kingdom. A new and unprophesied change has taken place. The very nature of the prophesied kingdom has been changed, for the superiority of Israel in the kingdom is destroyed. Israel is married to Jehovah.[2] The church is married to Christ and is His bride. West and Walvoord agreed that neither Christ nor Israel "acts without the other."[3] If this is the case, Israel, who is married to Jehovah comes between Christ and the church which is married to Christ. The bride of Christ the king will have less influence than Israel if Christ does not act without Israel. The church, though composed of redeemed Jews and Gentiles, will know that Israel is exalted even over the bride.

But how can this be, when the church as the bride of Christ is much closer to Christ than is Israel? Furthermore, Walvoord argued that Matthew 19:28 predicted the second advent and "that the Twelve Apostles will judge the twelve tribes of Israel."[4] The twelve apostles were set by God in the church. "And God hath set some in the church, first apostles..." (1 Cor. 12:28). The servants who were rewarded with rules over cities were Christians, part of the bride of Christ (Luke 19:12-27).[5] The apostles will be judging, in Walvoord's view of the millennium, the twelve tribes of Israel when Christ judges the earth at His second coming.[6] They will not step down from their throne immediately after the judging of Israel at the beginning of the millennium. The premillennialists view the regeneration as the millennial age when Christ rules in fulfillment of Old Testament prophecy. During this same regeneration, whenever it is, the apostles rule with Christ. "Verily I say unto you, that ye who have followed me, in the regeneration when the Son of man shall sit on the throne of his glory, ye also shall sit upon twelve thrones, judging the twelve tribes of Israel (Matt. 19:28). Peter and the apostles (members of the bride of Christ in which

---

[1] *Ibid.*

[2] *Ibid.,* page 303.

[3] *Ibid.,* 264.

[4] *Ibid.,* page 271.

[5] *Ibid.,* page 301.

[6] *Ibid.,* page 271.

there is neither Jew nor Gentile, Eph. 1:13-16; 3:3-6; Gal. 3:26-29) will have the keys of the kingdom and will tell Israel and the Gentiles what is binding and what is not binding (Matt. 16:19).

Faithful Christians of the entire gospel dispensation, who will out-number the Jews at least in the beginning of the millennium, will be ruling over cities. One parable even spoke of a faithful servant (during the gospel age) being placed "over all that he [the Lord] hath" (Matt. 24:45-47). There are not going to be many places left for Jews to fill in the millennium, for the bride of Christ will not be a part of Israel and the bride will have the place of honor and position and glory next to Jesus Christ the bridegroom. What a shock to Israel. The prophets knew nothing about the kingdom except the Messiah, Israel, and the Gentiles, but in the fulfillment of the kingdom prophecies there is the Messiah, the bride of Christ (the church), Israel, and the Gentiles. Walvoord stressed that the prophets knew nothing about a kingdom in which the Gentiles would be fellow-partakers, fellow-heirs, etc., with the Jews.[1] If the premillennialists are right, the prophets knew nothing of a kingdom in which Jews and Gentiles are in the church, with the Gentiles predominating (in fact West and Walvoord said "the Gentiles have [the kingdom in an inward form] under the New Testament," be-ing next to Christ and in a more exalted position than Israel who is not married to Christ. If they say that Israel is superior for she is married to Jehovah,[2] we reply that the Old Testament knew nothing of a king-dom in which Israel married to the Father is superior to Christ the Son who is married to the church. It knows nothing of a kingdom in which the bride of Christ will rule over both Israel and the Gentiles. This de-stroys the premillennialists' picture of the kingdom.

If the premillennialists are right, the kingdom prophesied by the prophets will never be established. *First*, it was not established in the first century. *Second*, the kingdom established during the millennium will be drastically different from the prophesied kingdom which had no place for the bride of Christ and in which Israel was to be exalted.

It would also be a strange situation where the Jews and Gentiles obey the temple laws in the millennium but the church, the bride of Christ, does not do so because Christ said those who serve the taber-nacle have no right to our altar. Christians did not abide in Jerusalem

---

[1] *Ibid.,* pages 236-237.
[2] *Ibid.,* page 303.

(Heb. 13:10-14).

Israel will no more be the superior people in the millennium than in the present kingdom. Therefore, the prophesied kingdom will never be established.

The Church will not Exist in the Millennium

"Any literal interpretation of the Old Testament will make plain that the purpose of God revealed for Israel in the millennial kingdom is quite different from the purpose of God in the present age in relation to the church as the body of Christ."[1] Walvoord was speaking in this context of Jew and Gentile being equal in one body, the church. "The idea that Jews and Gentiles might be united in one entity without any distinction whatever, with equal privileges, rights, and fellowship is foreign to the Old Testament."[2] In the millennial kingdom, the law, the middle wall of partition, will be restored and with it the distinction between Jew and Gentile. With the restoration of the law, and the distinction between Jew and Gentile re-established, why will not the Gentiles be "separate from Christ, alienated from the commonwealth of Israel, and strangers from the covenants of the promise, having no hope and without God in the world" (Eph. 2:12)? How can the law be restored without it bringing back the conditions which existed when it was the "middle wall of partition" (Eph. 2:14)?

Think of it: *God's eternal purpose* "to sum up all things in Christ" (Eph. 1:10); to enable all to see, through the embodiment in the church of the scheme of redemption, "the manifold wisdom of God" (Eph. 3:9-11). This church will come to an end with the second coming and an entirely different and contrasting (in so far as the position of Jew and Gentile is concerned) kingdom will be established. Paul should have said: "unto him be the glory in the church and in Christ Jesus until the second coming." Paul *actually* said: "Unto him be the glory *in the church and in Christ Jesus unto all generations for ever and ever. Amen"* (Eph. 3:21). The church has to be separated from the millennial kingdom, for Christ will then reign on David's throne (instead of from God's right hand), Israel will be exalted and the distinction between Jew and Gentile will be reestablished. No more will Gentiles be "fellow-heirs, and fellow-members of the body, and fellow-partakers of

---

[1] *Ibid.,* page 236.
[2] *Ibid.,* page 237.

the promise in Christ Jesus through the gospel" (Eph. 3:6). Christ would no longer be head of the church. And will not the body (the church) be dead without the head?

Church the Fulfilment of an Unrevealed Purpose of God

If the church does not fulfill the Old Testament predictions of the kingdom, "and in fact is the fulfilment of a purpose of God not revealed until the New Testament, then the [premillennialists] are right."[1] A mystery, said Walvoord, was something unrevealed and not something incomprehensible or obscure:

> it is rather that the truth relating to the church was once hidden, i.e., in the Old Testament, but is now revealed in the New Testament. Edwards correctly defines the word **mystery**, a secret imparted only to the initiated, what is unknown until it is revealed, whether it be easy or hard to understand.[2]

Walvoord said: "The church is never expressly called a mystery. The term *mystery* is used, however, of the distinctive elements of the truth concerning the church as the body of Christ."[3] There are some truths about the church which Walvoord says were a mystery. I shall discuss these. However, if every one of these things which he mentions was unrevealed, it would not mean that the church age was unrevealed. To say that some characteristics of the church age were not revealed does not prove that the church age itself was not revealed. The issue is whether the church age, and not whether everything about it, was revealed in the Old Testament.

Walvoord concluded that the central features of the church are unprophesied, therefore the church was unprophesied. In speaking of some things in Colossians concerning the church, as well as in Ephesians, he said:

> Again it may be seen that, while the church itself is not described by the term **mystery**, the central features of the church are. In other words, if the qualities observed here which are the very essence of the church in the present age are described as mysteries, it is not too much to regard the church itself as

---

[1] *Ibid.*, page 231.
[2] *Ibid.*, page 232.
[3] *Ibid.*, page 231.

unheralded in the Old Testament.[1]

This is as uncalled-for a conclusion as to maintain that if it was announced that the Masonic order was going to install a chapter in a community that it was not in reality announced because the people were not acquainted beforehand with the central features of the Masonic order.

None of These Prophesied!!

Premillennialism maintains that the church, therefore the church *age*, was not prophesied.[2] They appeal especially to some passages in Ephesians and Colossians. Let us scan Ephesians and see all the tremendous things which were unprophesied, if they are right. To put it briefly it means that the age of grace, when the law of Moses was not in force, was not prophesied. Justification through Christ without having anything to do with the law was not prophesied. In the millennium they believe the law of Moses with the Levitical system will be restored. That men would be children of God in Abraham, and Abraham's seed and heirs according to promise (Gal. 3:26-29) was not prophesied. A kingdom of earthly glory for Israel is of greater importance than the kingdom of grace, for the kingdom of earthly glory was prophesied but the kingdom of grace was not. But let us list some things in Ephesians.

First, all the wonderful things that are found in Christ were not prophesied. In Christ we have "every spiritual blessing" (1:3), we are chosen in Him (1:4), we are adopted as sons through Christ (1:5), His grace is "freely bestowed on us in the Beloved" (1:6), in Him we have redemption through his blood (1:7), in Him we have "the forgiveness of our trespasses, according to the riches of his grace, which he made to abound toward us in all wisdom and prudence" (1:7-8), "to sum up all things in Christ" (1:10), made a heritage in Him (1:11), "to the end that we should be unto the praise of his glory" (1:12), "the gospel of your salvation," sealed with the Spirit "which is an earnest of our inheritance, unto the redemption of God's own possession, unto the praise of his glory" (1:13-14). The glories of the so-called millennial reign fade into insignificance in comparison with these things, but ac-

---

[1] *Ibid.,* page 239.
[2] *Ibid.,* pages 230-231, 237-239.

cording to premillennialism none of them were prophesied. These things are as certainly characteristics of the church as are the characteristics discussed by Walvoord and on the basis of which he said the church was not prophesied.

God purposed these things "before the foundation of the world" (1:4), foreordained us unto adoption as sons through Jesus Christ" (1:5), He purposed it (1:9), "foreordained" (1:11), but all was unprophesied?!? If redemption was prophesied, forgiveness through the blood of Christ (1:6-8), how was it possible that the results of redemption—the church, the purchased possession—was not prophesied (1:6, 11, 14; Acts 20:28)?!? The blood of Christ was prophesied (Isa. 53), the lifting up of Christ was prophesied (John 3:14-15), but the purchased possession, the church which is redeemed by Christ's blood, was not prophesied!! The grandest truth in the Bible, that God so loved the world that He gave His only begotten Son, was not prophesied because if it were, salvation through faith in Him must have been prophesied. Surely the prophets did not prophesy the gift but indicated nothing about the outcome of the gift. The age of God's grace and great love was not prophesied, believe it he who can (1:6, 7; 2:4-8). Salvation in Christ is stressed in Ephesians (1:6-7, 11, 14; 2:4-8; 2:13, 16; 5:23), but the very salvation which we enjoy was prophesied by the prophets (1 Pet. 1:10-12). It matters not how much they understood about *when* it would be; the fact is *they knew it would be*. This salvation is preached to us in this church age and this salvation was prophesied.

Second, Christ's death for our sins (1:7) was prophesied (Isa. 53). Paul said, it was "according to the scriptures" (1 Cor. 15:3). How is it possible that our redemption through His blood was not prophesied (Eph. 1:7)?

Third, God raised Christ from the dead (Eph. 1:20). The resurrection was prophesied in the type Jonah, with reference to his experience in the belly of the great fish (Matt. 12:39-40), by Isaiah (Isa. 53:10-12), and by David (Acts 2:25-28, 31). Paul said the resurrection was "according to the scriptures" (1 Cor. 15:4).

Was the resurrection prophesied but not the age in which Christ's gospel, of the abolition of death through His gospel, is proclaimed (2 Tim. 1:10)? Walvoord admitted that certain feasts in the Old Testament prefigured "the death and resurrection of Christ."[1]

Fourth, God exalted Christ to His own right hand (1:20). This was clearly prophesied (Psa. 110:1, 4; Heb. 8:1-2), It followed Christ's making purification for our sins (Heb. 1:3, 13; Acts 2:34-36). Although Walvoord separates the reign of Christ in Psalm 110:1 with His reign in 110:2, he spoke of "the present position of the King at 'my right hand.'"[2]

Christ's present reign from heaven "far above all rule, and authority, and power, and dominion, and every name that is named, not only in this world, but also in that which is to come" (Eph. 1:20-20), is a far more exalted position of power and rulership than a reign on David's throne over Israel and over the earth. Think of it, if the premillennialists are right, the lesser reign (the premillennial kingdom) was prophesied but the greater reign was not prophesied.

Fifth, "for by grace have ye been saved through faith" (Eph. 2:8) is the central truth of the gospel age. This grace was prophesied (1 Pet. 1:10-1 2), and justification through faith in Christ was prophesied by the law and the prophets, otherwise they could not bear witness to it (Rom. 3:21-22; Gal. 3:8-11).

Sixth, premillennialism teaches that the promise of which the Gentiles are now partakers was not prophesied in the Old Testament. Paul said that the Gentiles, before the law was taken away, were "strangers from the covenants *of the promise*" (Eph. 2:12). Now in Christ they were "no more strangers and sojourners, but ye are fellow-citizens with the saints, and of the household of God" (2:13, 15, 19). As fellow-citizens they were "fellow-heirs, and fellow-members of the body, and fellow-partakers of the promise in Christ Jesus through the gospel" (3:6). The promise which the covenants made with the fathers and Israel contained ("covenants of the promise," 2:12) is the very promise of which "in Christ Jesus through the gospel" the Gentiles are "fellow-partakers of *the promise*" (3:6). What was this but the promise of salvation in and through the Messiah? As Abbott observed: "The promise is the promise of salvation, of a part in the kingdom of the Messiah; and to be partakers of the promise is to be joined with those to whom the promise is given."[3] This promise must refer to the promise in the

---

[1] *Ibid.*, page 229.
[2] *Ibid.*, page 266.
[3] Abbott, book, unspecified, page 83.

church age, for the premillennialists teach that the kingdom prophesied by the prophets was not one in which Jews and Gentiles were "united in one entity; without any distinction whatsoever, with equal privileges, rights, and fellowship." This, Walvoord said, "is foreign to the Old Testament."[1] Therefore, it was foreign to prophecies concerning the kingdom.[2]

Paul referred elsewhere to the promise. To Jews he said: "And we bring you good tidings of the promise made unto the fathers, that God hath fulfilled the same unto our children, in that he raised up Jesus; as also it is written in the second psalm" (Acts 13:32-33). He went on to speak of justification through Christ, justification which could not come through the law of Moses. Through Christ was "proclaimed unto you remission of sins" (13:38-39). Many of them thrust the word from them and thereby judged themselves "unworthy of eternal life" (13:46). In fulfilment of the prophecy that the Messiah was "for a light of the Gentiles" and *"for salvation* unto the uttermost part of the earth," Paul preached to the Gentiles (13:47-48). The Old Testament prophesied the Messiah, and salvation is found in the Messiah. Paul said that: "now I stand here to be judged for the hope of the promise made of God unto our fathers; unto which promise our twelve tribes, earnestly serving God night and day, hope to attain. And concerning this hope I am accused by the Jews, O king!" (Acts 26:6-7). The reason Paul was in prison was because he preached the gospel, but the reason he was in prison was "the hope of the promise made of God unto our fathers." But premillennialists tell us that this was not prophesied, since it is in the church that the Gentiles are fellow-heirs and fellow-partakers of the promise (Eph. 3:9). They affirm the Old Testament knew nothing of such a hope and promise.

Seventh, Gentiles were made nigh in the blood of Christ (2:13). The blood was prophesied, and the calling of the Gentiles was prophesied (Isa. 53; 49:6; Acts 13:47-48). Was neither the blood of Christ nor the salvation of the Gentiles prophesied?

Eighth, Christ abolished in His flesh, through His cross, the law which was the middle wall of partition between Jew and Gentile (2:14-16). The abolition of the law was prophesied when it was predicted that Christ, who was of the tribe of Judah, would be both king and

---

[1] Walvoord, *The Millennial Kingdom*, page 237.
[2] *Ibid.,* page 236.

priest on His throne (Heb. 7:1-22). It was also predicted when Jeremiah prophesied that the new covenant would not be like the old, and that under the new there would be no more offering for sins because sins would be forgiven—this implied the sufficiency of the sacrifice which sanctifies the new covenant (Jer. 31:31-34; Heb. 8:1-13; 7:22; 8:6; 12:24; 13:20).

Ninth, if premillennialism is right, the New Testament "household of God" (2:19), over which Christ the Son presides (Heb. 3:6), was not predicted (1 Tim. 3:16).

Tenth, if premillennialism is right, the holy temple, the church, God's promised new covenant were not prophesied (Eph. 2:20-22). It was prophesied that one would reign as king and priest (Zech. 6:12-13). However, the Messiah could not build Old Testament temple for He abolished it (John 4:20-24; Matt. 23:37-38; Heb. 2:14). He is building the spiritual temple today (Eph. 2:20-22; 1 Pet. 2:5, 9).

Eleventh, Paul did not say that the church was a mystery, but he did speak about the complete equality of Jew and Gentile in the church as a mystery which was not revealed in times past *as it is now* (Eph. 3:3-6). It is a far cry from saying that some characteristics of the church age were once a mystery and saying that the church age itself was a mystery. One could know that a Masonic Lodge was going to be built in a town without knowing the distinctive rituals which would take place in the lodge. Ignorance of these things would not mean one was ignorant of the fact that the lodge was coming.

Twelfth, the Gentiles were fellow-partakers "of the promise in Christ Jesus through the gospel" (3:6). The promise was jointly partaken of. What promise? The promise of salvation in Christ, the promised blessing; those who were in Christ were "Abraham's seed, heirs according to promise" (Gal. 3:29). The promise of justification through faith was prophesied (Gal. 3:7-14, 22-29; Rom. 3:21-22).

Thirteenth, the gospel through which they were "fellow-partakers" (Eph. 3:6) was the gospel of which Paul was a preacher (3:6-11). But the gospel which Paul preached was prophesied (Rom. 1:1-2; 3:21-22; 16:25-27; 1 Cor. 15:1-4). The church is the embodiment of God's eternal purpose to redeem men in Christ (Eph. 3:9-11), and regardless of how many aspects of the church age were not revealed (*or were not clearly revealed*) in the Old Testament, the church age *was* prophesied. Premillennialism in effect tells Paul that he was wrong when he said "that Christ *died for our sins according to the scriptures*; and that he was buried; *and that he hath been raised on the third day according to the scriptures*" (1 Cor. 15:1-4). This clearly show that the redemption in Christ through the gospel was prophesied (Eph. 1:6-7; 2:13), and that *it is through the same gospel that the Gentiles are "fellow-partakers of the promise in Christ"* (3:6). Poor Paul! He did not realize this was not possible, for this age was not prophesied! If it was not, then the gospel was not prophesied, for the age in which the gospel is preached is the church age. Furthermore, the "promise" of which the Gentiles partake was not prophesied. This "promise" was not promised in the Old Testament to the Gentiles in the gospel age, if premillennialism is right.

Fourteenth, if premillennialism is right, nothing was revealed in the Old Testament of the "unsearchable riches of Christ" which Paul through the gospel preached to the Gentiles (3:8). These unsearchable riches include "his grace, which he freely bestowed on us in the Beloved" (1:6), "our redemption through his blood" (1:7), "the forgiveness of our trespasses, according to the riches of his grace" (1:7), to make us a "heritage" (1:11), and "the redemption of God's own possession, unto the praise of his glory" (1:14). Again we stress that there is a vast difference between the mystery concerning the complete equality of Jew and Gentile, and the church itself being a mystery. This mystery was clearly revealed in the gospel Paul preached (3:9).

Fifteenth, if premillennialism is right, nothing was prophesied concerning the fact that "through the church the manifold wisdom of God" would be made known to earth and to "the principalities and the powers in the heavenly places" (3:10). Nothing was known of "the eternal purpose which he purposed in Christ Jesus our Lord" (3:11). I am not suggesting that all the details of the scheme of redemption in Christ were revealed in the prophecies. Ephesians 3:9-11 indicates that some things embodied in the scheme of redemption as unfolded in the church were not known to "the principalities and the powers in the heavenly places." The mystery, however, of which Paul speaks is the mystery concerning the complete equality of the Jews and Gentiles (3:3-6, 9). God concealed or revealed His purpose as and when He saw fit, but God did see fit to prophesy and promise in the Old Testament the redemption in Christ and therefore this present age in which we have the redemption in Christ.

Sixteenth, if premillennialism is right, no mention is made in the

Old Testament of the wonderful fact that "unto him be the glory in the church and in Christ Jesus unto all generations for ever and ever. Amen" (3:21). Nothing is said, if they are right, about the church.

Seventeenth, the Old Testament prophesied the ascension of Christ "on high," the leading of captivity captive, and His giving of gifts unto men after He ascended. "Wherefore he saith, When he ascended on high, he led captivity captive, and gave gifts unto men" (Eph. 4:8). There is a great deal of discussion concerning this use of Psalms 68:18. Whatever we may say about it should be said in the light of the statement by F. F. Bruce that:

> *New Testament quotations of Old Testament passages are also authoritative interpretations of the significance of these passages. The Spirit of God knows His own letter-press better than the most lynx-eyed modern critic, so often "all eyes and no sight." (It is noteworthy that the Aramaic Targum on the Psalter and the Syriac Peshitta both read "thou hast **given** gifts to men" in Ps. 68:18 in accordance with what was probably a long-standing oral interpretation. The Targum understands the words as referring to Moses, who **received** the Law on Sinai that he might **give** it to the people of Israel).[1]*

Bruce thought that:

> *The primary application of the passage relates doubtless to David's capture of the Jebusite acropolis and the triumphant ascent of the ark to Mount Zion ensuing thereupon (cf. Ps. 24). But that **epinicion** attains its germinant fulfilment in David's greater Son, the antitypical Ark of an auguster tabernacle than any made with hands.[2]*

David the king was a type of Christ the king. It would not be surprising if some of the events in the life of David typified some events in the life of Christ. Regardless of explanation of the passage which some may take or not take, Paul by the Spirit showed that this was a prophecy of Christ's ascension, and the giving of gifts from Him in heaven to men on earth after His ascension. He mentioned some of

---

[1] F.F. Bruce, *The New Testament Development of Old Testament Themes*, page 91.

[2] *Ibid.*, page 92.

these gifts in Ephesians 4:11. The exact nature of the gifts did not have to be specified by the prophet in order for the fact of gifts, when they were given, and from whence and to whom (men) gifts were given, to be made known. Since gifts given by Christ after His ascensionwere given in connection with the church and its perfection, it is obvious the church age was prophesied. "And he gave some to be apostles; and some, prophets; and some, evangelists; and some, pastors and teachers; *for the perfecting of the saints, unto* the work of ministering, *unto* the *building up of the body of Christ*" (4:11-12). These gifts were given to accomplish something concerning the church. They were to perfect, equip or adjust the saints (the saints mentioned here are the church, 1:1), in order that the saints or the church can carry on the work of ministering—and this ministering is in the gospel age, and unto the building up of the church which is the body of Christ (4:4, 12; 1:22-23). Regardless of how clear the prophecy was, it was a prophecy which concerned the ascension of Christ and gifts given for the benefit of the church.

Eighteenth, if premillennialism is right, the love of Christ for us and the love in which we are to walk were not prophesied by the prophets in any way. "Be ye therefore imitators of God, as beloved children; and walk in love, even as Christ also loved you, and gave himself up for us, an offering and a sacrifice to God for an odor of a sweet smell" (5:1-2). We are children of God today because of God's love (5:1-2; John 3:16). God's love was supremely demonstrated in His giving of Christ. Christ loved "you"—the Ephesians, both Jews and Gentiles. He "gave himself up for us"—Jews and Gentiles. All of this, including making possible our being children of God today, is so vastly superior to anything that can be given us in a millennial reign, that it makes it impossible to believe that the Old Testament is full of promises and prophecies of an earthly kingdom of a thousand years in duration, and yet promised and prophesied nothing concerning these marvelous things mentioned in Ephesians 5:1-2. Premillennialism cannot deny that the sacrifice of Christ was prophesied (Isa. 53; Eph. 5:2), but they deny that the consequences of that sacrifice (the creation of the church, Eph. 2:13-16; Acts 20:28) was prophesied. Believe it, if you have a veil over your heart as you read both the Old and New Testaments (2 Cor. 3:12-18).

Nineteenth, Paul spoke of those who did not have "any inheritance in the kingdom of Christ and God" (5:5). Did a kingdom of Christ exist at this time? Yes, Christians were (and are) in it. "Who delivered us out of the power of darkness, and translated us *into the kingdom* of the Son of his love; *in whom* we have our redemption, the forgiveness of our sins" (Col. 1:13-14). Christians were then receiving a kingdom which cannot be shaken (Heb. 12:28). To be in the kingdom was to be in Christ, for immediately after speaking of the kingdom of Christ, Paul said "in whom." To be in Christ is to be in His church, for it is in Christ that we have "our redemption, the forgiveness of our sins" (Col. 1:13-14; Eph. 1:7 says the same thing). But these premillennialists maintain that the "kingdom of Christ and God" mentioned by Paul (Eph. 5:5; Col. 1:13) was unknown to prophecy. We enter into the heavenly consummation of the kingdom when we enter the new heavens and the new earth (2 Pet. 1:11; 1 Cor. 15:24-28; Acts 2:34-35). This eternal consummation of the kingdom is not an earthly reign of just a thousand years, but the being with God and Christ and the redeemed forever in the new heavens and the new earth.

Twentieth, if premillennialists are right, the time when we put on the whole armor of God, in the church age, and stand against "the wiles of the devil" was not prophesied (Eph. 6:10-18).

Twenty-first, the mystery of the gospel of which Paul spoke in Ephesians 6:19 did not mean that the gospel was not prophesied. As has been shown in this book, it was clearly prophesied. The mystery which was not revealed in times past, *as it is now*, is the complete equality of Jew and Gentile in Christ (3:3-6). But the gospel itself was prophesied (Rom. 1:1-2; 16:25-27; 3:21).

By itself, the book of Ephesians refutes the contention of the premillennialists that the church age was not prophesied; and this is especially clear when it is considered in the light of related passages in other books.

Christ in You, the Hope of Glory

Walvoord agreed that the church is not called a mystery,[1] however, at least two of the distinctive features are. Therefore, the church was an unprophesied mystery. "The mysteries considered (the one body and the church as an organism)[2] are in sharp contrast to anything

---

[1] Walvoord, *The Millennial Kingdom*, page 231.
[2] *Ibid.,* pages 232, 237.

known to Israel in either history or prophecy."[1] Paul spoke of the mystery, now revealed, "which is Christ in you, the hope of glory" (Col. 1:25-28). Christ spoke of this in John 14:20 and 17:23. "Here is amazing condescension—the Lord of glory dwelling in vessels of clay."[2] "As far as the Old Testament foreview is concerned, Israel's hope of glory was the glorious return of Christ in His second advent. They were promised a share in His glorious government of the earth during the kingdom."[3] "There the glory of the Lord will be manifest to all the earth and His dwelling is with men. Here His glory is veiled, but His presence is the hope of future glory."[4]

One does not have to prove that this particular truth was prophesied in order to *know* the church age was prophesied. Walvoord agreed that in Colossians 1:25-28 the mystery is not the general truths relating to Christ or the gospel, but in the particular detail which is revealed in this context. The mystery is Christ indwelling."[5] One does not have to know distinctive features of the teaching of the Masonic lodge in order to know that it has been promised that a lodge will be built in one's town.

What are some of the things, mentioned in Colossians, which show that regardless of the mystery of the indwelling Christ, the church age was prophesied? What are some of the things in Colossians which show some of the unscriptural conclusions one is involved in when he maintains the church age was not prophesied?

First, Walvoord said that in contrast with Israel's share in Christ's glorious government of the earth in the age of the prophesied kingdom, "for the believer now the indwelling Christ is declared to be the 'hope of glory' (Col. 1:27). This thought is enlarged in Colossians 3… When Christ, who is our life, shall be manifested, then shall ye also with him be manifested in glory" (Col. 3:4). "The indwelling Christ is integral with the believer's hope. He is equated with our present existence as 'our life' and with our future as the promise of fully manifested glory when He is glorified. The ultimate goal of spiritual experience is reached in Colossians 3:11 when the believer enters into the truth that

---

[1] *Ibid.,* page 240.
[2] *Ibid.,* page 238.
[3] *Ibid.,* page 239.
[4] *Ibid.,* page 238.
[5] *Ibid.,* page 240.

'Christ is all, and in all.'"[1] Consider the following:

(1) When is our hope of glory fulfilled? "*When* Christ, who is our life, *shall be manifested, then* shall ye also with him be manifested in glory" (3:4). Is not Christ manifested in His second coming? If so, the second coming is when we shall be manifested in glory and the hope of glory will be then fulfilled. It is a veiled glory now, Christ in us, in so far as the world is concerned. We are children of God now although the world does not know us as such. "Behold what manner of love the Father hath bestowed upon us, that we should be called children of God; and such we are. For this cause the world knoweth us not, because it knew him not, Beloved, now are we children of God, and *it is not yet manifest what we shall be*" (1 John 3:1-23). This says in essence the same thing as Col. 3:4 which shows that we are not yet manifested but shall then be manifested in glory, and the hope of glory will give way to glory itself (Col. 1:27). What did John go on to say? "We know that, if *he shall be manifested, we shall be like him*; for we shall see him even as he is. And every one that hath *this hope* set on him purifieth himself, even as he is pure (1 John 3:2-3). This certainly is at least an essential aspect, if it does not entirely sum up, our hope of glory (Col. 1:27). When shall we be like Him? When He is manifested. It is our hope that then we shall be like Him, in some way or degree that we are not like Him now.

(2) We shall be like Him, and we shall be with Him. When He comes we shall "meet the Lord in the air; and *so shall we ever be with the Lord*" (1 Thess. 4:17). Walvoord believes that this is not the second advent, but that before that advent Christ comes in the air but not to the earth, receives the church, takes it to heaven with him, where the marriage feast between Christ and the church will take place.[2] The church will return with Christ when He comes to earth to rule.[3] Surely Israel will not be exalted over the church, the bride of Christ which will then be like Christ, having seen Him as He is. Israel will have to be subservient to Christ and His bride. This destroys the millennial kingdom, in the sense the premillennialists believe it was prophesied by the prophets, because the prophets knew nothing, if the premillennialists are right, of a kingdom in which any body of people was supe-

---

[1] *Ibid.,* page 239.
[2] *Ibid.,* pages 253, 245.
[3] *Ibid.,* page 246.

rior to Israel. But the church, God's spiritual nation, will be superior to Israel, for Israel will not be the bride of Christ. Israel will be married to Jehovah, not to Jesus Christ.[1] This destroys what the premillennialists view as the prophetic picture of the kingdom.[2] Israel will receive glory at the second coming, they say, but the church will receive greater glory. Just as the church is superior to physical Israel in this present age, it will also be in the millennial age!

(3) In speaking of our hope, Walvoord said: "The ultimate goal of spiritual experience is reached in Colossians 3:11 when the believer enters into the truth that 'Christ is all, and in all.'"[3] Walvoord may not have made himself clear, but this statement is made in connection with the glory which awaits the Christian when Christ is manifested (3:4). This ultimate in spiritual experience is experienced now in the church. "And have put on the new man, that is being renewed unto knowledge after the image of him that created him: where there cannot be Greek and Jew, circumcision and uncircumcision, barbarian, Scythian, bondman, freeman; but Christ *is* all, and in all" (Col. 3:10-11). If it refers to the millennium when Christ has already been manifested, and the hope of glory by Christians has been realized, it means that in the millennium there will be neither Jew nor Greek, etc. However, the premillennialists insist that in the millennium there will be the Jews, Israel, at the head of the nations of the earth, and the various Gentile nations will be there but be subordinate to Israel.[4]

Second, if the church age was not prophesied, the "hope which is laid up *for you* in the heavens, whereof ye heard before in the word of the truth of the gospel," which is contained in and based on the grace of God (1:5-6), the hope of glory (1:27), were all ignored by the Old Testament prophets. Our hope, our heavenly hope, is far superior to any hope of Israel for a kingdom on earth, but the prophets are full of the kingdom on earth for Israel but silent on the hope of eternal glory. Premillennialism teaches that the gospel was prophesied, but not the hope (which involves the hope of eternal salvation) which is based on the gospel, which is proclaimed in the gospel, and which is an outcome of the gospel. The central object of the gospel as it concerns men is their eternal salvation, which is the consummation of the hope. The

---

[1] *Ibid.,* page 303.
[2] *Ibid.,* pages 236-237, 264.
[3] *Ibid.,* page 239.
[4] *Ibid.,* page 264.

prophets overlooked this central object even though they prophesied the gospel. How could the gospel be prophesied and not its central meaning, message, and object? An earthly inheritance for one thousand years was prophesied by the prophets, but not "the inheritance of the saints in light" (1:12)?!? The heavenly hope of the church, so stressed by Peter was not prophesied (1 Pet 1:3-6)? Believe it he who can.

Third, if premillennialism is right, the deliverance in the church age "out of the power of darkness," the translating of us into the kingdom of the Son of his love" was not prophesied" (1:13). If the deliverance was prophesied, what we were translated into must be implied. The deliverance involves the translation, and if the deliverance was prophesied, the translation was also. The translation is into Christ's kingdom. If the translation was prophesied, the kingdom into which we were translated was prophesied. The deliverance was prophesied, for the gospel by which we are delivered was prophesied (1 Cor. 15:1-4). Premillennialism does not view these things as prophesied. The kingdom of God's Son in which there is no distinction between Jew and Gentile (Col. 4:11, Gal. 3:26-29) was not prophesied, but a kingdom in which Israel is exalted over the Gentiles was prophesied! As shown in the discussion on Ephesians, our redemption, our forgiveness was prophesied, therefore the kingdom, the body of Christ, in which we are redeemed and forgiven was prophesied (1:13-14, "in whom"; Eph. 1:6-7).

Fourth, the pre-eminence of Israel in the millennial kingdom was prophesied, if premillennialism is right, but the present pre-eminence of Christ was not prophesied (Col. 1:16-18). His authority as "head of the body, the church" was not foretold by the prophets (1:18), nor His present reign on the right hand of God" (3:1). However, the reign at God's right hand is also His reign as head of the church (Eph. 1:20-23). It is clear the reign at God's right hand was prophesied (Psa. 110:1-4; Acts 2:34-36). Even Walvoord maintains that Psalm 110:1 was a prophecy of the present reign of Christ from heaven, though he thinks Psalm 110:2 refers to a future reign on earth. "Psalm 110:1 speaks of Christ in heaven and Psalm 110:2 refers to His ultimate triumph at His second advent."[1] "Psalm 110 contrasts the present posi-

---

[1] *Ibid.,* page 229.

tion of the King at 'my right hand' (v. l) with His rule 'in the midst of thine enemies' (v. 2)."[1] But Christ's present pre-eminent position was prophesied (Psa. 110:1; Eph. 1:19-23; Col. 1:16-8; 2:10).

Fifth, the millennial age was prophesied but not the age in which "it was the good pleasure of the Father that in him should all the fullness dwell" (1:19). "For in him dwelleth all the fullness of the Godhead bodily, and in him ye are made full, who is the head of all principality and power" (2:9-10). The age of this type of fullness was unpredicted!! Believe it, he who is blinded by premillennialism!!

Sixth, surely the age of reconciliation was prophesied. This is of greater significance than a thousand year reign with Israel exalted. The reconciliation of Jew and Gentile in Christ is mentioned in Ephesians 2:13-16, but in Colossians its cosmic significance is stressed. "And through him to reconcile all things unto himself, having made peace through the blood of his cross; through him, I say, whether things upon the earth, or things in the heavens. And you, being in time past alienated and enemies in your mind in your evil works, yet now, hath he reconciled in the body of his flesh through death, to present you holy and without blemish and unreprovable before him: if so be that ye continue in the faith, grounded and steadfast, and not moved away from the hope of the gospel which ye heard..." (Col. 1:20-23). This is more glorious, spiritual, and significant than a thousand year reign with Israel exalted. This ties in with God's eternal purpose to sum up all things in Christ (Eph. 1:10). Paul's statement, "now hath he reconciled in the body of his flesh through death" (Col. 1:22), and through "the blood of his cross" (1:20), are elsewhere stated by Paul as the reason God sent His Son. "For what the law could not do, in that it was weak through the flesh, God, sending his own Son in the likeness of sinful flesh and for sin, condemned sin in the flesh; that the ordinance of the law might be fulfilled in us, who walk not after the flesh, but after the Spirit" (Rom. 8:3-4). Paul said "yet now hath he reconciled" (Col. 1:22); "'now,' i.e., in the present order of things, not 'at the present moment.' The aorist marks that the state of things followed a given event. It is correctly rendered by the English perfect."[2]

The object of His sacrifice for us is to present us holy and without blemish and unreprovable before him" (Col. 1:22; Eph. 5:27).

---

[1] *Ibid.*, page 266.
[2] Abbott, book unspecified, pages 225-226.

How strange it would be if the death of Christ was prophesied, but not the purposes, i.e., redemption, forgiveness, reconciliation, and presentation (Col. 1:14, 22, 28). That Christ in us, both Jewish and Gentile Christians, the hope of glory was a mystery in times past does not mean that the gospel age was a mystery (1:24-27).

Seventh, in Christ, and obviously therefore in His teaching, "are all the treasures of wisdom and knowledge hidden" (2:3). This is the reason we should not let anyone delude us into thinking that there are other moral and spiritual treasures which are found in philosophy (2 4-6, 8), the law (2:14-17), or pretended revelations (2:18-19), which are not found in Christ. Was a millennial kingdom prophesied but not the age in which all treasures and knowledge are hidden in Christ?

Eighth, the gospel age was prophesied in the types and shadows of the Old Testament. In speaking of the law and its observances (2:14-16; Eph. 2:14-15), Paul wrote: "which are a shadow of the things to come; but the body is Christ's" (Col. 2:17). By "the body is Christ's," Paul is not here referring to the church as the body of Christ. He is speaking of the body in contrast with the shadow the body casts. "The legal prescriptions of days gone by were but a shadow, of which the substance is Christ... This antithesis of the shadow and the substance is specially elaborated in the Epistle to the Hebrews"[1] (8:5; 10:1) "It is simply 'shadow,' having in itself no substance, but indicating the existence of a body which casts the shadow... The figure expresses both the unsubstantiality and the supersession of the Mosaic ritual."[2] Since that which pertains to Christ is the substance, to which the law gave way, it should be clear that the shadow (the Old Testament) pointed to and thereby predicted the reality, the substance, which is now found in Christ and His church; for Paul is speaking of those who are in Christ, thus in the church (Col. 1:1, 13, 18; 2:14-17). Regardless of how many mysteries are found in the church, the church age was prophesied.

The premillennialists think that in the millennial age the law with its rituals and festivals will be restored.[3] How could a millennial age in which the shadow is restored be something higher than the gospel age in which the substance, not the shadow, rules our lives?

---

[1] F.F. Bruce, *The New Testament Development of Old Testament Themes*, page 245.

[2] Abbott, book unspecified, page 264.

[3] Walvoord, *The Millennial Kingdom*, pages 311-315.

Ninth, where is Christ now? He is in heaven and is the head of the church (Eph. 1:20-23). Where is He? "…above, where Christ is, seated on the right hand of God" (Col. 3:1). When was this first proclaimed to the earth? Pentecost (Acts 2:30-36; Heb. 1:3, 13). Is He more than king? Yes, He is also high priest (Heb. 7:1-8:23). Was it prophesied that He would reign at God's right hand as king and priest? Yes (Psa. 110:1-4). Is it not obvious that the gospel age, when Christ reigns at God's right hand, was prophesied?

Tenth, was the gospel prophesied? Yes (1 Cor. 15:1-4). How does God call men today? Through the gospel (Acts 2:39; 2 Thess. 2:14). Into what does He call us? "...ye were called in one body" (Col. 3:15). The gospel was prophesied; was not that into which the gospel calls us (the saving relationship with God in Christ) unavoidably implied to say the least?

Eleventh, "... these only are my fellow-workers unto the kingdom of God, men that have been a comfort unto me" (4:11). What was Paul's work? "…to speak the mystery of Christ, for which I am also in bonds; that I may make it manifest, as I ought to speak" (4:3-4). His ministry was to preach the gospel and "to fulfill the word of God (1:24-28). It was to labor "that we may present every man perfect in Christ" (1:28). The ones who were mentioned in Colossians 4:11 were his fellow-workers. To be fellow-workers they had to work with him in the gospel and to further it. However, Paul said they "are my fellow-workers unto the kingdom of God" (4:11). This was the kingdom in which Christ now reigns at God's right hand (3:1), and it is "the kingdom of the Son of his love" (1:13), into which we are translated when we obey the gospel and are reconciled unto God in the one body, the church (Col. 1:13, 20-23; Eph. 3:13-16). The kingdom of God and of Christ was then in existence, and these were fellow-workers with Paul "unto the kingdom of God." "Unto" in some cases carries the idea of *with reference to*, or *in relation to*, or *in regards to*, something.[1] Paul wanted to "preach the gospel even unto the parts beyond you" (2 Cor. 10:16). Their labors concerned the gospel and the kingdom of God. They labored for the kingdom which now is, and taught people to persevere unto the kingdom in eternity (2 Pet. 1:5-11).

In the light of all these truths which are found in Colossians, how can anyone scripturally maintain that Paul's reference to the mystery

---

[1] Joseph H. Thayer, *Greek-English Lexicon of the New Testament*, page 134.

of Christ in us as the hope of glory (1:25-27) is one of the proofs that the church age was not prophesied by the Old Testament?

The Church a New Creation

Walvoord seems to think that when it is established the church is a *new* creation, one has proved something in favor of premillennialism. "Dispensational ecclesiology defines the church as a distinct body of saints in the present age, having its own divine purpose and destiny and differing from the saints of the past or future age."[1] The word "church" was used to refer to any assembly of people whether of Israel (Acts 7:38) or of citizens of a pagan city (Acts 19:39). However, it is also used of an assembly of Christians (1 Cor. 11:18, 20, 22, 34), of different congregations (Acts 12:1; 1 Cor. 16:19; Gal. 1:2; Rom. 16:16; 1 Cor. 12:13), and of the universal body of Christ (Eph. 1:20-23; 1 Cor. 12:13). In these last uses it is not used of literal Israel. It refers to the "saints of the present age." None of this proves anything in favor of premillennialism. That God's people served God in the Old Testament under a different dispensation than that of the church, and that heaven is different from earth, proves nothing with reference to whether the kingdom prophesied by the prophets has been established.

Walvoord stressed that in Matthew 16:18, the building of the church was future, for Jesus said "I will build," not "I am building." "... this is the first reference to the church in the New Testament, and is here regarded as a future under taking of Christ Himself... It did not exist before Pentecost." The fact that it is a new creation does not prove it was not prophesied. The fact that the word "church" is used does not prove that it cannot refer to the "kingdom" under a different designation. Walvoord said: "The concept of the body is foreign to the Old Testament and to Israel's promises."[2] That the word "church" was not used in Old Testament prophecy does not mean that the church as Christ's reign over His people was not prophesied. The fact that it is called the "church" does not mean that it is not also called the "kingdom of God's Son," the Messiah (Col. 1:13-14). To be in the kingdom was to be in Christ, and to be in Christ was to be in His body the church (Col. 1:13-14; Eph. 2:20-23; 1 Cor. 12:13; Gal. 3:26-27).

The kingdom, whether it has been established yet, or whether it

---

[1] Walvoord, *The Millennial Kingdom*, page 224.
[2] *Ibid.*, pages 224-226.

will be established in the future, is a new creation. The fact that it was prophesied does not mean that it is not something new. It is true the building of the church was future in Matthew 16:18, but it is also true that the kingdom was future in Matthew 3:2; 4:17; 10:17. In the very next verse, in which Christ mentioned that the building of the church was future, He also announced that the giving of the keys of the kingdom was future. "I will build my church... *I will* give unto thee the keys of the kingdom of heaven" (Matt. 16:18-19). Does this prove the kingdom was to be a new thing to be established in the future? Premillennialists do not believe the kingdom was already in existence, and that Christ instead of the apostles was using the keys and letting people into it.

Walvoord argued that the church was created on Pentecost by the Spirit. "It did not exist before Pentecost, as there was no work of the baptism of the Spirit to form it."[1] Although I do not agree with him that 1 Corinthians 12:13 refers to Holy Spirit baptism, it is still true that the church started on Pentecost. I shall turn Walvoord's argument against him. He referred to Acts 1:5 and 11:15 and said: "The baptism of the Spirit which is the subject of predictive prophecy in the Gospels and in Acts 1 finds its first fulfillment in Acts 2."[2] The Spirit then form the church.[3] The promise concerning the baptism of the Spirit on Pentecost was fulfilled when the apostles were baptized in the Spirit. The church then started and Christ was proclaimed as king—both Lord and Christ—ruling at God's right hand (Acts 2:34-36). It should teach Walvoord something when he realizes that on Pentecost, when the church was started, the word "church" was not used by Peter in his sermon, nor mentioned in the events which immediately followed Pentecost—as recorded in chapter two. Instead of Peter saying that Christ is now head of the church (Eph. 1:19-23), Peter said that Christ is Lord or ruler (Acts 2:36). He also proved that Christ is reigning at God's right hand in fulfillment of prophecy (Acts 2:34-36; Psa. 110:1-4). This reign, the New Testament makes clear, is Christ reigning as king and priest (Heb. 1:3, 13; 5:6; 7:1-2, 17, 21; 8:1). He cannot be like Melchisedek unless He is now both king and priest. In proclaiming Jesus as Lord in fulfillment of Psalm 110:1-4, Peter is proclaiming Christ as king. In so doing he is proclaiming the establishment of the

---

[1] *Ibid.,* page 226.
[2] *Ibid.*
[3] *Ibid.*

kingdom. Walvoord pointed out that the church was established on Pentecost and Peter pointed out the same reality though he proclaimed Christ as Lord, as King and Priest, as Psalm 110:1-4 makes clear, reigning at God's right hand. There could be no throne on which Christ could reign which is higher than the one at God's right hand unless He dethroned the Father, and no one believes that this will ever take place.

Walvoord said that: "The baptism of the Spirit which is the subject of predictive prophecy in the Gospels and in Acts 1 finds its first fulfillment in Acts 2." The first fulfillment formed or created the church. "...it becomes apparent that a new thing has been formed—the body of Christ. It did not exist before Pentecost, as there was no work of the baptism of the Spirit to form it."[1] Walvoord agreed that the Gospels predicted this baptism of the Spirit, and the passage in Acts 1:5, which he quotes carries us back in thought to John's statement, *before Christ began His ministry*, that the Christ would baptize in the Spirit.

> *I indeed baptize you in water unto repentance: but he that cometh after me is mightier than I, whose shoes I am not worthy to bear: he shall baptize you in the Holy Spirit and in fire: whose fan is in his hand, and he will thoroughly cleanse his threshing-floor; and he will gather his wheat into the garner, but the chaff he will burn up with unquenchable fire. (Matt. 3:11-12)*

This began its fulfillment on Pentecost. And it resulted in the formation of the church, Walvoord said. Therefore, Walvoord is shut up to the conclusion that John predicted, whether he understood it or not, the establishment or formation of the church when he said Christ would baptize in the Spirit. Again we emphasize that Walvoord said: "The baptism of the Spirit which is the subject of predictive prophecy in the Gospels and in Acts 1 finds its first fulfillment in Acts 2."[2] Of course, he does not think that the church was formed, created, again at the household of Cornelius although at that time it was made clear that the Gentiles were to come into the church through obedience to the gospel without having to be bound by the law of Moses.[3]

---

[1] *Ibid.*
[2] *Ibid.*
[3] See my book, *The Case of Cornelius.*

There are important consequences which follow the position which Walvoord has taken concerning the baptism of the Spirit and the formation of the church as a result of the fulfillment of the predictions concerning the baptism in the Spirit.

First, it means that John the Baptist predicted something (that Christ would baptize in the Spirit) which involved the formation of the church, the body of Christ. Although John did not use the word "church," its creation is tied in with what John here predicted. Therefore, although the word "church" was not used until Matthew 16:18, the church was predicted by John without using the word "church."

If the church was not predicted by the Old Testament, and if the kingdom has been postponed, John was involved in a contradictory situation. (1), he was proclaiming that the kingdom prophesied by the prophets was *at hand* (Matt. 3:2). (2), he was teaching, in effect, that the church was also at hand because Christ's work of baptizing in the Spirit was to begin within three years or so of the time that John began to proclaim the nearness of the kingdom. On the one hand John was plainly announcing the kingdom but on the other hand, in his reference to the baptism of the Spirit, he was making a veiled reference to the nearness of, and the establishment of, the church. How could John clearly announce the kingdom was at hand and in a veiled way announce the church was at hand? If they differ, as the premillennialists argue, why did John announce both of them as at hand? If one was established soon, the other could not be established soon, but John announced both as nearby in point of time.

Second, in the reference to fire, and the separation of the wheat from the chaff (and the wheat being gathered into the garner, and the chaff burnt), John announced that the Messiah would do a work of separation and destruction with reference to Israel, as well as of salvation. John announced this in three ways. (1) When he told the Jews not to rely on their relationship to Abraham, because God would raise up children unto Abraham from some source other than Israel (Matt. 3:7-9). (2) When he announced that the axe was at the root of the tree and the fruitful would be preserved, but the unfruitful be cut down and cast into the fire (3:10). (3) The preservation of the wheat and the elimination of the chaff. How much clearer could John have made the fact that no Jew would be in the kingdom just because he was a Jew?

Christ first baptized in the Spirit on Pentecost. Did He begin to use his fan then and there to separate the wheat and the chaff? Yes. The gospel separated the wheat from the chaff. The wheat was made up of those who obeyed the gospel, and they were gathered into the garner—the church. The chaff was made up of those who rejected the gospel and they were cut off from covenant relationship with God just as Moses prophesied (Acts 3:22-23; Rom. 11:20-24).

Walvoord recognizes that the baptism of the Spirit is connected in the Gospels, and Acts 1:5, with the beginning of the gospel dispensation or age. Therefore, he should recognize that John the Baptist in effect predicted the gospel age.

Walvoord's conclusion is: "The various mystery aspects of the church combined to form a united testimony. The features therein revealed are foreign to divine revelation given in the Old Testament. They are related to the church as a distinct entity in the present age. They mark out the church as a separate purpose of God to be consummated before the resumption of the divine program for Israel."[1]

Mysteries of the Kingdom of Heaven, Not a "Mysterious Kingdom."

The premillennialists know that the kingdom was prophesied by the Old Testament. They must also agree that Jesus spoke of mysteries of the kingdom, without thereby implying that the kingdom itself was a mystery! "And the disciples came, and said unto him, Why speakest thou unto them in parables? And he answered and said unto them, Unto you it is given to know the mysteries of the kingdom of heaven, but to them it is not given" (Matt, 13:10-11; Luke 8:9-10). In several parables Jesus said: "The kingdom of heaven is like unto…" (Matt. 13:31, 33, 44, 45, 47). Shall we argue that since so many things about the kingdom were mysteries, therefore the kingdom itself was a mystery which was not prophesied by the Old Testament prophets? Certainly not. All of us realize that the fact that there were "mysteries of the kingdom" did not mean the kingdom was not prophesied. Mysteries in connection with the church do not prove that the church age was not prophesied.

Why was it not given to some to know the mysteries of the kingdom? The reason was that they had closed their eyes (Matt. 13:15), and the reason it was given to others to know was because they saw

---

[1] *Ibid.,* page 247.

with their eyes and heard with their ears (13:16). It should be observed closely that Jesus is still speaking about the kingdom of heaven; the very one which was at hand (3:2; 4; 17; 10:7). He is not saying that the kingdom was a mystery, unknown to prophecy, but that there were certain things concerning the kingdom which were mysteries. Jesus said that in the parables He would, *in fulfillment of prophecy*, "utter things hidden from the foundation of the world" (13:35). But He did not say He was talking about a kingdom different from the one which He had said was at hand (4:17; 10:7). He was not saying that this kingdom was unprophesied. The fact that there were mysteries of the kingdom did not mean the kingdom was a mystery and unprophesied. The kingdom was clearly prophesied.

R. H. Boll identified this kingdom with the church age:

> *But one thing must have dawned upon us: the correspondence of these secrets with the present conditions in this **church-age**! These parables are really **an announcement of the new and unexpected aspect the kingdom would assume during an anticipated age of the king's rejection and absence from the world.** We have here the Savior's prediction of the circumstances as we find them unto this day.*[1]

He spoke of "the church dispensation."[2] The kingdom preached earlier In Matthew was not the church.[3] However, Jesus was not speaking of something *different* from the kingdom when He spoke of *mysteries* of the kingdom (Matt. 13:11), and stated several times what "the kingdom of heaven is like unto" (13:31, 24, 33, 44, 45, 47, 52). Jesus is still talking about the same kingdom.

However, Boll is right in saying that the parables describe the church age. In so doing they describe the kingdom of God's dear Son (Col. 1:13). Since the parables deal with the kingdom, and they deal with the church age, the church age must be the kingdom age.

It should also be observed that premillennialists maintain that the church age was not prophesied. However, Christ's speaking in parables, which they say describe the church age, was prophesied (13:35). Although this did not say "church," it prophesied this teaching in parables concerning the church. What are some of the things taught in

---

[1] R.H. Boll, *The Kingdom of God*, page 70.
[2] *Ibid.,* page 71.
[3] *Ibid.,* page 66.

these parables concerning the kingdom? How do these things harmo-nize with what was taught about the kingdom both before and after the parables?

First, the parable of the sower. (1) The kingdom is spread, con-verts are made, through teaching God's word (Matt. 13:19; Luke 8:11), and not through violence. Both John and Jesus taught people to prepare them for the kingdom, and Jesus said that the Father (John 6:44-45) through the Spirit (14:26; 17:12-15) would teach people and bring them to Christ. The great commission is a teaching program, and under it men preached the gospel, taught concerning the kingdom, and brought people, through teaching, into the kingdom (Matt. 28:19-20; Acts 2:30-42; 8:12; 28:31).

(2) The kingdom of heaven and of God are identical. Matthew spoke of the kingdom of heaven (13:11), and Luke in the same account spoke of the "kingdom of God" (8:10).

(3) The reception of the word of the kingdom depended not on na-tionality but on spiritual qualifications or lack of them (Matt. 13:14-23).

(4) Not everyone accepts the kingdom, nor do all who accept it remain faithful, nor do the faithful bear the same amount of fruit (13:19, 20-22). There is nothing here out of harmony with what John the Baptist taught (Matt. 3:1-12).

Second, the parable of the two sowers and two different kinds of seeds concerns the kingdom (Matt. 13:24). (1) The kingdom exists in the world (13:31, 38).

(2) "The good seed are the sons of the kingdom" (13:32) All Israel-ites, from the Old Testament standpoint, were "sons of the kingdom" (8:12), because the kingdom promises were made to them by the prophets. However, all Israelites who did not repent and accept Christ were cast out and did not enter the kingdom either in time nor will they in eternity (8:11-13; 3:7-12). The sons of the kingdom in the parable had received the word of God (Luke 8:11), and in the parable of the tares were "the good seed" (Matt. 13:38).

(3) Good and evil continue during the entire kingdom age. The evil does not wipe out the good and the good does not eliminate the evil. There is no period of the kingdom's existence when tares do not exist in the world. This ties in with the prediction that Christ would rule in the midst of His enemies. Enemies would exist during His reign and

the last one to be conquered is death (Psa. 110:1-2; Acts 2:30-36; 1 Cor. 15:24-28).

(4) The kingdom, spoken of in the parables, continues until the day of judgment. The harvest is the time of judgment when the final separation between the good and the bad seed is made (Matt. 13:30). When is the harvest—an expression in the Old Testament for a judgment of God (Jer. 51:53; Hos. 6:11; Joel 3:1)? "The harvest is the end of the world," or, as the margin translates it, "the consummation of the age." This consummation of this age is the end of the world and gives place to eternity. It is the final judgment, as is evident from not only the statement about the "end of the world" but also: (a) The wicked are gathered out, including out of His kingdom, and cast into eternal punishment. (Matt. 13:41 42; 25:46; 8:12). (b) "Then shall the righteous shine forth as the sun in the kingdom of their Father" (13:43). The millennial kingdom, envisioned by premillennialists, has in it good and evil, and is followed by a tremendous rebellion of the evil against the good (Rev. 20:7-10). Since premillennialists believe that the parables deal with the church, they cannot escape the conclusion that the church age extends to the final judgment, and the consummation of the kingdom in eternity. This fits perfectly with the fact that Christ's present reign continues until all enemies are conquered and then the kingdom is delivered to the Father (Acts 2:30-36; 1 Cor. 15:24-28). Death is not conquered until after the millennium, after the little season, and after the judgment when it is cast into the lake of fire (Rev. 20:11-15).

(5) There is no room for the premillennial rapture, since good and evil are not separated until the end of the world and the final judgment.

(6) See the perfect harmony between the fact that at the end of the world and judgment Christ delivers the kingdom to the Father (1 Cor. 15:24-28), and that in eternity the "righteous shine forth as the sun in the kingdom *of their Father*" (Matt. 13:43).

Third, the "Jewish expectations would have the kingdom appear with earth-shaking power. The wicked would be put down and the righteous vindicated."[1] The premillennialists believe the same thing. In the parable of the tares, Christ showed that the kingdom did not start with the separation of the good from the evil, and in the parables of the mustard seed and the leaven He showed that the kingdom had a small

---

[1] Jack P. Lewis, *The Gospel According to Matthew* (Living Word Commentary), Vol. 1, page 187.

beginning but an extensive growth (Matt. 13:31-33). If the kingdom was established in the way the premillennialists envision it, it would start as a large kingdom. Christ will return from heaven with the saints, a great company, and immediately bring all the world under His rule. Instead of working quietly like leaven and penetrating the world, it starts with the catastrophic overthrow of all worldly powers. Boll said:

> *The church was established in the days of Rome. But Rome felt no shock nor tremor. Neither was she broken up, neither did she begin to be broken up, or to decline. On the contrary she went on prosperously, conquering and to conquer.*

In speaking of Daniel 2:44, he continued by saying:

> *But the prophecy fairly taken represents, not a gradual process but a catastrophic event—a complete and radical demolition of the world kingdom by supernatural agency. The stone's effect upon the Image is due to violent impact, not to "peaceful penetration." The stone falls for judgment and destruction upon the world-power—not for the conversion and salvation of individuals. The Image is suddenly broken up—pulverized—by an act of God.[1]*

Boll is not enlightened by the mysteries of the kingdom revealed in the parable of the mustard seed and in the parable of leaven. Therefore, he concludes the kingdom has not been established. However, even Old Testament prophecy shows it was to have a small beginning (little stone, Dan. 2:44) and was not to start with the conquest of all enemies but that Christ would rule in the midst of enemies until all of them were conquered (Psa. 110: 1-2; Acts 2:30-36; 1 Cor. 15:24-28).

Fourth, the great worth of the kingdom is evident in the parables of the hidden treasure and the goodly pearl of great price (Matt. 13:44-47).

Fifth, the parable of the net shows that from the time the kingdom was let down from heaven it remained on earth (in the sea) until it was drawn up at the end of the world and the separation of the good and the bad (Matt. 13:47-50). There is no room left for another net, the millennial kingdom, to be let down into the sea (the world).

---

[1] R.H. Boll, *Lessons on Daniel*, pages 20-21.

Sixth, Jesus said: "Therefore every scribe who hath been made a disciple to the kingdom of heaven is like unto a man that is a householder, who bringeth forth out of his treasure things new and old" (Matt. 13:51-52). What are the things new and old? Some have said: "(1) the law and the gospel; (2) things hitherto unknown and those already known; (3) the old truths in new lights, new truths brought into proper according with the old. This is preferable."[1] For the explanation, we can start with the context Christ has taught them new things concerning an old subject—the kingdom of God. Things were prophesied about the kingdom, and John and Jesus had taught much about the kingdom, and now Jesus expounded unto them certain *mysteries* of the kingdom (Matt. 13:11). Christ's disciples would also learn more new things about the kingdom, as well as better understand old things, when the Spirit came and not only brought to their remembrance what Christ had taught, but also guide these inspired men into all the truth (John 14:26; 16:12-15). There were certainly things both old and new concerning the kingdom which differed with the Jewish and premillennial view of the kingdom. Certainly there were new things, such as the new birth being essential to enter the kingdom, and such as some things taught in the parables, which were quite different from what the Jews and the premillennialists expected concerning the kingdom.

Seventh, "therefore is the kingdom of heaven likened unto a certain king, who would make a reckoning with his servants" (Matt. 18:23). This parable, concerning forgiveness, was in answer to Peter's question as to how oft he should forgive a brother who sinned against him. This parable shows that forgiveness is an essential part of life in the kingdom. The kingdom is the kingdom of grace, and having received mercy we must show mercy. If we do not, we shall not receive mercy (Matt. 18:32-35; 6:14-15; James 2:13).

Eighth, "For the kingdom of heaven is like unto a man that was a householder, who went out early in the morning to hire laborers into his vineyard" (Matt. 20:1-16). Peter had asked the Lord what they would receive, for they had left all and followed Him (19:27). Christ stated that "in the regeneration when the Son of man shall sit on the throne of his glory, ye also shall sit upon twelve thrones, judging the twelve tribes of Israel" (19:28). They were to have this unique reward. However, there were others who would be rewarded. "And everyone

---

[1] Schaff, book unspecified, page 126.

that hath left houses, or brethren, or sisters, or father, or mother, or children, or lands, for my name's sake, shall receive a hundredfold, and shall inherit eternal life. But many shall be last that are first; and first that are last" (19:29-30). Then follows the parable of the house-holder, and it closes with the statement: "So the last shall be first, and the first last" (20:16).

Jesus shows that things can be the reverse from what some expect. There would be reversals. One thing that surprised the religious lead-ers was that Jesus taught that "the publicans and the harlots go into the kingdom of God before you" (Matt. 21:31). There were Jews who thought they would have a place in the kingdom because of the so-called merits of the patriarchal fathers. Whatever else the parable teaches concerning the kingdom, it does show that the Lord can do with His own as He determines. "Friend, I do thee no wrong: didst not thou agree with me for a shilling? Take up that which is thine, and go thy way; it is my will to give unto this last, even as unto thee. Is it not lawful for me to do what I will with mine own? or is thine eye evil, because I am good?" (20:15). God will reward men according to His grace and His divine sovereignty. He, not man, will make the decision. There is no claim by man to precedence on the basis of what he has done, or at what time in life he was called. The apostles who were with Christ in the personal ministry would not be guaranteed a greater re-ward than Paul who was called late, as a child born out of due season (Cor. 15:8-9). Jews were not to have precedence in the kingdom be-cause they were taught by Christ in the personal ministry, and called, when the church was established, before the Gentiles. It is true that the apostles had a unique position (Matt. 19:28). It is also true that men must respond to His call.

Ninth, "The kingdom of heaven is likened unto a certain king, who made a marriage feast for his son, and sent forth his servants to call them that were bidden to the marriage feast: and they would not come." They were again urged to come, but made light of it, and "the rest laid hold on his servants, and treated them shamefully, and killed them. But the king was wroth; and he sent his armies, and destroyed those murderers, and burned their city. Then saith he to his servants, The wedding is ready, but they that were bidden were not worthy. Go ye therefore unto the partings of the highways.... those servants went out into the highways, and gathered together all as many as were found, both bad and good; and the wedding was filled with guests" (Matt. 22:9-10).

One without the wedding-garment was cast into outer darkness. "For many are called but few chosen" (Matt. 22:1-14).

As mentioned before, it is the Messianic banquet to which they are invited. The invitation had been extended to Israel in the promises and prophecies of the Old Testament. John had summoned them to repent for the kingdom was at hand, and Jesus and the apostles had done the same (Matt. 3:2; 4; 17; 10; 7). Many were called, but few responded to the call. Those who were first bidden were not worthy, and the call then went out to others. Israel was first bidden, and those who accepted were saved, but the nation rejected Him, and although the call goes forth to all men, more Gentiles than Jews have accepted the invitation (Acts 13:46). The Israel who rejected the invitation does not have in store another call in the so-called millennial kingdom. Those who reject Him and persist in the rejection are lost. Sons of the kingdom were cast out (Matt. 8:12). Their city was destroyed (21:7). After the destruction of the city of Jerusalem, the church soon become predominantly Gentilish.

Tenth, "Then shall the kingdom of heaven be likened unto ten virgins… Watch therefore, for ye know not the day nor the hour" (Matt. 25:13). This parable is followed by the parable of the talents, and by the illustration of the sheep and the goats (25:14-46). The bridegroom may not come as soon as some expect. In fact, he did not come within the time for which the five foolish virgins had made preparation with reference to oil. We do not know when Christ will return, and therefore we should be ready at all times without setting a time in our thinking. We are also to work while the Lord is away. We have a responsibility for what we have, and our works must involve good deeds such as feeding the hungry, clothing the naked, and being helpful according to the needs of people. All of these parables teach that there is a time when it is too late, that the period of probation ends. Furthermore, when the absent one returns, and the absent one is "the Son of man" (25:31), He will not establish a kingdom on earth but will give the final judgment (25:12; 7:21-23; 25:30, 46). The church age, the kingdom of God's dear Son (Col. 1:13), continues until the return of Christ and is followed by the judgment and not another kingdom on this earth (1 Cor. 15:24-23).

These are parables in which Jesus illustrated some truths concerning the kingdom, and some of these truths were the revelation of mysteries concerning the kingdom (Matt. 13:11). The expression "the mysteries of the kingdom" does not mean that nothing of what was set forth in the parables was prophesied. It could include some things which were dimly set forth in prophecy or veiled in types and symbols. For example, Daniel's interpretation of the king's dream showed that the kingdom was to have a small beginning in comparison with its large outcome (Dan. 2:38-45). However, it is extremely clear that the existence up to that time of mysteries about some of the qualities and characteristics of the kingdom proves nothing at all with reference to the claim that this particular kingdom, the church age, was not prophesied; that it was a mystery.

Psalm 2—a Prophecy of the Present Reign

Walvoord maintained that Psalm 2 is a picture of Christ's enthronement after His second coming.[1] This interpretation is possible only if one clings to one's uninspired interpretation and ignores the teaching of the New Testament.

> *Why do the nations rage, and the peoples meditate a vain thing? The kings of the earth set themselves, and the rulers take counsel together, against Jehovah, and against his anointed, saying, Let us break their bonds asunder, and cast away their cords from us. He that sitteth in the heavens will laugh: the Lord will have them in derision. Then will he speak to them in his wrath, and vex them in his sore displeasure: yet I have set my king upon my holy hill of Zion.*
>
> *I will tell of the decree: Jehovah said unto me, Thou art my son; this day have I begotten thee. Ask of me, and I will give thee the nations for thine inheritance, and the uttermost parts of the earth for thy possession. Thou shalt break them with a rod of iron; thou shalt dash them in pieces like a potter's vessel.*
>
> *Now therefore be wise, O ye kings: be instructed, ye judges of the earth. Serve Jehovah with fear, and rejoice with trembling. Kiss the son, lest he be angry, and ye perish in the way, for his wrath will soon be kindled. Blessed are all they that*

---

[1] Walvoord, *The Millennial Kingdom*, pages 265, 299, 301, 306.

take refuge in him. (Psalm 2:1-12).

As shown elsewhere in this book, this passage, along with a statement in Acts, shatters the postponement theory. It proves that in spite of the rejection of the Messiah, God enthroned Him. Furthermore, it proves that the present reign of the Messiah was prophesied. *First*, Jews and Gentiles set themselves up against God and His anointed, or Messiah. They were going to successfully rebel against him, they boasted (Psa. 2:1-3). *Second*, the futility of their rebellion was made clear in the statement: "He that sitteth in the heavens will laugh; the Lord will have them in derision" (2:4). So puny are their efforts, that God holds them in contempt. *Third*, in spite of their opposition, God promised to enthrone His king, who was His son. "Yet, I have set my King upon my holy hill of Zion... Thou art my son... Kiss the son, lest he be angry, and ye perish in the way, for his wrath will soon be kindled. Blessed are all they that take refuge in him" (2:6-12). In spite of their opposition, God enthroned His Son, called for obedience to Him, promised punishment to those who refused to submit and that He would bless the obedient.

The New Testament makes clear that: *First*, the people who were in rebellion were the Jews and Gentiles of Jesus' day. "And they, when they heard it, lifted up their voice to God with one accord and said, O Lord, thou that didst make the heaven and the earth and the sea, and all that in them is: who by the Holy Spirit, by the mouth of our father David thy servant, didst say, Why did the Gentiles rage, And the peoples imagine vain things? The kings of the earth set themselves in array, and the rulers were gathered together, against the Lord, and against his anointed: for of a truth in this city against thy holy Servant Jesus whom thou didst anoint, both Herod and Pontius Pilate, with the Gentiles and the peoples of Israel, were gathered together to do whatsoever thy hand and thy counsel foreordained to come to pass. And now, Lord, look upon their threatenings: and grant unto thy servants to speak thy word with all boldness while thou stretchest forth thy hand to heal; and that signs and wonders may be done through the name of thy holy Servant Jesus" (Acts 4:24-30). *Second*. we know that God enthroned His Son in spite of their rebellion. They could not keep Christ from being raised and exalted to God's right hand. He went to the crown by way of the cross (Luke 24:25-27). Although they crucified Christ, God raised Him from the dead (Acts 2:22-28). He is king in His kingdom (Col. 1:13). *Third*, He reigns in Zion, but it is the new *heavenly* Zion, and not the old one on earth (Heb. 12:22; Acts 2 34-36). **Fourth**, He is God's Son. Paul showed that Psa. 2:7 was fulfilled in the resurrection and exaltation of Christ, God's Son. "That God hath fulfilled the same unto our children, in that he raised up Jesus; as also it is written in the second psalm, Thou art my Son, this day have I begotten thee (Acts 13:33). This passage, it seems to the author, does not refer to His virgin birth, but to His resurrection and exaltation wherein He was declared to be the Son of God with power by the resurrection from the dead (Rom. 1:4; Acts 2:27, 30-36).

The present rule involves the rod of iron, but not in that His day by day rule is enforced by the authorities in the power of an earthly-type of kingdom. (1) It is a rod of iron rule in that those who live contrary to the laws of God are sooner or later broken by these laws. (2) He can bring about judgments on people through His providence, though we do not know how minute is His providence and we cannot give an inspired interpretation of history. (3) This power will be seen in a visible way at His returning when all men are brought into judgment. He rules until all of His enemies are conquered (Acts 2:34-36, 1 Cor. 15:24-28). Those who are not conquered by the power of the gospel, or overthrown by the workings of His spiritual and moral laws and providence, will be conquered in judgment at the second advent.

David Prophesied the Present Reign (Psalm 110)

David made the prophecy of Christ's reign at God's right hand (Matt. 22:43-45). Walvoord destroyed all of his arguments designed to prove that the present reign of Christ was not prophesied when he wrote: "Psalm 110 contrasts the present position of the King at 'my right hand' (v. l) with His rule 'in the midst of thine enemies' (v. 2) His judgment upon the wicked in the future kingdom described in the words 'in the day of thy power' (v. 3) is given in verses 5-7."[1] Christ's present rule is at God's right hand, far above all principality and power (Eph. 1:20; Col. 3:1; Acts 2:30-36).

It is futile to try to make Psalm 110:1 and 110:2 refer to two different reigns—one now and the other after the second advent. Verse one said that he would reign at God's right hand, *until I make thine enemies thy footstool.*" This shows that He has enemies during His reign,

---

[1] *Ibid.,* page 266.

but that He will reign until all of them are conquered. Some of these enemies are described in Psalm 110:5-6, and all of His enemies will be conquered before His reign is over. The last enemy is death. The present reign, which Walvoord admits is now going on as prophesied in Psalm 110:1, continues until all enemies are conquered. This is not followed by another reign on earth, but by the deliverance of the kingdom to the Father (1 Cor. 15:24-28; Rev. 20:11-15). This leaves no room for a different reign which Walvoord thinks was described in Psalm 110:2.

Furthermore, Psalm 110:2 does not describe the type of reign which premillennialists say will exist in the future. "Rule thou *in the midst of thine enemies*" (110:2). If premillennialism is right, many of the enemies of Christ are destroyed in the unprecedented tribulation which they say precedes His coming and kingdom. The tribulation involves the entire population of the earth. All flesh on earth would have died if the second coming had not cut it short. When Christ comes after the tribulation, and judges Israel and the Gentiles, the saved are separated from the unsaved. Walvoord said that Matthew 25:31-46 represented the judgment for the Gentiles (in which, according to Walvoord,the unsaved Gentiles went into everlasting punishment, and the saved Gentiles into the millennial kingdom), and Ezekiel 20:34-38 represents "a judgment of God upon Israel,"[1] in which Israel is purged of rebels. "And I will cause you to pass under the rod, and I will bring you into the bond of the covenant; *and I will purge out from among you the rebels, and them that transgress against me*; and I will bring them forth out of the land where they sojourn, and they shall not enter into the land of Israel: and ye shall know that I am Jehovah" (Ezek. 20:37-38). The unsaved of both the Gentiles and Israel are separated from the saved. Where do the saved go? In speaking of both the passage in Matthew 25 and in Ezekiel, Walvoord said: "The righteous in both cases enter the kingdom and the land of Palestine as their immediate reward."[2] The premillennialists being our witnesses, the millennial reign of Christ will begin with the conquest of all of His enemies, and He will not rule in the midst of His enemies in the millennium. But Psalm 110:2, which Walvoord said refers to the millennial reign, said His reign would be in the midst of His enemies. In more than one

---

[1] *Ibid.,* page 253.
[2] *Ibid.,* page 244.

place Walvoord described the second coming as bringing destruction
(2 Thess. 2:8-10, for example) to Christ's enemies and the deliverance
of "the saved of both Jews and Gentiles, and to the nation Israel as
such."[1] The millennial reign is one of peace and prosperity, and not a
rule in the midst of His enemies, if premillennialism is right.

But let us consider, in additional detail, Psalm 110 as a prophecy of
Christ's present reign.

Christ's Present Reign as King and Priest (Acts 2:34-36)

"Jehovah saith unto my Lord, Sit thou at my right hand, until I
make thine enemies thy footstool. Jehovah will send forth the rod of
thy strength out of Zion: Rule thou in the midst of thine enemies. Thy
people offer themselves willingly in the day of thy power, in holy array: out of the womb of the morning Thou hast the dew of thy youth.
Jehovah hath sworn, and will not repent: Thou art a priest forever after
the order of Melchizedek" (Psa. 110:1-4).

We know that this was a prophecy of David, by the Spirit of God,
concerning Christ. When Jesus asked whose son the Christ was, the
Pharisees said, David's. "He saith unto them, How then doth David in
the Spirit call him Lord, saying, The Lord said unto my Lord, sit thou
on my right hand, till I put thine enemies underneath thy feet? If David
then calleth him Lord, how is he his son?" (Matt. 22:43-45). They
were unable to answer, but the answer is that He was David's son according to the flesh, but was David's Lord because He was God's Son
begotten by the Holy Spirit. He was the child who was born, and therefore was human, but he was also Divine (Isa. 7:14; 9:6-7; Matt. 1:20-
25; Rom. 1:1-4).

How do we know that Psa. 110 refers to the present reign of
Christ? *First*, the New Testament expressly states that it prophesied
Christ's present reign. Peter showed that the throne of David had been
promised to Christ, he unfolded by the Spirit the meaning of the promises, he showed its fulfillment in Christ's ascension to God's right
hand, and he concluded that this therefore proved that all Israel could
know that Jesus is both Lord and Christ. "Brethren, I may say unto you
freely of the patriarch David, that he both died and was buried, and his
tomb is with us unto this day. Being therefore a prophet, and knowing

---

[1] *Ibid.,* pages 272-273.

that God had sworn with an oath to him, that of the fruit of his loins he would set one upon his throne; he foreseeing this spake of the resurrection of the Christ, that neither was he left unto Hades nor did his flesh see corruption. This Jesus did God raise up, whereof we all are witnesses. Being therefore by the right hand of God exalted, and having received of the Father the promise of the Holy Spirit, he hath poured forth this, which ye see and hear. For David ascended not into the heavens: but he saith himself, the Lord said unto my Lord, Sit thou on my right hand, till I make thine enemies the footstool of thy feet. Let all the house of Israel therefore know assuredly, that God hath made him both Lord and Christ, this Jesus whom ye crucified" (Acts 2:29-36).

Peter clearly stated that Christ had been "by the right hand of God exalted," just as David prophesied (2:33-34). He expressly affirmed that Christ is now Lord or ruler, and Christ. As the anointed one, the Christ, He was prophet (Acts 3:22-23), priest (Heb. 7:17, 21-28), and king (Heb. 5:6; 7:1, 11-17; 8:1, 4; Col. 1:13; Eph. 5:5).

Second, we can know that Psa. 110:1-4 prophesied the present reign of Christ because it clearly describes His reign.

(1) He was to reign in heaven at God's right hand, and not on a throne on earth (Psa. 110:1). Christ now reigns from heaven (Acts 2:34-36; Col. 3:1-2).

(2) Enemies exist during His rule. He would not overthrow all of them at the beginning of His rule. "Rule thou *in the midst* of thine enemies" (Psa. 110:2). This is also indicated in the fact that He was to rule *until* all His enemies were conquered (110:1). Christ's present rule is in the midst of His enemies, and this is the reason that His disciples sometimes have to suffer for His sake (Matt. 5:10-12). The book of Acts records many examples of such persecution while Christ reigned, and He continues to reign, at God's right hand.

(3) "Jehovah will send forth the rod of thy strength out of Zion" (Psa. 110:2). Christ now rules in the heavenly Zion (Isa. 2:1-6; Acts 4:24-28; Heb. 12:22-24).

(4) Since Christ was to reign from heaven at God's right hand, He would be invisible to men on earth. And so He is in this gospel age. And so He shall be, until He comes a second time to take the redeemed to glory and to judge the world (Acts 2:34-36; Heb. 9:27-28; 2 Thess. 1:5-12).

(5) His people were to be a willing people who offer themselves to

Him (Psa. 110:3). No one is drafted into the kingdom of God. We must be willing to accept Christ (John 5:40; 7:17; Rev. 22:17-18).

(6) His rule could not be under the law of Moses. The law had to be abolished in order for Christ, who was of the tribe of Judah, to be both king and priest as David prophesied (Psa. 110:1, 4; Heb. 7:1, 7:11-8:4). The literal interpretation which some make of certain prophecies teaches that the law of Moses will be restored, along with the Levitical system. If this is true, Christ cannot then reign as king and priest. This was the reason He could not be a priest while on earth, because while He was on earth the law of Moses was in force. The change of the priesthood meant the change of the law (Heb. 7:11-19). "Now if he were on earth, he would not be a priest at all, seeing there are those who offer the gifts according to the law" (Heb. 8:4).

(7) Not only could his reign not be under the law of Moses—the Old Covenant (Rom. 7:1-6; Heb. 7:11-19)—but it could not be a reign which administered the law of Moses. The law was abolished that He might reign in His New Covenant: for His is the substance of which the Old was but the shadow (Col. 2:14-17; Heb. 10:1).

(8) The reign prophesied by David was to continue until all His enemies were conquered. "The Lord said unto my Lord, Sit thou on my right hand, until I make thine enemies the footstool of thy feet (Acts. 2:34). Who is the last enemy? Death. What happens when the last enemy is conquered? Christ delivers the kingdom to God in eternity (1 Cor. 15:24-28; Rev. 20:11-21:5). This leaves no room for another reign of Christ to succeed the present reign of Christ.

How can anything be clearer than that the church age, the age in which Christ rules at God's right hand, was prophesied by David?

The Gospel Age the Fulfillment
of at Least Two Abrahamic Promises

At least two of God's promises to Abraham are promises which are fulfilled in the gospel age. In *promising* the gospel age, God was *prophesying* the gospel age, for a promise partakes of the nature of a prediction. It tells you something God was going to do, and it tells you beforehand. If Jewish Rabbis did not know the significance of these promises, and if uninspired believers today do not know, all this counts for absolutely nothing in face of the fact that Jesus Christ through the apostle Paul clearly teaches that the gospel age is the fulfillment of these promises (John 16:12-15; 1 Cor. 14:37; Gal. 1:1, 6-12; 2:7-8; 3:6-29).

This proof is so crystal clear that any believer who does not see it, after studying the passages, has a veil over his heart when he reads these passages (Compare 2 Cor. 3:12-17). One of the promises God made to Abraham when He called him out of Ur was "in thee shall all the families of the earth be blessed" (Gen. 12:3). That uninspired men could not figure out from this passage alone how God was to do this in no way mitigates against the fact that the inspired apostle Paul tells us that God fulfilled this promise, and is fulfilling it, through justifying men by faith in Christ in this age—the gospel age. Paul was called by Jesus Christ to preach the gospel. Although he preached to Jews, his special mission was that of apostle to the Gentiles (Gal. 1:1, 6-16; 2:6-9). As Paul fought the Judaizers we fight the premillennialists: "*Know therefore that they that are of faith, the same are sons of Abraham. And the scripture foreseeing that God would justify the Gentiles by faith, preached the gospel beforehand unto Abraham, saying*, In thee shall all the nations be blessed. *So then* they that are of faith are blessed with the faithful Abraham* " (3:7-9).

Paul is speaking of those who are of faith, including Jews and Gentiles, for Jews and Gentiles are the nations to whom the blessing was promised (Gal. 3:26-28). Jews were the ones who had been "kept in ward under the law, shut up unto the faith which should afterwards be revealed" (3:23). They were the ones to whom the law "is become our tutor to bring us into Christ, that we might be justified by faith" (3:24). In the Old Testament people had to have faith, but Paul is here speaking of justification through faith in Christ who has already come. The entire context shows Paul is speaking of faith in Christ.

> *But the scripture shut up all things under sin, that the promise by faith in Jesus Christ might be given to them that believe. But before faith came, we were kept in ward under the law, shut up unto the faith which should afterwards be revealed. So that the law is become our tutor to bring us unto Christ, that we might be justified by faith. But now that faith is come, we are no longer under a tutor. For ye are all sons of God, through faith,_in Christ Jesus. For as many of you as were baptized into Christ did put on Christ. There can be neither Jew nor Greek... for ye all are one man in Christ Jesus. And if ye are Christ's, then are ye Abraham's seed, heirs ac-*

cording to promise" (Gal. 3:22-29).

Justification by faith in Christ is the fulfillment of the promise God made to Abraham in Genesis 12:3. Justification by faith in Christ is taught in the faith once for all delivered to the saints.

What about those who refused Christ and tried to continue under the law? And what about those who maintain that in the millennial age the law of Moses will be restored? If it is restored as a memorial, it would not be the restoration of the law of Moses for the law of Moses was never a memorial of the gospel age but contained many types, promises, and prophecies of the gospel age.

> *For as many as are of the works of the law are under a curse: for it is written, Cursed is every one who continueth not in all things that are written in the book of the law, to do them. Now that no man is justified by the law before God, is evident: for, The righteous shall live by faith; and the law is not of faith; but, He that doeth them shall live in them. Christ redeemed us from the curse of the law, having become a curse for us; for it is written, Cursed is every one that hangeth on a tree: that upon the Gentiles might come the blessing of Abraham in Christ Jesus; that we might receive the promise of the Spirit through faith" (3:10-14).*

Christ will not re-establish the law of Moses but without its curse. Its curse was a part of the law. How ridiculous it would be for Christ to place us under the tutor after He has come and established His covenant. He would not place us under guardians and stewards after the time appointed by the Father has long passed (4:1-7). "So that the law is become our tutor to bring us unto Christ... But now that faith is come, we are no longer under a tutor" (3:24-25). Hebrews told Christians, who were from the race of Israel and had been under the law, to leave the law and the city of Jerusalem for here we have no abiding city (Heb. 13:14-15). Those who serve the tabernacle have no right to our altar (3:10). Premillennialists maintain that in the millennium Christ will lead us back into the city, and into the law—at least the law will be bound on Jews, and the literal interpretation of parts of Ezekiel would bind it on Gentiles also.

It is true that in the Old Testament men had to have faith (Gal. 3:11; Hab. 2:4), but this was not faith in Jesus Christ—the faith which has now come (Gal. 3:22-29).

The gospel is the fulfillment of the promise of Genesis 12:3 (Gal. 3:7-14), therefore the gospel age, the age in which the gospel is preached, was prophesied.

Paul again emphasized that the inheritance was through the promise and not through the law (Gal. 3:15-29). The law did not *make void or add to* the promise, although it was not against the promises of God (3:15-21). "Now to Abraham were the promises spoken, and to his seed. He saith not, And to seeds, as of many; but as of one. And to thy seed, which is Christ" (3:16; Gen, 22:17-18). How do we benefit from the promise? *By being in Christ.* "And if ye are Christ's, then are ye Abraham's seed, heirs according to promise" (3:29), Could it be clearer? God said through Paul that "He saith not, And to seeds, as of many; but as of one, And to thy seed, *which is Christ*" (3:16). Do you want to know who is the seed to whom the promise was made? Why concern one's self with what the Rabbi thought, or what some scholar thinks today? The answer is crystal clear: "*And to thy seed, which is Christ.*" You do not like the answer? It does not harmonize with your uninspired interpretation of the Old Testament promise? What a shame that the Lord did not accommodate His Scriptures to your interpretations!!! Do you think this is a misappropriation of the promise? So much the worse for your thinking! Do you think this unfairly cuts some people off from the promise? They are invited to come to Christ and to be an heir (Gal. 3:29), but if they refuse to come whose fault is it (John 5:40)?

Second Coming Brings the End

John F. Walvoord thinks that the translation of the saints has a vital bearing on premillennialism, but that this has not always been recognized by even the premillennialists.[1] Walvoord said that the transformation of the corruptible body into the incorruptible comes by resurrection (which had already been revealed) or by translation which was a mystery not revealed until the days of Paul (1 Cor. 15:51-52).[2] There will be living saints when Christ comes "for His Church." He maintained that both the resurrection of the righteous and the translation take place *before the second advent* when Christ comes for the church but not to this earth because the saints meet Him in the air (1 Thess.

---

[1] Walvoord, *The Millennial Kingdom*, pages 240-241.
[2] *Ibid.*, page 241.

4:13-17).[1] The Old Testament saints, and the tribulation saints, are not promised translation. "In passages concerning the second coming to the earth, the separation of saints from the unsaved takes place uniformly *after* the return of Christ. Matthew 25:31-46 pictures this in regard to the Gentiles as taking place after a throne is established on earth subsequent to the Lord's return." Ezekiel 20:33-38 shows that the saved and the rebels in Israel are separated after the second coming and the gathering which is "a time consuming process."[2] Is Walvoord right?

First, the New Testament teaches that Christ brings eternal salvation to the Christians *at the second advent, not before*. Those that wait for Christ are the saints, the Christians. "So Christ also, having been once offered to bear the sins of many, *shall appear a second time*, apart from sin, to them that wait for him, unto salvation" (Heb. 9:28). The saints in Thessalonica were waiting for Him, as are the saints today (1 Thess. 4:18). Therefore, the coming of Christ mentioned in Thessalonians was the second coming. Walvoord is wrong, the saints are raised and the living saints translated at the second coming.

Second, Christ's present reign continues until all enemies are conquered and the last enemy is death (Acts 2:30-34; 1 Cor. 15:24-28). Death is conquered when Christ comes and the saints are raised and translated, as the case may be. "But when this corruptible shall have put on incorruption, and this mortal shall have put on immortality, *then* shall come to pass the saying that is written, Death is swallowed up in victory. O death, where is thy victory? O death, where is thy sting? The sting of death is sin; and the power of sin is the law: but thanks be to God, who giveth us the victory through our Lord Jesus Christ" (1 Cor. 15:54-58). This takes place after whatever the thousand years represents, as well as after the little season, when the resurrection and judgment take place and death and hades are cast into the lake of fire (Rev. 20:11-15).

Third, the resurrection of the departed saints and the translation of the living saints take place "*at the last trump*: for the trumpet shall sound, and the dead shall be raised incorruptible, and we shall be changed" (1 Cor. 15:52). The last trump sounds when Christ comes for

---

[1] *Ibid.*, page 243.
[2] *Ibid.*, pages 243-244.

His church. "For the Lord himself shall descend from heaven, with a shout, with the voice of the archangel, *and with the trump of God*: and the dead in Christ shall rise first; then we that are alive, that are left, shall together with them be caught up in the clouds, to meet the Lord in the air: and so shall we ever be with the Lord" (1 Thess. 4:16-17). This is the last trump. There will be no other trump to wake the dead, after the last trump, and unless all of the dead are raised at this time the rest of the dead will never be raised. The resurrection of the wicked takes place at the time of the last trump, although Paul did not mention the wicked in writing to the Thessalonians because he was dealing with a question concerning departed Christians and not concerning those who died out of Christ (1 Thess. 4:13-14: "fallen asleep in Jesus"). Jesus taught that the resurrection of the righteous and of the wicked takes place *the same hour* (John 5:28-29). Regardless of how long a period of time this "hour" includes, it is all in the same period of time. If the premillennialists are right, there are several hours between the resurrection of the righteous and of the wicked. The righteous are raised at the hour of the coming of the Lord for His saints, then there is the hour of the tribulation, then there is the hour of the second coming, then there is the hour of the thousand year reign, and then there is the hour of the little season, and then there is the hour of the resurrection of the wicked. These are too many hours or periods of time to get into one period (hour) of time. Furthermore, Jesus said that those who believed on Him would be raised on *"the last day"* (John 6:44, 54; 11:24). Unless the wicked are raised the same day there is no day after the last day on which they can be raised.

Fourth, it must also be stressed that the premillennialists contradict Paul who said: "Now this I say, brethren, that *flesh and blood cannot inherit the kingdom of God*; neither doth corruption inherit incorruption" (1 Cor. 15:50). He then goes on and explains that even the living saints will be transformed from flesh and blood into the heavenly, spiritual, body (15:42-49, 51-58). The premillennialists maintain that the church will not inherit the kingdom in a condition of flesh and blood. They will be changed before Christ's second advent. He will come for them, take them to heaven, the marriage of the Lamb will then take place, and then they will come with Christ to earth to reign with Him as glorified immortal beings with the spiritual and heavenly body.

However, the premillennialists believe that there will be people converted to Christ during the tribulation, and that these saints, who will not be a part of the church or body of Christ, *will inherit the king-dom in their flesh and blood state.*

> *Important events must occur between the rapture of the church and the establishment of the millennial kingdom such as the judgment seat of Christ (2 Cor. 5:10), the union of Christ and the church in the marriage relationship (Eph. 5:27), and the necessity of a program of salvation over a period of time to provide saints to dwell on the earth during the millennium who are not raptured but enter the millennium in their natural bod-ies (Isa. 65:20-25). This is further confirmed by the fact that the separation of the saved from the unsaved of those living on the earth at the time of the millennial return of Christ is ac-complished in a judgment of God upon Israel (Ezek. 20:34-38), and a judgment of the Gentiles (Matt. 25:31-46), judgments which would be unnecessary and out of chronological order if the rapture had already separated all the saved from the un-saved at the end of the tribulation. A post-tribulational rapture would leave no saints in their natural bodies to dwell upon the earth and fulfill millennial predictions.*[1]
>
> *The viewpoint of Old Testament prophecies is that saints on earth at the time of the second advent will enter the millennial kingdom in the flesh, an obvious contradiction of the idea of translation.*[2]

This means that there must be saints due to conversion after the church has been translated.

> *The normal premillennial position is that saints on earth at the second advent will enter the millennium and will be in the flesh, produce children, and have normal earthly experiences in contrast to the resurrected or translated saints who will have spiritual bodies.*[3]

After the judgments mentioned in Matthew and Ezekiel, which do not mention translation, the "righteous in both cases enter the kingdom

---

[1] *Ibid.,* pages 252-253.
[2] *Ibid.,* page 242.
[3] *Ibid.,* page 243.

and the land of Palestine as their immediate reward."[1]

This does not harmonize with the Scriptures. The judgment scene in Matthew says nothing about anyone entering Palestine. The kingdom is for those who are righteous and punishment is for the wicked. "Come, ye blessed of my father, inherit the kingdom prepared for you from the foundation of the world" (Matt. 25:34). This is equivalent to eternal life, and not to a millennial reign on earth in which there is still sin, and which is followed by a tremendous rebellion for a little season (little in contrast with the thousand years), and then the judgment and the eternal inheritance (Rev. 20:1-15). Inheriting the kingdom is equal to inheriting eternal life. "And these shall go away into eternal punishment *but the righteous into eternal life*" (Matt. 25:46). This does not sound like Palestine. This is the kingdom they were invited into (25:34, 46). If these Gentiles are in the fleshly state they enter into eternal life in the fleshly state.

Fifth, what is the program of salvation during the time of tribulation, which Walvoord mentioned?[2] If Matthew 25 is the total teaching on this judgment scene, salvation by grace through faith had nothing to do with inheriting the kingdom and going into eternal life. The only thing mentioned here was how they had treated the Lord's disciples (25:35-45). If this is the total picture, they enter eternal life on the basis of good works. If the church was not on earth during the tribulation, when did this non-Christian help Christ's "brethren" (25:40)? They must have done it before the rapture and thus before the tribulation. This would mean that in the church age there are two plans of salvation. (1) Salvation by grace through the only gospel (Eph. 2:8 Gal. 1:6-9). There is no other gospel. (2) Salvation by works and these works are done by non-Christians who treated Christ's brethren (Christians) with compassion. Surely Christ does not have brethren on earth other than Christians. One cannot harmonize this with the one plan of salvation which is in force in the gospel age. Premillennialism is wrong.

The Gentiles who live during the tribulation are saved by their good works if they did good works for the brethren of Christ. However, Jews must be saved by some other plan of salvation for they are not in the judgment scene in Matthew 25:31-46, if Walvoord is right. The

---

[1] *Ibid.,* page 244.
[2] *Ibid.,* page 252.

judgments on the Gentiles and on Israel are different judgments.[1] The scene in Ezekiel does not mention faith in Christ, it does not mention good deeds done to Christians. What is the plan of salvation for them? We do not know how God purged them. "And I will cause you to pass under the rod, and I will bring you into the bond of the covenant; and I will purge out from among you the rebels, and them that transgress against me; I will bring them forth out of the land where they sojourn, but they shall not enter into the land of Israel: and ye shall know that I am Jehovah" (Ezek. 20:37-38).

Salvation in the church age is by grace through faith, salvation in the tribulation age for the Gentiles is by good works which they had done previously during the church age to the saints, and salvation for the Jews is on some other and unspecified plan. Believe it, he who can.

---

[1] *Ibid.,* page 253.

CHAPTER 8:
ISRAEL WOULD HAVE ACCEPTED
THE PREMILLENNIAL KINGDOM

If the kingdom which was at hand was the type pictured by premillennialism, the Jews would have accepted Christ, They wanted the kind of kingdom wherein Israel would be freed from Roman rule and exalted over the nations of the earth with the Gentiles being blessed through and in subservience to restored and exalted Israel. If this was the kingdom which was at hand, it is impossible to explain why Israel rejected Jesus.

The New Testament shows that the devil tempted Christ with such an earthly rule and that Israel would have been willing to fight to make Jesus king in such a kingdom. "Jesus therefore perceiving that they were about to come and take him by force, to make him king, withdrew again into the mountain himself alone" (John 6:15).

There are several reasons why Israel rejected Christ. One of the basic reasons is pride, which is also basic in the rejection of Christ by others. Jesus said: "Blessed are the poor in spirit: for theirs is the kingdom of heaven" (Matt. 5:3). Since the kingdom is for the poor in spirit, and since the majority of Israel was proud in spirit, the kingdom did not belong to them. It was taken away from them and given to a spiritual nation, the church (Matt. 21:43; 1 Pet. 2:5-10). They were proud of their relationship to eminent ancestors—such as Abraham, Isaac, Jacob, and Moses. Jesus acknowledged that physically they were Abraham's children but they were not spiritually his children, for they did not have the faith and works of Abraham (John 8:37, 39-45). John the Baptist warned them against trusting in their physical relationship to Abraham. "And think not to say within yourselves, We have Abraham to our father: for I say unto you, that God is able of these stones to raise up children unto Abraham. And even now the axe lieth at the root of the trees: every tree therefore that bringeth not forth good fruit is hewn down, and cast into the fire" (Matt. 3:9-10).

Pharisees were proud of the righteousness which they thought they had attained. They trusted in themselves that they were righteous and set others at naught (Luke 18:9-19). They tithed small garden plants, but left undone the weightier matters of the law—justice, mercy, and faith (Matt. 23:23). They boasted they would not have persecuted the prophets, but they persecuted Him of whom the prophets spoke—Jesus the Messiah (Matt. 23:29-35). The kingdom cannot be received by the proud.

They prided themselves on their nation to the extent that their nation was a part of their religion, and they thought that true faith could not survive without the survival of the nation. Israel as a nation was to be the savior of the world. In speaking of the teaching of Paul that the law had given way to the gospel, Joseph Klausner wrote:

> *The abrogation of the ceremonial laws would necessarily have served to obliterate the distinction between Israel and the nations—and what would have happened then? One drop of wine—even of strong wine— will not give a taste to a great cask of water; and if Judaism had listened to the voice of Paul, it would have disappeared from the world both as a religion and as a nation, without leaving any influence whatever upon the great pagan world. But Judaism wished to endure as a religion, in order that in the course of time the pure ethical monotheism and the ethico-social Messianism of the prophets might prevail; and it wished to endure as a nation, in order that it might again be free upon its own soil to create there politiconational and economico- cultural values as do all other nations. For one simple fact must not be forgotten, although many Jewish scholars with a sense of "mission" and almost all Christian theologians neglect it either intentionally or unintentionally; this fact is that Judaism is **not only a religion, but a nation as well**—a nation and a religion at one and the same time. Hence, if it should surrender its characteristic religious faith, its nationality would also die; likewise, if it should give up its national existence, an end would also come to the particular religion and culture which we call collectively "Judaism." Therefore, only a small minority among the Jews accepted the teaching of Paul, and in the course of time, after a sharp struggle between Jewish Nazarenism and Gentile Christianity, this minority was swallowed up among the Gentiles.*[1]

The mistaken view that Israel is a messianic nation not only led them to reject Christ, but has been one of the driving powers behind

---

[1] Joseph Klausner, *From Jesus to Paul,* page 593.

the determination of many that at all cost Israel as a nation must exist.

Joseph Klausner also said: "Christianity was born within Israel, and Israel as a nation rejected it utterly. Why?"[1] Without suggesting that this was in every detail the view of all the Rabbis, Klausner said that Elijah would come before the Messiah and that then the Messiah would restore and exalt Israel.

> The "pangs of the Messiah" introduce the messianic age when there shall be a gathering together of the dispersed Jews after Elijah shall have appeared. Of him Ben Sira wrote that "he is ready for the time" not only to "turn the hearts of the fathers to the children" but also "to restore the tribes of Israel." Elijah shall blow the trumpet of the Messiah and the scattered Jews shall be assembled together from the four comers of the earth.
>
> Then shall come the Messiah, the "Saviour" full of the spirit of God, who shall overwhelm the heathen and restore the kingdom of Israel to its full power, rebuild Jerusalem and the Temple, and make them a spiritual centre for the whole world. Such nations as have not been destroyed, since they did not oppress Israel, shall become proselytes, and the world shall be reformed by the "kingdom of heaven," or, "the kingdom of the Almighty:" the Lord shall be the God of the whole earth, and righteousness, justice and brotherliness shall prevail. The Messiah will be the son of David.[2]

Klausner maintained that Jesus changed His view of the kingdom, and ended up with a spiritual kingdom. All of Israel looked for the Messiah to come but not all shared the same view or agreed on how the kingdom would come. The Essenes thought of the Messiah as a "mystical idea: it was bound up with a supernatural idea of social equality, of purity, of righteousness and of perfect worship." The Pharisees viewed the mission of the Messiah as both political and spiritual, but did not think they should try to hasten its coming. The Sadducees did not deny the belief in the Messiah, but "they disbelieved in all the post-Biblical accretions and took pains to belittle an idea which was politically dangerous." The Zealots were extreme nationalists who

---

[1] Klausner, *Jesus of Nazareth: His Life, Times, and Teaching,* page 9.
[2] *Ibid.,* page 200.

were willing to use, and did use, force in order to try to hasten the coming of the Messiah and His rule.[1] They hated foreign rule and "the rich, powerful and ruling classes... [T]hey were the finest patriots Israel knew from the rise of the Maccabaeans to the defeat of Bar Kckhba... Their one crime was that they acted according to their conscience."[2]

> Of these four parties the mystical and moral messianic belief of the Essenes was nearest that of Jesus, who, in the end, abolished its political aspect and made it purely mystical and ethical. Farthest removed from him were the Sadducees for whom the messianic idea was hardly more than an empty name. As we shall see later the more definitely political messianic idea of the Zealots was nearer the heart of Jesus at the beginning of his ministry [The devil tempted Him with it. J.D.B.]. But on the whole, he rather favoured the political-spiritual messianism of the Pharisees despite its lack of mysticism and its being too much "of this world" for his liking during the later period of his career, when his "kingdom" became definitely "not of this world."[3]

Klausner is saying that Jesus changed His teaching concerning the nature of the kingdom as time went on until it became a spiritual kingdom. Premillennialists believe that Christ first taught the Messianic kingdom and when Israel rejected Him, or was in the process of rejecting Him, He changed the message to one concerning the church, a spiritual kingdom. Klausner and the premillennialists are wrong. Jesus did not change the nature of the kingdom message which He preached. The fact is that as He more and more brought out the nature of the kingdom which He came to make possible, it became clearer that it was a spiritual kingdom, and not the kind that most Israelites wanted

Israel was and is blind when she reads the Old Testament and its prophecies of the Messiah (2 Cor. 3:12-18).

Joseph Klausner, and the Jews of Jesus' day, understood Jesus' kingdom no better than do the premillennialists. They rejected Him because He did not make Israel preeminent in a kingdom of this earth.

---

[1] *Ibid.,* pages 201-203.
[2] *Ibid.,* page 204.
[3] *Ibid.,* page 202.

They rejected Him because He did not offer them the premillennial view of the kingdom.

Missionaries, not Nationalists

If Israel as a whole had accepted Christ and His gospel, she would have become a spiritual nation sent out on a world-wide mission under the great commission. The nation would have been the first members of the new covenant. As the new covenant people of God, she would have been engaged in bringing men to God through the gospel that redeemed them from sin. If she had dedicated the time and energy to this work that she dedicated to a nationalistic struggle, what a powerful instrument she would have been in spreading this new nation throughout the world (1 Pet. 2:5-9).

But Klausner said that Israel did not accept Christ because it would have meant the death knell to their nationalistic hopes. As a matter of fact, their hopes were not realized even though they fought to death for them.

> *The Judaism of that time, however, had no other aim than to save the tiny nation, the guardian of great ideals, from sinking into the broad sea of heathen culture and enable it, slowly and gradually, to realize the moral teaching of the Prophets in* **civil life** *and in the* **present world** *of the Jewish state and nation.*
>
> *Hence the nation as a whole could only see in such public ideals as those of Jesus, an abnormal and even dangerous phantasy; the majority, who followed the Pharisees and Scribes (Tannaim), the leaders of the popular party in the nation, could* **on no account** *accept Jesus' teaching. This teaching Jesus had imbibed from the breast of Prophetic and, to a certain extent, Pharisaic Judaism; yet it became, on one hand, the negation of everything that had vitalized Judaism; and, on the other hand, it brought Judaism to such an extreme that it became, in a sense,* **non-Judaism.** *Hence the strange sight:— Judaism brought forth Christianity in its first form (the teaching of Jesus), but it thrust aside its daughter when it saw that she would slay the mother with a deadly kiss.*[1]

And so those who were offered a part in the building of Messiah's

---

[1] Klausner, *Jesus of Nazareth*, page 376.

kingdom, brought about the death of the Messiah. "...ye by the hand of lawless men (men without the law) did crucify and slay" (Acts 2:23; 4:11-12). "Therefore say I unto you, The kingdom of God shall be taken away from you, and shall be given to a nation bringing forth the fruits thereof. And he that falleth on this stone shall be broken to pieces: but on whomsoever it shall fall, it will scatter him as dust. And when the chief priests and the Pharisees heard his parables, they perceived that he spake of them" (Matt. 21:43-45).

Judaism into Non-Judaism

Christ fulfilled the law and the prophets, and in so doing He brought an end to the old covenant, of Israel as God's nation, and brought in the new covenant with the church as God's nation (Matt. 21:43; 1 Pet. 2:5, 9). It ended the Old Testament system of types (shadows) by fulfilling it in the new covenant realities. The church replaced Israel in the purposes of God. The church is to spread the gospel throughout the world.

Israel has in fact been engulfed by the "broad sea of heathen culture." Many of them today reject God and but a relatively few in Israel believe in the Old Testament. But belief in the Old Testament does not make them the Israel of God, for God long ago took away the old covenant and established the new (Rom. 7:1-7; Heb. 10:9-10). Indeed their house is desolate (Matt. 23:37-38).

Serve God Only?

Eleazar strengthened his companions for the final assault on Masada with the statement: "Since we, long ago, my generous friends, resolved never to be the servants to the Romans, nor to any other than to God himself, the time is now come that obliges us to make that resolution true In practice..."

"Next Eleazar recalled how the wind had changed direction and driven the fire against their inner wall, and he argued that 'this was the effect of God's anger against us for our manifold sins.'" Josephus also blamed the fall of Jerusalem on Israel's sins.

The diagnosis was right. Our Lord said:

> Wherefore ye witness to yourselves, that are sons of them that slew the prophets. Fill ye up then the measure of your fathers. Ye serpents, ye offspring of vipers, how shall ye escape

the judgment of hell? Therefore, behold, I send unto you prophets, and wise men, and scribes: some of them shall ye kill and crucify; and some of them shall ye scourge in your synagogues, and persecute from city to city: that upon you may come all the righteous blood shed on the earth, from the blood of Abel the righteous unto the blood of Zachariah son of Barachiah, whom ye slew between the sanctuary and the altar. Verily I say unto you, All these things shall come upon this generation. O Jerusalem, Jerusalem, that killeth the prophets, and stoneth them that are sent unto her! how often would I have gathered thy children together, even as a hen gathereth her chickens under her wings, and ye would not! Behold, your house is left unto you desolate. For I say unto you, Ye shall not see me henceforth, till ye shall say, Blessed is he that cometh in the name of the Lord" (Matt. 23:31-39).

Then followed Jesus' statement concerning the destruction of Jerusalem.

Israel had been in subjection to Rome for a long time, and Israel as a whole was not in subjection to God. Of the rejecters, Jesus said: "If God were your Father, ye would love me: for I came forth and am come from God; for neither have I come of myself, but he sent me" (John 8:42). To receive God, Israel had to receive Jesus (John 13:20).

Although the diagnosis was right (i.e., Israel's war against Rome failed because of her sins), they did not recognize that their sins were of such a nature that they led them to reject Christ, and this was their greatest sin. They did not receive the Son whom God sent (Matt. 21:33-46). Why did they fail to receive the Messiah? One basic cause was that their deluded view of the Messiah's mission led them to reject Jesus, because He offered them only a spiritual kingdom, and not nationalistic deliverance and the establishment of an earthly rule. This same attitude led them to rebel against Rome. They were not serving God only. They were serving their misconceptions of what it meant to serve God.

Religion Subservient to Nationalism

Israel in the first century rejected Jesus because they rejected His message of the kingdom, and His teaching and work as the Messiah. To them, the job of religion was to uphold Jewish nationalism. Nationalism became their religion in that all else was subservient to it. Again

Joseph Klausner said:

*Judaism is not only religion and it is not only ethics; it is
the sum-total of all the needs of the nation, placed on a religious basis. It is a national world-outlook with an ethico-
religious basis.*

*Thus like life itself, Judaism has its heights and its depths,
and this is its glory. Judaism is a national life, a life which the
national religion and human ethical principles (the ultimate
object of every religion) embrace without engulfing. Jesus
came and thrust aside all the requirements of the national life;
it was not that he set them apart and relegated them to their
separate sphere in the life of the nation: he ignored them completely; in their stead he set up nothing but an ethico-religious
system bound up with his conception of the Godhead.*

In the self-same moment he both annulled **Judaism** *as the*
life-force *of the Jewish nation, and also the nation itself as a
nation. For a religion which possesses only a certain conception of God and a morality acceptable to* **all**_mankind, does not
*belong to any special nation, and, consciously or unconscious-
ly, breaks down the barriers of nationality. This inevitably
brought it to pass that his people, Israel, rejected him. In its
deeper consciousness the nation felt that then, more than at
any other time, they must not be swallowed up in the great
cauldron of nations in the Roman Empire, which were decay-
ing for lack of God and of social morality.*

*Israel's Prophets had taught that man was created in the
image of God; they had proclaimed their message to all nations and kingdoms and looked forward to a time when they
would all call on the name of the Lord and worship him with
one accord.*

*Israel's spiritual leaders, the Scribes and Pharisees, also
looked for the time when "all creatures should fall down before
one God," and all be made "one society (a League of Nations)
to do his will with a perfect heart" (The Shemoneh-Esreh
Prayer for New Year and the Day of Atonement). And the people knew, if once they compromised their nationality, that that
ideal would be left with none to uphold it, and that the vision
would never be fulfilled. Religion would be turned to mere vi-*

sionariness, and morality would be torn and severed from life; while the manner of life of the Gentiles who were not yet capable of realizing such an ethical standard nor of being raised to the heights of the great ideal, would remain more barbarous and unholy than before.

Two thousand years of non-Jewish Christianity have proved that the Jewish people did not err. Both the instinct for national self-preservation and the cleaving to the great humanitarian ideal, emphatically demanded that Judaism reject this ethical teaching, severed, as it became, from the national life: the breach which, all unintentionally, Jesus would have made in the defenses of Judaism, must needs have brought this Judaism to an end.[1]

The attitudes, ambitions, and ideals which led them to reject Christ led them to rebel against Rome, and this led to the destruction of Jerusalem and Masada. Klausner's statement shows that nationalism is first, and religion is second. Judaism "is the sum-total of all the needs of the nation, *placed on a religious basis.*"

Israel, Klausner said, believed that she had a world-wide mission, but she rejected Jesus because He taught that Israel's function as God's nation had fulfilled its purpose and now the world-wide mission of Christ's kingdom was in force. The rejection of the concept of an earthly kingdom did not leave the Old Testament ideals without support but rather fulfilled them in the fuller revelation in the new covenant. Israel's special relationship to God in the Old Testament was contingent on her obedience to God. She disobeyed many times in the Old Testament, but her supreme disobedience was in the rejection of God's Son(Deut. 6:1-3, 13; 7:6-11; Isa. 1:2-23; Matt. 21:33-46). God said the land would vomit them out if they were not obedient to Him (Lev. 18:24-28).

Today's Israel is not even as obedient to God as was Israel in the first century. However, they continue to cling to the ideal of Jewish nationalism, and they would like for the U. S. to be dedicated to her defense.

Flee, not Fight

"When therefore ye see the abomination of desolation, which was

---

[1] *Ibid.,* pages 390-391.

spoken of through Daniel the prophet, standing in the holy place (let him that readeth understand), then let them that are in Judaea flee unto the mountains... and pray ye that your flight be not in the winter, neither on a sabbath: for then shall be great tribulation, such as hath not been from the beginning of the world until now, no, nor ever shall be" (Matt. 24:15-21).

Daniel the prophet had spoken of:

Seventy weeks are decreed upon thy people and upon thy holy city, to finish transgression, and to make an end of sins, and to make reconciliation for iniquity, and to bring in everlasting righteousness, and to seal up vision and prophecy, and to anoint the most holy... And after the threescore and two weeks shall the anointed one be cut off, and shall have nothing: and the people of the prince that shall come shall destroy the city and the sanctuary, and the end therefore be with a flood, and even unto the end shall be war; desolations are determined. And he shall make a firm covenant with many for one week: and in the midst of the week he shall cause the sacrifice and the oblation to cease; and upon the wing of abominations shall come one that maketh desolate; and even unto the full end, and that determined, shall wrath be poured out upon the desolate (Dan. 9:24-27).

The Roman armies with the idolatrous standards were the abomination which made desolation (Luke 21:20-24). And the fall of Masada was but one episode in the tragedy of a people who had rejected God's Son, who had been rejected by God, and who in their stubborn persistence to establish an Israelitish kingdom were destroyed.

The flight of the Christians, their refusal to fight for Jerusalem and the re-establishment of the kingdom of Israel, deepened the animosity between the Israel after the flesh and Israel after the Spirit (1 Cor. 10:18; Gal. 4:21-31).

It is this same nationalistic spirit (devoid even of faith in the God of the Bible for many Israelis) which led to the establishment of Israel today. But her struggles are no more blessed of God than were similar struggles two thousand years ago. And I have not seen the reversal of the Lord of His command to His people to flee, not fight for, Jerusalem. Should Christians have fled in the first century but fight in the twentieth century for the same delusion?

Begin visited a settlement on the West Bank and said: "We stand on the land of liberated Israel. There will be many many Alon Morehs,' Begin declared. Then, chiding reporters for their questions about his intentions in the West Bank, Begin said, 'We don't use the word annexation. You annex foreign land, not your own country."'[1] It is strange for Jews who do not believe in the Old Testament to talk about Palestine belonging to Israel. And even those who do believe in the Old Testament ought to realize that long ago the God-given lease on Palestine expired.

No King but Caesar

Pilate "saith unto the Jews, Behold, your King! They therefore cried out, Away with him, away with him, crucify him! Pilate saith unto them, Shall I crucify your King? The chief priests, answered, We have no king but Caesar!" (John 19:14-15). The response of the accusers of Jesus to Pilate's desire to release him, was, "If thou release this man, thou art not Caesar's friend: every one that maketh himself a king speaketh against Caesar" (19:12).

> Pilate had refused to carry out a sentence based upon Jewish opinion. The official chiefs of the theocracy converted themselves therefore into jealous guardians of the rights of the empire, and accused Pilate of negligence. The simple acceptance of the title of "king" is, they argue, a declaration of antagonism to the one emperor.[2]

Pilate acted now against Jesus, for he recognized the trouble he would be in with Tiberius if news reached the emperor that Pilate tolerated a rebel even when the Jews asked him to put him to death. In reply to Pilate's question, "Shall I crucify your King?" they said: "We have no king but Caesar!"

> [This was a] renouncing of their great national hope, the very idea of the Messiah, and a making themselves vassals of the empire. Such a victory was a suicide... [T]hey themselves pronounced the abolition of the theocracy and the absorption of Israel into the world of the Gentiles. They who cherished on-

---

[1] *Arkansas Democrat*, March 26, 1979, page 11A.
[2] Westcott, *The Gospel According to St. John*, page 271.

*ly one thought—the overthrow of the throne of the Caesars by
the Messiah—suffer themselves to be carried away by hatred of
Jesus so far to cry out before the representative of the emper-
or: "**We have no other king but Caesar.**"[1]*

*The official organs of the theocracy themselves proclaim
that they have abandoned the faith by which the nation had
lived. The sentence, "We have no king but Caesar" (the foreign
emperor), is the legitimate end of their policy, the formal abdi-
cation of the Messianic hope. The kingdom of God, in the con-
fession of its rulers, has become the kingdom of the world. In
the place of the Christ they have found the emperor. They first
rejected Jesus as the Christ, and then, driven by the irony of
circumstances, they rejected the Christ altogether.[2]*

They rejected the Christ. God rejected them (Matt. 21:43). They
are now in the world and therefore outside the kingdom, although they
still are invited into it.

---

[1] Godet, *Gospel of John*, Vol. 2, pages 378, 380.
[2] Westcott, *The Gospel According to St. John,* pages 272-273.

BIBLIOGRAPHY

Abbott, *Hebrews*[1]

E. D. Allen, *Armageddon, Studies In The Revelation of St. John*, Philadelphia: Presbyterian and Reformed Publishing co., 1964.

Jimmy Allen, *Survey of Romans*, Searcy, Arkansas: Harding College Bookstore, 1973.

J. Early Arceneaux, *The Bible Banner*, (March, 1947).

Arkansas Democrat, (March 26, 1979).

William F. Arndt and F. Wibur Gingrich, *A Greek-English Lexicon of the New Testament and Other Early Christian Literature*, Chicago: University of Chicago Press, 1979.

James D. Bales, *New Testament Interpretations of Old Testament Prophecies of the Kingdom*, Searcy, Arkansas: The Harding College Press, 1950.

Albert Barnes, *Commentary on Daniel*, Grand Rapids, Michigan: Baker Book House, 1950 reprint, Vol. 1.

Richard A. Batey, *The Letter of Paul to the Romans*. Austin, Texas: R.B. Sweet Co., 1969.

Joseph Agar Beet, *The Last Things*, New York: Eaton and Mains, 1898.

Joseph P. Berg, *The Second Advent of Jesus Christ, Not Premillennial*: Philadelphia: Perkinplne & Hlggings, 1859.

S.T. Bloomfield, *The Greek New Testament with English Notes*, Philadelphia: Henry Hopkins, 1843, Vol. 1.

Loraine Boettner, *The Millennium*, Philadelphia: The Presbyterian and Reformed Publishing Company, 1957.

---

[1] This is all the information included in Bales' manuscript. It is possible that a commentary on Hebrews by John H. Abbott is intended (date: 1976?); or it is possible that he is referring to the section on Hebrews in *Abbott's Illustrated New Testament Commentary* (1878).

R.H. Boll, *Lessons on Daniel*, Louisville, Kentucky: The Word and Truth, n.d.

——————, *The Kingdom of God*, Louisville, Kentucky: The Word and Work, n.d.

——————, *The Revelation*, Louisville: The Word and Work, 1947.

H. Leo Boles-R.H. Boll *Debate*, Nashville, Tennessee: Gospel Advocate Company, 1928.

Robert B. Boyd, *Maybe You Are Premillennial and Don't Know It*, Dallas, Texas: Good Tidings Broadcast, n.d.

John W. Bradbury, Editor, *Hastening the Day of God*, Wheaton, Illinois: Van Kampen Press, 1953.

John Broadus, *A Harmony of the Gospels in the Revised Version with new helps for Historical Study*, New York: Hodder and Stoughton, 1893.

David Brown, *The Apocalypse: Its Structure and Primary Predications*, New York: The Christian Literature Co., 1891.

——————, *Christ's Second Coming; Will It Be Pre-Millennial?* New York: Robert Carter and Brothers, 1879.

Charles E. Brown, *The Hope of His Coming*, Anderson, Indiana: Gospel Trumpet Co., 1927.

F.F. Bruce, *The Book of the Acts,* Grand Rapids, Michigan: Wm. B. Eerdmans, 1974.

——————, *The Epistle to the Hebrews*, Grand Rapids, Michigan: Wm. B. Eerdman's, 1964.

——————, *The New Testament Development of Old Testament Themes*, Grand Rapids, Michigan: Wm. B. Eerdmans, 1978.

G.B. Caird, *A Commentary on the Revelation of St. John the Divine*, London: Adam & Charles Black, 1966.

J. Estlin Carpenter, *The Johannine Writings*, New York: Houghton

Mifflin Co., 1927.

William Carpenter, *Popular Lectures on Biblical Criticism and Interpretation*, London: Thomas Tegg, 1829.

Lewis Chafer, *Satan: His Motives and Methods*, Grand Rapids, Michigan, Durham Publishing Company, 1919.

Christian News, "True Lutheran. Are Not Millennialists." November 3, 1980: 9.

Christianity Today, February 15, 1960:23-24.

——————————, March 28, 1960:36-37.

——————————, January 18, 1963:44.

——————————, May 8, 1964:19-20.

W. N. Clarke, *Commentary on the Gospel of Mark*, Philadelphia: Baptist Publication Society, 1881.

Robert C. Clouse, *The Meaning of the Millennium,* Downers Grove, Illinois: InterVarsity Press, 1977.

Burton Coffman, *Commentary on Revelation*, Austin, Texas: Firm Foundation Publishing House, 1979. I

William E. Cox, *The Millennium*, Philadelphia: The Presbyterian and Reformed Publishing Company, 1964.

J. T. Dean, *Visions and Revelations*, Edinburgh: T. & T. Clark, 1911.

D. R. Dungan, *Hermeneutics*, Cincinnati, Ohio: Standard Co., 3rd edition, 1888.

E. L. Eaton, *The Millennial Dawn Heresy*, Cincinnati: Jennings and Graham, 1911.

George P. Eckman, *When Christ Comes Again*, New York: The Abingdon Press, 1917.

Alfred Edersheim. *The Life and Times of Jesus the Messiah*, New York: Longmans, Green, and Company, 1925, Vol. 1.

Charles Ellicott, *A New Testament Commentary for English Readers*, London: Cossell and Co., 1901.

Patrick Fairbairn, *The Typology of Scripture*, New York: Funk and Wagnalls Co., 1900. Vol. 1 .

——————————, *Prophecy*, New York: Carlton & Porter, 1866.

Frederick W. Farrar, *Luke*, Cambridge: Cambridge Press, 1891.

George B. Fletcher, *The Millennium What it is Not and What it Is,* Hampton, Virginia: n.d.

A. G. Freed, *A Sermon On the Millennium*, n.d.

David Freeman, *The Bible and Things to Come*, Grand Rapids, Michigan: Zondervan Publishing House, 1939.

Cunningham Geikie, *Hours with the Bible*, New York: J. Pott and Company, 1893.

Frederich Godet, *Gospel of John*, New York: Funk and Wagnalls, 1886, Vols. 1, 2.

Gospel Light, "The Premillennial Fallacy," Delight, Arkansas: September, 1973:136.

Theodore, Graebner, *War In The Light Of Prophecy*, St. Louis: Concordia Publishing House, 1942.

P. W. Grant, *The Revelation of John*. London: Hodder and Stoughton, 1889.

J. Grier, *The Preterist and Comprehensivist Interpretation of Prophecy*, London: InterVarsity Fellowship, 1951.

Isaiah Boone Grubbs, *Commentary on Paul's Epistle to the Romans*, Cincinnati: F.L. Rowe, 1919.

Floyd E. Hamilton, *The Basis of Millennial Faith*, Grand Rapids, Michingan: Wm. B. Eerdmans, 1942. .

Alexander Hardie, *The World Program According to the Holy Scriptures*, Los Angeles: The Times-Mirror Press, 1923.

Harding College Lectures. Austin, Texas: Firm Foundation Publishing House, 1954.

E.R. Harper, *Prophecy Foretold, Prophecy Fulfilled*, Abilene, Texas: Ernest R. Haper. n.d.

Samuel Harris, *The Kingdom of Christ on Earth*, Andover: Warren F. Draper, 1838.

H.L. Hastings, *Plain Truths for Plain People,* Boston: H. L. Hastings, 1895.

William Hendriksen, *And So All Israel Shall Be Saved,* Grand Rapids, Michigan: Baker Book House, 1945.

——————, *More Than Conquerors*, Grand Rapids, Michigan: Baker Book House, 1980.

E.W. Hengstenberg, *Revelation of St. John,* New York: Robert Carter & Brothers, 1853.

George F. Holden, *Lectures on The Revelation of St. John the Divine*, London: Hugh Rees Ltd., 1903.

Victor E. Hoven, *Shadow and Substance*, St. Louis: The Bethany Press, 1934.

Archibald Hughes, *A New Heaven and a New Earth*, Philadelphia: The Presbyterian and Reformed Publishing Company, 1958.

Robert Jewett, *Jesus Against the Rapture,* Philadelphia: Westminster Press, 1979.

Ashley Sidney Johnson, *The Resurrection and the Future Life,* Knoxville, Tennessee: Knoarxville Lithographing Co., 1923

Raymond C. Kelcy, "Talking With a Premillennialist," *Firm Foundation.* November 8, 1977: 711.

J. Marcellus Kik, *Revelation Twenty*, Philadelphia: The Presbyterian and Reformed Publishing Company, 1955.

Joseph Klausner, *From Jesus to Paul*, London: George Allen & Unwin Ltd.

——————, *Jesus of Nazareth: His Life, Times, and Teaching*, New York: MacMillian Co,. 1953.

——————, *The Messianic Idea in Israel*, New York: The MacMillian Co., 1955.

George Eldon Ladd, "Church and Kingdom," *Christianity Today*, May 23, 1960:18-32.

——————, *Crucial Questions About The Kingdom of God*, Grand Rapids, Michigan: Wm. B. Eerdmans, 1952.

——————, *Jesus and the Kingdom*, New York: Harper & Row, 1964.

——————, *The Blessed Hope*, Grand Rapids, Michigan: Wm. B. Eerdmans, 1956.

G.H. Lang, *The Disciple*, Belfast: The Raven Publishing Company, 1956.

Moses E. Lard, *Comentary on Paul's Letter to the Romans*, Christian Board of Education, 1914.

William Lee, *The Revelation of St. John*, Grand Rapids, Michigan: Baker Book House, 1981.

Chester K. Lehman, *The Fulfillment of Prophecy*, Scottdale, Pennsylvania: Mennonite Publishing House, 1950.

R.C.H. Lenski, *The Interpretation of St. Matthews Gospel*, Minneapolis, Minnesota: Sugsburg Publishing House, 1964.

H.C. Leupold, *Exposition of Daniel*, Columbus, Ohio: The Wartburg Press, 1949.

Jack P. Lewis, *Matthew*, Austin, Texas: Sweet Publishing Co., 1976, Vol. 1.

Henry Liddon, *Explanatory Analysis of Paul's Epistle to the Romans*, New York: Longman, Green, 1899.

Nell Lightfoot, *Jesus Christ Today: A Commentary on the Book of Hebrews*, Grand Rapids, Michigan: Baker Book House, 1976.

Hal Lindsey, *The Late Great Planet Earth*, Grand Rapids, Michigan, Zondervan, 1970.

George Frederick Maclear, *A Class-Book of New Testament History*, London: The MacMillian Company, 1879.

George Preston Mains, *Premillennialism*, New York: The Abingdon Press, 1920.

H.G. Marsh, *The Origin and Significance of New Testament Baptism*, Manchester, England: Manchester University Press, 1941.

William Masselink, *Why Thousand Years?* Grand Rapids, Michigan: Wm. B. Eerdmans, 1953.

Philip Mauro, *Dispensationalism Justifies the Crucifixion*, Swengel, Pennsylvania: Reiner Publications, 1971.

——————, *Examination of Dr. Shailor Mathews' Pamphlet on Christ's Return*. Boston: Hamilton Brothers, n. d.

——————, *Of Things Which Must Soon Come to Pass*, Swengel, Pa: Reiner Publications, 1971

——————, *Paul and the Mystery*, Boston: Hamilton Brothers, n.d.

——————, *The Gospel of the Kingdom*, Boston: Hamilton Brothers, 1928.

——————, *The Gospel Promised Afore*, Boston: Hamilton Brothers, n.d.

——————, *The Kingdom Heresies of S. D. Gordon*, Boston:

Hamilton Brothers, n.d.

——————————, *The Ministry of Jesus Christ*, Boston: Hamilton Brothers, n.d.

——————————, *The Mission of Christ: What Was It?* Boston: Hamilton Brothers, n.d.

J.W. McGarvey and Philip Y. Pendleton, *The Standard Bible Commentary on Galatians*, Cincinnati: Standard Publishing Co., 1916.

Jim McGuiggan, *The Kingdom of God and the Planet Earth*, Lubbock, Texas: Sunset School of Preaching, 1978.

——————————, *The Reign of God*, Lubbock, Texas: Montex Publishing Company, 1979.

Jim McGuiggan and Richard Rogers, *A Synopsis of Dispensationalism*, Lubbock, Texas: Sentinel Bookstore, 1974.

S. D. Merrill, *The Second Coming of Christ*, Cincinnati: Walden and Stowe, 1879.

Harry Reigart Miller, *The Millennium*, Chickasaw, Alabama: The Biblicist Press, 1957.

John P. Milton, *Prophecy Interpreted*, Minneapolis, Minnesota: Ausgburg Publishing House, 1960.

Clifford H. Moore, Translator, *Tacitus: The Histories*, Cambridge: Howard University Press, 1931.

Robert Mounce, *The Book of Revelation*, Grand Rapids, Michigan: Wm. B. Eerdmans, 1977.

Dale Moody, *The Hope of Glory*, Grand Rapids, Michigan: Wm. B. Eerdmans, n. d.

Leon Morris, *The Revelation of St. John*, Grand Rapids, Michigan: Wm. B. Eerdmans, 1969.

Clayton A. Munro, *The Kingdom and Coming of Christ*, Boston: Richard G. Badger, The Gorham Press, 1919.

Charles Neal and Foy E. Wallace Jr., *Neal-Wallace Discussion*, Nashville, Tennessee: The Gospel Advocate Company, 1933.

Thomas Newton, *Dissertations on the Prophecies*, London: Isaac T. Hinton, 1829.

W. Robertson Nicoll, *The Expositor's Greek Testament*, Vol. 11. Grand Rapids, Michigan: Wm. B. Eerdmans Publishing Company, 1979.

W. L. Oliphant, John R. Rice, *The Oliphant-Rice Debate*, Austin, Texas: Firm Foundation Publishing House, 1935.

Bernard Orchard, *A Catholic Commentary on Holy Scriptures*, New York: Nelson, 1953.

Frank Pack, *The Gospel According to John*, Austin, Texas: Sweet Publishing Co., 1975, Vols. 1, 2.

—————————, *Revelation, Part 2,* Austin, Texas: R.B. Sweet Co., 1965.

J. Barton Payne, *Encyclopedia of Biblical Prophecy*, Grand Rapids, Michigan: Baker Book House, 1980.

W. Curtis Porter, "Notes on the Metropolis Debate." *The Bible Banner*, February. 1940:8-9.

Alfred Plummer, *A Critical and Exegetical Commentary on the Gospel According to St. Luke*, New York: Charles Scribner's Sons, 1902.

Harris Franklin Rall, *Modern Premillennialism and the Christian Hope*, New York: The Abingdon Press, 1920.

John C. Rankin, *The Coming of The Lord,* New York: Funk and Wagnalls, 1835

H. M. Riggle, *Christ's Kingdom and Reign*, Anderson, Indiana: Gospel Trumpet Company.

—————————, *The Kingdom of God and the One Thousand Years'*

Reign, Moundville, West Virgina; Gospel Trumpet Publishing Company, 1899.

Chas H. Roberson, "The Millennarian Conroversy," *Firm Foundation*, May 6, 1941:n.p.

John Roof, *Lectures on the Millennium,* Toronto: Sold by the Booksellers, 1844

Daniel-Rops, *Jesus and His Times*, New York: E.P. Dutton and Co., Inc. 1954.

M.F. Sadler, *The Epistle to the Romans*, London: George Bell and Sons, 1898.

T.H. Salmon, *Why I Left The Futurist School*. Auckland, New Zealand: The Anchor Printery, 1938.

William Sandy, *The Epistle to the Romans*, New York: Charles Scribner's Sons, 1904.

F.C.G. Schumm, *Essay on Revelation Twenty*, St. Louis: Concordia Publishing House, n.d.

Don Simpson, *Kingdom Prophecy in Review*, Fort Worth, Texas: Star Bible and Tract Corporation, 1977.

Eugene S. Smith, *Armageddon and Millennium*, Des Moines, Iowa: Gospel Broadcast Press.

Justin A. Smith, *Commentary on the Revelation*, Philadelphia: American Baptist Publication Society, n.d.

The Spiritual Sword, Vols. I and II, "The Millennium." Memphis, Tennessee: Getwell church of Christ, 1977.

Roy A. Stewart, *Rabbinic Theology*, London: Oliver & Boyd, 1961.

Ray Summers, *The Life Beyond,* Nashville: Broadman Press, 1959.

Henry Barclay Swete, *The Apocalypse of St. John*, Grand Rapids, Michigan: Wm. B. Eerdmans Publishing Company 1951.

Merrill C. Tenney, *The Book of Revelation*, Grand Rapids, Michigan: Baker Book House, 1963.

Milton S. Terry, *Biblical Apocalyptics*, New York: Eaton & Mains, 1898.

——————, *Biblical Hermeneutics*, New York: Eaton and Mains, 1890.

Joseph H. Thayer, *Greek-English Lexicon of the New Testament*, Nashville, Tennessee, 1977.

Alexander Thomson and T. Forester, Translators, *The Lives of the Twelve Caesars, by Suetonius Tranquillus*, London: G. Bell and Sons, Ltd., 1911.

Sylvia L. Thrupp, *Millennial Dreams in Action*, Den Hague, The Netherlands: Mouton & Co., 1962.

T.B. Tompson, *The Reign of Christ*, Austin, Texas: Firm Foundation Publishing House, n.d.

Peter Toon, *The Millennium and the Future of Israel: Puritan Eschatology 1600 to 1660*, Cambridge: James Clarke & Co, Ltd. 1970.

Peter J. Twisk, *The Peaceful Kingdom of Christ*, Elkhart, Indiana: Mennonite Publishing House, 1933.

Geerhardus Vos, *The Pauline Eschatology*, Grand Rapids, Michigan: Wm. B. Eerdmans, 1952.

Samuel Waldegrave. *New Testament Millennarianism, or the Kingdom and Coming of Christ as Taught by Himself and His Apostles*, Oxford: Bampton Lectures, 1854.

Foy E. Wallace Jr., *The Book of Revelation*, Nashville: Foy E. Wallace Jr. Publications, 1966.

——————, *God's Prophetic Word,* Fort Worth, Texas: Foy E. Wallace Jr. Publications, 1946.

Wilbur B. Wallis, "The Use of Psalms 8 and 110 in 1 Corinthians 15:25-

27, and in Hebrews 1 and 2." *Journal for the Evangelical Theological Society,* Winter 1972: 25-29.

John Walvoord, *The Blessed Hope and the Tribulation*, Grand Rapids, Michigan: Zondervan Book House, 1980.

——————, *The Millennial Kingdom*, Grand Rapids, Michigan: Zondervan Publishing House, 1959.

Michael R. Weed, *Ephesians*, Austin, Texas: Sweet Publishing Co.

Brooke Westcott, *The Gospel According to St. John*, Grand Rapids, Michigan: No publisher listed, 1958.

William Whiston, translator, *The Life and Works of Flavius Josephus,* Philadelphia: The John C. Winston Co., 1957.

Nathaniel M. Williams, *Commentary on the Epistles of Peter*, Philadelphia: American Baptist Publication Society, 1888.

John Wilmont, *Inspired Principles of Prophetic Interpretaion*, Swengel, Pennsylvania: Reiner Publications, 1967.

C.H. Woodruff and Arvil Weilbaker, *Biblical Analysis*, Omaha, Nebraska: Straub and Company, 1935.

Charles R. Wordsworth, *Lectures on the Apocalypse*, Philadelphia: Herman hooker, 1852.

Martin J. Wyngaarden, *The Future of the Kingdom In Prophecy and Fulfillment*. Grand Rapids, Michigan: Zondervan Publishing House, 1934.

Edward J. Young, *The Prophecy of Daniel,* Grand Rapids, Michigan: Wm. B. Eerdmans, 1953.

EL 50% DE LAS GANANCIAS DE

¡MI PERRO BOOSTER!

SE DESTINARÁ A LA UNIVERSIDAD BERGIN DE ESTUDIOS CANINOS PARA FINANCIAR LA CREACIÓN DE BECAS PARA ESTUDIANTES QUE DESEEN MEJORAR EL MUNDO UTILIZANDO EL VÍNCULO CANINO-HUMANO.

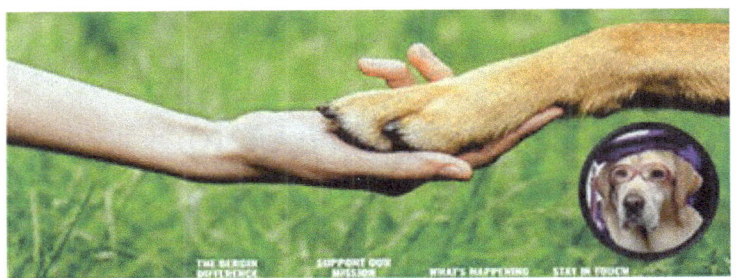

¡BOOSTER QUERRÍA ESTO!

¡MI PERRO BOOSTER!

ÉL SALVÓ MI VIDA . . .

y cambió la vida de otras personas
en todo el mundo!

DAVIS HAWN

DAVIS HAWN EDITOR
P.O. BOX 273
Pyatt, Ar. 72672

www.boosterelperrodeservicio.com

DERECHOS DE AUTOR 2024 DE DAVIS HAWN
Primera Edición -- 2024

www.boosterelperrodeservicio.com

ISBN
978-1—962832-12-0 (de tapa dura)
978-1-962832-10-6 (libro de bolsillo)
978-1-962832-13-7 (libro electrónico)

1.BIOGRAFIA Y AUTOBIOGRAFIA, MEMORIAS PERSONALES
Distribuido por Davis Hawn

Este libro está dedicado a Mi Booster, cuyo amor por la vida floreció cuando el mío flaqueaba. Él me enseñó que todo en la vida sucede por una razón, ya que inculcó la espiritualidad dentro de mi alma.

AGRADECIMIENTOS

Expreso mi agradecimiento sincero al programa Al-Anon, la luz del autoenfoque que trajo claridad y dirección a mi vida. Me enseñaron a creer en un poder superior a nosotros mismos, y para mí, es mi perro, Booster.

Doy las gracias con cariño a la Dra. Bonita (Bonnie) Bergin, quien fomentó mi educación canina, potenciando mi relación con Booster. Su abnegada dedicación a los perros y a las aulas cambió profundamente vidas, haciendo del mundo un lugar mejor.

La Dra. Elizabeth Pluhar despertó en mí la esperanza de un milagro en mis momentos más oscuros de desesperación y miseria. Al mismo tiempo, curó el cáncer de Booster y transformó mi depresión en optimismo. Booster logró mucho como resultado directo de su intervención médica que evitó su muerte segura.

La dedicación del Dr. Aubrey Beacham a la medicina veterinaria salvó la vida de mi Booster en innumerables ocasiones. Cuando otros se rindieron, él nunca lo hizo.

Los profesores Hwang-Woo-suk y Taeyoung Shin me concedieron la capacidad de seguir adelante en la vida cuando mi Booster cruzó el Puente del Arco Iris. Con su progenie, Boosted y Busted, a mi lado, tuve la nueva responsabilidad de fomentar el legado de Booster, mis estudios caninos y mi amor por la vida. Estoy profunda y eternamente agradecido.

La Dra. Pamela Tuli, mi oncóloga, me rescató cuando estaba a cuarenta y ocho horas de una muerte inminente. Gracias a ella, mi vida empezó de nuevo y tuve el tiempo precioso que necesitaba para terminar mi libro.

A mi amigo de toda la vida, Robert Bodenheimer, cuando las cosas iban mal, tú me ayudaste a levantarme, devolviéndome las ganas de vivir antes de tu fallecimiento. Te extraño mucho, amigo mío.

PREFACIO

La sociedad es cada vez más complicada, de ahí que recurramos con mayor frecuencia a los perros en busca de una solución. Cuando mi vida se tornó inmanejable, un cachorro entró sigilosamente y deshizo dos décadas de devastación emocional. Mientras el cachorro crecía, yo también lo hacía. En pocas palabras, le debo mi vida a un perro. Mi búsqueda de la autodestrucción codependiente se transformó en pasión por la superación personal y en deseo de ayudar a otras personas igualmente oprimidas. Mientras que una vez tuve una cita con la muerte y el suicidio, un perro me enseñó a vivir la vida en sus propios términos. Este libro explica la metamorfosis que se produjo en mí, cuando aprendí a comunicarme con un perro y a aceptar sus enseñanzas. En un momento parecido al de Helen Keller, tras haber estado a punto de suicidarme la noche anterior, ¡lo entendí!

A este perro tan especial no le bastó con cambiarme la vida. Viajó por el mundo, mejorando la vida de otros, ayudando a que se aprobaran leyes para los discapacitados. Muchos podrían pensar que no es posible que un perro tenga tanto impacto en el escenario mundial. Desde que falleció hace seis años, he luchado con montajes de recuerdos emocionales y turbulentos, que inmortalizan sus logros. Para los escépticos, internet ofrece pruebas de sus actos benevolentes de amor incondicional, que eran más grandes que la vida misma. Llamado involuntariamente Booster, cuando era un cachorro, hizo honor a su nombre. Él impulsó mi vida y la de otras personas en todo el mundo.

Es increíblemente difícil abrirse, compartir una vida destrozada y someterla al escrutinio de tus semejantes. Sólo lo hago para rendir homenaje a mi Booster, para que otros tengan la oportunidad de conocer la magnitud de sus logros caninos. Es lo menos que puedo hacer para rendir homenaje al perro que salvó mi vida, la cambió y transformó la vida de muchos otros. Con lágrimas en los ojos, les doy la bienvenida a nuestros corazones.

Davis Hawn Pass Christian,

Ms, Agosto 1, 2023

"He descubierto que cuando uno está profundamente atribulado, hay cosas que se obtienen de la silenciosa y devota compañía de un perro, y no es posible recibirlas de ninguna otra fuente".

— DORIS DAY

TABLA DE CONTENIDOS

PRÓLOGO

Por favor, no se deje engañar por este libro. Davis Hawn es uno de esos individuos excepcionales que atribuye a otros todas sus hazañas, emprendimientos y éxitos en la vida. Su generosidad (y su habilidad para dar crédito a otros) es lo que define quién es, lo que ha hecho y hasta dónde ha llegado para ayudar a que la vida sea un poco mejor para los demás.

Booster fue su compañero en estos esfuerzos, y los dos, en las buenas y en las malas, en la vida y en la muerte, con bondad y amabilidad, aportaron un legado de esperanza y ayuda a otras personas en todo el mundo.

Insistí en que escribiera este libro sobre estos recuerdos y momentos extraordinarios, y él, fiel a su naturaleza benevolente, dio crédito a otros por darle esta oportunidad. La generosidad fluye de su ser y cuando llegue el momento, como nos sucederá a todos, su legado será el de vivir para los demás y amarlos.

En este prólogo, soy la voz de miles de personas que habrían querido decir estas mismas cosas sobre él, quizá expresadas de manera diferente, en idiomas distintos, acompañadas de diversas experiencias, pero el resultado final habría sido el mismo – con Booster, él nos tocó a todos.

DRA. BONITA BERGIN,
UNIVERSIDAD BERGIN DE ESTUDIOS CANINOS, JUNIO 2023

INTRODUCCIÓN

"¿Qué vas a hacer con ese perro?", me preguntaron. Tardé más de una década en responder esa pregunta. Si hubiera respondido de inmediato, "El perro me va a salvar la vida (dos veces), me va a motivar para volver a la universidad y obtener un máster, va a promover las relaciones internacionales, va a participar en la búsqueda de una cura para el cáncer, me va a presentar con científicos de fama mundial y va a abrazar a niños con VIH, al tiempo que enseña a los niños con cáncer que pueden vivir con la enfermedad, todo ello mientras engaño a la muerte una y otra vez...", me habrían considerado loco. A decir verdad, mi querido perro, Booster, consiguió todo esto y mucho más. Levantó el ánimo de todos aquellos a quienes conoció. Sigue vivo de una forma poco habitual, propia de un perro traído a este mundo con un propósito divino. Te damos la bienvenida a nuestros corazones mientras compartimos nuestro increíble viaje, guiados y protegidos por un poder superior a nosotros... un poder supremo.

La manera en que *mi Booster* me rescató de las entrañas de la depresión y de una muerte inminente es incomprensible. Salvó mi vida y cambió la vida de otras personas en todo el mundo. Fue, sin lugar a dudas, el mejor maestro que he conocido. Sus lecciones de vida incluyeron la adicción, la codependencia, la espiritualidad, el amor incondicional y cómo vivir la vida misma. Inculcó en mí una pasión inquebrantable por compartir lo que me enseñó y mejorar la vida de los demás. Recurro a esa pasión para compartir los detalles más íntimos de mi vida, para que otros puedan entender la magnitud del milagro de *mi Booster*. Entra en el pozo oscuro de veinte años de estancamiento de mi vida, tal como era cuando la bomba de mi *Booster* se puso en marcha, y las mareas de efluentes emocionales cambiaron lentamente, convirtiéndome en el hombre que soy hoy.

CAPÍTULO 1
EN EL PRINCIPIO

"¿Qué vas a hacer con el perro? Sabes que no puedes cuidar de un perro", me advirtió mi hermano.

Mi vida había caído en un abismo de miedo, ¡y mi hermano se preocupaba por un maldito cachorro! ¿En serio? Llevaba mucho tiempo caminando sobre cáscaras de huevo, por años mi vida se había convertido en un cruel engaño. Inhalaba miedo y exhalaba el logro de haber vivido un segundo más. Vivir se había convertido en una maldición... en una carga. Luchar por sobrevivir el momento trascendía cualquier pensamiento sobre el mañana. *¿Qué voy a hacer con un perro? De verdad... ¿DE VERDAD?*

Lo que quedaba de mi vida era caos. Una bomba sucia de adicción había impregnado mi vida, hasta entonces sencilla. Mi adicción era hacia una persona necesitada, no a una droga. Me había vuelto adicto a los adictos. Sufría lo que clínicamente se denomina *codependencia.*

> La codependencia es un comportamiento aprendido que puede transmitirse de una generación a otra. Es un trastorno emocional y conductual que afecta la capacidad de un individuo para tener una relación sana y mutuamente satisfactoria. También se le conoce como "adicción a las relaciones" porque las personas con codependencia suelen formar o mantener relaciones unilaterales, emocionalmente destructivas y/o abusivas[1]

Cuando no estaba preocupado por que ocurriera algo malo o "revisando" cada comentario que pronunciaba a la persona adicta de mi vida, andaba preguntándome en qué me había equivocado. Había buscado

---

[1] "Codependencia," Mental Health America (Alexandria, VA: 2023). https://www.mhanational.org/co-dependency

el amor, lo había dado todo y había sufrido por ello. Sin saberlo, me había involucrado en dos relaciones con adictos merecedores del Récord Guinness, el primero adicto al alcohol, el segundo adicto al crack. No sabía que eran adictos cuando los conocí, pero supongo que me atraía ese tipo de personalidad. Dediqué una década de mi vida a cada uno.

Una vez involucrado en las relaciones, estaba decidido a curar a los adictos de mi vida. El amor lo vence todo, ¡o eso creía yo! El dolor y el sufrimiento, la confrontación física y la devastación emocional serían reparados por el caballero de brillante armadura. Después de todo, yo había cuidado de dos padres alcohólicos. Enfrenté a los médicos que recetaban Valium a mi padre alcohólico, escribiendo una carta a la Asociación Médica Americana y amenazando con enviarla por correo. Desde los ocho años, había consumido alcohol. Tenía un máster en adicciones mucho antes de que llegara la pubertad.

Hace poco, encontré un libro con garabatos en la portada que yo había escrito el 7 de febrero de 1969: "Mi papá se cayó". Había sido testigo de cómo mi padre, estando borracho, se caía por las escaleras a toda velocidad mientras le manaba sangre de la cabeza. A los cuarenta años, mi vida se volvió inmanejable, invivible e indeseable debido a la codependencia de mis adictos. Estaba atrapado, tan hiper vigilante que no podía tomarme el tiempo para concentrarme en una vía de escape. No podía ir a la tienda a comprar cuchillas de afeitar para acabar con todo sin sucumbir al mandato de mi adicto: "¿Adónde vas? . . . Será mejor que no hables de mí... Lo sabré si lo haces".

Una noche, mi adicto al alcohol estalló en furia y me exigió dinero que no tenía. Salí corriendo en la oscuridad de la noche con mi adicto detrás en plena persecución. De repente, sentí un golpe seco, un proyectil sólido impactó mi espalda causándome un dolor horrible. Más tarde supe que me había golpeado una barra de hierro. Si hubiera girado otros 90 grados, me habría apuñalado, liberándome de mi miseria. En retrospectiva, sé que habría agradecido esa nefasta libertad. Aquella noche dormí en el barro, bajo mi elevada cabaña de troncos, revolcándome en charcos de lágrimas, sollozando en silencio. Cualquier sonido habría revelado mi paradero.

Los mosquitos se deleitaban con mi cuerpo lleno de ronchas. Cuando terminaban su festín de sangre, yo aplastaba las lanzas ofensivas. Inmediatamente sentía remordimiento. Era un asesino. El dolor externo sucumbió al dolor interno, y lloré. Las ronchas de un yo quebrantado se dividían, multiplicaban y metastatizaban de forma cancerosa. Yo estaba en fase terminal, era un guerrero herido en el campo de batalla de la vida. Oré para que me llevaran en la camilla de Dios. No había vuelta atrás... ni pastilla... ni terapia... ninguna respuesta . . . y desde luego ninguna esperanza.

La noche se convirtió en un montaje mental de recuerdos de años pasados. Una vez más, me encontraba en un laberinto codependiente sin salida aparente. Nadie comprendería jamás la totalidad de la desesperanza en que se había convertido mi vida. Había caído en un profundo y oscuro agujero de desesperación y hacía tiempo que había renunciado a luchar para escapar. ¿Por qué yo? Me preguntaba. Recuerdos turbulentos bombardeaban mi conciencia mientras me encontraba aún atrapado en el peligroso campo minado de mi codependencia, impregnada de las adicciones de otros.

Recordé que hace años llevé a mi adicto al alcohol a acampar al oeste. Pensé que el esplendor de la Madre Naturaleza podría sanar a un alma maltratada por catorce botellas de 40 onzas de licor de malta al día. Junto con la tienda de campaña llegaron emociones reprimidas y cerveza. Una noche de nieve en un condado seco de Utah, me esforcé por dormir unas horas. Me despertó bruscamente un terremoto, o eso me pareció. Era la mano alcohólica meciendo la cuna del codependiente. "Se acabó la cerveza. ¡Tenemos que irnos!"

Completamente agotado, emocional y físicamente, estaba en una tienda de campaña sobre un lecho de nieve de 60 centímetros de profundidad, en un saco de dormir, congelándome. Le expliqué que no había cerveza a las 3 de la mañana en un condado seco, pero mi lógica cayó en oídos sordos y ebrios. Cuando me negué a responder, fue terrible para mí. En cuestión de segundos, tiró la tienda y me vi atrapado en un saco de dormir con camisa de fuerza dentro de una tienda colapsada. Al final salí en calzoncillos a una temperatura de 0 grados, con la cara azotada por los copos de nieve arrastrados por el viento. Iba a morir congelado.

De repente, salí corriendo hacia las duchas del camping. Una vez dentro, cerré la puerta metálica y me metí en una ducha caliente. Temblaba sin control, muerto de frío y consumido por el miedo. Planeaba dormir en el suelo y dejar que el vapor de la ducha me mantuviera caliente. Justo cuando mi adrenalina disminuía, oí un fuerte *BANG*, seguido de otro y otro. Mi adicto estaba pateando la rejilla de la parte inferior de la puerta.

"¡Voy a matarte!", gritaba una y otra vez en lo que parecía una grabación en bucle similar a las de Halloween. El final se acercaba una vez más. Me levanté a gatas del suelo de cemento, desnudo, lastimosamente resignado a esperar mi destino. El toro enfurecido y resoplando con esteroides saltó por la rampa. Con la determinación que Dios me había dado, levanté patéticamente la vista. "Estoy casi listo para salir. Si llamaste, no te escuché porque estaba en la ducha". El toro desconcertado soltó vapor como una olla a presión que estalla. Fue rápido y furioso, pero efectivo. Pronto, estábamos en el automóvil, rumbo a buscar bebidas. Mi adicto pensó que quedaba una lata de cerveza escondida en la guantera. Cuando la abrió, yo no tenía ningún as en la manga. El toro enfurecido tiró los papeles de la matrícula del auto por la ventanilla, al borde del precipicio.

Si dijera que aquella noche fue una excepción, estaría mintiendo. Los programas de doce pasos, como Alcohólicos Anónimos (AA) y Narcóticos Anónimos (NA), definen la locura como hacer las mismas cosas una y otra vez y esperar resultados diferentes. Yo estaba inequívocamente loco, por no decir otra cosa. *¿Qué es la cordura?* Me preguntaba. *¿Qué aspecto tiene? ¿Existe? ¿Está alguna vez libre de un dolor devastador?* Así era la vida cada día, cada hora, cada minuto. Estaba encerrado en un estado perpetuo de hipervigilancia y violencia, amortiguado por trampas explosivas de vestigios intermitentes y percibidos de amor falso. Esta fue mi vida durante casi dos décadas... un segundo a la vez... todos los días, por eternidades de 24 horas. Me dolía tanto que sentía el amor como el miembro fantasma de un amputado.

¿Qué vas a hacer con el perro? ¿Qué vas a hacer con el **perro**? ¡Mi hermano siente más amor por un perro que por su propio hermano! Supuse que él lo había deducido de mi estupidez por tener a un adicto en mi vida. En deferencia a mi hermano... y ruego que a muchos otros... él no podía saber por lo que yo estado pasando todos esos años catastróficos. Hacía años que él había huido de la catacumba familiar de la adicción y casi pierde la vida atravesando el tren subterráneo hacia la libertad. Pensé que él, entre todas las personas, lo entendería. No hay más ciego que el que se niega a ver. Quizás la falta de comprensión era negación y autopreservación.

Asistí a innumerables reuniones de Alcohólicos Anónimos (AA) y Narcóticos Anónimos (NA) con mis adictos. Se suele decir que la automedicación con alcohol y drogas preserva la vida del adicto hasta que está preparado para buscar ayuda y procesar el dolor. Con el tiempo conocí el programa Al-Anon, en el que aprendes a enfocarte en ti mismo y no en el adicto que hay en tu vida.

> Los Grupos de Familia Al-Anon, fundados en 1951, son una organización internacional de ayuda mutua para personas que se han visto afectadas por el alcoholismo de otra persona.[2] Los grupos de familia Al-Anon locales y virtuales proporcionan apoyo a las personas afectadas por el consumo de alcohol de otra persona. Además de las reuniones semanales y de la literatura escrita específicamente para la situación, los miembros encuentran nuevas formas de lidiar con los problemas que enfrentan. Las Tres C de Al Anon – Yo no lo causé, Yo no lo puedo controlar y Yo no lo puedo curar – son una de las cosas que muchos miembros encuentran útiles al principio del programa.[3]

---

[2] "Alateen," *Wikipedia,* https://en.wikipedia.org/wiki/Al-Anon/Alateen
[3] "Las tres C de Al-Anon," *Alcohólicos Anónimos*, https://al-anon.org/blog/al-anons-three-cs/

Cuando asistí a mi primera reunión de Al-Anon en Nueva Orleans y traté de contar mi historia como recién llegado, pronuncié una frase entrecortada y de repente fui sacudido por un tsunami incontrolable de emociones intensas y torrentes de lágrimas. Me sentía como carne derretida en el charco de los residuos de mi vida y no pude recuperar la compostura. Dos ángeles me acompañaron hasta mi auto y se ofrecieron a llevarme a casa, a más de 160 kilómetros de distancia.

Después de aquella reunión, me reencontré con mi adicto al alcohol, pagué el precio y volví a montarme en todas las atracciones. Pasaron años para que pudiera liberarme de las cadenas que me ataban, todo un drama al estilo Disney. La madre naturaleza no pudo liberar del alcohol a mi dependiente, él continuó con su candado de adicción, y acabó aferrándose a otra alma desprevenida, abandonándome. El respiro fue temporal, ya que más tarde me encontré en una relación con un adicto al crack.

Una noche calurosa en Florida, llevé a mi adicto al crack a casa de un amigo. El "amigo" resultó ser un consumado proveedor de drogas. Se abalanzó sobre mi camioneta y exigió el pago de la mercancía entregada. Pisé el acelerador mientras el adicto al crack me golpeaba y tomaba las llaves del encendido. El enfrentamiento físico se manifestó en forma de vapor en el parabrisas de la camioneta. (Años más tarde, cuando conducía y el parabrisas se empañaba, involuntariamente empezaba a temblar. Tenía que parar y relajarme antes de continuar). Mi adicto al crack encontró un cuchillo de mantequilla en el bolsillo de la puerta de la camioneta y se abalanzó sobre mí. No sé cómo evité mágicamente, la aguda realidad en qué se había convertido la vida, un aplazamiento momentáneo de una muerte prevista.

Con frecuencia me despertaba en la noche empapado en sudor y asustado, esquivando el cuchillo dirigido a mi alma. Las pesadillas recurrentes me hacían tenerles miedo a los sueños. Me cansé de casi morir noche tras noche. Sobreviví a las realidades cotidianas de la codependencia para sucumbir a los terrores de la noche. Una vez más, sentía desesperanza e incapacidad de seguir adelante.

¿Qué voy a hacer con un maldito perro? ¿En serio? Posteriormente reservé tres palabras para mi "amado" hermano, "vete al demonio".

Hacía tiempo que yo había muerto internamente y había experimentado una cremación lenta, metódica, calcinante y emocional. *¿Qué vas a hacer con el perro?* "Vete al d... tú y el maldito perro, ¿OK? ¿OK? ¿OK? Oh Dios mío, por favor... ¡que alguien me ayude... por favor... por favor!"

"¿Qué vas a hacer con el perro? No sabes cuidar de un perro".

A decir verdad, mi hermano tenía razón. Posteriormente tomé otra decisión equivocada, o eso fue lo que pensé, y me quedé con el maldito perro.

El perro al que se refería mi hermano era un cachorro que yo le había regalado a mi adicto al crack. En otro momento de desesperación, pensé que podría ser un catalizador para el cambio, un agente curativo. ¡La madre naturaleza no podía fallarme dos veces! El amor y la dependencia de un animal seguramente corregirían las frutas agrias de mi carrito emocional. *Qué idea tan brillante*, pensé. Empecé a buscar cachorros en el periódico de Nueva Orleans. Mi adicto al crack insistió en tener un labrador. Le sugerí un cachorro hembra, pensando que sería más apegado y afectivo. Tras ser reprendido por mi adicto, busqué obedientemente un cachorro macho, pensando que no sería tan apegado, ¡pero cualquier cosa era mejor que nada!

Para mi disgusto, sólo había dos anuncios de cachorros labrador en venta en el periódico. Llamé al primero y me dijeron: "Lo siento, vendimos todos los cachorros este fin de semana". Con mayor anticipación me dispuse a llamar al segundo número, temiendo una respuesta similar. Me atendió un tipo que me explicó que le quedaba un cachorro. Lo había guardado para un familiar que había cambiado de opinión en el último momento.

"¿Podría por favor, guardarme el cachorro mientras conduzco de Mississippi a Luisiana? Lo estaría recogiendo en unas horas", le pedí con desesperación. No había duda al respecto, ¡tenía una misión! ¡Iba a curar a mi adicto con el beso de la lengua canina!

A lo Sherlock Holmes, salí para hacer una llamada. En cuanto colgué, mi adicto salió y me preguntó: "¿Qué estabas diciendo?"

Le contesté: "Cosas de familia". En cuestión de minutos, estábamos en camino a una reunión de NA. Entramos en el edificio, corrimos hacia las máquinas de café y tomamos asiento entre los abatidos. Escuché innumerables historias de cómo sus vidas se habían vuelto inmanejables. Los veía como sirenas del mundo moderno, que atraían a los inocentes, para causar una devastación mucho mayor que la que ellos habían sufrido. Después de todo, ellos tenían el alcohol y las drogas para adormecer su dolor. Yo no tenía esa ventaja. Todos ellos experimentaban imprudentemente con las vidas por lo demás normales de otros. Escuchar todas esas historias deprimentes me hizo querer emborracharme lo antes posible. Pero esa no era una opción. Tenía la misión de conseguir un cachorro y curar a mi adicto al crack.

Tras la conclusión del ritual, le sugerí a mi adicto al crack que era un buen día para dar un paseo. Al no tener nada mejor que hacer, porque el trabajo no hacía parte de su vocabulario, avanzamos sin rumbo fijo por la accidentada autopista de la vida. Oré para que se convirtiera, como alude el poema de Robert Frost, en "El camino menos transitado". Seguramente, la cura canina transformaría el alma de mi adicto. Más tarde supe que NA/AA tiene un refrán: "Mantén viva una planta durante seis meses y entonces quizá puedas tener una mascota. Mantén a la mascota viva durante seis meses y tal vez puedas tener una relación con un ser humano".

"¿De verdad quieres un cachorro labrador?" le pregunté.

"Sí, ¿por qué?" fue la respuesta.

"Bueno, vamos de camino a ver uno, estamos a una hora en automóvil. ¿Estás seguro de que cuidarás de un cachorro si lo encontramos?" le pregunté. En mi modo de supervivencia cotidiana, no había caído en la cuenta de que un cachorro de labrador se convierte en una carga de responsabilidad de 45 kilos. Darle un cachorro a un adicto cuya vida se había vuelto inmanejable era una locura. Yo estaba loco. Mi vida era mucho más difícil de manejar; al menos mi adicto al crack conseguía drogas. En ese aspecto, mi adicto al crack tenía ventaja.

"¿En serio? genial", fue la respuesta. Como un adicto que busca esa piedra de crack que se le ha escapado, su entusiasmo floreció. "De verdad quiero un perro macho, ¿vale?"

Ya sabía que lo que el adicto quería, lo conseguía. Si me hubiera atrevido a sugerir un cachorro hembra, hubiera arriesgado no sólo la *cura* sino también el parabrisas de mi auto. "Bueno, no hay mucho de donde elegir. Sólo hay un cachorro, y es macho".

"¿Por qué sólo uno?" fue la respuesta rápida. Fue un glorioso ejemplo de intervención divina. Había buscado en toda la sección de clasificados de animales del periódico de Nueva Orleans y sólo había un cachorro labrador a la venta, *casualmente* macho.

"Vamos a verlo. Hace un buen día para dar una vuelta y podemos comer en algún sitio", dije.

Mi explicación fue recibida con suspicacia. Los adictos al crack suelen doblar las láminas de las persianas venecianas, asomándose al abismo del mundo exterior. Como dice el título de la canción de Elvis Presley, tienen "mentes sospechosas". Tuve que soportar los interminables comentarios. "Seguro que a ese cachorro le pasa algo. Deberíamos mirar más, antes de decidirnos por uno. ¿Por qué vamos a mirar sólo uno?"

Siempre dándole la razón a mi adicto al crack, le contesté, "Oye, estás en lo cierto, pero estamos a mitad de camino. Hace buen día y hay algo para hacer". Mi respuesta pareció apaciguar a mi adicto al crack.

Finalmente, nos detuvimos en la entrada de una modesta casa suburbana. Nos recibió un agradable y sonriente estudiante de posgrado. Él y su amigo habían criado a sus labradores. Habían logrado una conexión de suma importancia y buena intención. Ambos adoraban a sus perros y querían que otros experimentaran la satisfacción que ofrece el amor del labrador. Habían estado hablando de algunos cachorros cuando se les ocurrió la idea de criarlos. Seguro que los cachorros habían sido acogidos y amados desde el día en que llegaron al mundo de los humanos. Ojalá mi adicto al crack hubiera nacido en un mundo de inocencia y confianza. Tal vez el cachorro pudiera transformar de algún modo, el alma andrajosa pero redimible de mi adicto, en esas cualidades tan perdidas pero necesarias.

"Siempre ocurren milagros", leo con frecuencia en la literatura de NA/AA. Siguiendo esa ambiciosa ideología, mi adicto al crack no tardó en pasearse por el verde césped con un hermoso bulto de pelo amarillo persiguiéndolo a toda velocidad. Los programas de NA/AA también abogan por vivir "un día a la vez". El ansia de destrucción de mi adicto al crack lo redujo a vivir un momento a la vez. En este momento de serenidad concedido por Dios, mi adicto al crack se revolcaba en el pasto de la libertad, aferrado al amor, la aceptación y la necesidad inspirados por el canino.

"Tengo que ir al automóvil", le dije al grupo, ahora conectado con el perro. De algún modo llegué al auto, caí dentro y la represa de la condenación estalló. Temblaba y lloraba creyendo que me deshidrataría. Ya no podía aceptar lo bueno de la vida sin reaccionar emocionalmente de forma exagerada. *¿Qué me pasa?* me pregunté. *Ahora debería estar feliz, no llorando, ¡y se supone que los hombres no lloran!* Cuando la plétora de lágrimas se calmó, luché por recuperar la compostura. Cogí una camiseta vieja del suelo de la camioneta, le puse agua y me limpié con una esponja las secuelas del naufragio emocional.

Volví despreocupadamente a la escena que seguía desarrollándose en el jardín delantero.

"¿Cuándo nació? ¿Cuántos había en la camada? ¿Cuántos machos y cuántas hembras? ¿Qué le das de comer?" Las preguntas se sucedían rápidamente. *¡Recuerda El Álamo!* Una batalla de igual importancia se estaba librando en un campo suburbano. El cachorro estaba ganando por la gracia de Dios. Yo nunca había sido un hombre religioso, y hacía tiempo que la espiritualidad se había evaporado de mi mundo. Esto era lo más cercano a algo espiritual que había sentido en mucho tiempo. Tomé el dinero de mi cheque de desempleo y, sin darme cuenta, hice algo que resultaría muy complicado, ¡o que sería muy difícil para el cachorro!

"¿Cómo deberíamos llamar al cachorro?" me preguntó mi adicto al crack.

Antes de que pudiera responder, el adicto al crack respondió a la pregunta que él mismo había hecho. "Mamá tenía un perro que se llamaba Brewster, así que voy a llamarlo Boostie". Espera, exclamó mi adicto al crack, como si una revelación de proporciones incalculables, lo hubiera asaltado "¡quiero llamarlo Booster!"

Con una actitud temeraria, nos dirigimos a la tienda de animales más cercana para recorrer los pasillos de collares y correas. A continuación, se desató el debate sobre cuál era la mejor comida para perros, digna de un rey... ¡Rey Booster! El cachorro se regodeaba en el entorno afectuoso mientras mi adicto al crack enfocaba con orgullo su atención en las incesantes manifestaciones de un amor inocente e incondicional. De acuerdo con la ideología de NA/AA "sólo por hoy", mi adicto al crack encontró la felicidad, la aceptación y el amor.

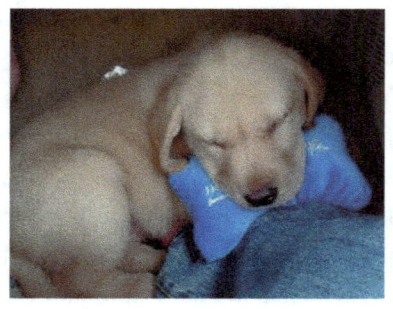

Podía bajar la guardia y relajarme por primera vez en mucho tiempo. Ajeno al mundo, el cachorro dormitó a los pies de mi adicto al crack durante todo el trayecto de vuelta a casa.

Una vez en casa, el pequeño Booster correteó en la hierba alta, saltando con gran ímpetu. Encontró una zanahoria en la hierba y corrió de un lado a otro, celebrando su nuevo hallazgo. La zanahoria fue la primera de muchas cosas que descubriría en la vida, ya que pronto se le abrieron las puertas de la realidad. ¿Era este inocente receptáculo de virtud, capaz de soportar los estragos del mundo humano en el que él había caído precipitadamente? *Sólo por hoy*, mi adicto al crack tenía una nueva adicción. Había un vínculo en desarrollo entre los indefensos, revelándose ante mis ojos. Abrazo tras abrazo curativo, se turnaban para disfrutar del afecto y la intimidad mutuos. El cachorro cuidaba de mi adicto al crack mientras yo veía cómo se desarrollaba la

Primera aparición de Booster en Televisión

escena en la gran pantalla de la vida.

De repente, el teléfono sonó. "Hola, soy mamá", dijo la voz al final de la línea.

"Mamá, tengo un cachorro, mamá. Este cachorro es especial. No lo entiendes, mamá. Es diferente".

De repente me preocupó que mamá, nada ajena a la adicción, se saliera por la tangente y no escuchara con la atención necesaria a mi adicto al crack. El castigo sería su frustración expresada en rabia. Justo la noche anterior, había esquivado un teléfono que me había lanzado por su frustración en respuesta a los comentarios de su mamá sobre su padrastro. La malla de la mecedora de caoba que le había regalado a mi madre años atrás, recibió el teléfono como una pelota de baloncesto lanzada a la canasta. El misil del teléfono no me golpeó en la cabeza, pero atravesó con facilidad el tejido

Aún no había aprendido c disfrutar del agua.

de la mecedora. Hasta una mecedora había sido presa de la furia de mi adicto al crack. De repente caí en cuenta de que había puesto a un cachorro en medio de un peligroso campo de tiro.

Inevitablemente, mi adicto al crack se frustró, ya que mamá prefería despotricar en lugar de escuchar. La conversación no fue a ninguna parte, como de costumbre. Sorprendentemente, mi adicto al crack dio por terminada la conversación y dijo: "Está enfadada otra vez. Bebiendo, como siempre".

En lugar de reaccionar y tirar algo, mi adicto al crack cogió al cachorro y entró en la casa. Pronto, el cachorro estaba bebiendo agua a lengüetazos como si llevara una eternidad perdido en el desierto. En cuestión de minutos, el cachorro orinaba en el suelo con un abandono temerario Alguien iba a tener que enseñar al cachorro a hacer sus necesidades afuera Contaba con que mi adicto al crack se responsabilizaría de su recién descubierta alma gemela. Al fin y al cabo, el cachorro era *especial*. A poco tiempo, el dúo dinámico estaba profundamente dormido en el sofá, ajeno al mundo exterior. Las semillas curativas estaban creciendo.

Por la mañana, me desperté con montones de desechos de perro en el salón. Mi adicto al crack roncaba sombríamente mientras el cachorro mordisqueaba los muebles. Ahora tenía dos fuerzas destructivas en mi vida. De repente me di cuenta de que el remedio podía ser peor que la enfermedad. Rápidamente, saqué al cachorro fuera y lo introduje en el concepto de regar el césped. Esperaba que de paso hiciera popó, pero no hubo suerte. Una vez dentro, le di de comer y empecé a limpiar el piso. Antes de que terminara de limpiar los charcos de orina, el cachorro se puso en cuclillas. "¡NO!" Le grité mientras el cachorro construía su pirámide de popó.

Mi adicto al crack se despertó, saltó y vociferó, "¡No le grites a mi cachorro!"

"Lo siento", dije disculpándome, preguntándome más tarde quién era más sumiso, si yo o el joven cachorro. Hace mucho tiempo me di cuenta de que era más fácil y seguro someterse que defenderse. *Nunca* cuestionas. Aprendes a elegir cada palabra para evitar el enfrentamiento que parece inevitable. La vida se convierte en un acto circense de caminar sobre cáscaras de huevo.

"¿Quieres desayunar?" me apresuré a preguntar para cambiar de tema.

"Vale, después de dar de comer a Booster", respondió mi adicto al crack.

Corriendo el riesgo de un nuevo enfrentamiento, le expliqué que había dado de comer al cachorro antes. Pasé por alto comentar que había fregado el suelo y recogido con éxito la pirámide de caca. Como era de esperarse, el adicto me amonestó, "Es mi cachorro y ése es mi trabajo".

"Lo siento", dije, "sólo intentaba ayudar". Enseguida serví el desayuno mientras mi adicto al crack jugaba con el cachorro y tomaba un sorbo de café. Pronto, el cachorro estaba comiendo huevos revueltos, ¡y yo acusé a mi adicto al crack de "incitarlo"!

"Eso es una estupidez", me contestó. En efecto, era estúpido, pero seguro.

Había aprendido a elegir mis palabras con cuidado, intentando inyectar humor siempre que fuera posible. El humor, cursi o no, era una cortina de humo que pronto envolvió mi vida. Me había convertido en el rey de los juegos de palabras sin gracia.

Sin mucho preámbulo, el dúo decidió dar un paseo. Yo vivía en el campo, en 20 acres de lo que había sido un terreno inservible. Era una colección de barrancos que había comprado en un anuncio clasificado. Más tarde compré un montón de materiales de construcción en mal estado y construí una cabaña de troncos. No tuve sistema séptico durante cinco años, y la maleza empezó a adorarme. A las serpientes les encantaban las malas hierbas, y no tardé en tener un auténtico ecosistema en mi pequeño mundo. Conseguí que me prestaran una excavadora, construí una presa en los barrancos y creé un estanque. Acabé teniendo una propiedad frente al mar en la Riviera redneck. Mi propiedad era mi arca. Tenía cabras, cerdos, ovejas y bichos.

La vida era una bendición hasta que introduje una especie humana... *Homo sapiens addicta*. La naturaleza depredadora de la especie dificultó la supervivencia de otras formas de vida. Al poco tiempo, éramos sólo yo y mis adictos. No hay tiempo para los demás cuando tienes un adicto en tu vida. A menudo dejaba de visitar a mi padre en la residencia de ancianos para dedicarme a curar de forma codependiente a mis adictos. Como lirios de agua que languidecen en un estanque obstruido, mi vida se estancó.

"Date prisa", me dijo una voz.

Corrí al patio delantero para ver al cachorro corriendo hacia mi adicto al crack.

"Ya sabe su nombre. Voy a enseñarle a dar la mano. Estoy deseando que mamá lo vea", retumbó la voz. En los días siguientes, la cara de mi adicto al crack se tiñó de carmesí por los días que pasaba jugueteando en el sol con el alegre manojo curativo. "Dame la pata... Dame la pata... Dame la pata", le hacía señas mi adicto al crack. El cachorro le obedeció antes de que acabara el día. O mi adicto al crack tenía un talento oculto, o el cachorro, con la paciencia de Job, aprendió que él también tenía que ser sumiso. En cualquier caso, tanto mi adicto al crack como el cachorro estaban aprendiendo.

De repente reflexioné sobre la dualidad del cachorro. Era a la vez alumno y maestro. Con sólo diez semanas de vida, el cachorro ya estaba enseñando a vivir a un humano. Supuse que el amor incondicional de un cachorro indefenso, trascendía la personalidad recelosa y desconfiada de un adicto desvalido. Superman era vulnerable a la kriptonita; quizá mi adicto al crack era sensible al amor canino incondicional. En lugar de juzgar, el cachorro simplemente aceptaba y daba amor.

¿Cómo era posible que mi adicto al crack, que había comido en contenedores de basura, dormido en el bosque y vendido zapatos con los pies cansados por el crack, de repente irradiara orgullo? El adicto al crack y el cachorro eran inseparables día y noche. El cachorro atraía a gente amable en las tiendas de animales, los parques y los patios de recreo. "¿Quieres acariciarlo?" preguntaba con frecuencia mi adicto al crack.

Una vez que los transeúntes acariciaban al cachorro, lo colocaban en el suelo para el gran final. "Dale la pata", ordenaba mi adicto al crack, y la pata del cachorro chocaba triunfalmente con la mano del desconocido, sin malicia. El cachorro sabía lo que se esperaba de él y parecía disfrutar de la oportunidad de complacer no sólo a su amo, sino a todos los que deseaban conocerlo. Más tarde aprendí que las personas que aman a los animales son especiales. Los que no, son mercancía defectuosa que debe devolverse a los vendedores para que la reprogramen.

El cachorro lo dio todo durante las primeras semanas, encapsulado en una relación simbiótica de la más alta magnitud. Era todo un espectáculo contemplar cómo mi adicto al crack se sentía orgulloso y se responsabilizaba de un alma canina indefensa. Tal era el milagro que se desarrollaba ante mis ojos inyectados en sangre. Sin embargo, al cabo de unas semanas, la novedad se desvaneció y me encontré ayudando a cuidar al cachorro. El cachorro crecía, al igual que el tiempo que yo dedicaba a su bienestar. Las pirámides de popó pronto se convirtieron en una expansión urbana.

A las pocas semanas, las cosas cambiaron. La novedad del amor y la aceptación incondicionales no era suficiente para justificar el esfuerzo de cuidar de un cachorro. Un día, mi adicto al crack gritó, "Destrozó otro juguete y tengo que limpiarlo... y me mordió los cordones de los zapatos, maldita sea... ¡los que acabo de conseguir!" Eran los zapatos robados de una tienda, por los que casi me arrestan. Mi adicto al crack había entrado en una tienda y cambiado los zapatos viejos por los nuevos. Una vez dentro del automóvil, me dijo que me diera prisa porque habían llamado a la policía. Una vez más fui cómplice de la adicción. Me sentí orgulloso del cachorro que acabó con el contrabando ilegal, fácilmente obtenido y fácilmente destruido. Tanto mi adicto al crack como el cachorro eran destructivos. Yo lo llamaba ¡igualdad de cachorros!

De repente, el cachorro gritó de dolor al ser golpeado duramente por la mano que había aprendido a amar y en la que había confiado.

"¿Por qué golpeaste al cachorro?" le pregunté.

"Porque me mordió y me dolió".

"Eso es lo que hacen los cachorros", le expliqué, "cuando mastican y afilan los dientes".

"¡Pues a mí no me va a morder! ¡Va a aprender!"

Por desgracia, el cachorro aprendió, y eso me entristeció. El humano al que había colocado en tan alto pedestal de admiración empezó a prestarle menos atención, a estar resentido con él y a hacerle daño físico. El proceso era lento, pero innegable. La dinámica estaba preparada para lo inevitable. No era una cuestión de si, sino de cuándo el cachorro recibiría un golpe demasiado fuerte o sería arrojado al otro lado de la habitación como el teléfono que había atravesado la malla de la mecedora.

Me odio, pensé. Era culpa mía lo que estaba ocurriendo. Había confiado en otra alma para que me ayudara con mi problema de codependencia. Un inocente estaba sufriendo y era probable que lo mataran. Tenía que encontrar una salida. Tenía que haber otra manera que no fueran las repetidas oraciones que quedaban sin respuesta. Incluso Dios me había abandonado a mi suerte. ¿Cuán cruel es un mundo sin Dios, lleno de codependencia y adicción, un mundo en el que un cachorro hermoso, inocente, confiado, incondicionalmente cariñoso y adorable paga el precio? Odiaba el mundo, me odiaba a mí misma y, sobre todo, odiaba la vida.

La noche siguiente, me desperté y mi adicto al crack y mi cachorro no estaban por ninguna parte. Sin duda, mi adicto estaba en otra carrera de crack en los barrios de la condenación... ¡esta maldita nación! Del crack a la metanfetamina, a la heroína, a Dios sabe qué... la gente sufría sin cesar. Vi el programa de televisión *Intervención* y fui testigo de abuelos llorando en brazos de niños, llorando en solidaridad con sus seres queridos caídos en los campos de batalla de la adicción. Los miembros de la familia cumplían con su deber en su propio mundo de codependencia. Yo no quería participar en la locura continua de la realidad. ¿Por qué iba a hacerlo? ¿Para qué? Empecé a llorar y a temblar, y luego vomité la poca comida que había ingerido horas antes. Había perdido peso, sueño y cualquier vestigio de amor propio que pudiera haber tenido alguna vez. Mientras mi vida caía en espiral, vi salir el sol. Lo único que estaba a punto de girar era el pomo de la puerta. Mi adicto al crack entró en la cabaña, y miró por las persianas para asegurarse de que la KGB ya no lo seguía.

"¿Dónde está el cachorro?" le pregunté.

"¿El cachorro? Está en la camioneta, pero no voy a salir".

Salí, llevé al maldito cachorro dentro y me acosté. No le di agua ni comida. Cuando me desperté horas más tarde, me apresuré a alimentar al cachorro, que movía la cola como un limpiaparabrisas en señal de gratitud, lavando el resentimiento que, con razón, podría haber albergado. Las cosas empeoraron progresivamente, como seguramente era de esperarse. Las noches y los días, como imanes que se atraen, pronto fueron uno solo. La luz se convirtió en oscuridad, y la oscuridad en luz. Buscaba conciliar el sueño cuando mi adicto al crack me bendecía con su desaparición. Sin embargo, también estaba preocupado por mi adicto al crack, las drogas, las armas, la policía y la muerte. No me inquietaba por el cachorro que también iba y venía. De alguna manera, el cachorro se perdió en mi conciencia. Sencillamente, ya no había sitio en la posada para las preocupaciones. Estaba mental y emocionalmente en bancarrota.

Mi vida pronto se tornó borrosa. No podía recordar lo que había sucedido el día anterior, y mucho menos ningún otro día. Los acontecimientos se mezclaban, se difuminaban e incluso desaparecían. Me esforzaba por conceptualizar lo que había sucedido y me preocupaba estar en las primeras fases del Alzheimer, o quizá en las últimas. Me asustaba la idea. Al día de hoy, no puedo establecer una cronología de los acontecimientos que tuvieron lugar. La vida se había convertido en un pozo negro que no podía aclarar. Me revolcaba en el sedimento de los excrementos de la vida. "Que Dios me conceda la capacidad de aceptar las cosas que no puedo cambiar, cambiar las que sí puedo, y la sabiduría para reconocer la diferencia", pregonan los programas de doce pasos. ¡Ése sí que es un concepto con el que me identifiqué con total claridad! No podía cambiar las cosas que sucedían precipitadamente en mi vida. Después de casi dos décadas de dominación, consideré seriamente poner fin a mi vida. Esperaba con impaciencia la libertad absoluta. Yo era un maestro en ayudar a los demás. Por una vez, ¡merecía hacer algo para mí mismo!

Un día, en el que me encontraba absolutamente desesperado, llamé a uno de los pocos amigos que me quedaban en el mundo. Curiosamente, era un chico con el que mi adicto al crack y yo habíamos entablado amistad en una reunión de NA. Solíamos asistir juntos a las reuniones, salíamos a comer o íbamos al cine. Éramos como los tres mosqueteros inadaptados, luchando juntos para mantener la cordura *día a día*. Buscar la sensatez en el mundo de la adicción era enloquecedor. Era una verdadera contradicción. Lo mejor que podía decirse era que la unión hace la fuerza. Ese día pedí a esa fuerza y a mi amigo que me ayudaran a escapar de mi Alcatraz. En el plazo de una hora, él llegó en su carro que humeaba como un tren diésel de mercancía. La carrocería del automóvil se parecía al cuerpo de mi amigo, ambos llenos de cicatrices y deteriorados.

"Hola, viejo, ¿cómo estás?" preguntó mi amigo.

"Un poco aburrido", respondí. "Vayamos al casino a pasar el rato, quizá nos ganemos unas copas gratis. ¡Podemos fingir que jugamos!"

Mi adicto al crack escuchó atentamente, pero optó por no unirse a nosotros. Obviamente, tenía un plan en marcha. Yo estaba agradecido de poder escaparme y no tener otro plan más que huir. Agotado una vez más, me subí al coche lleno de humo y nos fuimos. Mi amigo sabía que yo estaba sufriendo, ya que él, en las calles, se había enfrentado al agotamiento en innumerables ocasiones. Lo miré a los ojos y le dije: "Gracias, amigo". En los programas de AA/NA aprendí que "reforzamos nuestra recuperación compartiéndola con los demás", refiriéndose a la serenidad. Al hacer trabajos de servicio para ayudar a los demás, los adictos suplantan el sentimiento de inutilidad por la autoestima. Mi amigo valoraba ayudarme tanto como yo valoraba su ayuda y su amistad.

Pasamos la tarde en el casino, viendo cómo los que tenían dinero lo regalaban. Era otro peligroso campo de minas de adicción a punto de explotar. Al igual que las minas terrestres olvidadas en Camboya, algunos acabarían cayendo presa de los peligros del pasado. La estimulante dosis de hoy tendría que repetirse una y otra vez en el futuro. Para muchos, no era una cuestión de *si*, sino de *cuándo*. Dondequiera que miraba en mi mundo, veía adicción. Hicieron falta las maravillas del programa Al-Anon para enfocar mi mundo miope en *mí*.

Al final del día, no podía volver a casa. No podía quedarme con mi amigo, ya que él vivía en un centro de reinserción para adictos en recuperación. Llamé a una amiga que estaba en el programa Al-Anon. Ella y otra señora vivían juntas en una bonita casa a las afueras de la ciudad. Ella me invitó a quedarme en su casa. Hablamos durante horas sobre los estragos de la codependencia. Escuché repetidamente que "la codependencia mata".

"¿Puedo invitar a mi adicto al crack alguna vez?" le pregunté.

Ella respondió: "Nunca debes decirle a tu adicto al crack dónde vivimos. Queremos que siempre tengas un refugio seguro al que acudir y no queremos que tu drama invada nuestra casa".

Vaya, pensé, qué *comentario de doble filo*. Mi adicto al crack no era bienvenido, y me costaba entender por qué.

Aquella noche me quedé en su habitación de huéspedes. En mitad del sueño, tuve pesadillas que hacían que Freddy Kruger pareciera un filántropo. De repente, me levanté precipitadamente y vomité el contenido de mi estómago sobre la pared blanca. Luché por respirar, asfixiándome mientras el líquido obstruía mis conductos respiratorios. Finalmente, pude hacerlo. Fue horrible. Fue realmente horrible. No pude respirar lo que me pareció una eternidad antes de poder resollar y respirar lentamente. El aire no era suficiente y tenía que inspirar con fuerza.

Al final, empecé a toser y a despejar las vías respiratorias. De repente, se encendió la luz y miré a mis dos amigas. Empecé a sollozar. Una se sentó en la cama y me abrazó, apretándome introdujo amor en mis venas. Miré el vómito que ahora goteaba por la pared. Temblaba de vergüenza. Qué patético me había vuelto. Como solía decir mi padre, "Inútil como las tetas de un toro". ¡Yo era una gran teta de toro! Las señoras limpiaron la pared mientras yo permanecía sentado y temblando en la cama. Apagaron la luz y salieron de la habitación después de asegurarles que estaría bien.

Me desperté hacia el mediodía cuando llamaron a mi puerta. "El café está listo", fue el toque de corneta del día. Me vestí y me reuní a tomar el café con las señoras. Más tarde me indicaron que saliera al patio trasero y me acostara en la hamaca. Era un día cálido y soleado, así que me desnudé y me metí en la hamaca. Estas chicas nunca habían visto a un hombre entrar, desnudarse y tumbarse en su patio. En lugar de pensar de forma extraña, se alegraron de poder ayudarme y de que yo estuviera dispuesto a intentar ayudarme a mí mismo.

No podía vivir con ellas para siempre. Tenía que volver a la mazmorra de la depresión.

"Oigan chicas, aunque me gustaría quedarme con ustedes para siempre, tengo que volver a casa".

"Lo entendemos y si hay algo que podamos hacer para ayudar, llámanos".

"Bueno, para ser honesto, me temo que mi adicto al crack se va a enojar porque me quedé lejos. ¿Estarían dispuestas a ir conmigo para ayudar a suavizar las cosas?"

Cuando llegamos a mi casa, mi camioneta no estaba por ninguna parte. Me sentí aliviado, pero preocupado. No tenía que enfrentarme a mi adicto al crack, pero eso significaba que tendría que hacerlo más tarde. Las señoras me dieron un abrazo y se despidieron de mí. Encendí el televisor y, sin mucho entusiasmo, me puse a ver comedias. Horas más tarde, descubrí una pirámide de un día del cachorro. De repente, caí en cuenta de que el cachorro tampoco estaba en casa. Tanto el cachorro como mi adicto al crack habían desaparecido. Había que esperar a que volvieran y ver en qué condiciones llegaban.

Finalmente, me adormecí con la sinfonía de los grillos que retozaban en la maleza, la luz de la luna iluminaba lo que una vez había sido mi estanque Walden. Mi mente parecía una pista de NASCAR, con pensamientos compitiendo entre sí por el dominio. Finalmente, los pensamientos chocaron y las banderas a cuadros del sueño ondearon precariamente. De algún modo, hice una parada en boxes para dormir, sabiendo que el peligroso camino de mi vida podría reanudarse en cualquier momento. *Sólo por hoy*, dormí.

Por la mañana me desperté con una llamada telefónica. "Oye, viejo, ¿dónde está el cachorro?" Reconocí la voz, era el principal proveedor de drogas de mi adicto al crack. Semanas antes, el tipo y su señora habían sido invitados a dormir en mi cabaña por insistencia de mi adicto al crack. Se trataba de un tipo que llevaba a mi adicto al crack a los centros comerciales a hacer "devoluciones" para conseguir tarjetas de regalo por mercancía devuelta sin recibos. Por supuesto, no había recibos, ya que mi adicto al crack cogía descaradamente los artículos de las estanterías de las tiendas y se paseaba por los mostradores de devoluciones, devolviendo un regalo de cumpleaños tras otro. "Hay un cachorro que se supone que tengo que comprar".

Maldición... Maldición ... Maldición ... Maldición ... Maldición ... pensé. El cachorro se había ido, para ser sometido a pasar su vida en el extremo de una cuerda, estacado al suelo por una pieza de 3 pies de esclavitud. Los cretinos que hacen eso deberían ser atados al suelo con una cuerda de la misma longitud que la justicia.

Estaba preocupado por mi adicto al crack, y en menor medida, por el cachorro. No podía permitirme preocuparme por un maldito cachorro. El mundo estaba lleno de cachorros maltratados. Necesitaba concentrarme en una cosa a la vez. Tenía que curar a mi adicto al crack. El cachorro tendría que esperar. *¿Dónde está mi adicto al crack?* me pregunté. *¿Dónde está mi camioneta?* Por suerte, tenía un vehículo secundario. Intenté seguir con mi vida, pero pronto me di cuenta de que no tenía vida sin mí adicto al crack. Me había acostumbrado tanto a la montaña rusa de su estilo de vida, que un estilo de vida normal, fuera lo que fuera, me parecía anormal. Pasaban los días sin saber nada de él. Era Hansel sin Gretel y sin piedras que me guiaran, totalmente perdido en el camino de la autodestrucción. Había perdido todo propósito y dirección. No podía enfocarme. Faltaba el ingrediente primordial de la receta de mi vida. Inundado simultáneamente de preocupación y alivio, estaba totalmente perdido. En otras palabras, era un barco sin timón, una canoa sin remo. Los días se convirtieron en semanas, y al final tuve que presentar una denuncia policial por la desaparición de mi camioneta. No era la primera vez que mi adicto al crack me obligaba a presentar una denuncia por uso no autorizado de un vehículo.

La oficina del sheriff local se mostró reacia a tomar la denuncia. "Haremos un informe por última vez. Después de esto, ¡no vamos a perder el tiempo!" vociferó el oficial.

Lo entendí. No podía culpar a la oficina del sheriff. Al fin y al cabo, era mi adicto al crack, no el suyo. La denuncia se presentó y se avisó a la compañía de seguros.

Pasó un mes y ni adicto al crack, ni camioneta, ni cachorro. Yo había vuelto a trabajar en el parque de remolques que estaba construyendo. Por suerte, había contratado a una pareja de jubilados para que trabajaran para mí y se encargaran de eso. Ellos sabían lo que estaba pasando. Ellos gestionaban mi negocio del parque de remolques sin meterse en mis asuntos personales. Eran las piedras preciosas en el pozo de basura de mi vida; se preocupaban pero nunca criticaban. Tenían la sabiduría de la edad y sabían que el escenario tenía que desarrollarse, fuera como fuera. Ni el mismísimo Julio Verne podría haber imaginado los días que vendrían.

Una tarde, el teléfono sonó sin cesar. Sabía que era mi adicto al crack, cansado de vivir en el barrio, comiendo de nuevo en los basureros. Corrí hacia el teléfono.

"Hola, lo llama su compañía de seguros de automóvil. Nos gustaría saber si recuperó su vehículo", preguntó el representante de la aseguradora.

"No", contesté, "y vaya si lo echo de menos".

"Bueno, han pasado más de treinta días y estamos dispuestos a hacerle una oferta", exclamó la voz grave del hombre. Me hizo una oferta y acepté sin reparos. Al fin y al cabo, sólo me preocupaba mi adicto al crack, no la camioneta ni el dinero.

Al día siguiente, oí timbrar el teléfono. Una vez más, corrí como el atleta Jesse Owen para responder a la llamada.

"Hola, ¿está el Sr. Dave Hawn?"

"¿Quién lo busca?" pregunté bruscamente.

"Soy de Auto Wreckers. La policía estatal de Luisiana nos hizo remolcar una camioneta después de detener a la persona que la conducía. No lo llamaríamos si no fuera porque había un cachorro dentro", explicó el hombre. "Tiene que llamar a ese cachorro 'Le ahorramos dinero'. Normalmente, nos ponemos en contacto con la comisaría de nuestro estado, y ellos se comunican con la de su estado, y al final alguien de su estado lo llama a usted. Nos ganamos los gastos de depósito todo el tiempo".

Un policía de un estado vecino detuvo al camión en la madrugada. El conductor de Wrecker, que trabajaba en el turno de noche (de 6 de la tarde a 6 de la mañana), se despertó al día siguiente y recordó que había un cachorro en la camioneta que había transportado la noche anterior.

Qué extraordinaria **coincidencia,** pensé.

Llamó a su jefe, que salió corriendo hacia la camioneta en busca de un cachorro probablemente muerto. Hacía casi 40 grados en un día de verano abrasador en Luisiana. El jefe del deshuesadero rompió una ventana para acceder al camión cerrado. En unos instantes, encontró al cachorro jadeando desesperadamente en el asiento delantero, esperando pacientemente el regreso de su amo. El cachorro no era consciente de su muerte inminente, pues confiaba en que su amo volvería. Ambos esperábamos el regreso de nuestro humano para poder seguir con nuestras respectivas vidas. Irónicamente, la realidad dictaba que ambos nos enfrentábamos a la muerte por asociación. Resultó que el dueño del deshuesadero era un amante de los perros y casualmente su sobrino trabajaba en la cárcel. Hizo que su sobrino localizara al conductor del camión para averiguar un número de contacto para que alguien viniera a buscar al cachorro.

Llamé al encargado de mi parque de remolques, mi Peñón de Gibraltar, y le conté la noticia. El príncipe de los hombres insistió en llevarme a buscar mi camioneta y al cachorro abandonado que había escapado por poco de una muerte por abandono. Cuando por fin llegamos al deshuesadero, el dueño le dijo a un empleado que fuera a buscar al cachorro a la casa. Poco después, el cachorro salió, cargado en los brazos cubiertos de grasa del hombre. Aunque apenas me conocía, el cachorro respondió como si hubiera tomado una sobredosis de pastillas de la felicidad. Tomé posesión del animal, sin impresionarme de que me mirara a los ojos buscando escudriñar lo profundo de mi alma.

Cuando llegué a casa, dejé que el cachorro correteara por el jardín delantero mientras yo iba inmediatamente al teléfono para averiguar el horario de visitas de la cárcel donde se encontraba mi adicto al crack. Al día siguiente, fui a visitarlo. La conversación derivó rápidamente en un enfrentamiento verbal. Al parecer, era culpa mía que estuviera en la cárcel porque yo había presentado una denuncia por uso no autorizado, como exigía la compañía de seguros. ¡No era culpa de mi adicto al crack haberse fugado con la camioneta y haberse pasado un semáforo en rojo!

Sabía que no pasaría mucho tiempo antes de que mi adicto al crack fuera puesto en libertad anticipada por buen comportamiento. Los adictos son los mejores actores del mundo, pues han perfeccionado sus habilidades para tejer sus redes de engaño. Mi adicto al crack podía hechizar a una serpiente de cascabel infectada de rabia y, con el talento de Houdini, escapar de su confinamiento, legalmente o de otra manera. Yo estaba atrapado en una telaraña y quería salir. En cuanto los tentáculos traicioneros de la codependencia volvieron a apoderarse de mí, supe que podría ser la última vez. Llevaba veinte años con un estilo de vida autodestructivo y ya no quedaba mucho de mí. *¿Cómo era yo antes del problema de codependencia?* me pregunté en un ejercicio de interrogación e introspección. No podía seguir viviendo en mi casa. El miedo a que mi adicto al crack volviera, y las repercusiones que ello conllevaría, era demasiado para mí.

Llamé a mi amigo Charles y le pedí ayuda. Él había cambiado su vida tras años de abusos, aprendiendo a cuidar de sí mismo y a evitar las influencias negativas. Llegó a ser tan bueno en la autoprotección que solía desechar las amistades antes de que echaran raíces. Si Charles sospechaba algo, actuaba antes de reflexionar y, por lo tanto, las amistades potenciales a menudo quedaban en el olvido. Insistió en que me fuera a vivir con él a la habitación de huéspedes de su modesta casa móvil. Tenía una piscina en el patio trasero y a menudo celebraba fiestas en ella. Era un maestro en disfrutar de un estilo de vida sencillo. Lo envidiaba. Él de inmediato me acompañó a la cabaña para protegerme si mi adicto al crack aparecía sin avisar, como solía ocurrir. Tomé ropa, la puse en una bolsa de basura *Samsonite* y la metí en mi camión. Ah sí, también metí al cachorro. A Charles le encantaban los animales y tenía un rottweiler con correa en el patio trasero. Me preguntaba si el rottweiler devoraría al cachorro. Esperaba que no, pero tomar precauciones no estaban en mi lista de prioridades. Sólo la autopreservación. Me sentía como una carga para mi amigo. Después de todo, él había criado a sus hijos. No necesitaba criar a otro. Me sentía impotente, inútil y desesperado, como siempre. Yo era otro pezón de toro.

Una vez leí que cuando los indios americanos envejecían y se volvían improductivos, se iban a morir con dignidad en una cueva. Dispuesto a entrar en mi cueva, despojado de la dignidad que había tenido décadas atrás, me sentía desnudo y vulnerable. Vaya, pensé, *¡como un cachorro!* Hablando de cachorros, miré al gran arquitecto de la pirámide, una vez más construyendo un nuevo testimonio de su talento. *Rayos*, pensé, tiene que ser una broma, mientras el cachorro volvía a descargar sus intestinos dentro de la cabaña. Estaba enfadado, pero en el fondo, sabía que el cachorro no había tenido la oportunidad de adaptarse a nuestro mundo. Mis adictos al alcohol y al crack se habían ensuciado en mí día tras día, así que ¿por qué no lo haría el cachorro? ¡La vida era un proverbial cubo de excrementos con el asa por dentro! Salí de la cabaña, con el cachorro en la mano, y me fui a casa de mi salvador Charles.

Al día siguiente, me quedé sin material para construir pirámides, también conocido como comida para perros. Cogí al cachorro, lo metí en la camioneta y me dirigí a la tienda. Mientras conducía, vi un pequeño remolque tirado por una camioneta Ford pick-up blanca y desgastada. *Casualmente*, ¡era un clon exacto de la camioneta que yo conducía! En ese mismo momento, tuve una epifanía. Quizá podría comprar un pequeño remolque y llevarlo detrás de mi camioneta. Esa misma noche, como de costumbre, vi las noticias con Charles, con quien vivía desde hacía más tiempo del que podía recordar. Sentía que me estaba convirtiendo en una carga, pero Charles era muy buen amigo como para reconocerlo. Le comenté mi idea, y al día siguiente empezamos a buscar un remolque que pudiera arrastrar con mi camioneta. Iba a ser mi cápsula de escape. ¡Si los astronautas de la NASA podían tener una, yo también!

A los pocos días, encontramos un remolque apropiado que estaba bastante bien. *Casualmente*, unas semanas antes había recibido una tarjeta de crédito por correo, así que saqué un adelanto en efectivo de la tarjeta y lo compré. Llamé a los responsables del parque y les informé de mis planes de fuga. Nunca supieron la verdadera profundidad de la depravación que había rodeado mi vida. Ellos sabían que necesitaba escapar, pero no sabían que era literalmente una situación de vida o muerte. Yo era incapaz de explicar mi pérdida de identidad. Más tarde leí sobre el concepto de "vínculo de traición", en el que una persona queda atrapada, codependiente de otra, durante un periodo prolongado. La persona codependiente se niega a romper el vínculo enfermizo, ya que eso restaría sentido a toda la relación. Saber que todo lo que habías invertido en la relación, podía resumirse en que se habían aprovechado de ti, era una traición. Más que un compañero, tú eras un simple facilitador.

CAPÍTULO 2
RENDICIÓN Y ÉXODO

Al día siguiente, me puse en marcha, remolcando mi nuevo hogar, sin tener ni idea de adónde me dirigía. Me debatí entre la idea de llevarme o no al maldito perro, pero pensé que él ya había sufrido a manos del adicto al crack, igual que yo. No podía llevarlo a la perrera ni dejarlo para que mi adicto al crack acabara con él por negligencia. Lo más probable es que lo cambiaría a su proveedor por crack. Yo no quería al cachorro, pero tampoco quería que se convirtiera en parte integral de un ritual de sacrificio. Por fin era libre. Bajé la ventanilla de la camioneta y respiré profundamente el aire mientras iba a 110 kilómetros por hora. Miré a mi derecha y vi que el cachorro viajaba a mi lado y asomaba la nariz por la ventanilla. Los caninos tienen un agudo sentido del olfato, mucho mayor que el de los humanos. El cachorro olió la libertad a una edad temprana.

Yo me di por vencido... pero mi Booster nunca lo hizo. No sabía que viajar con un perro me complicaría la vida. Cuando paraba por combustible, tenía que pasear al maldito perro. Cada vez que comía en un restaurante en la carretera, tenía que dejar la camioneta en marcha con el aire acondicionado encendido. En raras ocasiones, en las que decidía quedarme en una habitación de hotel, solían denegarme el acceso porque tenía al perro. Algunos parques de remolques de todo el país no admitían mascotas. Con frecuencia alimentaba al cachorro con maravillosas sobras humanas y él, a su vez, me recompensaba con flujos de diarrea parecidos a la lava. Todo un detalle, ¿verdad?

Mi mayor resentimiento era el hecho de que cada vez que sacaba a pasear al maldito perro, a parques de remolques o a los campos detrás de las gasolineras, la gente *siempre* se me acercaba para que les permitiera acariciarlo. "Extraño a mi perro, ¿puedo acariciar al tuyo?"

"Qué perrito más lindo", decían con frecuencia.

Yo pensaba: ¿Qué tiene de lindo la diarrea, imbécil?

"Pasear al perro es un ejercicio estupendo", decían otros.

Mi respuesta preferida era: "Ojalá te ejercitaras alejándote de aquí, idiota".

La lista de comentarios agradables suscitados por la compañía de un perro, especialmente un cachorro, era asombrosa. *Maldito perro*, pensé, *¿cómo puede hacerme esto?* No quería hablar con nadie. ¡El cachorro tenía suerte de que le hablara! Normalmente, mis comentarios caninos eran duros. "Saca la cabeza de mi regazo. Me babeaste la pierna tratando de agarrar la patata frita. No puedo creer que te hayas tirado otro pedo". La lista era interminable. Me volví resentido con el perro. Pero él seguía ahí, irradiando amor incondicional, a pesar de todo.

Un día, mientras iba a toda velocidad por la autopista, recibí una llamada. Eran mis amigas, que estaban en el oeste y vivían en una casa rodante. Vendieron su casa, se desprendieron de la mayoría de sus posesiones terrenales y buscaban la iluminación espiritual en la carretera, en medio de la incertidumbre. Sabían que su "poder superior" las cuidaría... ellas "dejaron todo en manos de Dios", otro concepto de los doce pasos. Yo había decidido hace mucho tiempo que Dios no existía, si así fuera, mi vida no sería un infierno en la tierra, antes de ganarme un puesto en el asiento caliente del infierno final.

"Oye, estamos en Oregón. Ven y te reúnes con nosotras", me dijeron.

No quería hablar con nadie, y mucho menos unirme a nadie. Quería que me dejaran en paz. Las mujeres habían tejido un capullo alrededor de mi vulnerabilidad. Nunca me había sentido tan seguro como cuando me abrieron las puertas de su casa y de su corazón, a mí, un perfecto desconocido. Debería decir, un extraño *imperfecto*. Mi corazón seguía funcionando mientras mi cerebro fallaba. No podía "no ver" a los salvadores de mi alma y, sin darme cuenta, tracé una ruta de supervivencia.

"Tengo al maldito perro que le había regalado a mi adicto al crack", les expliqué.

"Genial, tu perro puede visitar al nuestro, Sunny", respondieron con entusiasmo.

"El perro es un verdadero fastidio", expliqué. Cometí un gran error cuando compré el cachorro. "¿En qué estaba pensando?" Mis quejas cayeron en oídos sordos.

"Simplemente ven aquí. Queremos verte a ti y al cachorro. Le diremos a nuestro perro Sunny que espere compañía".

¡Mujeres locas! pensé. Me preguntaba a qué jugaban. La vida no era tan fácil. La vida era un cubo de excrementos con el asa por dentro. ¿Qué ganaban ellas proyectando mi vida de una manera tan sesgada? *Iré al oeste, ¡pero no me uniré a esa locura!* pensé con toda seguridad.

El cachorro iba sentado en la camioneta, disfrutando del paisaje, ajeno al drama. Se sentaba a contemplar la vista y, luego, se quedaba dormido y relajado. Él estaba practicando el concepto de los doce pasos de "todo con moderación". En *mi* vida no había moderación. Había soportado dos décadas de situaciones extremas. ¿Cómo se atrevía el maldito cachorro a proclamar que un concepto como la moderación existía o era siquiera posible? Estaba celoso de un cachorro. Deseaba vivir la vida en sus términos y ser tan feliz como él, a pesar de haber sido abandonado alguna vez en una camioneta, en un caluroso día de verano. Él era increíblemente feliz. ¡Cómo se atrevía!

La vida pronto se convirtió en una licuadora de oscuridad. Me encontré apagando las llamas de la depresión con aguardiente, con la evidente ironía de que medicaba mi depresión al tiempo que alimentaba mi dependencia al alcohol, que lo cura todo. Una vez le ofrecí al cachorro un sorbo del remedio, sólo para ser reprendido con un "No, gracias" y un movimiento de la cola. El cachorro rechazó la pócima que yo había aprendido a valorar. Sin embargo, él era feliz. Era realmente feliz, resignado a sentarse a mi lado, babeando y tirándose pedos. Supuse que al cachorro le gustaba el sadomasoquismo, obtener placer infligiendo dolor a otros. ¡Maldito cachorro!

Al final, acabé en algún lugar del oeste con mis amigas. Eran fanáticas de Al-Anon y yo me estaba convirtiendo en esclavo de lo que ellas consideraban veneno. Algunos días, paseaba al maldito perro y le daba órdenes. Pronto aprendió a no provocar mi ira. Le decía: "Siéntate", y por Dios, ¡se sentaba! Le decía: "Espera", y él esperaba. Mientras tanto, mis amigas veían como controlaba al cachorro. Yo había tenido una vida fuera de control, y pronto me sentí cautivado por la capacidad de controlar con éxito a un ente vivo. Quería rescatar al pájaro herido controlando la vida de los demás, cuando en realidad, yo era el que necesitaba aprender a controlarme.

Mis amigas me lo reprocharon. "¿Por qué simplemente no lo dejas ser un *perro*?"

¿Qué demonios? pensaba yo. *El cachorro necesita una estructura en su vida, y yo se la voy a dar.* En retrospectiva, ¿qué demonios sabía yo de estructuras en la vida? Había dejado atrás a mi familia, mis amigos y mi negocio. Mi casa era un capullo sobre ruedas del que salía a regañadientes y periódicamente.

Cuando era niño, mi madre cultivaba perejil en el jardín. Aparentemente de la nada, las orugas aparecían milagrosamente en las hojas del perejil y se adherían al tallo. Mi madre colocaba el tallo cargado de orugas dentro de un tarro y nos mostraba cómo la oruga tejía su capullo. Una vez encapsulada dentro, cesaba todo signo de vida. Yo me preguntaba qué hacía la oruga dentro. Mágicamente, un día, el capullo se abría y emergía una hermosa mariposa.

Yo también vivía en un capullo. Por desgracia, *tenía* que salir periódicamente, y el maldito cachorro solía ser la causa. Estaba contento— no agradecido—de vivir mi existencia recluido en mi capullo. Estaba a salvo, como un bebé protegido en el saco embrionario rodeado de fluidos protectores, y nunca quería emerger. En mi caso, el fluido era el alcohol, pero igualmente protector. Nunca imaginé salir de mi capullo ni viajar por la corriente de la vida. El cachorro era el causante de mi muy frecuente surgimiento como mariposa. Aislarme simplemente no era una opción. El cachorro provocaba que me convirtiera en mariposa.

Yo percibía al cachorro como un irritante crónico, el mayor impedimento para cualquier cosa que estuviera pasando. Una mañana, me desperté con una bolsa de comida para perros abierta y esparcidas por el suelo del remolque. Jugué de mala gana 52 pickup y maldije una vez más al cachorro. Decidí poner la comida del cachorro en una caja de plástico afuera, en la lengüeta del remolque... ¡para mantenerla alejada del condenado cachorro! Él simplemente lo complicaba todo.

La noche siguiente, *casual* e inexplicablemente, me desperté de mi habitual borrachera y oí un extraño crujido en el exterior del remolque. Me asomé y vi a un cerdo barrigón intentando arañar la caja de comida para perros. Corrí hacia la puerta de la caravana, la abrí, me volví hacia el cachorro y le dije: "Ve por ellos, maldita sea". El cachorro se levantó de un salto y corrió hacia la puerta. De repente, experimenté una contracción involuntaria e inexplicable. Algo en mi interior me obligó a cerrar la puerta rápidamente, casi sobre el cuello del cachorro. Yo había ganado la carrera hacia la puerta con un milisegundo de ventaja. Estaba en control remoto. Nunca sabré cómo reaccioné de esa manera después de despertar de un sueño profundo.

Entonces oí *más* arañazos profundos, miré por la ventana y presencié cómo otro supuesto cerdo barrigón saltaba sobre la caja de comida para perros. En cuestión de segundos, llegaron más para deleitarse con el alimento de Chef Purina de cordero y arroz desmenuzados. Lo que en un principio pensé que era un cerdo panzudo que se había escapado de un remolque vecino, era algo llamado jabalí. Estaba en Ajo, Arizona, y una manada de jabalíes hambrientos, con colmillos de la mejor calidad culinaria, se había abalanzado sobre mi remolque en mitad de la noche. Si hubiera dejado salir al cachorro, los jabalíes se habrían dado un festín de cachorro labrador esa noche. *Maldito cachorro con suerte... ¿por qué yo nunca podía tener esa suerte?* me pregunté.

La noche anterior, al despertarme, vi que la puerta del remolque estaba abierta y que el cachorro no estaba por ninguna parte. Salí a tropezones del remolque y empecé a buscarlo. Pensé brevemente en abandonarlo a su suerte. Estaría mejor solo, que con un humano disfuncional, pensé. Caminé por el parque de remolques en la oscuridad con una linterna en la mano, en vano. Asunto resuelto, se acabó el problema con el cachorro y no había nada que pudiera hacer al respecto. Tropecé y me caí de camino al remolque. Por casualidad, divisé un objeto en movimiento a lo lejos. Era el cachorro, trotando por la autopista de la vida en medio de la carretera. Él estaba tan perdido e inconsciente como yo. Le grité: "¡VEN!" e hizo exactamente eso. Recordó la orden que le había enseñado la semana anterior, cuando mis amigas me reprendieron por no dejarlo ser un perro. Volvió corriendo a mi vida.

Mi ritual diario continuó... beber, comer un poco, beber, no comer, beber un poco más, todo mientras alejaba al cachorro que siempre volvía a hurtadillas a mi lado. Empecé a sentir resentimiento hacia el cachorro, que era tan codependiente como yo. Con frecuencia veía al cachorro arrastrarse sigilosamente por el suelo para poder estar conmigo. Por la noche, me despertaba para ir al baño y encontraba al  cachorro durmiendo en la cama de nuevo. Lo sacaba de la cama, hacía mis necesidades y me volvía a dormir. Cada vez que me despertaba, el cachorro estaba de nuevo en la cama, durmiendo a mi lado. El cachorro encontraba ingeniosamente formas de irritarme intencionalmente, o eso creía yo.

Estaba haciendo planes para un viaje a México. Tenía que asegurarme de que la camioneta y el remolque estuvieran en condiciones de circular y de que todos los sistemas funcionaran. Resultó que las luces traseras del camión no servían, así que, con disgusto, levanté el remolque y lo coloqué sobre bloques de hormigón. Un bloque se movió y el remolque cayó sobre mi pierna. Me clavó en el suelo y luché por liberarme. De repente, a mi locura mental se sumó el dolor físico. Regresé cojeando al interior de mi refugio, bebí unos tragos y me desmayé.

Cuando desperté, la pantorrilla izquierda me dolía y estaba hinchada. Pronto me di cuenta de que no podía doblar la pierna izquierda. Demonios, no podía alcanzar el calcetín izquierdo. Me quité los zapatos, pero me duché con el calcetín izquierdo puesto. Cuando salí de la ducha, el cachorro vino corriendo a saludarme con su alegría habitual. Yo le di una patada con gran fervor. Esta vez, él no aceptó un no por respuesta y empezó a jugar al tira y afloja con mi calcetín. Tú no puedes ganarlas todas, así que perdí el calcetín a manos del perro. Como represalia, le arrojé un zapato para enseñarle quién mandaba, ¡y el muy desgraciado lo cogió y me lo devolvió! Él estaba acostumbrado a traer cosas de vuelta a mi vida... cosas que necesitaba... cómo amor.

No me importaba en absoluto ver a un médico, siempre y cuando pudiera beber y adormecer mi dolor. Mis planes de viaje quedaron en suspenso hasta que mi pierna funcionara mejor... o eso creía. Al cabo de una semana, la hinchazón no disminuyó y tuve que aprender a lidiar con una pierna maltrecha. Es curioso. El perro empezó a llevarme los zapatos y a quitarme los calcetines. Al poco tiempo, el perro que me caía mal me estaba ayudando de maneras que ni siquiera era consciente. Simplemente no me daba cuenta.

CAPÍTULO 3
MI EPIFANÍA

Una noche, volví a beber hasta caer en el olvido. Estaba solo. El cachorro dormía y no había ruido. Me sentía en un vacío de inutilidad. La depresión me oprimía la cabeza. Me bebí el vodka de la botella y tomé un cuchillo. El telón final de la resolución se cerró. Era el acto final. La paz estaba cerca... ¿o debería decir mi muñeca? Era víctima de un esquema Ponzi emocional; cuanto más invertía, menos recibía. ¡Quería salir! De repente, todo se oscureció.

La tarde siguiente, experimenté un martilleo rítmico en mi cabeza. Las dolorosas pulsaciones de una horrible resaca asediaban mi cerebro, pero no explicaban todo aquel ruido. Alguien, o *algo*, golpeaba sin piedad la puerta de mi remolque. Me puse en pie con dificultad, sabiendo que probablemente dejaría un rastro de vómito en el camino. Tardé tres intentos en abrir la puerta, pero al final pude hacerlo y aparecieron dos humanoides... ¡niños malditos! Aquellos niños sujetaban el extremo de una cuerda con la que sujetaban a un perro. Entonces escuché una voz chillona como del infierno.

"Señor, ¿puede nuestro perro jugar con el suyo?"

Yo balbuceé: "Sí, llévate al maldito perro. Llévenselo. ¡Vayan!"

Los invasores consiguieron lo que querían (el cachorro), y yo conseguí lo que quería... expulsarlos de mi refugio. Aunque no lo suficientemente rápido, debo añadir que caí de nuevo en la cama y me quedé dormido. ¡Y entonces algo ocurrió! Treinta minutos más tarde, oí el grito más lastimero e inequívoco de dolor. Un alma se estaba muriendo. Era un grito desgarrador de angustia, inconfundible incluso para mi cerebro embriagado. Era el grito del cachorro. Sólo sabía que lo había atropellado un automóvil y yacía destrozado en la calle. En ese momento todo era sombrío, oscuro y premonitorio. Casi me había quitado la vida la noche anterior. ¿Por qué iba a pensar de otro modo? Me acerqué a la puerta del remolque y la abrí de un tirón. La noche anterior había estado dispuesto a enterrarme a mí mismo, así que sin duda estaba preparado para enterrar a un cachorro. Lo que ocurrió a continuación cambió mi vida para siempre. El cachorro estaba sentado, gritando con todas sus fuerzas y levantando la pata. Estaba sufriendo mucho, pensé. Los niños lloraban y lo abrazaban, lo consolaban de una manera que yo no conocía.

Empecé a llorar desconsoladamente.

"Está bien, señor. Está bien. Se golpeó la pata con un auto cuando jugaba con nuestro perro", me explicaron obedientemente. "Está bien, señor. Está bien. Se pondrá bien". Cuando los niños me vieron sollozar, se emocionaron aún más. Ellos también se echaron a llorar.

Lo que pasó después es confuso. Empecé a sollozar incontrolablemente. Temblaba mientras el cachorro respondía a mi emoción. El cachorro había acechado a su presa y saboreaba el final de la cacería. Era como si hubiera visto su primer arco iris. Puso mis necesidades por encima de las suyas. De algún modo, él sabía que ese día era especial. Los perros tienen emociones, son seres sensibles. Él estaba contento. Su cola se movía rápida y furiosamente, su lengua entraba y salía rápidamente, absorbiendo mis lágrimas, y sus patas tocaban mi rostro.

En cuanto a mí, ¡me puse a llorar aún más fuerte! Más tarde me pregunté si era capaz de distinguir entre las lágrimas de felicidad y las de tristeza. Ya no era "el maldito perro". Ahora era oficialmente "mi Booster". Me había abierto paso en la oscuridad de la vida gracias a la intervención divina de un perro. Dormí con mi Booster en brazos durante tres días. Cuando desperté, miré a Booster a los ojos y me sumergí en su alma, igual que él me había mirado a los ojos y se había adentrado en mi alma, el día que casi muere en el deshuesadero. Me despertaba todas las mañanas con una lamida alegre, algo que siempre hacía para expresar su amor incondicional... tirando de los hilos de mi capullo... esperando encontrar la mariposa dentro. Sin importar como lo tratara, él nunca se rindió. Yo me había rendido hacía mucho tiempo. Él nunca lo hizo.

Me volví hacia Booster con lágrimas en los ojos y lo abracé como si no hubiera mañana. Sabía en mi corazón que no habría un mañana sin Booster a mi lado. Le hice una promesa.

"Oye, amigo mío, nunca daré mi vida por sentada ni acabaré con ella dejándote solo en el mundo como alguna vez yo lo estuve. Voy a compartirte con el mundo para que puedas ayudar a otros como me ayudaste a mí".

De repente me di cuenta de que él había estado conmigo en las buenas y en las malas. Había recibido maltrato y devuelto amor. Me di cuenta de que él me había estado acercando a la gente... gente feliz... gente valiosa... que ama a los animales y es pura de corazón. Yo me había mantenido aferrado al precipicio de la vida mientras intentaba por todos los medios reintegrarme a la sociedad. Me molestaba su capacidad para soportar el maltrato y devolver amor. Me molestaba su felicidad. La epifanía se produjo cuando sentí que él estaba herido y era desdichado, igual que yo. De repente lo entendí, de manera similar a Helen-Keller.

Mientras yacía en mi cama con Booster a mi lado, ¡me pareció oírlo ronronear! Me levanté de un salto y pensé, *¡Gané un perro pero perdí la cabeza!* El cachorro sobresaltado, salió corriendo, pero se detuvo, se giró y miró hacia atrás. Cuando me vio reír, volvió alegremente a mi lado, marcando su camino con un chorro de orina. Yo muchas veces había huido, consumido por el miedo, sin detenerme lo suficiente para mirar atrás y reconsiderar la situación, confiando en que el cambio era posible. Yo también me había meado a mí mismo con una autocompasión sumisa. Las semillas de la devastación emocional sembradas hace mucho tiempo habían crecido hasta convertirse en un laberinto de telarañas enmarañadas que causaban una destrucción masiva en mi alma. Yo había creado con maestría un capullo protector, para luego encontrar que un cachorro no deseado mordisqueaba sus hilos, sin entender la importancia de lo que había ocurrido días antes. Estaba en el ojo del huracán de mi vida. Había sufrido una devastación de categoría cinco que me había puesto en peligro y, de algún modo, había sobrevivido. ¿Me dejé llevar por una sensación de seguridad falsa debido a un momento de calma en medio de la destrucción, en el ojo de la tormenta, mientras esperaba que la segunda parte de esta se manifestara? ¿Sería enterrado bajo los escombros de la desesperación que vendría?"

Me maravillé al ver cómo Booster dormía solemnemente a mi lado, inhalando y exhalando sin preocuparse por nada. Adapté mi respiración a la suya. Inspirando y espirando, imité la respiración de Booster hasta que ya no pude más. En algún momento, caí en un gran sueño, cuya profundidad nunca había alcanzado sin mi amigo "Jack" (Daniels) a mi lado. En aquel momento, sin que ninguno de los dos lo supiéramos, Booster había cortado los hilos de mi capullo, provocando una hemorragia del fluido brioso, protector y *vivificante* que me había rodeado y había impregnado mi vida. Mi dependencia del alcohol disminuyó. Después de dos décadas de destrucción emocional, nunca había encontrado mejoría hasta ese momento. Mi Booster me enseñó a dormir, una pesada tarea que me había resultado esquiva. "Respira hondo, aguanta la respiración, exhala, relájate y suspira con satisfacción. Repítelo cuando sea necesario".

Una mañana lluviosa, mientras navegaba por la web por aburrimiento, busqué "perros que ayudan a la gente". Pronto me encontré mirando una página web que describía a los perros de servicio. *¿Qué demonios es un perro de servicio?* me pregunté. Leí que ayudaban a personas discapacitadas. Algunos perros de servicio recogían cosas y se las llevaban a su compañero humano. Algunos ayudaban a la gente a vestirse o desvestirse. De repente, me di cuenta de que Booster había hecho muchas de estas cosas por *mí*. Entonces busqué "adiestramiento de perros de servicio" y apareció una página web que mostraba a la Dra. Bonita Bergin y el Instituto de Perros de Asistencia (ADI). Me pareció *muy interesante*.

Con el tiempo, mi relación con mi amigo Jack se desvaneció y lo saqué de la cama para dormir con mi Booster. Fue una rivalidad intensa. Era una justa olímpica de proporciones épicas. El ganador se lo llevaba todo; luchaban por mi alma. La transferencia de codependencia explotó, inconmensurable en la escala estándar Richter de la vida. El escenario que se desarrolló era demasiado para un alma perdida que vivía en un capullo. Tenía que escapar una vez más e irme a otro sitio; cuanto más lejos, mejor. Convencí a mis amigas para que me acompañaran a México. Sin saberlo, estaba buscando una *cura geográfica*... todos mis problemas no existirían si simplemente viviera en cualquier otro lugar.

En lugar de autodestruirme en la recién descubierta autorreflexión, ocupé mi tiempo socializando constructivamente con la ayuda de Booster. Ahora las cosas eran diferentes. Ya no estaba solo. Tenía un compañero, un amigo auténtico y cariñoso. De repente, había surgido en mí la necesidad de proteger y cuidar a un alma, que desprendía amor incondicional, y esperaba poco a cambio. Años más tarde aprendí, a través de la iluminación del programa Al-Anon, que necesitaba hacer lo mismo por mi alma. Incluso con la ayuda del programa Al-Anon, dudaba que alguna vez pudiera amarme a mí mismo como amaba a Booster.

Un día, mis amigas se acercaron a mi remolque y me preguntaron: "Amigo, ¿cuándo nos vamos a México?"

Como la espontaneidad es mi Santo Grial, respondí: "¿Qué tal ahora?"

"Necesitamos un poco de tiempo para desmontarlo todo e irnos", contestaron.

Las *mujeres*, pensé, *¡tienen que empolvarse la nariz antes de hacer cualquier cosa!* De repente, Sunny salió corriendo de la autocaravana para saludar a Booster. Estaban muy contentos juntos. Todos los días eran Navidad para los dos perros que se acababan de conocer. Uno había sido amado, el otro rechazado, y sin embargo ambos jugaban armoniosamente. ¿Podría ser que los perros tuvieran la capacidad de sobrellevar las cargas emocionales, mientras que los humanos no? me pregunté de repente. *Los perros viven el aquí y el ahora. ¿Quizá eso lo explique? No se obsesionan con el pasado y son incapaces de planear el mañana. Siguen la filosofía de los doce pasos de KISS... ¡Keep It Simple, Stupid (Mantenlo Simple, Estúpido)!*

Los perros jugaban mientras nosotros compartíamos un almuerzo de brotes de soja y hummus preparado por las chicas. Tuve la tentación de comer el cordero y el arroz de Booster.

"¿Dónde está la Coca-Cola light? pregunté.

"Esos productos químicos son muy malos para ti. Te matarán", fue la respuesta rápida.

No, pensé, *las relaciones son mucho más mortíferas.* Si hubiera habido una Coca-Cola, Booster me la habría traído encantado. No le interesaba controlar, sólo ayudar y amar incondicionalmente. *Lástima*, pensé, *que no se pueda tener una relación con un perro...* ¡o eso creía yo!

Como las damas eran miembros comprometidos de Al-Anon, yo no bebía en su presencia. Sin embargo, lo compensaba cuando volvía a mi refugio, automedicándome con el líquido embrionario mientras alimentaba y daba de beber a Booster. *Maldita sea*, pensé, *¡Booster bebe mucho!* El suelo se llenaba de salpicaduras de agua cuando él saciaba su siempre presente sed. De repente pensé, *¡Booster y yo tenemos más en común de lo que pensaba!*

Finalmente, me metí en la cama y me acurruqué con Booster a mi lado. Él siempre se dormía primero. Eso significaba que tenía que escuchar sus ronquidos, lo que me obligaba a beber más para poder dormir. Siempre cedía en esos momentos difíciles. Era lo menos que podía hacer por el cachorro que había soportado mucho durante tanto tiempo. Me tomaba las copas de más sin quejarme. Quizá yo también era capaz de sentir un amor incondicional. Ahí estaba la prueba... ¡86 pruebas, de hecho! Bebía por amor a Booster... ¿en serio?

La mañana llegó rápidamente y las damas estaban listas para partir. Despejé las nubes de mi cabeza y desmonté mi campamento. Una hora después, jugábamos a adelantarse el uno al otro en turnos en la carretera hacia México. Cruzamos la frontera en cuestión de horas y encontramos un precioso lugar para acampar en la playa de Puerto Peñasco. Era una ciudad fascinante y pequeña cerca de la frontera. Es la playa más cercana a Arizona. Pagué 5 dólares por el alquiler de la primera noche y me dijeron que al año siguiente el camping sería sustituido por un complejo de multipropiedad. *Qué triste*, pensé. La realidad dictaba que las pandillas se apoderarían de la zona en los años venideros. Las drogas, malditas drogas, impedirían que otros compartieran la utopía. *¿Alguna vez esto cambiará?* me preguntaba.

Dejé salir a Booster para que jugara con Sunny en la playa, agradecido de que tuviera una compañera con la cual jugar. Me apetecía beber algo, y las señoras me obsequiaron una botella de agua. Nos sentamos en nuestra Riviera de 5 dólares y contemplamos la puesta de sol mientras sus rayos se

transformaban en una panorámica de colores pastel. Después miré hacia abajo y Booster y Sunny estaban juntos a mis pies, cubiertos de arena. No teníamos suministro constante de agua, sólo 50 galones en un tanque de almacenamiento, ya que estábamos acampando en seco. Llevamos a los perros a las olas, les quitamos la arena y los secamos con una toalla. Luego nos retiramos a nuestras respectivas moradas con los perros en brazos.

Por la mañana, Booster me saludó como siempre. Estaba excitado y hambriento. Le di de comer y lo saqué a pasear. Salió corriendo a la playa y se echó ceremoniosamente arena entre las patas; lo haría todo el día si se lo permitiera. Luego, corrió hacia el agua y persiguió las olas mientras retrocedían hacia el océano, solo para huir de ellas cuando reaparecían milagrosamente instantes después. Era una lucha que nunca terminaba. Tuve que arrastrarlo lejos del agua que tanto amaba.

Más tarde, ese mismo día, paseamos por la playa y acabé hablando con un tipo mexicano al que le gustó mi camiseta. A mí me gustó su hierba. Se dibujó un compromiso en la arena; él se quedó con mi camiseta, ¡y yo con la hierba! Ya no era virgen a las maravillas de México. Tomé una siesta, y cuando la nube de distracción se disipó, Booster no estaba por ninguna parte. Mi corazón tuvo un sobresalto emocional y amoroso por primera vez en mucho tiempo. Miré frenéticamente hacia la playa y vi huellas de patas en la arena. A lo lejos, vi a Booster revolcándose sobre algo como si le estuvieran dando un masaje tailandés. Resultó que había encontrado una foca muerta hinchada al sol y cubierta de gusanos. ¡Estaba creando un vínculo!

Me llevó horas desprender el hedor a foca del espeso pelaje de Booster. *¿Por qué no podía ser uno de esos labradores de pelo corto?* me pregunté. Sólo tenía 50 galones de agua dulce para bañarme. Si la usaba con Booster, ¡seguro que iba a oler como si yo también me hubiera revolcado en una foca muerta! Con detergente y perseverancia, lavé a Booster como si no hubiera mañana. La realidad del día era que, por primera vez en décadas, esperaba un mañana. Me moría de ganas de ver el amanecer en la hermosa playa. Me imaginaba los rayos dorados del sol iluminando el pelaje dorado de Booster mientras trotaba por la playa, persiguiendo las incesantes olas.

Esa noche, paseé con las señoras y el dúo canino por la playa. La luz de la luna iluminaba nuestro camino mientras deambulábamos sin rumbo. "¿Por qué sigues estando alerta o en guardia?" me preguntaron de repente.

"No me había dado cuenta", respondí.

"Lo haces con mucha frecuencia. Es como si nunca estuvieras relajado".

Casi me rio en voz alta, ya que la palabra *relajado* nunca formaba parte de mi vocabulario.

"Ves, lo hiciste de nuevo", dijeron momentos después.

Abatido, me alejé del grupo y me senté en un tronco, para apreciar la inmensidad del océano. Empecé a llorar, lentamente al principio, y luego se abrieron las compuertas. Estaba ajeno a mi entorno hasta que un intruso interrumpió mi concentración. Booster entró corriendo a toda velocidad hacia mi regazo, casi me tumba y acabó con mi trance hipnótico. Su lengua secó frenéticamente mis lágrimas, igual que aquel fatídico día en el remolque en el que tuve mi momento de revelación. Con el paso del tiempo, Booster se convirtió en un experto en responder a mis emociones exageradas. Sorprendentemente, era igualmente experto en responder a la falta de emociones sacándome del trance. Las mujeres se acercaron y se sentaron a mi lado mientras Sunny yacía junto a Booster, y hablamos.

"Amigo, estás hecho un desastre... estás muy mal. La codependencia mata. No puedes seguir huyendo de ti mismo. No son los adictos los que te hacen esto... ¡eres tú mismo! *Sólo por hoy*, estás a salvo y con amigos; cuatro, para ser exactos".

Miré a mi alrededor para ver quiénes eran los otros dos amigos misteriosos. Entonces me di cuenta de que se refería a los miembros de nuestra familia canina. Tardé años en darme cuenta de la importancia de esas palabras. ¿Amigos? Yo no tenía amigos. Durante años, me había concentrado en curar a los adictos de mi vida, y mis amigos habían optado sabiamente por alejarse. Mi familia se fue distanciando mientras yo me sumergía en la locura. Ni siquiera me di cuenta de que mi manera de hablar se había visto afectada, ya que revisaba mis palabras antes de hablar y examinaba el terreno mientras caminaba. Mi sistema de defensa "AWAK" me llevaba a estar alerta las 24 horas del día, los siete días de la semana. Estaba en una playa con mis cuatro amigos, viviendo a salvo en un capullo móvil, y aun así estaba hipervigilante. Hasta el día de hoy, tengo espasmos en el cuerpo debido a un sistema nervioso hiperactivo. Años más tarde, en un crucero, mi hermano se sintió avergonzado cuando pensó que me estaba insinuando a alguien cuando parpadeé un ojo. Al principio, me enfadé, luego pensé... *Dios, ¡ojalá fuera tan sencillo!*

Las damas estuvieron maravillosas esa noche. Dijeron lo que quisieron sin rodeos. La elocuencia nunca fue un requisito para la Batichica y Robin. Se estaban convirtiendo en las superhéroes a las que recurría cuando la vida se volvía insoportable, como inevitablemente sucedía. Hablamos por horas esa noche. Todo el tiempo, la cabeza de Booster estuvo en mi regazo, y no sonó ni un gemido ni una queja. Él estaba en paz, contento de poder estar conmigo. De vez en cuando soñaba y se retorcía, igual que yo, pero ahí acababan las similitudes. Mi Booster era un ser social seguro de sí mismo y no agresivo. No tenía miedo de *relajarse en público* y ser él mismo. Buscaba atención, mientras que yo la rehuía. Era sensible, una cualidad que yo había perdido hacía mucho tiempo. Cuanto más pensaba en ello, más me daba cuenta de por qué había estado resentido con él. Éramos personalidades opuestas... como los polos norte y sur.

Muchos perros terminan en un refugio porque su dueño elige un perro con una personalidad contraria a las necesidades de la familia. Las estadísticas demuestran que cuando una familia elige a su próximo perro, rara vez acaba en un refugio porque la familia aprendió que la coincidencia de personalidad . . . canina-humana . . . es fundamental para el éxito de la adopción de un perro. El tipo de personalidad de Booster no encajaba, y era un candidato probable a ser dado en adopción si mi vida hubiera sido la típica. Milagrosamente, mi personalidad cambió para adaptarse a la de Booster, lo que dio lugar a una asociación que se desarrolló y cambió mi vida. Con el tiempo, me convertí en una persona extrovertida, como Booster, y mostré la misma confianza que él.

Regresamos al campamento y les di las buenas noches a las chicas y a Sunny. Me tomé unas copas y me fui a la cama a reunirme con Booster, que se había apoderado de mi almohada. Esa noche dormí sin almohada; se lo merecía. Había escuchado incondicionalmente todas mis tonterías durante horas. En realidad, se había ganado mucho más que una almohada, ¡se había ganado sus alas! Era un ángel enviado desde arriba.

Booster tenía una habilidad asombrosa para sentir las emociones humanas. Estaba totalmente en sintonía con mis cambios de humor en la playa. Instintivamente se quedaba tranquilo a mi lado y me ayudaba cuando yo necesitaba motivación. La primera vez que me di cuenta de esto fue cuando lo llevé a una residencia de ancianos en Truth or Consequences, Nuevo México, para visitar a enfermos de Alzheimer. Les pedí a las señoras que me acompañaran, pero se negaron rotundamente, aunque yo tenía miedo y necesitaba de su apoyo. En cambio, me aseguraron que aún tenía agallas y que estaba totalmente intacto, ¡aunque yo hubiera pensado lo contrario! El director de la residencia insinuó que la gente disfrutaría de una visita perruna, pero lamentablemente no la recordaría. Entré en una habitación con personas mayores sentadas en sillas formando un círculo. No estaba seguro de lo que iba a hacer, pero Booster sí lo sabía. Cuando me aseguré de que nadie tenía miedo de Booster, le di un conejito de peluche. Se acercó a un anciano, que le tendió la mano, tiró del juguete y le acarició enérgicamente la cabeza. Sin

más preámbulos, Booster se pavoneó, con el conejo en la boca, hacia una anciana de cabello canoso.

Booster no dejó de visitar a una sola persona de la sala aquel día, incluido el administrador. Antes de irme, salí al pasillo y agradecí al personal la oportunidad que me dio de visitarlos. El caballero que había tirado del conejito de Booster salió al pasillo. El administrador le preguntó: "¿Qué te pareció el perro?"

Sé que el administrador esperaba oír, ¿Qué perro?

Con voz alta, el hombre exclamó, "Un perro increíble, increíble... ¿viste lo que hizo? ¡Yo tuve un perro!"

Con Booster a mi lado, yo salí apresuradamente. Estaba llorando de nuevo, temblando y con movimientos nerviosos. Emociones enterradas brotaban de lo más profundo de mi ser. Me sentía como un bicho raro. Sólo un bicho raro reaccionaría así. Era un muerto emocional. Más tarde, esa misma noche, les conté a las chicas lo que había pasado. Sonrieron. ¡Se estaban riendo, maldita sea! Yo me enojé. "No tiene gracia", dije.

"Amigo, parece que Booster se divirtió", dijeron.

Estaba enfadado. Pensé que ellas se habían equivocado en esta.

Con la claridad del tiempo viene la reflexión. Booster se lo pasó en grande aquel día, junto con los pacientes, el personal y el administrador. Nos enseñó a todos la profundidad de la conexión entre los perros y los humanos. Al igual que sacó a la superficie los recuerdos de un paciente con Alzheimer, hizo lo mismo conmigo. Expuso mi vulnerabilidad y la necesidad de cambio que la acompañaba. ¡Yo quería lo que *él* tenía!

Estaba tan conmocionado por lo que había visto y aprendido que reuní el valor suficiente para llamar a un periódico y compartirlo con el mundo. Booster había dado lo mejor de sí. Ahora me tocaba a mí cumplir mi parte del trato. Le había prometido que lo compartiría con el mundo... el mundo que no me gustaba. Llamé al periódico local y expliqué lo que había pasado el día anterior en la residencia de ancianos. Estoy seguro de que mis sollozos y mis lapsus alertaron al periodista de que era algo muy emotivo... muy real para mí. Cuando la historia apareció en el periódico, se la mostré a Booster. "Como ves, estoy intentando cumplir mi promesa de compartirte con el mundo", le dije.

Cuando por fin llegó el día de Acción de Gracias, todos estábamos listos para celebrarlo. Hasta ahora, las celebraciones habían sido inexistentes en mi vida. En ese día soleado en la playa, nosotros y nuestros compañeros caninos simplemente disfrutamos del sol, el agua y el ambiente libre de estrés. Todos cantamos, ladramos, comimos, dormimos y nos relajamos. Éramos uno. Fue un momento armonioso. Las señoras prepararon una comida maravillosamente suave y sana. Nos deleitamos con alimentos que serían dignos de los dioses. Devoré mazorcas de maíz asadas y le di la mazorca a Booster. Quería que disfrutara de la delicia vegetariana. Masticó la mazorca durante lo que pareció una eternidad antes de dormirse por la tarde en la playa soleada. Escuchamos música y vimos las olas que serpenteaban dentro y fuera de la playa. Fue un Día de Acción de Gracias distinto a todos los que había vivido en los últimos veinte años. Yo era feliz en ese momento, al igual que Booster. De hecho, ¡todos éramos felices! Tuve que pellizcarme para asegurarme de que no estaba soñando. Al final, mi bebida cargada de vodka hizo efecto y tuve que echarme una siesta. Me acosté en la cama, Booster se unió a mí y caí en la antes esquiva zona de confort del sueño.

El tiempo pasaba y Booster me acercaba cada vez más a la gente, me veía obligado a hablar con completos desconocidos. Nunca me habría acercado a gente con el cuerpo cubierto de tatuajes o peinados rastafaris, y mucho menos a indigentes mexicanos borrachos de tequila y llenos de tacos. Booster nunca discriminaba; era un amante de la igualdad de oportunidades. Booster superaba con creces a Gandhi. Mi capullo acabó implosionando, abrumado por la positividad que ofrecía un perro. Pronto me di cuenta de que Booster tenía un máster en trabajo social. Hacía lo que yo nunca podría hacer. Saludaba a la gente, colaboraba con ella y la apreciaba por lo que era, de manera incondicional. Su filosofía era "inocente hasta que se demostrara lo contrario", ¡la mía era "culpable antes de poder demostrar la inocencia"!

Como séquito canino-humano, fuimos a pasear por la ciudad. Era genial ver esculturas de metal y souvenirs de colores brillantes de todas las variedades. El olor a sal marina impregnaba el aire cálido. Era muy profundo. Los mexicanos ofrecían sus mercancías... "Señor... "¡Señor!" De repente me sentí agobiado por el constante acoso de los vendedores ambulantes. Deberían haber aprendido de Booster, que tenía la extraña habilidad de atraer a la gente a su lado con adoración y no con resentimiento.

Un simpático niño mexicano se acercó a Booster y le tendió la mano para acariciarlo. Booster levantó una pata para estrechar su mano. *El lenguaje no es necesario para comunicarse,* pensé. Reflexionando, me di cuenta de que Booster se comunicaba constantemente con el lenguaje corporal. Hasta el ser humano menos instruido podría relacionarse con él. Cuando ofrecía una pata, el humano ofrecía una mano. Cuando estaba emocionado, compartía su entusiasmo saltando. Se convirtió en un maestro de la comunicación motivacional a través del lenguaje corporal. Caminaba entre las piernas de la gente y se detenía. Pronto alguien recibía un toque en el trasero de duración indeterminada. Cuando sabía que te tenía en el anzuelo, giraba lentamente sobre su espalda, y los humanos sabían instintivamente que debían darle un masaje en la barriga. Los británicos dirían que... ¡todo era brillante!

El niño mexicano se enamoró instantáneamente de Booster. Con el mayor de los respetos, el niño le dio a Booster su palito de helado para que lo lamiera. De un solo golpe, ¡el palito desapareció! Booster se había tragado el regalo entero. Agarré a Booster por la cabeza y le abrí la boca, y vi unos dos centímetros del palito de madera. Introduje frenéticamente la mano en la garganta, los dedos actuando como pinzas, y extraje el trozo de madera de 5 centímetros. Nunca sabré qué habría pasado si Booster se hubiera tragado el palito. Ese Día de Acción de Gracias, di gracias.

Caminamos por Puerto Peñasco, disfrutando de las maravillas de una ciudad extranjera. Más tarde, bajé la guardia y me relajé porque estaba cansado, habíamos caminado una larga distancia bajo un sol abrasador. De repente, la correa fue arrancada de mi mano. Pensé que alguien me había robado a Booster. Levanté la vista y vi a Booster corriendo por un muelle y saltando. Agarró un camarón que sostenía un mexicano en sus dedos, y que mostraba con la intención de venderlo. Sorprendentemente, Booster cogió el camarón, dejando los dedos del hombre totalmente intactos. El hombre se giró furioso al ver cómo Booster se daba un festín con sus camarones.

Un volcán de furia se transformó en una sonrisa de celebración. El hombre mexicano de dientes prominentes sonrió y dijo: "No hay problema". Quizás estaba contento de que alguien se esforzara tanto por apreciar sus camarones. Francamente, yo no estaba tan impresionado.

CAPÍTULO 4
NOS PUSIERON A PRUEBA

Cuando se está huyendo, la vida es agotadora. Llevaba dos décadas huyendo de la realidad y por fin me di cuenta de que ese estilo de vida no era sostenible. Emocional y económicamente, no era factible. Ahora era cuestión de hacerlo o morir. Con Booster a mi lado, elegí *hacerlo*. Pensé en la gente que había mantenido mi negocio en mi ausencia. Claro, recibían sus cheques, pero realmente se preocupaban por mí. Sabían por lo que estaba pasando, pero nunca interfirieron; me apoyaron, no se inmiscuyeron. Había eludido mis responsabilidades durante demasiado tiempo. Se acercaba la Navidad y decidí volver a casa y enfrentarme a mis demonios.

En una fresca mañana, Booster y yo subimos al remolque y nos dirigimos a casa. Cruzamos la frontera mexicana y mis rodillas empezaron a temblar. Mi cuerpo me traicionó. De repente, me invadió el miedo. Volvía a casa, deletreada *H a d e s*. Inconscientemente, mis emociones se aplacaban cuando paseaba a Booster, así que me detenía con mayor frecuencia de lo necesario para hacerlo. De algún modo, su confianza y calma se convirtieron en las mías. Crecíamos de forma simbiótica, y de manera muy positiva, debo añadir.

Mientras paseaba a Booster, noté que comía más hierba de lo normal. Días después, seguía comiendo hierba y empezó a vomitarla. Intentó defecar pero no pudo. Al día siguiente, me desperté con un montón de heces en la ducha. *Bueno, al menos es higiénico,* pensé. A medida que pasaban los días, me di cuenta de que el proceso de eliminación de Booster no estaba del todo bien. Vomitaba e intentaba hacer sus necesidades, pero no salía nada. Raro, pensé. Cuando estaba a un día de camino de casa, empecé a preocuparme.

Curiosamente, estaba en un pueblo donde vivía la madre de mi alcohólico. Era una de las mejores almas del planeta. La llamé y le expliqué que iba de camino a casa y que estaba preocupado por mi perro, Booster. Ella nos invitó a quedarnos en su casa mientras solucionaba todo. Como era Nochebuena en Lafayette, Luisiana, me preguntaba si mi adicto al alcohol vendría a visitarme. Y lo que es más importante, me preguntaba si Booster estaría bien. Cuando llegamos, me llevaron a mi habitación y a Booster a su patio. Salió obedientemente e intentó eliminar, sin éxito. Luego vomitó. Miré al otro lado de la valla y vi a una linda boxer. Booster no se fijó en ella, así que supe que estaba realmente enfermo. La boxer se llamaba Maggie y su dueña no tardó en acercarse.

"Hola, qué boxer tan linda", murmuré sin entusiasmo.

"Se llama Maggie y es un encanto", respondió la dueña de Maggie.

"Mi chico se llama Booster y acabamos de volver de México. Algo va mal, creo que está enfermo".

"Hay una clínica veterinaria no muy lejos", respondió ella.

"Pero es Nochebuena", contesté.

"Seguro que está abierto y si fuera mi perro, lo llevaría para que lo revisaran".

De vuelta a casa, mamá dijo: "Eso es lo que hacen los perros... comen hierba y vomitan".

Yo dije, "Eso no es lo que Booster hace."

"Bueno, prepárate para gastar un buen dinero", dijo.

Yo no tenía mucho dinero, pero sí una tarjeta de crédito con un límite parcialmente gastado. Le hice una seña a Booster y nos fuimos a la Animal Emergency Clinic de Lafayette.

Cuando entré, me encontré con el Dr. Moreau. "Mi Booster está enfermo", le expliqué, "estoy preocupado por él. La gente cree que estoy loco, pero algo no va bien". Con vergüenza, las lágrimas corrían por mis mejillas.

El Dr. Moreau me tranquilizó, "Vamos a dar un vistazo".

A Booster le dieron algo para que hacerlo defecar, pero no lo hizo. El Dr. Moreau dijo que haría algunas pruebas para determinar si había una obstrucción. Subieron a Booster a una camilla para hacerle una radiografía. Al revisar la placa, no había rastro de nada tangible que pudiera explicar un problema digestivo. Justo cuando empezaba a pensar que era sólo un problema dietético, el Dr. Moreau sugirió que hiciéramos una prueba con bario. Una radiografía con bario ilumina el camino por el sistema digestivo. Efectivamente, se detuvo abruptamente en un punto. Booster se estaba volviendo séptico y tenía como máximo cuarenta y ocho horas de vida a menos que se erradicara la obstrucción. Era necesaria una costosa operación.

Aunque en aquel momento era un hombre pobre, psicológica y económicamente, di el visto bueno y pagué un depósito con mi única tarjeta de crédito. No estaba seguro del saldo adeudado, ya que había estado de viaje, pero sirvió para que Booster entrara en el quirófano más tarde ese mismo día.

De vuelta en casa, tejí un nuevo capullo. Yo no quería hablar ni comer. Más ebrio que nunca, no había consumido ni una gota de licor. Sentía frío y soledad y me preocupaba por cómo se estaría sintiendo Booster. Él también estaba solo en una habitación de concreto fría y extraña y llena de jaulas. *Este mundo sin duda apesta. ¿Por qué Booster había prolongado mi agonía sólo para que se lo llevaran cuando más lo necesitaba?* Yo sentía mucho dolor. Aunque no había comido hierba, yo también vomité. Sin energía, me quedé sentado por horas, pasando de una vida de hipervigilancia a un trance hipnótico. Ya no estaba en un capullo; estaba en una tumba.

De repente llamaron a la puerta. "Oye, tienes una llamada", dijo mamá.

¿Quién demonios quiere hablar conmigo? me pregunté. Escuché la voz en el teléfono. "Hola, soy el doctor Moreau. ¿Puede venir a la clínica, por favor?" preguntó el veterinario al que había conocido horas antes.

Grité de dolor, lloré, sollocé y dejé caer el teléfono.

Mamá corrió a mi lado y me abrazó.

"¡Me duele!" grité. "Hasta Booster me ha traicionado. Se ha muerto, maldita sea".

Con la fuerza que sólo una madre tiene en los momentos difíciles, cogió el teléfono y dijo: "Hola". Luego se volvió hacia mí y me dijo: "Se va a poner bien".

Me senté y esperé a que se detuvieran los temblores. No estaba en condiciones de conducir, así que mamá me llevó a la clínica. Entré en la sala de espera y los minutos se convirtieron en horas, o eso me pareció. El Dr. Moreau salió con una sonrisa y me invitó a pasar al consultorio. "Me tomó dos intentos encontrarlo, pero aquí está el problema", dijo con determinación. Me mostró un trozo de mazorca de maíz. "Las mazorcas de maíz pueden ser mortales para un perro. Los veterinarios las extraen del estómago de los perros todo el año. Sin embargo, no siempre se trata de una mazorca de maíz. Hace un mes, una señora trajo un perro que se había tragado una hebilla metálica de zapato. Se la quité, pero volvió dos semanas después y el perro volvió a tener los mismos síntomas. Volví a operar y le saqué la hebilla del otro zapato".

"Ese fue un par de zapatos costosos", bromeé con desgano. Como siempre hacía, utilicé el humor para ocultar mis abrumadoras y dolorosas emociones. *Sólo por hoy*, la vida volvería a ser buena porque tenía a mi Booster. Pagué la factura con la tarjeta de crédito que tenía el límite justo para cubrir el costo de la operación. WOW, otra *coincidencia*, pensé.

Llevé a Booster a casa de mamá. Tenía la barriga llena de puntos, pero nunca se quejó. Lo llevé a mi habitación y le acaricié su barriga. De repente se levantó, gimió de dolor y me lamió la cara. Volví a sollozar. La lengua de Booster absorbía las lágrimas más rápido de lo que podía atraparlas. Él estaba más preocupado por mí que por su propio dolor. Pronto me levanté para irme, pensando que se tranquilizaría en la cama. Caminé dos pasos y él saltó al suelo. *Dios mío, se van a romper los puntos, pensé.* No le importaba nada excepto estar conmigo. Otra vez me puse a llorar.

Las horas se convirtieron en días mientras Booster se curaba en la seguridad de la casa de mamá. Me seguía de habitación en habitación y se negaba a perderme de vista. Con frecuencia, cuando iba a hacer mis necesidades, me bajaba los pantalones y descubría que habían aterrizado sobre la cabeza de Booster. Una relación simbiótica de la mayor importancia se estaba desarrollando a una velocidad asombrosa. Yo no iría a ningún lado sin Booster, y él no se iría a ningún lado sin mí. No había nada que no hiciera por él, y él lo sabía. A su vez, él permaneció a mi lado mientras yo navegaba peligrosamente por los campos de minas de la vida con un sistema de navegación defectuoso.

Un día, antes de irme de la casa de mamá, ella me miró y me dijo, "Dave, ese perro es especial... te quiere... de hecho, te adora". Yo no supe qué decir, pero ciertamente no me sentía merecedor de ser amado. Como un ser humano emocionalmente agotado, un cascarón vacío, no sabía lo que era el amor, y mucho menos cómo reconocerlo.

De camino a casa, me lamenté por haberle dado a Booster una mazorca de maíz para masticar, pensando que era un gran hueso vegetariano. *No lo sabía*, me repetía una y otra vez, mientras sostenía a Booster en mis brazos con él sentado en mi regazo. Me sentía muy culpable. Hacía mucho tiempo que no sentía emociones, y ahora me estaban afectando. Lo curioso era que a Booster no parecía importarle la experiencia. Estaba feliz simplemente de estar en mis brazos. Yo estaba más que feliz porque estaba vivo. La habilidad de sentir de esa manera simplemente no era humana, ¿o sí? No sabía lo que era, pero me parecía algo nuevo.

Por suerte, había contratado un seguro médico para Booster. La compañía ofrecía una póliza con un calendario de pagos rígido y una tasa de reembolso limitada. Lo justificaban diciendo que era una póliza económica. "Entonces, ¿por qué no cobrar un dólar y pagar cincuenta centavos, idiotas?" les pregunté, totalmente convencido de que la mayoría de la gente no tenía la capacidad para pagar la parte restante de la factura y las mascotas perdían la vida con rapidez. Presenté una reclamación por la extracción del cuerpo extraño (mazorca de maíz), y el agente me exigió todos los registros veterinarios relacionados con Booster desde hace una eternidad.

"¿Para qué los necesita?" le pregunté.

"Señor, si su perro se tragó algo alguna vez, eso es una afección psiquiátrica, y no cubrimos ese tipo de condiciones", respondió el imbécil.

Perdí la paciencia y le dije amablemente al agente, "Vete al diablo, idiota. Todos ustedes son iguales... toman el dinero, luchan contra las reclamaciones y tratan de demostrar que es una preexistencia como excusa para no pagar".

Aunque tengo mis reservas sobre los políticos, aplaudo la lucha del presidente Obama por eliminar la palabra "preexistente" de las entrañas de los ejecutivos de las compañías de seguros de salud. HECHO: Un perro nunca trataría a otro perro de la manera en que muchas aseguradoras tratan a sus asegurados. Una vez leí sobre una compañía de seguros que daba primas a los empleados que denegaban reclamaciones legítimas y se salían con la suya. Booster acabó teniendo más vidas que un gato, y sus gastos veterinarios de por vida superaron los 40.000 dólares, de los cuales, la aseguradora pagó aproximadamente la mitad. Disfruté del hecho de que vencí a la compañía de seguros en su propio juego. Irónicamente, Booster salvó mi vida, la elevó, y como resultado, más tarde pude pagar los copagos exorbitantes.

Después de lo que me pareció una eternidad, llegamos a casa, a una granja llena de maleza. Apagué el motor de la camioneta y me quedé sentado con las puertas cerradas. Después de mirar al norte, al sur, al este y al oeste, bajé cautelosamente la ventanilla de la camioneta hasta la mitad y olí el aire. No olí comida cocinándose ni rastros de vapor de crack flotando en la brisa. Tardé un rato, pero finalmente abrí la puerta de la camioneta y salí. Ajeno a todo, Booster corrió hacia un árbol, levantó la pata, orinó en charcos y reclamó su territorio. Este era su hogar ahora. Estábamos en casa. El águila había descendido y yo estaba con respiración asistida, alimentado por el amor incondicional de mi perro. Me dirigí a la cabaña y abrí la puerta sin llave. Envié a Booster a inspeccionar los alrededores, pero no estaba preparado para lo que ocurrió a continuación. ¡Nada, absolutamente nada! ¡Nada! ¡Nada! ¡Nada!

Qué hermosa era la nada. Rodeado de un mar de tranquilidad, mi mente se quedó completamente en blanco por primera vez en décadas. Me senté en medio del suelo en un trance hipnótico. De repente, Booster corrió y saltó sobre mi regazo. Lo abracé tan fuerte que creí que reventaría, pero no se quejó. Lo miré a los ojos, me adentré en su alma una vez más, y lloré, sabiendo que, pasara lo que pasara, no estaba solo. Esperando a que apareciera uno de mis adictos, inconscientemente inspeccioné mi entorno con el piloto automático. Sencillamente, no sucedió.

Poco a poco fui pegando los pedazos de mi vida. Lo que una vez se había hecho añicos se volvió a ensamblar, unido por una capa de pegamento canino. *No puede durar*, pensé. La única constante en mi vida era Booster. Él celebraba cada momento de su existencia. Me maravillaba lo mucho que le encantaba oler el estiércol de ciervo. ¡Simplemente orinar para dejar su marca lo emocionaba al máximo! No estaba afiliado a ninguna pandilla, sin embargo, su graffiti estaba en todas partes, proclamando algo. A menudo salía corriendo al patio, se tiraba al suelo y se revolcaba bajo el sol. Booster sabía vivir la vida a su manera y le sacaba el máximo partido. *¿Cómo es posible?* me preguntaba.

Resultó que mis adictos se habían marchado. No tenía forma de saber por cuánto tiempo o si volverían. Probablemente habían encontrado a otros inocentes codependientes carentes de autoestima e igual de necesitados que yo. Mi hipervigilancia aumentaba en lugar de disminuir. No era posible estar tan seguro. Había algo terriblemente erróneo en esta imagen. De alguna manera, con el talento de Booster, perseveré y la vida se hizo llevadera. No estaba solo. Tenía a Booster y a Al-Anon. Con frecuencia, buscaba en Internet información sobre mis adictos. Mantenía mis escudos en alto, al estilo Star Trek. Lamentablemente, hace poco me enteré de que mi adicto al alcohol murió solo, en las calles de San Diego, California.

CAPÍTULO 5
CONDOMINIO INFERNAL

La vida se calmó al no tener a un adicto que alimentara la montaña rusa. Justo cuando las cosas parecían estabilizarse, una mañana recibí una llamada telefónica. El suegro de mi adicto al crack me llamó para comunicarme que uno de sus empleados se había encontrado con mi adicto al crack, que vivía en un condominio en Destin, Florida. Años atrás, yo había comprado un condominio de vacaciones en la comunidad turística de la playa. Mi adicto al crack quería estar cerca de su familia, así que compré un condominio allí. No había nada que no hiciera por mis adictos. Con el tiempo, descubrí que mi adicto al crack estaba viviendo en *mi* condominio, al que yo no había visitado en mucho tiempo.

Llamé a la oficina de seguridad del condominio. Más tarde me informaron que el individuo que vivía en mi condominio afirmaba ser residente, presentaba una llave y mostraba ropa en un armario para demostrarlo. Se trataba de mi llave oculta. Mi adicto al crack se trepó por el balcón exterior de mi condominio en el segundo piso y rompió la cerradura de las puertas corredizas del patio. Los de seguridad se negaron a intervenir, así que llamé al departamento del sheriff. Ellos tampoco se habrían involucrado, pero mi adicto al crack tenía órdenes de detención pendientes.

Después de que me aseguraran repetidamente que mi adicto al crack estaba encarcelado, conduje hasta mi condominio. Los guardias de seguridad me dijeron que habían visto a mi adicto al crack escondiendo algo debajo del sofá. Cuando moví el sofá, encontré una pipa de crack. Más tarde, encontré otras pipas de crack esparcidas por mi preciosa casa de vacaciones, cuya posesión siempre me había llenado de orgullo. El apartamento era lo único hermoso en mi vida, que por lo demás estaba contaminada. Miraba por las ventanas las olas que golpeaban la playa. Me acordé de cuando Booster perseguía las olas en México. Cómo deseaba que Booster y yo pudiéramos disfrutar de Destin como habíamos disfrutado de México. Rara vez ingresábamos a los sagrados terrenos del condominio, debido a la egoísta y egocéntrica junta directiva de la asociación de condominios que se regodeaba en su política de no permitir mascotas.

Cuando regresé a mi cabaña, el miedo volvió a apoderarse de mí. La morada de mi adicto al crack volvía a ser una celda. Yo sería el culpable y sufriría las consecuencias. No era cuestión de si ocurriría, sino de cuándo. Acaricié tanto a Booster que pensé que se le caería el pelo. Él percibió mi inquietud y se mostró más apegado que nunca. De repente me pregunté por qué la comunidad de propietarios no permitía perros en el edificio. Resulta que, aunque en un principio era una urbanización que admitía perros, una nueva junta había tomado el control antes de mi compra. De repente se prohibieron las mascotas y se construyeron casas adosadas en terrenos que antes habían sido senderos para pasear mascotas. *¡Qué astutos!* pensé.

Se ha afirmado que, mientras nuestra sociedad crece, nos alejamos de la Madre Naturaleza y creamos entornos urbanos de frío hormigón y acero. Los niños han sufrido daños inconmensurables como consecuencia directa. En el siglo XIX, una joven británica llamada Florence Nightingale rescató a un perro moribundo y lo cuidó hasta que se recuperó. Fue un acontecimiento que cambió su vida y que inició el vínculo entre humanos y caninos. Más tarde se la conoció como la madre de la enfermería. La llegada de las viviendas sin mascotas creó una desconexión con la naturaleza, y los niños dejaron de aprender lo que era la empatía, el cariño y la responsabilidad de cuidar de otro ser. Era la generación del yo. Las consecuencias se manifestaron en jóvenes que no tenían ningún problema en robar un bolso o sacar una pistola y matar a alguien. *Cuando uno de estos chicos de sangre azul se convierte en víctima de un delito,* pensé, *contribuye a perpetuar su propia desaparición debido a un egoísmo desmedido.*

De repente pensé que debería poder disfrutar de las cosas bonitas de la vida, como la arena, el sol y la playa. Mi apartamento era lo mejor que había tenido en mi vida. Quería disfrutar de mi condominio, por el que pagaba una hipoteca exorbitante. Me había esforzado mucho para comprarlo y luchaba cada mes para pagarlo, así que pensé que más valía que intentara usarlo. Cuando lo compré, no me había preocupado por la política de no mascotas porque no tenía ninguna. Sólo tenía que cuidar de mi adicto al crack. Demonios, no había pensado en nada cuando lo compré, excepto que mi adicto al crack estaría cerca de su familia.

Un día, escribí una carta a todos los propietarios de condominios, pidiéndoles que me explicaran por qué no se permitían mascotas. Añadí fotos con humor y envié ciertos de cartas. Al fin y al cabo, Booster me había salvado la vida. Estoy seguro de que no todas las mascotas poseen tal mérito, pero la mayoría lo merecen por el amor incondicional que profesan a sus dueños. Esto desencadenó una tormenta de consecuencias. Sin darme cuenta, provoqué un baño de sangre con respecto a la política.

Las élites del condominio se llenaron de indignación y la junta directiva se quejó profusamente ante la idea de que los perros caminaran por los terrenos sagrados y venerados de los dioses. Enardecidos por la ignominia, los aristocráticos miembros de la junta se quejaron del tipo que quería permitir la presencia de miembros caninos en los terrenos. Uno de los miembros de la junta era tan odioso que hacía que Lucifer pareciera un pacifista. ¡Su sangre era tan azul que en realidad era púrpura!

Recibí cartas de todo tipo. Muchas personas agradecieron mis esfuerzos. Algunas eran desgarradoras, como la del hombre que había vivido en su condominio durante más de veinte años y había tenido que abandonarlo porque la asociación no le había permitido tener a su perro, que había sido prescrito. Otra propietaria me envió un email encantador en el que contaba que su esposo, moribundo, le había comprado un perro mientras estaba en su lecho de muerte en el hospital. Me explicó que nunca iba a ningún sitio sin ese perro porque era su última conexión con su esposo, ya fallecido. La junta del condominio nunca le permitió llevar a su perro, su *razón de ser*. Derramé lágrimas entonces, como lo hago ahora. Nunca la olvidaré y siempre recordaré lo amable que fue al tomarse el tiempo de compartir detalles tan íntimos de su vida. ¡Condo country era una audaz dicotomía entre egoísmo y altruismo!

1/26/2005

Estimado Mr. Hawn,

Soy propietaria de una unidad y he recibido su carta de fecha 5 de enero de 2005. En aquella época se admitían mascotas. . . En 1999 me diagnosticaron hepatitis "C" debido a una transfusión de sangre. . . El tratamiento fue como si me introdujeran clavos en todas las articulaciones del cuerpo y me golpearan con un bate de béisbol. . . Mi esposo fue diagnosticado con cáncer... Recibió quimioterapia, radiación y cirugía.... En la Navidad de 2003, me regaló otro border collie (Dakota). . . Aunque me gustaría mucho pasar tiempo en el condominio, no dejaré a ninguno de mis perros. . . Perdí a mi esposo en noviembre de 2004 y él amaba a los dos miembros de nuestra familia tanto como yo... Tiene todo mi apoyo, ojalá algún día todos conozcan y experimenten el amor de una mascota, Buena Suerte.

Después de un tiempo, la ebullición de los calderos se calmó. Nunca pedí formalmente permiso para tener a Booster en mi condominio. Por aquel entonces, evitaba la confrontación a toda costa y simplemente no estaba dispuesto a librar esa batalla. Las cosas se calmaron lo suficiente como para que la siguiente catástrofe entrara en mi vida aproximadamente un año después. Se llamaba Katrina. El huracán Katrina, de categoría 5, arrasó con mi vida y mi negocio. Tomé a Booster en brazos y me dirigí al único refugio que tenía. Me dirigí a los sagrados terrenos del condominio, fuera de peligro. Cuando llegué, me recibió una marioneta. Era la administradora de la propiedad que estaba bajo las órdenes de la junta directiva. Era su trabajo y no tenía nada contra ella. Sólo detesto cómo algunas personas se ven obligadas a ser más sumisas que un perro encadenado. Se acercó y me dijo, "Sr. Hawn, sabe que no puede tener un perro en la propiedad".

"Tuve que evacuar mi casa y mi perro Booster es mi hijo canino. Booster significa todo para mí. La junta puede proceder a desalojarme, pero será después de que pase la tormenta, cuando estemos a salvo y fuera de peligro."

Ella replicó, "Así que estamos de acuerdo en discrepar".

Yo repliqué cortésmente, "Sí, señora, así es". Como un davidiano de Waco, me mantuve firme.

Otros propietarios, que también buscaban refugio para sus familiares caninos y felinos, se acercaron a la junta y dijeron, "¡Bueno, si el señor Hawn puede tener a su perro, nosotros también podemos tener a nuestras mascotas!"

Finalmente, la junta accedió y notificó a los propietarios que, de momento, podrían tener a sus mascotas. ¡Un paso para mi Booster, un gran salto para la humanidad! Aquella tarde, la puesta de sol era preciosa, una vista panorámica del púrpura más vivo que uno pueda imaginar. *Los humanos podían encontrar la manera de complicar hasta un movimiento intestinal; ¡la junta tenía un control excesivo sobre todo el mundo!* pensé.

Lo que Booster y yo vivimos en Condo Hell fue el resultado de la ignorancia egocéntrica y miope de los de "sangre azul". En los días y años que siguieron, aprendí cuán ignorantes e insensibles eran muchos funcionarios *públicos* en este mismo sentido. Estos funcionarios, en puestos de confianza, no comprendían la profundidad del vínculo entre  mascotas y seres humanos. Es en esos momentos cuando las personas necesitan urgentemente los atributos únicos, terapéuticos y cariñosos que proporcionan incondicionalmente los animales.

No entendieron que la gente no abandonaría a sus miembros peludos de la familia, a sus hijos caninos, especialmente durante acontecimientos catastróficos como los huracanes. Como resultado directo, innumerables personas perdieron la vida.

Un reportero que asistía a una rueda de prensa preguntó a un supervisor de la Agencia Federal para la Gestión de Emergencias (FEMA), "¿Qué pasa con los perros y gatos que quedaron atrapados?" Su respuesta empezó con: "No son de nuestra incumbencia".

Tras el huracán Katrina se documentaron muchas historias trágicas relacionadas con animales. Un rescatista declaró, "La FEMA nos ha dicho que no podemos llevarnos a las mascotas. Nos dijeron que no podíamos llevar ni un gato ni un perro en nuestros botes. . . Es una norma estúpida. Va a morir más gente debido a eso". Recuerdo haber leído sobre un niño que estaba refugiado en el Superdome de Nueva Orleans. Cuando intentó subir a un autobús hacia Houston con su pequeño perro blanco, un agente de policía tuvo que quitarle el perro. Cuando leo las historias del Katrina relacionadas con mascotas, todavía derramo lágrimas. Ayudé a dar forma a una política temporal y transformadora en los terribles terrenos del condominio. Sólo desearía que otros que actúan en un cargo oficial hubieran tenido el beneficio de un *Booster* en sus vidas. De alguna manera, *se quedaron atrás*. Este es otro ejemplo flagrante de lo que sucede cuando se corta el vínculo entre la Madre Naturaleza y los seres humanos. Las viviendas sin mascotas conducen a la insensibilidad, a seres humanos ignorantes y a la falta de sentido común. Esto me hizo estar aún más agradecido de tener a Booster en *mi* vida.

En los años transcurridos desde Katrina, se han aprobado muchas leyes estatales y federales para garantizar que ya no se considere el vínculo entre las mascotas y los humanos con la misma insensibilidad. En 2006, el Congreso aprobó la *Ley de Normas de Evacuación y Transporte de Mascotas* (PETS, H.R. 3858). El Presidente Bush la firmó y se convirtió en ley. Incorporaba el bienestar de los animales en los planes de catástrofes, incluido el transporte, rescate, recuperación, seguimiento, etc. Felicitaciones al Congreso y al presidente por promover la sensibilidad, el liderazgo y lo que yo llamo "sentido común".

Después de que pasara el huracán, empecé a ir al condominio, pero acaté las normas y alojé a Booster en casa del suegro de mi adicto al crack en Destin. Tenía un bonito patio con cerca, pero me destrozaba tener que abandonar a Booster. Por la noche, lo buscaba en una cama vacía. Sin Booster a mi lado, simplemente no podía disfrutar de nada de lo que la vida tenía para ofrecer. Hércules tenía su cabello y yo

tenía a Booster. Lo que es... ¡es! Ya no podía justificar ir a mi condominio sin Booster. No era saludable para mí, y lastimaba a Booster, que no podía comprender por qué lo abandonaba.

La Junta colocó carteles en la propiedad que mostraban su arrogancia. Tenía un efecto escalofriante e intimidatorio. Pensar que cualquier ser humano haría algo así con respecto al acceso para personas discapacitadas me dejó completamente desconcertado. Cuestiono la legalidad de la redacción, ya que para el acceso no se requiere documentación de apoyo que demuestre que el perro está adiestrado o que la persona está cualificada para tener un perro de servicio. En algunos casos, podría ser razonable presentar una cartilla de vacunación. NO SE ADMITEN ANIMALES DE COMPAÑÍA, EXCEPTO ANIMALES DE SERVICIO CON LA DOCUMENTACIÓN APROPIADA; SE RECOMIENDA AVISAR CON ANTELACIÓN PARA ASEGURARSE DE QUE TODA LA DOCUMENTACIÓN ESTÁ EN REGLA. ¿Aviso previo? ¿Qué documentación? ¿Era necesario un sello presidencial para entrar en el recinto sagrado con un perro de servicio?

En ese momento, decidí que nunca volvería a mi condominio sin Booster. Fui a casa del suegro de mi adicto al crack a recoger a Booster para llevarlo a casa. Me recibió con saltos y carreras, como de costumbre. Poco después, estábamos de camino a casa, a la cabaña. Los dos estábamos tranquilos excepto por la tos intermitente de Booster. Una vez en casa, la tos de Booster empeoró. Lo llevé a un veterinario rural, que dijo que probablemente era tos de las perreras. Le recetó un antibiótico y eso fue todo. Booster siguió tosiendo durante una semana y, de repente, empezó a caminar por las sombras. Se negaba a caminar bajo la luz directa del sol. Me llevaba a la sombra. Era extraño. Volví a llevarlo al veterinario y le recetó otro antibiótico.

Esa noche me desperté de repente a las 4 de la mañana sin motivo aparente. Booster no estaba en mi cama, así que supe que algo andaba mal. Éramos siameses... nunca nos separábamos; simplemente no era posible. Entré en la cocina y estaba en el suelo. Se esforzaba por levantar la cabeza. Las babas caían al suelo como plástico líquido. Me miró con unos ojos que nunca, nunca olvidaré. Era como si dijera: "Me estoy muriendo. Ayúdame si puedes, pero si no, lo entiendo".

Entré en pánico. Mi corazón latía tan fuerte que no creía que mi pecho pudiera resistir el ataque. Tomé a Booster por las patas, lo arrastré hasta mi camioneta y conduje a 160 kilómetros por hora por la autopista hasta la clínica que atendía urgencias las 24 horas. Entré y ofrecí mi alma canina a los desconocidos que había dentro. Una vez más, fui reducido a escombros. La recepcionista estaba más preocupada por mí que por Booster. El veterinario más tarde me informó que Booster tenía 107 grados de fiebre y los pulmones llenos de sangre. Yo no podía soportar el sádico balanceo de la vida. *¿Por qué torturan mi alma?* me pregunté.

"Vete a casa. Te llamaremos", dijo la recepcionista.

En la cabaña, oía a las cucarachas pedorrear. Me senté solo y lloré, temblé y lloré aún más. Pensé en las veces que había echado a Booster. Recordé la sonrisa del mexicano cuando Booster le *quitó* los camarones de la mano. Pensé en el momento en que se incorporó, a pesar de sus puntos, para besarme después de la operación en la que le sacaron la mazorca de su estómago. Recordé el aullido desgarrador cuando se lastimó en Ajo jugando con otro perro.

Booster se moría. Si él moría, yo también moriría con él. No sería capaz de vivir la vida sin Booster a mi lado. Ese mismo día, más tarde, sonó el teléfono. Me estremecí. Esta vez, la madre de mi adicto al alcohol no estaba para atender la llamada. Tenía que hacerlo yo mismo. Una mano invisible tomó la mía y me ayudó a contestar el teléfono. "Hola, soy la Dra. Sutton. Booster va a estar bien, pero estuvo cerca. Parece que ingirió veneno para ratas, que impide la coagulación de la sangre. Por suerte, se trata de un veneno para ratas que podemos contrarrestar con Vitamina K. Está débil pero estable. Vamos a tenerlo aquí y le sugerimos que lo lleve a su veterinario cuando le demos de alta, con suerte mañana".

Dejé caer el teléfono y respiré hondo. Si hubiera dormido toda la noche y me hubiera despertado como la mayoría de las mañanas, Booster estaría muerto en el suelo de la cocina. *¿Por qué me había despertado? ¿Quién me despertó?* Era una gran **coincidencia**... una más en una cadena de **casualidades**. Me dormí llorando de incredulidad. Cuando desperté, me pregunté de dónde demonios había sacado Booster el veneno para ratas. Me di cuenta de que debía de estar en la casa del suegro de mi adicto al crack. Lo llamé para contarle la historia y me enteré de que, efectivamente, había puesto raticida en el jardín el año anterior, pero no donde había estado Booster... o eso creía él. Entonces me estremecí y recordé las palabras de mi adicto al crack, "Si descubro que te preocupas más por ese perro que por mí…" Después de todo, Booster era lo único que impedía a mi adicto al crack vivir a tiempo completo en una preciosa casa en la playa cerca de su familia. Nunca sabré la realidad de lo que pasó. ¿Booster encontró por casualidad el veneno para ratas o se lo dio mi adicto al crack? Si nos hubiéramos quedado en el condominio del que estaba tan orgulloso, esto nunca habría pasado.

A Booster ya no le gustó caminar bajo la luz directa del sol por el resto de su vida. Mostraba un comportamiento aprendido. Había caminado en la sombra cuando se vio afectado por el veneno para ratas. El calor había exacerbado su capacidad de respirar debido a sus pulmones llenos de líquido. ¡El sol era su enemigo! Vendí mi bote porque Booster no quería estar al sol. Por amor a Booster, cambié un precioso BMW Z4 convertible de color marrón y negro por un Honda Element verde lima. Cuando estaba entregando el BMW, una amable anciana del concesionario de Honda me preguntó, si había comprado el perro color marrón para que hiciera juego con la capota marrón de mi anterior coche. Rápidamente respondí, " No, señora, compré ese automóvil para que hiciera juego con mi perro!" Los vendedores de Honda se quedaron sorprendidos de que estuviera cambiando un BMW Roadster por un Honda Element. ¡Simplemente no había nada que no haría por el bienestar de Booster!

CAPÍTULO 6
EL INICIO DE LA EDUCACIÓN

Un día, pensé en mi promesa incumplida a mi Booster de darlo a conocer al mundo. Me di cuenta de que necesitaba educarme y algún tipo de credencial para hacerlo, así que empecé a leer todo lo que pude sobre el adiestramiento canino. Había enseñado a Booster a sentarse, agacharse, quedarse quieto y calmarse. Él había aprendido a abrir la nevera y a traer agua. Había sido muy sociable en parques de remolques alrededor de EE.UU. y México. Era hora de una educación más avanzada para mí y mi Booster. Leí sobre Camp Gone to the Dogs, donde los dueños acompañan a sus perros a un campamento de verano. ¡En lugar de enviar a tu hijo humano al campamento, llevas a tu hijo canino!

Llamé a la dueña del negocio, que me explicó que se había jubilado de Corporate America y había montado el negocio años antes. Subarrendaba una parte del campus del Marlboro College, situado en Marlboro (Vermont). Los asistentes podían alojarse en los dormitorios  o alquilar una habitación de hotel. Acabé llevando a Booster y a mi caravana a Vermont. La mayoría de los participantes humanos eran mujeres, pero había algunos hombres dispersos. Entrenadores de perros de todo el país acudieron al campamento para adiestrar a los dueños y a sus perros. Había una plétora de actividades para elegir. Podías llevar a tu perro a recuperar patos de goma de un estanque, enseñarle a hacer bonitos trucos, aprender órdenes de obediencia y mucho más.

Por la noche daban conferencias sobre temas veterinarios, nutrición canina, etc. Muchas personas disfrutaban haciendo *retratos de patas.* Se elegían colores de pintura y se aplicaban a una cartulina. Luego animabas a tu perro a caminar por la cartulina y voilà, había nacido un artista. Pronto apareció un Booster Van Gogh. Booster tenía la costumbre de tirar de mí. Un instructor se dio cuenta de que Booster era quien  me llevaba de paseo y me enseñó un collar para perros llamado Gentle Leader. No era un bozal, pero lo parecía. El Gentle Leader era útil para evitar que el perro tirara. Mi Booster era más fuerte que yo, así que en un instante mejoró nuestra relación para pasear. En el campamento, aprendí la forma correcta de dar una orden a un perro y la importancia del refuerzo positivo. Aprendí a utilizar eficazmente la comida para atraer a un perro y moldear su comportamiento. También le pagué a un instructor para que me diera clases individuales.

El American Kennel Club (AKC) tenía representantes en el campamento. Realizaban una prueba llamada Examen de Buen Ciudadano Canino (Canine Good Citizen - CGC), que evaluaba la respuesta del perro a las órdenes y su comportamiento en público y con otros perros. Fue una prueba dura, pero Booster la superó y recibió un parche CGC, que luego llevó en su chaleco durante años. En lugar de dejarlo ser simplemente un perro, yo había trabajado con él todos los días cuando estuvimos en el oeste. Booster había aprendido de una relación simbiótica con un humano al que cuidaba y quería ayudar. Eso le fue de gran ayuda para pasar el examen CGC. Los perros tienen una ética de trabajo y Booster tenía más que la mayoría. Nos enseñábamos el uno al otro, sin tener ninguno de los dos credenciales formales de enseñanza. Me sentí muy orgulloso cuando Booster aprobó el examen de CGC gracias a los conocimientos y experiencias adquiridos en las calles. Si Booster hubiera podido hablar, estoy seguro de que también habría expresado su alegría por *mi* progreso social.

Le pagué a un instructor para que fuera con nosotros a un supermercado, evaluara a Booster en público y escribiera una valoración porque yo quería hacer las cosas de la manera correcta. Booster sobresalió en todos los aspectos posibles. Él era natural y siempre se comportaba bien en público. Yo, en cambio, cuando era confrontado, solía perder la compostura, pasando de la calma a la furia en cuestión de segundos. Aunque a veces usaba un lenguaje impropio cuando encaraba a alguien, Booster nunca ladraba en público. Cuando se producían mis arrebatos, solía mirar a Booster y empezaba a respirar lenta y metódicamente. Salía de la situación y daba un paseo con Booster para calmarme. Pronto me volví reacio a ir a lugares sin él a mi lado. Necesitaba que me acompañara a todas partes.

Después de diez días en el campamento, regresamos a casa en nuestro remolque. Totalmente motivado por haber asistido al campamento canino, leí historias sobre cómo los perros ayudan a la gente. Leí en Internet una historia sobre una organización llamada Asociación Internacional de Perros de Asistencia (Association of Assistance Dog Partners – IAADP). Me enteré de que fue fundada en 1993 por el Dr. Ed Eames, un profesor que se quedó ciego debido a una retinosis pigmentaria a los cuarenta años. Posteriormente, él decidió tener un perro guía que le ayudara a superar los retos de la vida en Manhattan, Nueva York. Llamé a la IAADP y Ed contestó al teléfono. Respondió a mis preguntas con la paciencia y la comprensión de Job. Me explicó que uno de los mayores impedimentos para mantener su independencia no era su falta de visión, sino la incapacidad de los demás seres humanos para *ver* la importancia de Perrier, su perro guía benefactor. El magnífico labrador negro guiaba a Ed en las buenas y en las malas y permanecía resueltamente a su lado. El largo bastón blanco es una gran herramienta para los ciegos; sin embargo, no tiene un corazón que late como el tuyo mientras te consuela, dejándote saber que la vida va a ir bien".

El empático hombre me explicó que, los taxis solían pasar de largo porque iba acompañado de un perro guía. Si el conductor de taxi tenía miedo a los perros o pertenecía a una religión que enseñaba que los perros eran de alguna manera impuros e inmundos, el problema empeoraba. La *Ley de Estadounidenses con Discapacidades (Americans With Disabilities Act* – ADA) exige que todos los taxis permitan el acceso a los perros guía, pero no impide que los taxis los ignoren y sigan de largo.

Ed explicó además que, en ocasiones, fingía estar de compras mirando la vitrina de una tienda. Pedía a un desconocido que llamara a un taxi. Una vez que le abrían la puerta, se metía dentro con Perrier. Con frecuencia, el taxista gritaba, le decía que se bajara y lo amenazaba. En una ocasión, un taxista lo agarró e intentó sacarlo del taxi. A menudo, la policía tenía que intervenir para ayudar a Ed a conseguir un taxi.

La IAADP se fundó para ayudar a las personas que tienen perros de asistencia. Durante generaciones, la asociación actuó como una especie de mediador cuando surgían disputas entre las empresas y los discapacitados que se desplazaban con perros de asistencia. Ed era imparcial. Decía las cosas tal como las percibía, era ciego a la parcialidad. Me comentó que se iba a celebrar una conferencia de la IAADP en Baltimore dentro de unas semanas. Yo podía llevar a mi perro educado en casa, pero si causaba algún problema, me pedirían que abandonara la conferencia. "Sr. Hawn", me explicó, "entrenar perros de asistencia puede costar más de 100.000 dólares, y las personas dependen de sus perros. Si su perro actúa de forma agresiva o muerde a otro de los perros, podría asustarlo y volverlo inútil para el trabajo de perro de asistencia." Le aseguré a Ed que comprendía la magnitud de la situación. Le di las gracias, colgué el teléfono y empecé a pasearme por la cabaña.

Booster se levantó y corrió a mi lado, pensando que íbamos a dar un paseo. No tenía ni idea de que estaba pensando en llevarlo en avión a Baltimore para asistir a una conferencia repleta de perros. Booster adoraba ¡demasiado a otros perros! Sabía que estaría bien a mis pies en un avión, pero entrar en un edificio público y comportarse como un caballero era otra cosa. Demonios, ¡yo no sabía si podría actuar como un caballero bajo tanta tensión! Me angustié y seguí angustiándome aún más por la oportunidad.

Al darme cuenta de que era una *oportunidad*, decidí aprovecharla. Booster era un perro de servicio en entrenamiento. Él había aprobado el examen CGC y yo había recibido capacitación en el campamento. Como los dos habíamos sido entrenados, estaba seguro de que teníamos las credenciales para volar juntos en avión. Cuando llegó el fatídico día de viaje, Booster se puso su chaleco y entró conmigo en el aeropuerto de Nueva Orleans. Pronto entramos en el avión y nos sentamos en el asiento de la parte delantera, el asiento elegido por quienes viajan con perros de asistencia. El vuelo fue tranquilo. Booster durmió, pero yo no. Estaba preparado por si un gato caía del techo o un conejo corría por el pasillo.

Cuando aterrizamos, pedí un taxi y me preparé para una posible confrontación. Un señor mayor abrió la puerta del taxi a Booster, que saltó dentro sin ningún problema. Llegamos al puerto de Baltimore y sin tardar nos registramos en nuestra habitación de hotel. *¿Podría ser que, mientras mi actitud empezaba a mejorar, mi vida seguía el mismo camino? ¿Fue mi búsqueda de educación humana y canina la responsable de que mi actitud cambiara?* Reflexioné. Al día siguiente, asistimos a la conferencia. Entramos tímidamente en el centro de conferencias y nos dirigieron a un pasillo del segundo piso que conducía a la sala de conferencias.

Había mesas a ambos lados del pasillo. A mitad del pasillo, dos señoras con perros de asistencia estaban una al lado de la otra, observando los artículos que estaban a la venta en las mesas. No estaba dispuesto a pasar entre dos perros por miedo a la interacción canina. *¡Qué egoísmo el de estas señoras al crear un bloqueo tan peligroso!* Yo era novato en cuanto a los perros de asistencia, así que me senté y esperé a que se despejara el camino. En el momento en que me senté, otra señora entró con su perro y pasó por el pasillo. En cuestión de segundos, su perro se comportó de forma amenazadora con uno de los otros perros. Ed le dijo con autoridad que se marchara con su perro. La mujer culpó al otro perro de haber incitado al suyo, pero Ed no le creyó.

Cuando el camino se despejó, Booster y yo entramos en la sala de conferencias. Quedaban pocos asientos y nos sentamos entre dos Golden Retrievers que descansaban tranquilamente a los pies de sus adiestradores. Yo sabía que Booster iba a portarse mal... ¡pero no lo hizo! Casi decido marcharme, pero no permití que el miedo nos impidiera crecer como equipo.

Al final del día, las mujeres se volvieron hacia mí y me preguntaron: "¿Te gustaría cenar con nosotras?"

Como el idiota que era, pregunté, "¿Llevan a sus perros al restaurante?"

La respuesta fue un rotundo *"Sí, por supuesto"*.

Con voz temblorosa, dije: "Um… um… No sé, porque mi perro nunca ha estado en un restaurante y le encanta la comida".

Las mujeres se rieron y dijeron, "¿De qué te preocupas? Estarás con dos entrenadoras de perros".

Bueno, diablos, pensé, *si ellas están dispuestas, yo también iré.*

Nunca olvidaré el paseo por el puerto de Baltimore de camino al restaurante con los dos ángeles adiestradores y nuestros compañeros caninos. No estaba muy seguro de haber tomado la decisión correcta y de estar preparado para la tarea. Al poco tiempo, entramos en el restaurante y acabamos disfrutando de una comida estupenda y de muchas risas. Incluso olvidé que Booster estaba debajo de la mesa junto con las "Chicas de Oro". Les dije a las adiestradoras que era raro, pero cuando Booster llevaba su chaleco de perro de servicio, parecía saber que estaba trabajando. Debe ser psicosomático, les expliqué.

Las entrenadoras me miraron y me dijeron con toda naturalidad, "Los perros distinguen perfectamente entre el tiempo de trabajo y el tiempo de juego. Cuando les pones el chaleco, saben que es hora de trabajar". Lo comparé con un agente de policía que salía de fiesta en su día libre pero actuaba con profesionalismo cuando llevaba el uniforme.

Al final de la cena, expresé mi más sincero agradecimiento. ¡Había perdido mi virginidad como dueño de un perro de servicio! Una vez perdida, ¡nunca la recuperas! Estaba entusiasmado. Volamos a casa al día siguiente y un amigo nos recogió en el aeropuerto. Insistí en que fuéramos a comer a un restaurante cercano. Entramos como un grupo de tres. Booster estaba contento, descansando a mis pies. Rara vez volví a entrar en un restaurante sin Booster y estaba muy contento de poder vivir mi vida con él a mi lado dondequiera que fuera. Tenía sed de más enriquecimiento canino.

Recordando lo que había leído sobre la ADI cuando estaba en mi remolque en Arizona, cogí espontáneamente el teléfono, llamé a la escuela y hablé con gente que entendía de "perros". Fue como compartir un nuevo idioma. Por primera vez en veinte años, sentí pasión por algo que no eran mis adictos. Iba a ir a California con Booster, contra viento y marea.

En cuestión de días, hice los preparativos para asistir al seminario de adiestramiento de perros de servicio de siete semanas en la ADI de la Dra. Bergin y reservé una habitación en el Hotel Flamingo de Santa Rosa, California. Quería recibir capacitación y reforzar mis credenciales con respecto a la tenencia de perros de servicio. Me subí a un avión, con Booster a mis pies, y volé a California, sin saber muy bien qué esperar. El primer día, Booster encontró una tarjeta de crédito en la hierba y la llevó en la boca a la recepción. Resulta que la tarjeta pertenecía a uno de los empleados y Booster era un héroe. Por supuesto, yo ya lo sabía, pero era increíble que otros se dieran cuenta. La mayoría de los días me acompañaba a clase y se echaba fielmente a mis pies. Otros días, contrataba a estudiantes para que pasearan a Booster en mi ausencia.

Nací en el infierno de una familia de clase media, pero tuve la suerte de recibir una excelente educación secundaria. Mi madre trabajaba en la Universidad de Tulane en la época en que los salarios de las mujeres no estaban a la par con los de sus homólogos masculinos. No estoy seguro de que hoy sea muy distinto. Lo bueno era que si trabajabas a tiempo completo en la universidad durante cinco años, tus hijos podían matricularse gratis. Nunca terminamos de apreciar lo que se nos da y, en ese sentido, tardé diez años en graduarme. Más tarde asistí a la Facultad de Derecho de la Universidad Howard y fui elegido representante estudiantil de primer año. Estoy seguro de que fui el primero, si no el único, estudiante blanco elegido por el alumnado negro. Fue un honor. Lamentablemente, no terminé mis estudios porque tenía un padre con una enfermedad terminal a quien tenía que cuidar, así que abandoné.

Nunca utilicé mi educación formal. A menudo trabajaba con mis manos, haciendo tareas temporales. Durante muchos años, transporté a actores de compañías locales de producción cinematográfica que filmaban en ubicaciones en Luisiana. Mi padre me dijo una vez que preferiría verme trabajar con la cabeza que con las manos, pero él sabía que tendría éxito en la vida. Más tarde, construí un parque de casas móviles, reuniéndome con ingenieros y arquitectos por la mañana y operando grúas y bulldozers por la tarde. Esa fusión de aptitudes, utilizando mi educación para conocer a gente profesional y a la vez trabajando codo con codo con obreros, fue un regalo. Todo era educación. Dicen que si te gusta lo que haces para ganarte la vida, no volverás a trabajar otro día. Disfruté aprendiendo y construyendo el negocio. No se trataba simplemente de dinero.

En el seminario de ADI, de repente me di cuenta de que estaba teniendo la mayor experiencia educativa de mi vida. Asistí a clases en silla de ruedas y aprendí cómo las distintas enfermedades afectan al cuerpo. Algunas enfermedades afectan la movilidad, otras el razonamiento y otras influyen en ambos. Me enseñaron a adiestrar perros. ¡Ellos estaban ansiosos por aprender, y eran los mejores alumnos! Me dieron una correa y un perro y me dijeron que no soltara la correa durante siete días. Se llamaba el *proceso del cordón umbilical*. Igual que una madre está atada a un feto, yo estaba atado a una dulce Golden Retriever llamada Tatiana, que dependía de mí para alimentarse y nutrirse. Después de siete días de encierro emocional y físico, entré en un gimnasio con mis compañeros. Nos dijeron que soltáramos a nuestros perros, que empezáramos a caminar por la pista y que no los miráramos.

Sorprendentemente, cada perro caminaba al lado de su respectivo compañero humano. Un vínculo de la mejor calidad se había creado después de una semana. Cuando terminó el ejercicio, nos sentamos. Le entregué mi correa y mi perro a mi compañero y le dije, "Discúlpame". Salí y seguí andando. *¡Dios mío*, pensé, me acordé de mi Booster, que nunca se negaba a separarse de mí, incluso cuando lo apartaba y estaba resentido con él! El ejercicio del cordón umbilical fue más conmovedor para mí que para la mayoría. Mis compañeros nunca habían echado a su perro ni habían mostrado animadversión hacia él. Yo sí lo había hecho con Booster y, sin embargo, ¡la recompensa fue la misma! El amor y la lealtad caninos son incuestionables. Sí, lloré y caminé, caminé y lloré. Más tarde volví al gimnasio, cogí la correa de mi perro y miré a Tatiana a los ojos. Ella saltó a mi regazo y esbozó una hermosa sonrisa—creo que percibió que lo había *entendido*.

Aprendí cómo motivar a un perro utilizando golosinas como refuerzo positivo, con comida y elogios emocionales. Aprendí que la psicología utilizada para motivar a los humanos suele ser la misma que se emplea para motivar a los perros. A mitad del seminario, la clase fue llevada a un centro comercial donde te daban una lista de tareas para realizar con tu perro mientras permanecías en una silla de ruedas. Nos instruyeron para que lleváramos a nuestro perro a una tienda, hacer que tomara un par de calcetines de la estantería y los llevara al mostrador. Luego, le indicábamos que se pusiera en dos patas y dejara los calcetines en el mostrador. En ese momento, hacíamos que nuestro perro llevara nuestra tarjeta de crédito al cajero. Se enumeraron muchas tareas en una hoja de asignaciones. Sin que lo supiéramos, cada uno de nosotros estaba siendo observado por un *comprador secreto* que tomaba notas sobre nuestro desempeño. Por supuesto, no teníamos idea de que nos estaban siguiendo. Más tarde, ese día en el instituto, conocimos a la persona que nos había seguido y escuchamos las críticas.

Debo compartir algo que ocurrió aquel día. Me ordenaron que entrara en un baño con Tatiana y aprendiera a utilizar las instalaciones junto con mi perro. Entrar en un baño con un perro expone al perro a gran cantidad de olores y posibilidades. Por suerte, el baño de hombres estaba vacío cuando ingresé. Entré en la cabina de puerta ancha para discapacitados y le di la orden de sentarse. Ya estaba enamorado de Tatiana; era mi princesa dorada. Le dije: "Siéntate, chiquita".

Tatiana se negó a moverse.

Volví a decirlo pero más fuerte: "*Siéntate*, chiquita".

Tatiana, como la perra que era, se me quedó mirando.

Volví a darle la orden: "Siéntate chiquita... siéntate chiquita".

De repente, oí unos pies que se arrastraban y miré debajo de la partición. Había un tipo cuyos pies estaban delante del orinal. *¿De dónde demonios había salido?* me pregunté, pensando erróneamente que estaba solo con mi *chiquita*. Entré en pánico cuando repetí mis palabras en mi mente... *¡Siéntate chiquita, siéntate!* Me levanté de un salto, abrí de golpe la puerta y miré a un señor mayor muy desconcertado. "Señor", le expliqué, "estoy en la universidad aprendiendo a adiestrar perros de servicio y esta es mi *preciosa chiquita*, Tatiana. ¿Verdad que es linda?" ¡Él debió haber pensado que yo era un tipo muy raro!

Otro día empezamos a trabajar con adolescentes en situación de riesgo. Me llevaron a un centro de detención juvenil para chicas, donde les enseñé a socializar y adiestrar perros de servicio. No sabía absolutamente nada de trabajar con este tipo de población, pero el instructor de ADI me dijo que tuviera paciencia, que diera un paso atrás y que dejara que los perros hicieran su magia. En poco tiempo, las chicas se habían encariñado con *sus* perros. ¡Pidieron tiempo adicional para trabajar con ellos! Durante una excursión a la tienda con los perros, varias de ellas me pidieron dinero para comprar bocadillos... ¡para los perros! Esas chicas encontraron amor incondicional. Algunas contaron historias sobre sus padres maltratadores, o cosas peores, y yo me limité a escucharlas. Abrazaron a los perros y después compartieron un sinfín de pensamientos profundos. La experiencia fue tan terapéutica para mí como para las chicas. Todos tenemos una cruz que llevar; ¡sólo que algunas cruces son más pesadas que otras!

Recordé el día en que lo *entendí* y abracé a mi Booster en Ajo, Arizona. Mi vida cambió para siempre, y ahora era testigo de una transformación similar. La tasa de reincidencia entre los participantes en programas de adiestramiento canino en prisiones es significativamente menor que la de los no participantes. Bonnie me había introducido en un

"círculo de educación". Tuve la experiencia de trabajar con perros y adolescentes en situaciones de riesgo. Los adolescentes aprendían a adiestrar a los perros (una futura vocación), y las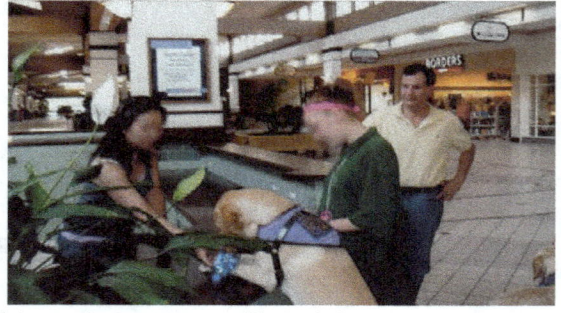

personas discapacitadas recibían a los perros, utilizándolos para aumentar su independencia en la vida. Era una tormenta perfecta de benevolencia.

Durante la segunda mitad del seminario, te conviertes en instructor y se te pide que pongas en práctica las habilidades de adiestramiento que acababas de adquirir. Enseñas a una persona discapacitada a usar el perro de servicio que va a recibir de la universidad. Se utilizaba una fórmula elaborada de coincidencia de personalidades para seleccionar qué perro se entregaba a cada discapacitado como perro de servicio. ¡Era fascinante!

Tuve que enseñar a una joven en silla de ruedas eléctrica a utilizar el perro de servicio que le iba a dar la universidad. Tuve que estrechar la mano a una persona cuya mano no funcionaba. Había hecho muchas cosas en mi vida, pero esto era diferente y poderoso. Por primera vez, estreché la mano que no funcionaba de una persona discapacitada. Se llamaba Elise.

Durante una salida de clase, Bonnie nos llevó a una ferretería para que aprendiéramos a elegir un mosquetón especial para atar la correa a la silla de ruedas y evitar que una rueda la atropellara y se enredara. Después enseñé a Elise a atar la correa de su perro a la silla. También le enseñé a entrar en un ascensor con su perro de la forma correcta. Si no lo hacía bien, la puerta del ascensor se cerraba, el perro se quedaba fuera y podía perderse o lesionarse. Ésta fue sólo una de las innumerables tareas que me encomendaron.

A veces, Elise estaba triste y se echaba a llorar. Yo también tenía que lidiar con eso. No, perdón; quería lidiar con eso. Yo también había experimentado lágrimas de frustración en la vida, y recurrí al pasado para mejorar el presente. ¡Fue verdaderamente un *regalo* para los dos! Cuando Elise recibió el perro que habíamos elegido para ella, se sintió muy decepcionada. Tenía la vista y el corazón puestos en otro perro. Por decirlo suavemente, estaba destrozada. Lloró mucho; sentí su dolor. Conocía muy bien el dolor de la decepción y la consolé lo mejor que pude. Al final de cada día, yo contaba con Booster para aliviar mi carga emocional y reemplazarla con vigor renovado, como sólo él podía hacer.

Mientras tanto, en el campus, una de mis compañeras sucumbió a la presión. Me explicó que tenía un umbral bajo de tolerancia al estrés debido a problemas en su vida. Yo tenía una tolerancia exagerada debido a todo lo que había pasado... una existencia de maldita zona de guerra. Le pedí que me acompañara a dar una vuelta. Yo conducía y ella hablaba. Ella lloraba y yo la escuchaba. Paramos en una cafetería y nos tomamos un refresco. Nos abrazamos durante lo que me pareció una eternidad. Me abrí a ella y ella se abrió a mí. De algún modo, ese día nos *fusionamos.*

A la mañana siguiente, me desperté con una misión en mente. Decidí tomar una foto de cada uno de mis compañeros e instructores en acción, trabajando con su perro. Quería regalarles un recuerdo de 8x10 para que recordaran la experiencia verdaderamente única de ADI y a su perro. Es difícil despedirse de tus compañeros de clase, pero aún más difícil es despedirse de tu perro. Realmente, tu perro ADI se convierte en un compañero de clase y miembro de la familia. Estábamos todos juntos en esto, y a muchos estudiantes les costó separarse. Yo fui uno de ellos. Aunque Booster era parte de mi vida, iba a extrañar a mi *chiquita* Tatiana, más conocida como Tattie. Fue duro dejarla atrás. Todavía tengo videos de mi chiquita Tattie, y Booster saltando de cama en cama.

Tomé un montón de fotos de mis compañeros, elegí las poses más expresivas y las amplié. Además, mandé hacer una de tamaño billetera y la introduje en un llavero de plástico al que puse una etiqueta que decía, "Aprender es la clave". Estaba deseando ver las reacciones de mis compañeros cuando les entregara los regalos. Por primera vez en años, había hecho nuevos amigos... amigos amantes de los perros... amigos especiales. Tenía ganas de hacer algo. Me preocupaba ir a California y ser capaz de afrontar una experiencia escolar, así que no lo había esperado con entusiasmo. Dar regalos a mis compañeros de clase era *un paso de gigante para Davis, ¡un gran salto en mi vida!* Recordé mis enseñanzas de Al-Anon... la serenidad... *sólo la mantienes en tu vida, si la das.*

Un día en clase, oí que Bonnie se había dirigido al Estado de California expresando su deseo de fundar una universidad en la que los estudiantes pudieran aprender sobre perros. A menudo le pido a la gente que se imagine a Bonnie entrando en alguna oficina estatal en el otoño de su vida. Puedo oír al empleado estatal preguntando, "¿Puedo ayudarla, señora?"

"Sí, quiero fundar una universidad", seguramente habría dicho Bonnie.

"¿Qué tipo de universidad quiere fundar, señora?" sería la pregunta más probable.

Ella explicaría: ¡"Va a ser una universidad donde la gente aprenda sobre perros"!

Se me ocurre que probablemente pensaron que consumía marihuana medicinal antes de que se pusiera de moda en California.

Bonnie hipotecó literalmente todo por lo que había trabajado en la vida para lograr su objetivo. Hoy en día, la BUCS es la única universidad acreditada del mundo dedicada a enseñar a los estudiantes las Ciencias de la Vida Canina. Vienen estudiantes de todo el mundo, a un alto costo, debo añadir, para aprender de Bonnie en ADI y BUCS. Muchos de los estudiantes son mayores, en busca de una ocupación más significativa, con lo que se pretende marcar una diferencia significativa en su país y en el mundo. Me interesé por la posibilidad de entrar en el máster como una persona mayor con deficiencias físicas y mentales.

Mi hermano me dijo que sería un despilfarro de dinero espantoso. Hacía tiempo que había aprendido que si él decía que no debía hacer algo, entonces ¡*DEBÍA* hacerlo! Él era la prueba de fuego. Me había dicho que no debía poner casas rodantes en mi propiedad, y eso terminó dándome independencia económica. Cuando sus pensamientos negativos surgieron y se desbordaron, me inscribí sin demora. Le había prometido a Booster que compartiría con el mundo lo que había hecho por mí. Necesitaba de educación para cumplir mi promesa a Booster, independientemente de lo que pensara mi hermano. Después de todo, Booster salvó mi vida, ¡no mi hermano! Contemplé la posibilidad de asistir a la universidad futurista, igual que una vez había contemplado el suicidio. Mi decisión de no suicidarme me permitió vivir. Contemplar la posibilidad de seguir una educación canina podría permitirme *vivir*... un bien antes desconocido.

Después de lo que pareció una eternidad, el día de la graduación del seminario de verano (también conocido como campamento de entrenamiento) estaba cerca. Booster y yo, habíamos hecho amigos, tanto hombres como perros, y pronto tendríamos que separarnos. Mi nuevo y valiente mundo pronto llegaría a su fin y tendría que regresar a la realidad. Estaba haciendo la transición de un mundo en el que había perdido mi individualidad y no tenía relaciones saludables, similar al *"Mundo feliz"* de Aldous Huxley. En él se describe el temor a perder la identidad individual en un mundo orientado a la ciencia que está por venir. De repente me sentí triste y al mismo tiempo deprimido, estaba cansado y me encontraba pasando más tiempo en la cama con Booster que relacionándome con mis compañeros. Booster seguía saltando emocionado cuando escuchaba a los demás perros jugando afuera con sus dueños, quienes les enseñaban nuevas habilidades. Me daba pena por Booster; le tocó la peor parte al tenerme como su humano. Yo lloraba, dormía, me despertaba y repetía el proceso.

Un día, mi antes estresada compañera de clase llamó a mi puerta. Lo primero que pensé fue en alejarla. *¿Quizá necesita mi apoyo otra vez?* pensé. No podía abandonarla, como tampoco pude abandonar a Booster en el deshuesadero. Abrí la puerta y me encontré con una sonrisa alegre y un abrazo. "Vamos a celebrar", me dijo al oído. "Estoy muy contenta de haber terminado el curso, y no podría haberlo hecho sin ti. Quiero invitarte a tomar unas copas para celebrarlo. ¡Llevemos a Booster y a Tatiana a pasar una tarde en la ciudad!" me dijo.

Acepté a regañadientes y, en cuestión de minutos, nos llevamos a nuestros caninos a un pub local.

Booster y su dulce Golden se comportaron perfectamente. Mi compañera de clase me levantó el ánimo al instante, y hablamos, hablamos y hablamos aún más. Me dijo que yo era muy fuerte, pero que me sentía muy débil. No dejaba de darme las gracias, y yo le decía una y otra vez que era su fuerza interior la que le había permitido completar el difícil curso. En pocas palabras, le dio la vuelta a la situación y me dijo que yo también tenía una fuerza interior que me ayudaría a superar los días venideros. Tras horas de melancolía y risas entremezcladas, dejamos el pub y sacamos a pasear a los perros. Cuando volvimos a los dormitorios, le di las buenas noches, miré a Booster y le pregunté, "¿Listo?" Corrió hacia la puerta de mi dormitorio, y golpeó la manija. La puerta se abrió y Booster saltó a la cama en señal de celebración. Al poco rato, los dos estábamos profundamente dormidos.

Días después, estaba en el escenario con Booster a mi lado. ¡Nos estábamos graduando! Nuestros compañeros estaban a nuestro lado con un sentimiento mutuo de logro. Juntos habíamos trabajado con perros, discapacitados, adolescentes en situación de riesgo y otros, para adquirir una habilidad especializada. Pocos no participantes podrían entender la cantidad de trabajo y dedicación invertidos en el campamento de entrenamiento de ADI. Todos pagamos para aprender una habilidad que ayudaría a los discapacitados a tener una vida mejor. Nos sentimos orgullosos. Hubo un asistente que debería haberse sentido más orgulloso que los demás. Era mi Booster. Él había roto las cadenas de la codependencia y me había motivado para asistir al seminario de ADI. Miré a mi Booster que sonreía a mi lado. Lo miré a los ojos. Él sabía muy bien lo que yo sentía.

Una vez recibidos nuestros diplomas y carnés de graduación de ADI, nos sentamos en el escenario para la segunda parte de la ceremonia. Los asistentes discapacitados con los que trabajamos iban a recibir a su perro de servicio. Los perros y su compañero discapacitado se graduaban juntos. No estaba preparado para lo que estaba a punto de presenciar. Una joven subió al escenario con un precioso Golden Retriever que ella, junto con su familia, había criado en su casa durante más de un año. Eran *criadores de cachorros* que patrocinaban perros de servicio en entrenamiento hasta que tuvieran edad suficiente para recibir adiestramiento a tiempo completo en la universidad. La niña miró al veterano de guerra en el escenario y dijo, "Quiero a Missy. La he paseado y he hablado con ella... ¡es una perra estupenda! Es muy dulce. Ahora quiero que sea tuya". La valiente niña tomó la correa y la apretó contra la mano destrozada del veterano de guerra. En cuestión de segundos, el auditorio se inundó de lágrimas, sacudido por un tsunami de emociones. La máquina de matar que era aquel hombre lloraba desconsoladamente, reducido a escombros emocionales. Yo estaba temblando. Mientras escribo estas palabras, lágrimas de recuerdo corren por mis mejillas.

A continuación, Elise fue llamada al escenario para recibir a su perra, Kate. Condujo su silla eléctrica por el escenario con una sonrisa cuyo resplandor opacaba el de la estrella más brillante. Era la joven que había estallado en lágrimas el día en que estaba tan estresada. Había compartido detalles íntimos de su vida como parapléjica, viviendo en un cuerpo que no funcionaba como debía. Su madre había ido a la universidad con ella para que pudiera obtener su título al lado de sus compañeros. *Qué héroes*, pensé. Ojalá yo hubiera tenido la fuerza, la fortaleza y la convicción que ella tenía. Aunque a Elise no le funcionaban las piernas, ese día se ganó sus alas. ¡Se elevó!

Cuando concluyó la ceremonia de graduación, me apresuré a colocar las fotos 8x10 en sus marcos sobre una mesa que había comprado para este fin. Mientras mis compañeros de clase salían con sus amigos y familiares, les dije que tenía un regalito para ellos en la mesa. Se acercaron a la mesa y encontraron sus respectivas fotos 8x10 y el llavero que las acompañaba.

"Así que por eso has tomado tantas fotos últimamente", comentó uno.

"Davis, qué genial", dijo otro.

Entonces, de reojo, vi a Elise y a su familia que venían hacia mí. Elise hizo que Kate se levantara, tomara la foto con el marco de plástico y se la llevara. Me acerqué a ella, tomé su mano y cuando la solté me pareció que había pasado una eternidad. Yo tenía lágrimas en los ojos y su madre se me acercó y me agradeció por enseñar a su hija y ayudar a que todo fuera posible.

La primera vez que trabajé con Elise, le tendí la mano a su perra Kate y ella me dio su pata. Entonces me di cuenta de que yo no había estrechado la mano de Elise. Me sentí mal y le tendí la mano, ¡sin saber cómo estrechar una mano que no puede "moverse"! Mi mano no tardó en apretar la suya y todo mi cuerpo empezó a temblar. Se convirtió en el mejor apretón de manos que he experimentado en mi vida. Desde ese momento, nunca he dejado de acercarme a una persona con discapacidad física para estrecharle la mano o establecer un contacto físico.

Miré a Elise, me volví hacia su madre y le dije: "Antes de la experiencia con ADI, nunca había conocido ni trabajado con un parapléjico. No sabía cómo acercarme a una persona así y nunca le habría tendido la mano a alguien que no podía encontrar la mía. Su hija me enseñó mucho más que yo a ella". En una ocasión coloqué las piernas de Elise en su silla de ruedas. El destino la había obligado a exponer su vulnerabilidad y a confiar en los demás a una edad

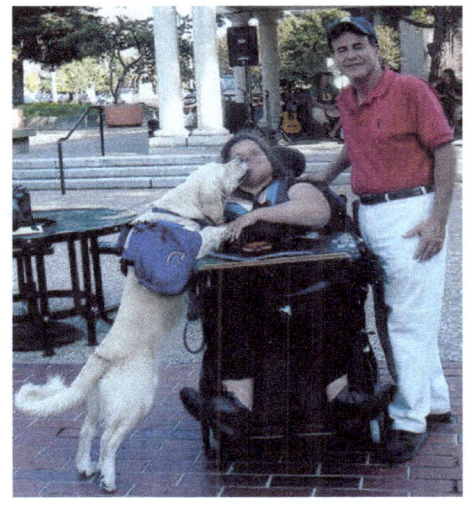

temprana. Los estudios han demostrado que un perro de servicio hace más accesible a una persona discapacitada. La gente suele recordar más el nombre del perro que el de su compañero discapacitado. Lo aprendí de primera mano en ADI. Raro es el día que no extrapole algo que aprendí con alegría en ADI.

Trabajar con Elise me enseñó que hay otras personas en este mundo que también luchan a diario y, sin embargo, están a la altura de las circunstancias. Sin saberlo, me enseñó que está bien confiar, ser vulnerable y aceptar la ayuda de los demás. Lo recordé cuando pedí ayuda física y psiquiátrica a los médicos en los años siguientes. El primer día, después de conocer a Elise, de alguna manera me sentí menos diferente. Si Elise podía hacerlo, ¡entonces yo también podía! Confiaba en que la vida sería un poco más fácil para Elise con Kate a su lado. Esperaba que a mí me ocurriera lo mismo con Booster a *mi* lado.

Al final del día, me palpitaba mucho la pierna. Me metí en la bañera, tomé la regadera y rocié agua caliente en la zona afectada sin parar, por horas. Mandé a Booster que me trajera agua de la nevera y la bolsa de medicinas. Mis compañeros se habían ido y ya no tenía a Tattie. Ahora estábamos solos, Booster y yo. Con frecuencia miraba por encima del borde de la bañera para asegurarme de que él seguía ahí. Nunca me abandonó. Nunca se separó de mí en el suelo del baño. Derramé algunas lágrimas que cayeron en una bañera de contentamiento. Aunque sentía dolor físico, me estaba esforzando por manejar un dolor psicológico que era discapacitante y tortuoso. Me recordé a mí mismo que si Elise podía hacerlo, yo también, sobre todo con Booster a mi lado.

A la mañana siguiente, tomé el chaleco de servicio de Booster y le dije: "Vístete", y él entró en él. Bonnie me explicó una vez que uno se viste a sí mismo, y tú perro también debería hacerlo. Es cuestión de responsabilidad. Todo en ADI se enseña en el contexto de la relación entre caninos y humanos. Vestirse era otro ejemplo. Sí, los perros pueden vestirse solos. También pueden ayudar a los humanos a vestirse y cambiar sus vidas para siempre de formas inimaginables. Solo hay que preguntar a nuestros veteranos. En Estados Unidos mueren más veteranos por suicidio que en combate; una ramificación lamentable del trastorno de estrés postraumático (TEPT). Casi cada hora del día muere un veterano por suicidio; veintidós al día, para ser exactos. Al hacer que los veteranos con problemas psiquiátricos entrenen perros para ayudar a veteranos con problemas físicos, los efectos del TEPT y la tasa de suicidios disminuyen, ¡y el veterano regresa a casa!

De repente me di cuenta de que yo también volvería a casa pronto. La verdad es que no me ilusionaba mucho. De hecho, tenía miedo. Aunque me había fortalecido, seguía siendo frágil, habiendo caminado sobre cáscaras de huevo durante tanto tiempo. Booster y yo subimos al automóvil alquilado por última vez. Él abrió la puerta con entusiasmo y saltó adentro. Yo entré, lleno de inquietud. Estuve en piloto automático hasta que entregué el vehículo en el aeropuerto. Horas después, Booster y yo estábamos en casa. La cabaña estaba vacía y desolada. Judy Garland en *El Mago de Oz* dijo una vez, "No hay lugar como el hogar. No hay lugar como el hogar". Para nosotros, nunca se dijo algo más verdadero. Un hogar es lo que tú haces de él, ¿verdad? Había convertido mi hogar en un infierno en la tierra. Ahora sentía que podría convertirlo en un paraíso en la tierra, con la ayuda de Booster.

En los días siguientes, necesité que Booster me ayudara física y emocionalmente. Me sostenía cuando no podía tocar el suelo con el pie debido al dolor insoportable de la gota. Se acostaba sobre mi pierna cuando palpitaba sin piedad durante la noche. Booster abría la nevera y me traía agua. Abría la puerta del automóvil y me traía la bolsa de las medicinas. Encendía los interruptores de la luz por la noche cuando tenía pesadillas. Cuando tenía imágenes del cuchillo acercándose a mí, en mi último segundo de vida, Booster respondía a mis gritos. Saltaba a la cama y me despertaba. Al instante sabía que no estaba siento atacado realmente... después de todo, ¡había un perro de 45 kilos a mi lado!

Booster me mantenía conectado con la realidad. Mantenerse conectado con la realidad es una forma de calmar a una persona que experimenta ansiedad durante un ataque de pánico. La persona toma conciencia de su entorno. La familiaridad resultante genera una sensación de tranquilidad. También me avisaba cuándo alguien estaba cerca. Siempre confiaba en Booster para que entrara en mi casa, en un hotel y en mi automóvil antes de atreverme a entrar yo.

Fortalecido por mi formación en ADI, empecé a entrenar a Booster para que se convirtiera en mi *perro de servicio*. Mucha gente lo llama así para poder viajar con su *mascota*. Yo consideraba eso egoísta y detestable. Había completado lo que consideraba el mejor curso de adiestramiento de perros de servicio del mundo. Mi instructor creó el concepto de perro de servicio. Booster y yo habíamos pasado más de un año preparándonos para el acceso público. Llegaría el día en que lo llevaría en público sin que un adiestrador, un compañero o un amigo me acompañara. Me preocupaba recaer en un comportamiento inaceptable y vergonzoso si me enfrentaba a humanos ignorantes que rechazaban a Booster.

La primera vez que llevé a Booster a un lugar público con fines de adiestramiento, estaba solo, y tenía un miedo terrible. Ya no era un estudiante practicando bajo supervisión o rodeado de compañeros. La gente se quedaba mirando al hombre del perro grande. Era una tienda por departamentos de mi ciudad natal y dos niños pequeños empezaron a gritar cuando vieron a Booster Era como si un monstruo del espacio exterior hubiera aterrizado. El director de la tienda de fotografía me dijo que sacara al perro. En lugar de arriesgarme a una confrontación, no dije ni una palabra. Simplemente me fui. Booster no había hecho absolutamente nada malo. Pensé, *Si los padres de los niños hubieran educado a sus hijos tan bien como yo había educado a mi Booster, los niños no habrían reaccionado de una manera tan absurda.* Si hubiera dicho algo, mi TEPT me habría afectado y habría pasado de la calma al exceso de forma instantánea.

Con frecuencia, no recordaba las batallas que había librado. Un amigo que me había acompañado una vez, me dijo, que yo no era la misma persona cuando las ramificaciones del TEPT se manifestaban. Tuve que aprender a controlarme ante la agresión humana. Al final del día, estaba bastante deprimido por haber defraudado a Booster. No logramos crecer como equipo. Me llevó mucha práctica incorporar con éxito mis lecciones de ADI a las lecciones personales de la vida real. Con el tiempo, el número de episodios de confrontación disminuyó, al igual que la gravedad de los eventos. Booster buscaba atención en lugares públicos, algo a lo que me fui acostumbrando e incluso llegué a apreciar. Después de todo, ¡era mi Booster!

Cuando aprendí a controlar mis emociones, a menudo me divertía dando la vuelta a la situación, cuando los empleados de las tiendas me desafiaban al entrar en un local con Booster. Una vez en Flippin, Arkansas, entré en unos grandes almacenes en Halloween. Los empleados estaban disfrazados y, como era de esperarse, al entrar en la tienda nos esperaba un enfrentamiento. El Zorro se acercó. "Oiga, señor, no permitimos perros en la tienda", gritó el joven héroe, salvando a la humanidad de la presencia de un perro.

"Es un perro de servicio", le expliqué a aquella persona, suponiendo que no podía leerlo por sí mismo aunque estaba escrito en el chaleco de Booster.

"¿Es un perro de servicio de verdad?" dijo.

Le contesté intencionadamente, en voz lo bastante alta como para atraer la atención de todos: "Oye, chico, es un perro de servicio real, pero tú no eres el Zorro, así que ¿podrías quitarte de en medio para que pueda comprar y gastar mi dinero?"

El joven metió el rabo entre las piernas y se escabulló. En ese momento, un guardia de seguridad de aspecto algo cómico se acercó para salvar la situación.

"Necesito hablar con el gerente", le expliqué. "¿Dónde está el gerente? pregunté con firmeza.

Antes de que pudiera responderme, el director de la tienda saltó como un perro San Bernardo con sobrepeso.

Le expliqué, "Señor, este joven me desafió al entrar en su tienda simplemente porque soy discapacitado y voy acompañado de un equipo médico duradero llamado perro de servicio. Todas las miradas estaban puestas en mí, y yo era el centro de atención. No me gusta, pero, en realidad, no es culpa de él... ¡es culpa suya! Usted tiene carteles que dicen "se admiten animales de servicio" porque su empresa perdió un pleito hace años y ese fue parte del acuerdo. De hecho, su tienda perdió un juicio posterior relacionado con los perros de servicio que exigía la colocación de un número específico en todas las puertas de entrada, explicando: "Si tiene problemas, llame al 1-800...". Sr. gerente, usted no capacitó adecuadamente a este joven y, por tanto, sometió a su empresa a otra posible demanda. Nos debe una disculpa a los dos".

Después de que el gerente murmurara una disculpa fingida, la gente sonrió y yo fui a hacer más compras sin impedimentos. Detestaba la confrontación, disfrutaba de la soledad y muchas veces temía por mi seguridad cuando estaba solo. Parecía que cada vez que bajaba mi escudo protector, mi cabeza rechazaba la idea y la consideraba totalmente inaceptable. Por suerte, sabía que Booster me avisaría si alguien se acercaba y eso me consolaba. En realidad, no habría podido quedarme en mi casa si no fuera por mi Booster, mi amigo, mi medicina, ¡mi roca!

Después de un tiempo, me di cuenta de que Booster no tenía compañía canina. Era totalmente feliz conmigo siendo el centro de su universo, pero yo quería más de la vida para él que para mí. Un día, entré en Internet y busqué un cachorro labrador, una novia para Booster. Vi la fotografía más increíble de un perro que se parecía a un Weimaraner, pero era un Labrador plateado. Booster había fertilizado mi tenue regreso a la vida, y yo quería plantar otra semilla. Decidí redoblar la apuesta y me prescribí otra receta canina. Booster y yo nos beneficiaríamos.

Llamé a mi amigo Charles y le dije, "Oye, hace un día soleado y hermoso, vamos a Carolina del Norte".

"¡Eh!" fue la respuesta.

Me reí y le expliqué que pensaba que mi Booster se sentía solo. ¡Por una vez, yo quería ser *su* apoyo! Charles siempre estaba dispuesto a vivir aventuras y quería a Booster como si fuera suyo. Estuvo totalmente de acuerdo en que Booster se merecía una compañera canina. Al día siguiente, Booster, Chuck y yo nos subimos a mi camioneta y nos fuimos a Carolina del Norte. Visitamos a un criador de labradores cuyas instalaciones eran absolutamente impresionantes. De hecho, ¡te quitaba el aliento cada vez que inhalabas! Si alguna vez hubo un criadero de cachorros, ¡era éste! No me sentí desanimado, sino más decidido que nunca a rescatar un alma canina. Mi necesidad de rescatar al pájaro herido se activó y elegí al cachorro labrador plateado más necesitado. La llamé Grecian, como el tinte para el cabello Grecian Formula... ¡para quitar las canas!

Mientras paseaba por las instalaciones, vi por casualidad a una preciosa hembra labrador blanca blockhead. Pregunté por ella y me dijeron, "Se llama Penny, es mi favorita, pero estoy dispuesto a dejarla ir". En un criadero de cachorros *TODO* tiene un precio y efectivamente, regresé a casa con las dos cachorras. Penny siguió siendo Penny, ya que no podía despojarla de la única dignidad que había tenido al crecer en un criadero de cachorros. Mi familia crecía a pasos agigantados. No podía ser más feliz. Es una afirmación increíble viniendo de un alma torturada. Pensé en el mítico personaje Tántalo, quien buscaba alcanzar frutos en los árboles y agua, pero los árboles y el agua se alejaban continuamente. Me sentía como un Tántalo moderno; la felicidad a veces parecía posible, pero siempre estaba fuera de mi alcance.

Mi vida con un trío de labradores floreció. Seguí entrenando a Booster para que realizara tareas de perro de servicio y se comportara correctamente en público, como yo también aspiraba a hacerlo. Mientras tanto, jugaba con Penny y Grecian en su tiempo libre. Booster era feliz. Aprendí a apreciar la felicidad del perro que antes había rechazado.

Grecian y Penny eran el harén de Booster. Grecian era una diva, y Penny era absolutamente la perra labrador blockhead más hermosa del planeta. No necesitaba joyas porque ella misma era una joya.

Un día, llegué a casa y encontré a Booster y a Grecian, pero no a Penny. El trío era inseparable. Las alarmas se encendieron de inmediato. Busqué a Penny, pero no estaba por ninguna parte. Busqué con pánico durante todo el día, pero no la encontré. Al día siguiente, Charles vino por su propia cuenta. Me llamó por la tarde y me dijo, "Dave, encontré a Penny. Está muerta en el bosque".

Entré en erupción espontáneamente como un volcán expulsando emociones. Conduje para encontrarme con Charles y mi querida Penny. Tenía un agujero en el pecho que parecía de bala. Lógicamente, especulé que algún lugareño podría haberle disparado. Tomé a Penny en brazos y la llevé a mi veterinario, el Dr. Beacham. Le expliqué que necesitaba saber qué le había pasado a Penny. Si había un asesino canino en mi barrio, necesitaba saberlo. Más tarde ese día, llamó y dijo que no era una herida de bala. Era más bien una pinchazo.

Unos días después, paseaba por mi propiedad y vi una gran roca en el campo. No tenía idea de dónde había salido. Cuando la examiné, vi un alambre que sobresalía de la parte superior. De repente me di cuenta de que era un resto de la losa de hormigón que había formado parte de mi garaje antes de que el huracán Katrina lo destruyera. Había nivelado la losa con una excavadora y colocado los escombros resultantes en la parte trasera de mi represa para fortificarlo. Penny debió cruzar la presa, resbaló y cayó sobre la roca que la lastimó. Probablemente continuó en el campo con Booster y Grecian hasta que la roca se desprendió. Se desangró más adelante en el camino. Yo estaba destrozado, igual que las rocas de la represa.

Caminé hasta la represa y miré todas los restos. De repente me di cuenta de que había barras de acero y fragmentos de metal que sobresalían de los escombros de hormigón. Era una pesadilla a punto de ocurrir. Me sentí estúpido. Entre lágrimas, me agaché y rompí todas las barras. Pedí perdón a mi difunta Penny con cada barra que se rompía con mi mano. Dicen que el tiempo lo cura todo, pero nunca he olvidado a Penny, aunque he intentado hacerlo para disminuir mi sentimiento de culpa. Como un hombre que lloró después matar a un mosquito que lo picó, deshacerse de la culpa no es tarea fácil. Sé que Booster y Grecian echaban de menos a Penny tanto como yo.

La depresión se apoderó de mí, pero la vida continuó. Más tarde, cuando estaba fuera de la ciudad por trabajo, pasé tiempo navegando en Internet y buscando cachorros de labrador que estuvieran a la venta. Vi un hermoso labrador hembra de color rojo zorro que era simplemente precioso. No me atraían las perras pelirrojas, pero estos cachorros eran sencillamente preciosos. Llamé al criador e impulsivamente gasté el sueldo de esa semana en un nuevo cachorro. Luego tomé el teléfono y llamé a mi amigo Charles. "Necesito tu ayuda, como siempre. Acabo de enamorarme de una perra pelirroja".

Charles no supo cómo responder a eso. Simplemente dijo, "¿En serio?"

Le transmití mi intención de comprar un cachorro labrador rojo zorro a un criador de Michigan. Charles, siendo Charles, aceptó de inmediato recoger a mi pelirroja, acertadamente llamada Scarlett, en el aeropuerto, una semana más tarde.

Cuando llegué a casa, fui en seguida a casa de Charles y conocí a Scarlett. Era tan pelirroja cómo podía serlo, una labradora de color rojo zorro que había sido criada para cazar y buscar a la presa, por lo que tenía mucha energía y entusiasmo. Era todo un desafío, seguramente mantendría ocupados a los demás. Tenía más energía que un Terrier Jack Russell. Conduje a casa y sostuve a Scarlett en mis brazos durante una hora. Le presenté a Booster. Él gruñó y se alejó. Grecian, por otro lado, de inmediato amó a Scarlett y la cuidó. Me recordó a una reunión de recién llegados de Al-Anon. La manada ladró como bienvenida y la nueva cachorra reaccionó con serenidad, pero expresó temor a lo desconocido. En una hora, la recién llegada se había integrado y la familia había crecido. Éramos uno. La manada me necesitaba y yo los necesitaba a ellos. La dinámica de la dualidad se puso en marcha y floreció. En poco tiempo, solía ver a Booster durmiendo con Scarlett. Era el líder dominante de la manada, a veces gruñón pero siempre cariñoso. Me recordaba a mi padre.

Esa noche, dormí con todos los "niños" en mi cama. Me abrazaron, me besaron, me arroparon y me amaron sin preguntas ni planes. Los niños no tardaron en roncar y estoy seguro de que yo también. Mis chicos sabían aceptar, agradecer y apreciar. Eran enérgicos, entusiastas y querían ser complacientes por razones altruistas. Fue una curva de aprendizaje para mí. Fue una de las mayores curvas de aprendizaje que he experimentado en mi viaje por la tierra. Éramos como uno solo.

Todos los días la manada socializaba en el campo cercado de 5 acres contiguo a mi cabaña. Corrían, saltaban y se zambullían en el estanque. Se revolcaban en la hierba y perseguían pájaros. Solían meter la cabeza bajo el agua persiguiendo a los peces que, de alguna manera, siempre se escapaban. ¡Mi manada celebraba la vida con la misma energía de un adicto a la bebida energética Red Bull! Algunos días, veía a uno de los perros lamer y limpiar las orejas del otro. Había aprendido en ADI que esto se llamaba allogrooming. Vi cómo los perros se comunicaban entre sí. Cuando Booster perseguía a Scarlett, ella saltaba y ladraba triunfante. Era la animadora de la manada. Con los años, Scarlett y Grecian se hicieron inseparables. A menudo bromeaba diciendo que eran mi cariñosa pareja de divas lesbianas.

No querían ir a buscar una pelota y rara vez querían nadar. Les encantaba ser ellas mismas. Al principio, me sentí decepcionado por no poder entrenarlas para realizar tareas de perro de servicio. Al menos, no sería tan fácil como lo fue con Booster. Con el tiempo, aprendí de Grecian y Scarlett que estaba bien ser uno mismo. No todos marchamos al ritmo del mismo tambor, ni actuamos de la misma manera, ni en el mismo nivel que los demás. Scarlett se amaba a sí misma y siempre estaba contenta... ladraba animando a los demás en cuanto tenía ocasión. Ella y Grecian compartían un vínculo especial innegable. Aprendí a valorar el amor en cualquiera de sus formas. También aprendí a apoyar y aceptar a los demás y a animarlos. Tardé mucho tiempo en aprender a aceptarme tal como soy. Aún estoy aprendiendo a amarme. Tengo que agradecérselo a Scarlett y a Grecian. Al-Anon me enseñó que sólo consigues conservar la serenidad dándola. ¡Me preguntaba cuándo Scarlett y Grecian habían asistido a reuniones de doce pasos!

Los animales están legítimamente preocupados por la supervivencia y por las actividades que mejoran la vida. La capacidad de incorporar el amor incondicional a la propia vida parecía funcionar con los perros. Utilizamos el amor incondicional canino para ayudar a los humanos a vivir mejor. Tal vez podamos aprender de los animales a incorporarlo directamente, y así permitir que los perros vivan menos agobiados por los humanos. El tiempo dirá si el hombre alguna vez puede bajar la nariz lo suficiente como para ver el mundo tal y como es y necesita ser. Booster me bajó la nariz y me abrió los ojos. Hasta el día de hoy me esfuerzo por emularlo. Aprender a dar para mantener la serenidad es un gran regalo. Nunca habría sido posible de no ser por Booster. Sólo tenía mi vida gracias a él. Yo estaba destinado a perderla y había intentado hacerlo. Con la intervención divina de Booster, disfruté de la oportunidad de salvar mi vida de una manera beneficiosa en lugar de desperdiciarla en un instante con un corte de cuchillo. Con la ayuda de mi Booster, quise ayudar a otros a salvar sus vidas, como Booster lo había hecho por mí. No estaba seguro de cómo hacerlo, pero estaba aprendiendo.

CAPÍTULO 7
RUMBO A TAILANDIA

Un día leí que Bangkok (Tailandia) estaba sufriendo terribles inundaciones. Tras haber sufrido las consecuencias del huracán Katrina, conocí de primera mano la carga emocional que esta tragedia supuso para la vida de la gente, especialmente para los niños. Después de una inundación, no queda nada. Sabía que Booster tenía un lugar especial en su corazón para los niños. También sabía que había trabajado muy duro para entrenarlo para el acceso público. Por capricho, decidí volar a Tailandia para llevar a Booster a visitar a las víctimas de las inundaciones. Él me había sacado de un abismo emocional y sabía que podía ayudar a los demás como solo él sabía hacerlo. Una vez más, tenía más fe en Booster que en mí mismo.

Averigüé los requisitos para llevar a un perro a Tailandia. Se requería la documentación adecuada e inspecciones de entrada y salida. Todo era bastante razonable. Al cabo de un mes, Booster y yo abordamos un avión con destino a Bangkok vía Tokio (Japón). No le di comida ni agua a Booster, sabiendo que si nada entra, nada sale. En realidad, es muy sencillo. Durante veintiséis horas de vuelo, oriné con frecuencia, debido al síndrome del hombre viejo. Booster no orinó ni una sola vez en el avión, aunque yo estaba preparado con almohadillas absorbentes por si acaso.

Aproximadamente en mitad de camino hacia Tokio, le di a Booster un trozo de hielo para que lo lamiera, como había aprendido en un curso de adiestramiento, pero no lo hizo. Me preocupaba que estuviera deshidratado. Expresé mi preocupación a la azafata, que era amante de los perros. Me trajo un tazón con agua, pero mi Booster se negó a beber. En ese momento, empecé a entrar en pánico. La amable señora me dijo, "Espere un momento. Ahora vuelvo". Volvió unos minutos más tarde con un nuevo tazón de agua, y Booster bebió hasta la última gota. Con una cálida sonrisa, explicó que había cocinado un filete y había echado los restos en el agua. Al instante se transformó de azafata en superheroína.

Al cabo de unos minutos, regresó con otro tazón. Explicó que había cortado el filete y preguntó si podía dárselo a Booster, que no paraba de babear. En mi vida había visto a un perro devorar algo tan rápido. El filete desapareció en un abrir y cerrar de ojos. Nuestra superheroína volvió de nuevo y explicó que se sentía culpable. Le pregunté que cómo era eso posible si me había salvado el día. Dijo que se sentía culpable porque Booster había obtenido un filete y yo no. Entonces me preguntó cómo quería que me prepararan "el mío". Booster y yo fuimos los únicos que volamos en clase turista y comimos filetes durante el vuelo. "Imagine", como dijo John Lennon alguna vez.

Estábamos sentados en la primera fila del avión junto a un caballero increíblemente amable. *Nos* invitó a reunirnos con él en la sala VIP a nuestra llegada a Tokio. La cola para entrar en la sala era larga y yo estaba esperando a que un auxiliar me ayudara a acceder a una zona de descanso para Booster, que seguramente estaba a punto de estallar en cualquier momento. De repente, la parte trasera de Booster descendió, y yo a toda prisa abrí el bolso de mi computador y le tiré la almohadilla absorbente debajo de su cuerpo. Se dejó ir con temerario abandono. La gente miraba, pero nadie se inmutó. Me deshice de la almohadilla y entramos en la sala VIP sin más preámbulos.

Al llegar a Bangkok, tomé una furgoneta privada para ir a Tui's Place, un pequeño hotel boutique en la cercana Pattaya (Tailandia). Había hecho arreglos para quedarme con Booster en el hotel. Era la primera vez en la historia del hotel que permitían que un perro se quedara con un huésped. Le expliqué mi misión al reservar la habitación, y el dueño expresó su deseo de ayudarme en todo lo que estuviera a su alcance. Una vez instalados, hice llamadas para concertar visitas de terapias con perros. Al final del primer día, había muchas visitas programadas. Una era quizás un poco más especial que las demás. Se trataba de un orfanato situado en Rayong, Tailandia, a una hora de camino. A nuestra llegada, me informaron que todos los niños tenían algo en común, o tenían SIDA o eran VIH positivos. *Casualmente*, yo iba a demostrar los talentos de

Booster a jóvenes discapacitados, tal y como había sido entrenado para hacerlo en ADI. Sabía que estábamos en el lugar apropiado y, al instante, fui divinamente consciente de por qué habíamos emprendido este viaje.

Al principio, los niños tenían miedo del perro de 45 kilos. Él demostró sus habilidades, los conquistó y terminó rodeado de admiradores que lo abrazaban. Era un espectáculo maravilloso. Los niños no apartaban la vista de Booster. Estaban hipnotizados. Él, por su parte, no paraba de mover la cola de alegría. Booster enseñó a los niños lo que un perro puede hacer para ayudar a personas discapacitadas. Tiró de mí en una silla de ruedas, abrió un frigorífico y les trajo una botella de agua, me quitó los calcetines de los pies, me trajo los zapatos y mucho más. Booster era todo un artista. Le puse la gorra de lado en la cabeza, al estilo gángster, y los niños se volvieron locos.

Aquel día, los niños me enseñaron que podían vivir la vida en sus términos y aún ser felices. Yo había vivido la vida que había *elegido*, por insidiosa que fuera, mientras que estos niños vivían con una sentencia de muerte potencial, sin elección propia. Aquel día aprendí de los niños una valiosa lección de vida que nunca he olvidado. Era como el círculo de educación en el que tuve la suerte de participar en ADI.

Cuando llegó la hora de irse, todos los niños querían abrazar a Booster. La escena era hermosamente caótica; sonrisas y risas exuberantes llenaban el aire. El fotógrafo del centro giró rápidamente en innumerables direcciones, captando imágenes especiales de Booster interactuando con los niños. Fue tan emotivo que me quedé sin palabras y sin lágrimas. En aquel momento no quedaban más lágrimas por derramar. Inconscientemente, me resigné al hecho de que la vida era vivible en sus términos. Nunca olvidaré aquella visita ni lo que el centro hizo por nosotros.

Al final de la visita, Booster y yo estábamos agotados y a la vez entusiasmados. El día había sido tan especial que no podía procesar mis pensamientos. Booster se quedó dormido a mis pies en el viaje de regreso. Me había hecho sentir muy orgulloso. La buena gente del orfanato me dio las gracias profusamente, pero el verdadero agradecimiento era para Booster. Llegamos a Tui's Place, entramos en el edificio y subimos las escaleras hasta nuestra habitación del segundo piso. Le di a Booster sus croquetas habituales y me dormí temprano sin cenar. De todos modos, necesitaba perder unos kilos. ¡Me preguntaba quién roncaría más fuerte! Al día siguiente teníamos que visitar otro orfanato y los dos necesitábamos descansar.

A la mañana siguiente, tomamos un buen desayuno y llamé a nuestra furgoneta para que nos llevara a una fundación que albergaba a más de 800 niños necesitados o discapacitados. Aquello iba a ser una empresa enorme, y la duda mermó mi confianza por un momento. Miré hacia abajo y Booster sonreía, asegurándome que estaba preparado para el reto. No podía decepcionarlo, ni a él ni a los niños, así que me animé, hice las maletas y me subí a la furgoneta. Cuando llegamos a la fundación, una amable señora nos recibió y nos explicó que quería presentarnos a alguien.

Entramos en una sala de reuniones cercana, donde conocimos a una amable mujer que era ciega y tenía una sonrisa cautivadora. Trabajaba y vivía en el centro y nos contó que había tenido un perro durante muchos años, pero que se le había muerto y era demasiado vieja para tener otro. "No sería justo para el perro", explicó. Luego me dijo, "me enteré de que iba a venir un perro a visitarnos, así que le pedí a un amigo que me llevara en moto a una tienda de animales. Espero que no te importe que le dé un juguete a tu perro".

Quedé en estado de shock cuando la escuché. Me la imaginaba con ochenta años en una moto, sin poder ver nada. Era ciega de nacimiento, pero se las arregló para traerle un regalo a Booster. Buscó en su bolso y le regaló a Booster un coche de carreras de peluche. Luego le dio una pelota chirriante. Booster cogió la pelota y ¡chirrió! Estaba extasiado. Entonces ella se acercó y abrazó al perro. Mi Poder Superior estaba trabajando horas extras. Al instante me sentí abrumado por lo que la vida me ofrecía. Después de todo, había bondad en el mundo.

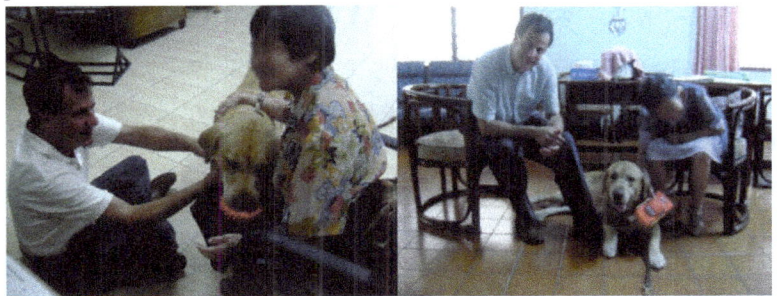

Tras una larga y agradable visita, llegó el momento de saludar a los niños. Entramos a un aula y de repente nos vimos rodeados por los niños más dulces. Sus profesores los ayudaron a cada uno de ellos, ya que querían saludar, tocar y abrazar a mi Booster... y ese día, ¡también era *su* Booster! Estos niños eran mucho más pequeños que los que habíamos conocido el día anterior, así que fue más una visita de perro de terapia que una demostración de perro de servicio. A mí me pareció bien, porque todavía estaba dolorido por las actividades del día anterior. Me sorprendió la rapidez con que los niños aceptaron a Booster, mientras él se sentaba, y disfrutaba pacientemente de su cariño. Pensé que *realmente hay belleza en la simplicidad.*

Todas las cosas buenas eventualmente llegan a su fin, y llegó el día de irnos. El vuelo de regreso a casa no tuvo ninguna novedad. Una vez en casa, la vida volvió a la normalidad rápidamente. Un día me dirigí a la oficina de correos y saqué sin entusiasmo un paquete de mi apartado postal. Lo abrí y todo se descontroló, como si me hubiera golpeado un agente

nervioso ruso. Me desmoroné como el día en que acepté a Booster en mi vida en Ajo. Ese paquete había sido entregado en secreto por un poder superior. El mismo poder que había entregado a Booster lo estaba haciendo de nuevo. Como el agua que corre cuesta abajo desde la cima de una montaña arraigada en el cielo, las lágrimas brotaron. Era otro regalo espiritual concedido a mi alma perdida.

En cámara lenta, como congelado en el tiempo, pasé una hora en la oficina de correos mirando veinte de las páginas más hermosas y llenas de amor, jamás concedidas al hombre. Escritas en un lenguaje inocente, compuestas por mentes puras como las de los dioses, los documentos no estaban corregidos. Todos los símbolos, palabras y objetos expresaban amor y gratitud, compuestos por almas del oro más puro. Los autores seguramente no tenían experiencia, pero esgrimían una mezcla homogénea de sabiduría terrenal y celestial. Me encontraba en el lugar equivocado para semejante acontecimiento; debería haber estado en la cima de una montaña en Nepal, tomado de la mano de otro hombre, uno que perteneciera al Dalai Lama. Me derretí emocionalmente como una "vela en el viento", como alude la canción de Elton John. La Princesa Diana habría donado lágrimas si se le hubiera otorgado el honor de hacerlo.

El director de la fundación en Rayong, Tailandia, me envió dibujos hechos por los niños tailandeses que Booster había visitado el mes anterior. Los dibujos eran de Booster, con su nombre escrito y palabras como "amor" en inglés y tailandés. Dudo que haya algún ser humano vivo hoy que no se haya preocupado por el temible cáncer o las enfermedades infecciosas, y me duelen las almas jóvenes que se enfrentan a la dura realidad de la vida a una edad que ya no es inocente. En otro tiempo, yo fui culpable de arruinarme en vida, mientras que estos niños, mucho más valientes que yo, poseían tal valentía *y alegría*, para vivir la vida en sus propios términos. Los niños tailandeses tomaron el regalo de los lápices de colores, los convirtieron en cañones de amor y me devolvieron el fuego con una artillería que poseía la eficacia del karma. Este fue un *disparo de Booster* de proporciones épicas.

LOVE . . .

. .รัก Rạk

CAPÍTULO 8
VIDA FAMILIAR – LA MÍA – LA SUYA – LA NUESTRA

Mientras tanto, en el rancho, observar a mi manada interactuar era como presenciar a artistas de circo bajo la gran carpa. La actuación de cada perro aportaba singularidad al espectáculo ¡y no había dos presentaciones iguales! No había nada en la vida que me gustara más que tumbarme en la hierba en un día soleado y jugar con mis hijos caninos. Disparaba pelotas de tenis como si fuera una ametralladora y ellos las devolvían en segundos. Veía a mis hijos caninos chapoteando en el estanque que era alimentado por un manantial. Les encantaba el estanque, pero también las mocasines de agua que aparecen en los días cálidos. Todos los perros habían sido mordidos alguna vez por esta serpiente venenosa y llevados a la clínica veterinaria que había salvado la vida de Booster. Siempre los mordía en la boca porque intentaban atrapar a la serpiente. El único perro que se apartaba de ese plan de ataque era Booster.

Un día, mientras paseaba por el campo, Booster se adelantó y saltó sobre una serpiente mocasín de agua justo cuando yo estaba a punto de pisarle la cabeza. Fue mordido en la pata y recibió eso por mí. Me sentí culpable una vez más. Booster regresó a casa cojeando y tuve que llevarlo a la clínica de urgencias. Cuando un perro es mordido por una serpiente venenosa, el riesgo inmediato es la hinchazón. El collar puede asfixiar al perro cuando se le hincha la cabeza. Por suerte, les había quitado los collares a todos mis perros mucho antes. Un policía me contó una vez, que cuando estaba en la secundaria, había tenido un pastor alemán. Un día llegó a casa y vio a su amado perro colgado, con el collar atascado en una alambrada. El perro había saltado y su collar se enganchó en la valla. Después de escuchar esta triste historia, compré collares que se rompen en caso de que ocurra algo así. Esos collares duraron dos días. Los perros tiraron de ellos, estos se rompieron como estaba previsto y acabaron en el campo. ¡No fue una buena inversión!

Con el paso del tiempo, me dediqué más a los miembros de mi familia canina. Cuanto más tiempo les dedicaba, más serenidad y curación obtenía. Una tarde en la que me encontraba aburrido, me puse a navegar por Internet en busca de información sobre labradores. Vi una fotografía maravillosa de un hombre de Tennessee con una carretilla que contenía doce cachorros labrador blancos en venta. Instantáneamente me enamoré. Y, al igual que antes, llamé a mi amigo Charles y surgió otro viaje por carretera. Al día siguiente. Booster, Charles y yo conocimos al hombre y a su mujer. Me presentaron a la cachorra que habían elegido para mí. Era una de doce, nacida en lo que debía ser una familia canina muy prolífica. ¿De qué otra manera se explican las doce crías? Me quedé mirando a la más adorable de las cachorras. Era una bolita de pelo llena de alegría que no paraba de dar saltitos.

La puse en el suelo, ¡y Booster no quería saber nada de ella! Le gruñó, igual que cuando conoció a Scarlett. Lo aparté de ella. La cachorrita gorda era muy linda. La abracé y ella me besó por todas partes. Me babeó de arriba abajo y ¡me encantó! La llamé Puffy porque parecía una gran bola de pelo. Más tarde, mi veterinario la llamó Piggy porque estaba muy gorda. A lo largo de su vida, mantuvo su peso, aunque le daba menos comida que a sus hermanos. Un estudio que leí en la BUCS afirmaba que un 25% de los labradores tienen un gen que les hace retener el peso; no me cabe duda de que Puffy pertenecía a ese selecto grupo.

Después de dar unas vueltas en el automóvil, nos dirigimos a casa con Puffy dormida en mi regazo, y la cabeza de Booster apoyada en mi muslo. Su cabeza me calentaba la pierna y aliviaba el dolor punzante que sentía con frecuencia. Cuando llegué a casa, me di cuenta de que tenía que volver a pasar por el ritual de domesticación, pero esta vez no había intromisiones, ni agentes dominantes contraproducentes dirigiendo desde un sofá, ni interferencias de adictos. Puffy aprendió rápidamente lo que se esperaba de ella y pronto se unió a Booster como una siamés inseparable. Era todo un espectáculo verlos jugar. Booster gruñía con la pelota en la boca cuando Puffy se le acercaba. La soltaba para provocarla. Cuando ella iba por la pelota, Booster la agarraba de nuevo, ¡para su disgusto! Era un espectáculo maravilloso. El disgusto de Puffy era el deleite de Booster.

Unos dos años más tarde, Booster veía a Puffy desde una perspectiva distinta. Adoraba su perfume acalorado y agradecía la oportunidad de conocerla más íntimamente. Por alguna razón, no parecían conectarse, y no me refiero psicológicamente. Busqué consejo veterinario y Puffy fue inseminada artificialmente. Nació una camada de cachorros, pequeñas bolas de pelo tipo mini-Booster. Vendí los cachorros a hogares amorosos a un precio bajo, en algunos de ellos sus mascotas habían muerto y los hijos estaban de luto. De la mejor manera posible, a los niños que estaban sufriendo, se les había explicado el concepto de la muerte. Me sentí muy orgulloso de ayudar a las familias a consolar las almas heridas de sus inocentes hijos.

He mantenido el contacto con una de las familias a lo largo de los años. Recuerdo la mañana en la que respondí a una emotiva llamada de socorro SOS. La gravedad de la llamada al 911 no daba espera. Unos padres amorosos habían llevado recientemente a sus hijos al veterinario para sacrificar a su perro. Los padres inscribieron a sus hijos en una lección avanzada de la vida. No sabían cómo manejar el dolor de sus hijos. Sus hijos habían perdido a su mejor amigo, la única mascota que habían conocido desde que nacieron. Sentí mucho dolor tanto por los padres como por los hijos. Los padres sufrían por sus hijos y, al mismo tiempo, por la pérdida de su perro. El vínculo entre caninos y humanos no tiene límite de edad. Muchos me han dicho que la única vez que vieron llorar a su padre fue el día que sacrificaron al perro de la familia.

El patriarca de la familia dictó los requisitos que debían cumplirse, era un enfoque radical que buscaba sanar el singular dilema emocional. El hombre lanzó un pase desesperado hacia la zona de incertidumbre. "Queremos un cachorro labrador macho, grande y de color blanco. Seguro que no tienes ninguno y vives a 160 km de distancia". Él no estaba preparado para mi respuesta.

"Tengo justo el cachorro que buscas". Mi Booster se convirtió en "su" Booster ese día, ya que había sido el padre de una camada de cachorros que incluía a un precioso cachorro macho, gordo y blanco que me encantaba. Tuve la tentación de quedármelo, pero no hubiera sido justo para él negarle la entrada a una familia amorosa, así que le dije al padre que me reuniría con la familia a mitad de camino en un área de descanso de la autopista. No iba a permitir que nadie hiciera todo el trabajo. Después de todo, ¡ahora era miembro de Al-Anon!

Ya fuera por esperanza o desesperación, el padre aceptó el trato. Al día siguiente conocí a una familia preciosa. Los niños estaban impecablemente vestidos y desinteresadamente dispuestos a conocer a un nuevo cachorro. Al igual que los huérfanos tailandeses, eran niños que se enfrentaban a la vida a una edad temprana. Hicieron un mejor trabajo para sobrellevar la situación de lo que yo había logrado a una edad avanzada. Quizá algún día pudieran sentarse conmigo y contarme cómo lo consiguieron. Quería aprender con oídos abiertos, sin los prejuicios asociados a la edad. Observé como los niños se integraban con el cachorro. Se abrieron los corazones, tanto caninos como humanos, y nació una relación simbiótica y juvenil. Una pizca de normalidad regresó a los niños afligidos y a los padres perdidos. Ese día, la manada volvió a casa llena de optimismo por un nuevo comienzo.

En otra ocasión, un día que vivirá en la infamia, como lo habría expresado el Presidente Roosevelt, recibí una llamada que cambió mi vida y validó mi propia existencia. "Hola, me llamo Joseph. Vi su anuncio en el periódico. . . Se venden cachorros de labrador, el padre es un perro de servicio."

"Tengo diecinueve años. El año pasado me tiré a una piscina y me rompí un disco del cuello. Quedé paralizado al instante. Estaba seguro de que moriría, pero alguien me vio debajo del agua, inmóvil. Soy cuadripléjico y tengo movilidad limitada. Puedo mover un poco la mano y las yemas de los dedos. Fui al Shepherd's Center de Atlanta, Georgia, para recibir rehabilitación. Me sugirieron que podría interesarme tener un perro de servicio. Les dije que me gustaría entrenar al mío.

Señor, ¿cree que yo podría entrenar a mi propio perro de servicio? Entrené perros en el 4H cuando era más joven..."

Después de recuperar la compostura, sentí que tenía la responsabilidad de ser honesto y al mismo tiempo reconfortante. En mi cautelosa respuesta, le conté que una vez había estado a punto de quitarme la vida y que mi perro Booster había hecho cosas por mí que yo no podía hacer por mí mismo. Le expliqué además que ni Booster ni yo habíamos recibido ningún tipo de adiestramiento, sino que todo era fruto del vínculo único que existe entre un perro y una persona.

"Joseph", profeticé, "creo sinceramente que puedes entrenar a tu propio perro de servicio si construyes ese vínculo. Tengo cachorros que genéticamente serán los mejores perros de servicio".

Esa misma semana, una furgoneta se detuvo frente a mi cabaña. Se abrió una puerta lateral y se extendió una rampa para sillas de ruedas. Salió un joven muy apuesto atado a una silla de ruedas motorizada. "Hola, soy Joseph", me saludó con voz suave pero segura.

Me acerqué, le tomé la mano que no funcionaba y se la estreché con entusiasmo. Me acordé de cuando conocí a Elise en la BUCS. "Hola, soy Dave, y este es mi Booster", exclamé mientras le acariciaba la cabeza. "Si miras allí, verás a sus cachorros, ¡todos están deseando conocerte!"

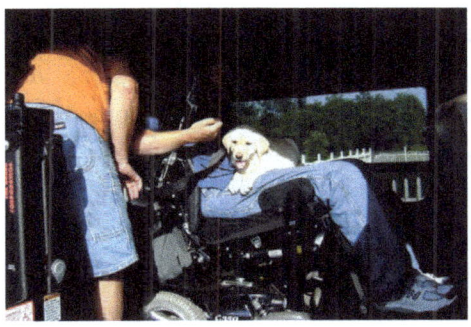

Joseph impulsó su silla motorizada hacia el corral y se detuvo. Abrí la puerta, saqué uno a uno los cachorros y los puse en el regazo de Joseph. Después de jugar con cada cachorro lo mejor que pudo, le sugerí que tal vez quisiera el cachorro macho grande. Me miró y dijo con firmeza: "No, quiero esa hembra de ahí".

"¿Estás seguro?"

Me miró y dijo de manera tajante: "Sí, estoy seguro".

Nunca había cobrado mucho por mis hijos caninos, ya que el dinero no era el objetivo. Quería ayudar a la gente a incorporar el amor canino a sus familias. Así que le expliqué que pedía 350 dólares por cachorro, pero que aceptaría 100, ya que tenía muchos cachorros y necesitaba encontrarles hogar. Aunque quería regalarle el cachorro, el patetismo no era una opción en este glorioso día. Como yo mismo soy discapacitado, era muy consciente de que las personas discapacitadas son fiables, trabajadoras y quieren ser lo más autosuficientes posible. Una discapacidad no inhabilita el orgullo. Cuando puse a la cachorra en el regazo de Joseph, él se impulsó de regreso a la furgoneta y le dijo a su tío: "¡Págale al hombre!" Todo eran sonrisas mientras los dos se alejaban por el camino de entrada rumbo a un nuevo comienzo, tanto para la cachorra como para Joseph. Abracé a Booster con determinación y el alma renovada.

Aproximadamente un año después, recibí una llamada de Joseph y le pregunté cómo estaba. Me dijo entusiasmado, "Jill y yo estamos muy bien".

Entonces le pregunté: "¿Tienes novia, amigo?"

Su respuesta fue de asombro. "NOOOO Dave, le puse Jill a mi perra". Cuando le pregunté por qué Jill, me explicó que la primera especialista en rehabilitación que trabajó con él en el centro Shepherd se llamaba Jill y ¡nombró al cachorro en su honor! Dios mío, una vez más mis ojos se llenaron de lágrimas al oír esas palabras de homenaje. Luego le pregunté cómo estaba Jill y me dijo, "Cuando mando a Jill a la nevera para que me traiga agua, me la trae. Cuando le digo Gatorade, me lo trae". Mis lágrimas se convirtieron en torrentes al final de la frase, aunque hice todo lo posible por ocultar mis emociones. Le comenté a Joseph que lo que él había logrado era mucho más grande que cualquier cosa que yo hubiera hecho jamás y que además se lo decía sintiéndolo profundamente.

Al concluir la llamada, contacté de inmediato al periódico de la ciudad natal de Joseph. Le expliqué que había un héroe entre ellos. "¡Un joven cuadripléjico me compró un cachorro labrador y lo entrenó con la punta de los dedos para que fuera su propio perro de servicio! ¿Pueden imaginar algo así?" pregunté. La semana siguiente, la historia se publicó con Joseph en su silla de ruedas motorizada y con Jill, Booster y yo orgullosos a su lado. Joseph explicó más tarde que sus amigos lo llamaron después de leer el artículo. Le dijeron que "¡no sabían que Jill era así de talentosa!" Joseph no sólo le enseñó a Jill, sino también a muchas personas. Una vez más, ¡la educación genera educación!

En otra llamada, tiempo después, Joseph compartió pensamientos sinceros.

"Dave, hubo tres acontecimientos importantes en mi vida. Recibí a Jill, me casé y tuve una hija... me convertí en padre".

"¡Vaya! No sabía que te habías casado y que tenías una hija, Joseph. ¡Felicidades! De verdad, felicidades. Te mereces eso y mucho más".

"Cuando te conocí, no quería vivir. Me mantenía en la cama y dejaba que me vistieran y que pasaran los días. Luego, recibí a Jill y tenía que hacer lo correcto con ella. Tenía que alimentarla, jugar con ella, enseñarle. Tenía un nuevo propósito para vivir".

Mi silencio al otro lado de la línea fue más poderoso que cualquier comunicación verbal.

"Dave, el acontecimiento que más cambió mi vida de los tres fue tener a Jill".

Me quedé sin palabras. *¿Cómo podría formular una respuesta? ¿Quieres adivinar lo que sucedió después?* Un tsunami es una sequía comparado con el deshielo glaciar de mis emociones en ese instante. ¿Me estaba convirtiendo en un caso emocional perdido o estaba recuperando mis sinapsis emocionales? La vida cambió para Joseph y para mí gracias a una intervención canina divina y milagrosa. Sencillamente, no había palabras. Cuando me recuperé del momento, dije: "Espero que no le digas a tu esposa que Jill fue el acontecimiento más importante de los tres en tu vida".

Él respondió: "Oh, ella lo sabe, Dave".

Recientemente, tuve el honor de invitar a cenar a Joseph, su esposa y su hija. Fue un reencuentro asombroso; doce años después, Joseph me enseñó un video de Jill en su móvil realizando las tareas. Cuando Joseph decía "Linterna", Jill la buscaba y se la traía. Cuando él le decía "Zapatos", ella volvía con sus zapatos. Las peticiones parecían interminables y Jill nunca se equivocó. Yo estaba totalmente asombrado. Nunca jamás, había logrado algo así. Era un testimonio del amor mutuo y de la unión entre caninos y humanos. Yo había escrito sobre mi experiencia al conocerlo y le pedí a su esposa que por favor lo leyera en voz alta en la mesa. Quería el permiso de Joseph para incluirlo en mi libro y quería asegurarme de que todo estuviera cómo debía ser. Mientras su esposa leía, las lágrimas empezaron a rodar por las mejillas de Joseph. En ese instante me vi reflejado en él. La descendencia de Booster, Jill, había hecho por él lo que Booster había hecho por mí.

Aproximadamente dos semanas después, me desperté con un mensaje de texto que sacudió mi mundo. Estaba escrito por un alma valiente llena de amor y gratitud desbordantes. No pude asimilarlo. Después de leerlo, me senté en el suelo y llamé a todos mis perros. Los abracé, acaricié, lloré, apreté y lloré un poco más. El desastre de Chernóbil, cuando se fundió el reactor nuclear de la URSS, no era nada comparado con esto. Me dolió porque sentí el dolor ajeno con mucha intensidad. Y aunque quería tender la mano y ayudar, me sentía impotente para hacerlo. Leí el hermoso mensaje tantas veces que casi lo había memorizado.

Hola Dave,

Sólo quería decirte que tuve que dormir a Jill esta tarde. No puedo hablar de ello, pero quería darte las gracias porque en un principio, tuve una razón para levantarme de la cama, y ella fue mi mejor amiga durante los últimos 12 años. Realmente no podría haber pedido una compañera mejor. Siempre esperé no llegar a ver este día, pero aquí estamos. Sinceramente, cuando la compré, no tenía intención de vivir más que ella, pero esa maldita perra me hacía levantarme cada día y seguir adelante. Ahora tengo una mujer y una hija que me mantendrán en marcha. No hay palabras para expresar lo mucho que esa perra cambió mi vida y la de muchos otros. Realmente fue la mejor amiga en los buenos y malos momentos, me vio en mis peores momentos y también en los mejores. No estaría aquí si no fuera por ella. Desde el fondo de mi corazón, ¡GRACIAS!

Joseph

Incluso el Presidente de Estados Unidos encontró consuelo en la compañía canina. Una vez leí que durante la crisis de los misiles cubanos, llegaron consejos de todas partes. Se investigó, pero no hubo una respuesta perfecta. Mientras los halcones de la Casa Blanca se apresuraban a bombardear Cuba, el joven presidente Kennedy llamó al dueño de la residencia canina de la Casa Blanca y le pidió que le trajeran a su perro.

Pocos seres humanos han tenido la vida en sus manos como Kennedy aquel día. Acarició resueltamente a su perro mientras el Secretario de Defensa McNamara exudaba una retórica bélica sin igual. Kennedy no sucumbió al veneno, al igual que mi manada no lo hizo cuando se enfrentó a las mocasines de agua. Al final, el joven presidente, como una paloma, adoptó un enfoque más suave. Ordenó el bloqueo de Cuba, evitando una respuesta de consecuencias inimaginables. Los rusos en Cuba tenían órdenes de tomar represalias en caso de que Estados Unidos lanzara sus bombas, y los cubanos ya habían acumulado mucha más potencia bélica de la que éramos conscientes. Se puede argumentar que el presidente tomó una decisión tranquila ese día debido a la influencia tranquilizadora de su perro. Mientras John Kennedy acariciaba a su perro, la energía emocional cinética fluía desde su cuerpo, a través de sus brazos, hasta un alma capaz de procesar las emociones de la misma manera que el hígado purifica el torrente sanguíneo.

Historias que cambian la vida como estas dieron sentido a mi vida y validaron la cría de cachorros con un propósito más elevado. La alegría asociada a los adorables cachorros contribuyó sustancialmente a mi recuperación y a que aprendiera a vivir la vida en sus propios términos. Una mañana me desperté y me di cuenta de que de mi camada de ocho cachorros se había reducido a dos machos. Les había enseñado a ambos a abrir la puerta de la nevera y a realizar tareas de perro de servicio. Uno era grande, como Booster, y el otro más pequeño. Ese día, mientras barría el suelo de la cocina, observaba que el más grande le tenía miedo a la escoba. El pequeño era confiado y atrevido. Decidí quedarme con el pequeño y vendí el grande a una familia de Arkansas que me tomó en alquiler una cabaña. Vi crecer a ese cachorro hasta convertirse en un hermoso perro grande como Booster. Siempre me he cuestionado la decisión que tomé aquella mañana. *¿Debería haberme quedado con el más grande y no venderlo en lugar de quedarme con el más pequeño?* En honor al programa que se había convertido en mi salvaguarda, bauticé al cachorro más pequeño con el nombre de Al-Anon y más tarde lo llevé a las reuniones de Al-Anon, a veces junto con Booster. A menudo bromeaba diciendo que lo llamaba Al en público para no avergonzarlo. En realidad, estaba orgulloso de él, ya que se destacaba en las tareas de perro de servicio, y yo estaba orgulloso del programa Al-Anon.

Con el paso del tiempo, una tormenta de resentimiento se apoderó de mi alma. Me molestaba el hecho de no poder ir a mi condominio en Florida simplemente porque tenía un compañero canino, uno que literalmente me había salvado la vida. Hacía más de un año que había enviado una carta preguntando por qué no se permitían mascotas en la propiedad. En resumen, encontré un abogado para que me ayudara a obtener acceso a mi condominio. Sin duda no iría a ninguna parte sin Booster. Lo había entrenado durante más de un año y no había ninguna razón por la que no pudiera acompañarme.

La ley estaba de mi parte, o eso creía. La ley permitía que los perros de servicio y los animales de apoyo emocional (emotional support animals - ESA) entraran en viviendas donde no se permitían mascotas. Me dirigí a la montaña de los dioses y pedí permiso en una reunión de la junta aristocrática, sólo para ser reprendido por Lucifer, el señor de la junta, "¿Sabes qué? El último hombre que pidió permiso para tener un perro de servicio se mudó".

Más tarde hablé con ese hombre, que había vivido en el edificio durante más de veinte años. Él tuvo un ataque de depresión severa y pidió permiso para tener su perro de servicio prescrito. Cuando se lo denegaron, acabó mudándose. Me dijo: "Lucifer me avergonzó públicamente frente a los demás propietarios de condominios. Sabía cómo hacerlo con mucha habilidad". ¡Increíble! Lucifer era más que solo una cavidad de salida del cuerpo humano. Era un tumor canceroso.

Después de que mi abogado pidiera formalmente permiso, en mi nombre, para tener a mi perro de servicio Booster, en mi apartamento, seguí recibiendo cartas de los abogados de los ricachones solicitando más y más documentos. Me pidieron historiales médicos con declaraciones de médicos bajo juramento. Esto fue antes de cualquier mención de una posible demanda. Se hizo evidente para todos que la junta del condominio estaba dando largas. La junta nunca dijo que sí, pero tampoco dijo que no. Tenían los mejores asesores legales a quienes se les pagaba muy bien y, sin duda, conexiones políticas. En poco tiempo, me vi envuelto en una demanda federal. Fui arrastrado por las brasas ardientes de las declaraciones y me ridiculizaron. Rompí en llanto, para regocijo de Lucifer, que apareció para presenciar mi angustia. Lucifer no formaba parte del equipo legal defensor. Simplemente estaba allí para añadir su queroseno al fuego, escupiendo arrogancia con cada movimiento de su cuerpo. Sentí lástima por sus hijos, que tenían que vivir con semejante padre. Me enviaron a médicos para que me diseccionaran psicológicamente sin anestesia y me hicieran sentir como un pedazo de basura esperando a ser arrojado por el retrete de la vida.

Me enviaron a un psiquiatra a sueldo, que me entrevistó. Hacia el final de la sesión, el imbécil me amenazó diciendo, "Vamos a traer a tu adicto al crack a la sala". Mi corazón se detuvo. Entré en pánico, me estremecí y sentí náuseas al instante. El juramento hipocrático que supuestamente hizo cuando se convirtió en un supuesto médico, se convirtió en un juramento *hipócrita*. Quedé mentalmente paralizado. Aquella bomba atómica emocional me hizo retroceder en la vida. Nunca más volví a confiar plenamente en los "profesionales" de la salud mental. Necesitaba toda la ayuda posible, pero ya no podía confiar en esos seres humanos. Booster nunca habría hecho algo tan espantoso. Mi confianza en los caninos estaba fortalecida y grabada en granito.

Mis temores crecían con cada día que pasaba, y con frecuencia sostenía a Booster en mis brazos durante horas. Me sentía herido, había sido mutilado por mi codependencia y por los adictos que habían llegado a mi vida. ¿Por qué la gente aparentemente educada se sumaba a la pira funeraria? Era como si estos tipos de "sangre azul" tuvieran tanto miedo de un perro como yo de un drogadicto con amigos armados que tenían una vendetta que saldar. De forma insensible, al estilo de los abogados, estas bestias de la alta sociedad pidieron historiales médicos, fotografías, el ADN mismo de mi existencia. Si hubieran podido citar mis válvulas cardíacas, lo habrían hecho sin dudarlo.

Busqué ayuda, tanto física como mental, de profesionales de la salud. Los especialistas en ortopedia me hicieron una radiografía de la pierna palpitante y determinaron que tenía un hematoma a raíz del remolque que me cayó encima años atrás. Desde entonces se había calcificado. Era evidente en una radiografía. El dolor insoportable que experimentaba a menudo cuando tocaba el suelo con el pie era algo que no aparecía en una radiografía. Me impedía caminar y se presentaba en momentos imprevistos. Los médicos de salud mental me explicaron que padecía un trastorno de estrés postraumático. Hasta el día de hoy, cuando conduzco de noche, si se empaña el parabrisas, tiemblo y tengo que detenerme. Mi mente recuerda instantáneamente la calurosa noche de Florida en mi camioneta, cuando mi adicto al crack se abalanzó sobre mí con un cuchillo. Todavía me da miedo entrar en mi casa, a un estacionamiento o en una habitación de hotel sin que mi perro de servicio se aventure a entrar antes que yo.

Tenía pruebas concretas de lo que ya sabía, y tenía discapacidades físicas y mentales legítimas. Sin embargo, eso no fue suficiente para que la sangre fría y azul se volviera cálida y roja. Nunca sería suficiente. La empatía y la comprensión hacia otro ser humano dejaron de existir. El juez concedió un fallo sumario a favor de lo que yo consideré la aristocracia "conectada", afirmando que yo sólo había buscado ayuda profesional una o dos veces antes de presentar la demanda. El juez, ante quien nunca tuve la oportunidad de comparecer, me cuestionó por haber esperado para buscar ayuda y por haber recibido solo unos pocos tratamientos, antes de solicitar que se permitiera a Booster entrar en la zona azul prohibida de mi condominio, por el que pagaba diligentemente una hipoteca pero que no podía usar.

El noble príncipe de la IAADP, Ed Eames, me dijo que llevaba años ciego. Ciego es ciego. Si hubiera ido al médico cinco años después de perder la vista, no significaría que no hubiera estado ciego todo el tiempo. No se me permitió hablar de mi vida. Estuve bajo el control total de mis adictos durante décadas, nunca se me permitió acceder a ayuda. Nunca, nunca fue posible. Haber buscado ayuda habría comprometido mi vida. Una estadística del Instituto Nacional de Salud afirma que las mujeres maltratadas mueren con mayor frecuencia al dejar al abusador que por permanecer en la relación disfuncional. Comprendí perfectamente esa increíble conclusión.

El juez justificó mi imposibilidad de acceder a un tribunal porque consideró que la junta nunca dijo que no. Eso es cierto. La defensa legal de la junta seguía pidiendo más y más documentos mientras astutamente aumentaba los costos de la defensa a 350 dólares la hora. En Estados Unidos todo gira en torno al dinero, y los estadounidenses lo saben. La junta nunca, ni en un millón de años, diría que sí. Así que, básicamente, no me quedaba más remedio que empezar de nuevo y probablemente debería haberlo hecho, pero tenía otras ideas en mente. Mi abogado reconoció más tarde, que debió haber hecho que la junta simplemente dijera sí o no. Lo que realmente me dolió, y me sigue doliendo, es que la decisión sirvió de precedente legal a los miembros de las juntas de condominios de todo el país. Mi abogado apeló más tarde, pero la apelación corrió la misma suerte. Los de "sangre azul" lo controlaban todo. Fidel de Cuba controlaba a los infieles y lo mismo hacía la junta igualmente "compasiva" del condominio.

Me han dicho que la defensa de mi demanda costó más de 100.000 dólares. Es probable que estos adoradores del dinero no hayan incurrido en ningún gasto porque tenían una póliza de responsabilidad por errores y omisiones que los cubría en caso de que fueran demandados. Para mi satisfacción, en el futuro tendrían que responder afirmativamente cuando se les preguntara si alguna vez habían sido demandados. Como un perro que limpia su saco anal, arrastrando su trasero por el suelo, la maldad de los de "sangre azul" dejó un rastro. Su mayor error fue nacer en familias que adoraban más el dinero que el vínculo entre animales y personas. La lección aprendida se redujo, una vez más, al dinero, como la mayoría de las cosas en Estados Unidos.

Lo que tenía que haber hecho era ignorar a los de "sangre azul". Habrían tenido que desalojarme y pagar el costo de desalojar a un propietario. Las compañías de seguros no financian los costos asociados con el desalojo de inquilinos. La asociación de propietarios habría tenido que recaudar miles de dólares aprobando gravámenes especiales sobre la propiedad. En Estados Unidos no se trata de lo que está bien o mal. Se trata de quién tiene el dinero para ganar. Como estadounidense que vive en la supuestamente mayor democracia del mundo, nunca tuve mi oportunidad en los tribunales. Podría haber aceptado perder mi caso en la corte (aunque dudo que lo hubiera hecho, dada la profundidad de las pruebas que tuve que presentar). Lo que todavía no puedo aceptar es no haber tenido la oportunidad de acceder a la sala del tribunal. También fui culpable por contratar a un abogado con poca experiencia en leyes de discapacidad. Goliat había asomado su poderosa cabeza azul. El poderoso juez de OZ había hablado.

Algún tiempo después de la decisión del tribunal, llamé a la oficina de alquiler de condominios y reservé un alquiler. Muchos de los propietarios participaban en un programa de alquileres en el que los peces gordos utilizaban una sub-corporación para alquilar las viviendas y obtener ingresos extra. Llamé a la *señora* de la oficina y reservé un apartamento, para disgusto de todos. El día del juicio, llegué con el joven Al-Anon en mis brazos como perro de servicio en entrenamiento. Yo tenía mis credenciales de entrenamiento de perros de servicio, ya que había sido adiestrado bajo la tutela de *la* Dra. Bonita Bergin.

Cuando entré en una reunión de propietarios con Al-Anon, los de "sangre azul" volvieron a ponerse morados. Un exmarine gordo, tipo "Pillsbury Dough Boy", me miró y dijo con arrogancia, "¿No tenemos un fallo judicial?"

Le respondí: "Sí, lo tienen, pero se refiere a un hombre discapacitado y su perro de servicio. Hoy estoy aquí como entrenador de perros de servicio con un cachorro en entrenamiento".

"Bueno", dijo Pillsbury Porky, "tal vez tengamos que llamar al departamento del sheriff".

Le ofrecí mi teléfono móvil y le dije, "Toma, por favor, usa mi teléfono. ¿Los llamas tú o los llamo yo? Por cierto, en el estado de Florida es un delito menor interferir en el adiestramiento legal de un perro de servicio en lugares públicos".

Porky se calló y probablemente más tarde se fue a comer y se pegó un atracón.

En una ocasión anterior, cuando fui a mi condominio sin Booster, había ido a Blockbuster Video. Alquilé unas cuantas películas y, en mi camino de regreso, vi a Porky. Al entrar por la puerta de seguridad de la propiedad, el guardia me detuvo. Miró atentamente mi camioneta. Al instante supe que algo andaba mal.

"Hola, ¿qué pasa?" le pregunté.

"Sr. Hawn, ¿lleva a su perro con usted?"

"No, pero ojalá lo tuviera. ¿Por qué busca con tanto detalle?"

"Recibí una llamada de Porky diciendo que lo vio en la tienda de videos con su perro".

"Sí, efectivamente, estábamos *juntos* en la tienda buscando películas, como lo permite la ley federal que *algunos* no respetan".

"Me advirtió que yo podría estar intentando entrar a mi perro en la propiedad".

"Gracias por explicármelo. Sólo haces tu trabajo, lo entiendo".

Cuando llegué a casa, le envié a Porky una tarjeta de agradecimiento por correo que decía: "Gracias por poner tu vida en pausa para preocuparte por la mía. . . Con mucho amor, Booster".

Después de eso, intenté ganarme la vida lo mejor que pude, aunque con frecuencia experimentaba mucho dolor en la pierna y un miedo repentino sin razones aparentes. Empecé a trabajar como contador para un hombre de mi ciudad que llevaba a una cuadrilla de chicos a realizar trabajos de mantenimiento en fábricas. Ataviado con casco, gafas de seguridad y botas con puntera de acero, llevaba mi remolque a las comunidades rurales con Booster de copiloto. Lo dejaba en la caravana, a regañadientes, hasta que regresaba a casa todos los días. Tenía que ganarme la vida. Booster tendría que entenderlo.

Un día, cuando se completó un trabajo de seis semanas, llevé a Booster al lugar de trabajo. Mi jefe y amigo, se sintió avergonzado. Le expliqué sobre ADA y le pedí que confiara en mí. Pronto llegó Charlie, el supervisor de la planta. Yo tenía a Booster equipado con un casco, gafas y una pequeña lonchera colgando de su cuello. Charlie sonrió y dijo, "¡No puedo esperar para escuchar *esta* historia!" A todos los chicos les encantó Booster.

Demostré sus habilidades a gente que nunca se había imaginado que un perro pudiera hacer esas cosas. Iba por agua y me traía los zapatos. Me quitaba los calcetines y encendía los interruptores de la luz. Si giraba el dedo índice hacia la derecha, él también lo hacía. Si lo giraba hacia la izquierda, Booster giraba hacia la izquierda. Pronto se convirtió en parte del equipo. ¡Era un **verdadero** *perro de trabajo*! "Pronto Booster fue conocido de forma cariñosa como *Bootie* (trasero). Los chicos bromeaban, "¡Dave consiguió un lindo trasero!" Para que conste, ¡fue el mejor trasero que tuve! Booster me ayudó a liberar más endorfinas que *ningún otro*".

Desde cachorro, Booster atraía a gente de todas las clases sociales y seguía haciéndolo cada día que pasaba. Aprendí *algo* de cada persona que me presentó. El perro al que alguna vez rechacé *seguía* cambiando mi vida. Insidiosamente, inculcó sus cualidades caninas en mi alma. Yo no lo sabía entonces, pero esa era la inequívoca realidad del día. Al fin y al cabo, era mi Booster. Con el paso del tiempo, me involucré más en la vida. Aprendí poco a poco a aceptar la vida según sus términos. Como cabe imaginar, no me resultó fácil. Había adquirido conocimientos callejeros relacionados con los perros y ahora me daba cuenta de que necesitaba una educación formal.

¡MI PERRO BOOSTER!

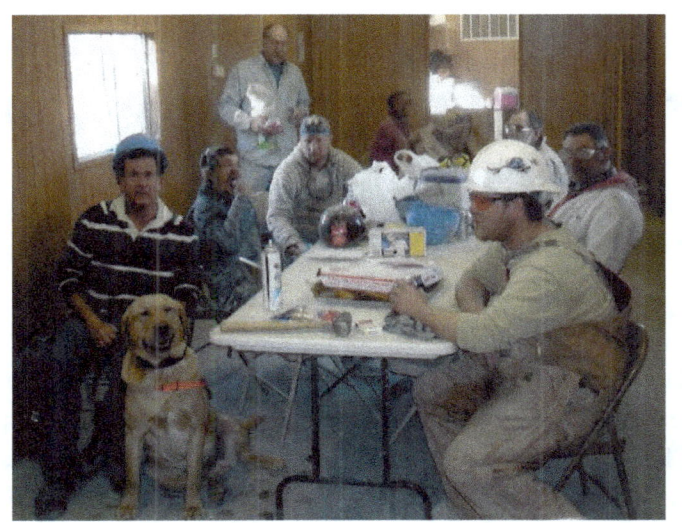

CAPÍTULO 9
AUTO INVERSIÓN – DÓLARES PARA LA BUCS

Cuando se trataba de hacer grandes inversiones, mi hermano siempre intervenía. Yo tenía un as en la manga. Cada vez que él decía que no debía invertir en algo, yo sabía inmediatamente que debía hacerlo. ¡Tanto él como mi hermana tiraban monedas como si fueran tapas de alcantarilla! No podía imaginar mi vida de esa manera. Me planteé asistir a la BUCS para obtener un máster en Ciencias de la Vida Canina. Cuando compartí eso con mi hermano, su respuesta fue, "Qué desperdicio de dinero". Cuando bromeó diciendo que yo le estaba "ladrando al árbol equivocado", ¡al instante tuve luz verde! Aprendí a invertir en mí y a tener confianza en mí mismo. Booster me enseñó a tener confianza y que no hay extraños en la vida. Scarlett me animó. Puffy me enseñó el valor de amar por el puro y simple propósito de amar. Al-Anon, el programa y el perro, ¡me mantuvieron enfocado en mí mismo! Mi vida de Yugo se estaba convirtiendo en un Lamborghini. Aceleré el motor, solté el pedal del freno, quemé los neumáticos y salí al mundo real para dar un vistazo a lo que muchos otros daban por sentado.

Me lancé con una fuerza nunca antes experimentada y nunca miré atrás. El programa Al-Anon me enseñó que *si dejas ir el pasado, él te dejará ir a ti*. El Lamborghini de mi vida no tenía espejo retrovisor. Una mañana tomé el teléfono e informé a la universidad que estaba empacando las maletas y que Booster y yo pronto estaríamos allí. Luego, conseguí a una persona para que viviera con mi manada e hice todos los preparativos para mejorar mi vida. Aunque tendría que viajar a California durante semanas, varias veces al año, sabía que podría soportarlo con Booster a mi lado.

Cuando finalmente pisé el campus universitario, me sentí como si hubiera regresado a Oz. Tenía ganas de chasquear los talones y decir: "No hay lugar como el hogar, no hay lugar como el hogar...". Había vivido en los suburbios, en el centro de Nueva Orleans, en Washington DC y en una cabaña de madera en el bosque, pero me sentía más en casa, más aceptado, más a gusto en mi universidad que en cualquier otro lugar del planeta. Entre mis compañeros de clase, experimenté el calentamiento global más rápido de lo que Al Gore lo imaginó ambientalmente. Bonnie Bergin, presidenta de la universidad y Maga de Oz, me abrazó a mi llegada. Sí, sí, lloré un poco más, pero estas lágrimas eran dulces. Bonnie había trabajado con discapacitados toda su vida. Tenía un doctorado en educación y en la vida misma. No juzgaba a nadie. Igual que yo había aprendido de mi manada de perros, ella aprendía de su grupo de alumnos. Bonnie consideraba la educación como una calle de doble sentido.

Un día, hubo desavenencias en el aula. Tuve una sobrecarga emocional y salí. Un compañero, una persona empática como la mayoría de la familia BUCS, corrió a buscar a Bonnie. Me alejaba de la universidad y oí una voz tenue que me decía, "Davis, vas en la dirección equivocada". Me giré y vi nada menos que a la propia Bonnie. Encontramos un espacio verde y nos sentamos en la hierba. Bonnie simplemente me explicó que la universidad nos necesitaba a Booster y a mí. La universidad era un bebé prematuro con respiración asistida, luchando por la acreditación, y los estudiantes eran el cordón umbilical. Bonnie me explicó que necesitaba estudiantes con experiencia vital, que quisieran aprender y mejorar la vida de los demás. Al instante me reconforté, como una víctima de un shock envuelta en una manta cálida. ¿Realmente me necesitaban?

¿Quieres adivinar si lloré? ¿Quieres adivinar si tengo lágrimas en los ojos mientras comparto estas palabras? Muchos en todo el mundo tienen a Bonnie en gran estima. En una ocasión, Oprah Winfrey la invitó a su escenario y le entregó un cheque para apoyar su labor humanitaria. Al principio de su carrera, Bonnie daba clases en Asia, y un día vio a un burro que ayudaba a un hombre sin piernas a cruzar la calle. De repente tuvo una epifanía, los perros podrían contribuir a mejorar la calidad de vida de los discapacitados, de más formas que simplemente guiando a los ciegos. Para asombro de sus colegas condescendientes, ella creó el concepto de perro de servicio. Apostaría a que algunos de sus amigos de entonces eran como mi hermano... hacían proselitismo de la pérdida de tiempo, dinero y recursos que suponía su idea.

A sus sesenta años, Bonnie hipotecó todo lo que tenía para fundar una universidad en la que personas de todo el mundo pudieran recibir una educación completa relacionada con los caninos. Los estudiantes podían desarrollar sus propios pensamientos, objetivos y aspiraciones para hacer del mundo un lugar mejor. Ella imaginaba a los estudiantes aprendiendo a motivar a los perros para que ayudaran a la sociedad de formas nuevas y novedosas mediante la creación de programas caninos. Uno de ellos era "Paws for Purple Hearts", en el que veteranos con problemas psiquiátricos entrenaban perros para ayudar a otros veteranos con deficiencias de movilidad. Otro programa utilizaba perros para oler y localizar gusanos que estaban diezmando los queridos cultivos de uva de California, lo que repercutía negativamente en la industria vinícola. Los estudiantes, los programas que desarrollaron y sus contribuciones a la sociedad eran diversos, pero se basaban en el denominador común del amor y el deseo ferviente de utilizar atributos caninos únicos para ayudar a otros.

En la BUCS, los estudiantes pueden obtener un título de asociado, una licenciatura o un máster. Es una universidad de artes liberales que ofrece una amplia variedad de cursos, todos relacionados de alguna manera con los perros. Aprendí sobre la historia de los perros en la sociedad, la psicología del perro, datos sobre diversas razas, discapacidades humanas, medicina veterinaria, cómo utilizar Internet e investigar en revistas médicas... y mucho, mucho más. Aprendí cómo se entrena a los perros para detectar bombas, productos agrícolas, niveles bajos de azúcar en la sangre, ataques inminentes y mucho más. La facultad de veterinaria es una experiencia educativa enfocada exclusivamente en mejorar la salud de los perros y de los animales en general. También recibí lecciones prácticas de entrenamiento de perros impartidas en un formato de interacción entre humanos y caninos. No se golpea a un niño y no se golpea a un perro. ¡No se asfixia a un niño ni se coloca un collar de eslabones metálicos a un perro! Me enseñaron metodología positiva en su máxima expresión.

Una vez, cuando entré en clase, Bonnie me agarró de la manga de la camisa y tiró de ella con tanta fuerza que casi me caigo. La clase estalló en risas. Pensé que se había vuelto loca y me alejé de un salto. Bonnie se volvió hacia la clase y preguntó, "¿Vieron lo que hizo? Davis saltó hacia atrás cuando tiré de él, tenía una mirada de incredulidad y desconcierto ¿Quizás estaba resentido?" Luego, explicó de manera sucinta que cuando las personas tiran de la correa de un perro, a menudo crean el mismo escenario en los ojos de sus adorados caninos. Cuando tiras de la correa, le estás enseñando a resistirse. Quizá de ahí venga la expresión en inglés "don't yank my chain" que en español significa "no bromees conmigo". Bonnie continuó diciendo que esperaba no ver nunca a una persona tirando de la correa de un perro o utilizando un collar de eslabones metálicos en el campus. Los estudiantes se quedaron atónitos, fueron iluminados y se dieron cuenta al instante de que estaban en el lugar adecuado para aprender lo que no podrían aprender en ningún otro lugar del mundo. Bonnie me llevó ese día... a su corazón... mientras yo experimentaba su pasión práctica por la educación. Combinaba la pasión con la compasión al asociar su amor por los perros con un amor igual por los discapacitados y sus alumnos.

Un día entró en el aula un psicólogo infantil. Explicó detalladamente cómo trabajaba con niños de tres años. Me pregunté de qué se trataba todo esto. Después de todo, estaba sentado en un aula con doce adultos y ninguno... permítanme repetir... ¡ninguno de nosotros tenía hijos! Ni siquiera la propia Bonnie tenía descendencia. No, no era un festival del arco iris, ¡y nadie se llamaba Dorothy! Era más como un Festival de la Esencia… Esencia porque no todos los humanos procrean por motivos de validación o de otro tipo. Algunos estudios sugieren que las personas solteras, las parejas sin hijos o las parejas homosexuales tienen perros en su unidad familiar como sustitutos de los niños. Para mí, los niños gritan y los perros ladran... no hay mucha diferencia. Cuando crecen, algunas personas se convierten en modelos de conducta, mientras que otros se vuelven asesinos. Estoy seguro de que los padres se sienten desolados cuando su hijo acaba con la vida de otro ser. Yo sentiría lo mismo si mi perro hiciera algo así".

Bonnie explicó que un perro tiene una capacidad mental equivalente a la de un niño tres años. Nos dijo que trabajáramos con los perros utilizando las metodologías psicológicas que funcionaban para los niños de tres años, que escribiéramos un trabajo sobre nuestros hallazgos y que lo entregáramos por la mañana. ¡Me pareció *genial*!

En la BUCS, los perros son emparejados con los estudiantes, socializados y enseñados a realizar tareas de perro de servicio. Finalmente, los perros adiestrados son asignados a una persona discapacitada el día de la graduación. Un semestre, Bonnie nos asignó la tarea de adiestrar a nuestro perro para que realizara una tarea complicada o una recopilación de varias tareas sencillas. Yo fui el primer alumno al que le tocó demostrar para qué había adiestrado a Booster, así que invité a Bonnie y a toda la clase a que me acompañaran al balcón del segundo piso. Entonces miré a Booster y le dije, "Carro". Bajó corriendo los escalones, abrió la puerta de la camioneta de Bonnie, saltó dentro y encontró mi maletín médico. Luego saltó fuera y corrió a traérmelo. Le dije, "Llévaselo a Bonnie". Booster me miró a los ojos y se dirigió hacia Bonnie, y después de esquivarme puso la bolsa en la mano de Bonnie. Le había mostrado a Booster la puerta de la camioneta de Bonnie durante los descansos de clase. Él sabía hacia qué vehículo tenía que correr, ya que era el único que tenía una cuerda de juego atada. Yo me sentí orgulloso.

De vuelta al aula, mis compañeros estaban molestos. Me acusaron de elevar las expectativas. "Davis, ¿cómo demonios se supone que vamos a enseñar a nuestros perros a hacer algo así?... ¡Ahora Bonnie esperará lo mismo de nosotros!" No estaba seguro de cómo tomar eso y simplemente dije, "Chicos, están aquí para aprender. Estoy seguro de que pueden hacer algo mucho más emocionante". Con Booster a mi lado, estaba aprendiendo a creer que todo era posible en la vida. Incluso podría aprender la tarea de vivir.

Otro día, uno que nunca olvidaré, entré en clase y vi a una señora de cincuenta y tantos años en una silla de ruedas eléctrica. Marcia, nuestra instructora de la clase de discapacidades, la invitó a dar una conferencia en clase. Yo había aprendido en el seminario de verano de ADI a saludar y comunicarme verbal y físicamente con personas con discapacidades graves. Esta mujer entraba en esa categoría. Tenía mi edad y bien podría haber sido yo. Me acerqué a ella, puse mi mano sobre la suya y simplemente la saludé. Mi miedo al rechazo estaba siempre presente; sin embargo, nunca había experimentado el rechazo de una persona discapacitada. Con cada nuevo encuentro, mi autoestima y valor aumentaban.

La dama tenía la enfermedad de Lou Gehrig, esclerosis lateral amiotrófica (ELA). Yo había aprendido en una clase anterior sobre discapacidades que se trata de una enfermedad de las neuronas motoras que deteriora insidiosamente el sistema nervioso y acaba provocando la muerte. Como estudiantes, tomamos asiento con una libertad de movimientos que antes dábamos por sentada. Eso estaba a punto de cambiar... para siempre. ¿Puedo pedir prestado un Kleenex a un lector en este momento? ¿Por favor?

La increíble señora vivía cerca y se impulsaba en su silla de ruedas eléctrica por la acera para llegar al campus de la BUCS. Entró sola en el ascensor y llegó a la escuela puntualmente, como estaba previsto. Llevaba una pantalla de proyección acoplada a su silla de ruedas eléctrica. Cuando miraba un objeto en la pantalla, ésta decía el nombre del objeto. Contó a la clase que antes había sido una abogada corporativa de alto nivel que ejercía su profesión por todo el mundo. Ella era una de esas personas. Un abogado inexperto había fallado en mi intento de permitir que mi Booster viviera conmigo en mi apartamento de Florida. Un abogado con experiencia en condominios me había destrozado. Yo era una víctima en todos los sentidos y tenía poca capacidad para apreciar a un traficante de drogas o a un abogado, ya que con frecuencia sentía el mismo desprecio por ambos.

Ella explicó cómo su enfermedad había transformado su vida. Con mis compuertas emocionales abiertas de par en par, ella compartió las ramificaciones de la transformación de su vida. Yo estaba a punto de sufrir otro colapso emocional al comprender la transformación y la impotencia que me acompañaban, aunque en un contexto muy diferente. Justo cuando estaba a punto de perder el control, ella explicó que ¡ESTABA AGRADECIDA POR SU ENFERMEDAD! Pensé que estaba soñando despierto. No recordaba haberme emborrachado antes de la clase y no era un diabético entrando en un coma eufórico, como el que había estudiado en la clase del día anterior. Con honestidad, queriendo claridad, levanté la mano. Simplemente dije: "Repita... eso... por favor". Ella dio la misma respuesta.

Miré a Booster y le pedí que se "subiera" y me diera un "abrazo". Hizo lo que le pedí y pronto se sentó a horcajadas sobre mi regazo con total abandono. Apreté a Booster porque estaba en el ojo de una tormenta y necesitaba su ayuda para atravesarla. Mi alma herida se preparaba para enfrentar algo para lo que quizás no estuviera preparado. Mi única defensa era sujetar a Booster y prepararme para la erupción volcánica de lava emocional que seguramente fluiría. Yo era alérgico a las emociones y estaba a punto de ser mordido y sometido a un shock inminente. La mocasín de agua de la vida estaba a punto de inyectarme su veneno. Estaba fascinado y al mismo tiempo hipnotizado. No me moví, y Booster tampoco lo hizo. Él percibía la energía que fluía a través de mi cuerpo hacia su alma empática.

La abnegada dama, explicó además, que había estado tan ocupada en su existencia corporativa que nunca se había dado cuenta de las cosas importantes de la vida. Durante años había estado dedicada a ganar dinero y reconocimiento. Expresó su resentimiento por haberse perdido las cosas buenas de la vida debido a la falta de perspectiva. La enfermedad de Lou Gehrig fue el faro de su alma, que redefinió los últimos años de su vida. El regalo que recibí al instante, fue el deseo espontáneo de encontrar el éxito y la aceptación que ella había logrado. Como un infomercial de televisión, "¡Espera, y sí, hay más!" Nunca había escuchado realmente al predicador cuando iba a la iglesia de niño. Había estado en la iglesia porque tenía que estar allí. Ahora, sin embargo, estaba en la BUCS porque *quería* estar allí. Había invertido en una educación y, por Dios, ¡esta vez sí que la había recibido!

Continuó diciendo que, después de todo lo que había experimentado, vivía con cinco centavos al día. Su historia era tan única como su alma. Amplió su afirmación diciendo que vivía con cinco centavos de *energía* al día. Si se movía para vestirse, gastaba dos de sus cinco centavos y sólo le quedaban tres de energía, insuficientes para ir a ver a su nieto jugar al béisbol con su equipo en el parque. Se sometió a que la bañaran y vistieran para preservar la energía y poder ir al parque.

A partir de ese momento, cada vez que veía un centavo, pensaba en esta experiencia de aprendizaje verdaderamente única. Un penique ya no vale un penique, dicen. Yo estoy de acuerdo. No tiene precio. Recordé el día en que perdí a "Penny" (mi perro). ¡Nunca lo superé! Es curioso cómo funciona la vida cuando la trabajas. "Sigue viniendo. Funciona si la trabajas, así que ¡trabájala porque tú lo vales!" solía cantar junto a desconocidos en innumerables reuniones de los doce pasos de Al-Anon. De repente lo entendí como nunca antes. Después de conocer a la dama milagrosa, nunca volví a ver el dinero de la misma manera. De hecho, lo desprecié por completo y a quienes lo acumulan, despilfarrando al mismo tiempo lo que realmente importa en la vida. Mientras construía mi parque de caravanas, utilicé todas las tarjetas de crédito, transferencias de saldo y cupones que pude encontrar para invertir en mi negocio. La pareja jubilada y conservadora que había dirigido mi negocio durante mis tiempos turbulentos, llamaba a las tarjetas de crédito "palas", ya que, a su juicio, me enterrarían en deudas. Me reí de su actitud conservadora, ya que para mí el dinero significaba poco, desde el momento en que salí de la clase de la BUCS aquel día. El éxito de la valiente oradora al encontrar lo que de verdad importa en la vida encendió un fuego en lo más profundo de mi ser, una combustión espontánea sin igual. Me compadecí de los que tiraban los centavos en lugar de invertirlos en aprendizaje para ayudar, de alguna manera, a los menos afortunados. Luego tomé esa filosofía adquirida, viajé por el mundo y aprendí a asimilar y respetar otras culturas y apreciar la *diversidad*.

Como resultado directo, devalué la importancia del dinero y, por ello, lo invertí en mi negocio sin preocuparme por las consecuencias. Usé el dinero como si se tratara de un tablero de Monopolio. Creé una empresa y luego la vendí por millones de dólares, a pesar de que alguna vez viví una semana con una bolsa de patatas de dos kilos, cuando se me acabaron los cupones de alimentos del gobierno. Con todo derecho, yo, más que la mayoría, debería haber valorado el dinero y la seguridad que proporciona. Tengo amigos y familiares que son conservadores con el dinero, es decir, tacaños. Hasta cierto punto, confían en que la estructura de su vida los guíe, un concepto que yo nunca conocí. Siempre me ocupaba de mis cosas, necesitaba libertad para explorar, como expresó el poeta Robert Frost en su poema "El camino menos transitado", y rara vez pasaba el tiempo siguiendo las directrices de otros en un entorno estructurado. Por tanto, tuve la suerte de contar con Booster, Bonnie y la BUCS como mentores, que me enseñaron cuales eran las inversiones importantes de la vida, y a confiar en las propias capacidades para obtener el mayor rendimiento de la inversión (ROI). Fue mejor haber aprendido tarde en la vida que no haber aprendido nunca.

Un perro y una educación única cambiaron el estilo de vida devastador que había tenido por décadas. Hasta este mismo momento, estoy comprometido y eternamente agradecido con Bonnie Bergin y la BUCS. ¡Supongo que soy como una enfermedad de la que no se pueden librar! Asisto a las graduaciones y me mantengo en contacto. En el fondo de mi corazón, espero que Bonnie me vea como una enfermedad de la misma manera que la maravillosa dama con ELA veía su enfermedad. Me veo a mí mismo como un receptor de transfusiones de sangre de Bonnie Bergin. Todo por lo que ella trabajó en la vida lo invirtió en la BUCS y, por tanto, en mí. Viajo por el mundo aspirando a hacer la única cosa que Bonnie espera de sus alumnos... la única cosa... *cambiar el mundo a través de la utilización del vínculo entre caninos y humanos.* Permítanme afirmar simple y sucintamente que amo a Bonnie y a la BUCS... porque ella y su/nuestra universidad, junto con mi Booster, realmente transformaron mi vida para siempre. La vida a la que una vez intenté poner fin, ahora la atesoro.

La verdad es que me encantaban todas las clases. Fue increíble. Aprendí mucho. La BUCS ofrece una educación amplia, no un enfoque estrecho, y me sentí agradecido por ello. Doy crédito a mi Booster por haberme devuelto la vida. Fue un nuevo comienzo. Sin ADI y BUCS, nunca habría podido hacer crecer mi relación con Booster, ni tener los conocimientos necesarios para que ambos pudiéramos desarrollar todo nuestro potencial.

A los perros de servicio se les enseña a "calmarse" cuando están en lugares públicos. Con el tiempo, mi vida también pareció calmarse, pero yo no. Seguía preocupado de que algo malo pudiera ocurrir a donde quiera que iba. Con frecuencia, buscaba los nombres de mis adictos en Internet para saber dónde estaban y qué hacían. Nunca dejé atrás mi pasado. El miedo estaba inequívocamente tatuado en mi alma. ¿Acaso un esclavo olvida alguna vez su pasado? ¡Yo no podía! Dependía de Booster para minimizar el miedo en mi vida, siempre que fuera posible. Continuaba enviándolo a mi automóvil y a mi casa antes de entrar. Si oía ruidos extraños por la noche, sacudía a Booster y le preguntaba de manera sugerente, "¿Quién es?" Booster siempre se levantaba, miraba a su alrededor, olfateaba el aire y escuchaba resueltamente. En las ocasiones en que ladraba, me ponía a la defensiva y tomaba el teléfono, listo para llamar al 911 ante la más mínima provocación.

Siempre supe que algún día llegaría a casa y encontraría a uno de mis adictos durmiendo dentro. La historia se repite. En el pasado, mis adictos desaparecían durante un mes. Algunos días yo regresaba a casa, y encontraba a uno de ellos, con su alma igualmente perdida, durmiendo dentro de la cabaña. Si la puerta estaba cerrada, mis adictos rompían una ventana e ingresaban o dormían en un automóvil viejo en el patio. ¡La única certeza en mi vida era la incertidumbre! Cada vez que tenía la oportunidad de salir de casa, me sentía más seguro en algunos aspectos, pero más temeroso en otros. Sabía que en otro lugar no tendría que enfrentarme a los fantasmas del pasado; sin embargo, en el mundo exterior me acechaban nuevos fantasmas.

El único consuelo que tenía era Booster. Él era mi única y constante "cosa agradable". Me sentía protegido, amado y más seguro de mí mismo con él a mi lado. Booster representaba el 90% de mi sana interacción social. Realmente no quería hacer amigos ni arriesgarme a conocer a nuevos humanos y confiar en ellos. Pero, con Booster a mi lado, no tenía elección, ya que él atraía a la gente y la conversación era inevitable.

CAPÍTULO 10
LA VIDA EN CALMA
RUMBO A LAS BAHAMAS

Un día, decidí hacer un crucero por el Caribe. No era capaz de ir solo, así que invité a la pareja de jubilados que había administrado mi parque de casas móviles y, por supuesto, me llevé a Booster. Desde el momento en que nos paramos en la fila para abordar, todas las miradas estaban *puestas*

en él. Los pasajeros miraban fijamente a Booster y al hombre del perro. En cada paso que daba, las manos se extendían y la gente preguntaba, "¿Puedo acariciar a su perro?" Con el efecto tranquilizador de Booster a mi lado, ya no respondía mordazmente, "Quiere decir,

¿Me da *permiso* de acariciar a su perro?" pues ahora me sentía menos miserable en la vida. Me sentí agradecido de que Booster desviara la atención de mí. Estaba en el punto de mira porque tenía un perro, pero de alguna manera era diferente. Las preguntas no iban dirigidas a mí, sino a Booster. Empecé a tener lo que yo llamaba "conversaciones seguras". La

gente compartía historias felices sobre sus vidas y sus perros.

La línea de cruceros preparó una bonita caja para que Booster depositara sus desechos de agua y comida. Estaba llena del material más estéril y no provocador de orina del mundo. El problema era que no tenía idea de qué demonios era… ¿un corral de juego, una obra de arte o un minigolf? Por mucho que lo intenté, no logré que usara la caja. Incluso llegué al extremo de orinar en un par de mis calcetines y tirarlos a la misteriosa caja. Booster se limitó a mirarme como diciendo, "¡Caramba, esto cada vez es más divertido!" Él intentaba devolvérmelos. Yo no quería que él explotara, ni que lanzara una bomba en el barco delante de todo el mundo.

Recurrí al internet y envié un correo electrónico a una adiestradora de perros, y ella me sugirió poner una cerilla de madera con la cabeza roja en el recto. La verdad es que estuve a punto de encender una cerilla para lograr que mi Booster hiciera popó. Me sentía desesperado. Meses después, me enteré de que algunos adiestradores en las exposiciones caninas introducen la cabeza de una cerilla roja en el recto del perro porque el azufre funciona como una especie de enema, lo que provoca la defecación. ¡Mi Booster casi arde en llamas! ¡No defecaba!

Fui a buscar hierba de verdad. Le pregunté a la florista de a bordo si tenía hierba (no de la mala) o flores olorosas. Me contestó que no. Le expliqué mi dilema y me dijo amablemente, "En mi país, Rumanía, era veterinaria". Sí, otra *coincidencia*. Con un marcado acento europeo, añadió, "Sube a tu perro a la cubierta superior y pon su nariz contra el viento y él hará su trabajo". A las 3 a. m., los borrachos caminaban por la pista del barco para irse a dormir. A las 6 de la mañana, los marchadores olímpicos senior salían a pavonearse. Me preparé y llevé a Booster a la cubierta delantera superior (con la bolsa de desechos en la mano) y puse "su nariz contra el viento". En menos de un minuto, orinó en la almohadilla lo suficiente como para apagar un incendio forestal. Luego, enjuagué la zona con un trapo y agua que había traído, y seguimos adelante... pero no por mucho tiempo... Las caderas de Booster se hundieron, y la más maravillosa y voluminosa pila de desechos de perro llegó a la almohadilla número dos. ¿He dicho *NÚMERO 2*? ¡Porque así fue! Booster se sintió aliviado y yo también. ¡Los milagros nunca cesan! Él encontró la manera de hacer sus necesidades.

Poco después, el barco atracó en Freeport, Bahamas. Todos fuimos a dar un paseo por Port Lucaya. Un caballero bahameño nos saludó y nos ofreció una comida gratis si accedíamos a visitar un proyecto de tiempo compartido. Ya conocen el procedimiento. Nuestro amigo bahameño nos llevó al Island Seas Resort. Era un complejo donde *no se admitían mascotas*, pero me aseguraron que podía visitarlo con mi perro de servicio Booster. Mientras recorríamos la propiedad, Booster hizo amigos. Lo puse a recoger la basura, y a que la depositara en las papeleras de la propiedad. Aunque no le ofrecieron trabajo a Booster, sí le permitieron acompañarme si decidía comprar una semana de tiempo compartido. No compré una semana de 12.000 dólares al vendedor, pero sí compré una semana de segunda mano en eBay por unos cientos de dólares. La decisión de asistir a la presentación cambió mi vida. No tenía forma de saber hasta qué punto esa decisión transformó mi vida. "Sigue viniendo. Funciona si lo trabajas, así que trabájalo porque tú lo vales", el tema de Al-Anon de los doce pasos resonaba en mi psique.

Al año siguiente, Booster y yo regresamos a Island Seas Resort. Como me había hecho socio por Internet y no a través de un vendedor, me preguntaba si se cumpliría la promesa de permitir la entrada a mi perro de servicio. Volamos a Freeport y el taxista nos llevó al complejo sin ningún problema. Entramos en el vestíbulo del complejo, fuimos a registrarnos y les recordé que me habían dicho que podía llevar a mi perro de servicio. La señora del mostrador nos dijo, "Sr. Hawn, ¿recuerda que nos mostró las habilidades de su perro a mis hijos y a mí cuando estuvo aquí el año pasado? Mis hijos llevaron su historia en el periódico a su colegio y les dijeron a sus compañeros, "¡Conocimos a Booster, conocimos a Booster!" Luego afirmó, "Por supuesto, usted y Booster son bienvenidos aquí en Island Seas". ¡Casi me desmayo!

Al día siguiente, el autobús me transportó a mí y a Booster al mercado de la paja. Mostré las habilidades de Booster en Port Lucaya frente a turistas y bahameños. Quería poner en práctica mi recién descubierta confianza en la humanidad, a la que tenía acceso gracias a mi Booster. Un policía bahameño se me acercó y me dijo, "Señor, sé lo que hace, pero tenga cuidado con los niños". Le preocupaba que el perro grande pudiera morder a un niño. Me alegró ver que un policía se tomaba en serio su trabajo. Después reservé una excursión por la isla con una empresa turística local. Era la misma empresa con la que el complejo había contratado el servicio de transporte de ida y vuelta al puerto.

A la mañana siguiente, el autobús turístico vino a recoger a los pasajeros de la excursión. "No señor, no puede llevar a su perro en el autobús", explicó el conductor con su bello acento bahameño.

"Pero señor, es un perro de servicio y lo necesito por razones médicas".

"No señor, podría morder a alguien y perderíamos nuestro seguro".

"Todos los pasajeros son de mi resort de tiempo compartido, y han estado jugando con mi perro de servicio toda la semana.

¿Puedo hablar con el dueño de la compañía, por favor?"

El conductor llamó a su jefe y amablemente me pasó al teléfono. Le expliqué al jefe, "Yo también tengo un negocio y nunca querría que perdiera su seguro, pero me gustaría tener unos minutos de su tiempo".

Él accedió amablemente a escucharme.

"Un perro de servicio es, por poder, parte del cuerpo humano. Si eres ciego, el perro guía es tus ojos. Si eres sordo, el perro guía es tus oídos. No puedes separar las partes de tu cuerpo para subir en un autobús turístico. Soy discapacitado y, como tal, soy una minoría. Una de mis heroínas en la vida es Rosa Parks. ¿Sabes quién era?"

"Por supuesto, sé quién era Rosa".

"Estados Unidos tiene un pésimo historial de derechos civiles. A las minorías se les hacía viajar en la parte de atrás del autobús. Rosa era una minoría porque su color de piel era negro. La discriminación basada en la pigmentación de la piel era ignorante, errónea y repugnante. Yo también soy una minoría porque soy discapacitado. Injustamente hicimos que una minoría viajara en la parte trasera del autobús por el color de su piel. Con mucho gusto ocuparía el asiento de Rosa en la parte trasera de su autobús. Pero lo que me acaba de hacer hoy, señor, es mucho peor porque acaba de echar a la minoría del autobús. Pero yo sé que usted no tiene un hueso discriminatorio en su cuerpo. Al fin y al cabo, se dedica al turismo. Es un concepto nuevo y lo entiendo. Quiero agradecerle de todo corazón que haya sacado tiempo de su ocupada agenda para atender mi llamada y escuchar mis palabras."

"No hay problema".

Antes de abandonar el resort, llamé a una reportera del periódicc y le propuse hacer una historia para agradecer a los bahameños su hospitalidad. Cuando llegó la reportera, le presenté a Booster y le mostré algunas de sus habilidades. Ella tomó muchas fotos y escuchó atentamente mis palabras de agradecimiento. Fue un encuentro feliz. Unos días después, la historia apareció en *The Freeport News*, "Visitante aplaude el servicio recibido". Estaba seguro de que la buena gente del resort lo vería, ya que Freeport es una comunidad relativamente pequeña.

Meses después, busqué "discapacidades en Bahamas" en Internet y me enteré de que en Nassau se celebraba la Semana de Concienciación sobre Discapacidades. Llamé a muchos números de teléfono para obtener información. Me dijeron que llamara a una señora llamada Sheila Culmer. Era la presidenta del Consejo Nacional de Discapacidades de las Bahamas. Hablé con ella después de lo que me pareció un siglo de esfuerzo. Era una bahameña encantadora que me explicó que llevaba años luchando por conseguir que se aprobara una ley para los discapacitados, pero que había perdido toda esperanza. Luego, nos invitó amablemente a Booster y a mí a asistir a las actividades de la Semana de Concienciación sobre la Discapacidad de Bahamas. Llamé a mi amiga ciega, Toni Eames, y le pedí que me acompañara a Bahamas, y ella aceptó la invitación. Sheila se encargó de que yo apareciera en un programa de televisión llamado *Bahamas at Sunrise* y de que hablara en la iglesia baptista Native Golden Gates de Nassau. Compré boletos de avión para volar a Nassau con Booster, con la intención de visitar poco después mi recién adquirido tiempo compartido en Freeport.

Todas las aerolíneas que vuelan a Estados Unidos deben permitir la entrada y salida de perros de servicio. Es competencia del Departamento de Transporte estadounidense. Sin embargo, una vez que aterrizas en un país extranjero, estás sujeto a la discreción de las aerolíneas extranjeras. En este viaje compré boletos para Nassau. Busqué un alojamiento que aceptara mascotas, pero no tenía ni idea de cómo iba a llegar a Freeport. Como estaba acostumbrado a vivir al límite, decidí improvisar y tomarme cada día como viniera. Pensé que podría tomar un barco si fuera necesario.

Llegamos a Nassau y necesitábamos un taxi que nos llevara a nuestro resort. Estaba preparado para suplicar el acceso, pero no tuve ningún problema. Fuimos recibidos por el director del complejo, que nos explicó que él y su mujer habían levantado la restricción de no admitir mascotas para que pudiéramos asistir a la Semana de Concienciación sobre Discapacidades. Lo miré a los ojos y le agradecí su amabilidad. Me estrechó la mano y se acercó para acariciar a Booster, que inmediatamente se puso de espaldas. Booster no tardó en recibir un masaje en la barriga y los visitantes del resort se apresuraron a saludar al simpático perro. Mi miedo se disipó momentáneamente. Con Booster a mi lado, yo era Superman, ¡sin kriptonita en el planeta!

Al día siguiente, Booster, Toni y yo nos encontramos con Sheila. El resort reservó un taxi para llevarnos a la iglesia. Nos invitaron a demostrar las habilidades de un perro de servicio a un grupo de bahameños discapacitados que asistían al servicio dominical. Booster y yo entramos en la iglesia y conocimos al predicador. Le expliqué que nunca antes me había dirigido a una audiencia y que tenía problemas. Él tomó mi mano temblorosa y me dijo, "Todo estará bien". Una gran calma entró en mi cuerpo, como si estuviera conectado a una bomba de morfina. Nos llevaron a un asiento en la primera fila y poco después nos llamaron al escenario. Booster abrió una nevera y trajo agua. Me quitó los calcetines de los pies y me trajo los zapatos. Miré al público, muchos de los cuales eran discapacitados, y vi caras asustadas. Al instante pensé, *"En la cultura bahameña, los perros se utilizan para pelear, no para ayudar a los discapacitados"*. El público sentía temor por el perro de 45 kilos.

El predicador me pidió entonces que me dirigiera al público. Estaba indeciso, pero entonces una nube de serenidad me envolvió, así que me levanté y caminé hacia el atril con Booster. Necesitaba su apoyo. Él era mi roca. Yo no era nada sin mi Booster. Mientras observaba al público y veía ojos tan grandes como platillos, mi boca se abrió involuntariamente y empezaron a brotar las palabras.

"Veo miedo en esta sala esta mañana", dije. "Le tengo respeto al miedo. Sueño en la noche con un cuchillo que viene hacia mí, y me queda un segundo de vida. Tengo flashbacks de una agresión por un enfrentamiento anterior. Estoy cansado de estar a punto de morir noche tras noche. Quiero que sepan que le tengo respeto al miedo. Tengo miedo de sucesos en sueños que parecen reales pero no lo son. Ustedes tienen miedo de un perro de 45 kilos y eso es mucho más real. La gente pelea con perros y un perro de 45 kilos puede hacer daño. Lo entiendo. Pero quiero que sepan que esta mañana leí en su periódico que este año ha habido más de noventa asesinatos en Nassau. ¡Ninguno de ellos fue cometido por un perro! Quizás debieran temer más a las personas que están sentadas a su lado en este salón que al perro que se encuentra aquí enfrente. Es la inhumanidad del hombre hacia el hombre lo que deben temer. Mi Booster trabajará para mí el resto de su vida sin un céntimo de pago".

El público se quedó en silencio. Booster y yo tomamos asiento. Bajé la mirada, por temor de mirar al público, sin saber cómo habían sido recibidas mis palabras. Seguramente había ofendido a alguien o había dicho algo equivocado. Booster lo había hecho todo bien, como siempre. Yo había metido la pata. Pensé *que había decepcionado a mi Booster.* Me sentía triste mientras seguía acariciando a Booster con un celo incontrolable, con la mirada fija hacia abajo, lleno de incertidumbre.

El predicador subió al escenario. Empezó con una parábola sobre un perro. Cambió su sermón previsto para ese día. Improvisó y fue tan genuino cómo podía ser. Me maravillé de la parábola que se desarrolló espontáneamente como resultado del impacto de Booster sobre los fieles. Pensé en cómo Booster nunca me había defraudado. Él también era fiel, y aquel día renové mi promesa de compartirlo con el mundo y no defraudarlo nunca. Hércules tenía su cabello y yo tenía a mi Booster. Su confianza y su amor impregnaron insidiosamente mi vida. Yo estaba cambiando, pero no me daba cuenta. Mi desprecio por el prójimo disminuía. Después de todo, no me había equivocado. Mis palabras, unidas al talento de Booster, habían sido bien recibidas. Sí, lloré en el momento.

Cuando terminó el servicio, Booster y yo salimos a pasear. Toni y su perro guía Keebler nos acompañaron para estirar las piernas. Al cabo de unos instantes, nos saludaron los simpatizantes de la embajada estadounidense. "Fue increíble", dijeron los funcionarios que vinieron a saludarnos a Booster y a mí.

"Nos encanta todo lo que hay en las Bahamas, excepto que no tienen una ley para discapacitados", les dije.

Nunca conseguiremos que se apruebe una ley de discapacidad en nuestro país; llevamos años intentándolo", comentó Sheila con cierto pesimismo.

NASSAU.USEMBASSY.GOV
2011 Press Releases | Embassy of the United States Nassau, Bahamas

El 2 de diciembre, el Consejo Nacional de Bahamas para la Discapacidad (BNCD) inició actividades en conmemoración de su Semana anual de concienciación sobre la discapacidad con un foro de un día enfocado en "Vida independiente y legislación para todos". El tema de la semana era "capacidades diferentes", con el objetivo de crear conciencia sobre los problemas de la discapacidad, abordar los derechos fundamentales de las personas con discapacidad y la integración de los discapacitados en los ámbitos social, político, económico y cultural de la sociedad. (Bahamas Local, 6 de diciembre de 2011).

United States Embassy Nassau, The Bahamas ✓
December 5, 2011 ·

Más tarde, nos deleitamos con una maravillosa sopa de almejas, caracolas fritas y ensalada de caracolas. No pedí langosta, ¡me la guardé para la cena! Me encantaba el marisco y las Bahamas, ¡una combinación perfecta! Después de una comida digna de un rey, tomamos un taxi rumbo a una emisora de radio local, donde Sheila y yo hablamos de cómo un perro puede ayudar a una persona discapacitada. Hice notar el hecho de que los perros de servicio se convierten en minusválidos si no tienen acceso público. "¿Por qué un ciego tiene que suplicar para entrar en un restaurante o en un hotel con un perro guía?" pregunté. Aunque yo no era ciego y Booster no era un perro guía, seguía recordándome que esta sociedad no estaba familiarizada con los perros de servicio. Era un concepto extraño en un país extranjero. La mayoría de la gente había oído hablar de los perros guía para ciegos, y esa familiaridad fue útil para introducir el concepto de perro de servicio.

Al día siguiente, Sheila consiguió que apareciéramos en un programa de televisión. Yo estaba muy emocionado, pero Booster estaba mucho más

acostumbrado que yo al estatus de celebridad, así que se limitó a dormitar con su amiga, Minnie Mouse. Más tarde visitamos escuelas bahameñas. La primera que visitamos fue la Stapledon School for the Mentally Disabled. Me impresionó ver a un

reportero de prensa acompañado por un camarógrafo. Les pregunté a los niños, cuántos tenían miedo de mi Booster de 45 kilos. Casi todos los niños levantaron la mano. Pregunté si alguien tenía un perro en casa, y varios levantaron la mano. Pregunté si alguien dejaba que su perro entrara en la casa, y algunas manos se alzaron. Los niños bahameños, como los adultos de la iglesia el día anterior, se mostraron aprensivos para relacionarse con un perro de 45 kilos. Entonces di un paso atrás y dejé que Booster hiciera lo suyo.

El entusiasmo de los niños era difícil de contener. Fue conmovedor. Booster mostró a los niños cómo un perro puede cambiar vidas humanas.

Luego les expliqué que, en lugar de pelearse con un perro, quizá quisieran adiestrarlo para ayudar a su anciana abuela.

Booster actuó ante la mirada de los profesores y la prensa. Al final de la visita a la escuela, hice una pregunta a los niños. Inmediatamente pensé, *"¡Qué pregunta más estúpida!* Y empecé a recriminarme por hacerla. *¡Qué pregunta más tonta!* Había preguntado a unos niños asustados, "¿Alguien quiere acariciar a Booster?"

Los niños gritaron ceremoniosamente SÍ, y las manos tocaron el cielo al unísono. Saltaron y corrieron al lado de Booster. De repente sentí claustrofobia, pues ya no veía la luz del día. Estaba rodeado de niños, todos tendiendo la mano para acariciar a mi Booster con una adoración estrepitosa. Durante la conmoción que se produjo, un niño me miró y me preguntó inocentemente, "¿Por qué lloras?"

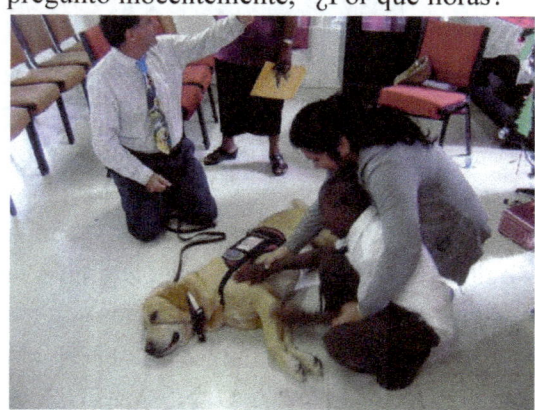

"Porque ustedes son muy especiales", le dije. Era sólo una lágrima solitaria, pero no pude ocultarla del astuto alumno. Mis emociones habían vuelto a aflorar. En ese momento, supe que estaba cambiando internamente. Después de dar las gracias a los niños y a los profesores por habernos invitado, regresamos al resort.

Al día siguiente, visitamos otra escuela. Los niños iban impecablemente vestidos, algo que es normal en Bahamas. Estaban concentrados en Booster y escucharon atentamente lo que les conté. Las preguntas planteadas eran realmente sorprendentes para niños de esa edad. Un joven se mostró reacio a acariciar a Booster, pero la maestra intuyó que quería hacerlo. ¿Quizá sus compañeros se burlaban de él? La maestra lo acompañó al lado de Booster. Acarició a Booster varias veces y luego, despreocupadamente, juntó su mano con la de él y acariciaron a Booster simultáneamente. El vínculo entre canino y humano se había perfeccionado.

Esa maestra fue puesta en esta tierra para enseñar. Me quedé asombrado. Los profesores dijeron que les vendría bien tener un perro como Booster en su escuela, un perro en las instalaciones. Al día siguiente, fuimos al aeropuerto, con la duda de si me permitirían llevar a Booster en el avión.

Mi plan alternativo era tomar un ferry. Booster y yo esperamos en una zona lo más alejada posible del personal de la aerolínea. Fiel a su costumbre, Booster hizo amigos mientras esperaba. Cuando llegó el momento de subir al avión, presenté mi tarjeta de embarque, tomé la correa de Booster y salí corriendo. Me senté en mi asiento con Booster a mis pies. Las azafatas estaban desconcertadas. El piloto se acercó por el pasillo para hablar conmigo. Me explicó que no llevaban perros dentro del avión. Le pregunté, "¿No llevarían a un ciego con un perro guía?"

Me contestó: "Yo sé que usted no es ciego, señor".

Le repliqué: "Sí, señor, tiene razón, pero mi perro de servicio especialmente adiestrado me equilibra cuando mis piernas no funcionan. Me ayuda con la movilidad y a mitigar los horribles efectos del TEPT".

El benévolo capitán me miró a los ojos y me dijo: "Señor, lo llevaré en el avión, pero le pido que me envíe información y documentación para poder explicar a mis supervisores por qué decidí llevarlo en el avión hoy". Anotó su correo electrónico personal y el de su superior en una servilleta y me la entregó.

El aura de Booster estaba trabajando a toda marcha. Me sentía orgulloso. Se confiaba en mí porque mi Booster actuaba con profesionalismo y ¡era digno de confianza! Cuando regresé a casa, envié al capitán y a su supervisor información sobre los perros de servicio/perros de asistencia. También les envié copias de artículos de prensa de las Bahamas en los que aparecían niños abrazando a Booster y profesores bahameños elogiándolo, y afirmando que podrían utilizar perros de este tipo en sus escuelas. Incluí fragmentos de apariciones en televisión que habíamos hecho.

A los pocos días apareció un artículo en el periódico de Nassau sobre la valiente decisión del capitán de ayudar a un semejante. Al principio, me sentí un poco avergonzado por haber causado tanto alboroto en un país que me había tratado con tanta amabilidad. Los bahameños no merecían ser molestados por mis problemas. Sheila me llamó más tarde para felicitarme por haber hecho historia en Bahamas. Yo no sabía qué pensar. Booster me miraba y sonreía. Era como si dijera, "Te dije que no todos los humanos son malos. Puede que no sean tan buenos como un perro, pero no todos son malos".

THE TRIBUNE   MONDAY, MAY 30, 2011, PAGE 7

LOCAL NEWS

Bahamasair eases travel policy curb on animals who help people with disabilities

Traveller with Post Traumatic Stress allowed to take dog on board

By AVA TURNQUEST
Tribune Staff Reporter
aturnquest@tribunemedia.net

THE compassion of a Bahamasair pilot, and determination of a disabled traveller, has effected changes to the airline's operational policy concerning animals

POLICY CHANGE: Bahamasair

The pair also appeared on many television programmes, including Bahamas at Sunrise and Conversations with Estelle Pinder.

"The Bahamian people gave me the confidence to associate with people again in my life," said Ms Haven.

Siete años después, otro piloto de Bahamasair puso en duda mi capacidad para volar con un perro de servicio. Fue bastante embarazoso, pero yo estaba acostumbrado a tratar con los que querían salvar el día protegiendo al mundo de un perro de servicio. Le indiqué al piloto que consultara el manual de operaciones de Bahamasair y que llamara al magnífico capitán que me había ayudado en el pasado. Fue molesto, pero al final nos sentamos en el avión. Lo que ocurrió a continuación fue increíble.

Cuando volví a casa, hice lo de siempre: documentarme y crear un diálogo con la esperanza de evitar que se repitieran tales transgresiones. Escribí un correo electrónico al director general de Bahamasair, poniendo de manifiesto el valor de los perros de servicio en la sociedad. Además, le expliqué que me habían faltado al respeto y me habían tratado injustamente por el simple hecho de contar con la ayuda de un equipo médico duradero, mi perro de servicio especialmente adiestrado. "Una vez sentados los pasajeros", expliqué, "el capitán salió de la cabina con su teléfono móvil en la mano. Nos tomó varias fotos mientras TODOS los pasajeros nos miraban incrédulos. Me fotografiaron como a un delincuente siendo fichado en una cárcel. Mi perro de servicio y yo actuamos con el máximo profesionalismo, mientras que su capitán no lo hizo... y en violación del manual de operaciones de Bahamasair".

Al año siguiente, regresé a Island Seas con Toni, su amiga ciega Lyn y sus perros guía. Toni y Lyn querían subir al autobús turístico... el mismo autobús que me había denegado el acceso el año anterior. Compramos los boletos. Cuando el autobús llegó al día siguiente, nos hicieron señas para que subiéramos. Dudé y dije: "No, por favor llama al dueño del negocio y pídele permiso para que subamos al autobús". Hablé con él por teléfono y me dijo escuetamente, "Son bienvenidos al autobús". Miré a Booster y, una vez más, las lágrimas brotaron. La respuesta del empresario resonó en lo más profundo de mi ser. Nunca hubo ofensas ni se pronunciaron palabras duras. El respeto mutuo, unido a la educación, dio como resultado una respuesta muy valiosa. Nuestro viaje a las Bahamas fue un acontecimiento que cambió mi vida. Yo no era feliz entre seres humanos en mi propio país, y mucho menos entre extranjeros en una tierra que no era la mía. Me sentía inseguro. En lugar de trabajar junto a otros, la mayoría de las veces prefería trabajar solo. Tenía más prejuicios contra mí mismo por *ser* diferente que contra los demás por *parecerlo.*

Ir a las Bahamas y hablar en público fue un gran reto. De hecho, fue uno de los *mayores* retos a los que me había enfrentado en la vida. Resultó ser una *gran* experiencia, ya que aprendí mucho de la aceptación que recibí del pueblo bahameño. Me aceptaron y me escucharon mientras contaba lo que había aprendido de un perro. En una cultura en la que el amor por los perros suele ser secundario frente al interés por luchar contra ellos, yo había conectado. Regresé a mi tiempo compartido de Freeport todos los años. Siempre llamaba al periódico, visitaba una escuela o escribía cartas a los primeros ministros.

Meses después, estaba hablando por teléfono con mi amiga Peggy y le mencioné que tenía un crédito de tiempo compartido. Tenía que usarlo o lo perdería. Era una bonita época del año y Peggy sugirió que fuéramos a algún lugar de Nueva Inglaterra. Encontramos una unidad disponible en Vermont y la reservamos unos días después. Le dije a Peggy que había un lugar muy especial llamado Dog Mountain que teníamos que visitar cuando estuviéramos allí. Peggy, como era Peggy, sonrió alegremente, aplaudió y dijo, "¡Qué genial!", antes de que yo pudiera explicarle su significado.

Dog Mountain fue la inspiradora creación del renombrado artista Stephen Huneck, cuya vida era muy parecida a la mía. Stephen estaba en coma en la cama de un hospital cuando su mujer, Gwen, lo visitó con uno de sus queridos perros. Stephen despertó del coma y atribuyó a su perro la metamorfosis. Posteriormente dedicó su talento artístico a pintar perros, representando la espiritualidad y la virtud. Algunos de sus cuadros muestran ángeles caninos con alas. Mi Booster también era un ángel canino.

Stephen también construyó una increíble capilla canina donde los perros podían entrar y salir por una puerta en mitad de la noche. Yo había visitado la capilla años antes, cuando Booster era sólo un cachorro. Incluso a una edad temprana, Booster se enfrentó a la muerte, por lo que una capilla canina era especialmente significativa para un perro al que se le salvó la vida en numerosas ocasiones. Peggy y yo leímos sombríamente muchas de las notas escritas por amantes de los perros de todo el país que querían inmortalizar los recuerdos de los miembros más queridos de su familia canina.

Por desgracia, Stephen sucumbió a la depresión y se suicidó cuando la economía se desplomó y no pudo pagar a los empleados a quienes tanto quería.

Con el apoyo de Peggy, más tarde hice una entrevista en el periódico con su esposa, Gwen, y le expliqué que seguramente habría seguido los pasos de Stephen de no ser por el impacto de Booster en mi vida. Ella sonrió y dijo, "Stephen siempre estaba pintando (aislado) y rara vez llegó a experimentar el amor de quienes lo admiraban a él y a su obra". Las lágrimas brotaron espontáneamente de mis ojos porque yo podría haber corrido la misma suerte "de no ser" por la intervención de un perro al que en un principio rehuía. Yo también había querido aislarme, pero Booster seguía llevándome hacia la gente; aislarme no era una opción. Mientras mi relación con Booster florecía, también lo haría mi vida en los años venideros, aunque tardé mucho en darme cuenta de lo importante que era. Hasta el día de hoy, vivo basándome en los principios que me transmitió mi Booster.

CAPÍTULO 11
PROYECTO FIDELITY

Durante dos años viajé a California para asistir a mis clases de maestría de la BUCS. Bonnie nos pidió que mantuviéramos la mente abierta con respecto a lo que haríamos para la tesis. Yo era un discípulo de Bonnie como ninguno, pero ya sabía lo que iba a hacer para mi tesis. Quería demostrar que una mujer codependiente que sufría el síndrome de mujer maltratada podía transferir su codependencia del maltratador a un perro. El amor fingido de un maltratador sucumbiría ante el amor incondicional de un perro. Me imaginaba llevando a mujeres maltratadas desde su refugio a visitar a otras almas probablemente maltratadas, igualmente hipervigilantes y aparentemente indefensas. Las mujeres podrían realizar una labor de servicio rescatando a perros de refugios, cuyas vidas también estuvieran en peligro. Planeaba enseñar a las mujeres a adiestrar a los perros para que se convirtieran en perros de terapia. Los dúos dinámicos entrarían en hospitales, residencias de ancianos y hospicios para aprender lo que eran el aprecio verdadero y el amor incondicional. Eso es lo que Booster había hecho por mí. Fue algo personal.

Una noche, mientras estaba en el dormitorio, leí por casualidad un artículo de una revista titulado "El sueño de La Habana". Aludía al día en que los estadounidenses podrían volver a viajar a Cuba. Los cubanos estaban atrapados en una isla, sin poder viajar libremente, ¡pero también lo estaban los estadounidenses que deseaban viajar a Cuba! Booster había sido el artífice de mi libertad mental y de la capacidad de comunicarme con los demás. *Me reí a carcajadas al pensar, apuesto a que un perro puede hacer lo que los humanos no pueden... promover una comunicación que conduzca a la fidelidad.* Sabía en mi corazón que si alguien podía fomentar el amor, la armonía y la fidelidad, era un perro, particularmente Booster.

Esa noche, no tuve un sueño en forma de flashback relacionado con el TEPT que pusiera en peligro mi vida. Soñé que estaba en La Habana, rodeado de extraños que querían acariciar a Booster. Estaba en La Habana, mostrando las habilidades de Booster a una población educada que nunca había visto a un perro realizar tareas de ayuda a los discapacitados. Ese sueño se convirtió en una obsesión. Se acercaba rápidamente el momento de seleccionar mi proyecto de tesis, y yo estaba en conflicto como la relación entre Estados Unidos y Cuba. ¿Cómo elegir entre ayudar a personas que sufren el mismo tormento que tú sufriste una vez, y unir a dos pueblos que sufren una desconexión disfuncional de décadas?

Sabía que Booster era el único diplomático en el mundo que podía proyectar de forma única la fidelidad entre Estados Unidos y Cuba. Booster tenía una extraña habilidad como embajador para conocer, saludar y transmitir un amor incuestionable e incondicional. Era el equivalente canino de John Lennon. Con total despreocupación por las normas establecidas, decidí abordar la *nave estelar Booster* e ir a donde "ningún hombre había ido antes con éxito"... al menos no un ciudadano estadounidense normal (durante décadas). Estaba decidido a ir a Cuba para proyectar fidelidad. Mi tesis afirmaba que los perros son un lubricante social, un puente que une a las personas de una manera única. Con esta idea en mente, concebí el Proyecto Fidelity para fomentar la fidelidad entre dos países que parecían incapaces de hacerlo, a pesar de los numerosos intentos llevados a cabo por individuos de todo el mundo.

Casualmente, fue en esa época cuando el presidente Obama incentivó los intercambios culturales entre ciudadanos estadounidenses y cubanos. Si realizabas una investigación en colaboración con una universidad estadounidense acreditada, unido a la probabilidad de que se publicaran tus hallazgos, se te concedería el todopoderoso permiso de viajar como hombre  libre, para visitar a otras personas que vivían a 90 millas de distancia, en

Cuba. Sin embargo, seguía existiendo un problema. La BUCS aún no estaba acreditada. Era una universidad incipiente que buscaba la acreditación del gobierno. *¿Por qué los seres humanos complican tanto las cosas aparentemente fáciles?* Los perros enfrentan obstáculos, pero siguen con sus vidas sin que sus compañeros se los impidan. Forman manadas porque saben que la unión hace la fuerza.

Los humanos suelen distanciarse de los demás, e incluso adoptan posturas provocativas, que con frecuencia acaban en guerra.

Dejé en pausa mi idea del Proyecto Fidelity mientras proseguía mis estudios. Volví a pensar en ayudar a las mujeres maltratadas a superar la codependencia con apoyo canino. Era inútil ir a Cuba a pregonar los méritos de un perro si no podía publicar mis hallazgos sin someterme a juicio. Según Wikipedia, Estados Unidos ya tenía la tasa de encarcelamiento más alta del mundo. No quería aumentar esa estadística. Seguí en mi callejón sin salida hasta que un día Bonnie hizo un anuncio en clase. Con una sonrisa radiante, ella explicó que la BUCS había superado los requisitos para obtener la certificación de ACIS, un consejo de acreditación para las universidades estadounidenses. *Casualmente...* la BUCS había obtenido la acreditación en el momento perfecto. La acreditación me permitió trabajar de lleno en el Proyecto Fidelity. Mi Poder Superior me acechaba. *¿Quizá Mi Poder Superior también es codependiente?* pensé.

Tomé mis recién adquiridas habilidades de investigación de la BUCS y me metí de lleno a aprender todo lo que pudiera sobre Cuba. En concreto, quería averiguar qué se necesitaba para ingresar a un perro, mi Booster, en Cuba. No es de extrañar, que un país que no permite a sus ciudadanos el acceso a Internet o la libertad de viajar, publicara poca información en la web. Había mucha historia sobre la crisis de los misiles cubanos, pero poco de otros temas. Sin embargo, me enteré de que algunos canadienses viajaban a Cuba y exaltaban sus virtudes. Hace poco leí la historia de un canadiense que se aventuró a ir a Cuba cuando murió su querido perro Spanky. Se compadeció de los perros callejeros cubanos y quiso ayudar. Fundó el Proyecto Spanky y coordinó la entrada de veterinarios canadienses y donaciones a La Habana, y también inició un programa de esterilización que tuvo mucho éxito.

Un día lo llamé y me dio el nombre de su socia, una canadiense que vivía en La Habana y trabajaba como traductora. También me dio el nombre de un hombre en quien podía confiar para que fuera mi guía. No tardé en comunicarme con ambos por correo electrónico. La comunicación estaba limitada por el tamaño de los archivos. Con frecuencia, mis correos electrónicos eran rechazados por extrañas razones. No sabía si se debía a la primitiva Internet cubana o al Gran Hermano cubano que escuchaba. No me importaba, lo único que quería era darle a Booster la oportunidad de hacer su trabajo.

Yo le tenía un miedo inherente al comunismo. Cuando estaba en primer grado, me enseñaron a meterme debajo de un pupitre en caso de que los cubanos lanzaran los misiles. Si estaba en el pasillo cuando sonaba la sirena de defensa civil, debía tirarme en un rincón, juntar las manos detrás de la nuca y apartar la vista del fogonazo. A los estudiantes de todo Estados Unidos se les enseñó a *agacharse y cubrirse* para protegerse de la lluvia radiactiva. Años más tarde, escuché a Walter Cronkite en las noticias de la noche, "Otros 100 muchachos estadounidenses perdieron la vida a manos de los "comunistas" norvietnamitas". Tenía miedo de entrar en Cuba, mi terapeuta me aconsejó que no fuera, pero confié en Booster y su capacidad terapéutica y diplomática.

No pude encontrar ninguna información sobre cómo llevar un perro *a* Cuba. Los grupos de rescate habían sacado perros. No había embajada de EE.UU., a la que pudiera llamar para obtener información. Llamé a la Sección de Intereses Cubanos en Washington, DC, y nunca conseguí hablar con una persona. Más tarde, llamé a la Misión Cubana de Nueva York y hablé con una secretaria que tenía una amiga que trabajaba en la Sección de Intereses. Me dio un número privado al cual llamar. Cuando hablé con su amiga, me dijo que conocía a un diplomático que siempre viajaba con su perro a Cuba. Aquella chispa encendió mi esperanza. Le envié una canasta con frutas y un caluroso agradecimiento. Con el tiempo, obtuve suficiente información para diseñar mi proyecto, pero casi había renunciado a llevar a Booster a Cuba. Había investigado en vano durante meses sobre cómo llevar a un perro a Cuba, si las autoridades cubanas lo permitirían y qué se necesitaba. Encontré una empresa turística canadiense, Cuba Educational Tours, que llevaba estadounidenses a Cuba. No admitían perros en sus autobuses turísticos ni en los hoteles cubanos. Yo me encontraba dolido y completamente desanimado. Me inscribí en el tour y decidí ir sin Booster y limitarme a investigar sobre temas caninos en Cuba. Después de todo, necesitaba graduarme, pasara lo que pasara.

Unos días antes de mi partida, recibí una llamada de una compañera de clase, Dailyah. Los dos éramos almas incomprendidas y nos habíamos convertido en compañeros de la BUCS. Hablábamos como queríamos, tanto si la otra persona quería oír lo que cada uno tenía que decir como si no. Yo criticaba a menudo a Dailyah, y ella me criticaba a mí. Era un diálogo honesto entre adultos educados que tenían una mentalidad abierta y apreciaban el respeto íntimo sin inyectar dramatismo emocional. Las palabras de Dailyah aquella noche resuenan hasta hoy. "Dave, eres un gran tipo, ¡pero no eres nada sin tu perro!" Me sorprendió oír eso, ¡pero tenía razón! Se trataba de Booster, no de mí. Si tenía que nadar hasta Cuba con Booster a la espalda, ahora estaba decidido a hacerlo.

Esa noche, después de que me dijeran que no era nadie sin Booster, me acordé del piloto de Bahamasair que me había ayudado. Su dirección de correo electrónico seguía archivada y apareció cuando la solicité. Envié un correo electrónico al capitán, sin saber si la dirección seguía siendo válida. Le pregunté con cautela si Bahamasair podría ayudarme con mi trabajo universitario llamado Proyecto Fidelity. Los bahameños valoran la educación y envían a sus hijos a la escuela con uniformes limpios y orgullosamente vestidos. Sospeché que el buen capitán podría ser comprensivo y solidario. Él conocía de primera mano mi devoción por Booster y la educación, así como mi agradecimiento por la aceptación que me había brindado la sociedad bahameña. Al día siguiente recibí un correo electrónico del capitán en el que me decía, "Bahamasair está familiarizado contigo y con Booster; por lo tanto, no veo ningún problema en que vuelen con nosotros". Qué halago pensé... ¡un testimonio del profesionalismo de Booster!" El correo electrónico además decía, "Si decides volar con Bahamasair, por favor, dime la fecha y la hora, y yo avisaré a mis colegas, para asegurarme de que tú y Booster tengan una experiencia increíble con nosotros." No dijo "tú y tu perro". ¡Recordó el nombre de Booster!

Yo estaba absolutamente asombrado. Era simplemente un hombre con un perro. Una vez más, en estado de shock, derramé lágrimas de cocodrilo. Era abrumador. El amor de una compañera de clase, un piloto de otro país, y canadienses y cubanos se unieron para ayudarme a perseguir mi pasión en la vida. *¿Qué demonios estaba pasando?* me preguntaba. *¿Por qué la gente necesita drogarse cuando la vida ofrece semejantes estímulos?* Terminé de leer el correo electrónico del capitán y, de algún modo, mantuve la compostura el tiempo suficiente para escribir un correo electrónico al guía cubano que se había ofrecido a ayudarnos. Le pregunté si él, su mujer y su hijo cuidarían de mi posesión más valiosa en la vida, mi Booster. Él aceptó y se ofreció con empatía. Me explicó que su mujer se tomaría una semana libre y cuidaría a Booster.

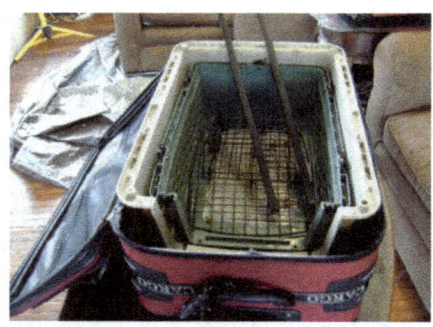

Sí, sí, las lágrimas fluían. *¿Por qué estos actos de bondad me ocurren a mí, que no lo merezco?* me preguntaba una y otra vez. *¿Existe **realmente** la bondad y el karma?* Rápidamente me enfoqué en prepararme para volar hacia lo desconocido. Compré antibióticos caninos para los perros cubanos y jaulas para alojarlos. Como sólo podía llevar dos maletas, utilicé el cerebro que me había dado Mi Poder Superior (MPS) y empaqué por capas. Empezando con una maleta grande, metí dentro la mitad de un huacal grande, con la mitad de una maleta más pequeña, y luego metí mi ropa y las cosas que necesitaba. Repetí el proceso con la maleta número dos.

A la mañana siguiente, contacté a mi veterinario y corrí a su consultorio para que inspeccionara a Booster. Él rellenó el formulario APHIS del Departamento de Agricultura de Estados Unidos

para el transporte internacional de animales. También le pedí que rellenara otro formulario que había encontrado en Internet y que estaba escrito en español. Reuní copias de los registros de vacunas, sin saber si los cubanos aceptarían los documentos estadounidenses o el hecho de que Booster había recibido la vacuna antirrábica de tres años. Muchos países, e incluso mi condado local, exigían la administración de vacunas *anuales* contra la rabia. En una clase de veterinaria de la BUCS, aprendí que la vacuna antirrábica de un año era idéntica a la vacuna antirrábica de tres años. Era una cuestión del periodo de garantía de un año frente al de tres. Exigir vacunas anuales contra la rabia era sobre dosificar innecesariamente a los perros. Leí que una facultad de veterinaria estaba realizando un estudio que pretendía demostrar que la vacuna antirrábica proporcionaba protección por siete años.

Cuanta más documentación tuviera, mejor. Si las autoridades cubanas no dejaban entrar a Booster en Cuba, volaría a casa. Sin embargo, me preocupaba mucho que pudieran poner a Booster en cuarentena en quién sabe qué instalaciones, o posiblemente destruirlo si no hubiera una opción de cuarentena disponible. Como siempre, empecé a agobiarme. *¿Por qué arriesgaría la vida de Booster para facilitar mi educación? ¿Soy un monstruo por permitir tal posibilidad? ¿Qué hizo Booster para merecer un compañero humano tan horrible?* Salté por los aros de los campos minados mentales, esperando explotar en cualquier momento. Bajo presión, tanto real como percibida, sentía dolor. Volvía a estar en mi montaña rusa mental, viendo en un momento el cielo y en el siguiente el infierno. Coexistían la adrenalina y el dolor.

Tres días más tarde, abordé un avión con destino a Cuba vía Miami y luego Nassau. Al llegar al aeropuerto de Miami, una amable agente de Bahamasair me vio, se acercó y me dijo, "Usted debe de ser el señor Hawn, y éste debe ser Booster".

"Sí, señora, es mi Booster", respondí.

Enseguida subimos al avión y poco después aterrizamos en Nassau. Durante las dos horas de escala, Booster entretuvo a niños y adultos en la sala de espera. Nos indicaron que subiéramos al avión primero y nos sentáramos en los asientos asignados. Nos sentaron en el centro del avión, aislados. Los asientos de adelante y detrás de nosotros estaban bloqueados para proteger a los demás pasajeros de un perro y limitar posibles quejas.

Una vez acomodados, los pasajeros empezaron a caminar por el pasillo. La gente se apresuraba a sentarse junto al amistoso labrador amarillo que ya era su amigo personal. Booster sonreía y movía la cola. Las azafatas, posiblemente asustadas por la visión de un perro de 45 kilos, no tenían palabras para describir su asombro. Yo podía leer su lenguaje corporal, "¿La gente quiere sentarse al lado de un perro?"

El avión despegó con las manos acariciando a Booster. Los cinturones de seguridad sujetaban las cinturas de los pasajeros, pero sus manos adoradoras estaban fuera de control. Yo me sentía muy feliz. ¿OISTE ESO? ¡ESTABA FELIZ! Mi felicidad pronto se unió a las lágrimas. Una vez más, Booster me hizo llorar. Aterrizamos en el aeropuerto internacional José Martí de La Habana. Cuando entré en el aeropuerto, un hombre con aspecto de funcionario, con chaqueta azul y corbata, me tomó del brazo y me dijo, "Venga conmigo".

Empecé a temblar sin control. *¡Voy a ir a la cárcel! ¿Qué será de Booster cuando me lleven?* El hombre me miró y me dijo tranquilamente, en un inglés casi ininteligible, "Soy el veterinario del aeropuerto y debo inspeccionar a su perro. Yo también tengo un labrador amarillo". Él no podía saber lo asustado que yo estaba. Empecé a acariciar a Booster a tal punto que pensé que perdería el pelo por la fricción. Booster posteriormente drenó mis emociones como sólo él podía hacerlo. Yo estaba muy asustado.

Víctima de mis emociones y atrapado en Cuba, no tenía ninguna agencia estadounidense a la cual pedir ayuda ni ningún terapeuta en quien confiar. Simplemente tenía a mi Booster. De manera inexplicable, dicen que la muerte suele convertirse en una experiencia placentera. De alguna forma, yo también me vi envuelto en una nube protectora de serenidad mientras Booster se comportaba como siempre, no se inmutaba. La calma que proyectaba me permitía ver que mis emociones estaban desequilibradas, fuera de control con la realidad. Sonrisas amistosas se irradiaban por todo el aeropuerto mientras las cabezas se giraban para ver al perro amarillo que llevaba al universalmente conocido Mickey Mouse. Viví lo que estaba seguro sería una experiencia al límite.

El veterinario me explicó entonces que tenía un consultorio privado y me invitó sutilmente a visitarlo en su clínica. Me dio su información de contacto y me pidió que no le contara a nadie de su maravillosa invitación. Los cubanos temían las repercusiones gubernamentales de las interacciones con extranjeros, especialmente estadounidenses. Luego, se ofreció a ayudarme a pasar mis dos maletas por la aduana. Lo miré y le dije, "Tengo drogas en mi equipaje". Él quedó estupefacto.

Pero entonces le expliqué que había traído frascos de antibióticos para perros como donación para el Proyecto Spanky, pero que ahora quería que él se quedara con la mitad Me acompañó por la aduana y señaló la maleta que no contenía medicamentos. La abrieron y la inspeccionaron, ¡pero la otra no! *¿Coincidencia?* Más bien, *conexiones*, pero nunca lo supe.

Salí de la terminal y no estaba preparado para lo que vendría después. Había cientos de cubanos rodeando el aeropuerto. Yo estaba en medio de una revuelta, o eso creía. La verdad era que estaban esperando la llegada de los envíos de sus familiares en Estados Unidos. Estaban desesperados por recibir sus mercancías. Fue la primera de muchas lecciones aprendidas en Cuba.

Un hombre se acercó de repente, se presentó y dijo en un inglés entrecortado, "Tú debes de ser Dave. Hola, Booster". Nos llevó a conocer a la familia cubana que acogería a Booster. Entramos y Booster pidió atención, que recibió de inmediato. Luego se acercó a la mujer del hombre, con Mickey Mouse en la boca, y se congració con ella. Su hijo adolescente entró en la habitación, un poco temeroso de saludar al monstruo amarillo de 45 kilos. No dijo ni una palabra. Booster tomó la iniciativa y llevó a Mickey a saludar al joven. Al poco rato, el chico estaba lanzando una pelota y Booster no paraba de devolvérsela. ¡La guerra fría canino-humana terminó tan rápido como empezó! Tomé fotos, pero me pidieron amablemente que no las compartiera por miedo a las represalias, ese era un tema que se estaba desarrollando rápidamente.

Hicimos planes, me despedí de Booster con una caricia y un abrazo, y el taxista me llevó al hotel. Conocí al director del tour y a mis compañeros de viaje. La mayoría eran profesoras de California. Esa noche me enteré de que el camarero del hotel ganaba más en una noche con las propinas de los turistas que un médico en un mes. Estábamos escuchando a un pianista tocar cuando de repente, empezó a tocar una canción nueva de John Lennon, "Imagine". Al instante pensé en mi tesis de la BUCS, en la que aparecía una foto de Booster vestido de John Lennon con el subíndice *"imagine"*. Casi me desmayo. ¡Mi Poder Superior seguía persiguiéndome como si estuviera verificando una tarjeta de puntuación!

Al final de la velada, entré en el ascensor para subir a mi habitación. Era de estilo antiguo, como casi todo en Cuba. El hombre cerró la puerta metálica y giró una rueda para animar al viejo ascensor a subir. Me dio la bienvenida en inglés. Había aprendido que a los cubanos no se les permitía hablar con los turistas en la calle. Si los atrapaban haciéndolo, se arriesgaban a ir a la cárcel. Le pregunté al hombre que si le daba una lista de preguntas sobre perros, ¿me las contestaría? Subí a mi habitación, preparé la lista y regresé al ascensor. La noche siguiente, detuvo el ascensor entre pisos y respondió todas mis preguntas. Me entregó un trozo de papel con notas garabateadas. Lo hizo en secreto. Me encontraba realmente en una población controlada por los comunistas, donde atreverse a cuestionar o violar las normas establecidas tenía severas consecuencias.

Al día siguiente, la agencia de viajes canadiense revisó nuestro itinerario. Habían preparado una impresionante lista de lugares para visitar en La Habana. El primer día fuimos a la Escuela Latinoamericana de Medicina. Conocí al administrador, el médico jefe, y le expliqué que en Estados Unidos utilizamos a los perros como forma de medicina. Además, le comenté que entrenamos a veteranos con problemas mentales para que adiestren perros para veteranos con discapacidades físicas, y esto ha hecho que la tasa de suicidios disminuya. Estados Unidos tiene fama de ser un país agresivo, especialmente en Cuba. El médico me miró inmediatamente a los ojos y me dijo, "¡Mejor perros que balas!" Nunca olvidé sus sabias palabras, con las que estoy totalmente de acuerdo.

Después visitamos un gran proyecto urbano de jardinería hidropónica patrocinado por una organización alemana, que los cubanos llamaban Organopónicos. Nos enseñaron sobre el cultivo de alimentos sanos. La mayoría de mis compañeros caminaban sin rumbo por los campos, observando la flora y la fauna. Mientras otros recorrían los campos, yo opté por visitar a mis compañeros caninos. Una miríada de perros y cachorros languidecían en los campos, igual que los trabajadores Cubanos atrapados en un sistema social que rara vez recompensaba la productividad. Los granjeros adoraban a los perros de la granja y les habían puesto nombres a todos. Me preguntaba si alguno de los rusos de años atrás había traído sus perros a Cuba. En la BUCS aprendí que los investigadores rastreaban la migración histórica del hombre por los continentes basándose en muestras de ADN tomadas de caninos actuales. Cuando los humanos viajaban, se llevaban a sus perros con ellos.

Los trabajadores cubanos nos prepararon una comida que fue la mejor que tuve. La comida en Cuba es un asco, ya que el gobierno no tiene dinero para hacer muchas importaciones y gran parte de las tierras de cultivo están ociosas por falta de incentivos para trabajarlas. ¿Vas a tirar de un arado en un calor de 100 grados por 25 dólares al mes? Aprendí rápidamente de un cubano, "El gobierno finge pagarnos y nosotros fingimos trabajar". Al final de la comida, todos dejamos una pequeña muestra de agradecimiento en forma de propina. La mayoría de las señoras dejaron un peso convertible cubano (CUC), pero yo opté por dejar dos. De repente, una señora tendió su mano para retirar su propina y me dijo: "No quieres estropearlo dejando demasiado... esperarán más en el futuro". Estaba molesto, ya que quería mostrar gratitud como sabía hacerlo, y no basándome en la idea preconcebida de otra persona. Así que metí la mano en el bolsillo y puse otro CUC sobre la mesa. Ella se levantó y se marchó. ¡Ya no podía retirar nada de la mesa!

Años antes, en la época en que los rusos retiraron su apoyo a Cuba, se le llamó Periodo Especial. La vida era difícil. Los cubanos con frecuencia no tenían electricidad.

Muchos comían animales para sobrevivir. Me dijeron que comían más gatos que perros. Aquel día en el jardín, representó el segundo *período especial* cuando una gratificación vital fue egoístamente retirada. Los caninos no actúan así; destilan amor incondicional, no egoísmo. Me alegré de viajar

acompañado de un perro. Mi vida había estado alguna vez bajo cero, pero con Booster a mi lado, aprendí a tener confianza día tras día. Ese día manejé la confrontación por primera vez en mucho tiempo. Estaba cambiando, ¡para bien!

Días después, en la ciudad rural de Vinales, vi a una perra anciana sufriendo en la acera bajo el ardiente sol. Un cubano me ayudó a perseguir y capturar a la indefensa *perrita* mientras su amigo traía un carro para llevarnos al veterinario local. Su cuerpo lleno de sarna no tenía ni un pelo. No tenía pelaje que la protegiera del calor del sol. En la BUCS aprendí que el pelo de un perro puede ayudarlo a refrescarse. Muchas personas los afeitan en verano, pensando que así se refrescan, cuando en realidad agravan la situación al exponer la piel del perro a los rayos del sol. Pagué el tratamiento y dejé a la preciosa perra en manos cariñosas que prometieron cuidar de ella.

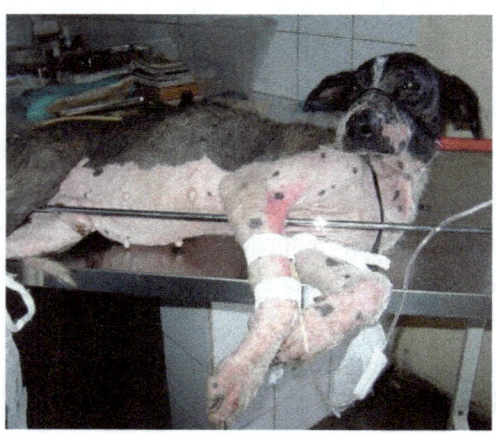

Esa noche, decidí ir a Chinatown a comer algo. Booster subió al taxi con Mickey Mouse en la boca. Cuando llegamos, nos dirigimos a un bonito restaurante chino donde disfrutamos de una comida muy buena. Unos artistas callejeros disfrazados de dragón interpretaron una rutina bien ensayada. Cuando llevaba una hora comiendo, oí a un hombre gritar, "Señor, señor". Levanté la vista y vi al taxista que me había traído, llevando a Mickey. Se inclinó y se lo dio a mi (agradecido) Booster, que lo cogió al instante. Me explicó que había llegado a casa, ¡vio el juguete en el taxi y vino a buscarme por todo Chinatown!

Los cubanos no tienen dinero para la gasolina. Ese hombre condujo una hora, ida y vuelta, para devolver el juguete de Booster. Me levanté y le di un abrazo. Saqué mi billetera y le di 20 dólares. Estoy seguro de que a mi egoísta compañera de viaje le habría dado un infarto en ese mismo instante si lo hubiera visto. Fue otro momento reparador en mi vida. Quizá para algunos no fue nada, pero para mí lo fue todo. Significó el mundo para mí. Este hombre eligió proyectar fidelidad de la manera más simple, más pura. Yo estaba listo para regresar a casa. El benévolo taxista nos llevó a la casa de acogida de Booster. Abracé a Booster para darle las buenas noches y el taxista me llevó al hotel. Se negó a aceptar más dinero.

Más tarde, esa misma noche, caminé por la principal calle turística de La Habana. Era como Bourbon Street en Nueva Orleans.

Luego de caminar unas pocas cuadras, me puse a hablar con un estudiante universitario. Al cabo de unos minutos, un agente de la policía cubana se me acercó y me preguntó, "¿De dónde lo conoces?"

El joven asustado dijo, "Dile que conoces a mi familia".

Le expliqué que nos habíamos conocido mientras hacía una demostración con mi perro en la calle el día anterior. El insensible policía anotó su nombre en un libro y lo mandó a casa. Sentí el mayor miedo de mi vida. Fue peor que la situación del aeropuerto. Agradecido por mi libertad, regresé al hotel. Un canadiense me explicó que yo nunca había corrido peligro de ser detenido, pero el cubano sí. No se les permite hablar con turistas en la calle. Si los atrapan haciéndolo, su nombre va a parar a un libro. ¡Si vuelven a hacerlo, pueden ir a la cárcel! Yo no tenía idea. Había caminado por esa calle durante el día con Booster y realizado tareas de perro de servicio muchas veces, y grandes multitudes a menudo nos rodeaban. Parecía como si un gran negocio de drogas estuviera teniendo lugar allí.

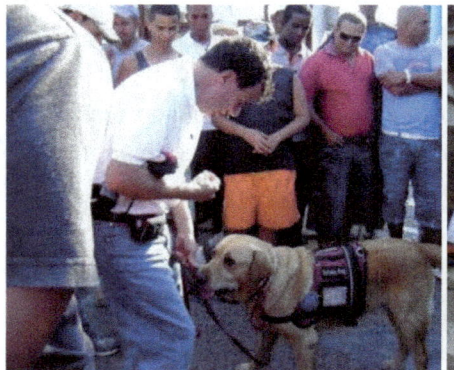
La multitud se agolpaba; la policía vigilaba.

Éramos observados.

Esa perra me asusta. ¡No tiene pelo!

¡Hemingway me mira!

Mi Booster fue testigo de cómo los perros cubanos trabajaban en red. Uno mira mientras el otro consigue la mercancía.

Yo sabía muy bien que la policía cubana y los funcionarios del gobierno habían visto a la multitud de cubanos hablando conmigo y con Booster en la calle. Siempre había un policía o cinco en cualquier esquina. Yo pensaba que los oficiales permitían que los cubanos hablaran conmigo en la calle porque era una forma de educación. Me preocupaba que pensaran que intentaba promover la democracia utilizando un perro como estratagema. En aquella época, un contratista estadounidense fue condenado y estuvo en prisión por intentar supuestamente promover la democracia introduciendo teléfonos satelitales pieza por pieza. Supuestamente formaba parte de una operación del gobierno estadounidense. Estoy bastante seguro de que yo estaba en la mira y de que me dieron cuerda suficiente para ahorcarme.

Los cubanos son astutos. Probablemente sabían que iba a ir, antes de que llegara. Nadie necesitaba cuestionar *mi* decisión... ¿o sí? Fui a La Habana con pureza de alma y propósito. Fui como un perro... viviendo el aquí y el ahora... sin agobiarme por el pasado ni planear el futuro. A menudo me acostaba temblando, preguntándome si el gobierno comunista podría malinterpretar las cosas y encarcelarme. Temblaba y llamaba a Booster en mitad de la noche para que me consolara, ¡pero no estaba allí! Era terrible. Mi terapeuta tenía razón. No estaba preparado para soportarlo. Simplemente no podía afrontarlo. ¡*Oh, MPS ayúdame*, oré!

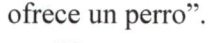

Con la ayuda del proyecto canadiense Spanky, me presentaron al presidente de AINCI, el grupo cubano de ciegos. Él me preguntó, "¿Para qué quieres un perro guía si puedes usar un bastón?"

"El cincuenta por ciento del beneficio de un perro guía", le expliqué, "es el componente emocional, la comodidad que ofrece un perro".

"Señor, estoy seguro de que ha llorado en la oscuridad de su cama por la noche. Yo con frecuencia he hecho lo mismo. El bastón no te lame la cara, se acuesta en tu pecho y te hace saber que la vida irá bien. Nunca estás

solo en la oscuridad cuando tienes un mejor amigo, que te transmite amor incondicional, las 24 horas del día".

¡Él entendió!

Al día siguiente, visité al presidente y al vicepresidente de ACLAFIM para discapacitados. Después de hablar durante una hora, Booster demostró algunas de sus tareas y se quedaron asombrados. La traductora canadiense dijo, "Dave, haz que Booster le quite los calcetines de los pies". Pensé, Estupendo. Si algo sale mal, quizás no pueda salir de la isla. ¿Por qué pidió eso sin preguntarme? Estaba en apuros, miré a Booster y le dije, "Calcetines/tira". Mi Booster corrió hacia el hombre, le quitó los calcetines, ¡y se los entregó! Conté medio en broma los dedos de los pies del hombre para comprobar que estaban todos. Mi miedo infundado impedía a Booster crecer o utilizar el conjunto de habilidades en las que era tan experto. Yo tenía que trabajar más con el miedo.

Más tarde visitamos a la presidenta de ANIPLANT, la organización para las plantas y los animales de Cuba. La presidenta, Nora García, expresó su deseo de tener un perro como el mío cuando se jubilara. Con su ayuda, salí *EN VIVO* en la televisión y la radio cubanas. Ellos tenían cosas buenas que decir del americano y su perro doctor (término utilizado por un niño cubano que conoció a Booster en la calle).

Un día, en el que tenía tiempo libre, me acordé del veterinario cubano del aeropuerto y decidí llamarlo. Me invitó a encontrarnos en un parque para almorzar. Fui, recogí a Booster y tomé un taxi para ir al parque, como me había indicado. Me senté en un banco a esperar a mi nuevo amigo veterinario. A mi lado estaba la estatua de bronce de un hombre que me resultaba familiar. *¡Bam!* Al instante me di cuenta de que estaba sentado junto a nada menos que ¡John Lennon! Me asusté muchísimo. Booster y yo estábamos en las afueras de La Habana, *casualmente* sentados junto a John Lennon en el Parque Lennon. Realmente estaba siendo acosado por MPS No cabía la menor duda. Empecé a temblar y agarré a Booster.

En los años sesenta y setenta, los cubanos no podían escuchar música rock and roll estadounidense. Si eran sorprendidos haciéndolo, se exponían a ir a la cárcel. Muchos jóvenes la escuchaban en los sótanos con los auriculares puestos. Algunos ponían música rock americana discretamente, a sabiendas de que podían ser encarcelados. Con el tiempo, alguien explicó a los funcionarios cubanos que el mensaje de paz, armonía y de *compartir que transmitía John Lennon al mundo,* era sinónimo del mensaje comunista de igualdad.

Según la doctrina comunista, todos somos iguales. Según la realidad exhibida en los países comunistas, incluida Cuba, todos son iguales, ¡pero algunos son *más* iguales que otros!

Mi amigo veterinario llegó y compartimos un cálido abrazo. Le expliqué que estaba siendo perseguido, y se rio. Me explicó que el día que Fidel Castro inauguró el parque, vinieron personas de todo el mundo a arrojar flores a la estatua. Al final del día, la estatua no se veía porque estaba enterrada bajo dos metros de flores que polinizaban amor. ¡Ya podía *imaginarlo*! Le pedí a mi nuevo amigo que nos tomara una foto a Booster y a mí sentados con nuestro amigo John. Aunque quería incluirlo, esto lo habría expuesto a posibles represalias. Estoy bastante seguro de que se habría negado, para preservar el anonimato en la dura cultura comunista de la época.

Más tarde, fuimos invitados a la casa de mi nuevo amigo para visitar su clínica veterinaria. Booster tuvo la oportunidad de conocer a su labrador amarillo. La noche siguiente, el señor nos invitó a su casa. Conocí a su mujer y a sus hijos. Su hermano había venido a visitarlo desde Miami, adonde había viajado durante el éxodo del Mariel. Fue un círculo completo de intercambio y amor incondicional.

No esperaba menos de un hombre que se dedica a ayudar a los oprimidos animales cubanos. Con frecuencia he dicho que se puede confiar en un ser humano que ama a un animal. Lo contrario también es cierto. Rápidamente hice amigos de calidad en Cuba. Irónicamente, mi amigo veterinario cubano ganó más tarde la lotería de inmigración y ahora vive en el sur de Florida.

Un día, mientras paseaba por el centro de La Habana, me encontré con un perro callejero que se me acercó corriendo. Era un lindo perrito, mitad de color cobrizo y mitad con sarna sin pelo. Parecía muy amistoso. Supuse que los turistas le daban de comer, así que estaba muy bien socializado. Me senté en el pavimento sucio y él saltó a mi regazo. Me lamió la cara. Sé que no suena muy higiénico, pero un perro me salvó la vida, así que para mí, ¡los perros no pueden hacerte nada malo! Cada momento de mi vida era un *extra* gracias a un perro. Me senté allí durante veinte minutos, tomando el sol cubano, jugando con el perro, cuando me sorprendió la emoción. Como una tonelada de ladrillos cayendo desde la cima de una montaña, fui golpeado por otra epifanía.

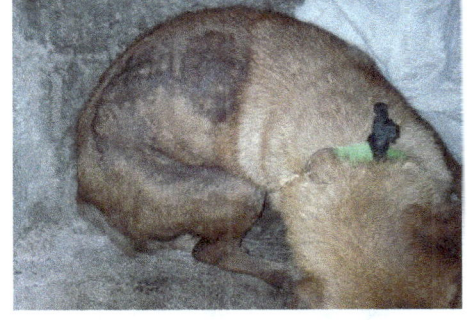

Yo también había vivido sin rumbo, y aparentemente abandonado. Había estado solo y había luchado por sobrevivir contra viento y marea. Cuando miré al perrito a los ojos, me vi a mí mismo, yo también había estado en la miseria alguna vez. Me eché a llorar, acunando al perro, sin darme cuenta de que la mitad trasera de su cuerpo no tenía pelo y estaba ennegrecida por la sarna. No estoy seguro de lo que ocurrió después. Me perdí en rayos de reflexión. Sólo recuerdo

que miré a un adolescente cubano en un taxi de pedales. "Señor, señor, ¿está usted bien?"

Temblando, le dije: "Yo... Quiero ayudar al perrito". En lugar de cuestionar mi cordura, que habría sido lo correcto, corrió y cogió una bolsa de yute que encontró en un montón de basura. Se acercó al perrito, lo envolvió y lo tomó en sus brazos. "Suba", dijo, "lo llevaré al veterinario".

En pocos minutos estábamos en el consultorio de un veterinario, pero estaba cerrado. La clínica de mi amigo estaba al otro lado de la ciudad y posiblemente también estuviera cerrada. Se hacía tarde y me preocupé. El joven leyó mi expresión y me dijo, "No se preocupe, mi hermano es barbero y le encantan los perros". Peluquero o Mickey Mouse, habría aceptado ayuda de cualquier fuente disponible en ese momento. Nos paseó por La Habana y acabamos en el apartamento de su hermano. ¡Sólo MPS sabía dónde! Entró, le explicó a su hermano que yo quería ayudar al perro y el hermano puso al perrito sarnoso en un rincón de su sala. Luego lo ató con una correa.

Le di al hermano algo de dinero para que le comprara al perro comida y vitaminas. Después de lo que me pareció una eternidad, el hermano menor me llevó de vuelta al hotel. Subí a mi habitación, me duché para quitarme la baba pegajosa y me dormí en la cama. No necesitaba contar ovejas para dormirme, ¡podía contar perros!

Al día siguiente, nuestra visita nos llevó a una escuela de primaria en el centro de La Habana. Había acordado de antemano con el organizador del tour hacer una presentación de Booster como perro de servicio. El grupo entró en la escuela y mis ojos se posaron en la foto de Booster que había enviado días antes para decirles a los niños que los visitaríamos y les llevaríamos algunos juguetes divertidos. La esposa de mi guía nos recibió en la escuela, como estaba previsto, acompañada de Booster. Yo estaba sentado en el aula cuando Booster entró corriendo entusiasmado y me llenó de besos toda la cara. Los niños se rieron mientras yo caía de espaldas. Miré alrededor de la clase y no vi a ningún niño discapacitado. Entonces les expliqué que algunas personas tienen discapacidades y que un perro puede ayudarles a hacer cosas que no pueden hacer por sí mismos.

Hice que Booster corriera a una pequeña nevera y trajera a uno de los niños una botella de agua. Luego me quité los zapatos y él me los trajo de vuelta. Luego me quitó los calcetines. Até un trapo a una silla y le pedí que me lo trajera. Booster nunca había sido adiestrado para hacer eso, pero se le daba bien *generalizar* y a menudo aplicaba las tareas aprendidas de formas nuevas y novedosas. Recordé por un momento la vez que entré en un avión y no pude salir debido a un ataque de gota. La compañía aérea me trajo una silla de ruedas, y Booster tiró de mí por el aeropuerto, sin haber sido entrenado para ello.

Los niños cubanos, los líderes del mañana, estaban aprendiendo una valiosa lección. Fui testigo de mentes abiertas, deseosas de aprender de un nuevo maestro... ¡un perro! Hacia el final de la visita, los niños se reunieron alrededor de Booster para tomarse una foto. Pasamos en la escuela más tiempo del previsto y nos retrasamos el resto del día. *Pensé que era un pequeño precio a pagar,* pero estoy bastante seguro de que *mis compañeros de viaje estaban empezando a digerir suficiente Dog 101 en este momento.*

Más tarde comenté con unos amigos que los niños de Cuba parecían muy maduros para su edad. Cada vez que paseaba a Booster en Cuba, los niños cubanos corrían hacia el gran perro, se detenían, me miraban a los ojos y preguntaban tranquilamente, "¿Muerde?"

Yo siempre respondía: "¡Nunca!" Los niños solían mirarme directamente a los ojos para evaluar mi respuesta. ¡Eran como pequeños adultos de treinta años!

En otra visita a la isla, me invitaron a una escuela para niños

discapacitados cubanos. Entré en el edificio de la escuela y fui recibido por niños de todas las edades que clamaban por conocer al nuevo visitante... ¡y no era yo! Al instante, Booster fue inundado de amor en forma de caricias y palmaditas en la cabeza. Los niños se fijaron de inmediato en el hecho de que Booster tenía una zona negra hundida en la cabeza donde le habían extirpado un tumor. Le señalaron la cabeza y el lado de la cara donde no tenía pelo debido a los efectos secundarios de la radioterapia (RT). Los niños discapacitados eran sensibles al hecho de que Booster también era discapacitado. Estaban tan entusiasmados que se olvidaron de preguntar, "¿Muerde?" El vínculo instantáneo fue más hermoso que cualquier arco iris que hubiera presenciado jamás.

Los abnegados profesores cubanos organizaron a los niños en un aula central. Le pedí a Booster que demostrara sus singulares habilidades caninas. Mientras los niños observaban al perro, yo miraba a los niños de la clase.

Estaban equipados con modernos aparatos médicos para ayudarles con su discapacidad. Vi cables que conducían a modernos implantes cocleares para niños sordos. Otros usaban nuevos bastones y muletas. Algunos se sentaban en relucientes sillas de ruedas. Cuando terminó la demostración, pregunté a los niños si alguien quería acariciar a Booster. ¡Las manos se alzaron y una cola se movió orgullosa!

Los maestros cubanos calmaron a los niños con una facilidad sorprendente. No se trataba tanto de disciplina como del respeto que los niños tenían por sus profesores. Una de las maestras acercaba a los alumnos de tres en tres para que conocieran y abrazaran a Booster. Todos acariciaron a Booster con gran entusiasmo. De repente, ¡un coro de manos se alzó hacia el cielo! Querían saber si podían volver a acariciar a Booster. "Sigue viniendo. Funciona si lo trabajas". Recordé el dicho de Al-Anon. Cada vez que compartía a Booster con otras personas, y realmente quiero decir *cada vez*, la vida funcionaba como debía. Con frecuencia, yo ganaba y aprendía más de la experiencia que aquellos a los que había ido a visitar. ¡Esto me ponía a pensar y pensar un poco más!

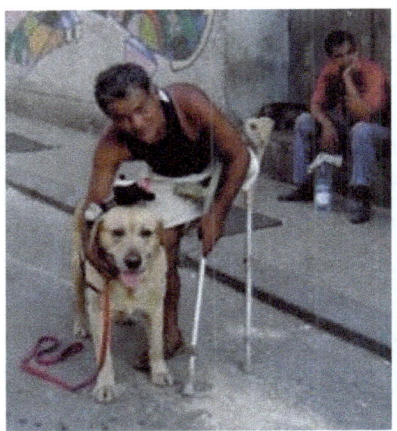

El gobierno cubano se ocupa de sus ciudadanos discapacitados. Los dispositivos médicos utilizados para ayudar a los discapacitados eran relativamente nuevos y estaban en buenas condiciones. Nunca vi a personas sin hogar en Cuba, aunque estoy seguro de que las hay. La única vez que fui testigo de personas sin hogar en viajes a Cuba fue cuando hice escala en San Francisco y fui a pasear por los parques. Hablé con las personas sin hogar y me enteré de que varios eran veteranos incapaces de lidiar con las atrocidades en las que habían participado en ultramar. Nuestros veteranos de guerra dependen de un Hospital de la Administración de Veteranos Me pregunté si Cuba proporcionaría una atención sanitaria mejor a sus militares. Recordé que después de que el huracán Katrina arrasara la zona donde vivo, el gobierno cubano se ofreció a enviar cientos de médicos para ayudar. El gobierno estadounidense rechazó la ayuda.

La gente quería acariciar al perro que llegó a Cuba, para demostrar cómo los perros pueden ayudar a los humanos a los que aman incondicionalmente. Al igual que los cubanos, Booster nació con hermanos negros. No tenía prejuicios, como tampoco los tenían la mayoría de los cubanos. Los cubanos blancos y negros crecieron juntos, eran simbióticos. Todos luchaban por sobrevivir en un país pobre.

Era obvio para todos los que tenían los ojos abiertos que la discriminación era difícil de encontrar en Cuba. Los cubanos no tenían la capacidad de amar el dinero, así que en su lugar *amaban al prójimo*, sin importar su color. Me pareció fascinante que el comunista Castro prohibió la religión para consolidar el control, pero aun así, la doctrina religiosa del amor al prójimo floreció. Estoy seguro de que existían algunos prejuicios, porque todos somos humanos, ¿no?

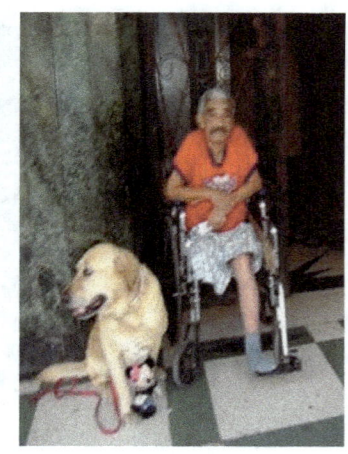

Un día llevaron a nuestro grupo a visitar la casa de Ernest Hemingway en Cuba. Todos los días hay colas de turistas. Al entrar en la propiedad, te saludan perros y gatos callejeros que nunca se alejan demasiado. Los cuidan cubanos interesados en el bienestar animal, así como personal afiliado al Proyecto Spanky. Ves un cementerio donde están enterrados los queridos perros de Hemingway. Es fácil imaginar al viejo bebiendo, escribiendo y acariciando a sus perros. Desde luego, me identifico. Hemingway sabía que se estaba muriendo debido al alcohol. Sin duda fue consolado por quienes lo querían incondicionalmente. Dejó tras de sí sus obras literarias y homenajes en las lápidas de sus perros. Ambos siguen siendo visitados a diario por personas de todo el mundo.

Después de pasar semanas en Cuba, llegó la hora de volar a casa. Tuve que conseguir un permiso de salida para Booster. El gobierno cubano inspecciona a los animales antes de que salgan del país. Por supuesto, Booster pasaría la inspección, pero mi perrito callejero no. Me reuní con Nora y me dijo que encontraría un hogar de acogida para el perrito, y que yo podría darle algo de dinero para su comida y medicinas. Agradecido, recogí al perrito cubano del peluquero y lo llevé a la sede de Aniplant. Al final del día, ya no era el perrito. Se llamaba Fidel...ity ¡y con razón! ¡No me atreví a ponerle Fidel por miedo a que no me dejaran volver a Cuba por faltarle al respeto al líder cubano, poniéndole su nombre a un perro callejero!

¡Dios mío, más turistas!

Me quedaba una tarea pendiente antes de abandonar la isla. Semanas antes, había entrado en la Galería de Artistas Cubanos de la calle Obispo, donde siempre paseaba a Booster. Compré una cabeza de bulldog tallada en madera de teca y encargué al artista que me tallara una cabeza de perro

Lápidas en honor a los perros de Hemingway

labrador. El artista accedió a tenerla lista el día antes de mi salida de Cuba. Cuando fui a recoger mi cabeza de labrador, me dijeron que el artista estaba en camino. Venía en una motocicleta Harley-Davidson bajo la lluvia para entregar la escultura, como había prometido. Me pidieron que esperara un poco.

Crucé la calle hasta una cafetería y pedí una taza de café cubano. Un hombre demacrado de unos ochenta años se me acercó. Sabía que iba a intentar venderme algo, pero no estaba de humor, ya que estaba repasando mi lista mental antes de salir de la isla. Le hice un gesto con la mano para que se alejara, pero o no entendía el lenguaje de signos o prefirió ignorarlo. Pronunció palabras en español que no entendí. Intentaba dirigirse respetuosamente al americano en inglés. Me puso en las manos cuatro páginas de un cuaderno rayado y escrito en inglés. Esto *va a ser interesante*, pensé. Lo leí, tristemente, más por curiosidad que por respeto.

En un inglés entrecortado, intentaba explicarme algo sobre los escritos. Cuanto más leía, más me fascinaba. Era poesía. Era hermosa en su contexto, intelectual en su compostura, ¡y escrita en inglés! Llegué a la última página y vi una frase que contenía un asterisco. Mis ojos se dirigieron al asterisco explicativo de la esquina superior derecha. Lloré... sí, maldita sea, ¡OTRA VEZ! Perdí el control. Sí, maldita sea, ¡otra vez!

¡El asterisco estaba unido al nombre JOHN LENNON! Tuve que sentarme para no caer. Me agarré la cabeza con las manos. Nunca sabré lo que el hombre estaba pensando.

Tal vez pensó que lo veía como la prosa más bella que había conocido jamás. Si pensaba eso... ¡tenía razón! Era una afirmación de MPS, de que con Booster, yo había aprendido de alguna manera a traer fidelidad a mi vida. Pueden decir que soy un soñador.

Dicen que con tres strikes estás fuera. En mi caso, tenía tres John Lennon y la casa llena. Había visitado a niños y adultos ciegos y discapacitados físicamente, me había hecho amigo de caninos cubanos, había aparecido en directo en la televisión y la radio, me habían permitido el acceso a las aulas y había hecho amistades duraderas a través del *contacto persona a persona*, tal y como lo concibió el Presidente Obama. Aunque nunca sabré si estuve bajo la vigilancia del Gran Hermano del gobierno cubano, sí sé que estuve bajo la vigilancia de Mi Poder Superior, documentado por John Lennon. Booster me había presentado una espiritualidad como nunca antes había existido en mi vida. Hablando de *contactos entre personas*, Booster, BUCS, canadienses, cubanos e incluso el propio John Lennon fueron todos instrumentos utilizados por Mi Poder Superior para dar vida a mi alma desgarrada. La vida a la que una vez traté de poner fin experimentó un renacimiento. A los predicadores Dios les dio la Biblia; Mi Poder Superior me dio un perro. "¿Qué vas a hacer con un perro?" me había preguntado una vez mi hermano. Aún me quedaba mucho camino por recorrer para responder completamente esa pregunta.

El día antes de partir, llevé a Booster a visitar al pequeño Fidelity. Fuimos a la sede de Aniplant, y Nora nos recibió con su habitual sonrisa. Entramos, y antes de que pudiera siquiera saludarla, me puso una taza de café cubano en las manos. Nos sentamos a charlar y, de repente, entró corriendo el pequeño Fidelity. Le ladró a Booster como un marinero borracho. *¡Yap yap yappy yap!* Booster mantuvo la calma con el más fino decoro. Por un momento pensé que tendría que implementar un nuevo bloqueo cubano. Fue todo lo que pude hacer para mantenerlos lo suficientemente cerca como para sacarles una foto. Esa noche fuimos a un bonito restaurante cubano. Las paredes estaban adornadas con grafitis escritos por visitantes de todo el mundo. Muchas de las inscripciones eran de visitantes estadounidenses, así que, sin dudarlo, ¡mi Booster y yo nos unimos al grupo! "Booster y BUCS estuvieron aquí", escribí en la pared.

En cuanto llegué a casa, empecé a trabajar en un plan para traer a Fidelity a mi vida. No podía traerlo a Estados Unidos en un vuelo de Bahamasair porque la normativa bahameña no permitía la entrada de animales cubanos en Bahamas. La aerolínea bahameña tampoco tenía un acuerdo de carga con el gobierno cubano, así que Fidelity no podía volar en un huacal. No tenía ni idea de si los servicios de inmigración y aduanas de Estados Unidos aceptarían los documentos veterinarios cubanos que certificaban la buena salud de Fidelity cuando estuviera arreglado y listo para volar por los amistosos cielos. Me puse en contacto con grupos protectores de animales mexicanos y canadienses. De alguna manera, el grupo mexicano había hecho una alianza con un grupo canadiense para llevar a los perros cubanos sin hogar a manos de quienes los habían conocido y se habían enamorado de ellos en Cuba.

Un día recibí un correo electrónico de la asociación canadiense para el bienestar animal Cats and Dogs International (CANDI). Su presidenta y

fundadora, Darci Galati, me informó que se había contactado con APAC-Varadero, una alianza canadiense-cubana para la defensa de los animales. Las dos organizaciones habían colaborado para que la aerolínea canadiense Air

Transat transportara a Fidelity a Toronto (Canadá). Habían oído hablar de mi amor por un perrito cubano. La aerolínea era conocida por apoyar el bienestar de los animales y hacerlos volar gratis para mejorar sus vidas. Me preguntaron si podía volar a Toronto y recogerlo. Mi respuesta inmediata fue, "¡Claro que sí!" aunque lo expresé de manera un poco diferente. Me tomó meses, pero finalmente abordé un avión a Toronto para recoger a mi pequeño Fidelity, sin saber si pasaría la aduana en el aeropuerto internacional O'Hare de Chicago.

El avión procedente de La Habana aterrizó a las 3 de la madrugada en Toronto. Conocí a una dulce voluntaria canadiense que saludó a las tres personas que habían venido a reclamar a sus huérfanos caninos cubanos. Nos llevó al hangar del aeropuerto, donde los perros esperaban en sus respectivas jaulas. Los tres padres adoptivos tuvieron que pasar a sus canes cubanos por la aduana canadiense. Nos advirtieron de que el gobierno canadiense querría algún tipo de impuesto. Prepárense... ¡no es sólo la canción de marcha de los Boy Scouts!

Me reuní con el funcionario de aduanas canadiense y, como si fuera una señal, me preguntó, "¿Cuánto vale el perro?"

Lo miré fijamente a los ojos y le dije: "No vale nada *económicamente*".

El hombre gruñón dijo entonces, "Bueno, debe valer *algo*, o usted no estaría aquí".

Le respondí, "Tiene razón, señor. Ahora que lo pienso, entre los vuelos a Cuba, el alojamiento veterinario y los gastos médicos, ¡el perro vale unos 2.000 dólares negativos!" Debo admitir que el tacto no fue exactamente la mejor manera de manejar la situación. Llegamos a un acuerdo por un valor declarado de 100 dólares, sobre el que pagué un pequeño porcentaje. Pagué la "fianza" de Fidelity y fui con los demás a recoger a nuestros presos en libertad condicional.

Los huacales se abrieron uno a uno y cada inmigrante canino cubano corrió hacia su respectivo humano. Era un espectáculo digno de contemplar... una afirmación del poderoso vínculo canino-humano. Fidelity fue el último en ser liberado. Yo estaba sentado frente a su jaula, y él  dio un gran salto y se sentó a mi lado. Una vez más, me besó como lo había hecho cuando sentimos que nuestras vidas eran miserables en La Habana. La voluntaria captó el momento con una foto. Esta vez había lágrimas a raudales, pero recuerdo cada precioso segundo. Se estaba gestando una variante del poema de Robert Frost " El camino no tomado". En lugar del verso "Dos caminos se bifurcaron", era "Dos cunetas se bifurcaron". Curiosamente, de joven, mi madre tuvo a Robert Frost como profesor de inglés. Ni en sus sueños más locos podría haber imaginado este corolario.

Nos llevaron con Fidelity al hotel de Toronto que admitía mascotas. Estaba seguro de que Fidelity estaba hambriento, ya que había pasado todo el día en una jaula en La Habana antes de volar a Toronto. Me disgustó bastante que el perrito no hubiera podido simplemente volar de La Habana a Nueva Orleans debido al embargo estadounidense contra Cuba. El embargo de Estados Unidos a Cuba, justificado o no, perjudicó a muchas personas. Que conste que también hizo daño a un perrito que encarnaba la fidelidad. Le puse a Fidelity una correa, pero él se resistió de inmediato. Los cubanos supuestamente lo habían acostumbrado a una correa y lo habían paseado por La Habana. ¿Lo habrían hecho realmente, o Fidelity era tan rebelde como el líder cubano Fidel Castro? Más tarde, llevé a "pequeño Fidel" en mis brazos hasta mi habitación. Puse comida en mis manos y lo alimenté. Luego sostuve al pequeño en mis brazos y le di agua Quería establecer el nexo canino-humano asociando mi olor, mi presencia, y la provisión de alimentos. Después de dar de comer a Fidelity, decidí bajar al vestíbulo para alimentarme. No quería abandonar al perrito ni un momento, así que le puse la correa y "luchamos" para llegar al ascensor, y descendimos al oasis de las máquinas expendedoras a las 4 de la mañana. Encontré las máquinas y me di un festín de Coca-Cola y papas fritas, la cocina tradicional estadounidense.

Volvimos con dificultad al ascensor. Cuando se abrió la puerta del ascensor, Fidelity se precipitó hacia delante y solté la correa. Salió corriendo a la velocidad del rayo y de repente se perdió de vista. Nuestra habitación estaba a cuatro pasillos de la puerta del ascensor. Al llegar a la habitación, el perrito estaba sentado frente a la puerta, mirándome, moviendo la cola. *¿Era arrogancia u orgullo?* me pregunté. Abrí la puerta, me senté en una silla y el pequeño bastardo saltó a mi regazo y volvió a besarme la cara. Lo llevé al baño, le lavé el trasero y lo sequé con una toalla. Saltó a mi cama y los dos nos quedamos profundamente dormidos.

Por la mañana, le puse a Fidelity un chaleco de Perro de Servicio en Entrenamiento. Dimos un paseo largo y combativo por el recinto del hotel. El perro, antes salvaje, se acostumbró poco a poco a llevar su uniforme oficial. Al poco tiempo, estábamos en el autobús de enlace hacia el aeropuerto. La vida cambió para siempre para el pequeño Fidelity. Aprendió rápidamente a caminar con correa. Se sentó pacientemente en la escalera mecánica, lo que me dejó completamente asombrado. Practicamos "sentarse" y "esperar" en el aeropuerto. Mientras avanzábamos, insistía en pararse a saludar a los nuevos amigos que encontrábamos por el camino.

Aunque las aerolíneas canadienses no reconocen a los perros de servicio en adiestramiento, abordamos el avión sin problema. Antes de embarcar, le di a Fidelity varias galletas de carne para perros. Los cubanos alimentan a los perros con órganos de vaca triturados mezclados con arroz hervido. Era caviar fino para un perro. Las galletas secas convencionales habrían sido tan apetitosas para Fidelity como un ladrillo, pero los perros callejeros rara vez dicen que no a cualquier tipo de comida. ¡Expresó su deseo de más, siguiéndome servilmente como un niño sigue a Papá Noel!

Cuando aterrizamos en Chicago, el inmigrante canino cubano se sentía muy seguro de sí mismo mientras salía del avión con todo su atuendo. Me recordó a un Clydesdale en miniatura mientras trotaba por el pasillo del avión y saludaba a los asistentes de vuelo y a los pasajeros por igual. Su chaleco lucía las banderas cubana y estadounidense "juntas". Mi declaración de aduanas daba fe de que traía un animal vivo al país. Nos desviaron a la zona de aduanas. Era el día del juicio final en el OK Corral. Era el momento de la verdad. Me encontré con un agente de aduanas algo desconcertado, que no sabía muy bien cómo manejar la situación. No sabía si la documentación veterinaria y los certificados sanitarios cubanos se aceptarían en EE.UU., así que había llevado a mi perro recién llegado, que pagaba impuestos canadienses, a un veterinario local para que le diera su certificado sanitario canadiense. *Casualmente*, la veterinaria era una señora cuya familia había emigrado de Cuba años atrás. Dejando a un lado toda la "comida procesada" de toros, se nos permitió entrar en EE.UU.

Mi vuelo a casa desde Chicago se retrasó, así que tuve que caminar para liberar la energía de Fidelity. Resultó ser una tarea insuperable ¡Pronto aprendí a hacer lo que el pequeño dictador exigía! Como es lógico. Fidelity no estaba acostumbrado a caminar con correa. En BUCS aprendí a no tirar nunca de la correa de un perro, ya que esto genera resentimiento. Recordé el día en que Bonnie me agarró de la camisa. Cuando Fidelity quería ir a la izquierda, yo iba a la izquierda. Cuando él elegía ir a la derecha, yo obedientemente iba a la derecha. Si hubiera optado por pelearme con él, el mundo habría sabido que no estaba lo bastante adiestrado para volar en cabina como perro de servicio en entrenamiento. Para que conste, a los perros de servicio en adiestramiento no se les permite viajar en cabina en los aviones. Fidelity llevaba un chaleco que decía claramente Perro de servicio en adiestramiento. Si se comportaba adecuadamente, supuse que se nos concedería el privilegio de volar juntos.

Llevé a mi pequeño dictador al baño del aeropuerto para que tomara agua. Junté las manos y el inteligente perrito sabía que le esperaba un refresco, pero sólo le di un puñado de agua porque no quería que orinara en el avión. Más tarde ese mismo día, nos apresurábamos para alcanzar nuestro vuelo de salida, y sin comprometerse, Fidelity insistió en ir a la derecha cuando teníamos que ir a la izquierda. Cedí, no quería montar una escena de último momento. Me llevó al baño de caballeros, donde horas antes le había dado agua. Tenía sed, ¡y sabía *dónde* conseguirla!

Mi mente tenía una sobrecarga sensorial. Como un minero en busca de oro, había encontrado la veta madre de la educación. Recordé mi clase en la BUCS, en la que aprendimos que los perros tienen habilidad cartográfica.

¡Así es como los perros perdidos encuentran el camino a casa, a veces cruzando todo el país! Recuerdo que de joven aprendí la teoría de Charles Darwin sobre la *supervivencia del más apto*. Un perrito callejero cubano acababa de enseñarme una lección que requería una síntesis educativa. Fidelity era un perro callejero que recorría las calles de La Habana a 100 grados de calor. Sin duda sabía dónde se encontraban los contenedores de basura con restos de comida. Conocía los lugares donde los turistas se congregaban, ya que era increíblemente sociable. Me lo imaginaba con un cartel colgado del cuello que proclamaba, "Besos a cambio de comida". Debía de saber cómo ir a los aires acondicionados que goteaban agua procedente del húmedo aire cubano, o al Malecón, donde el agua salpicaba la orilla y se acumulaba en charcos. Era un gran ejemplo de supervivencia del más fuerte. Su inteligencia y sus habilidades cartográficas le habían permitido sobrevivir en un entorno hostil.

Con asombro, había visto a Fidelity encontrar el camino de vuelta a nuestra habitación de hotel la noche anterior. Estaba en el baño de un aeropuerto con un perro que recordaba dónde había encontrado agua horas antes. Una vez más, estaba aprendiendo de un perro. También sabía que si no hubiera asistido a la BUCS, nunca habría visto la realidad de ese día. Era una forma muy novedosa de ver el concepto de supervivencia del más apto en el mundo real. Yo era un perro viejo al que un perro joven, que supuse que sólo tenía un año, le enseñaba trucos nuevos. Había aprendido en mis clases de veterinaria de la BUCS que se puede juzgar la edad de un perro por sus dientes.

Finalmente abordamos el vuelo a casa sin problemas. Llegamos y presenté a Fidelity a mi manada. Los problemas surgieron cuando el pequeño dictador aprendió que no podía imponerse a una manada con una jerarquía ya establecida. Fidelity introdujo la agresión, un concepto relativamente desconocido en mi manada. El hijo de Booster, Al-Anon, siendo bastante pacifista, se opuso a la agresividad de Fidelity. Al-Anon era mucho más grande, pero Fidelity era más rápido y tenía inteligencia callejera. Al sufrió un desgarro en una oreja y una herida en un testículo debido a la agresividad de Fidelity. Hubo un golpe de estado cuando mi labrador Savior (el otro hijo de Booster), aún más grande, defendió al perrito cuando los demás enfrentaron su agresividad.

Había facciones enfrentadas entre las filas. Mi pequeño Fidel introdujo luchas similares a las que se vivieron en Colombia en tiempos pasados. Era una versión canina del Che Guevara, un revolucionario cubano asociado al grupo rebelde colombiano Fuerzas Armadas Revolucionarias de Colombia (FARC). Tenía una familia nuclear que sufría una agresión extranjera no deseada. Las "Fidelity Activist Revolutionary Canine (FARC)" entraron en mi antes pacífica patria.

A los pocos días de estar en casa, Fidelity aprendió a realizar tareas de perro de servicio. Abría la nevera y traía agua. Aprendió a recuperar objetos. Para mí fue una lección de primera mano. Tenía un lindo perrito callejero que podía realizar tareas pero que era agresivo con los otros perros. Cuando Bonnie desarrolló por primera vez el concepto de perro de servicio, entrenó a un perro de un refugio. Estaba a punto de colocar a ese perro con un compañero humano discapacitado cuando el perro reaccionó de forma adversa a un conductor de reparto.

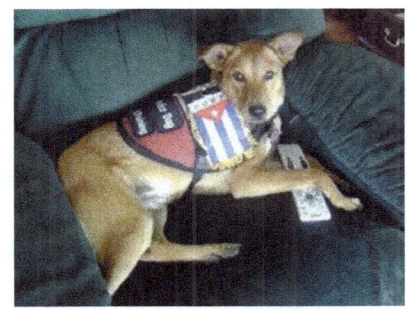

El perro del refugio, como yo, tenía cargas emocionales. El repartidor llevaba barba y Bonnie supuso que el perro podría haber sido maltratado por un hombre con barba. Fue entonces cuando decidió que era mejor adiestrar a los perros desde el nacimiento, cuando las *páginas están en blanco*. Todos tenemos equipaje en nuestras vidas. ¡Yo tengo más que la mayoría! Nos enseñan a adiestrar a los perros en un contexto canino-humano. ¿Por qué esperaríamos que los perros no tengan también equipaje emocional? Debes repetir una lección positiva treinta veces para intentar borrar una experiencia de aprendizaje negativa, y aun así es probable que haya recaídas.

Poco después de mi regreso de Cuba, la empresa turística canadiense publicó una sinopsis de mi viaje.

El propietario de la empresa me pidió permiso para redactarla como si yo la hubiera escrito. Se lo concedí encantado. Era un artículo muy positivo, probablemente escrito para generar nuevos negocios, apaciguar al gobierno cubano y pintar una imagen favorable de la Cuba socialista. El periódico bilingüe californiano *LaVoz* también publicó un extenso artículo en inglés y español. Meses después, me puse en contacto con el periódico de Nueva Orleans *The Times-Picayune*. Una periodista estaba interesada en escribir una historia sobre un hombre que fue a Cuba con un perro. Era un artículo destacado en la sección Living del periódico. La periodista hizo un gran trabajo e incluyó numerosas fotografías. Unos días después de su publicación, la periodista se puso en contacto conmigo. Me dijo que un compañero de clase de la secundaria con el que yo no había tenido contacto en más de treinta años leyó la historia y quería ponerse en contacto conmigo.

Poco después, recibí un correo electrónico. Mi compañero y yo nos pusimos al día sobre los últimos treinta años. De repente, abrió sus compuertas emocionales y las agitadas turbinas de su vida generaron interés. Yo quería reunirme en persona en lugar de compartir emociones por teléfono. El fin de semana siguiente nos reunimos en un popular restaurante de Nueva  Orleans. Por supuesto, tenía a Booster a mi lado. Mi compañero me miró y me preguntó, "¿No intentarás entrar con tu perro, verdad?" Le contesté, "¡No entraría sin él! Oye, es la ley... no pueden negarnos el acceso". En su favor, me siguió la corriente sin expresar su inquietud. Estoy seguro de que se sentía avergonzado de entrar en un restaurante con un perro. Le dije que nos recibirían con más aceptación de la que se imaginaba. El personal del restaurante ni se inmutó. Fue una experiencia perfecta. Nuestra camarera nos saludó y fue todo risas.

En pocos minutos, ella compartió sus historias perrunas y sacó un móvil para enseñarnos sus fotos con su compañero canino. Booster recibió una palmadita en la cabeza y se quedó tranquilo a mis pies, debajo de nuestra mesa.

Entonces compartí una comida caliente con un corazón cálido. Mi amigo me explicó que había trabajado con perros de Búsqueda y Rescate (SAR) como hobby. Me dijo que tenía una esposa cariñosa, dos hijas, una bonita casa y una gran profesión. Después de la secundaria, se alistó en la Marina y se hizo médico. Después fue a la escuela de medicina y se hizo cirujano ortopédico. ¡Tenía la vida bajo control! (Palabras mías, no suyas). Un día su vida cambió para siempre. Tenía dos hijas en la universidad, una gran casa en la parte alta de la ciudad, préstamos estudiantiles y un montón de deudas. Una mañana se despertó con un problema de visión. Tenía un desprendimiento de retina y había perdido la vista en un ojo. Sin percepción de la profundidad, ya no podía realizar cirugías.

Dicen que Dios nunca nos da más de lo que podemos manejar, pero creo que en su caso sobrepasó el límite. Incluso los acaudalados experimentan dificultades. Yo no era el único que lidiaba con la vida en sus términos. Comprensiblemente, él experimentó una depresión aguda. Nunca le pregunté si había "considerado opciones de salida", como yo había hecho alguna vez. Le pregunté cómo lo superó. Me miró a los ojos y me dijo, "Fue Messie", refiriéndose a su querido perro SAR y compañero canino. Una vez más, el vínculo humano-canino sostuvo a un ser humano en tiempos difíciles. Tuve que creer que ambos teníamos ángeles caninos enviados desde el cielo.

Curiosamente, en lugar de detenernos en las historias de horror de nuestras vidas, empezamos a hablar sobre cómo nos habían ayudado nuestros perros. El perro de mi compañero estuvo a su lado en las buenas y en las malas. Hay algo en un perro que nos sostiene y que es diferente de un ser humano. Con frecuencia, nuestros compañeros humanos no entienden el apego a un perro. Cuando una persona discapacitada adquiere un perro de servicio, el cónyuge o el familiar se queda sin trabajo de cuidador y se siente defraudado. Ya no se les necesita igual que antes. El perro de servicio permite la independencia. Muchas veces nos piden que expliquemos nuestra conexión canina. Fiel a su estilo, él dijo que no creía que su amada esposa lo entendiera del todo.

Después de compartir una excelente comida, nos despedimos. Años más tarde, le envié un correo electrónico para preguntarle cómo estaba. Me enteré de que acababa de regresar de un resort con su actual labrador. Me explicó que Messi había fallecido años atrás. Había abierto su corazón a un nuevo perro al que había adiestrado para que fuera un perro de servicio que le ayudara a superar las deficiencias de su día a día. Se había incorporado a un grupo de ortopedia y hacía trabajos de consultoría. La mayoría de los días llevaba a su perro al trabajo. ¡Para orgullo de sus compañeros humanos, su perro de servicio fue aceptado como un compañero más del grupo! Hoy en día, rara vez viaja sin su medicina canina, su perro de servicio labrador. Una vez más, pude mantener mi serenidad al darla. Booster cambió mi vida años antes y cambió la de mi compañero años después.

Un día, abrí mi cuenta de correo electrónico y encontré un e-mail maravillosamente inspirador de un hombre cubano. Incluía una foto suya con su perro en brazos mientras disfrutaba de un día de playa. Me dijo que ojalá hubiera tenido la oportunidad de conocernos a Booster y a mí cuando estuvimos en La Habana. Me hizo prometer que me pondría en contacto con él cuando volviera a la isla. De alguna manera, había visto algunos de mis artículos y noticias en Internet. Al principio sospeché un poco, ya que los cubanos de a pie no tenían acceso a Internet en aquella época.

Cuando regresé a Cuba meses después, él me recibió en el aeropuerto. Me llevó a su casa a conocer a unos amigos y a su querido rottweiler. Me presentó a un médico internista que me dio las gracias en nombre de los ciudadanos cubanos, que podrían utilizar un perro de servicio, para mejorar sus vidas y ayudar a generar independencia. No estaba muy seguro de poder procesar la palabra *independencia* en la misma frase que contenía la palabra *Cuba*. La Revolución Cubana dio lugar a la independencia de Cuba del control del gobierno estadounidense y el dominio de la mafia, pero los cubanos perdieron toda independencia al no poder salir de la isla durante más de cincuenta años, como ratones atrapados en una jaula.

En mi tercera visita a Cuba, volví a encontrarme con él. Había desarrollado un proyecto para mejorar el vecindario y ayudar al pueblo cubano. Me presentó a su equipo de voluntarios. Esa noche asistí a una fiesta en su casa, conocí a profesores universitarios estadounidenses y me sumergí en profundas discusiones filosóficas. Prácticamente todos estaban de acuerdo en que si se ponía fin al embargo y los estadounidenses acudían en masa a Cuba, el país sufriría las consecuencias. ¡Los estadounidenses volverían a arruinar a Cuba! Podía imaginar a multitudes de jóvenes estadounidenses en Cuba, bajándose los pantalones y mostrando sus calzoncillos floreados. A los cubanos no se les permite hacer tal cosa. Me reía al pensar en niños estadounidenses preguntando a un agente de policía cubano "¿qué dices?" y siendo llevados a la cárcel, muchos aprendiendo el concepto de disciplina por primera vez.

Entonces pensé en ayudar a los cubanos a aprender a adiestrar perros de servicio. En un país donde el salario promedio mensual es de 25 dólares, se podrían adiestrar muchos perros a un costo mucho más razonable que 50.000 dólares cada uno. El gobierno cubano concedía becas a estudiantes de todo el mundo para que se convirtieran en médicos. Me imaginé al gobierno cubano apoyando el entrenamiento de "perros médicos" y exportándolos por todo el mundo como parte de su modelo comunista. Para mí era obvio. Podría escribir un libro sobre lo que ocurrió a continuación, pero no fue agradable.

Como parte del Proyecto Fidelity, entregué becas a dos cubanos para que viajaran a la BUCS. Uno era un hombre de unos cuarenta años y la otra una joven de unos treinta. Eran los hijos adultos de unos amigos de Nora. El gobierno cubano les dio permiso para salir de la isla, pero el gobierno estadounidense, a través de la Sección de Intereses Cubanos en Cuba, dirigida por Suiza, no les permitió venir. Escribí cartas muy duras e hice muchas llamadas, y en el verano siguiente los estudiantes vinieron. El cubano que supuestamente amaba a los perros no soportaba su olor en la habitación y se apropió del ambientador del baño para rociar su dormitorio, donde se encontraba el perro que le habían asignado. No seguía las normas, pero lo que si hacía era perseguir la comida hasta la cocina y devorarla más rápido que su canino asignado. Le retiré mi apoyo y le di un boleto de avión a Miami para que tomara su vuelo de regreso a Cuba. Debería haberlo hecho caminar... ¡en cuatro patas! El arrogante hombre exigió un billete sin escalas a Miami que costaba el doble que uno con conexión. *¡Casualmente,* hubo un problema mecánico en el avión y tuvo que hacer una escala al día siguiente! Resultó que todo el tiempo había estado hablando con amigos cubanos en Miami y no regresó a La Habana. ¡Me sentí traicionado y utilizado!

A la joven le iba bien en la escuela y le encantaban los perros. Le compré dos Golden Retriever costosos para que se los llevara a Cuba y pusiera en marcha el Booster Center, el primer centro de adiestramiento de perros de servicio de Cuba. Apoyé sus esfuerzos, pero cuando más tarde visité a los perros, ¡eran unos salvajes! Uno de ellos perseguía a los niños y transeúntes que caminaban por la acera junto al patio vallado.  La primera noche que estuve allí, un perro saltó y se robó el asado crudo de la encimera. La carne es un bien preciado en Cuba, ¡pero no para un perro estadounidense mimado! Me sentí avergonzado.

Más tarde gasté miles de dólares rescatando a los perros de Cuba. Fue difícil quitárselos a la señora, que de todos modos sabía que iban a ser entregados a una persona discapacitada en el futuro. Fue terrible, y pagué mucho para conseguirlo. Hoy, uno de los perros vive con una familia y tiene una piscina donde refrescarse. El otro fue adoptado por un adiestrador de la BUCS y lo está haciendo muy bien, trabajando como perro de demostración en un programa de ayuda a veteranos. La historia es mucho más larga, como cabe imaginar, pero esto es lo esencial de los acontecimientos.

Me esforcé mucho y nunca defraudé a nadie. Hasta el día de hoy, tengo una excelente reputación en la isla. Realmente intenté ayudar a los ciudadanos de Cuba, pero al final, los cubanos defraudan a los cubanos. Fui a Cuba durante el deshielo de las relaciones internacionales. No me cabe duda de que Booster sembró semillas de salvación. Volví muchas veces. El presidente Obama promovió acertadamente los contactos de persona a persona. Él no podía saber que los contactos entre personas y caninos podían ser mucho más fructíferos. Tomé la delantera, llevé a Booster a Cuba e hice contactos que perduran y crecen hasta el día de hoy.

Cuando llegué a la isla, no hablaba ni una palabra de español. La noche anterior al viaje bajé a mi computador un programa de traducción llamado Jibbigo. Una vez descargado, no necesitaba acceso a Internet. Sabía que no tendría fácil acceso a Internet en el país comunista. El programa me ayudó a comunicarme con los cubanos de La Habana y sus alredededores. Cuando regresé a Estados Unidos, me sentí obligado a expresar mi agradecimiento al creador del programa. Booster me había enseñado el valor de expresar gratitud en lugar de negatividad. Envié un correo electrónico a los creadores del programa explicándoles que su programa había contribuido a mi éxito en Cuba. Les dije: "Por cierto, es un gran país con gente maravillosa".

Recibí una respuesta rápida. "Gracias, señor, me alegra haberle sido de ayuda. Gracias también por sus bonitas palabras sobre Cuba, ¡porque soy cubano!" Una y otra vez, ¡Mi Poder Superior me enseñó que no existen las *coincidencias!*

Después de llegar a casa, fui a visitar a un amigo. Cuando regresé, vi una caja abierta en mi patio delantero. Al acercarme, empecé a temblar. Era una caja que contenía medicinas y pastillas para doce o más meses, eran para prevenir el parásito del corazón. Habían desaparecido. Están hechas con un sabor apetitoso para los perros, que deben masticarlas y digerirlas. Las ingirieron. *¿Uno de mis perros se las comió todas... o fueron ingeridos por varios?* Entré en pánico. *¿Se habían envenenado mis "hijos"? ¿Iban a morir por sobredosis?* La empresa que envió la MEDICINA incluyó en la caja un CARAMELO en forma de galleta grande y sabrosa para perros. Los perros tienen un gran sentido del olfato. El conductor había dejado el paquete en el jardín. Mis "hijos" lo encontraron, olieron la galleta y se comieron todo. Devastado, llamé a una línea de ayuda en caso de envenenamiento. Fue horrible. Imagina que tus hijos hubieran hecho lo mismo.

Llamé a la empresa y le pregunté a una supervisora, "Señora, ¿por qué demonios envían galletas para perros en cajas que contienen medicamentos?"

"Lo siento, señor, pero nuestros clientes esperan con impaciencia la galleta gratis y se quejan si no las incluimos", respondió.

"Oiga, señora, ¿cree que se quejarían si llegaran a casa y encontraran a un perro muerto? Si el VA o la farmacia le enviaran medicinas en cajas con caramelos y palomitas de maíz, y sus hijos se comieran las golosinas y las medicinas y enfermaran o murieran, ¿cómo se sentiría?"

Por mucho que lo intenté, no pude convencer a la empresa de que corrigiera sus prácticas. Lo mejor que hicieron fue poner *"no incluir hueso"* en el pedido. Recibí otras dos cajas de medicamentos con caramelos porque el almacén los envió a pesar de que las instrucciones estaban CLARAMENTE IMPRESAS EN LA PROPIA ETIQUETA. Nunca volví a pedir nada a esta empresa. Incluso sus propios farmacéuticos estaban de acuerdo conmigo. Semejante estupidez e insensibilidad por el bienestar de los perros a los que pretendían ayudar me dejó estupefacto. Llamé a la empresa por capricho justo antes de la publicación para averiguar si se había rectificado la insensata política.

Para mi absoluto asombro, el representante de la empresa me explicó que ya no enviaban huesos en cajas. *Casualmente*, el cambio de política entró en vigor pocos días antes de que yo hiciera lo que me pareció una llamada inútil. Pedí hablar con un miembro de la dirección y por fin tuve una conversación con un adulto racional que comprendía mi frustración. Resulta que se acordaba de mis llamadas de antaño, pidiendo un cambio de política. Me explicó que a otros clientes les había pasado lo mismo y que la dirección por fin había entendido el mensaje. Yo ya no tenía nada que *objetar* a esa empresa. ¡¡¡¡SIGUIENTE!!!!

Con el tiempo, mi vida se estabilizó, pero me costó adaptarme a un estilo de vida que ya no giraba en torno al drama. Me resultaba extraño. Años más tarde, recibí una llamada de mi amiga Sheila Culmer, reelegida Presidenta del Consejo de Bahamas para la Discapacidad. "¡Dave, tenemos nuestra ley!" dijo Sheila con entusiasmo. "Dave, hemos recibido más notoriedad y prensa gracias a ti y a tu Booster que en los veinte años anteriores". Yo estaba en estado de shock. Mi Booster había fallecido seis meses antes y no estaba a mi lado para oír la gran noticia. Empecé a temblar, incapaz de hablar.

"Dave, ¿estás ahí?" preguntó Sheila.

Conseguí pronunciar: "Uh huhhh". Respiré profundamente como Booster me había enseñado años atrás. Con el habla entrecortada, dije, "Sheila, me da miedo preguntar, ¿está incluido el acceso de perros de servicio y perros guía en la nueva legislación?"

Sheila respondió emocionada, "¡Oh, sí, Dave, está todo ahí!"

Rayos, la maldita presa se rompió de nuevo, y sollocé, orgulloso de los logros de mi Booster y muy triste de que no estuviera cerca para compartir el protagonismo de su éxito.

Unos meses más tarde, decidí visitar de nuevo mi tiempo compartido en Freeport, Bahamas. Invité a mi amiga Sharon, y a su esposo a acompañarme. Un fatídico día, salimos a pasear por la zona portuaria. Por la tarde, pedí un taxi para que nos llevara de vuelta al resort. El conductor se negó a que mis perros de servicio, Boosted y Busted, entraran en el taxi. Le expliqué que estaba infringiendo la nueva ley de discapacidades de las Bahamas. No le importó lo más mínimo.

Nos dirigimos a la comisaría de policía más cercana para solicitar ayuda para mis perros de asistencia. Le pedí a Sharon que se quedara con Busted mientras yo entraba con Boosted. Al entrar en la pequeña y modular comisaría, un agente de policía me abordó verbalmente de inmediato. "Saque al perro", retumbó la voz del megáfono.

Entonces respondí, "Es un perro de servicio".

Otro agente se sumó y gritó, "¿Escuchó lo que dijo?"

Un tercer oficial intervino y dijo: "Será mejor que saque al perro". El Presidente Roosevelt se habría referido a ello como "una fecha que permanecerá en la infamia". Fue mi día de Pearl Harbor. Estaba devastado. Salí del edificio antes de arriesgarme a que me detuvieran. Llamé a Sheila y le expliqué lo que había ocurrido. Me devolvió la llamada ese mismo día y me dijo que había estado en contacto con el subjefe de policía de las Bahamas. Nos invitó a asistir a una conferencia, *casualmente* programada para dos días después, en la isla de Freeport. Cuando llegó ese día, Sharon y su esposo se reunieron conmigo, Boosted y Busted. Entramos tímidamente en una gran sala de conferencias de un juzgado. Había unos veinte jefes de policía de todas las Bahamas sentados en mesas de conferencias ordenadas. También había una cámara de vídeo que retransmitía la conferencia para los jefes que se encontraban en otros lugares y no podían asistir en persona.

Nos saludaron cordialmente. Observé a todos los presentes, hombres y mujeres, ataviados con trajes marrones que denotaban su rango. Les expliqué lo que había ocurrido dos días antes. "A la gente le preocupa ser atacada por una jauría de perros, pero a mí me atacó una jauría de agentes de policía, en una comisaría, violando su legislación nacional. ¿De qué sirve una ley si la policía la viola? ¿A quién recurres? No estoy enfadado, sino agradecido por poder compartir mi educación con una población dispuesta a escuchar y aprender. Estoy muy orgulloso de su país por aprobar una ley relacionada con la discapacidad". A continuación expliqué que los perros de servicio y los perros guía son una extensión del cuerpo de una persona discapacitada y no pueden separarse. A continuación, hice una demostración de cómo Boosted y Busted realizaban tareas relacionadas con los perros de servicio, porque ver para creer.

Al poco rato, las sonrisas y las preguntas se entremezclaron rápidamente. La temperatura volvió a subir en un entorno policial, pero esta vez debido al calor de la amabilidad y la comprensión humanas. Los funcionarios se disculparon e insistieron en tomarse una foto de grupo en las escaleras del juzgado. A día de hoy, sé que una persona discapacitada acompañada de un perro de asistencia será recibida calurosamente en todas las Bahamas. Cuando volvimos al Island Seas Resort, era hora de que mis perros y yo nos relajáramos y socializáramos... ¡mis niños caninos se habían ganado sus alas una vez más!

Un año después, Boosted, Busted y yo regresamos a Freeport con mi amigo Rocky. Volví a llamar al periódico y repetí la historia de la vida de Booster a un periodista que estaba al otro lado de la línea telefónica. Lo primero que pensé fue que a esa persona no le importaba, pero luego recordé que en Bahamas, siempre me habían recibido con mucha calidez. Solía pensar que era allí donde se había originado el concepto de amabilidad. Me estremecí al contar mi historia y pude sentir el cariño del alma que se encontraba al otro lado de la línea. Esa calidez se transformó en la siguiente historia a toda página, en la que aparecía la foto de mi Booster: Lágrimas, lágrimas y más lágrimas.

Buscar un cambio positivo es fundamental. Expresar gratitud es igual de importante y contribuye al cambio. Cada vez que le daba un premio a Booster, él me expresaba su gratitud moviendo la cola, dándome un beso en la mejilla y ladrando enérgicamente. Aprendí de él a hacer lo mismo, ¡quizás utilizando un formato diferente!

CAPÍTULO 12
TANTEANDO EL TERRENO

Con el tiempo, disfruté yendo de crucero con Booster. Solía aislarme en mi camarote y pasearlo en los momentos menos concurridos. De vez en cuando, me gustaba compartirlo con otras personas, dependiendo de mi estado de ánimo.

Las compañías de cruceros siempre envían un sinfín de documentos en los que se explican las responsabilidades de viajar con un perro de servicio a bordo. Dada la proliferación de perros de servicio falsos que son llevados a lugares públicos por personas egoístas e ignorantes, lo entendí perfectamente.

Como defensor profundamente orgulloso de los perros de servicio, me sentí obligado a promover a quienes no podían promoverse a sí mismos. Para dar fe de la aptitud canina, envié una foto de Booster orinando en su caja asignada que aprendió a usar fielmente. También envié fotos tomadas de la señalización que vi en un país al que visité en cruceros anteriores. En la

isla de Santa Lucía, el gobierno colocó señales en los edificios públicos con palabrería elocuente. Sugerí no muy humildemente a la compañía de cruceros que si alguno de sus clientes era de esa isla, tal vez deberían enfocarse en las personas y enviarles documentos similares para que los firmaran.

Además, compartí que "Mi Booster tiene una educación de 50.000 dolares y sabe cuándo... y dónde... no orinar". Cuando estaba de un humor especialmente sarcástico, añadía, "¡A Booster le gusta mucho la buena música, especialmente la de cuerda! Por favor, no se preocupen, él sabe que tiene que hacer sus necesidades antes de subir al escenario". En un crucero, el personal con orgullo, colocó un dibujo de la cabeza de un perro encima de mi caja de alivio de mi Booster.

Posteriormente adorné la pared con fotos de Booster, tomadas por todo el mundo. Solía incluir una sección titulada, "Cartas de referencia". Adjunté la siguiente carta recibida de la Oficina del Presidente de Carnival Cruise Line:

Feb 1, 2007

Sr. Davis Hawn Mississippi

RE: VACACIONES, 11/11/06, M21, 2N431.6, 005030541B

Estimado Sr. Hawn:

Gracias por tomarse el tiempo para contactarnos con respecto a sus vacaciones a bordo del crucero HOLIDAY. Sabiendo que nuestro éxito depende de la satisfacción de nuestros huéspedes, agradecemos la oportunidad de responder a sus amables palabras. Es un verdadero placer recibir comentarios de huéspedes que disfrutaron de sus vacaciones en el crucero. Carnival se esfuerza por ofrecer a cada uno de nuestros huéspedes un producto excelente y un servicio superior. Le agradecemos que se haya tomado el tiempo para decirnos que cumplimos nuestro objetivo. Como muestra de agradecimiento, nos gustaría ofrecerle un regalo especial para su próximo crucero. Por favor comuníquese con el Departamento de Relaciones con los Huéspedes, 45 días antes de la salida, llamando al 1-800-929-6400 y nos encargaremos de que tenga un regalo de Bon Voyage en su camarote a su llegada.

Gracias de nuevo por tomarse el tiempo de ponerse en contacto con nosotros. Esperamos darle la bienvenida a usted y a Booster a bordo nuevamente pronto.

Atentamente, Susan Cohn
Asesora Especial,
Oficina del Presidente

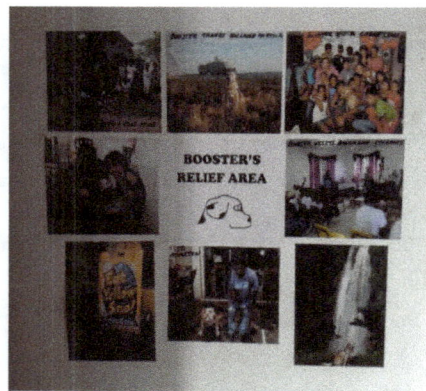

Siempre era una gran experiencia pasear con Booster. Ya fuera en los salones de baile o las playas, en los parques o las calles de la ciudad, siempre tenía un séquito. Adoraba a la gente de todas las clases sociales. Ojalá todos los humanos lo imitaran. "What a Wonderful World", ¡cómo lo expresó maravillosamente Louis Armstrong en su famosa canción!

En un crucero, mi grumete indonesio me preguntó si tenía una foto con Booster. Yo tenía una que había sido tomada en un crucero anterior (la foto de la portada), y se la di, pensando que probablemente sería una especie de recuerdo, debido a lo novedoso de tener un perro a bordo. El último día del crucero, oí que llamaban a la puerta de mi camarote. Cuando abrí la puerta, mi grumete me entregó un documento enrollado. Sabía que no era un aviso de desalojo, pero no tenía ni idea de qué esperar. Acepté el documento con

cautela y lo desenrollé lentamente. De repente, me encontré en la zona de impacto de una bomba atómica de emociones. Mis ojos incrédulos se elevaron automáticamente para encontrarse con los del joven. Me quedé estupefacto, sin palabras. Al instante pensé, *"Qué gesto tan amable"*.

Los empleados de un crucero trabajan un número inimaginable de horas, y este joven dedicó su tiempo libre a dibujar un boceto de mi Booster y yo.

"¡VAYA, no tienes idea de lo mucho que esto significa para mí! Gracias por compartir tu talento. Estoy deseando enmarcarlo y colgarlo en la pared de mi casa", le dije.

"Espero que le guste, señor", dijo con una sonrisa llena de confianza.

Le dije, "Eres increíble", y le di una propina. No había propina suficientemente generosa. Se lo agradecí de la mejor manera que pude, dado el estado emocional en que me encontraba.

En otro crucero, llevé a Booster a la playa. Le lancé la pelota al mar y él saltó a las olas para cogerla. Otros pasajeros del crucero pidieron tirar la pelota, y fue un momento muy divertido. Esa misma noche, de vuelta en el barco, Booster empezó a vomitar sin contemplación. Estaba enfermo, muy enfermo. Estábamos indefensos en medio del océano con mi querido Booster. Llamé a la recepción, pidiendo ayuda. El personal angelical logró que un veterinario viera a Booster en el siguiente puerto de escala en Roatán, Honduras. Oré hasta más no poder para que Booster sobreviviera a la noche. Supuse que había ingerido una cantidad peligrosa de agua salada.

Cuando el barco atracó, tomé un taxi con Booster hasta la clínica veterinaria. Debo admitir que estaba llorando cuando entré a la clínica. Estaba limpia y tenía un aspecto moderno. Booster caminaba con dificultad. Al poco rato estaba en la camilla. No recuerdo lo que me dijeron porque estaba completamente fuera de mí. Mis emociones me dominaban. El veterinario irradiaba confianza y empatía. Le puso una inyección a Booster y me aseguró que se pondría bien. También me preguntó si podía tomarnos una foto juntos.

Un año después, tenía previsto asistir a una de las conferencias veterinarias. Envié un correo electrónico al veterinario hondureño y le invité a asistir. Le expliqué lo mucho que había impactado mi vida aquel día y que nunca lo olvidaría. Me devolvió el correo y me dijo que él también asistiría a la conferencia. Entonces me ofrecí a proporcionarle boletos de avión para que él y su mujer volaran a Estados Unidos para asistir a la conferencia. Estaba todo previsto hasta que su veterinario de apoyo canceló a último momento y no pudo ir. *Qué lástima,* pensé.

Años más tarde, llevé a Booster a un crucero y compré el paquete termal. Te daba acceso a una preciosa sala de cristal con vista al mar mientras estabas sentado en una tumbona de cerámica con calefacción.

Era el lugar perfecto para leer, relajarse y, en mi caso, escribir un libro. También había un gran jacuzzi para varias personas y varios más pequeños. Entré en la suite termal con Booster, que se sentó en el rincón más alejado mientras yo utilizaba el jacuzzi. Más tarde se sentó

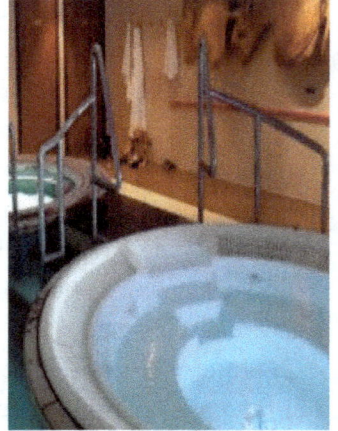

estoicamente a mi lado cuando yo estaba en una tumbona.

Aquella tarde me llamaron para reunirme con uno de los oficiales del barco.

"Señor, lo siento pero no puede entrar en la suite termal con un perro", declaró con autoridad.

El oficial estaba preocupado por la higiene de tener un perro cerca de los jacuzzis. En lugar de enfadarme, fingí reírme. Como suele ocurrir, utilicé el humor para calmar una situación conflictiva. La cabeza del desconcertado agente empezó a oscilar como la de un perro de juguete que se encuentra sujeta con un resorte al tablero de un automóvil. Cuando recuperé la compostura, le dije con franqueza:

"Señor, mi perro de servicio, Booster, estaba a 15 metros de los jacuzzis. Estos tenían vello corporal de, como diría el chef viajero Anthony Bourdain, "partes desconocidas". Algunos podrían haber sido negros, marrones, rubios o rojos. Podrían haber venido del estómago, la espalda o tal vez de un pene o una vagina. ¿Le preocupa que un pelo de perro flote a 15 metros por el aire y entre en el jacuzzi? ¿En serio?

Sus jacuzzis están llenos de productos químicos esterilizantes que me quemaron los ojos. Mi perro de servicio Booster ha estado debajo de la mesa en todos los cruceros que he tomado, incluido éste, y a ustedes no les preocupa que su pelo entre en la comida de la gente y pueda ser ingerido".

Su respuesta fue que la oficina central de la compañía de cruceros había tomado esa decisión. Me devolvieron el importe de la sala termal. Entonces envié un correo electrónico a la oficina central con copia a una agencia gubernamental. Cuando hablé con un funcionario de la oficina de origen, me dijeron que la decisión dependía del barco. Eso me enfureció mucho... *Un círculo vicioso de policía bueno y policía malo.* Regresé con el funcionario del barco y le expliqué lo que me habían dicho. Alguien no estaba diciendo la verdad sobre quién había tomado la decisión discriminatoria. Le expliqué que presentaría una queja ante el gobierno estadounidense y que, puesto que el barco zarpaba de un puerto estadounidense, estaba sujeto a la ADA y a sus disposiciones. ¡Estaba indignado y furioso!

Dos días después, me citaron de nuevo en la oficina del funcionario. Me explicó que había tardado algún tiempo en solucionarlo todo. Luego se disculpó y dijo:

"Sr. Hawn, esto es una curva de aprendizaje para nosotros. Le pido disculpas por el malentendido y las molestias. Puede utilizar la suite termal con Booster, su perro de servicio, y será gratuito durante el resto del crucero. Le otorgaremos un crédito de $100 en su cuenta del barco como un gesto de buena voluntad. También lo invito a usted y a su perro de servicio a unirse a nosotros en la mesa de los oficiales en la cena de esta noche, para ver a los acróbatas actuar en el espectáculo del cirque du soleil".

Por si fuera poco, a continuación le pedí que me hiciera un favor. Le expliqué que el chico de la piscina había traído voluntariamente agua a Booster en un día caluroso y que el grumete siempre lo saludaba amablemente. Le pregunté, "Señor, ¿podría citar mañana a esos dos caballeros en su oficina para que pueda agradecerles su amabilidad? Me gustaría darles las gracias en su presencia y una propina de 50 dólares a cada uno". Lo que vale, vale. Los 100 dólares que me otorgó, quiero dárselos a ellos".

Una vez más, mi educación de BUCS, junto con mis habilidades sociales inculcadas por Booster, crearon una maravillosa interacción social. Amaba a Booster y empezaba a amarme a mí mismo. Realmente no hay palabras para describir la transformación que tuvo lugar. Como demuestra la foto, los dos éramos felices. ¡Mi vida cambió de manera *épica*!

CAPÍTULO 13
MI QUERIDA PEGGY

En poco tiempo, llegó la hora de regresar a casa. Cuando entramos, se desató la locura canina. Los otros perros estaban extasiados de que estuviéramos en casa. Habían pasado años, pero por fin tenía tranquilidad y una vida hogareña como se supone que debe ser.

Un día sonó el teléfono. Era mi amiga Peggy. Nos invitaba a Booster y a mí a visitarla. Estaba emocionado de pasar tiempo con Peggy. Si había alguien con los *cojones* bien puestos, como dicen en McAllen, Texas (cariñosamente conocido como el norte de México), era ella. Con tres pensiones y una casa libre de deuda a sus cincuenta y tantos años, tenía su vida asegurada. Dicen que si algo parece demasiado bueno para ser verdad, probablemente lo sea. Tal era el caso de Peggy. Recientemente le habían diagnosticado cáncer de mama... ¡por segunda vez! Había luchado con éxito contra la enfermedad unos diez años atrás y lamentaba no haberse sometido a una mastectomía radical.

Tras su primer enfrentamiento con el cáncer, se matriculó en la BUCS para obtener un título relacionado con los caninos y así poder ayudar a los veteranos a hacer frente al TEPT. Sin saberlo, ella era una veterana a punto de enfrentarse a la mayor batalla de su heroica vida.

Mucha gente piensa que el TEPT es simplemente una puerta de entrada para conseguir un cheque por discapacidad. Yo nunca elegí ese camino, pero probablemente habría cumplido los requisitos. Antes pensaba que nuestras tropas eran débiles, hasta que leí que mueren más veteranos por suicidio que en combate. Cité esa estadística de suicidios a un caballero en el Barrio Francés de Nueva Orleans. Él me dijo, "Señor, no hace falta que me lo diga. Mi hijo volvió de la batalla y se suicidó hace seis meses".

Entonces relató una historia sobre cómo la noche anterior se había encontrado con un joven soldado, vestido de uniforme. El soldado estaba llorando y el hombre le preguntó por qué. El soldado le explicó que lo habían robado y que no tenía dinero para divertirse y conocer a unas jóvenes. Además, dijo que iba a "suicidarse".

"¿Se va a suicidar porque no puede divertirse?" le preguntó el hombre.

El soldado dijo con toda naturalidad que iba a suicidarse porque ya no se soportaba a sí mismo. El valiente soldado se había hecho amigo de un niño afgano con quien jugaba a la pelota casi todos los días. "El chico era como un hijastro. Un día, los talibanes le pusieron una bomba y vino corriendo a nuestro campamento. Lo vi, levanté mi fusil y tuve que dispararle. Todavía puedo ver su cerebro explotando. No hay pastilla o medicina que pueda borrarlo. La única forma de liberarme del dolor es el suicidio".

En otra ocasión, un hombre explicó que su hijo conducía camiones militares en convoyes. A los conductores se les decía que no se detuvieran nunca, porque si lo hacían, el enemigo se abalanzaría sobre ellos. Los talibanes, o el enemigo de turno, arrojaban a los niños bajo los neumáticos o las orugas de los vehículos. El hijo del hombre miró por el retrovisor de su vehículo y vio la cabeza de un niño aplastada, apenas unida al cuerpo sin vida. Había atropellado al niño y la cicatriz emocional le dolió durante años.

Me preguntaba, cuánta gente sabía a qué eran sometidos nuestros jóvenes. Había sido muy ingenuo en asumir automáticamente que nuestros héroes eran débiles, y estoy seguro de que no soy el único. Estaba muy equivocado.

Lo que había experimentado en mi vida, palidecía comparado con esto, pero aun así me pasó factura. Mi mente solía jugarme malas pasadas. Por la noche, soñaba y revivía el momento en que el cuchillo se acercaba a mí. Conduciendo por una autopista, en una noche oscura y calurosa, el parabrisas se empañaba con frecuencia. Me temblaban las manos y tenía que parar. Me acercaba a Booster y lo abrazaba con fuerza. Era una reacción emocional a aquella noche en la Florida en la que tuve el enfrentamiento físico y se empañó el parabrisas de mi camioneta.

Peggy y yo luchamos contra las ramificaciones mentales de eventos erróneamente procesados por el cerebro humano. Su mayor batalla aún no había terminado, ya que le habían diagnosticado un cáncer de mama en etapa IV. A ella le dolía y a mí también. El cáncer de mama amenazaba con llevarse a uno de los pocos seres humanos a los que amaba de todo corazón y en los que confiaba sin reparos... como lo hacía con un perro. La vida volvía a ser un asco. Irónicamente, Peggy me apoyaba más a menudo que yo a ella. Ella era una valiente guerrera y yo un cobarde.

Peggy apreciaba mi disposición a compartir detalles íntimos de mi vida para ayudar a otros. Le expliqué que no me importaba lo que los demás pensaran de mí. Le conté el dicho que había oído en una reunión de Al-Anon, "Lo que los demás piensen de mí no es asunto mío". Además, le expliqué que cada momento de cada día era tiempo extra, ya que debería haber muerto hace mucho tiempo. Mi voluntad de exponer mis fragilidades se basaba en mi relación con mi Booster. Él me había ayudado, y yo estaba decidido a ayudar a otros con él a mi lado.

Un día, mientras Peggy y yo hablábamos sobre conceptos básicos del cuidado de los perros, me di cuenta de que ella también podía ayudar a otros, al igual que yo me esforzaba por hacerlo.

"Oye Peggy, sabes que eres mi experimentada heroína en la batalla y en la vida. Puedes conectar con otros veteranos y mujeres que sufren codependencia y abusos mucho mejor que yo. Hagamos un reportaje en el periódico de tu ciudad y compartamos cómo nuestros perros de servicio han cambiado nuestras vidas."

"¡Oh Dios mío, no sé si podría hacer eso! ¡No quiero que mis vecinos piensen que soy una loca del Cuerpo de Mujeres del Ejército (Women's Army Corps - WAC)"

"Respeto totalmente tus sentimientos, es solo que eres muy especial. ¡Eres mi Peggy! "Desde el momento en que nos conocimos en BUCS, me inspiraste. Te abriste y me apoyaste mucho. Tuviste un impacto en mi vida. Sé en mi corazón que puedes hacer lo mismo por los demás".

El silencio se apoderó de la sala. Peggy, como la guerrera que era, respondió con altruismo, "Al diablo con eso. Si puedo ayudar a otros a sobrellevar la porquería con la que yo he lidiado y promover los perros de servicio, ¡cuenta conmigo, amigo!"

Antes de una de mis visitas a casa de Peggy, tomé el teléfono y llamé al *Monitor Newspaper* de McAllen. Expliqué que tenía un perro de servicio al que atribuía el mérito de haber salvado mi vida y haberla cambiado por completo. Luego le conté que tenía una amiga íntima que era veterana de guerra, una heroína de McAllen, que tenía una historia importante que contar. Tras compartir un sinfín de detalles, la reportera sugirió que nos reuniéramos en el aeropuerto de McAllen a mi llegada.

El día que llegué, la reportera nos recibió y vio con asombro cómo Booster tiraba del carro de mi equipaje. Tomó muchas fotos de Peggy con su perra, Tara, y a mí me fotografió con Booster. Luego nos acompañó a casa de Peggy. La periodista era toda una dama, respetuosa y empática. Yo sabía que haría un buen trabajo y presentaría la historia de forma positiva. A los pocos días, el reportaje apareció en el periódico.

THE MONITOR

Los perros de servicio ya no son sólo para ciegos

Esa noche, Peggy y yo fuimos a cenar a un restaurante mexicano para celebrar y relajarnos. Entramos con nuestros perros de servicio y nos dijeron que no podíamos llevarlos adentro. Les explicamos que tenían que dejarnos entrar al restaurante con nuestros perros de servicio, así lo estipulaba la ley. Los idiotas nos llevaron al patio trasero, encendieron una luz que colgaba de un cable e intentaron sentarnos en una mesa de picnic vieja y tambaleante. ¡Perdí el control! ¡Mi trastorno de estrés postraumático superó al de Peggy aquella noche! "Mira, ¿es aquí donde metes a los gringos? ¿Expulsas a los discapacitados y minorías al campo para que se los coman los mosquitos?" No iba a ser devorado vivo debido al TEPT como lo había experimentado escondido en mi casa años atrás. "Mira, Poncho", le dije irrespetuosamente, "¡eso no va a pasar en los Estados Unidos". Miré a Peggy y grité, "¡Sígueme!"

Peggy parecía asustada. Nos dirigimos al centro del restaurante y nos quedamos allí de pie mientras marcaba al 911 desde mi teléfono móvil. El departamento del sheriff local respondió cuando les dije que las cosas se estaban saliendo de control. Llegaron dos agentes y escucharon mi historia. Tuve que calmarme. Si parecía agitado o hablaba en voz alta, les daría la excusa apropiada para echarnos del restaurante.

Con todos los ojos del restaurante fijos en nosotros, les expliqué, "Vine a este bonito restaurante con mi veterana amiga Peggy, sin esperar hacerla pasar otra vez por una batalla. El camarero nos expulsó del restaurante y nos llevó a una mesa de picnic en el patio trasero. Ambos somos discapacitados y vamos acompañados de perros de servicio profesionales".

"Señor, les explicaré que la ley permite el acceso a las personas acompañadas por perros de servicio, pero no puedo obligarlos a atenderlos".

Lo dije con firmeza para que todos me oyeran, "Oficial, lo entiendo perfectamente. Simplemente le pido que levante un acta, para tener pruebas cuando presente la demanda. ¡Necesitaba documentación en el país de los indocumentados! ¡Estaba enfadado!

Miré al personal y les dije, "Nunca he querido ser dueño de un restaurante mexicano pero, en este caso, me sentiría muy orgulloso de ser el dueño de este lugar debido a la gran multa que pagarán por haber infringido la ley federal. Daré de comer a los perros adentro y a los humanos en el patio trasero donde nos llevaron". Entonces tomé aire y les pedí que llamaran al propietario para poder hablar con él.

Posteriormente, el dueño se disculpó y nos sentaron en el centro del restaurante.

Al día siguiente, Peggy me preguntó dónde quería comer. ¿Quieres adivinar dónde elegí comer? Fuimos al restaurante donde habíamos comido la noche anterior. Cuando estábamos entrando, le dije a Peggy que se detuviera. Había una máquina expendedora de periódicos cerca de la puerta principal. Nuestro artículo había sido publicado ese día y aparecía en el encabezado de la primera página. *Vaya*, pensé, otra *coincidencia*. "Mi Poder Superior sí que tiene sentido de la oportunidad", le dije a Peggy. Compré un ejemplar y entramos. El gerente nos saludó y mostró un comportamiento aprendido, ¡como el de Fidelity años atrás! Abrí el periódico con orgullo y desafío y le enseñé el artículo. "Anoche evité que su personal infringiera la ley, y sé que el dueño del restaurante está agradecido". Recibimos un postre de cortesía, que saboreamos como nunca.

Miré a Peggy y le dije, "Estoy orgulloso de ti. Te quiero". Luego me dirigí a mi Booster y al perro de servicio de Peggy, Tara, y los abracé. Dije con equidad, como había aprendido a hacer en la BUCS, "Y los quiero a los dos por igual". Peggy se rio con su resplandeciente sonrisa que me encantaba ver. "Eres realmente increíble, amigo mío", dijo.

Yo respondí, "Y tú eres realmente mi mejor amiga, ¡sólo superada por mi Booster!" Ella sonrió aún más.

En otra ocasión, llamé a Peggy y le pregunté si a ella y a su perra de servicio, Tara, les gustaría asistir a la conferencia de la Asociación de Adiestradores Caninos Profesionales en Covington, Kentucky. A ambos nos encantaba ampliar nuestra formación canina en cuanto teníamos oportunidad. Peggy aceptó entusiasmada. Volamos a Kentucky, nos reunimos en el hotel, cenamos juntos y nos acostamos temprano. Después de tomar un desayuno rápido en la mañana, salimos y llamamos a un taxi para que nos llevara a la conferencia. Nos acercamos con calma al conductor, pero se negó rotundamente a llevarnos porque íbamos acompañados de nuestros perros de servicio. Me esforcé por mantener la compostura. *Aquí vamos de nuevo*, pensé. *¡Reprodúcelo de nuevo, Sara!*

Le expliqué repetidamente que el acceso era una obligación de ley. Pronto me di cuenta de que estaba orinando al viento, por expresarlo de forma educada. Le dije, "¡Voy a llamar a la policía y tú no irás a ninguna parte!"

Marqué al 911 antes de que las cosas se me salieran de las manos. Mi Booster y yo nos pusimos delante del taxi, impidiendo que se fuera. Peggy dijo que iba a tomar otro taxi y yo asentí con la cabeza. A los pocos minutos llegó un agente de policía.

"Agente, estoy asistiendo a una conferencia con una amiga. El taxista nos negó el acceso porque ambos llevamos perros de servicio que nos ayudan a superar las discapacidades que tenemos."

"Entiendo señor", respondió el oficial.

El agente le explicó al taxista, "Debe transportar a un pasajero acompañado de un perro de servicio a menos que el pasajero o el perro estén fuera de control. Si no desea permitir que un perro suba a su taxi, quizá debería buscarse otro oficio".

Le pedí al oficial que me diera el número del reporte policial. Entonces, el taxista dijo cortantemente, "Suba".

Le respondí, "¿De verdad cree que voy a subir a su vehículo después de lo que acaba de suceder? En primer lugar, no me sentiría seguro y, en segundo lugar, ¡no voy a recompensarlo con un pago por violar nuestra ley nacional!"

El oficial, amablemente, esperó a que llegara otro taxi para llevarnos a la conferencia. Más tarde conseguí una copia del informe, escribí una carta de agradecimiento al oficial y se la envié a su superior. Sorprendentemente, recibí un correo electrónico de respuesta del agente. Me dio las gracias y me explicó que su tío era ciego y que conocía las leyes de acceso para perros de servicio. También me dijo que estaba igual de disgustado y que se alegraba de poder ayudar. Qué coincidencia que ese oficial en concreto respondiera a mi llamada.

MANCOMUNIDAD DE KENTUCKY

SINOPSIS:

Un taxista negó el servicio al demandante porque éste tenía un perro de servicio. El perro estaba claramente marcado y tenía licencia.

FECHA Y HORA DE LA OCURRENCIA: 21/10/2012 a las 16.28 horas INVESTIGACIÓN:

El señor Hawn sufre una discapacidad y tiene un perro de compañía/servicio de 8 años. El perro tenía las credenciales apropiadas, llevaba un chaleco que lo identificaba como perro de servicio. Además del chaleco, el perro llevaba correa y se comportaba bien. El Sr. Hawn intentó entrar en el taxi comunitario amarillo Nº XXX que conducía el Sr. A. El Sr. A negó rotundamente la entrada del Sr. Hawn a su vehículo. El Sr. A dijo al Sr. Hawn que no permitiría que el perro entrara en su taxi. A pesar de que el Sr. Hawn le explicó que se trataba de un perro de servicio y que la Ley de Estadounidenses con Discapacidades le prohibía denegar el servicio a causa del animal, el Sr. A siguió negándoselo.

Un vehículo aparcado detrás del taxi impidió al Sr. A dar marcha atrás, y el Sr. Hawn se quedó delante del taxi con su perro mientras esperaba a la policía. Al llegar, el especialista C y yo, le explicamos la ley al Sr. A y que no podía negarse a prestar el servicio. El Sr. A nos comentó

que tenía miedo a los perros y que desconocía dicha ley. El
Sr. Hawn decidió esperar a otra compañía de taxis.

Cuando me encontré con Peggy en la conferencia, me miró fijamente a
los ojos y me dijo que estaba orgullosa de mí. Además, me explicó que
había librado sus batallas en el ejército y que no era capaz emocionalmente
de enfrentarse a otros debido a su trastorno de estrés postraumático.

La entendí y aprecié su franqueza. Yo había tardado años en ser capaz
de resolver conflictos sin una confrontación excesiva. Tenía que
agradecérselo a mi Booster.

Peggy luego tomó una foto de mi Booster abrazándome en la
conferencia. La guardo con mucho cariño.

CAPÍTULO 14
EL ENEMIGO INTERIOR

Al regresar de Tailandia al año siguiente, me informaron que mi Booster había sido llevado al veterinario porque tenía dolor en la mandíbula. El diagnóstico fue trastorno de la articulación temporomandibular (ATM), dolor muscular asociado a la bisagra que conecta la mandíbula con el cráneo. A mi Booster le encantaba portar un peluche y llevarlo a saludar a la gente con gran exuberancia. Lo había entrenado desde cachorro para hacerlo. Me dijeron que sentía dolor cuando abría la mandíbula lo suficiente para soltar el peluche. Le recetaron relajantes musculares y parecía estar bien. Yo también experimentaba dolor asociado a la ATM que aparecía y desaparecía. No es para tanto, ¿verdad? Quizás mi Booster sólo necesitaba unas vacaciones.

Tras mi regreso de Tailandia, había planeado durante meses asistir a la Conferencia Veterinaria de América del Norte (NAVC) en Orlando, Florida. Invité a Peggy y a Tara a que nos acompañaran a Booster y a mí a la conferencia. Reservamos un maravilloso "crucero canino" después de la conferencia. Un organizador del evento había dispuesto que especialistas caninos impartieran una serie de conferencias a bordo. Uno de los ponentes era el Dr. Aubrey Fine, que formaba parte de mi comité de tesis de la BUCS. Habíamos hablado con frecuencia e intercambiado muchos correos electrónicos, pero nunca nos habíamos visto en persona. Contaba los días que faltaban para conocer al Dr. Fine y presentarle a Booster.

Cuando llegó el momento de volar a Orlando, Booster y yo subimos al avión sin contratiempos. Casualmente me senté al lado de un caballero que se presentó como el Dr. Frederic Gaschen, especialista en gastroenterología canina de la Universidad Estatal de Luisiana (LSU). Mencioné la ATM de Booster durante nuestra conversación. Cuando aterrizamos en Orlando, me acerqué a la cinta de equipajes para recoger mi maleta. Casi nunca facturo equipaje, pero casualmente lo hice en este viaje. El veterinario especialista se acercó a reclamar el equipaje y me preguntó si podía examinar a Booster y revisar su mandíbula adolorida. Miró la garganta de Booster, le olió sus oídos y palpó su cabeza. Encontró un pequeño bulto en la cabeza detrás de su ojo derecho. No se notaba antes del vuelo. Me sugirió que lo hiciera ver y me recomendó una clínica especializada en la cercana Maitland, Florida.

Tomé un taxi hasta el resort donde nos alojábamos. Peggy me recibió con un cálido abrazo. Mi Booster corrió a jugar con Tara. Nos reímos mientras los perros retozaban, jugaban y corrían en círculos. Le di a Booster su peluche y él y Tara jugaron al tira y afloja. Cuando terminó el ritual, Booster abrió la boca para soltar el juguete y gritó de dolor. Saltó por los aires y corrió como si un cable eléctrico de 240 voltios le hubiera tocado la lengua. Ambos entramos en pánico y la preocupación se apoderó del momento. Tenía que hacer algo de inmediato.

Tras localizar la clínica que me había recomendado el Dr. Gaschen, concerté una cita para el día siguiente. Esa tarde, Booster agarró uno de los juguetes de Tara y se negó a soltarlo. Sabía que le dolería si abría la boca lo suficiente para soltarlo. Tuve que abrirle la boca para quitarle el juguete y volvió a gritar horriblemente. Oré para que no pensara que yo era el causante del dolor. Mantuve a Booster alejado de todos los objetos que cogía "automáticamente" para saludarme. Era un comportamiento aprendido tan arraigado que, aunque al final le provocaba un intenso dolor, lo hacía de todos modos. Prácticamente no sentía dolor hasta que abría la boca de par en par. Yo sentía tanto dolor emocional que tampoco podía abrir la boca. ¡Era horrible!

Peggy y Tara nos acompañaron a la clínica al día siguiente. Los especialistas de Maitland Veterinary Specialists determinaron con un TAC y una resonancia magnética que el bulto que había encontrado el Dr Gaschen era un tumor. Se había comido el cráneo de Booster como un globo de agua que explota a través de una galleta salada. El experimentado oncólogo sospechaba que era canceroso, probablemente un carcinoma de células escamosas. Este tipo de cáncer suele aparecer en los dedos de los pies y de las manos, pero a veces también se encuentra en la cavidad sinusal. El agresivo cáncer se había iniciado en el revestimiento del cráneo, se había alimentado del hueso y lo había atravesado. Si la patología confirmaba el diagnóstico, a Booster sólo le quedaban tres semanas de vida, y cada día que pasara prometía un dolor más atroz.

Nos sugirieron que le diéramos a Booster una fiesta con pastel y helado antes de sacrificarlo. ¡Yo quería que Booster comiera helado allí mismo! Peggy me llevó a comprar un litro de helado de vainilla. Fue surrealista. Fue peor que horrible. Estaba viajando con las dos almas a las que había aprendido a amar más que a la vida misma. A mi Booster le diagnosticaron una enfermedad terminal y Peggy tuvo que acompañarme. Ella fue abofeteada bruscamente con un recordatorio de su tenue mortalidad, de camino a nuestro fabuloso, todo para olvidar crucero.

El dolor emocional de aquel día hundiría el barco de guerra más fuerte que el mundo haya conocido jamás. Mi Peggy era una enferma terminal de cáncer, ¡igual que mi Booster! Ella tuvo que escuchar todos los horribles detalles.

"El tumor está afectando un nervio cercano al cerebro. Es probable que el dolor sea intenso, y debe decidir pronto por el bien de Booster", me dijeron.

Dios, no quería que Peggy reviviera su propio diagnóstico y su probable mortalidad. Yo estaba fuera de mí por el dolor y el resentimiento. *¿Por qué? ¿Por qué? ¿Por qué? ¿Por qué? ¿Por qué? ¿Por qué? MPS, ¿por qué?* Estaba casi listo para poner a dormir a mi Booster cuando *casualmente* recibí un correo electrónico de un ángel ubicado en lo que muchos en los Estados Unidos llaman "territorio enemigo".

Mi amigo cubano Rodrigo me envió un correo electrónico desde La Habana. "Davis, los cubanos somos luchadores. Lucha por Booster. Él luchó por ti". Cuba es conocida por la medicina y la educación, unidas a la disciplina. Era un intelectual y no me orientaría mal.

¡Maldita sea! ¿Qué se suponía que hiciera? Recordé las palabras de mi hermano hace tiempo, "¿Qué vas a hacer con el perro?" Ahora sí que tenía que responder a esa misma pregunta, y cuanto antes. No era capaz de manejar esto, a pesar de la terapia y los medicamentos. Me desplomé y caí en una silla. Mi Booster corrió a mi lado, lamiéndome la mano. *Por favor, mátame a mí, no a mi Booster. Me rindo. Me rindo por completo, pensé.*

Mi Booster siempre quiso vivir, mientras que yo a menudo no. Él apreciaba la vida y yo con frecuencia la odiaba.

Peggy se sentó a mi lado mientras yo entraba en trance hipnótico. Me abrazó, me apretó y me dijo, "Llévate a Booster a casa y tómate tiempo para pensar". Ese mismo día hice una reserva para el último vuelo que tomaría mi Booster, el vuelo al infierno, y luego le sugerí a Peggy que una amiga ocupara mi lugar para que pudiera disfrutar del crucero. Con la fuerza transmitida por Peggy y las palabras desafiantes de Rodrigo, de algún modo me las arreglé para abordar el avión ese mismo día. Como si llevara el piloto automático, Booster se dirigió directamente al asiento del compartimento que él conocía. Era un viajero experimentado, que no sabía lo que estaba a punto de vivir.

Me mintieron. Yo había tenido razón todo el tiempo. La vida apestaba y NO valía la pena vivirla. Estaba tomando el penúltimo vuelo con mi Booster. En el último y definitivo vuelo, él dejaría este mundo. Mentiría si no pensara en reservar yo misma los boletos para ambos vuelos. ¿Cómo podría sobrevivir sin mi Booster y por qué demonios querría hacerlo? *Al demonio. Al demonio todo. ¡Al diablo la vida!*

Llegué a casa y saludé a mi manada. Mi Booster fue recibido en casa con todos los honores. Los otros miembros de la manada se acercaron y le lamieron la boca... un signo de respeto y sumisión hacia el líder. Booster mantuvo su papel, aunque su papel en la vida era de repente tenue. Me preguntaba cómo se adaptaría la manada a la vida sin *nuestro* Booster. Después de abrazarlo durante casi una hora, le di varias golosinas. La preocupación por su peso ya no era un problema. Era el peso sobre mis hombros el que soportaba la realidad. No estaba seguro de poder manejarlo, pero se lo debía a los demás miembros de mi "familia". Después de todo, una vez había rechazado a Booster, pero él me había apoyado en las buenas y en las malas. Me había salvado inequívocamente de mí mismo. No podía abandonar a mi Booster. Quizás, egoístamente, sabía que no podría vivir sin él.

Pensé en los padres humanos a cuyos hijos se les diagnostica una enfermedad terminal. *¿Cómo demonios lo hacen? ¿De dónde sacan la fuerza? ¿Cuál es su booster (estímulo)?* me preguntaba. No lo entendía entonces y sigo sin entenderlo. Supongo que viene de la necesidad de mantener al resto de la manada, si es que la hay.

Después de levantar cualquier objeto que Booster pudiera recoger, intenté ver la televisión. También podría haber intentado escalar el Monte Everest. Inevitablemente, acabé conduciendo hasta el hospital veterinario de la Universidad Estatal de Luisiana (LSU). El viaje fue una completa pérdida de tiempo, ya que la clínica veterinaria no contaba con un neurólogo en plantilla. El internista dijo que lo más probable era que no se tratara de un carcinoma de células escamosas, ya que esa forma de cáncer rara vez se encuentra en la cavidad sinusal.

Casualmente, en ese momento, sonó su buscapersonas y el departamento de oncología de Maitland Veterinary Specialists transmitió la patología de mi Booster. Efectivamente, tenía un tumor de carcinoma de células escamosas. Sacudí la cabeza, abracé a Booster y supe que tenía que ponerme en contacto con el especialista de inmediato. Era de vida o muerte, *quizás* sólo para mi Booster.

Cuando regresé a mi cabaña, me senté en mi escritorio, mirando atentamente mi computador. Utilicé las habilidades de investigación que había adquirido años atrás en la BUCS. Investigué sobre el carcinoma de células escamosas, los ensayos y los tratamientos. A mis más de cincuenta años, apenas sabía manejar un computador antes de ir a la universidad. Busqué en Internet como si no hubiera un mañana, porque podía no haberlo. Uno tras otro, leí artículos científicos publicados en PubMed e interpreté datos estadísticos. Me invadió una fuerza que sólo MPS sabía de dónde había sacado. Pasé los dedos por mi computador portátil como un detector de tesoros buscando oro. Leí con determinación todo lo que pude encontrar sobre el carcinoma de células escamosas. Había tratamientos convencionales y alternativos. Llamé a todo el mundo haciendo preguntas. Permanecí en mi escritorio durante los dos días siguientes... sólo abandonaba el barco el tiempo suficiente para alimentar a mi familia canina. Entonces hice una lista de los diez tratamientos más probables que podrían ayudar a Booster, convencionales y no convencionales. Estas opciones eran oro para mí, pero ¿era oro de tontos? ¿Eran reales? Reuní diez paquetes con desesperación. Cada paquete contenía una copia de la resonancia magnética y la tomografía computarizada de Booster, junto con fotos de él rodeado de niños cubanos en un aula y de huérfanos infectados por el VIH en Tailandia. Adjunté una nota, "Mi Booster ha hecho mucho por los seres humanos de este mundo, y le gustaría participar en su investigación por el bienestar de la humanidad.

¿Pueden ayudarle? ¿Puede participar en su ensayo?"

Entonces ayudé a Booster a subir a mi camioneta. Juntos, fuimos a FedEx en un esfuerzo desesperado por solucionar el problema. Lloré profusamente por el camino mientras la cabeza de Booster, que contenía al enemigo interior, yacía sobre mi regazo. Las recurrentes punzadas en mi pierna se disiparon con el peso de la cabeza de Booster. ¡Ambos teníamos enemigos internos! No debería haber conducido aquel día. Fue egoísta de mi parte y me arrepiento de haberlo hecho. Mi Poder Superior de alguna manera me permitió hacer el viaje. Volví a casa y traté de pensar en una vida sin mi Booster. Por mucho que lo intenté, no pude hacerlo.

El dolor era tan agudo que ni siquiera intenté beber para adormecerlo. En el pasado me hice daño debido a mi percepción errónea del amor. Esta vez me dolía el amor REAL. Este dolor era excepcional y exponencial; yo estaba entumecido hasta los huesos, hasta lo más profundo de mi existencia. No comía, no veía la televisión y, desde luego, nunca escuchaba la radio. La música era lo peor, ya que siempre giraba en torno al amor, la desesperación y el tormento, o eso parecía.

Tres días después de enviar los paquetes, sonó el teléfono. NO quería contestar. Sorprendentemente, no lo hice y dije, "Quienquiera que seas, lárgate". La voz melódica de un ángel estaba en la línea. En ese momento, supe que se trataba de una intervención divina, de un poder superior desconocido para mí. "Hola, soy la Dra. Elizabeth Pluhar, llamo desde la Universidad de Minnesota. Quiero ayudar a Booster". El ángel tocó su arpa de esperanza y dijo, "Quiero extraer un trozo del tumor de Booster y hacer una vacuna para luchar contra su cáncer. Hemos tenido éxito con otras formas de cáncer, pero nunca habíamos trabajado con células escamosas. Estaré disponible en tres semanas". La realidad dictaba que a Booster no le quedaban tres semanas de vida.

Al instante, todo mi ser se subió a la montaña rusa de la vida. Lloré en los oídos de aquella señora con temerario abandono. Estaba en lo profundo de un pozo sin fondo, catapultado a la mayor altura del cielo, sólo para saltar en bungee hacia abajo sin cuerda. Le expliqué, "A mi Booster no le quedan tres semanas de vida. Tiene dolores agudos, y yo también".

La conversación telefónica llegó a su fin, la ventana de la vida se cerró de golpe. Para este momento, Booster me había inculcado la creencia en un poder superior, más grande que yo. No había *coincidencias, ¿*verdad? Me senté en mi silla, abrazando a Booster como si no hubiera un mañana porque *no lo había.*

De algún modo, mi subconsciente recurrió a mis clases de veterinaria de la BUCS. Inmediatamente cogí el teléfono y llamé al cielo. Una operadora de la Universidad de Minnesota contestó el teléfono y me puso en contacto con "nuestro" ángel.

"Habla la Dra. Pluhar. ¿En qué puedo ayudarle?" repicó la voz del optimismo. "Dra. Pluhar, le llama el dueño de Booster. ¿Sería posible enviarle un trozo del tumor para intentar desarrollar la vacuna?" imploré. "Estoy pensando que la radioterapia (RT) reducirá el tumor y podría proporcionar alivio a corto plazo. Creo, basándome en mi formación en la BUCS, que el tejido irradiado será inútil para el desarrollo de la vacuna. Tenemos que extirpar una muestra del tejido afectado antes de la radiación. ¿Es correcto?"

"Eso funcionaría, Sr. Hawn", fue la respuesta del ángel. Los engranajes de mi mente se aceleraron rápidamente, engrasados por el amor y la desesperación. En ese momento, la espiritualidad, la confianza, el amor y todo lo bueno de la vida se fusionaron. Le dije a la Dra. Pluhar que esperara una muestra en breve. Una vez calmado como dictaba la necesidad, llamé a Maitland Veterinary Specialists. Pedí hablar con el oncólogo, el Dr. Lurie. "Dr. Lurie, soy Davis Hawn y 'necesitamos' su ayuda. Llevo días en Internet buscando la fórmula salvadora. He sabido de varias terapias prometedoras aún no probadas. ¿Nos ayudaría, por favor?" le pregunté.

El Dr. Lurie, siendo el caballero que era, dijo con palabras que nunca olvidaré, "Les ayudaré en todo lo posible, pero deben hacerlo rápido". Le pregunté dócilmente, "¿Estaría dispuesto a extirpar un trozo del tumor antes de comenzar la radiación?" El Dr. Lurie contestó, "Estoy certificado en cirugía, así que sin duda puedo hacerlo".

Vaya, ¡otra *coincidencia*! Concerté una cita con ese ángel y luego volví a llamar al *otro* ángel. "Dra. Pluhar, mañana vuelo a Florida para ver al radiólogo de Booster, el Dr. Lurie. Él extirpará un trozo del tumor de Booster y se lo enviará y guardará una muestra extra por si acaso. Me trasladaré temporalmente a Florida para que mi Booster pueda recibir radioterapia durante un mes". Mis conocimientos informáticos adquiridos en la BUCS ofrecieron un arco iris de oportunidades de investigación para Booster, que tenía como destino al Rainbow Bridge. Lo llevé al aeropuerto al día siguiente para un vuelo que nunca pensé que llegaría. Era "otro" vuelo para Booster después de haber tomado su "último" vuelo. Aterrizamos en Orlando, condujimos hasta Maitland y entramos en el consultorio de la oportunidad.

El Dr. Lurie sonrió y habló con un relajante acento británico. Me prescribió un plan de radioterapia compuesto por 18 sesiones diarias. Firmé el formulario de información que incluía la posibilidad de ceguera en el ojo derecho, situado dentro del campo de radiación. Alquilé un apartamento durante un mes, y conduje cuarenta y cinco minutos diarios con mi querido Booster, yendo y viniendo del tratamiento. Al cabo de cinco tratamientos, mi Booster ya no gritaba de dolor cuando abría la boca para soltar el preciado juguete, que tanto le gustaba entregar a cualquier persona que se acercaba a su perímetro personal.

El Dr. Lurie me explicó que las células cancerosas estaban respondiendo bien a los tratamientos de radiación. Yo también estaba respondiendo a los tratamientos de radiación;

así como iba mi Booster, iba el reino de las emociones de Davis. Le mostré al Dr. Lurie cómo Booster corría hacia mi camioneta, agarraba la cuerda atada al tirador de la puerta, y la abría con orgullo para traerme agua o medicinas. El perro que una semana antes no podía sonreír debido a un dolor insoportable, volvía a tirar para abrir una puerta, esta vez hacia el futuro. Me quedé momentáneamente congelado en un ambiente de gratitud y libre de dolor por el amor de otro. Mi Booster y mi Peggy estaban bien, "solo por hoy", y me esforcé por vivir el momento.

Decidí llevar a Booster a Disney World para celebrar la vida, ¡sólo por hoy! Nos montamos juntos en algunas atracciones, pero la mayor parte del tiempo Booster entretenía a los niños que corrían a saludarlo. Tanto Booster como los niños eran ajenos a la línea de tinta negra en la cabeza rapada de Booster. Era el lugar de aterrizaje del armamento atómico que en su momento se utilizó para destruir miles de vidas, pero que hoy se usaba para salvar una. Los niños apuntaban sus pistolas de burbujas hacia Booster, y éste saltaba e interceptaba las bombas de burbujas entrantes mejor que el más eficiente escudo de defensa de la Guerra de las Galaxias jamás diseñado.

Mientras observaba a Booster, vi por casualidad a un artista haciendo caricaturas. Al instante supe que quería inmortalizar ese día y a mi Booster. Nos reunimos con el amable hombre y le encargamos un dibujo. La caricatura resultante no me favorecía, pero Booster se veía genial. Resumía nuestra relación en tiempo real. Booster estaba feliz, ya que podía jugar con niños a los que adoraba mientras yo me preguntaba continuamente si alguna vez podría volver a hacerlo.

Después de dieciocho sesiones diarias de radiación, con fines de semana libres, Booster y yo regresamos a la cabaña. Volvió a ser él mismo y jugaba alegremente con su manada como si nada perjudicial hubiera ocurrido. Me tendí bajo el sol con Booster a mi lado como nunca antes. Lo abracé como si no hubiera mañana porque sabía que el mañana era ahora un lujo para Booster. Durante las seis semanas de radioterapia, empezó a perder el pelo de la cabeza. La radiación había reducido el tumor, pero el aspecto radiante de Booster era ahora diferente. En efecto, parecía un superviviente del cáncer, un héroe, pero era ajeno a su aspecto exterior. A diferencia de los humanos, que pueden desanimarse cuando su aspecto exterior cambia, Booster conservaba su confianza. Era un mártir y un modelo a seguir. ¡Más tarde le dije a Peggy que si Booster podía hacerlo, ella también!

Después de dos semanas de recuperación, Booster y yo volamos a la Universidad de Florida en Gainesville. Estábamos de nuevo, en otro vuelo, que no esperaba que ocurriera. Esta vez volábamos para que le abrieran el cráneo para extraer los restos del agresivo tumor. El Dr. Lurie nos citó con el Dr. Nicholas Bacon, un prestigioso neurocirujano inglés. El Dr. 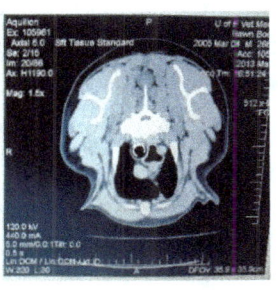 Bacon accedió a operar para extirpar lo que quedaba del tumor. Dejé a Booster en las sabias manos del Dr. Bacon y regresé abatido a mi apartamento vacío.

No podía soportar estar sin Booster. Él estaba en una jaula luchando por su vida. Yo tenía que hacer *algo*, así que fui a ver una película al campus de la universidad. Se titulaba *El último vuelo de Petr Ginz*. Las palabras "último vuelo" me obligaron a ir a ver la película. Para entonces, era más que consciente de que la *coincidencia* era una palabra clave que MPS utilizaba para decirme que iba por buen camino en la vida, junto con mi Booster.

Entré en la sala de proyección y vi a gente distinguida y bien vestida... era gente de mi edad y mayor. La película contaba una historia emocionalmente devastadora sobre un joven llamado Petr (Peter) que vivía en Praga. Fue encarcelado por los nazis durante el Holocausto. Petr tenía un talento asombroso y, a los dieciséis años, había hecho circular un periódico en el campo de prisioneros y pintado más de sesenta cuadros al óleo. Uno de sus cuadros de la Luna era una imagen especular de las primeras fotos de la Luna tomadas por los astronautas décadas más tarde.

Peter tenía un compañero de litera llamado Sydney que ayudaba a su padre a herrar los caballos para los soldados nazis. Un día, un soldado nazi vino a llevarse a los dos chicos a la cámara de gas. El padre de Sydney intervino y explicó que su hijo era el único que sabía ayudar a herrar los caballos. Sydney se salvó, pero el joven Peter, cuya imaginación lo llevó a la luna, y que pintaba tan maravillosamente, emprendió su "último vuelo" y murió prematuramente en una cámara de gas nazi.

Los escritos de Peter sobre el campo de prisioneros fueron encontrados más tarde, cuando su campo fue liberado. Acabaron en un desván de Holanda y sirvieron de base para la película que documenta su vida. Al final de la película, un anciano subió al escenario. Se llamaba Sydney Taussig. Fue compañero de litera de Peter décadas antes, un superviviente del Holocausto. Eché un vistazo al público, ¡y había pocas almas menores de treinta años en la audiencia de educación superior! El Sr. Taussig se había aferrado tenuemente a la posibilidad de vivir un día más, uno a la vez, igual que Booster.

Regresé a mi apartamento estéril sabiendo que Booster también estaba en el último vuelo de su vida. Empecé a castigarme a mí mismo—sí, maldita sea, otra vez—¡porque era tan cobarde! *Después de escuchar la historia del Sr. Taussig, ¿cómo me atrevía a pensar que la vida de un perro era igual de importante?* Había sido egoísta al pensar en esos términos. Yo era un hombre mayor que había escapado a una muerte potencial provocada por mis malas decisiones en la vida. El Sr. Taussig había escapado a la muerte por acontecimientos sobre los que no tenía control. Mucho más devastadora fue la muerte de Petr siendo joven. "Como una vela en el viento", su vida terminó prematuramente. Mi mente estaba con una sobrecarga sensorial. Empezaba a preocuparme de nuevo por los demás.

No sabía qué pensar ni cómo hacerlo. El mundo era malvado y no se suponía que funcionara así. ¿Por qué estaba ocurriendo esto? Seguramente se avecinaba una gran decepción, acechando a la vuelta de la esquina. Recibía actualizaciones periódicas sobre el estado de Booster por parte del personal del Dr. Bacons. Dos días después, sonó el teléfono y supe que iba a ser "ESA" llamada. "Sr. Hawn, el Dr. Bacon dice que puede venir a recoger a Booster por la mañana". Me quedé helado. No sabía que decir. Estaba en sobrecarga sensorial una vez más. El interruptor instalado por mi Poder Superior se activó antes de que yo entrara en cortocircuito.

Una hora más tarde, me recompuse y llamé al periódico Gainesville Sun. Les dije, "Quiero informar de un milagro". La Universidad de Florida coordinó una visita con un reportero del *Gainesville Sun.* Todos estaríamos presentes para visitar a mi Booster cuando saliera de la sala de recuperación. Más como un dron que como un ser humano, entré en las instalaciones veterinarias de la Universidad de Gainesville. Un funcionario de la universidad y el reportero del periódico me saludaron.

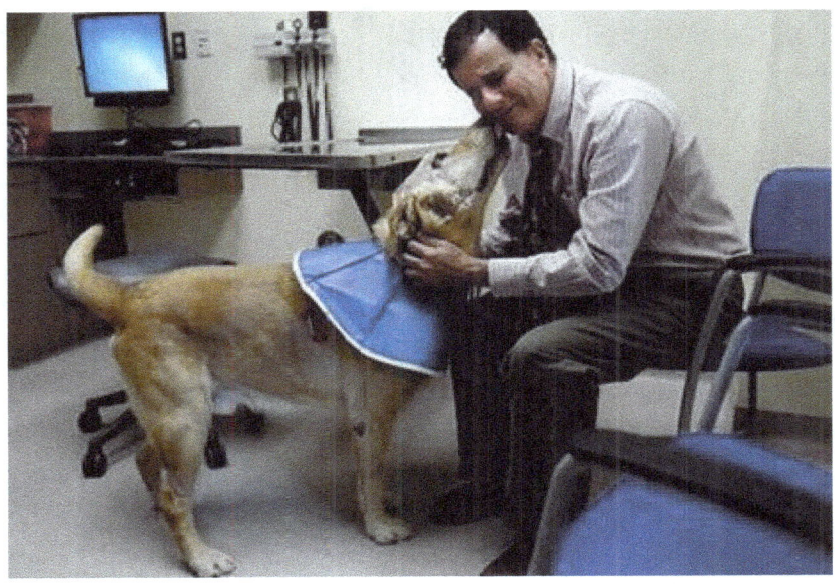

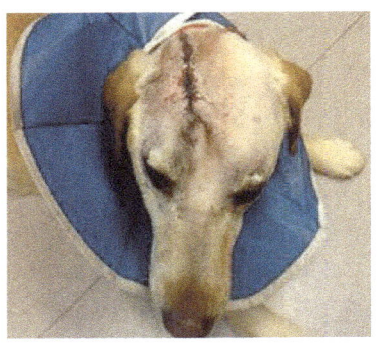 Poco después me llevaron a una habitación. Me senté en una silla y esperé. De repente, entró el Dr. Bacon con Booster, que llevaba un cono alrededor de la cabeza afeitada y cosida. Lloré y seguí llorando. Me caí de la silla al suelo y Booster se acercó y me besó en la cara. Estaba preocupado

por "MÍ". La cámara del fotógrafo parpadeó. Levanté la vista del suelo y busqué los ojos del Dr. Bacon, sin palabras. Con un esfuerzo hercúleo, pronuncié la palabra "gracias" con labios temblorosos. Mi cuerpo era como mantequilla derretida al sol.

El Dr. Bacon me explicó, "Puede que le den seis meses, quizá un año más", mientras Booster me lamía las lágrimas de los ojos.

Tenía puntos de sutura en la frente y no tenía pelo en el lado derecho de la cara. Parecía una creación de Frankenstein. Yo seguía mirando a Booster y él no dejaba de sonreír. Había aprendido mucho de él y sabía que tenía mucho más que enseñarme. Él y Bonnie fueron mentores milagrosos.

El día que Booster fue dado de alta del hospital veterinario de la Universidad de Florida, recibí una llamada de Bonnie. "¿Cómo está Booster y cómo estás *tú*, Davis?" Le dije a Bonnie que no sabía cómo responder a esa pregunta, "Estoy entumecido, y mi Booster está aparentemente sin dolor y continúa siendo 'Booster'". Seguía 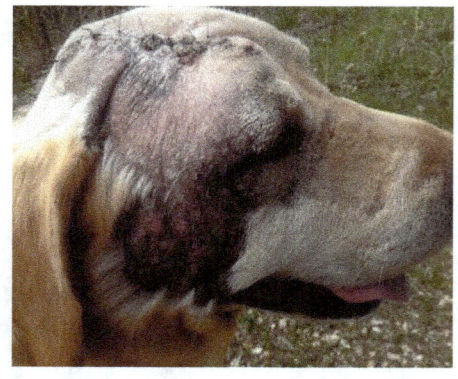 buscando cambios de personalidad por la operación cerebral, pero no encontré ninguno. El Dr. Lurie y el Dr. Bacon habían realizado una hazaña asombrosa y habían salvado la vida de un perro que había estado a pocas semanas de una muerte segura y dolorosa.

Unos días más tarde, mi Booster y yo volamos a casa. Me preocupaba que un empleado de la aerolínea pudiera pensar que tenía algún tipo de enfermedad. Le pedí al oncólogo que escribiera una carta con membrete oficial explicando el estado de salud de Booster. Cuando llegamos a casa, nos recibieron con abrazos y besos, unos sabuesos alegres que no conocían límites. Yo era feliz en ese momento. NOSOTROS éramos felices en ese momento. La vida era buena. ¡Entonces sonó el teléfono!

"Hola Davis, soy Liz Pluhar." Me explicó que las células cancerosas de carcinoma escamoso de Booster habían crecido prolíficamente dentro de los confines de la "placa de Petri de promesa".

"Por favor, dígame que tiene buenas noticias", le supliqué.

"¡Claro que sí!" exclamó con entusiasmo. Las células han crecido prolíficamente, parece prometedor.

"¿Cómo procedemos a partir de aquí?" pregunté.

"Dejemos que Booster, y su sistema inmunológico, se recuperen de la operación. Dentro de un mes, le enviaremos una dosis de la vacuna cada dos semanas hasta un total de seis dosis."

"Dra. Pluhar, no existen palabras que puedan expresar adecuadamente mi sincero aprecio, usted ha impactado dos vidas, no sólo una. Se lo agradecemos".

Otro rayo de esperanza iluminaba las oscuras nubes de la desesperación. ¿Cómo era posible que tales magnitudes mentales estuvieran trabajando para salvar la vida de mi Booster? Era divino. Nunca pensé que la humanidad tuviera dentro de sí la capacidad de proyectar semejante vista de arco iris panorámica sobre un telón de fondo de desesperanza.

Mi dedicación a los estudios en la BUCS no había sido una pérdida de tiempo y dinero, como predijo mi hermano adivino. De hecho, con los años, aprendí a consultarle las ideas a mi hermano. Si él pensaba que eran una locura, yo seguía adelante a toda máquina. El dinero invertido, junto con las horas de investigación iluminadora, culminaron aparentemente en un esfuerzo coordinado para salvar la vida de un perro que tanto lo merecía. Fue como si Mi Poder Superior se convirtiera en un contratista general, un director de orquesta de los mejores instrumentos conocidos por el hombre, para dirigir la salvación de mi Booster. Yo era un simple peón, moviéndose por el tablero de ajedrez de la vida.

Pasé cada momento con Booster. Mi corazón contaba los segundos que me quedaban para compartir con el bien más preciado que me ofrecía la vida. La realidad dictaba que no nos quedaba mucho tiempo, y yo quería estar ahí para Booster como él siempre había estado para mí. Me encantaba verlo coger los juguetes de peluche, guiando a los demás miembros de la familia en un juego de "sigue al líder". Corría alrededor del sofá con sus leales súbditos, solo para detenerse y correr en la dirección opuesta. A veces, el magnánimo gobernante se dejaba atrapar intencionadamente para provocar el inevitable juego de tira y afloja. La mayoría de las veces, la criatura de peluche perdía la vida. El relleno volaba, quedando mitad de un juguete en una boca y el resto en la otra.

Yo lanzaba pelotas de tenis al estanque y veía con alegría cómo Booster nadaba y las recuperaba triunfalmente. Lo mejor de todo es que era capaz de abrir la boca para soltar la pelota. Me había dolido mucho verlo el mes anterior. Nunca olvidaré cómo mi Booster cogía algo y de repente entraba en pánico. Había sido algo horrible. El miedo al dolor era posiblemente tan malo como el dolor mismo, pensé. Prefería haber sido objeto de tal destino que someter a mi Booster a él. Tal vez yo mereciera lo que la vida me había deparado, pero mi Booster, desde luego, no.

La vacuna que la Dra. Pluhar desarrolló ayudó a curar el cáncer de mi Booster. Fue el milagro de todos los milagros. Un año después, la Dra. Pluhar me explicó en un correo electrónico que, debido al rotundo éxito de la terapia con la vacuna, el gobierno federal había aprobado su uso en ensayos con humanos.

Me preguntaba si la respuesta de Booster a la vacuna había contribuido a obtener la aprobación del gobierno. Así que le pregunté a la Dra. Pluhar, "¿Puedo suponer que esta terapia que salvó la vida de Booster, puede ayudar a los humanos en un futuro próximo?"

Respondió a mi pregunta con dos letras mayúsculas... "SÍ!"

Muchos años después, fui al supermercado local. Mientras compraba, noté que una señora me miraba fijamente. No siendo un regalo de Dios para las mujeres, fue una sensación extraña. Estaba bajo vigilancia por alguna razón desconocida. *¿Quizás mi cremallera estaba abierta?* me pregunté. Después de unos quince minutos, mi acosadora gritó, "¡BOOSTER!"

¡Casi me caigo!

Ella empujó su carrito de compras junto al mío y dijo con toda naturalidad, "Mi esposo es el veterinario que le salvó la vida a su cachorro cuando ingirió veneno para ratas hace años. Ese cachorro tenía algo especial y nunca lo olvidé."

Con una sonrisa en mi rostro, le dije, "Si tomas ese móvil que tienes en la mano y haces una búsqueda en Internet de *Davis Hawn Booster*, obtendrás más de 10 páginas de historias de todo el mundo".

Luego pasé a explicarle que "cuando Booster tenía ocho años, le diagnosticaron un cáncer de carcinoma de células escamosas (CCE) y le dieron solo tres semanas de vida. Un tumor canceroso le había perforado su cráneo y pinchado un nervio".

En ese momento, ella se emocionó y empezó a llorar. "Me sorprende que eso te afecte tanto, sobre todo siendo la esposa de un veterinario. Seguro que sabes que uno de cada cuatro perros tendrá cáncer a lo largo de su vida, uno de cada dos después de los diez años."

"No, no lo entiendes, Dave. Mi esposo está luchando contra un CCE", me dijo con lágrimas en los ojos.

Otra *sorprendente coincidencia*, pensé en silencio. Adivinen quién tenía lágrimas en los ojos en ese momento. Como un pseudo-Paul Harvey, *le conté el resto de la historia*. Le expliqué cómo la Dra. Pluhar había tomado un trozo del tumor de Booster y había fabricado la primera vacuna CCE del mundo para un perro y que había curado su cáncer junto con RT. Luego le conté que la Universidad de Minnesota obtuvo más tarde la aprobación federal para realizar ensayos en humanos basándose en el éxito con los perros. Por último, le dije que le había preguntado a la Dra. Pluhar si la experiencia de mi Booster había contribuido a la aprobación de los ensayos en humanos y me dijo sin rodeos que sí, y que hoy en día se conoce como inmunoterapia. En ese momento, la mujer se emocionó aún más y empezó a llorar. "¿Qué te pasa?" le pregunté. Cuando recuperó la compostura, me explicó entre lágrimas, "Dave, mi esposo recibió recientemente un tratamiento de inmunoterapia para su carcinoma de células escamosas".

Con Buster en mi vida, la norma para mí era ver *coincidencia* tras *coincidencia*. Cuando me enteré, me quedé en shock, en shock absoluto. Booster podría haber contribuido a salvar la vida del veterinario que le había salvado la suya años atrás.

Parece una vez más, que lo que va vuelve, al menos en un mundo perfecto. Así veía el mundo mi Booster, que dedicó su vida a mejorar la de los demás. Con un ojo, veía el mundo mejor que la mayoría con dos. ¡Él se había convertido en el booster del mundo!

CAPÍTULO 15
PERÚ PARA NOSOTROS DOS

El cáncer de Booster se convirtió en mi cáncer. El diagnóstico de cáncer de mi Booster me dejó absolutamente destrozado. Ahora mis dos mejores amigos, mi Booster y Peggy, tenían la temida enfermedad que seguramente me los arrebataría en cualquier momento. Mi frágil mundo de recuperación sucumbió a un terremoto jamás experimentado en la escala Richter. Estaba aprendiendo a vivir la vida en sus términos, pero esto era algo totalmente fuera de lo común. De repente, sólo quería irme con mi

Booster. Necesitaba un respiro, así que reservé un boleto a Perú y me alojé en una casa de huéspedes de un hombre que adoraba a los perros. ¿Por qué Perú? ¿Por qué no?

Cuando llegamos a Lima, Perú, Booster fue inspeccionado por el veterinario del aeropuerto, que miró la cabeza de Booster, parecida a la de Frankenstein, envuelta en suturas.

El veterinario me miró como diciendo, ¿Qué diablos pasa aquí? No podía culparlo, ya que Booster parecía haber escapado de la morgue en medio de una autopsia. Miré al hombre con lágrimas en los ojos y le expliqué sobre el cáncer de Booster y la posible cura milagrosa. El caballero peruano me miró con empatía y selló los papeles, ya estábamos libres... o eso creía yo. Después de convencer a un taxista para que transportara a un perro en su taxi, llegamos a la casa de huéspedes.

Pronto nos enteramos de que me había equivocado de fecha y no había sitio en la posada hasta el día siguiente. Entré en pánico, absolutamente en pánico. Estábamos en un país extranjero sin un lugar donde alojarnos, pero recordé que la mayoría de las propiedades Hilton admiten mascotas. Pregunté si había un Hilton en Lima. El encargado de la pensión me dijo que sí. Llamé al Hilton en el hermoso distrito turístico de Miraflores, les expliqué mi dilema, que tenía a mi perro de servicio Booster, y que esperaba dormir en una habitación y no en la calle. La joven al otro lado del teléfono me aseguró al instante que me acogerían a mí y a mi Booster. Me quedé estupefacto. No podía hablar. Un meteorito de asombro golpeó mis cuerdas vocales.

"Señor, ¿está usted ahí?" preguntó la dulce voz.

"Sí, estoy aquí. Estoy sorprendido y muy agradecido", le dije. Yo no hablaba español en aquel momento, pero *casualmente* ella hablaba inglés con fluidez. Lo esencial de la conversación era que ella entendía el concepto de perro de servicio, y a Booster y a mí nos dieron la bienvenida en el Hilton. Nunca sabré cómo demonios una recepcionista de un país extranjero sabía algo así. Tal vez fuera por la excelencia del programa de formación del Hilton en acción. Tras llamar a un taxi y educar al conductor, llegamos al Hilton. ¡Nos recibieron con entusiasmo!

Pedí hablar con la persona que había respondido mi consulta telefónica. Una joven se me acercó tímidamente. Le expliqué mi asombro por su conocimiento del concepto de perro de servicio y le pedí que llamara al director para expresarle mi gratitud. Cuando llegó el director, hice todo lo posible por explicarle mis sentimientos. Le pregunté si tenían un departamento de relaciones públicas. Más tarde, ese mismo día, me senté con una representante de relaciones públicas, que realmente "lo entendió". Me citó con una periodista que hablaba poco inglés. Con la ayuda de su amiga traductora, le expliqué entre lágrimas lo que significaba para mí la políticas de puertas abiertas del Hilton, estando acompañado de mi perro de servicio Booster.

Esa misma noche, el conserje del Hilton nos consiguió entradas para ver la obra Annie. Estaba muy emocionado. Cuando intentamos entrar, nos pararon. *"Lo siento señor, no se le permite entrar al teatro con un perro"*, retumbó la voz. Estaba destrozado y enfadado. No sabía si gritar o llorar. Por un lado, nos trataban como a miembros de la realeza y, por otro, como a ciudadanos de segunda clase. Era como si nos hubieran preparado para una decepción. El colmo de la ironía era que tenían a un perro como artista, ¡acurrucado en los brazos del discapacitado Presidente Roosevelt! ¡Mirando hacia atrás, debería haber hecho lo que fuera necesario, incluso ir a la cárcel, para acentuar la repugnante ironía! El problema era, ¿qué habría pasado con mi Booster? A veces hay que poner un límite, aunque uno desearía no tener que hacerlo. Todo fue muy decepcionante, pero mantuve la compostura, como la BUCS y Booster me habían enseñado a hacer a lo largo de los años.

En otros tiempos, habría luchado por entrar. Habrían tenido que representar otra obra, *"Annie Get Your Gun"*, de Irving Berlin, la historia ficticia de una francotiradora. Tales circunstancias me brindaron la oportunidad de iluminar a los no ilustrados y educar a los ignorantes, sabiendo que "ignorancia" no es una palabra fea. Reflexioné sobre la entrevista que me habían hecho esa mañana, en la que me abrí y compartí detalles íntimos de mi vida. Ahora estaba más agradecido que nunca por haberlo hecho.

Al día siguiente, el reportaje apareció en el periódico más importante de Lima. Incluía innumerables fotos de mi Booster en acción. Una vez más, un reportero encontró mérito en el viaje de mi vida con Booster a mi lado. Fue una validación de la más alta magnitud. Sí, reaccioné con lágrimas de emoción, pero ¿fue esa una reacción desmedida?

Después de leer la última línea de la noticia del periódico, me emocioné totalmente. Hacía referencia a la Ley de Concientización 29830 del Perú que establece que los *perros de asistencia pueden ingresar a todos los lugares públicos y privados, incluidos los medios de transporte.* Tomé el periódico en la mano y me dirigí a un cine local. Cuando entré en el cine, el guardia de seguridad intentó detenernos, pero lo esquivamos rápidamente. Compré caramelos y palomitas y entré en la sala de proyección. Un empleado del cine entró corriendo, diciendo que no se permitían perros en la sala.

"¿Me venden palomitas y luego quieren echarme?" le pregunté. Le enseñé nuestra historia en el periódico y se la llevó a su encargado, que se enfrentó a mí poco después. El gerente quería echarme del cine. Le pedí amablemente que llamara a la policía para que documentaran la discriminación y la violación de la ley. El gerente me entregó mi periódico y se marchó. No tenía ni idea de lo que iba a ocurrir a continuación, pero con Booster a mi lado y mi periódico en la mano, no tenía miedo. Booster tenía un ángel sobre sus hombros una y otra vez. La película era en español y yo no tenía ni idea de lo que se decía. Pensé, *¡gané la batalla pero perdí la guerra!* Después de la película, armados con el periódico, visitamos un restaurante Chili's local y no encontramos resistencia.

Investigué la ley con la ayuda de unos peruanos amables, que se disculparon por los problemas que enfrenté mientras visitaba su ciudad. Resulta que la ley se aprobó para el acceso de los perros guía, sin incluir a los perros de asistencia. Con frecuencia, se permite el acceso a los perros guía antes de que se apruebe una ley más inclusiva para los perros de asistencia. La discapacidad de la ceguera es más evidente y suele suscitar más simpatía, comprensión y voluntad de adaptación.

Más tarde, una señora encantadora se puso en contacto conmigo y me explicó que tenía un blog a través del cual promocionaba Lima. Le  expliqué que mi respeto por la ciudad había decaído al ser fríamente rechazado la noche anterior, al no poder ver una obra de teatro por ser una persona con discapacidad. Ella publicó con empatía mi historia en su blog. Revelar al mundo tu alma dañada, sobre todo si eres una persona que ha hecho silencio durante mucho tiempo, no es fácil. Su blog se llamaba LimaEasy. Cuando leí nuestra historia en el blog, ¡me sorprendió el tiempo que invirtió en escribirla! Todo estaba allí, con lujo de detalles.

Más tarde, fui invitado a visitar una escuela veterinaria mientras estaba en la ciudad. El director era un caballero afable y cortés. Consiguió que Booster fuera visto por uno de los pocos especialistas en óptica canina del país,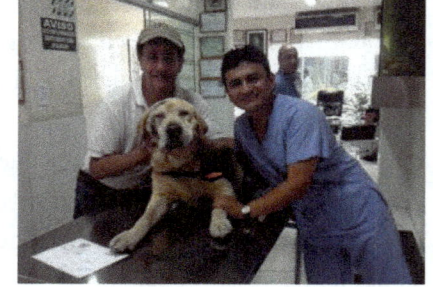

que *coincidencialmente* ejercía en la facultad de veterinaria de Lima. Le expliqué que había estado poniendo gotas en el ojo seco de Booster cinco veces al día como resultado de la radioterapia. El examinó a Booster y me explicó que el ojo había muerto como resultado de la radioterapia que había recibido. También me dijo que, cuando está seco, es doloroso, y sugirió que se lo extirpara. "Los perros se desempeñan muy bien con un solo ojo", me aseguró. Lamentablemente, Booster necesitaría otra cirugía transformadora.

En Lima experimenté más cosas buenas que malas, y estoy agradecido de que Booster y yo pudiéramos dejar huella en otra sociedad distinta a la nuestra. Fue un gran honor poder compartir con el alma y con pasión y que respondieran con empatía. Mis experiencias en Lima fueron parte de un proceso de sanación mayor que tuvo lugar, como resultado directo de la bendición de tener a Booster en mi vida.

CAPÍTULO 16
ENOJADO

Cuando regresé a casa, pedí a mi veterinario de Arkansas que extrajera el ojo muerto de Booster. Me aseguró que era un procedimiento relativamente fácil, y todo salió bien. Ya no tenía que poner gotas lubricantes en su ojo cinco veces al día. Estaba seguro de que se sentiría más cómodo. El veterinario peruano estaba en lo cierto, ya que nunca pareció hacer una diferencia para Booster. Era el mismo Booster, positivo y enérgico de siempre.

Continué trabajando en mi parque de casas móviles y seguí adelante con mi vida y mi familia canina. Con el tiempo, compré un terreno en la cima de una montaña en Arkansas y construí una gran casa de madera de tres pisos. Pronto me di cuenta de que las niguas y garrapatas de la propiedad tenían un apetito voraz. Eran como pequeños tanques y portaban enfermedades potencialmente mortales que afectaban tanto a animales como a humanos.

Mientras caminaba con mi grupo por los senderos, me di cuenta de que las caderas deterioradas de Booster le estaban causando dolor, como lo evidenciaba su cojera. Pensé que podría ser el momento para otra inyección de células madre en la cadera, ya que sabía que los beneficios de la implantación de células madre no eran permanentes. Llamé a Medi-Vet America y conseguí que Booster recibiera otra ronda de terapia con células madre. La semana siguiente fuimos a una clínica de nuestro estado natal, Mississippi. Invité a la prensa. Cuando llegaron, les expliqué que mi perro de servicio Booster iba a verse obligado a jubilarse debido a una displasia de cadera. También les expliqué que lo iban a someter a una segunda ronda de terapia con células madre para mejorar su movilidad y aliviar el dolor, en un esfuerzo por prolongar su vida laboral. Booster demostró sus habilidades mientras las cámaras tomaban fotos y videos.

Booster abrió la puerta de mi camioneta y entró a buscar una botella de agua. Le susurré al oído, "Sé que duele". Uno de los reporteros escuchó mis palabras y las citó en un artículo del *USA Today* e incluyó imágenes de video. El astuto y empático reportero comprendió que mi relación con Booster era realmente especial. Tanto Booster como yo experimentábamos dolor en nuestra vida cotidiana y en nuestros rituales. Cada uno conocía el sufrimiento del otro. Estoy seguro de que es un concepto difícil de entender para muchos, pero es muy cierto. No hay nada que mi Booster no haría por mí, y nada que yo no haría por mi Booster. Nuestra relación era puramente simbiótica. Todos somos animales, seres sensibles, capaces de amar y cuidar.

Después de la demostración, a Booster le inyectaron células madre derivadas de tejido adiposo en sus caderas displásicas, con la esperanza de reconstruir el tejido afectado. Los milagros siempre ocurrían en la "vida sin coincidencias" de mi Booster, así que esperaba que el procedimiento le ayudara como lo había hecho antes. El procedimiento salió bien y regresamos a casa ese mismo día.

Unas semanas más tarde, Booster y los miembros de su familia canina subieron a la camioneta y nos dirigimos a nuestro refugio en la cima de una montaña en Arkansas. Tiempo después, recibí a Booster con mi habitual y recién descubierta alegría de vivir. Él estaba enfermo. Movía la cola, pero no podía levantarse. Se me paró el corazón y entré en pánico. Llamé a mi veterinario de Arkansas, quien nos atendió enseguida y le puso una inyección. Booster estuvo bien durante un día, y luego volvió al mismo abismo de impotencia. Se hundía rápidamente.

Volví a visitar a mi veterinario y él me remitió a una clínica de urgencias en Springfield, Missouri. Los veterinarios de la clínica de urgencias me enviaron al Hospital de Enseñanza Veterinaria de la Universidad de Missouri (MIZZOU). Inmediatamente llamé a la universidad y les informé que estábamos en camino. Horas más tarde, llegamos al hospital. Miembros voluntarios del personal nos ayudaron a subir el cuerpo lánguido de Booster a un carro.

Llevamos a Booster a la sala de espera. Caminaba en círculos y luego empezó a darse cabezazos contra la jaula. Tenía encefalitis y el cerebro inflamado. Mientras la Dra. Melissa Carpentier examinaba a Booster, le expliqué que había viajado por el mundo y que había estado expuesto a toxinas, lo que complicaba cualquier posible diagnóstico. La Dra. Carpentier dijo que tomaría medidas inmediatas para intentar ayudar a Booster. Ordenó antibióticos y pruebas de todo tipo. Por supuesto, tenía que ser un fin de semana festivo, ¿no? Era el Día de los Caídos, y los resultados de las pruebas se retrasarían. La Dra. Carpentier le ordenó todo lo que pudo, sin saber a qué nos enfrentábamos.

Esa noche, me fui a una habitación de hotel vacía y lloré a lágrima viva. Dudaba que Booster sobreviviera esa noche. Llamé a mi hermano, quien me sugirió suavemente que "lo dejara ir". Mi hermano compartió su opinión, me dijo que Booster estaba cansado, ya había sufrido bastante, y yo necesitaba dejarlo ir.

Le expliqué con determinación, "Quiero a mi Booster con todo mi corazón y yo, más que nadie, no quiero causarle dolor y sufrimiento". Los especialistas aún no han determinado qué le pasa, y no voy a abandonar prematuramente a mi mejor amigo. Yo no le diría a 'tu' médico que dejara de tratarte sin saber siquiera qué te pasa . . . ¡y tú eres mucho mayor que Booster!" Había aprendido a hablar claro y a no tener tanto miedo a la confrontación, pero sólo cuando se trataba de defender a mi Booster. Pasaron años para poder incorporar esa fuerza interior a mi vida personal. Booster me enseñó a luchar por las cosas que más importaban en la vida. También pensé en todas las veces que después de escuchar el consejo de mi hermano, había hecho lo contrario, ¡lo que resultaba ser la decisión correcta!

Le recordé a mi hermano la vez que nuestro padre estuvo gravemente enfermo. Mi padre tenía neumonía y estaba al borde de la muerte. Su internista de entonces sugirió que lo dejáramos marchar. Mi padre había firmado la orden de "no reanimación". ¡Le expliqué al internista que mi padre no quiso decir que lo dejaran morir si estaba resfriado! Encontré a un neumólogo que dijo que, con la medicación apropiada, mi padre probablemente sobreviviría. Una vez consumada la batalla de jerarquías médicas, el neumólogo se hizo cargo y mi padre vivió muchos años con una calidad de vida mejor que la que tenía antes.

A la mañana siguiente, llamé a Medi-Vet America y les pregunté si habían tenido casos en los que la terapia con células madre hubiera fracasado. "¿Alguna vez han tenido un perro que contrajera una infección, o tuviera una reacción adversa grave, como resultado de los procedimientos de implantación de células madre?" pregunté. El personal médico de la empresa me habló sin rodeos, fueron empáticos y sinceros. Investigaron en su banco de datos y me explicaron que se trataba de una anomalía total que muy probablemente no estaba asociada al procedimiento. Por el tono de sus voces, confié en ellos. Llamé a la Dra. Carpentier y le transmití la respuesta recibida del personal de Medi-Vet. Luego, le envié fotos de excrementos de rata que había encontrado dentro de mi casa, donde almacenaba comida para perros. Le expliqué que había investigado en Internet y había descubierto que los perros pueden contraer enfermedades por ingerir excrementos de rata. Algunos de los síntomas de las enfermedades asociadas se parecían a los que presentaba Booster.

Luego de escucharme pacientemente, me dio las gracias por la información. Después de todo, mi Booster no era un perro corriente. Había viajado por todo el mundo, a países exóticos que tienen enfermedades que rara vez, o nunca, se ven en los EE.UU. Me explicó que Booster no estaba mejor, PERO tampoco estaba peor.

Entonces le conté que me había puesto en contacto con otro veterinario que una vez le había salvado la vida a Booster cuando sólo le quedaban tres semanas debido a un carcinoma de células escamosas. Tras explicarle que la Dra. Pluhar había desarrollado la primera vacuna del mundo, hecha a la medida, para tratar el carcinoma de células escamosas en nombre de Booster, le pregunté a la Dra. Carpentier si estaría dispuesta a hablar con la Dra. Pluhar. *Casualmente*, ¡resultó que la Dra. Pluhar le enseñó a la Dra. Carpentier cuando era estudiante de veterinaria en la Universidad de Minnesota! ¿Quieres adivinar mi respuesta al oír esas palabras? por supuesto. Lloré y supe que MPS estaba actuando en mi vida. El factor *coincidencia* fue totalmente *borrado*, ya no era una posibilidad. Muchos pensamientos asaltaron mi cerebro hasta el máximo de su capacidad.

Visité a Booster más tarde ese mismo día y disfruté el contacto con su cálido pelaje. Mientras lo abrazaba con fuerza, le susurré al oído, "Te amo". Mi corazón ardía. Estaba solo, en otro estado, y me sentía desesperado. *¿Qué demonios está pasando y por qué?* Peor aún era el hecho de que no habría respuestas, ya que la calamidad de Booster ocurrió un fin de semana festivo. ¡Vaya vacaciones!

Milagrosamente, Booster luchó como siempre lo hacía. Pronto supe que tenía Fiebre Maculosa de las Montañas Rocosas (FMMR) por una picadura de garrapata. Días después, la Dra. Carpentier me llamó y me dijo que podía ir a visitar a Booster esa tarde. Me dijo que creía que estaba un poco mejor. Fui al hospital y Booster me reconoció de inmediato. Su lengua azotó mi cara con amor y agradecimiento innegables. De alguna manera, sabía que yo luchaba junto a él, siempre presente a su lado. Al instante supe que estaba mejor. Conocía a Booster así como él me conocía a mí. Éramos realmente simbióticos. Éramos uno.

Más tarde, mi disgusto se convirtió en enojo cuando pensé en cómo el medicamento contra pulgas y garrapatas en el que confiaba para proteger a mi Booster falló y puso en peligro su vida. Llamé al "principal fabricante estadounidense" del producto defectuoso y le expliqué, "Su medicamento contra las garrapatas falló y mi perro casi muere por ello. Creo que lo menos que pueden hacer es cubrir sus facturas médicas, si sobrevive". En la típica negación corporativa, recibí una llamada unos días después: "Nuestro producto no garantiza la protección contra la FMMR". Fue una respuesta de lo siento y vete al carajo. "¡Oye idiota, si su producto hiciera la ÚNICA COSA para la que fue diseñado, prevenir las picaduras de garrapatas, no sería posible contraer la FMMR y otras enfermedades transmitidas por garrapatas!"

Al cabo de una semana, Booster, que una vez más había estado a punto de morir, se iba a casa. Posteriormente supe que la Dra. Carpentier había sacrificado a su propio perro el día que salvó la vida de Booster. Más tarde me confesó que no estaba segura de que Booster fuera a sobrevivir. En el fondo de mi corazón, sabía que salvar la vida de Booster había servido de consuelo a la doctora, que había tenido que despedirse de su mejor amigo canino. Mentiría si no dijera que derramé lágrimas por la Dra. Carpentier. Conocía ese dolor único. El pegamento del amor es muy fuerte. El Puente del Arco Iris cobra un alto peaje emocional.

Sorprendentemente, unas semanas después, un representante de relaciones públicas de MIZZOU se puso en contacto conmigo para hacer un reportaje sobre la experiencia de Booster en el Hospital Veterinario Universitario. Aparecería en la página web del Centro de Salud Veterinaria de Mizzou. Estuve encantado, ya que era lo menos que podíamos hacer por la institución que salvó la vida de mi Booster. ¡Mi Booster pronto se convertiría también en su *Booster*!

Cuando llegamos a casa, la manada vino corriendo a ver a su exaltado pero agotado líder. Corrieron de un lado para otro y Booster cogió un peluche y jugó al tira y afloja. Después de unos minutos, puse fin al juego e hice que Booster se relajara. Booster estaba en casa y viviría para ver otro día. Pensé en lo prolíficas que eran las garrapatas en Arkansas y en muchas partes del país, y en la cantidad de enfermedades que transmiten. Después de cada excursión por el bosque, veía garrapatas en mis hijos caninos y en las perneras de mis pantalones. En ocasiones, las garrapatas se caían de mis perros dentro de la casa. La garrapata que casi mata a Booster podría haberme infectado y matado con facilidad. Muchos lugareños de Arkansas contrajeron la "fiebre de las garrapatas" cuando eran niños. Aprendí que era insoportablemente dolorosa. Un hombre dijo que era como si tuvieras la cabeza en una prensa y alguien estuviera apretando el tornillo cada vez más.

Muchas familias deciden no atender a sus mascotas por costo o ignorancia. Mis vecinos del campo tenían varios perros con garrapatas hinchadas por todo el cuerpo. "Es sólo un perro y las garrapatas les salen. No voy a arrancar ninguna garrapata de ningún perro", me dijeron desafiantes cuando les sugerí que quitaran las garrapatas de sus sufridos perros. Me correspondía a mí intentar hacer algo después de presenciar el sufrimiento potencialmente mortal que acompañaba a algo tan simple como una picadura de garrapata.

Como por control remoto, tomé el teléfono, llamé a mi veterinario de Arkansas y le pregunté si estaría dispuesto a hacer un reportaje conmigo. Quería mejorar las vidas humanas y caninas. La gente debía saber que, al utilizar medicamentos contra garrapatas y pulgas para sus perros, también protegían la vida de los miembros de su familia. El Dr. Mark Whitmore aceptó ayudar a transmitir el mensaje. Luego, llamé al periódico *Harrison Daily News* de la cercana Harrison, Arkansas. Dos días más tarde, nos reunimos con un reportero, y la historia se publicó poco después. Si la historia de Booster evitaba que un solo animal o persona (niño o adulto) contrajera una enfermedad potencialmente mortal y sufriera un dolor insoportable, su terrible experiencia habría servido de algo.

Con una decidida determinación de vivir, un perro de servicio vence a la fiebre maculosa de las Montañas Rocosas.

Por DAVID HOLSTED davidh@harrisondaily.com 19 de junio de 2014

Davis Hawn (derecha) agradece al Dr. Mark Whitmore y al personal de la Clínica Veterinaria del Condado de Boone por salvar a Booster, su labrador dorado de 10 años, de un caso de fiebre maculosa de las Montañas Rocosas. Lee H. Dunlap/Staff

Aproximadamente un año después, asistimos a la Conferencia sobre Bienestar Animal en el Caribe, celebrada en Trinidad y Tobago.

No tuvimos ningún problema para que nos llevaran y trajeran en taxi. Booster y yo conocimos a todo tipo de gente interesante, incluido un profesor universitario de Costa Rica que nos invitó a dar una conferencia en la Universidad de Costa Rica. Me dio el nombre de una señora con la que debía reunirme para organizar la conferencia, así que Booster y yo tomamos un taxi y nos reunimos con la señora, que estaba en el campus. Me explicó que los estudiantes estaban de vacaciones y que no se explicaba por qué nos habían invitado a dar una conferencia cuando no había estudiantes. Estaba avergonzada y yo simplemente le seguí la corriente.

Entonces nos dijo que tenía un contacto en el sistema escolar de una pequeña ciudad llamada Manuel Antonio y que podíamos visitar a los niños allí. Le pregunté, "¿Estás segura?" y ella me confirmó que así sería. Al día siguiente, Booster y yo hicimos un viaje de dos horas en taxi hasta el pueblo. Nos alojamos en un complejo que no aceptaba mascotas dirigido por un alemán que entendía el concepto de perro de servicio y nos permitió quedarnos en su resort. Por la mañana, tomamos un taxi hasta una escuela primaria donde nos recibieron los profesores.

Booster hizo lo de siempre y se ganó el corazón de los niños que terminaron adorándolo. Hacía mucho calor y los dos estábamos un poco abrumados. Cuando terminamos nuestra demostración, un profesor me informó que teníamos que hacer otra presentación para otro grupo de edad. Booster estaba cansado y yo sabía que le dolían las caderas. Le expliqué mis preocupaciones e hice una demostración más corta al segundo grupo de niños. Hacia el final de la demostración, a Booster le fallaban las caderas y se deslizó en el suelo para recuperarse. Invité a los niños a acariciarlo y nos fuimos poco después.

Al día siguiente, tomamos un taxi para ir a ver la famosa Reserva Natural y Refugio de Fauna de Manuel Antonio. Fuimos hasta la entrada para comprar un boleto, pero no querían dejar entrar a Booster. Le expliqué el concepto de perro de servicio y por qué necesitaba un perro. El hombre sonrió y dijo, "Señor, usted no entiende". Milagrosamente, mantuve la boca cerrada. Escuché y aprendí. "Señor, aquí hay muchos monos. Están en lo alto de los árboles y suelen alterarse al ver un animal extraño; son territoriales. No quiero que los monos le hagan daño a su perro". Esta fue la explicación más lógica y razonable que había oído en más de diez años para denegar el acceso a Booster.

También dijo que los visitantes debían caminar mucho para llegar a la playa. Ninguno de los dos éramos capaces de caminar, sobre todo bajo un sol abrasador. El hombre permitió entonces que el taxi nos llevara. Fue una idea maravillosa, y se lo agradecí enormemente. Poco después llegamos a la playa. Efectivamente, los monos que había encima empezaron a parlotear como un grupo de ancianas jugando bingo. Se habían agitado ante la presencia del intruso canino.

Caminamos rápidamente hasta la playa, que carecía de árboles y monos emocionados. En el fondo, los monos seguían expresando su descontento. Yo pensé que los monos nos arrojarían cosas, pero llegamos a la playa antes de que se dieran cuenta. Booster corrió un par de veces hacia las olas que entraban y salían. Arañó la arena y la lanzó hacia atrás entre sus patas. En veinte minutos estaba cansado pero feliz. Llamé al taxista y volvimos a nuestro hotel. A la mañana siguiente, dimos un largo paseo hasta el aeropuerto y volamos a casa. Cuando entramos en la cabaña, la manada vino corriendo a saludar a Booster.

Dos días después, me desperté y encontré a Booster en el suelo de la sala. Al instante supe que si no estaba a mi lado, algo debía ir mal. Tuve una sensación de pesadumbre, igual que la vez que me desperté a las 2 de la madrugada y encontré a Booster abatido en el suelo de la cocina cuando había ingerido veneno para ratas. Cuando me acerqué a Booster, que movía cariñoso su cola y tenía esa sonrisa que tanto adoraba, ¡¡¡BOOM, me di cuenta!!! Oh, MPS, me sentí muy golpeado. Las patas de mi Booster estaban paralizadas. Sus piernas eran como fideos flácidos, 100% inútiles.

Rompí a llorar y abracé a Booster con fuerza. No podía entender lo que le había pasado. Estaba tan indefenso. Yo también había estado indefenso alguna vez, pero no así. Fue devastador. Mi Booster yacía en el suelo, incapaz de moverse, despojado de su dignidad mientras orinaba y defecaba en su posición necesariamente boca abajo. Llamé a mi amigo Chris para que me ayudara a meter a Booster en la camioneta para ir al veterinario de urgencias.

Sabía que esto era "todo". Incluso un gato sólo tiene nueve vidas. ¿Booster sobrevivió al cáncer para morir parapléjico sumergido en orina y heces? ¿EN SERIO? De nuevo, la vida era un engaño cruel. Esto estaba mal. Sentí que Booster era la encarnación del dolor y de las experiencias cercanas a la muerte. Quería tanto a mi Booster y no podía entender por qué MPS le había hecho pasar por tantas cosas a él y a los mortales que lo amábamos. Llegamos al consultorio del veterinario y llevamos a Booster dentro. El Dr. Beacham y su ayudante miraron a Booster y luego me miraron a mí. No, miraron *mi* interior. Sabían muy bien todo lo que yo estaba sufriendo. Booster recibió una inyección y mi veterinario, el príncipe de los hombres, me dijo que no me rindiera con Booster.

El Dr. Beacham me sugirió que me pusiera en contacto con la Dra. Pluhar y la Dra. Carpentier quienes me habían ayudado en el pasado. Seguí su consejo y llamé a la Dra. Carpentier. Me dijo que condujera hasta Missouri y que nos vería enseguida. Llamé a mi amigo Warren y me acompañó en el viaje. Warren y yo condujimos toda la noche con mi Booster incapacitado. Alquilamos una habitación de hotel con un patio de césped y una puerta exterior. Llevamos a Booster afuera, y yo dije, "Vacía", la orden para decirle a Booster que orinara y defecara. Booster orinó y defecó tumbado de lado. Me dolió por Booster ya que él sabía que no había "vaciado" donde debía. Booster siempre defecaba levantando el trasero y arrojándolo a un arbusto. Nunca le había enseñado a hacerlo. Era genial porque no tenía que sacar la bolsa de plástico cuando sus heces caían sobre la flora.

Al día siguiente, fuimos a la consulta de la Dra. Carpentier. Trabajaba para la Universidad de Missouri (MIZZOU), pero también era socia de un consultorio privado. Llegamos a la puerta de su clínica y una joven nos recibió con un carrito. Subimos el cuerpo incapacitado de Booster al carro y lo introdujimos en la

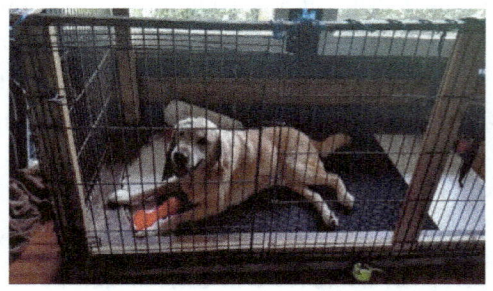

clínica. La Dra. Carpentier nos saludó, examinó a Booster y ordenó una resonancia magnética. Los resultados evidenciaron una pequeña contracción que afectaba las vértebras del cuello, pero nada que explicara la tetraplejia que sufría Booster. La Dra. Carpentier sugirió suavemente que "podría ser ese momento". Yo respetaba mucho su opinión. Después de todo, había salvado la vida de Booster el día en que tuvo que sacrificar a su querido perro. Era una heroína incuestionable de proporciones inconmensurables.

Llamé a mi veterinario, el Dr. Beacham. Él me sugirió que pusiera a Booster en un régimen de esteroides a pesar de que había recibido medicamentos contraindicados para los esteroides. Le di las gracias a la Dra. Carpentier y llevé a Booster a casa. Creo que no se dijo ni una palabra. Aunque Booster no podía mover sus extremidades, estaba agradecido de que no tuviera dolor. Cuando llegamos a casa, construí un bonito ático para mi Booster. Si alguna vez alguien merecía una vivienda tan especial, era mi Booster. Construí un corral de alambre de 5x12 en mi sala, instalé un bebedero que se rellenaba automáticamente, forré el suelo

con linóleo impermeable y taladré un agujero de media pulgada en el suelo de mi cabaña.

Booster nunca me había fallado y no había nada que no hiciera por él. Me había salvado la vida y lo quería más que a la vida misma. Debo decir que Booster sabía que yo haría lo que fuera necesario. Por mucho que lo dudara, él había engañado a la muerte en tantas ocasiones que había llegado a saber que yo lo rescataría. No lo relacionaba con la codependencia y el fenómeno de "rescatar al pájaro herido". Booster sabía que yo estaría ahí para él, como yo sabía que él estaría ahí para mí. Muchos dirán que se trata de un ejemplo extremo de antropomorfismo, pero yo les aseguro que no es así.

Un día, metí a mi Booster en mi camioneta y conduje hasta una tienda de suministros local. Compré un carro que se suele utilizar para arrastrar las macetas del jardín y lonas de plástico. Luego pasé por un Mickie D's y le compré a Booster dos hamburguesas, le di un poco de agua y nos fuimos a casa. A la mañana siguiente, construí una rampa en el lateral de mi porche elevado. Clavé una lona en la parte delantera de la cabaña y la extendí hasta el patio. Booster ahora tenía entrada y salida con un carro tirado a mano, y sombra para que pudiera tumbarse en el patio.

Cada mañana me levantaba y subía el cuerpo de Booster al carro verde de la salvación. Lo sacaba por la puerta principal por la que había caminado durante más de una década. Luego lo llevaba por los campos que una vez había recorrido cargando una zanahoria cuando era cachorro. Tiraba del carro de mi Booster arriba y abajo, a izquierda y derecha, como si fuera el Rey del Carnaval. Ni una sola vez se quejó, ni gimoteó, ni se rebeló. Era un príncipe en todo el sentido de la palabra. Oh, MPS, amaba tanto a mi Booster. ¿Cómo podía ser tan valiente cuando yo había sido un cobarde en mi vida?

Había escuchado el mantra de Al-Anon durante años: *Dios concédeme la serenidad para aceptar las cosas que no puedo cambiar, cambiar las cosas que puedo y la sabiduría para conocer la diferencia.* Booster encarnaba lo que Al-Anon exaltaba. Aceptó su destino y nunca se rindió. A su vez, yo respetaba tanto a Booster que nunca me rendí. Pensé en un adhesivo que adornaba el cuarto de baño de mi madre cuando tenía cáncer de pulmón terminal, "Los milagros siempre ocurren". Ese adhesivo animaba a mi madre a seguir adelante y hacer frente a la adversidad. Me quedé con el recuerdo de ese adhesivo y seguí adelante en la vida con Booster.

Semanas después, me desperté y vi cómo Booster arrastraba el cuerpo por el suelo con sus patas delanteras para saludarme cuando me dirigía a su corral. Pensé que estaba soñando. "Hola, Booster, buenos días", le dije con entusiasmo. Abrí la puerta del corral y Booster arrastró su cuerpo a través de la puerta. Lloré con mucha fuerza, quizás nunca en mi vida había llorado así. Empecé a hiperventilar al verlo luchar con su recién encontrada independencia, tal como era. Me senté en el suelo y Booster volvió a lamerme las lágrimas de los ojos.

Booster era muy valiente. Era un luchador sin límites. Se negaba a darse por vencido. Corrí al teléfono y llamé al Dr. Beacham, a la Dra. Carpentier y a la Dra. Pluhar. Les dije que "Booster había recuperado el uso de sus extremidades delanteras". Los tres doctores estaban asombrados por el progreso de Booster. Les pregunté si también podría recuperar el uso de las extremidades posteriores. "Sólo tenemos que esperar y ver", respondieron. El Dr. Beacham me contó un caso en el que una familia no podía pagar una operación cuando su perro sufrió una parálisis. Le dio esteroides y se recuperó totalmente. Al instante pensé en el adhesivo de mi madre que tenía en su cuarto de baño, "Los milagros siempre ocurren". Al cabo de un mes, Booster recuperó el uso de todas sus extremidades, aunque su manera de andar se vio afectada. Nunca sabremos cuál fue la causa de la parálisis. Booster se negó a rendirse y a dejarme solo en el mundo. Sabía que lo necesitaba; su trabajo en la tierra aún no había terminado.

CAPÍTULO 17
EL CORAZÓN Y EL ALMA DE LA CLONACIÓN

Mientras vivía con Booster, experimenté un renacimiento educativo personal. La BUCS fue un catalizador para mi enriquecimiento educativo. La Dra. Bergin fue la alquimista que proporcionó la mezcla justa de estrés y estímulo para encender la pasión educativa que llevaba dentro. Mientras investigaba para una clase de genética en la BUCS, encontré por casualidad un artículo relacionado con la clonación. Quedé fascinado con un tema que había oído discutir a menudo en la prensa. Había ido a la BUCS como un viejo chocho, ansioso por aprender. Como una esponja seca que es sumergida en agua por primera vez, absorbí todo lo que pude en todas las direcciones. Pronto me di cuenta de que la clonación era única en el sentido de que involucraba ciencia, política y religión, todo ello envuelto en un polémico paquete.

Cuanto más leía sobre la clonación, más me fascinaba y motivaba. Leí sobre el profesor coreano Hwang Woo-Suk. Con el intelecto de Einstein y el entusiasmo de un niño en la mañana de Navidad, publicó un trabajo de investigación en el que ensalzaba su supuesto éxito en el establecimiento de una línea de células madre. Cuando otros científicos se maravillaron de su trabajo, pero no consiguieron replicarlo, sus hallazgos se consideraron fraudulentos. También se le acusó de apropiarse de dinero en el camino, pero eso no es precisamente algo único en la investigación médica y la venta de productos farmacéuticos. Algunos dicen que era auténtico y altruista, pero otros afirman que era egocéntrico y usurero. Aunque supuestamente soñaba con devolver la movilidad a los discapacitados y curar las enfermedades que asolaban a la humanidad, sin duda se adelantó a su tiempo al no respetar lo políticamente correcto, ya que compró óvulos a una de sus estudiantes de posgrado para establecer una línea de células madre y tal vez intentar clonar un embrión humano.

Con el tiempo, el otrora respetado profesor cayó en el ostracismo mientras asociados, estudiantes y funcionarios del gobierno se distanciaban de un hombre que personificaba la fragilidad humana. Al sucumbir a la presión internacional de la comunidad científica, el gobierno coreano presentó cargos contra él para salvar las apariencias. Cuando estaba en su peor momento, recibía limosnas en la calle. Un hombre paralítico le dio un donativo y le dijo, "Sé que algún día su trabajo me ayudará a volver a caminar".

Yo también había caído en picada en la vida, era débil, me rendí y estuve a punto de tomar el camino fácil. En la cultura coreana, el suicidio es una opción honorable. Hasta el día de hoy, creo que el querido profesor no optó por esa salida porque quería mejorar la vida de los demás. Sufrió humillaciones de proporciones épicas y amenazas de cárcel, y aun así se vio fortalecido por su sed de conocimientos y el deseo desinteresado de ayudar a los demás. Mientras investigaba sobre el hombre, comencé a identificarme con él. Sentí una conexión con un alma gemela en Seúl que nunca había conocido… un alma que no sabía que yo existía.

Una mañana, miré a Booster y me eché a llorar. Se levantó con dificultad y caminó hacia mí. Me incliné para acariciarlo y me rozó la mejilla con amor. Me llenó de babas a las que pronto se unió un afluente de lágrimas. Mi roca se estaba erosionando; mi Booster estaba envejeciendo. Había sobrevivido a una posible insolación abandonado en un camión, al ataque de una manada de jabalíes, al veneno para ratas, a la parálisis, a la RMSF, al cáncer y a la ineptitud de su dueño. Booster era un testimonio andante del extraordinario potencial del vínculo canino-humano que florece bajo la tutela divina de un poder superior... ¡y mucho más! Con un historial tan innegable y consolidado, pensé que podría vivir otra gran experiencia. Booster estaba destinado a convertirse en el primer perro que viviría para siempre. Me esforcé por encontrar la solución para superar la muerte por si acaso sucumbía al destino final al que estamos sometidos todos los seres vivos.

En la locura del momento, envié un correo electrónico al célebre profesor coreano. Como ameba extranjera, prácticamente un don nadie, le expliqué que mi perro Booster me había salvado la vida cuando me ahogaba en un mar de desesperación. Además, le prometí a Booster que lo compartiría con el mundo cada vez que viajara. Le pedí al profesor que investigara nuestros nombres –Davis Hawn Booster– para que viera nuestras historias en todo el mundo. Esas historias eran una afirmación de la promesa que le había hecho a mi amado Booster años atrás. Le dije, "Se está haciendo mayor y me preocupa mi futuro sin él. Mi Booster es una forma de vida, y no estoy seguro de poder soportar el vacío sin él".

Sabía que nunca habría otro Booster, pero necesitaba algo en lo que creer, para llenar el inevitable vacío que vendría. La clonación podía reproducir las características físicas de un animal, pero la personalidad no era clonable. También le expresé mi devoción por la educación y el hecho de que volví a estudiar a los cincuenta años para obtener un título en Ciencias de la Vida Canina. Mi pasión me consumía, al igual que la suya. Pulsé el botón de enviar de mi computador, sin esperar respuesta.

A los pocos días, abrí un correo electrónico de Taeyoung Shin, uno de los amables colaboradores del querido profesor. Me explicó que al profesor Hwang le había conmovido mi historia y mi relación con Booster. La conversación derivó rápidamente hacia el tema de la clonación. Inmediatamente me advirtió que la clonación no es una forma de devolver la vida a un animal muerto. Yo no tenía expectativas tan ingenuas; sin embargo, estoy seguro de que hay quien podría pensar de esa manera. Sólo podía asegurarme que el clon se parecería al perro original en la *mayoría* de los aspectos.

Clonar un animal con manchas no siempre produce crías con manchas en los mismos lugares. Un gato calicó clonado no tendrá las manchas del mismo color ni en el mismo lugar que su predecesor. Esta aberración se debe a que el proceso de clonación se ve afectado por el ADN residual localizado en las mitocondrias (el centro neurálgico de la célula). Mi Booster era un Labrador retriever amarillo sólido con una tenue mancha blanca en el pecho, por lo que estaba seguro de que era un candidato ideal para la clonación en cuanto a atributos físicos. Mi *Booster* clonado tendría un aspecto idéntico, con la posible excepción de la mancha blanca en el pecho que tienen muchos labradores.

Entonces le pregunté al Dr. Shin si los caninos clonados eran tan sanos como los nacidos de forma natural. Había oído que Dolly, la oveja clonada, murió prematuramente, lo que dio pie a la idea de que los animales clonados eran poco saludables. En realidad, Dolly murió de una forma de neumonía común en las ovejas. El Dr. Shin explicó que, históricamente, algunas crías habían nacido más pequeñas de lo normal pero, al cabo de un año, crecían hasta alcanzar el mismo tamaño que otros compañeros de camada. En los inicios de la clonación, algunas crías nacían con anomalías, pero hoy en día son raras.

A largo plazo, los caninos clonados tienen prácticamente la misma esperanza de vida que los nacidos de forma natural. El profesor Hwang clonó el primer perro en 2015 tras una acalorada competencia con Texas A&M. Llamó al perro Snuppy, acrónimo de Seoul National University Puppy, y vivió hasta una edad avanzada de doce años. Nunca sabré si el cáncer de Booster fue ambiental o hereditario. Si hubiera caído presa del cáncer a una edad temprana, habría llegado a la conclusión de que era hereditario y no le habría considerado candidato a la clonación. A los ocho años, era más probable que influyera el entorno. La realidad dicta que uno de cada cuatro perros morirá de cáncer. Después de los diez años, uno de cada dos perros muere de la temida enfermedad.

La verdadera preocupación era que Booster tenía problema de caderas. La displasia de cadera es frecuente en los perros labradores. Una vez asistí a una conferencia veterinaria en la que un ponente afirmó que quizá sólo el 10% de los labradores tienen caderas excelentes. El gurú de la genética aconsejaba mezclar sólo labradores con caderas excelentes, hablaba mal de los "criadores caseros" que juntaban perros indiscriminadamente.

Desde luego, yo *no* era un gurú de la genética ni un veterinario, pero *sí* un graduado de la BUCS formado bajo la tutela de Bonnie, que me enseñó a ser objetivo y a pensar de manera no convencional. Levanté la mano y me permitieron hablar. "Disculpe, ¿está diciendo que criemos el 10% de una población entre sí? Eso me sugiere que estamos eliminando el 90% de la reserva genética. ¿Seguiremos teniendo un perro labrador? Ante semejante circunstancia, doy gracias a Dios por el criador casero". Como hombre que había vivido dos décadas de sumisión, me levanté y desafié la norma establecida, arriesgándome a enfrentarme a ella. El amor de un perro y una universidad fundada por uno de los pocos seres humanos a los que tenía en alta estima me habían fortalecido. Había adquirido confianza en mí mismo y autoestima gracias a un perro al que antes rehuía y guardaba resentimiento. Todo empezó con Booster.

El genetista hizo una pausa para reflexionar. Lo esencial de su respuesta fue, "Bueno, todo con moderación".

"Bueno, ¿dónde trazas la línea?" pregunté. Quería profundizar, pero preferí evitar una posible confrontación. Tuve que trazar mi propio límite en ese sentido.

Cuando me enfrentaba a cuestiones caninas, me mantenía firme. Una vez asistí a una conferencia de Assistance Dog International (ADI). Solicité asistir con mi perro de servicio, pero me rechazaron porque Booster estaba "intacto". Asistí a la conferencia sin Booster. Cuando me llamaron para hablar, me levanté y cogí al toro por los cuernos, o mejor dicho, ¡al perro por las pelotas! Expliqué que mi perro de servicio había sido excluido de la conferencia porque tenía testículos, como la mayoría de los machos de esta sala. Dije además que había aprendido sobre perros desde una perspectiva canina-humana, habiendo estudiado bajo la tutela de las mejores autoridades caninas, en la única universidad del mundo dedicada a los estudios caninos (BUCS). No castramos a los machos humanos, ¡aunque creo que a menudo deberíamos hacerlo!

Continué explicando que las últimas investigaciones demuestran que los caninos machos castrados sufren una mayor incidencia de rotura de ligamentos cruzados debido a la falta de cantidades suficientes de testosterona. También experimentan mayores tasas de incidencia de cáncer, excepto el cáncer testicular, que se erradica fácilmente mediante la castración en el momento del diagnóstico. La castración es uno de los temas más candentes que se pueden discutir.

En otra conferencia hice la misma afirmación. La conferencia estaba patrocinada por una compañía de seguros para mascotas que limitaba los beneficios de la póliza si el perro no estaba castrado al año de edad. Planteé la hipótesis de una familia que pagaba mensualmente las primas del seguro de las mascotas. A continuación, presenté la situación de un perro en el patio vallado de la familia y un conductor ebrio que se estrella contra la cerca hiriendo al inocente perro. El querido perro de la familia es llevado al veterinario y necesita una operación. La familia está muy agradecida por tener un seguro médico para mascotas. Pero el veterinario abre las patas del perro de un año y ve que tiene testículos, así que la aseguradora no cubre el costo de la operación porque el perro está intacto. La familia no podía permitirse pagar la costosa operación; de ahí que el perro perdiera la vida por no haber sido castrado al año de edad. La ignorancia humana siendo impuesta a los clientes que pagan.

Hablé con uno de los ostentosos ejecutivos de la empresa en una conferencia veterinaria. Le expliqué que castrar a un perro no es sano por las razones antes aludidas. Además, le dije que en la cultura latina, la castración con frecuencia no es aceptada. Le pregunté por qué su compañía de seguros condenaría a muerte a un perro por la decisión de su familia humana. "¿Por qué ejecutan a un can inocente por la decisión de un humano?" El arrogante hombre justifica la política de la compañía diciendo que los perros no castrados suelen mostrar más agresividad, persiguen automóviles, etc.

En otra conferencia veterinaria, se me acercaron dos mujeres. "¿Por qué tu chico no está castrado?" me preguntaron. "Porque quiero lo mejor para mi perro. No es saludable castrar a un perro joven y en la edad adulta no disminuye la agresividad porque la testosterona ya está en el cuerpo", dije con firmeza. "Los perros no castrados hacen que los castrados se vuelvan agresivos en su presencia", me dijeron. Miré a las personas que se quejaban, sonreí y les dije, "No me culpen por la agresividad de su perro. No voy a aumentar las posibilidades de que mi Booster contraiga cáncer o se rompa un ligamento cruzado porque su perro puede estar insuficientemente entrenado o restringido y fue sometido a castración." La decisión de castrar es una decisión personal, y no condeno a la gente por ello, pero no quiero que me condenen por no hacerlo. El problema es de los humanos irresponsables, no de los animales. En algunos países es ilegal esterilizar a un animal. En Alemania y Escandinavia, se considera mutilación y es ilegal. La responsabilidad humana es la clave del éxito de la asociación canina.

Yo era, y sigo siendo, un defensor de los caninos. Antepongo el bienestar de un animal al mío propio. Cuando me planteé clonar a Booster, tuve un conflicto. Desde luego, no quería traer al mundo un perro que sufriera una displasia de cadera extrema. En la BUCS me habían hablado de un procedimiento llamado sinfisiodesis púbica juvenil (SPJ), una sencilla intervención quirúrgica, realizada de forma óptima a las doce semanas, que probablemente garantizaría que un cachorro tuviera mejores caderas de adulto. Una prueba especial llamada estudio Penn HIP había determinado que las caderas de Booster eran peores que las del 70% de todos los demás labradores sometidos a la prueba. Pensé que sería asombrosamente valioso realizar la cirugía SPJ en el duplicado genético de Booster para erradicar potencialmente la displasia de cadera mientras ayudaba a determinar la eficacia del procedimiento.

En la BUCS, aprendí que el peso adicional afecta negativamente las caderas de un perro y leí un estudio de Purina que mostraba que los perros obesos mueren dos años antes que aquellos cuyo peso se mantiene dentro de parámetros aceptables. Recuerde, todo en la BUCS se enseña en el contexto canino-humano. ¿Alguien cree que los humanos obesos son más saludables que aquellos que son delgados, están forma y se ejercitan regularmente? He luchado contra la obesidad toda mi vida. Los humanos obesos suelen tener hijos obesos y perros obesos. A menudo se citan factores genéticos como causa de la obesidad; realidad o ficción, no puedo juzgarlo. Yo era dolorosamente culpable de sobrealimentar a Booster hasta el punto de que pesaba 105 libras en lugar de las 87 apropiadas. En la BUCS aprendí a enmendar mis errores por el bien de Booster. Con el tiempo, Booster adelgazó hasta pesar 87 libras, pero el daño a sus caderas genéticamente inferiores ya se había manifestado.

El Dr. Shin pasó muchas horas en el teléfono respondiendo mis preguntas, muchas veces provocadoras. Se maravillaba de mis conocimientos básicos sobre temas caninos. Más tarde supe que él, al igual que la Dra. Bergin, era profesor. Fue paciente, amable y atento. Me sinceré con él y le expliqué la importancia de clonar a Booster. Mi familia y mis amigos estaban preocupados por cómo afrontaría el eventual fallecimiento de Booster, o si sería capaz de hacerlo. Sabían que siempre existía la opción de que me "diera por vencido". Lo que no sabían era que años antes le había prometido a Booster que nunca consideraría esa posibilidad.

Le pedí información al Dr. Shin porque quería aprender todo lo relacionado con los caninos. No disponía de los 100.000 dólares necesarios para clonar un perro. ¡Mi médico habría duplicado la dosis de mis medicamentos psiquiátricos si hubiera considerado gastar esa cantidad de dinero en clonar un perro! Buscaba una educación única, algo que valoraba más que nunca gracias a Booster, Bonnie y la influencia de la BUCS en mi vida. Estaba desarrollando la confianza y la autoestima que acompañan a la educación, ¡estaba viviendo para aprender y aprendiendo a vivir! Lamenté el hecho de que tal renacimiento se produjera tan tarde, pero me sentí muy agradecido por haberlo experimentado. Muchas almas se pierden en el mar turbulento de la vida y nunca llegan a la orilla para descubrir el fruto de la abundancia.

Mi conversación con Taeyoung se dio sobre la base del respeto mutuo. Hablamos en muchas ocasiones. El hecho de que estuviera dispuesto a compartir su ajetreada vida con un completo desconocido daba testimonio de él. Él percibía mi entusiasmo por vivir y sabía que emanaba de Booster. Un día le dije que me gustaba Asia y que pronto iría a Tailandia. Le pregunté si sería posible visitar el laboratorio del profesor Hwang, SOOAM Biotech. A los pocos días, Taeyoung me llamó y dijo que el Profesor Hwang me había extendido una invitación para recorrer las instalaciones de clonación en Seúl, Corea del Sur.

Celebré en el fondo de mi corazón que el elogiado, aunque castigado, profesor Hwang sintiera mi dolor. ¡En pocas semanas, estaba en un avión con destino a Seúl! Con temblores emocionales similares a los de un terremoto, me aventuré a entrar en territorios desconocidos, personales e internacionales. ¿Sería lo suficientemente buen estudiante como para ser aceptado por un centro de investigación tan profundo? ¿Considerarían clonar a Booster? No tenía el dinero necesario para clonar a un perro. Había vaciado mis arcas personales meses antes para preservar las células de Booster y enviarlas a Corea. Era una utopía que se mantenía viva gracias a una inversión inicial. Sin duda, me estaba preparando para un daño y una devastación personal de proporciones nucleares. Nunca podría darme el lujo de clonar a Booster.

Justo cuando empezaba a cuestionarme lo que había hecho, aterricé en Seúl. Como un cachorro que sale de un vientre protector, o una mariposa de un capullo, emergí del aeropuerto de Corea. Miré tímidamente a mi alrededor y vi a un hombre de aspecto distinguido que sostenía un cartel Davis Hawn Booster. Me acerqué y estreché su mano. Era un empleado de SOOAM Biotech enviado para darme la bienvenida. Después lo seguí, como el cachorro que era, hasta un Mercedes negro tan pulido como su porte. Me recibió como si se tratara de un familiar al que no veía hace mucho tiempo. Al instante me sentí como en casa. Ojalá Booster hubiera estado conmigo en ese momento para ayudarme a procesar mi sobrecarga emocional.

Booster fue el responsable de otro increíble viaje. Estaba viviendo la oportunidad de mi vida, a una edad avanzada, en una nueva cultura. Me trataban como a un intelectual gracias a un perro y una universidad especiales. Todo era bastante surrealista, por no decir otra cosa. ¿Cómo sucedió? Era el humano más afortunado de la tierra porque mi Poder Superior me había presentado a un alma canina única, al programa Al-Anon y a la BUCS. La poderosa combinación me había introducido en la espiritualidad y me había inculcado la fe. Sin la fe restaurada en mi prójimo, nunca habría podido experimentar un momento tan mágico; nunca, de ninguna manera.

Finalmente, mi anfitrión coreano se detuvo en la entrada de mi hotel. Me miró y me preguntó, "¿Cómo elegiste este hotel?" Le dije que había conseguido una buena oferta por Internet. Aceptó mi explicación con una sonrisa. Me registré y subí a mi habitación. Había un jacuzzi en medio de la habitación. Había reservado el hotel porque el agua caliente del jacuzzi solía aliviarme la pierna, que a veces seguía dando problemas. En la pared, frente a la cama, había dos computadores con pantallas grandes. ¡Es algo *diferente*! Pensé. Más tarde me enteré de que era un "hotel del amor", ¡donde los jóvenes enamorados coreanos despliegan sus alas y copulan bajo la atenta mirada de Cupido!

Volví al vestíbulo y mi anfitrión me invitó a una barbacoa coreana aderezada con todo tipo de guarniciones, como kimchee y ¡sólo ellos sabían qué más! Devoré lo desconocido mientras mis sentidos no se centraban en el sabor sino en mis pensamientos. Como un viento frío que se encuentra con una ola de calor, fui golpeado por un rayo emocional. Echaba de menos a Booster, me sentía solo, fascinado, aprendiendo, y deseaba que Bonnie estuviera a mi lado para disfrutar de la vista y cuidarme. Pero, por desgracia, estaba solo, valiéndome por mí mismo, y eso adquirió una importancia única. Disfruté de la comida y de la compañía, y pronto regresé a mi hotel.

Por la mañana, mi anfitrión llegó en el Mercedes negro para llevarme a SOOAM Biotech. Cuando llegamos a las instalaciones, entré y me quedé helado. Levanté la vista y vi un letrero electrónico que me daba la bienvenida. En luces de neón se leía, "Bienvenido a SOOAM Biotech, Sr. Davis Hawn". Me recibieron como a un rey y me trataron como tal. Me dieron un recorrido general por las instalaciones y me dijeron que estaba invitado a presenciar el proceso de clonación al día siguiente. Después de una maravillosa cena coreana con el profesor, un miembro del personal me llevó de vuelta al hotel. Estaba demasiado agotado para usar el jacuzzi. Tuve que esperar al otro día.

A la mañana siguiente, el Mercedes negro volvió a recogerme. Disfruté de una cálida conversación de camino a la biotech. Cuando llegamos, me quité los zapatos y me calcé unas higiénicas sandalias de plástico como había hecho el día anterior. Pronto me convertí en parte integrante de una comitiva que incluía estudiantes en prácticas de investigación de París. Entramos en un ascensor para subir al trono de la investigación científica. Al

salir del ascensor, sonó una radio. "Han venido dos miembros de los medios de comunicación para hacer un reportaje sobre el estadounidense que está clonando a su perro".

El día anterior me había contactado por teléfono con la prensa para proponerles un reportaje. Expliqué mi amor por un perro que me había salvado la vida, mi amor por mi universidad y mi aprecio por el científico coreano que me había concedido semejante honor. El personal de SOOAM no creía que un miembro de la prensa fuera a cubrir la noticia. El profesor Hwang había rehuido las entrevistas y yo percibía cierta animadversión hacia la prensa. Aquel día, un empleado del SOOAM se me acercó y me dijo, "Sr. Davis, dos periódicos quieren cubrir la noticia. ¿Qué vamos a hacer?" Yo respondí, "Estupendo, ¡por favor, dígales a los dos que vengan!" Mi capacidad para transmitir a los demás la importancia de Booster en mi vida creció exponencialmente con el tiempo. *Casualmente*, ¡los dos periódicos enviaron a sus reporteros a SOOAM al mismo tiempo! Cuando llegaron, aseguré a mis anfitriones que podía manejar la situación. Confiaron en mí y se sometieron a mi criterio.

Con los periodistas en fila, nuestra comitiva entró en el laboratorio. Miré por un microscopio y presencié cómo una aguja extraía ADN de una célula de perro y posteriormente implantaba ADN de un donante. Entonces sonó una radio que avisaba que había llegado la entrega. Momentos después, un hombre con un

carrito de mano entró con una jarra de metal que parecía una jarra de leche de los años cincuenta. Me explicaron que contenía las células de Booster que había enviado desde Estados Unidos. *Casualmente* llegó al mismo tiempo que yo. Debería haber estado usando un pañal porque casi me hago encima de incredulidad. Entre lágrimas, extendí la

mano para tocar simultáneamente a Booster y a mi futuro clon de Booster, ambos encapsulados en la jarra plateada de la promesa. Era un concepto difícil de entender. Perdí el control emocional y las cámaras de los periodistas lo captaron. Temblaba y las lágrimas fluían; estaba emocionalmente desnudo entre extraños en un país extranjero. Una mano cálida y reconfortante no tardó en llegar a mi hombro. Era sólo una mano, pero irradiaba calidez. Era la del profesor Hwang. Me sentí "conmovido" más allá de lo imaginable. Aumentó la intensidad de las lágrimas y la trascendencia del momento que estaba viviendo.

El profesor Hwang desapareció y poco después reapareció tras una pared de cristal en un quirófano. Implantó células embrionarias en el útero de una perra de alquiler mientras hablaba por un micrófono, explicando el procedimiento. Yo también hablé por un micrófono. Le hice preguntas al profesor y él las respondió. Fue una experiencia tan enriquecedora que me sentí indigno. Al conocer a varios miembros del personal, me llevaron a un salón para ser entrevistado por los dos reporteros surcoreanos asignados a cubrir mi historia. Me hicieron preguntas perspicaces y compasivas que hicieron que se me quebrara la voz. A menudo tenía que parar y recuperar la compostura. Todo el tiempo pensaba en Booster. *Debería estar aquí, pensé, tiene que estar siempre conmigo. No necesito clonarlo, ya que vivirá para siempre.* El siempre engaña a la muerte. Con Booster en mi vida, todas

las cosas eran posibles. ¡Hércules tenía su cabello, y yo tenía a Booster! No podía concebir una vida sin él. Simplemente no era una opción.

La semana anterior, mientras recorría Asia, encontré un cuadro de varios perros en una escena campestre. Tres cachorros de aspecto similar estaban sentados en una cesta de mimbre en el campo. Le pedí al artista que pintara "SOOAM" en el lateral de la cesta. Lo enmarqué en Seúl y lo envié a SOOAM. *Casualmente* llegó el día de la entrevista.

El periodista se marchó cuando terminó la entrevista. Cuando se enteró de que yo estaba a punto de entregar un regalo al profesor, volvió para tomarme una foto entregando el regalo de *Booster* al profesor Hwang. Apareció a todo color en la *portada* del periódico *Korea Herald*. En la página seis aparecía un reportaje sobre el Presidente Obama. Pensé con picardía: *¡Labrador de pura raza página uno, mestizo autoproclamado página seis!*

Presidente Obama: página 6

Los clones de mi Booster: portada

Unos días después, dejé el hotel. La persona de la recepción me dijo que había leído las noticias en el periódico. Le pedí que llamara a un taxi. Me explicó que el autobús de la esquina iba directamente al aeropuerto. Insistió en acompañarme a la parada a las 5 de la mañana para asegurarse de que cogiera el autobús correcto al aeropuerto.

Mientras caminaba, entró en una cafetería y me invitó un café. Cuando se acercaba el autobús, me puso un pequeño sobre en la mano. Tenía un adhesivo de un perro en la parte delantera. Lo metí en la maleta del computador y me olvidé de él. Días después, lo encontré en mi bolso y lo abrí.

El sobre contenía una nota escrita a Booster en coreano. La envié a mis amigos de SOOAM y les pedí que me la tradujeran. Cuando me la devolvieron en inglés, concluí que había sido escrita por mi Poder Superior y entregada por un ángel mensajero coreano. Empecé a llorar y a temblar mientras leía cada palabra en cámara lenta. Cuanto más leía, más me emocionaba. No podía entender que un desconocido hubiera dedicado parte de su juventud a escribir una carta tan hermosa, cariñosa e inspiradora. Los jóvenes no hacen eso en el mundo de hoy, ¿o sí? Todavía hoy releo la carta y lloro lágrimas de cocodrilo. Uno de mis objetivos en la vida es volver a encontrarme con el joven autor algún día, abrazarlo, mirarlo a los ojos y decirle simplemente, "Gracias". También quiero conocer a los padres que criaron a un joven tan increíble. Hice duplicar esa carta y la enmarqué dos veces. Una copia adorna la pared de mi casa. La *copia* clonada está expuesta en un lugar destacado de la oficina principal de la BUCS. Ambas llevan la misma declaración introductoria irrefutable:

El vínculo canino-humano es un poderoso tsunami de energía capaz de transformar el mundo de formas insondables. Prueba de ello es la siguiente nota de un humano a un perro que nunca conoció y que vive a 7.000 millas de distancia en un país lejano.

¡¡Hola Booster!!

No estoy seguro si puedo escribir esto justo después de saludarte pero. . . Realmente quiero decirte.... ¡¡¡Gracias!!! Puede ser muy repentino, pero escuché que fue gracias a ti que el Sr. Hawn pudo recuperar su fuerza, vivir una nueva vida y abrirse de nuevo a los demás... y lo apoyaste en sus momentos más difíciles... Al principio sólo te veía como un caso más, pero sin saberlo me emocioné tanto que incluso te escribí esta carta, y además en coreano. ^^ Es porque soy coreano. . . El hecho de que hayas sido capaz de conmover a un completo desconocido que no conoces y que vive en un país muy muy lejano... es muy impresionante. Si fueras una persona, creo que serías una celebridad. . . lo que quiero decirte es:

No sé qué es exactamente el "carcinoma de células escamosas" pero sé que estás sufriendo por ello. . . y que no te queda mucho tiempo.

Pero aun así... Tus sentimientos, tus pensamientos, tus recuerdos... Todo lo que sentiste mientras viviste, todos los pensamientos que tuviste y todos los recuerdos...

Si guardas todo esto en tu corazón, ni siquiera la muerte podrá asustarte . . .

El hecho de que no pueda hacer nada por ti me entristece mucho. Aun sabiendo que no sabes leer te escribo esta carta, esperando que seas capaz de entenderla con tu corazón. . .

Aunque te hayas ido tus huellas permanecerán ¡Booster!

Tengo la esperanza de que reencarnes y te reúnas con el Sr. Hawn.

Estaré esperando buenas noticias en internet.

2014/11/10

Tu fan desde Jong-ro, Corea del Sur

Una vez más, reflexioné sobre lo que Booster me enseñó, que no hay *casualidades* en la vida. Hasta el día de hoy, me maravillo por el hecho de que, sin saberlo, me registré en un hotel del amor... ¡y, en consecuencia, encontré el amor! Estaba predestinado. Mi vida siguió cambiando exponencialmente. Y lo que es más importante, aprendí que el amor no es sólo un concepto ideado para infligir dolor al alma. En su forma más pura, es una energía de positivismo incuestionable, que preservará a la humanidad.

Meses después, hablé con Taeyoung. Me explicó que el profesor Hwang y su abnegada familia de empleados se habían conmovido con mi experiencia. Habían leído la carta del *ángel* a mi Booster y querían ayudarme a hacer realidad mi sueño de clonar a mi compañero de vida. Tras unos meses de intercambios sentimentales, SOOAM me hizo una oferta especial que nunca antes habían hecho a nadie. Hicieron posible la clonación de mi Booster. ¡Sí, maldita sea, más lágrimas! Juro que los coreanos saben muy bien cómo hacer llorar a un hombre adulto... ¡una y otra vez! Me dieron el mejor regalo que el mundo podía ofrecerme. Me había tocado la lotería de la empatía humana y era incapaz de sentir, pensar y utilizar mis sentidos. Me senté en el sofá y me balanceé de un lado a otro como un metrónomo, con los brazos agarrados a los costados, ajeno al mundo exterior. Me llevó horas romper el trance hipnótico. Me sentía cansado. No, agotado. No sabía qué había pasado ni por qué.

Después de mucho buscar en mi alma, me di cuenta de que la noticia era abrumadoramente hermosa. Acabé radiante de orgullo como un arco iris después de un huracán. Había vivido una tormenta y otros habían encontrado algo rescatable en mi otrora lamentable yo. Ya no estaba en bancarrota emocional; había encontrado la autoestima. La oferta de clonar a Booster era mucho más que simplemente clonar a un perro, era reparadora. Entonces recordé la carta de amor del joven coreano. Yo había sido el destinatario de un *golpe de gracia*. Aunque no me sentía digno, sí sentía mucha gratitud, más aún con el paso del tiempo. Cuando me enteré de que Booster iba a ser clonado, llamé a todos mis conocidos, ¡e incluso a algunos que no conocía! En el séptimo cielo, compartí con entusiasmo las historias de amor coreanas.

"¿Qué vas a hacer con un perro?" me había preguntado mi hermano años atrás. Ese día respondí a su pregunta con determinación, "¡Voy a clonarlo!" Como era de esperarse, él replicó, "Qué pérdida de dinero más tonta".

Otros me dijeron que hipotecarían su casa para clonar a un perro o un gato al que hubieran amado mucho. En su mayoría, la gente se mostró abrumadoramente positiva. El consenso era, "Oye, es tu dinero. Trabajaste por él, disfrútalo". Cuando estaba considerando si debía clonar a mi Booster, leí sobre una pareja que había clonado a su perro. Decían que habían ahorrado dinero para un Land Rover nuevo, pero que luego lo gastaron en clonar a su querido perro. Explicaron además que decidieron gastar su dinero en algo que ganaría valor en lugar de depreciarse. Esas palabras resuenan hoy con perfecta claridad. Estoy totalmente de acuerdo.

Meses después, asistí a la fiesta de mi sobrina, que se iba a casar. Le regalé fotografías ampliadas y enmarcadas de su infancia y le canté la canción de Harry Belafonte "Turn Around" ante la mirada de los invitados. Había practicado la canción cientos de veces en casa y mientras viajaba por el mundo. Ahora me arriesgaba a hacer el ridículo, con la esperanza de compartir el amor como Booster me había enseñado, incondicionalmente y sin miramientos. Por suerte, salió bien. A mi sobrina se le llenaron los ojos de lágrimas y los invitados aplaudieron. Me alegró el corazón.

Mencioné a algunos de los invitados que estaba clonando a mi perro y se mostraron fascinados. Un anciano me explicó que había tenido un perro al que seguramente habría clonado. Le conté a una señora que me había quedado con uno de los cachorros de Booster, que lo había llamado Al-Anon y que me acompañaba a las reuniones de Al-Anon. Le comenté que lo llamaba "Al" en público para no avergonzarlo. Ella se rio y compartió que asistía a las reuniones de Hijos Adultos de Alcohólicos. Fue un intercambio cálido que ambos valoramos. Alabamos la capacidad del programa para ayudar a quienes se ven afectados por los estragos de la adicción de otros.

Al día siguiente recibí una llamada de mi hermana, "¡No puedo creer lo que hiciste en la fiesta!

"¿Qué hice?" pregunté.

"Le dijiste a la gente que ibas a clonar a tu perro. ¿Sabes lo vergonzoso que es eso?"

Le contesté, "Oye, yo estudio a los perros y los entreno para ayudar a los demás. La clonación es una oportunidad educativa única, y es posible que me proporcione estabilidad en mi vida cuando Booster ya no esté.

"También hablaste del programa Al-anon, y se supone que eso es secreto y privado", dijo.

Le contesté, "El programa Al-anon también tiene que ver con ayudar a la gente. Los programas de doce pasos salvan vidas. Todo el mundo podría beneficiarse de algún tipo de programa de doce pasos. Lo que las personas comparten en las reuniones es confidencial, pero el programa es muy conocido en todo el mundo. Deberías plantearte trabajar para el gobierno chino, ayudar a censurar Internet y controlar el acceso a la realidad". Mi explicación cayó en oídos sordos.

Mi hermana y su esposo son personas maravillosas. Son banqueros, muy conservadores, y han criado con éxito a su familia. Francamente, me parece extraño que la gente pueda trabajar en torno a algo tan carente de valor como el dinero, pero nunca los condené por ello. Ni siquiera lo hice en 2008, cuando millones de personas perdieron sus casas debido a irregularidades bancarias. Como contribuyente, había rescatado a los sinvergüenzas de los bancos. ¡Sólo un perro, mi Booster, me rescató y me sacó de apuros! Tener la oportunidad de trabajar con perros, compartir amor incondicional y ayudar a personas con discapacidades, en comparación con trabajar con dinero y bancos codiciosos, me parece una elección obvia. Al fin y al cabo, según el apóstol Pablo, el amor al dinero es supuestamente la raíz de todos los males. El vínculo canino-humano es la encarnación del amor incondicional, probado a lo largo del tiempo, y muy a menudo venerado. ¡Hay que clonarlo!

Más tarde recibí una llamada de mi querida hermana. Se disculpó por intentar decirme lo que podía y no podía decir. Me reí para mis adentros, pensando, *"Seguro que nuestros padres nos miran desde el cielo y dicen: "¡Clona al perro, pero no clones a nuestros hijos!""* Que conste que quiero mucho a mi hermana. Doy crédito al amor incondicional de Booster por fomentar mi amor incondicional hacia mi familia. Una vez más apliqué lo que aprendí en la BUCS al ver las cosas en un contexto canino-humano. Mi Booster me enseñó a celebrar la vida con canciones y a tener una interacción juguetona en grupo.

Unos cuantos aficionados a los perros me criticaron por gastar *mi* dinero en clonar a un perro cuando ese dinero podría alimentar *su* interés... perros de refugio. ¿Saber qué vino después? Los humanos, incluida mi hermana, preguntaron, "¿Por qué gastas tu dinero en perros cuando hay niños hambrientos en el mundo?" Algunos me acusaron de jugar a ser Dios. Me sentí obligado a decir que amaba tanto a la criatura única que Dios había creado que simplemente quería otra... una fotocopia. ¡No estaba alterando ni un ápice el ADN que Dios creó y puso en mi vida en forma de perro que se convirtió en mi Booster!

Cuando un perro *hace sus necesidades*, otros perros lo olfatean porque contiene información, es la versión canina de investigar o leer un libro. Los humanos meten las narices en los *asuntos* de los demás para condenar o imponer sus propios intereses. Los perros suelen seguir adelante cuando no se les provoca. Los humanos se detienen para provocar, comentar, juzgar y luego publicar en las redes sociales. Los daños colaterales suelen adoptar la forma de intimidación, que a veces resulta en muerte. No es de extrañar que recurramos a los perros para que nos ayuden a resolver nuestros problemas.

Mientras esperaba con impaciencia noticias sobre el día en que comenzaría la clonación, me enteré de la existencia de un libro que relataba la historia de la clonación de principio a fin. Me pareció bastante negativo. Las revelaciones del libro me fascinaron. Sabía que la gente probablemente tendría una opinión negativa sobre la clonación después de leerlo. Me pareció poco objetivo y, francamente, bastante sesgado. Booster me enseñó que en la vida no hay *casualidades*, así que pensé que encontrar y leer el libro estaba predestinado. Era como una advertencia previa del enfrentamiento que se avecinaba. Una vez más, iba a tener que educar a una población ignorante que defendía teorías sobre un clon cuando nunca había compartido su vida con uno. No iba a permitir que me disuadieran. ¡Estos seres humanos pierden el tiempo ladrando al árbol equivocado!

Por capricho, envié un correo electrónico a Taeyoung preguntándole si estaría dispuesto a compartir sus conocimientos con los estudiantes de la BUCS. Él accedió filantrópicamente a dar una conferencia gratuita en la universidad. Más tarde supe que se había subido a un autobús desde su ciudad natal, Wisconsin, con destino al aeropuerto de Chicago. Se tomó tiempo libre en su trabajo y viajó hasta California para enriquecer las mentes de los estudiantes. Había organizado el envío por correo de un ejemplar del libro sobre clonación a todos los estudiantes de la BUCS interesados. Cuando Taeyoung llegó a la BUCS, había mucha negatividad basada en las conclusiones extraídas de la información presentada en el libro.

Los estudiantes escucharon amablemente e hicieron preguntas durante dos días. El ambiente cambió cuando Taeyoung presentó información actual y objetiva sobre la clonación y la replicación del ADN. Él no defendió la clonación, sino que se mantuvo neutral y pidió opiniones. Justo antes de que abandonara el campus, los estudiantes le preguntaron si podían tomarse una foto con él, le regalaron una parka de la BUCS y le agradecieron efusivamente su presencia. En Seúl, yo había experimentado el amor y la dedicación coreanos. Los estudiantes de la BUCS aprovecharon esta experiencia, y tuvieron la oportunidad de darse un festín con el intelectualismo de un coreano y la educación resultante.

Los días iban y venían. ¡Lo que parecía una eternidad era una eternidad! Prácticamente todos los días me despertaba esperando noticias de que Booster había sido clonado. Solía enviar correos electrónicos pidiendo actualizaciones, preguntando, "¿Empezó la clonación?" Siempre recibía respuestas amables, pero nunca una respuesta positiva. Un día, más de un año después, ¡recibí la noticia! "Sr. Hawn, hemos comenzado la clonación de Booster." Me quedé helado en ese momento. Me quedé mirando el correo electrónico en la pantalla del computador. *¿Realmente? ¿En serio? ¿En serio? ¿En serio?* me pregunté. Como un padre expectante, sonreí con orgullo y esperé con impaciencia la llegada del nuevo miembro de la familia y la siguiente fase de mi vida. ¿Oíste bien? ¡ESPERABA CON IMPACIENCIA LA SIGUIENTE FASE DE MI VIDA! Mi Poder Superior había respondido a mi llamado una vez más. Mi vida cambió en ese momento, ¡y cambió rápidamente! Las ramificaciones de lo que había hecho, de repente se hicieron evidentes. Empecé a analizar mis acciones y me bombardeé con introspección.

Tendría que ir a Corea a trabajar con el clon y dejar atrás a Booster. ¿Cómo podría estar pendiente de Booster en sus últimos días y, al mismo tiempo, dedicar al cachorro clonado toda mi atención y educación durante el periodo de socialización, es decir, las primeras doce o catorce semanas de vida? ¿Sería un traidor? Me había autoimpuesto el requisito de adiestrar al futuro clon como el mejor perro de servicio del planeta. De repente me sentí desgarrado, y con razón, ya que tenía aproximadamente sesenta y tres días para resolverlo. Sería un periodo de gestación moral que coincidiría con el del cachorro clonado. Me concentré en preservar mi bienestar mental, como había aprendido en Al-Anon. Por el momento, me enfoqué en mí mismo, no en el clon. Resultaron ser los sesenta y tres días más largos de mi vida.

Había vivido con mucha aprensión, ¡no con anticipación! Nunca había tenido la posibilidad de un arco iris después de la tormenta, sino de una nueva tormenta. Esto era nuevo para mí. En lugar de obsesionarme con el mal inevitable y la recaída segura en una depresión destructiva, iba a tener que vivir la vida en sus términos. Tenía que tomar decisiones de adulto, antes obstaculizadas por la falta de opciones en una relación codependiente. Como había aprendido en las reuniones de Al-Anon, "Si dejas ir el pasado, él te dejará ir a ti". Había trabajado duro y me había centrado en dejar el pasado en el retrovisor, pero había perdido de vista el parabrisas. La verdad es que ni en mis mejores sueños pensé que viviría lo suficiente para mirar hacia *adelante*, ¡y mucho menos que *podría* o *querría* hacerlo!

Era el amanecer de un nuevo día y de un nuevo amigo. Me desperté abrazando a Booster y sonriendo. Jugaba con todos los miembros de mi familia canina con renovado vigor y gran exuberancia, y acariciaba como nunca a los perros y gatos que encontraba en público. En lugar de odiar a los que encontraban felicidad en saludar a Booster, cuando era cachorro, me convertí en *uno de ellos*. Mi balance de la vida había cambiado. Mientras que antes valoraba la economía de palabras, ahora mostraba diarrea verbal. Ya no lloraba cuando luchaba contra la depresión. Mis emociones recién adquiridas se presentaban como lágrimas, debido a un concepto antes esquivo llamado felicidad. Quería huir y unirme al circo. ¡Había aprendido a hacer malabarismos con mis emociones!

Así que decidí volar a Corea para presenciar el nacimiento del cachorro clonado. Los días pasaban como imágenes de cartas moviéndose lentamente en los primeros días de los dibujos animados. Un día, de repente, recibí un correo electrónico con una foto bastante particular. "Sr. Hawn, hemos detectado un latido fetal en una de las madres de alquiler. Vigilaremos su evolución 24 horas al día, 7 días a la semana, y le informaremos periódicamente. ¡Felicidades!" Visité mi meca de las emociones. Me pellizqué para confirmar la realidad del momento. Era más que un clon, era la confirmación del karma.

Mi Booster se había abierto camino en el mundo haciendo el bien a los demás. Le gustaba complacer a la gente y le encantaba la interacción.

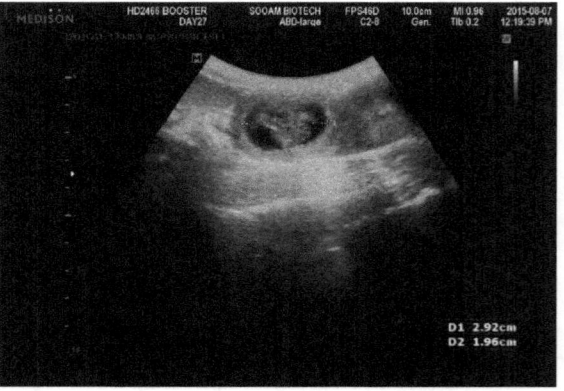

Yo era su humano favorito y, como tal, él quería que yo fuera feliz y continuara su trabajo en el mundo, y para ello ¡necesitaba un *Booster*! Una vez le había impedido la interacción humana que tanto le gustaba. Con el tiempo, no pude contener su amor por los demás. Su personalidad eclipsó mi sombrío pasado y cambié. Yo también me convertí en alguien que disfrutaba complaciendo a la gente; me encantaba dar y me sentía culpable recibiendo.

La familia SOOAM me había hecho una oferta única, trabajó sin descanso para cumplirla, mantuvo su compromiso y utilizó una gran cantidad de conocimientos acumulados para hacer realidad un sueño. Fue algo monumental y especial para mí. Unos absolutos desconocidos hicieron una promesa increíble y la cumplieron. Fue una novedad, ya que mis adictos rara vez hacían algo así.

En mi vida "anterior", se hacían promesas que nunca se cumplían. Aquellos en quienes confiaba fielmente, me decían desde una edad temprana, "Nunca volveré a beber, nunca volveré a tomar esa pipa, nunca volveré a ponerme violento..." Mi padre prometía cambios por la mañana, y ese mismo día, manifestaba un comportamiento descarado y repetitivo. Aquellos con los que más tarde forjé relaciones, mis adictos, siguieron ese precedente. Estaba acostumbrado a que me mintieran, me defraudaran y a quedarme sumido en el dolor. Si preguntaba, "¿Estás seguro?" la respuesta era, "¿Qué, no confías en mí? Entonces, ¿por qué estoy contigo?" Recuerdo que una vez fui al banco y cubrí la tarjeta del cajero automático al sacar el poco dinero que tenía. Inmediatamente, con la intensidad de una explosión sónica, "¿Por qué diablos tienes que *ocultarme* tu código PIN?" Yo en seguida respondí de manera sumisa, "Lo siento, fue un acto reflejo... ¡es el 2345!" Al mes siguiente recibí mi extracto bancario y descubrí retiros realizados en mitad de la noche con mi tarjeta de cajero automático.

Finalmente, llegó el día de abrazar a Booster y abordar el avión rumbo al corazón de Corea, a Seúl. Con inquietud, Booster y yo subimos a mi camioneta y unos amigos nos llevaron al aeropuerto. El día estaba soleado, pero experimenté ráfagas de emoción interna. Booster me miraba a los ojos como si fuéramos al parque cuando, en realidad, iba a estar ausente por un tiempo. Estaba muriendo por dentro, ya que el clon estaba a punto de nacer. Como solía suceder, sentía dolor. Mi inspirador Booster se convirtió en la fuente de mi espíritu abatido. Me estaba castigando, desaprender conductas es difícil. Por eso la mayoría de los centros de adiestramiento de perros de servicio empiezan con cachorros y no con perros adultos. Aprendí en la BUCS que se necesitan por lo menos treinta repeticiones correctas de una tarea positiva y correctamente enseñada para deshacer el daño de una inculcada erróneamente. Tenía miles de lecciones erróneas que necesitaba desaprender, y no tenía tiempo suficiente para hacerlo.

Mis lecciones de la BUCS me ayudaron a sofocar el levantamiento interno de mi campo de batalla emocional. Utilicé para mí, la psicología que había aprendido a aplicar en los perros, en la escuela canina. Me dije una y otra vez que Booster querría esto para *mí*, que yo lo necesitaba y que el mundo necesitaba un *booster*. Pensé en la condena de los demás por intentar clonar a Booster, pero repasé mentalmente mis enseñanzas de Al-Anon. "Lo que los demás piensen de mí no es asunto mío".

El personal veterinario y de investigación de SOOAM es uno de los mejores del mundo. Sus cachorros clonados suelen venir al mundo por cesárea para disminuir el riesgo asociado al parto. De hecho, algunas razas no pueden parir de forma natural. El hombre había invadido la santidad del mundo canino, mediante la selección artificial y la cría por ingeniería, a menudo en detrimento de la especie. Los clones de SOOAM estaban valorados en 100.000 dólares, era la culminación de enormes inversiones económicas y emocionales, que justificaban garantías adicionales para asegurar el nacimiento sin problemas del cachorro. Hice un llamamiento ad hominem a la buena gente de SOOAM para que permitiera que el clon de Booster naciera de forma natural. Bonnie me enseñó que era beneficioso para un cachorro experimentar una estimulación neurológica temprana en forma de estrés natural durante el proceso de parto. Muchas asociaciones de perros de asistencia y criadores introducían estímulos estresantes para preparar a un cachorro para el estrés que se experimenta en el mundo humano. ¡Ojalá yo hubiera recibido este tipo de adiestramiento cuando era un bebé!

Cuando se crían perros de asistencia, se seleccionan perros de alto rendimiento, con la esperanza de que su progenie tenga la misma capacidad. El adiestramiento posterior de los cachorros recién nacidos en un entorno controlado es aún más crítico. La mezcla adecuada de atención a la naturaleza frente a educación es lo que garantiza la mayor probabilidad de adiestrar al mejor perro de asistencia. En los años 70, el ejército de los Estados Unidos diseñó el Programa Bio Sensor, conocido coloquialmente como el Programa Superperro. Los cachorros eran sometidos a estimulación sensorial, tanto física como ambiental, con la esperanza de mejorar la capacidad de los perros militares de manejar el estrés en tiempos de guerra. Hoy en día, muchos criadores siguen los principios del programa y continúan aplicándolo.

Llegué a Seúl el día antes del nacimiento del clon. El empleado de SOOAM, con el que ya había entablado amistad, en el Mercedes Benz de costumbre, me transportó al hotel. Esta vez había renunciado al hotel del amor en favor de un hotel de larga estancia cerca de SOOAM. Al fin y al cabo, no *buscaba* el amor. Había venido a recibirlo con el nacimiento. Le había pedido permiso al personal del SOOAM para trabajar con el cachorro clonado en el centro de investigación, ya que necesitaba hacerlo quince minutos dos veces al día. Dado que sería molesto que un extraño estuviera merodeando mientras se llevaba a cabo una intensa investigación en el SOOAM, no sabía qué esperar como respuesta. El profesor Hwang respetó mi amor por Booster y mi deseo de ampliar mis estudios y me concedió amablemente el acceso. Decidí incorporar el programa de biosensores al régimen de adiestramiento de perros de servicio del cachorro clonado.

A la mañana siguiente, me recogió un investigador del SOOAM que era mi persona de confianza y mi nuevo amigo. "Sr. Hawn, tenemos noticias para usted", me dijo. "Ha habido un avance". Mi corazón implosionó. Sabía que mi futuro Booster había nacido muerto. Al presumir lo peor, automáticamente volví a mi antiguo comportamiento, como un perro que ha sido sometido a muchas repeticiones de adiestramiento positivo para cambiar un comportamiento no deseado, pero recae. Se puede cambiar un comportamiento previamente aprendido, pero no se puede borrar. Por lo tanto, muchas escuelas de adiestramiento de perros de asistencia, prefieren empezar con cachorros para eliminar la posibilidad de recaer en un comportamiento anterior, que podría ser problemático para su compañero discapacitado. Un perro al que se le enseña a no perseguir a los gatos que una vez cazó, podría volver a hacerlo al ver a un "gato ladrón" que le roba la comida. En mi caso, recaí instantáneamente en un tsunami de pensamientos negativos. En los centros de tratamiento se suele decir que las recaídas forman parte de la recuperación. Aunque siempre había considerado que ese concepto era una gran excusa, de repente tuve que revisar esa interpretación. Del mismo modo que "sabía" (conjeturaba erróneamente) que Booster había sido atropellado por un automóvil cuando era cachorro, supe que el cachorro clonado debía de haber muerto durante el proceso de parto. En un nanosegundo, ¡la vida volvió a ser un asco!

"Sr. Hawn, ¿recuerda cuando le enviamos una copia de la ecografía que mostraba el latido del corazón del feto?"

Me están preparando lentamente para la decepción; ¡qué considerados son, musité, sin gracia!

"Estamos avergonzados. Deberíamos haber hecho una segunda ecografía de seguimiento". Reviví la crisis de los misiles cubanos y esperé la bomba y la subsiguiente explosión.

"No vimos el *otro* latido del feto", me explicó.

Me perdí en el ritual emocional. El "seguro" cachorro muerto era, de hecho, ¡dos cachorros sanos! La madre de alquiler se había adelantado un día, así que me perdí el parto, pero me sentí aliviado. Sigo sin saber por qué se me concedió tal dualidad de grandeza. ¿Por qué dos? Con negatividad, me pregunté si uno de ellos estaba destinado a morir en el futuro, así que mi Poder Superior estaba cubriendo todas las bases. Mi estado mental todavía no era lo que debería haber sido.

Esa mañana entré en SOOAM rodeado de una plétora de simpatizantes. Como era costumbre, me dirigieron al estante donde cambié mis zapatos por zapatillas desinfectadas. Me acompañaron a la planta donde estaban los perros clonados y sus cachorros. En un puesto de cristal había un cartel con una bandera estadounidense y la fecha de nacimiento. ¿ESTÁS PREPARADO PARA ESTO? ¿ESTÁS LISTO PARA ESTO? Los cachorros nacieron posiblemente el día más emotivo de la historia de Estados Unidos, el 11 de septiembre. Antes de que pudiera asimilar el

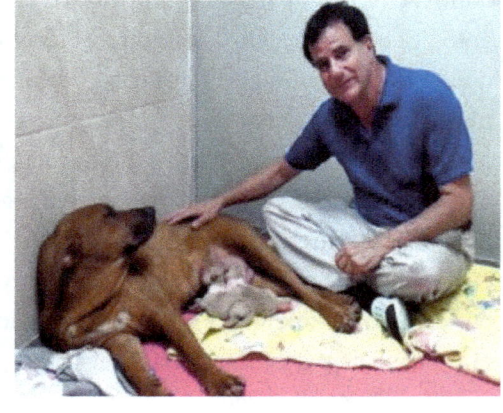

significado, me hicieron señas para que entrara en la cabina estéril. Me acerqué a la madre de alquiler a nivel del suelo, desde una ligera distancia, y hablé con ella tranquilamente. Era grande y cuidaba de sus hijos como debe hacerlo una madre. Leí su lenguaje corporal como había aprendido a hacer en la BUCS.

Cuando sentí que la aceptaba, me acerqué, me senté a su lado, la acaricié y le hice saber que había hecho un gran trabajo. Estaba cansada, pero era paciente y tolerante... mucho más de lo que habría sido yo, un viejo gruñón ¡habiendo dado a luz unas horas antes!

Entonces extendí la mano y simultáneamente la acaricié a ella y a su cría. Era una familia dentro de mi familia SOOAM. Estaba en las nubes. Era como si el Imodium 86 hubiera sanado mi diarrea verbal. Estaba verbalmente en quiebra, absolutamente sin palabras. Estaba flotando en una nube, en otro mundo. Los coreanos hablaban un inglés perfecto, pero yo no los oía. Me introdujeron en un estrés asombroso, y yo estaba... ¡feliz ¿DE VERDAD? ¿HABÍA APRENDIDO A MANEJAR EL ESTRÉS Y SER FELIZ? (OMPS). En el pasado, había hecho todo lo posible por ocultar mis extrañas emociones a mi familia y amigos. Me esforcé por hacerlo cuando estaba acompañado de los miembros del personal coreano. Fue duro, muy duro. Necesitaba a mi Booster, allí y en ese momento.

Gran parte de lo que ocurrió aquel día está borroso. Recuerdo haber hablado largo y tendido con los investigadores y haber entrevistado a los cuidadores de los clones. Cuando las instalaciones estaban a punto de cerrar, pregunté al agotado personal si podía ver a los clones una vez más antes de abandonar SOOAM. En lugar de negarse, sonrieron con sinceridad, rezumando la leche de bondad que llegué a conocer como SOOAM. Con los clones acurrucados en mi pecho, comparé el desamparo de los cachorros recién nacidos y la necesidad de su madre, con mi vida y mi necesidad de Booster. En ese momento, me di cuenta de que ambos cachorros tenían la característica mancha blanca de Booster en el pecho. De repente obtuve una fuerza hercúlea proveniente de la más frágil de las criaturas. Me sentí místicamente envuelto en una serenidad que no podía explicar. Era de naturaleza divina, tranquilizadora y reconfortante.

Más tarde deduje que no sólo había clonado a Booster, sino también mi creencia en las cualidades curativas que él confería a mi maltrecha psique. Fue medicinal y curativo en el momento. Animado y cauteloso, me levanté y miré los ojos de los que me rodeaban. No necesitaba palabras; mis emociones lo expresaban todo. Una cacofonía de estridentes dialectos asiáticos me felicitó mientras me escoltaban jubilosamente hasta las puertas de salida del cielo. ¿Mi interpretación del cielo? Un lugar seguro, rodeado de Boosters, liberando endorfinas como nunca antes las había experimentado. Había encontrado el cielo en mi Seúl.

Antes de embarcarme en el viaje a mi Seúl, había decidido asistir al nacimiento del cachorro clonado y luego tomarme un tiempo para alejarme y reflexionar. En Al-Anon, aprendí a cuidarme. Sabía que tendría una sobrecarga sensorial. Tenía previsto regresar a SOOAM unas dos semanas más tarde para enseñar a los clones y darles clases de quince a treinta minutos dos veces al día hasta que tuvieran la edad suficiente para volver a casa.

Antes de irme de Seúl, repasé el protocolo del biosensor con los cuidadores de los clones, y ellos aceptaron trabajar con los clones en mi ausencia. Les di una grabadora y les pedí que pusieran mi voz grabada y ruidos ambientales a los cachorros varias veces al día, a partir de las dos semanas y media. Los cachorros nacen sordos y empiezan a oír alrededor de las tres semanas de vida. Sabiendo que los cachorros nacen con una capacidad olfativa totalmente funcional, les llevé camisetas sudadas para que pudieran percibir mi olor corporal a una edad temprana. Podían captar el olor de mi cuerpo, que era diferente al del personal asiático. También les di comida especial para bebés y aceites de pescado para mejorar su desarrollo cerebral.

Durante la Segunda Guerra Mundial los perros fueron adiestrados para "olfatear al enemigo". Estadounidenses de segunda generación de ascendencia japonesa se ofrecieron como voluntarios para ser localizados por los perros rastreadores, donados por dueños de mascotas de todo el país. Los perros podían ser adiestrados para oler y alertar sobre un ser humano basándose en la transpiración. El olor que desprende una persona viene determinado por la dieta. A menudo se puede oler la transpiración de un alcohólico, o quizá la de una persona que ha comido mucho ajo. Los estadounidenses tenían una dieta basada en el trigo, mientras que los asiáticos tenían una dieta basada en el arroz. El problema era que los japoneses americanos de segunda generación comían una dieta "americana" basada en el trigo, por lo que no había una diferenciación perceptible. El proyecto fracasó.

Dejé Seúl unos días después del nacimiento de los clones. Era un desastre mental y viajé por Asia con doble propósito. Aprendí mucho sobre otras culturas y aún más sobre mí mismo. Monté en elefante en Tailandia y aprendí del adiestrador del animal, la dura realidad del entrenamiento. Conocí los horribles sufrimientos que padecen los osos bailarines de la India para aprender a bailar... ¡a bailar! Lloré a lágrima viva cuando supe del cultivo de bilis de oso en China. Los osos eran mantenidos durante décadas en pequeñas jaulas, exprimidos como una naranja en una prensa de zumo para extraer su bilis, utilizada con fines medicinales... aunque la bilis de oso genérica está fácilmente disponible. Supe que despellejaban a los gatos con un soplete antes de cocinarlos. Visité un restaurante vietnamita que servía carne de perro, ¡aunque yo nunca la probaría! Fue un viaje educativo. Después de todo, tal vez no era tan malo, ser tan emocional en un mundo aparentemente muy cruel. Adoraba tanto a Booster que intenté conseguir otra copia, un clon. Otros sometían a los animales a torturas increíbles, animales para los que una cámara de gas habría sido mucho más benévola.

En mi viaje de introspección, pensé mucho en los nombres de los clones. Quería ponerles un nombre que rindiera honor a su padre. Booster había robado un juguete de una tienda de mascotas... era un ladrón... ¡un *booster*! Yo, por mi parte, potencié las células de su piel y las envié a Corea para clonarlas. Mi hermano y mi hermana no lo aprobaron, así que me *descubrieron*. De ahí que llamara a los cachorros clonados Boosted y Busted (Potenciado y pillado). "¿Qué hay en un nombre?" se preguntarán. En este caso, es un legado. Una búsqueda en Internet de nuestros nombres, Davis Hawn Booster, revela historias en todo el mundo. Las mismas historias aparecen si se sustituye el nombre por Boosted o Busted; por lo tanto, los clones heredaron el legado de su padre al nacer. Imaginé una noticia en el periódico, "Cachorros clonados reciben un legado clonado".

Me preocupaba, sin embargo, que los clones no pudieran diferenciar entre los dos nombres de sonido similar. Si alguien podía responder a esa pregunta de forma irreprochable era Bonnie. Ella, literalmente, escribió el libro sobre el comportamiento canino. Le envié una pregunta por correo electrónico y me aseguró que serían capaces de hacerlo. También me dijo que podían ser clones, pero eran seres individuales por derecho propio. Así que llamé a los clones Boosted y Busted. Rápidamente aprendieron sus respectivos nombres. El problema surgió cuando de repente me di cuenta de que no podía diferenciarlos. ¡Yo era el que tenía el problema de diferenciación! Al final, puse un gran punto de tinta roja en la cabeza de Boosted. ¡Me preguntaba si los padres de gemelos idénticos harían lo mismo!

Mientras viajaba por Tailandia, durante dos semanas, recibía constantemente noticias escritas y fotografías de los dedicados empleados de SOOAM en Seúl. Boosted y Busted estaban muy bien. Los pesaban a diario y crecían al mismo ritmo. Sus cuidadores no detectaron diferencias notables en sus personalidades. Pedí que Boosted y Busted estuvieran con otros cachorros de tamaño similar durante un rato cada día para fomentar su socialización. Me entristecía que no tuvieran compañeros de camada con los cuales interactuar socialmente. Los cachorros aprenden a interactuar correctamente jugando. Si son demasiado agresivos, pueden recibir un mordisco de vuelta. Es una curva de aprendizaje. La observación de la socialización entre compañeros de camada es vital. El cachorro más grande de una camada suele ser el agresor, y el más pequeño el más molestado. Esto puede afectar su personalidad en los años venideros. Podríamos no elegirlos como candidatos para perros de asistencia debido a esto. Observamos a los cachorros "intermedios" y hacemos una selección.

En otro orden de cosas, ¿se han dado cuenta de que a los humanos nos da vergüenza mostrar nuestro cuerpo desnudo, pero a los perros les da igual? Amamantar a un bebé en público suele ser rechazado. ¿Qué podría ser más natural? Siempre había querido conocer una playa nudista y tuve la oportunidad de hacerlo años más tarde, cuando visité Barcelona (España). Un día cogí un autobús hacia una playa nudista, me quité el traje de baño y planté mis "cocos" en la arena. Pronto me aburrí. La decepción fue más impactante que bajarme el bañador. Decididamente, me levanté, me volví a poner el bañador y me fui a tomar una copa o dos o tres a la cantina de la playa. Pedí una piña colada, me senté y observé cómo dos españoles tiraban migas de pan a los pájaros de la playa. El pájaro más pequeño saltó tímidamente para coger una miga, pero sus esfuerzos fueron superados por un pájaro más grande y agresivo. De repente, un pájaro aún más grande se apareció de la nada y la batalla de Normandía en la playa comenzó de nuevo.

Desconcertado, observé a los pájaros durante más de una hora. Algo me impactó y empecé a reírme. Los espectadores probablemente pensaron que las drogas que había ingerido habían hecho efecto. Había empleado inconscientemente mi formación de la BUCS y observaba la interacción de los pájaros como si fuera una camada de cachorros. Sorprendentemente, el encanto de ir a una playa nudista por primera vez en mi vida duró como quince minutos como máximo. Ver a los pájaros perseguir migas de pan duró más de una hora. Todavía hoy me río de ello. Reflexioné que las lágrimas, que antes emanaban por depresión, se transformaron en lágrimas de asombro y felicidad debido a la intervención de Booster.

Más tarde, regresé a Seúl con emoción desenfrenada. El día de mi llegada, cogí el metro hasta SOOAM, me acerqué a la puerta principal y pulsé el timbre. El joven investigador que me había acompañado desde mi hotel hasta SOOAM el día que nacieron Boosted y Busted me saludó con una enorme sonrisa. "Boosted y Busted lo estaban esperando", me dijo en un inglés perfecto. Era un joven brillante que cumplía con su obligación militar trabajando para el centro de investigación. Me recordó que debía quitarme los zapatos y ponerme las zapatillas sanitarias. Nos dirigimos a la sala donde estaban todos los cachorros clonados.

Miré a Boosted y a Busted, habían crecido mucho. Alcé a uno y luego al otro y los sostuve durante el mismo tiempo. En la BUCS, aprendí que los perros tienen sentido de la equidad. Si tienes a dos perros en una habitación, debes recompensar a cada uno de ellos por darte su pata. Si dejas de recompensar a uno mientras sigues con el otro, el perro que dejó de recibir golosinas dejará de ofrecer su pata. Tuve mucho cuidado de no mostrar favoritismo. Todos los días les cantaba a los cachorros, mientras los miembros del personal entretenidos observaban. Cantaba como Frank Sinatra y rugía como Elvis Presley. "I Can't Help Falling in Love with You" y "Love Me Tender" eran mis canciones favoritas. En serio, ¡les cantaba esas canciones a Boosted y Busted todos los días! Quería que se acostumbraran a los distintos tonos de mi voz y bromeaba con el personal coreano diciéndoles que no les pagaban lo suficiente para escuchar todo eso.

Empecé a llevar gafas y barba postiza cuando trabajaba con los cachorros y de vez en cuando caminaba amenazadoramente, como un espantapájaros con mala postura. Muchos de los perros ladraban, pero Boosted y Busted nunca lo hicieron. Les expliqué a los coreanos lo vital que es la socialización de los cachorros. Tiraba de su cola y las orejas y les hacía cosquillas en la barriga. Les hablaba en voz baja y alta, pero nunca lo suficiente como para asustarlos, ya que los cachorros se asustan más a las ocho u once semanas. Tenía un gato de juguete que *maullaba* y un reloj que hacía *tictac*. Ponía las grabaciones de portazos, gritos de gente y conciertos musicales. Cuando había visitantes, les pedía que cogieran a los cachorros en brazos o jugaran con ellos un rato.

A las seis semanas, los cachorros abrieron de un tirón un portón infantil que bloqueaba una puerta. Se les enseñó a sentarse, quedarse, ir, bajar, dejarlo y, sobre todo, a venir. Soy muy sensible a esta orden, ya que quiero que mis compañeros caninos dejen de hacer lo que están haciendo y vengan corriendo cuando se les ordena. Puede ser una cuestión de vida o muerte, ya sea una serpiente venenosa o un automóvil en la carretera. Desde el principio me di cuenta de que estos cachorros tenían lo necesario para convertirse en perros de servicio. Me miraban a los ojos. Se concentraban. Y lo mejor de todo, les encantaba aprender. Yo les enseñaba y ellos me enseñaban a mí. Los miembros del personal de SOOAM visitaban la sala de adiestramiento para presenciar mis sesiones. Me

alegraba ver su interés. Todos compartíamos el aprendizaje. ¡Era como trabajar en una fábrica de Mensa!

Muchas veces trabajaba descalzo, y los coreanos me decían: "Está bien que uses zapatillas". Entonces yo decía, "Zapato", y los cachorros de seis semanas corrían a buscar mis zapatillas. Era consciente de que siempre estaba en el escenario, y quería que el personal viera tareas de perro de servicio realizadas por cachorros. Además, quería que Boosted y Busted olieran mis pies mientras entregaban las zapatillas que cubrían por completo sus jóvenes narices. Mientras enseñaba a Boosted y Busted a buscar mis zapatos (también conocidos como zapatillas), un miembro del personal de SOOAM me enseñó cómo NO hacerlo. Tenía un par de zapatillas que eran mis favoritas en el vestuario de la sala de llegada. Me las ponía todos los días al entrar en el centro. Un día, un miembro del personal se acercó y me dijo, "Sr. Hawn, está sacando las zapatillas de la sección equivocada del armario. Esas zapatillas proceden de la sección de empleados y pertenecen al profesor Hwang". ¡Hoy vino a buscar sus zapatillas!" Muchas veces se dice que puedes entender mejor a una persona si caminas en sus zapatos. Me imaginé que en esas primeras semanas había caminado al menos una milla en esos zapatos/zapatillas. Me acordé al instante de una canción que Joe South escribió en 1970, "Walk a Mile in My Shoes".

El profesor Hwang era tenido en tan alta estima que el Papa podría haber palidecido en comparación. Cayó en desgracia debido a un escándalo relacionado con su investigación, pero de algún modo resurgió del abismo para recuperar su prestigio. Tras ser perseguido por la justicia, fortaleció su vida con la convicción de su propósito. Él, como yo, había llevado una vida difícil. Yo había caminado una milla en sus zapatos. ¿Qué posibilidades había de que cogiera unas zapatillas de la sección equivocada de un armario y pertenecieran a mi benefactor? ¿Coincidencia? Mi Booster me habría dicho educadamente, ¡"Helllllllll no!" en inglés, o 안돼 en coreano.

Pasé mucho tiempo enseñando a Boosted y Busted a no chillar cuando los metía en una jaula rodante para perros. Iban a volver a casa en avión y no quería que chillaran. Empecé metiéndolos y luego sacándolos. Al cabo de una semana, se acostumbraron a su hogar rodante. Luego, cerré la cremallera superior por un momento. Con el tiempo, dejaba la tapa cerrada y los cachorros permanecían a gusto en el interior. Entonces empecé a rodarlos por los pasillos para que aprendieran a aceptar el movimiento y no temerle. Boosted y Busted iban a estar conmigo en un avión durante más de catorce horas de Seúl a Dallas. Estaban en una edad en la que podrían tener miedo al regresar en avión a casa. Por ese motivo, nunca llevamos a los cachorros de perros de servicio en una jaula en la bodega del avión. Necesitaban estar cómodos en su jaula durante mucho tiempo. Cuando llamé a la compañía aérea para reservar mi boleto de regreso a casa, me dijeron que no podía viajar con un cachorro en una jaula en un vuelo de más de ocho horas de duración. Me quedé atónito. Eran demasiado jóvenes para ser considerados perros de servicio, y las compañías aéreas no suelen volar con perros de servicio en fase de adiestramiento. Estaba verdaderamente estresado. Mi última opción era considerarlos como animales de apoyo emocional (Emotional Support Animal - ESA).

Siempre había dicho que los ESA eran una responsabilidad potencial. Simpatizaba con las aerolíneas que se veían obligadas a transportarlos por ley. ¿Qué son? Son simplemente mascotas de la que alguien depende debido a una discapacidad emocional reconocida. El perro pitbull podría haber perdido una pelea feroz y estar desanimado. Con una nota de un profesional médico, se podría llevar a ese perro a bordo del avión, y las aerolíneas tendrían que transportarlo. El peleador de perros no tiene experiencia en adiestramiento canino de cara al público. El perro está entrenado, pero sólo para matar y mutilar. ¡Qué engaño y qué problema de seguridad! Cuando la FAA abrió un periodo de comentarios públicos sobre posibles cambios en la política de los ESA, presenté mis ideas.

De repente me di cuenta de que, en mi caso, Boosted y Busted me apoyaban emocionalmente. La *línea roja en la arena* estaba a punto de cambiar. No pasaba un día sin que pensara en la muerte de Booster. Las mascotas ayudan a sus dueños a liberar endorfinas. Los cachorros probablemente liberan más que los perros adultos. Llamé a la compañía aérea y pregunté si había alguna especificación de edad para un ESA. Me dijeron que no. Entonces pregunté si una persona puede tener dos ESA. La agente me dijo que no, pero que lo comprobaría. Le expliqué que ya había volado con dos perros de asistencia. Tras una larga espera, volvió a la línea y dijo que no habría problema si el profesional médico declaraba por escrito que necesitaba a los dos cachorros por razones de apoyo emocional. Llamé a mi cuidadora de perros. *Casualmente*, ella iba al mismo psiquiatra que yo y su cita mensual casualmente era unos días después de mi llamada.

Nuestro psiquiatra escribió encantado la carta requerida. *¡Dios bendiga a Estados Unidos y a la ESA!*

Reservé un boleto en la última fila del avión, frente al lavabo, y luego fui a una ferretería coreana e intenté explicar que necesitaba láminas de plástico Visqueen. Tardé un poco, pero conseguí un rollo. Luego fui a la tienda de comestibles e intenté explicar que necesitaba ambientador y NO en aerosol (ya que lo llevaba en un avión). Intenta pedir un ambientador en aerosol como una persona de habla inglesa en Corea. Pensé en el programa de televisión y la película *Misión Imposible*. "Su misión, señor Hawn, es explicarle a un coreano que necesita ambientador y en un envase con bomba". De forma clara y concisa pedí un *ambientador con bomba*. El dependiente coreano simplemente se negó a entender. ¡Yo pensaba que había expresado claramente mis deseos en Korenglish! No lograba hacerme entender, pero una atenta compradora coreana escuchó mi conversación y sintió mi frustración. Me explicó en coreano lo que necesitaba y el problema se resolvió allí mismo. Para que conste, si alguna vez necesita un ambientador sin aerosol en Corea, se pronuncia *bi eeolojol gong-gicheongjeongje*. Etiqueté las botellas con la palabra "smell" (olor) con la esperanza de que el personal de seguridad de la aerolínea entendiera lo que había en la botella.

A medida que se acercaba la hora de regresar a casa, me volvía más receloso de volar con cachorros que hacían sus necesidades y defecaban dentro de sus jaulas en el avión. Envié a un amigo un boleto de avión a Seúl para que me ayudara con los cachorros. Si yo estaba durmiendo y un cachorro hacía sus necesidades y el olor se extendía por el avión, seguramente me echarían a 30.000 pies de altura. Supuse que podríamos turnarnos para dormir, así ninguno estaría demasiado agotado para refrescar el aire rápidamente si las bombas de comida usada de perro caían. Esperaba que los demás pasajeros estuvieran durmiendo y soñando que visitaban una granja en casa, si el olor

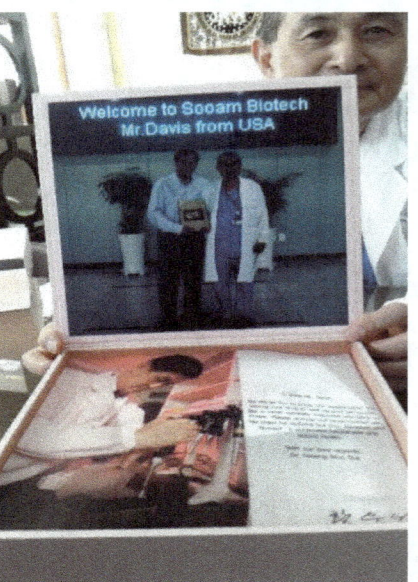

ambiental empeoraba. Además, compré un tercer asiento, con la esperanza de que los demás permanecieran vacíos. A menudo, los asientos vacíos se colocan estratégicamente junto a compañeros que viajan con sus perros de servicio.

Unos días antes de que voláramos a casa, un equipo de *Dateline NBC* acudió a los pasillos sagrados del SOOAM. Uno de los productores me entrevistó y quería respuestas de una sola frase a preguntas difíciles y delicadas. Por mucho que lo intenté, no pude dar respuestas concisas de una sola línea. No fue fácil clonar a Booster. Y aún más difícil era explicar por qué lo había hecho, en una sola frase. Tal vez por eso mis imágenes nunca salieron al aire. Los productores optaron por emitir una entrevista que habían realizado a un adiestrador de perros del ejército estadounidense que estaba en el SOOAM al mismo tiempo que yo. Explicó que había clonado uno de los mejores perros del ejército, un belga malinois. Yo tenía mis dos cachorros Booster y él tenía sus cinco cachorros militares. Cuando le preguntaron sobre sus expectativas con respecto al cachorro clonado, el adiestrador dijo que pensaba que sería como los demás cachorros. "¿Lo era?" preguntó el entrevistador. La asombrosa respuesta fue: "Oh, no, no... el cachorro clonado estaba más centrado, era más maduro y parecía mostrar una experiencia vital previa".

Por fin llegó el gran día y pronto estaríamos volando por los cielos (con suerte) amigables. SOOAM organizó una fiesta de graduación para celebrar el momento. Todos los empleados se unieron a nosotros en una gran sala de conferencias y vimos una presentación en video que documentaba la evolución de Boosted y Busted desde el día en que llegaron a este mundo. Acompañada de una música conmovedora, fue la gota que colmó el vaso. Mi maldita presa se rompió una vez más cuando mi serenidad se vio afectada por el calentamiento global extremo dentro de la sala. Las cámaras de *Dateline NBC* llegaron a la escena mientras Boosted y Busted eran colocados cuidadosamente sobre mi pecho palpitante, uno a uno, entrando en mi corazón. De algún modo, me recompuse el tiempo suficiente para pronunciar un *discurso* de agradecimiento que me aseguré de dirigir a los ojos coreanos que me observaban pero que probablemente no podían entender.

Expliqué al personal de SOOAM que el profesor Hwang era conocido por decir a sus estudiantes de posgrado de la Universidad Nacional de Seúl que esperaba que trabajaran lunes, martes, miércoles, jueves, viernes, ¡viernes y viernes! Con lágrimas en los ojos miré a cada uno de los treinta pares de ojos que había en la sala y les dije, "Quiero darles las gracias de todo corazón por trabajar lunes, martes, miércoles, jueves, viernes, ¡viernes y viernes! para clonar a mi Booster y hacer todo esto posible".

Los creanos me enseñaron mucho más que la clonación de perros. Fue una lección de vida y un honor innegable. Como perro viejo, aprendí nuevos trucos que llevaría adelante en la vida y nunca olvidaría. El climax final llegó justo cuando salíamos del edificio.

Cuando terminó la fiesta de graduación, Derek y yo llevamos a Boosted y Busted a la furgoneta de biotech. Entonces me dieron un regalo de despedida único. El profesor Hwang me entregó una caja con una foto de recuerdo y muestras de cosméticos que él había ayudado a desarrollar. Recuerdo que pensé en lo elegante que había sido toda la experiencia en

SOOAM. Desde darme libre acceso a biotech para entrenar a Boosted y Busted, hasta obsequiarme videos y regalos muy preciados. Una vez que los clones tomaron asiento, partimos. Sinceramente, no recuerdo el recorrido al aeropuerto aquel día. Sólo me acuerdo de haber llevado a Boosted y a Busted en sus *maletas* hasta la sala de pasajeros, que probablemente nunca había tenido un visitante canino. Mientras mi amigo Derek vigilaba a mis *futuros Boosters*, me hice amigo del personal del mostrador de la aerolínea. Con los ojos hinchados, me acerqué a ellos y les compartí el legado de Booster y por qué sentía que los coreanos tenían un alma especial. Había mecanografiado un dossier de varias páginas sobre la historia de mi Booster, que culminaba con la clonación. Con empatía y comprensión, nos permitieron abordar el avión primero.

Una vez dentro del avión, presenté mi dossier de Booster a las azafatas que nos recibieron. Encontré nuestros tres asientos y rápidamente coloqué la lámina de Visqueen, rodé los transportines de los cachorros y nos sentamos. Desafortunadamente, el avión estaba lleno. El único asiento que quedaba en nuestro grupo estaba ocupado por una señora que olía a Durian en mal estado y que, sin embargo, se quejaba de estar sentada junto a perros. Boosted y Busted olían mucho mejor; los habían rociado ligeramente con colonia Polo Blue de Ralph Lauren.

Tuve suerte de que mis compañeros de viaje fueran humanos y no perros. Si hubiera sido al revés, habría tenido problemas. El olfato humano palidece en comparación con el de un perro, que puede oler entre diez mil y cien mil veces mejor. Según los científicos, un perro puede oler una cucharadita de azúcar en un millón de litros de agua, o una manzana podrida en dos millones de barriles. Quería asegurarme de que, si mis compañeros de vuelo tenían que oler algo que emanara de mí dirección, fueran flores de manzano brotando del spray desodorante que había comprado para este acontecimiento especial. ¡Si se me salía un gas, no quería que Boosted y Busted sufrieran el impacto! Me tiro un pedo, roció, ¡salvo el día! Como siempre, era muy consciente de que mis acciones afectarían la capacidad de otros, que seguirían nuestras huellas.

Abrí los transportines, acaricié a Boosted y a Busted y les di una golosina a cada uno. Me miraron con una mirada que conocía demasiado bien. Era una mirada de adoración que al instante me hizo pensar en su

origen. Era la sonrisa y la mirada de confianza de mi Booster multiplicada por dos. Al instante me sentí abrumado, dominado e hipnotizado. Me iba a casa con un séquito canino de amor, y con un amigo que decidió ayudarme en esta empresa aparentemente imposible. Booster me había enseñado a reconocer el amor y a no tener miedo de usar la palabra. Me volví hacia mi

amigo Derek y le dije, "No podría haber hecho esto sin ti...amigo mío".

Cuando el vuelo ya estaba en marcha, una azafata se acercó a nosotros y con una sonrisa, nos dijo, "Sr. Hawn, todos hemos leído su periódico. Estamos aquí para ayudarle, pero debo hacerle una pregunta". Ella preguntó si podía acariciar a los cachorros. De repente supe que todo iba a salir bien. Puse a Boosted en mi regazo y su adorable mano acarició su cabeza. Inmediatamente movió la cola en reconocimiento del honor concedido. Entonces le expliqué que era importante que Busted tuviera la misma oportunidad debido a la equidad. Entonces puse a Busted en mi regazo y el proceso se repitió. Durante todo el vuelo, las azafatas se desvivieron por Boosted y Busted. Nunca olvidaré su amabilidad.

Una hora antes de aterrizar, insistieron en trasladarnos a primera clase para que pudiéramos desembarcar más rápido. Las azafatas tenían un requisito, insistieron en llevar a Boosted y Busted en brazos a la cabina de primera clase. Una vez sentados, los hombres de negocios dejaron lo que estaban haciendo, preguntaron por los cachorros y algunos de ellos pidieron acariciarlos. Cloné a mi Booster, y fui reprendido por mis familiares, mientras otros me acusaban de jugar a ser Dios. ¡Milagrosamente acabé en un avión que descendía de una visita celestial! ¡OMPS! (Oh, Mi Poder Superior) ¡OMB! (Oh, Mi Booster).

Pasar por la aduana fue otra historia. Estaba preocupado, aunque no tenía una razón válida para ello. Cuando me acerqué al inspector, le pregunté dócilmente, "¿Ha visto alguna vez cachorros de 100.000 dólares? Son clones de un perro al que quiero mucho", le dije.

"¿Tiene certificados de rabia?" preguntó.

Con la mano algo temblorosa le entregué los papeles veterinarios coreanos esperando que no surgiera ningún problema.

El inspector me miró a los ojos y dijo, "Disfrute de sus cachorros. Bienvenido a casa, señor". Casualmente, compartió con entusiasmo, "Yo entreno perros".

Volví a sentir gratitud.

Mi amigo me miró y dijo, "¡En Inglaterra, de donde soy, no creo que la Reina reciba mejor trato que el que recibieron los cachorros en todo este viaje!"

Llevamos a los cachorros en sus carritos hasta el mostrador de alquiler de automóviles del aeropuerto de Dallas. Alquilé una minivan espaciosa y nos dirigimos a nuestra habitación de hotel para descansar. Llevé a Busted y Boosted fuera para que retozaran libremente en una zona de hierba poco frecuentada por otras mascotas o animales. Los cachorros son muy susceptibles al parvovirus canino, que tiene una tasa de mortalidad del 50% y cuyo tratamiento puede resultar costoso. Descubierto en los años setenta, el virus se extendió por todo el mundo en pocos años. El parvo puede vivir en los entornos más duros hasta un año, sin que exista una forma 100% segura de erradicarlo en suelos contaminados.

¿Cómo socializar a un cachorro de perro de asistencia, algo de vital importancia durante las primeras doce a catorce semanas de edad, y protegerlo al mismo tiempo del parvo? Es una decisión que hay que tomar con sentido común. Son más los perros que pierden la vida por falta de socialización que por parvo. Los perros no socializados suelen terminar en refugios, sin posibilidad de ser adoptados, sujetos a la eutanasia. Tuve que arriesgarme a exponer a Boosted y Busted al parvo antes que exponerlos al fracaso por falta de socialización. Este es el caso de todos los cachorros de perros de asistencia en fase de adiestramiento.

Esa noche puse a Boosted y a Busted en el cuarto de baño con baldosas de cerámica y no en sus transportines. Quería que pudieran estirar sus jóvenes patas y no llorar. Por la mañana, tuve que ir a una tienda a comprar lejía y amoniaco para limpiar el suelo. No me alegré de haberles dado una libertad que se tradujo en un suelo sucio y un retraso en la salida. Sin embargo, estaba feliz de haber enfrentado el caos en el baño en lugar de un desastre más tarde en el avión. Con el baño más limpio de lo que estaba al principio, partimos hacia casa, con Boosted y Busted en el regazo de Derek. Era el compañero ideal para los nuevos bebés. El hogar estaba donde estuviera mi Booster. Mis pensamientos se aceleraron como en la NASCAR. Booster pronto estaría de nuevo en mis brazos, aunque no lo suficientemente pronto.

Me sentía culpable por haber estado fuera tanto tiempo. Una vez más, empecé a castigarme. Mi abusivo yo interno me atormentaba. Me detuve, cogí a Boosted y lo senté en mi regazo mientras conducía. Lo acaricié y, para mi sorpresa, se quedó dormido. Después de mirar a Busted para darle mi reconocimiento, miré a mi sonriente amigo Derek, empecé a explicarle y me di cuenta de que él sabía que necesitaba consuelo. Él sabía... que era mi amigo.

Cuando llegamos a casa, estallé en llanto y abracé a Booster. Lo acuné y lo miré profundamente a los ojos. Él miró a Boosted y a Busted con desconcierto. Inclinó la cabeza hacia la derecha y luego hacia la izquierda. Él no podía entender la aparentemente inexplicable conexión que sintió. Era sutil, pero siempre presente. Mantuve a los clones a distancia durante un tiempo, presentándolos lentamente a Booster y a la manada. Todo salió bien. Yo me sentía muy vivo por dentro; experimenté una explosión festiva del Cuatro de Julio dentro de *mi alma.*

CAPÍTULO 18
CLONACIÓN:
PRUEBAS Y TRIBULACIONES

Los clones eran una copia anatómica exacta de Booster, que tenía unas caderas terriblemente displásicas. Sabía que los había traído al mundo, y que necesariamente desarrollarían caderas defectuosas. ¿Por qué haría algo así? Una ventaja de la clonación es que sabes hasta cierto punto lo que vas a obtener... lo bueno y lo malo. En la BUCS me habían hablado de la cirugía JPS y sabía que tenía que hacerse pronto, ya que pierde eficacia con cada semana que pasa, así que era imperativo operar de inmediato. Había llamado a clínicas en todo el país para que realizara el procedimiento y recibí respuestas desde un simple "No sabemos qué es eso", hasta "No podemos hacerlo porque tienes un clon valorado en 100.000 dólares, y nuestro seguro de mala praxis no nos cubrirá esa cantidad". También me dieron cotizaciones de hasta 3.000 dólares por perro. Después de una investigación exhaustiva, hablé con la gente del Centro de Salud Veterinaria de la Universidad de Missouri (MIZZOU). Hablé con el Dr. Torres, especializado en cirugía ortopédica de pequeños animales, con interés en la artrosis y la medicina deportiva. Estaba muy bien informado e irradiaba confianza; sin duda, era el médico apropiado para el trabajo.

A los pocos días, Derek y yo, junto con Boosted y Busted, nos pusimos en camino hacia el Centro de Salud de la Universidad de Missouri. Al llegar, nos trataron con guantes de seda. Un sonriente Dr. Torres nos hizo señas para que entráramos en una sala de examen. Le fascinó mi historia y no pudo ser más amable. Nos explicó que la cirugía era mínimamente invasiva y nos citó para el día siguiente. Me preocupaba que anestesiaran a Boosted y a Busted, ¡pero más me preocupaban sus caderas! Al día siguiente, todo salió según lo planeado. Un día después, Boosted y Busted fueron dados de alta. Sugerí que hiciéramos un reportaje para promocionar el procedimiento. Se organizó una sesión fotográfica. El costo de los procedimientos fue increíblemente razonable y me quedé helado cuando vi que me habían hecho un descuento porque los cachorros eran perros de servicio en adiestramiento o iban a ser utilizados como perros de servicio. Significó mucho para mí.

Mi(s) Booster(s).   *Viendo doble.*

Un trío de felicidad.   *¿Quién soy? preguntó Boosted, mirándose en un espejo.*

(Fotos cortesía de Karen Clifford Centro de Salud Veterinaria de la Universidad de Missouri, MIZZOU)

Booster disfrutaba a diario de su progenie. Jugaban y correteaban todo el tiempo mientras los clones se disputaban su atención. Con frecuencia, los otros niños caninos se unían. Un año después, fui a un festival que se celebraba en un parque de la ciudad. Caminaba con Boosted y Busted uno al lado del otro. Conocimos a todo tipo de gente, jóvenes y mayores. Decir que un perro es un lubricante social es quedarse muy corto. Nunca olvidaré cuando Busted se acercó a un hombre que se destacaba entre la multitud. Muchos perros se habrían sentido incómodos o habrían ladrado ante un hombre que llevaba un gorro y un gran palo en la mano. Busted mantuvo la calma. Yo había aprendido en la BUCS a introducir "activadores ambientales" a una edad temprana y el entrenamiento dio sus frutos. De repente, el hombre se arrodilló, y surgió el amor. Él recibió calurosamente los fervientes besos de Busted. Se trataba de un veterano sin hogar que utilizaba el palo para mantener el equilibrio debido a una lesión sufrida en combate años atrás. Aunque a Busted le resultó mucho más fácil conectar con el hombre que a mí, me enteré de que el veterano tenía dos cosas muy cerca de su corazón... la bandera de EE.UU. que llevaba con orgullo en el pecho y el amor incondicional de un perro de servicio.

Me acordé de mis estudios en la BUCS. Había aprendido cómo los perros cambiaban la vida de los veteranos de todo el mundo y reducían la tasa de suicidios. Fue una experiencia de la vida real que corroboró mi educación en el aula. Reflexioné sobre lo mucho que mi educación en la BUCS había influido en mi vida cotidiana y, posteriormente, en la de muchas otras personas. Al instante pensé en la vez que mi buen amigo Charles me  informó de que había estado en el hospital de veteranos y le habían diagnosticado una dolencia hepática. Era candidato a un trasplante de hígado, pero necesitaba a alguien que lo cuidara en caso de ser operado. Booster y yo acompañamos a Charles al hospital de veteranos de Houston (Texas), donde iban a evaluarlo para la intervención.

Llegamos al hospital y nos registramos en la VA Fisher House, que ofrece alojamiento gratuito para pacientes y sus familias. Al entrar en la habitación, el teléfono empezó a sonar. Charles contestó la llamada e inmediatamente me pasó el teléfono. "¿Tienes un *perro* en la habitación?" preguntó la voz con tono autoritario.

Le respondí, "Tengo un perro de servicio en la habitación, ¡igual al que aparece en los folletos de su recepción!" No estaba preparado para la conversación que siguió.

"Ese perro tiene que irse", dijo la mujer de manera dictatorial.

Le respondí cortésmente, "No señora, el perro de servicio no tiene que irse".

"¿Tiene sus papeles?" (Esto no tenía nada que ver con la cartilla de vacunación, que ella habría tenido derecho a pedir).

Estuve a punto de perder los nervios y le dije, "¿Quiere el título de bachillerato, el GED o el certificado de notas de la universidad?"

Ella colgó y evitó una crisis de proporciones nucleares.

Al día siguiente, en trío, entramos en el hospital. Charles iba a someterse a innumerables pruebas. Algunos médicos sonreían, pero una doctora de origen extranjero parecía consternada y agitada. Era evidente que no le gustaba ver a un perro en el hospital. En algunas culturas, los perros son rechazados. Más tarde ese mismo día, cuando Charles terminó una prueba, una enfermera se acercó a nosotros y nos dijo que Charles tenía una cita con el Jefe de Personal. Supuse que era para verificar que tenía un cuidador.

Las primeras palabras que salieron de la boca del hombre fueron, "¡Señor, estamos aquí para hablar del perro!"

"Estupendo", respondí, recordando mi formación en la BUCS para mantener la calma ante la adversidad o la ignorancia (ignorancia no es un término despectivo). Le expliqué, "Señor, tiene usted aquí unas instalaciones preciosas. Tengo una maestría en Ciencias de la Vida Canina con énfasis en Educación de Perros de Servicio. Asistí a la aclamada Universidad Bergin de Estudios Caninos. La universidad fundó un programa llamado Paws for Purple Hearts para ayudar a reducir la tasa de suicidios entre nuestros veteranos. Como probablemente sabrá, mueren más veteranos por suicidio que en combate, aproximadamente uno cada hora. Si sus hombres terminan en bolsas para cadáveres, no hay mucho que usted pueda hacer por ellos. Señor, estamos de acuerdo en salvar vidas".

El caballero explicó que su trabajo era informarse. Le aplaudí por su diligencia y salimos de la oficina. Mi Booster y yo fuimos directamente a la unidad de rehabilitación física, con Charles siguiéndonos tímidamente. Al llegar a la unidad, pregunté si sería posible que mi Booster hiciera una visita como perro de terapia–él estaba certificado por Therapy Dogs International–y demostrara tareas de perro de servicio. La señora me explicó que ya tenían visitas de organizaciones de perros de terapia, pero que si estuvieran interesados, me llamarían más tarde.

Efectivamente, sobre las cinco de la tarde sonó el teléfono y me invitaron a visitar al personal al día siguiente. "¿Podrían venir usted y su perro Booster sobre las 12, durante nuestro periodo del almuerzo?"

¿Cómo sabía ella el nombre de mi Booster? Le hice esa pregunta.

"Señor, hice una búsqueda en internet y lo encontré en varias páginas de todo el mundo".

"¿Me investigaste?" pregunté asombrado.

"No creerá que voy a dejar que cualquiera que venga de la calle hable con mi personal, ¿verdad?"

¿No es genial? Una vez más, la educación engendra educación... el trabajo duro y la dedicación cosechan recompensas. Yo sólo tenía una maestría, pero mi Booster se doctoró en Perro Fenomenal. Pasar de "ese perro tiene que irse" a "por favor, visite a nuestro personal", ¡todavía me asombra!

¡Al mes siguiente, un vecino invitó a Boosted y Busted a unirse a los Scouts! Habrían sido excelentes Scouts, sin embargo, se trataba de una invitación para unirse a los Scouts en una reunión para demostrar las tareas  de los perros de servicio. Se turnaron para demostrar sus habilidades, y con el mismo talento realizaron las tareas solicitadas. Booster se habría sentido muy orgulloso de ver a su progenie rendir a su altura. Los clones heredaron el conjunto de habilidades únicas necesarias para ser los mejores perros de servicio, ya fuera ofreciendo apoyo emocional o abriendo un frigorífico o la puerta de una camioneta.

Como dice el refrán, obtienes lo que pagas. Aunque no siempre es cierto, sí lo fue en el caso de la clonación de Booster. Mi hermano me reprendió por gastar mucho dinero en clonar un perro. Como siempre ocurría, esa fue la luz verde que necesitaba para seguir adelante con el proceso de toma de decisiones. Era la prueba de fuego que utilizaba a menudo para decidir. Si él decía "no", yo escuchaba "¡sigue adelante! Cada día que pasaba, daba gracias a mi Poder Superior por poner un "booster" en mi vida. ¡Había recargado mi *potenciador* clonando a mi Booster!

Meses después, vi un anuncio en televisión. *Dateline NBC - La Zona de Clonación, ¿Clonarías a tu perro?* aparecía en un lugar destacado de la pantalla. Más tarde lo sintonicé y vi el reportaje algo sesgado. Entrevistaron a un especialista en clonación y a una pareja británica que había clonado a su querido perro. El debate que siguió cuestionaba si la clonación se aprovechaba de los vulnerables dueños, haciéndoles creer que podían recuperar a su mascota fallecida. Estoy seguro de que ninguno de los comentaristas había clonado nunca un perro y probablemente tenían más experiencia en tonterías que en la clonación de perros y la conexión canino-humana. La pareja británica explicó que al principio estaban un poco recelosos, pero que estaban muy contentos con la experiencia.

Mientras estaba en SOOAM, me hice amigo de un caballero japonés que había clonado a su perro en SOOAM. El gobierno japonés impone una cuarentena de seis meses a la importación de perros al país. Sorprendentemente, el señor volaba de Japón a Corea casi todos los fines de semana para jugar con su amado cachorro clonado. Que conste que nunca he conocido a nadie desencantado con la decisión de clonar a un ser querido canino.

Además de clonar mascotas, SOOAM desarrolló modelos para clonar cachorros que desarrollarán ciertas enfermedades como Alzheimer y diabetes. Como resultado directo, los investigadores disponen ahora de una valiosa herramienta para buscar tratamientos médicos preventivos o curativos. La clonación de órganos humanos para su implantación es un objetivo prioritario, ya que estos órganos, fabricados a partir de células propias, no deberían ser rechazados ni obligar al receptor a tomar de por vida medicamentos debido al rechazo. ¿Qué pensaría mi hermana de la clonación si un miembro de su familia recibiera un trasplante de órganos clonados que le salvara la vida? No me atrevo a preguntárselo. Ella no podría soportar semejante "activador ambiental".

El ADN humano y el canino son muy similares, por lo que suelen utilizarse perros en experimentos científicos. ¡Estoy seguro de que esto, comprensiblemente, tiene a PETA molesto! Hoy en día, los humanos reciben tratamientos contra el linfoma basados en los conocimientos adquiridos en estudios realizados con sangre donada de Golden retriever. En Estados Unidos los Golden retriever tienen una alta tasa de incidencia de linfoma, y suelen sucumbir a esta forma de cáncer a partir de los ocho años de edad.

Personalmente, considero que utilizar animales para probar cosas como las reacciones a los perfumes es inaceptable. Cuando se trata de curar el cáncer, la diabetes, el Alzheimer y otras temibles enfermedades, es motivo de consideración adicional. Booster participó en la *primera investigación clínica* de este tipo en el mundo para el tratamiento de su carcinoma de células escamosas; los seres humanos se beneficiaron directamente de ello. La investigación puede realizarse de forma ética y beneficiosa, aunque a menudo se considera en un contexto negativo con respecto a la participación de animales. Mientras aprendía a amar la vida gracias al amor incondicional de un perro, aprendí a apreciar las cosas que la preservan. La investigación ética es una herramienta para hacer precisamente eso. Por supuesto, la definición de "ética" es tema para otro libro.

Para que conste, soy un gran defensor de la clonación, sobre todo con un fin razonable. En mi caso, se trataba de evitar una depresión profunda y la posibilidad de consecuencias catastróficas. También necesitaba lo que comúnmente se denomina un *perro sucesor*, un nuevo perro de asistencia cuando el perro actual es muy viejo para trabajar o ha fallecido. Booster era una parte integral de la persona en la que me había convertido. Fue mi estímulo evolutivo que transformó mi vida para mejor, proporcionándome seguridad, dirección y un propósito. Bajo su tutela, aprendí a vivir y, lo que es más importante, deseé hacerlo. Clonar a Booster fue esencial para mi bienestar.

La clonación puede no ser atractiva para algunos, y respeto eso. Suelo compartir mis pensamientos sobre el tema porque siento que estoy adoptando una postura defensiva cuando, en realidad, debería sentir justo lo contrario. Estoy orgulloso de mi decisión y mi trayectoria vital posterior da fe de ello. Apareció un artículo algo negativo en *Psychology Today* y tuve que contribuir al diálogo en línea:

PSICOLOGÍA ACTUAL

CLONACIÓN DE LA REALIDAD

Enviado por Davis Hawn y Booster el 2 de agosto de 2016 - 4:57pm

Cloné a mi perro Booster, que una vez me salvó la vida. Prometí compartirlo con el mundo. ¡Para poder hacerlo, obtuve una maestría en Ciencias de la Vida Canina en la Universidad Bergin de Ciencias Caninas de California! Booster fue clonado en SOOAM, Seúl, Corea del Sur. Sufro de depresión y alguna vez estuve a punto de darme por vencido. Booster cambió mi vida 180 grados. Busca en Google, Davis Hawn Booster y verás lo que un perro hizo por un hombre y por otros en todo el mundo. Sus clones Boosted y Busted encarnan sus cualidades: confianza, cero agresividad, sensibilidad y una aguda ética de trabajo. La clonación me permitió avanzar en el mundo del mismo modo que lo hizo Booster. ¡La concordancia de personalidad entre un can y un humano lo es todo! En realidad, los clones evidencian experiencias vitales previas. Los cachorros abrieron la puerta de mi camioneta, encontraron una botella de agua y me la entregaron en la mano ¡SIN HABER SIDO ENTRENADOS NUNCA ANTES PARA HACERLO! Habían sido entrenados para abrir una nevera. TODAS las personas que he conocido han estado contentas con los resultados de la clonación de su mascota. Alguien dijo que tuvo que decidir si invertir en un Land Rover nuevo, o en un clon. El automóvil se deprecia, ¡mientras que los clones se revalorizan con el paso de los días! Clonar es la mejor decisión que he tomado. Ojalá todos los dueños de mascotas tuvieran esa opción. Los detractores hacen gran daño a quienes necesitan las cualidades únicas de los animales que cambiaron sus vidas. Karen dio en el clavo. Lo hizo bien. Booster estuvo a mi lado durante 12 años como mi perro de servicio. Los clones empezaron con un año de madurez e inteligencia heredada. Si alguien quiere hablar con un individuo que clonó a su perro . . . y quiere una opinión imparcial . . . por favor envíeme un correo electrónico.

Davis Hawn

PD Al menos conserve las células de sus mascotas para futuras clonaciones si tiene algún interés en hacerlo.

Mis esfuerzos por explicar mi experiencia de clonación, basada en la vida real y no en conjeturas por ignorancia, dieron sus frutos.

ME ALEGRO MUCHO POR DAVIS

Enviado por Karen en Agosto 2, 2016 - 10:46pm

Me alegro mucho por Davis, Booster, Boosted y Busted por haber encontrado un amor incondicional y sin límites. Deberíamos documentar información como la de Davis para mejorar nuestra comprensión. He guardado todos los juguetes y camas de Baby para ver si su clon reconoce los olores. El amor es energía que trasciende los límites físicos. ¿Quiénes somos nosotros para imponer limitaciones a cosas que no comprendemos del todo? Sólo podemos observar, documentar y estudiar para ser más conscientes en el futuro. Estoy muy agradecida por la ciencia y la tecnología, que han abierto puertas y mentes a nuevos descubrimientos y posibilidades.

Enviado por <u>Jessica Pierce Ph.D.</u> el 2 de agosto de 2016 - 5:18pm

Davis – Gracias por compartir tus experiencias personales. ¡Tres hurras por Booster y sus clones por haber cambiado tanto tu vida! [4]

Años más tarde, me entrevistó un periodista local de la emisora de televisión WLOX de Gulfport, Mississippi. Hizo un trabajo extraordinario y filmó a Boosted y Busted en acción, trayéndome una botella de agua de la nevera. Sorprendentemente, ese día ambos cogieron la botella al mismo tiempo y me la trajeron. Fue un bonito trabajo en equipo, perfecto para el reportaje. Más tarde, el reportero me envió una foto que había tomado con su móvil en el patio delantero. Años después, cuando estuve en Tailandia, la convertí en un óleo (contraportada).

En 2016, cuando Boosted y Busted tenían alrededor de año y medio, decidí asistir a la Western Veterinary Conference en Las Vegas. Llamé a mi amigo Warren y aceptó acompañarme para ayudarme. Cuando entré en la conferencia con Boosted y Busted, la gente vio la palabra CLONE en sus chalecos de perro de servicio. Muchos pensaron que era el nombre del perro. Veterinarios y otros asistentes pedían a gritos conocer a los clones y escuchar mi historia. Asistí a una conferencia tras otra, absorbiendo conocimientos como una toalla de papel en una inundación. Warren y yo paseamos a Boosted y Busted por la sala de exposiciones, donde los

---

[4] Davis Hawn, "Todos los perros van al cielo," *Psychology Today* (Febrero 2016), https://www.psychologytoday.com/ie/blog/all-dogs-go-heaven/201602/cloning-pets#comments_bottom. [enlace inédito]

vendedores ofrecían sus productos para perros. No sé quién disfrutó más paseando, si nosotros o los perros.

Una de las conferencias veterinarias corrió a cargo de un especialista en ortopedia canina, que mostró en pantalla una radiografía de un cachorro con caderas en evidente mal estado. A continuación, ofreció tres opciones de tratamiento: (1) monitorear las caderas, (2) administrarle medicamentos para las caderas y (3) operarlo de inmediato. Cuando preguntó a los asistentes qué opción recomendarían a los padres de sus mascotas, casi todos los veterinarios presentes eligieron las opciones uno o dos. Mi mano se levantó al instante, casi tocando el techo, optando por la opción número tres, operar inmediatamente. El especialista me preguntó por qué operaría al cacharro.

Le respondí con entusiasmo, "Con la cirugía mínimamente invasiva del JPS, realizada de forma óptima entre las doce y las catorce semanas de edad, las caderas del perro adulto se habrán beneficiado enormemente". De hecho, estos dos perros sentados a mi lado son clones de un perro que tenía unas caderas excepcionalmente malas. Ambos clones se sometieron a la cirugía JPS a la edad apropiada. Las radiografías de sus caderas tienen muy buen aspecto. Es como si hubiera cogido a mi perro original de más edad, lo hubiera metido en una máquina del tiempo, lo hubiera devuelto a su etapa de cachorro y le hubiera practicado la cirugía JPS. Luego, como en la película *Volver al futuro*, lo devolví a la edad adulta y le hice nuevas radiografías. Los clones son anatómicamente el mismo perro original. Aunque puede haber algunas diferencias ambientales sutiles, en general, es indiscutible que el procedimiento benefició a los clones."

Una vez captada la atención del público, expliqué lo difícil que era encontrar un centro capaz de realizar el procedimiento. Terminé diciendo que yo no era veterinario, ni siquiera técnico veterinario, pero que tenía un máster en Ciencias de la Vida Canina de la aclamada BUCS, donde había estudiado bajo los auspicios de muchos educadores e investigadores caninos de renombre. En ese momento, me sentí increíblemente orgulloso de mi formación en la BUCS y de la Dra. Bergin, fundadora de la universidad y creadora del concepto de perro de servicio. Me incliné y abracé a Boosted y Busted.

A la mañana siguiente, llamé a una cadena de televisión local para ver si querían cubrir el reportaje, ya que había miles de personas en la ciudad asistiendo a la conferencia que probablemente estarían interesadas. Aceptaron enviar un reportero esa tarde. Efectivamente, un joven se puso en contacto conmigo y llegó con una cámara en la mano. Me pareció un poco cursi, pero agradecí el esfuerzo. Esa noche, el reportaje no se emitió. Llamé a la emisora a la mañana siguiente y el director pensó que estaba intentando cometer un fraude. Le expliqué que la historia de mi vida se encontraba en Internet.

El director explicó con naturalidad, "Ahí es donde se producen la mayoría de los fraudes hoy en día". Casualmente, la emisora estaba afiliada a la NBC.

Entonces le pregunté, "¿No están ustedes afiliados a la NBC?" Él respondió, "Sí".

"¿Confiarías en un productor ejecutivo de la NBC?" le pregunté. "¿A dónde quieres llegar?"

"Llame a la oficina de Nueva York y pregunte por la productora de *Dateline NBC*. "Ella me entrevistó en biotech, Seúl, y dará fe de mi autenticidad", expliqué alegremente.

Aquella tarde, un equipo de televisión "de verdad" nos filmó en la emisora. Fue una entrevista maravillosa y cálida. Cuando se emitió el reportaje, abría con un cartel en el centro de conferencias y la presentadora era *casualmente* una entusiasta coreana. Aluciné cuando vi el reportaje en la televisión, ya que incluía imágenes tomadas años antes en SOOAM Biotech que habían sido filmadas durante la entrevista de *Dateline*. ¿No es genial?[5]

---

[5] Gabby Hart, "El hombre que clonó a un perro de servicio fallecido comparte su historia," *NBC News* (May 19, 2016). https://news3lv.com/news/local/man-who-cloned-deceased-service-dog-shares-his-story

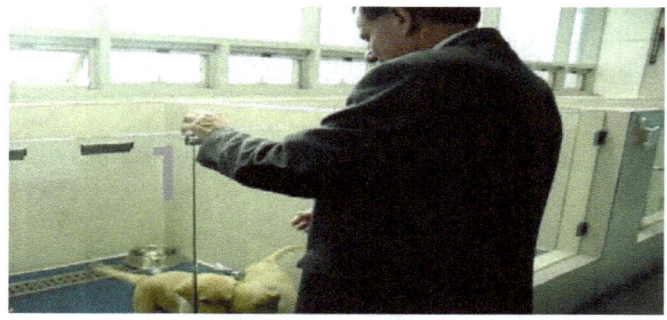

Boosted, Busted y yo volvimos a casa unos días después. ¡Fue agradable volver a ver a la manada! Compartí el video de televisión con amigos y me di cuenta, más que nunca, de cómo mi Booster, Boosted, Busted y los niños caninos había transformado mi vida. Mi pasión por compartir la medicina canina con el mundo crecía exponencialmente, impulsada por un sentido de la espiritualidad cada vez mayor. La vida volvió a la normalidad... hasta que estando de viaje en Asia, recibí una llamada telefónica de un fiscal adjunto del condado en el que vivía en Mississippi.

Habían encontrado el cadáver de un hombre en descomposición en el bosque de mi propiedad. Se había emitido una orden de inspección y mi casa fue registrada a profundidad. La señora que vivía en mi casa y cuidaba de mis hijos caninos mientras yo estaba fuera, tenía un hijo recién salido de la cárcel. El treintañero, parecido a *Hannibal Lector*, con la cara tatuada que lo hacía irreconocible, había pedido drogas y se había encargado de que se las entregaran en mi casa, a la que se había mudado sin que yo lo supiera. Acababa de salir de la cárcel, así que no tenía ni un céntimo. Cuando llegó la droga, sacó una escopeta y mató al traficante. Luego condujo el automóvil del traficante hasta la parte trasera de mi propiedad de 20 acres y lo cubrió con ramas. Meses después, su novia lo delató y los detectives vinieron a buscar el cadáver.

No soy un defensor de las armas, pero entiendo por qué la gente las necesita para protegerse. Yo tenía una pequeña escopeta calibre .410 para matar a las serpientes venenosas que parecían estar siempre presentes en mi propiedad, sobre todo en las orillas del estanque que había justo detrás de mí cabaña. El arma utilizada para cometer el asesinato no era otra que la mía. El monstruo de carne humana había encontrado mi escopeta debajo de las escaleras, en una bodega. Yo era el legítimo propietario del arma, así que me pidieron que me presentara a rendir declaración a mi regreso al país. Me enfadé al instante porque me habían usado.

Aunque no había hecho nada malo, los miedos y temores del pasado se apoderaron instantáneamente de mi psique. ¿Cómo iba a testificar contra *Hannibal*? Empecé a temblar y a balancearme. Hacía mucho tiempo que no lo hacía. El miedo estaba arraigado. No tenía a Boosted ni a Busted conmigo, así que tenía que valerme por mí mismo sin una gota de medicina canina. Sabía que me pedirían que testificara en el juicio del monstruo, y me sentía obligado a hacerlo. ¿Pero cómo? Salí a pasear, busqué el bar más cercano y me tomé unas cuartas copas.

Cuando regresé a Estados Unidos, me puse inmediatamente en contacto con el fiscal adjunto. Quedó en verme al día siguiente y me llevé a Boosted. Cuando entré en una oficina llena de caras sonrientes, con Boosted trotando alegremente a mi lado, me tranquilicé, aunque solo fuera por un momento. Mientras me interrogaban, no paraba de abrazar a Boosted. ¡Debo haber parecido un niño abrazando un osito de peluche! El arma del crimen fue encontrada entre el somier y el colchón de mi cama. Me preguntaron si dormía con el arma, y les expliqué que realmente no me gustan las armas y que nunca lo haría.

Hannibal había estado durmiendo en mi cama, haciendo el amor con mi escopeta. OMG, pensé. Tiré el colchón y el somier y dormí en otra habitación durante meses.

Le dije al fiscal adjunto que testificaría en el juicio a pesar de mi trastorno de estrés postraumático (TEPT). Él lo entendió perfectamente, como alma empática que era. Entonces le pregunté si podría tener a mi perro de servicio, Boosted, a mi lado cuando testificara, ya que sabía que *Hannibal* me estaría mirando. No estaba seguro de poder soportarlo en el tribunal, pero era más probable que lo hiciera con Boosted a mi lado.

Me explicó que nunca habían permitido que un perro acompañara a un testigo en la sala del tribunal, así que tendría que consultar al juez. Unos días más tarde, me llamó y me explicó que el juez había aceptado la presencia de mi perro de servicio en el juicio. Sí, lo has adivinado... me brotaron las lágrimas. Sentía gratitud por el fiscal adjunto y el juez, quienes entendieron mis necesidades y concedieron la adaptación.

Más tarde entré en la sala y subí al estrado. Boosted estaba tranquilamente a mis pies. Respondí lo mejor que pude las preguntas de ambos abogados mientras me hipnotizaba el rostro tatuado de *Hannibal*. El mismo mal, tenía la mirada puesta en mí. Estaba entumecido mientras acariciaba constantemente a Boosted en busca de consuelo y apoyo. Me lamió la mano como si supiera que estaba estresado. Sabía que lamería mis heridas emocionales incondicionalmente hasta que la infección psicológica sanara. En poco tiempo, el calvario terminó y me permitieron retirarme. Salí de la sala del tribunal y fui recibido en la calle por un abogado amante de los perros que vino a ver al perro en el juicio. Siguió una cálida conversación, y luego caminé con Boosted hasta un banco y me senté tranquilamente durante una hora antes de intentar volver a casa.

A la mañana siguiente, leí en el periódico lo que había ocurrido en el juicio. Resulta que era la primera vez que un perro de asistencia acompañaba a un testigo a un tribunal en la historia del Estado de Mississippi. Pensé que Booster estaría muy orgulloso. En ese momento de reflexión, estaba destrozado emocionalmente. Busted se levantó, cruzó la sala y se sentó a mis pies. Yo era un desastre emocional.

HARRISON COUNTY

Cloned dog accompanies witness testifying at Mississippi murder trial

BY PAUL HAMPTON

Hawn, an expert in service-dog training and a worldwide

Por si fuera poco, el juicio acabó siendo nulo porque un detective testificó sobre lo que la novia de *Hannibal* le había contado. Ella originalmente accedió a testificar pero luego cambió de opinión. Nadie había informado al detective. ¡Eso significaba que yo tendría que pasar por todo ese calvario otra vez! Estaba en Arkansas cuando recibí una llamada diciendo que me necesitaban para testificar la semana siguiente. Contraté a una niñera canina para cuidar de mi manada. Boosted y yo tomamos un avión a Mississippi para testificar una vez más. Resultó que el juicio se aplazó porque el sumario estaba lleno. Regresamos a Arkansas y nos reunimos con nuestra manada, sin resolver el problema. El juicio fue programado de nuevo para una fecha posterior. Por suerte, *Hannibal* conectó los puntos... cómo esas lágrimas tatuadas debajo de sus ojos. Finalmente aceptó un acuerdo con la fiscalía. Yo quedé exento. De alguna manera, mantuve la calma durante todo el calvario. Había aprendido de un perro, del programa Al-Anon, y de la BUCS. Sabía cómo interpretar las señales y vivir la vida en sus términos, buenos y malos. Además, había aprendido a vivir el presente, a dejar atrás el pasado y a no obsesionarme con el futuro. En otras palabras, ¡aprendí a vivir como un perro! Mi vida había alcanzado alturas nunca imaginadas. Me preguntaba si podría llegar más alto. Al igual que un adicto, temía volver a caer. Estaba eufórico por la vida. ¿OÍSTE ESO? ¡ESTABA EUFÓRICO!

Meses después, decidí visitar a mi querida amiga Peggy. Necesitaba inspiración, y ella era una de las personas más inspiradoras que conocía. Peggy me invitó amablemente a su casa, aunque yo sabía que estaba casi postrada en cama. Se había sometido a tratamientos de quimioterapia y había perdido la batalla del cabello, pero no la guerra. Hacía poco que había perdido la movilidad y sabía que tenía que verla mientras pudiera.

Yo había criado a uno de los cachorros de Booster, llamado Savior, que se convirtió en mi salvador en ausencia de su padre. Es curioso cómo funciona la vida. Nunca supe que le había puesto un nombre tan apropiado cuando no era más que un bulto blanco de energía que brincaba por la cabaña. Desde muy pequeño, Savior aprendió a recibir órdenes y a hacer tareas con facilidad. Era muy cariñoso como Booster y conquistaba a la gente a su manera. Era mucho más pegajoso que Booster, pero eso era exactamente lo que yo necesitaba en aquel momento. Peggy había visitado mi casa cuando Savior era sólo un cachorro. Me miró y me dijo, "Dave, es un guardián". Con tal estímulo, lo conservé. Llevé a Savior conmigo a visitar a Peggy.

Había perdido a Booster y estaba perdiendo a Peggy. Estaba desesperado por visitarla. *¿Estaba siendo egoísta* por necesitarla cuando se enfrentaba a la muerte? Me tranquilicé pensando que, conociendo a mi Peggy como la conocía, ella querría estar allí para mí. Después de pensarlo dos, tres y cuatro veces, decidí ver a Peggy y luego visitar a unos amigos en Ciudad de México. Reservé un boleto de ida y vuelta desde Nueva Orleans a Ciudad de México con United Airlines. En aquella época, United permitía a sus clientes volar y regresar más tarde con un boleto de ida y vuelta.

El sistema de boletos de United me llevó a McAllen, Texas, donde Savior y yo nos bajamos para visitar a Peggy. Nunca olvidaré cuando, acostado junto a Peggy en su cama, nos reímos y charlamos como un grupo de colegiales (que, por supuesto, éramos). Todo el tiempo, Savior estuvo en la cama a nuestro lado junto con Tera, la benefactora canina de Peggy. Todos estábamos compenetrados unos con otros, humanos y caninos por igual. Fue nada menos que glorioso. Era justo lo que necesitaba en ese momento.

Al cabo de unos días, Savior y yo regresamos al aeropuerto internacional de McAllen para tomar nuestro vuelo a Ciudad de México. United nos había reservado un boleto en una aerolínea asociada, Aeromar Airlines de México. Fuimos al mostrador y el agente de Aeromar se negó a emitir mi boleto. "Sólo transportamos a perros pequeños en una caja, señor".

"Pero deben llevar perros de servicio", le contesté. "Es la ley. Por favor, llame a su oficina en Ciudad de México", le pedí. El agente llamó, pero la oficina de origen le indicó que no me permitiera abordar con mi perro de servicio. Nos miramos con Savior. Sabía que debía mantener la calma, ya que gritar me convertiría en el malo de la película y justificaría la negativa de la aerolínea a volar con un *hombre peligroso.*

Pensé en mi Booster, que había cojeado de dolor para defender los derechos de acceso y visitar a niños igualmente doloridos.

Tenía que pensar con claridad y con convicción de propósito, ya que no podía defraudar a Booster, ni a otros que seguirían mis pasos, tratados de forma similar por una compañía aérea que viola la ley establecida. Así que respiré hondo y me serené lo mejor que pude, luego llamé al departamento del sheriff de McAllen y les expliqué la situación. Enviaron a un funcionario, que hizo todo lo posible por explicar la ley a los representantes de la aerolínea, pero fue en vano. Hizo un informe claro y conciso. Aunque se solidarizó con nuestra situación, él no podía obligar al personal de Aeromar a llevarnos.

Entonces llamé a una cadena de televisión local. En treinta minutos llegaron un reportero y un camarógrafo para realizar una entrevista. *Casualmente,* su cadena los había llamado justo antes de realizar un reportaje en otro sitio. Me explicaron que mi historia sonaba más interesante, así que empacaron todo y se dirigieron hacia mí. Les expliqué con firmeza, "A mi perro de servicio, Savor, no lo van a meter en una jaula, en la bodega de un avión a 100 grados de temperatura... ¡eso no va a pasar!" El aeropuerto estaba cerrando al concluir la entrevista, pero pude alquilar un automóvil en el último momento. Volví a encontrarme con Peggy y su cálido abrazo mientras me explicaba con regocijo que mi historia había aparecido en la pantalla de televisión, "Sigan sintonizados a las 5 p.m. ¡Se niega el acceso a un hombre con perro de servicio en el aeropuerto de McAllen!" A las pocas horas, sonó el teléfono de Peggy. Era un representante de United Airlines, disculpándose por las acciones de su socio, Aeromar Airlines. El representante nos consiguió un vuelo con United Airlines para la mañana siguiente. También se ofreció a pagar el alquiler de mi automóvil y el dinero perdido en la noche de hotel en Ciudad de México. ¡Fue un buen arreglo por no habernos llevado! ¡UNITED nos apoyó!

17 de agosto de 2015

Estimado señor Hawn,

Permítame disculparme por mi respuesta tardía y por el inconveniente que experimentó para viajar en el vuelo 0799 de Aeromar Airlines el 30JUL2015. Hemos recibido su solicitud y los recibos de reembolso. Tal y como le comenté en nuestra conversación telefónicas, le adjunto un cheque por valor de 259,42 USD, que representa el reembolso del alquiler del automóvil (56,86 USD) y los gastos de hotel (159,85 USD) en McAllen, TX, y 42,71 USD en Ciudad de México la noche del 30 de julio de 2015. Se ha procesado un reembolso de USD$50.00 a su tarjeta visa terminada en xxxx que representa una entrada al United Club. Por favor, espere de siete a diez días *hábiles para que se complete el proceso de reembolso. Tenga la seguridad de que United Airlines ha remitido su queja a Aeromar Airlines, ya que, según el apartado 382 del Departamento de Transporte de Estados Unidos, la compañía operadora está obligada a gestionar las quejas relacionadas con discapacidades que afecten a sus vuelos. Esperamos tenerle a bordo de los vuelos de United/United Express en el futuro.*

Atentamente,

Servicio de atención al cliente

A la mañana siguiente, regresé al aeropuerto y abordé el vuelo de United sin inconvenientes. Al llegar a Ciudad de México, me recibió inesperadamente un directivo de Aeromar que me saludó y tomó mi maleta. Me llevó a un restaurante del aeropuerto, donde hablamos. Me explicó que había un problema legal por entrar a México con un perro en el avión. Le expliqué que no era mi primera vez y que ya había volado a México muchas veces con mi perro de servicio. Estaba seguro de que él era el hombre que respondió la llamada en Ciudad de México que dio lugar a la negativa de Aeromar de llevarnos. Le expliqué que Aeromar había discriminado a los discapacitados violando la ley, y esperaba una disculpa. En lugar de una disculpa, lo que hicieron fue tergiversar la verdad.

Al día siguiente, en las noticias de televisión de McAllen, el presentador citó a un funcionario de Aeromar que dijo, "Sentimos el incidente, pero el Sr. Hawn no tenía la documentación necesaria". Esa denigrante tergiversación me motivó a buscar una solución legal que acabó costándole a Aeromar mucho dinero y años de disgustos. Para que conste, era exactamente la misma documentación que United utilizó para llevarme en avión a Ciudad de México al día siguiente. Conocía los requisitos. De Cuba a Tailandia, de México a las Bahamas y más allá. . . Estaba bien informado en lo que respecta a los viajes internacionales con un perro, ya fuera de servicio o mascota. Estaba preparado para la lucha. Todos los perros tienen su día... y *¡Savior eventualmente tendría el suyo!*

Como hombre que ha volado a varios países del mundo (y a México muchas veces), me ofendió que Aeromar no reconociera su error. Me sentí menospreciado hasta el punto de temblar de rabia. Me habían hecho quedar como un novato. Cuando llegamos a casa, una cadena de televisión local nos entrevistó. Me preguntaron, "¿Es justo decir que se metieron con la persona equivocada?" Sin dudarlo ni un momento, exclamé emocionado, "¡Oh no, se metieron con la persona correcta!" Tenía a mi Booster en mi corazón, mi educación de la BUCS en mi cabeza y a mi Savior a mi lado. Esta era una batalla que estaba destinada a suceder.

Al final presenté una queja de veinte páginas ante el Departamento de Transporte de los Estados Unidos (DOT) explicando las transgresiones de Aeromar. Más tarde tuve que tratar con una abogada de Nueva York contratada por Aeromar. Esa abogada se refirió a mi perro como *perro de comodidad*. Le expliqué que no estaba seguro de lo que era un perro de comodidad, pero que mi *perro de servicio* estaba adiestrado y vestía como tal. Si mi perro era un perro de comodidad, ¡la abogada de Nueva York era una Girl Scout!

El asunto tardó más de un año en resolverse. En un momento dado, la abogada presentó el manual de Aeromar en el que se explicaban los requisitos para que un perro fuera reconocido por la compañía aérea como perro de servicio. Se refería a requisitos especiales que violaban absolutamente los requisitos de la ADA y el DOT. Reforzaba mi argumento de que la compañía aérea era ignorante en materia de perros de servicio, al igual que la abogada de Nueva York. Eran la pareja perfecta. Además, Aeromar publicó más tarde en su sitio web lo siguiente:

Animal de servicio.

Si tiene un animal de servicio, como un perro guía, puede viajar con él. Si su animal requiere viajar hasta su próximo servicio, recuerde que **usted no puede ocupar un asiento**, aunque esté desocupado, ni obstaculizar la circulación de otros transeúntes ni su comodidad. Si viaja con un perro guía se le asignará un **asiento en el pasillo.**

Si viaja en un vuelo internacional tenga en cuenta que la mayoría de los países aplican políticas estrictas respecto a la llegada de animales salvajes extranjeros, tome todas las precauciones para evitar contratiempos y malentendidos en la aduana. Algunas medidas incluyen un pasaporte que acredite que el animal es un animal de servicio y una cartilla oficial de vacunas aplicadas.

Los animales de servicio *que no sean perros guía, como los de apoyo emocional, no podrán viajar en cabina con usted,* salvo que se acredite con documentación médica (carta del psicólogo o psiquiatra tratante) que es imprescindible que viaje con ellos. De no disponer de la documentación necesaria serán tratados como mascotas y deberán viajar en la bodega de equipajes, asumiendo el costo del transporte y cumpliendo los requisitos necesarios.

(http://www.aeromar.com.mx/politicas/pasajeros-particulares/) (enlace no publicado).

El sitio web decía, "Un perro de servicio no puede sentarse en un asiento, y **USTED DEBE PERMANECER EN EL SUELO**". Un niño de preescolar podría haber escrito mucho mejor... ¡y sin embargo Aeromar Airlines era responsable de la vida de miles de pasajeros aéreos a diario! Halloween daba menos miedo. Le expliqué al DOT que esto evidenciaba la completa falta de comprensión de Aeromar sobre el tema de los perros de asistencia, perros guía y ESAs, y que esto ha causado problemas a las personas discapacitadas. Los perros de servicio NO necesitan una carta para viajar a bordo de un avión y es ilegal pedirla. Los ESA sí.

La andanada legal parecía no acabar nunca. Escribí muchas cartas largas en respuesta a las preguntas planteadas, y corregí las preguntas y respuestas legales ignorantes presentadas por la abogada de Nueva York. No estoy seguro de dónde obtuvo su educación, pero no estaba a la altura de mi educación en la BUCS sobre los perros de asistencia. La abogada tuvo que haberle costado a Aeromar una buena suma. ¡Me encantó el hecho de que su incompetencia seguramente haría perder el caso a la aerolínea discriminadora y les haría pagar más! Parecía que con cada nuevo comunicado, la abogada empeoraba aún más el caso de su cliente.

La abogada puso en duda que Savior estuviera identificado como perro de servicio. Le expliqué la ley a la abogada, con copia enviada al Departamento de Transporte:

> Efectivamente, el Departamento proporciona un medio para que una compañía aérea identifique a un perro de servicio. En la página 68 del Registro Federal, 24875-24876, el Departamento de Transporte afirma: Los transportistas aceptarán como prueba de que un animal es de servicio identificadores tales como tarjetas de identificación, (Mi perro de servicio tenía esto) otra documentación escrita, (Mostrada al funcionario y al personal de Aeromar como se indica en el informe del sheriff) la presencia de arneses (mi perro de servicio tenía esto), etiquetas (mi perro de servicio tenía esto), o las garantías verbales creíbles de una persona cualificada con una discapacidad que utiliza el animal (Registro Federal, DOT). (Tanto un funcionario de la ley como yo dimos innumerables garantías).

Cumplía todos los requisitos del DOT. Tenía el informe del funcionario y las imágenes de televisión para corroborarlo. Todo estaba documentado, como me habían enseñado a hacer renombrados instructores de la BUCS. Tanto Savior como yo actuamos de forma tranquila y profesional, sin reproches. En mi respuesta al Departamento de Transporte, expliqué que Aeromar discriminaba a una clase minoritaria llamada discapacitados al no permitirme abordar su avión. En lugar de disculparse, Aeromar me culpó por no "tener la documentación apropiada". Su abogado también me culpó por llamar a la policía/TV/prensa para documentar la práctica discriminadora de la aerolínea. También comentaron que yo debería haber abordado un vuelo de United que saliera de McAllen. Me sugirieron que, como hombre discapacitado que depende de un perro de servicio, no era lo bastante bueno para volar en el avión de Aeromar. El hecho de que quisieran enviarme en otra aerolínea era inconcebible e inaceptable.

"En lugar de inventar excusas para discriminar a los discapacitados", pregunté, "¿no sería correcto que Aeromar reconociera su error y simplemente se disculpara? ¿Es mucho pedir?

"En un futuro próximo viajaré por la misma ruta. Seré el mismo hombre y tendré el mismo perro de servicio con la misma apariencia. ¿Se me permitirá embarcar en un vuelo de Aeromar como a los miembros no minoritarios?"

Curiosamente, el sheriff de McAllen que redactó el informe del incidente, citó a funcionarios de Aeromar diciendo que no vuelan con perros de servicio labradores de gran tamaño. Yo estaba en Tailandia cuando el Departamento de Transporte me informó de que iban a cerrar el caso porque se trataba de una cuestión relacionada con el peso del perro grande. Exigí ver el manifiesto de carga/peso de ese vuelo, ¡no había forma de que el peso de mi perro impidiera que el avión despegara!

Así que le expliqué al Departamento de Transporte que si una compañía aérea puede negarse a embarcar a un perro guía o de servicio debido al término subjetivo "grande", entonces debería aplicarse a todas las compañías aéreas por igual. Luego exigí que enviaran esa decisión a TODAS las compañías aéreas de inmediato. ¿Se imaginan cuántos pasajeros ciegos o discapacitados se quedarían tirados, a escala nacional e internacional, si prevaleciera esa orden? Era una decisión absurda. Les expliqué que era bueno publicando comunicados de prensa y les sugerí que me buscaran en Google a mí y a mi perro, Booster. Las autoridades hicieron una "reconsideración" y, al cabo de dos años, por fin se resolvió la cuestión. A pesar de los esfuerzos de la abogada de Aeromar, ¡el Departamento de Transportes de Estados Unidos citó a Aeromar por dos infracciones de la ley!

***163

Departamento de Transportes de EE.UU.

ABOGADO GENERAL

1200 New Jersey Ave. S.E. Washington, DC 20590

Oficina del Secretario de Transportes

HOJA DE RESUMEN DE LA INVESTIGACIÓN

Queja/Asunto: Una aerolínea se negó a transportar a un perro de servicio.

Sección aplicable de 14 CFR Parte 382:   382.117(a)(d)(e)

Resumen de la sección: (a) Como transportista, debe permitir que un animal de servicio acompañe a un pasajero con discapacidad.

(d) Como prueba de que un animal es de servicio, el transportista debe aceptar tarjetas de identificación, otra documentación escrita, la presencia de arneses, etiquetas o las garantías verbales creíbles de una persona cualificada con una discapacidad que utilice el animal.

(e) Si un pasajero desea viajar con un animal que se utiliza como apoyo emocional o animal de servicio psiquiátrico, usted no está obligado a aceptar al animal para su transporte en cabina a menos que el pasajero le proporcione documentación actualizada con el membrete de un profesional de la salud mental autorizado.

¿Regla infringida? Si

Por las razones expuestas anteriormente, consideramos que Aeromar violó la sección 382 117 en este caso por no permitir el animal de servicio del Sr. Hawn en su vuelo originalmente programado. Si decidimos emprender acciones de cumplimiento contra Aeromar con respecto a esta cuestión, esta queja se considerará, lo que podría llevar a la emisión de una orden de cese y desistimiento y a la imposición de sanciones civiles.

Sección aplicable de 14 CFR Parte 382: 382.41

- -

Resumen de la sección: 382.41 Como transportista, debe proporcionar la siguiente información, previa solicitud, a las personas cualificadas con discapacidad o a las personas que pregunten en su nombre sobre la accesibilidad de la aeronave, prevista para realizar un vuelo determinado. La información que facilite debe ser específica para la aeronave que prevé utilizar para el vuelo, a menos que le resulte inviable hacerlo (por ejemplo, porque circunstancias impredecibles como las condiciones meteorológicas o un problema mecánico requieran la sustitución por otra aeronave que pudiera afectar a la ubicación o disponibilidad de una acomodación). La información requerida es:

Cualquier limitación relacionada con la aeronave, con el servicio o de otro tipo que afecte a la capacidad de acomodar a pasajeros con discapacidad.

Regla infringida? Si

En este caso, Aeromar infringió el artículo 382 41 al no facilitar información exacta al Sr. Hawn sobre su política relativa a los animales de servicio. Si decidimos emprender acciones legales contra la compañía aérea en relación con este asunto, esta denuncia será una de las que se examinen, lo que puede dar lugar a la emisión de una orden de cese y desistimiento y a la imposición de sanciones civiles.

Confiar en que Aeromar haría lo correcto era como pedirle lo mismo a una ex pareja enojada. Por eso, una vez tomada la decisión, reservé un boleto con el mismo itinerario. Quería estar seguro de que Aeromar dejaría de discriminar a los discapacitados que optaran por utilizar perros de servicio. Por desgracia, mi Peggy había fallecido y no pudo compartir la historia de David contra Goliat. Savior y yo volvimos al mostrador de Aeromar donde ya nos habían rechazado antes. Esta vez nos trataron cordialmente. La agente era la misma que nos había denegado el abordaje. Nos explicó que sólo había hecho su trabajo según las instrucciones. Le dije que la entendía perfectamente, ya que había estado presente cuando llamó a la oficina central ese día por solicitud mía.

El amor incondicional de mi Booster fue el impulso que me hizo salir de mi capullo de autoexilio. Recuerdo la enseñanza de mi madre sobre cómo una oruga se convierte en mariposa. Booster transformó la lección de vida de mi madre en una realidad vital. Gracias a Booster y a mi graduación de la BUCS, fui capaz de defenderme a mí mismo y a los que no eran capaces de hacerlo. Uno de los mayores deseos de Bonnie era que sus alumnos salieran y cambiaran el mundo, utilizando el vínculo canino-humano. Yo había cumplido mi promesa a Booster, hecha años atrás, de compartirlo con el mundo. De repente me di cuenta de que cumpliendo esa promesa, cumplía también el deseo de Bonnie. Yo tenía la pasión necesaria para viajar por todo el mundo y promover el vínculo canino-humano, además de la educación requerida para hacerlo. Cuando viajaba, siempre me acordaba de hacer las maletas con gratitud, como Booster me había enseñado.

Un día, me desperté y me tomé mi habitual taza de café. Siendo el maravilloso laxante que es, posteriormente utilicé el baño. Por casualidad presencié lo que parecía ser sangre en la taza y, en consecuencia, pedí cita con un proctólogo. Resultó ser una simple hemorroide que de alguna manera había molestado, pero el médico ordenó una prueba de PSA para el cáncer de próstata para estar seguro. Ya me habían hecho una, años atrás y una biopsia. Todo salió bien. Esta vez mi PSA era de 7, lo que suponía un 25% de probabilidades de tener cáncer de próstata. Tuve que someterme a otra biopsia. Después de la intervención, me fui a casa dolorido y me acosté temprano, con Boosted y Busted al pie de mi cama.

A la mañana siguiente, me desperté y bajé las escaleras. Boosted y Busted solían correr hacia la puerta principal para salir y bendecir el jardín con lluvia amarilla. Busted salió corriendo como de costumbre, pero Boosted se quedó dentro, frotándose contra mi pierna. Miré hacia abajo y ¡tenía un pequeño libro en la boca! Yo tenía un montón de libros en una estantería del dormitorio que me llegaba hasta la cintura. Por casualidad, Boosted había cogido una Biblia. Asombrado, me deslicé lentamente sobre el suelo y lo abracé. Luego lo abracé un poco más... ¡y lo volví a abrazar! Ore para que yo estuviera bien y poder seguir cuidando de mi familia canina.

El informe patológico tardó más de una semana en llegar, pero resultó que estaba bien. Años más tarde, estaba desayunando en un hotel de Bangkok (Tailandia) cuando oí a un hombre que contaba que hacía años le habían extirpado la próstata. Le pregunté cómo había descubierto el cáncer. Me dijo que se había hecho una prueba rutinaria de PSA. Le pregunté si recordaba su resultado y me dijo, "¡Sí, era 7!" ¡Otra *coincidencia*! Casi me desmayo. Cómo hubiera deseado tener a mi lado a Boosted o a Busted para aferrarme a él.

CAPÍTULO 19
AMA A TU PRÓJIMO: MÉXICO

Mientras el nuevo año 2015 transcurría sin sobresaltos, yo disfrutaba más que nunca jugando con mis hijos caninos. Disfrutaba de la vida en sus propios términos. Era como si hubiera aterrizado en la luna. "¡Un pequeño paso para mí; un gran salto para mi vida!" Un día, leí un artículo que promocionaba una conferencia de la Sociedad Humanitaria de los Estados Unidos (Humane Society of the United States) que se celebraría en la cercana Nueva Orleans. Le envié un correo electrónico a mi amigo Les, antiguo presidente de la HSUS, y él organizó mi asistencia a la conferencia en marzo.

Cuando llegó la fecha de la conferencia, llevé a Booster y enseguida me vi rodeado de compañeros amantes de los animales. Para deleite de todos, llevaba su peluche de Mickey Mouse en la boca y se acercaba a un transeúnte tras otro. Era un maestro de las relaciones públicas, habiendo perfeccionado ese arte. Recordé su viaje a la residencia de ancianos de Truth or Consequences, Nuevo México, donde no dejó de saludar a ningún residente.

De repente, Booster me acercó a una señora muy atractiva cuyo inglés era ligeramente mejor que mi español, ¡que era inexistente! Dependíamos de una aplicación de traducción del móvil para comunicarnos. Se presentó gentilmente como Doctora Claudia Edwards, DVM. Me explicó que trabajaba para Humane Society International (HSI) en México. También era la Directora de la Escuela Veterinaria de México en la Universidad Nacional Autónoma de México (UNAM), ubicada en Ciudad de México. Le conté la historia de mi Booster y nos hicimos amigos al instante. Éramos dos guisantes en una vaina, compartiendo la pasión y el amor por los animales. Nuestra amistad se mantiene hasta el día de hoy, un vínculo hecho del pegamento más fino.

A las pocas semanas de nuestra "reunión coordinada por Booster", propuse llevar a Booster a Ciudad de México para explicar a la sociedad el valor de los perros de servicio. El concepto de perro de servicio era relativamente nuevo en la mayor parte de Latinoamérica. La Dra. Edwards estaba tan entusiasmada que abracé emocionado a Booster cuando leí su respuesta a mi sugerencia enviada por correo electrónico. En pocas semanas, la Dra. Edwards organizó una conferencia para Booster y para mí en la Facultad de Veterinaria de la Universidad de México bajo los auspicios de la Humane Society International HSI. Había hermosos carteles promocionales expuestos de manera destacada por todo el campus de la UNAM anunciando mi presentación, se titulaba, "Cambiando el mundo a través del vínculo canino-humano".

Fue una oportunidad única para compartir a Booster y hablar de temas caninos con estudiantes de veterinaria, profesores y el público amante de los perros. Era una especie de trifecta canina. Me imaginaba compartiendo mi pasión en México, al igual que lo había hecho durante años en otras partes del mundo. Si nos recibían bien en la conferencia, sería un buen augurio para ayudar a la comunidad mexicana de discapacitados a aprobar una ley de acceso para perros de asistencia.

A pesar de haber sido aceptado en las Bahamas y en Cuba años atrás, me seguía poniendo nervioso de hablar en público en un país extranjero. Volví a confiar en Booster para que me ayudara a *reforzar* mi confianza como sólo él sabía hacerlo. Nunca me había enfrentado al rechazo, al ridículo o al desprecio con Booster a mi lado. De hecho, siempre encontraba aceptación y parecía que no podía equivocarme. La fuerza y la autoestima que obtenía de nuestra asociación eran simplemente indescriptibles. La transformación de mi vida, de tener pensamientos suicidas a abrazar la pasión por compartir a Booster y mejorar la vida de los demás, sólo podía explicarse como un milagro.

De inmediato me puse a trabajar en la crónica de mi vida, decidido a construir una autopista hacia mi alma; el único peaje a pagar era el mío. Era como si me acercara a la mesa de juego de la vida y apostara con todas mis fuerzas. ¡Escribí día y noche, agarrando a Booster tantas veces que pensé que se le caería el pelo! Tenía que hacerlo *bien*. No habría una segunda oportunidad. Si lo arruinaba, si parecía poco sincero, no volvería a embarcarme en una expedición tan emotiva.

Cuando estaba a punto de terminar de escribir mis pensamientos, me entró el pánico. Por absurdo que parezca, de repente me di cuenta de que iba a un país donde mis palabras no podrían entenderse, incluso si hacía mi mejor esfuerzo por transmitir su significado sincero. Llamé de inmediato a la Dra. Edwards y le expliqué mi dilema. Con calma, sugirió que intentara relajarme y que su jefe, Anton, era bilingüe y seguramente me ayudaría. Me pregunté si esta dama era un ángel disfrazado de humana. Me encontré balanceándome hacia adelante y hacia atrás. Con la fuerza de Job, me levanté, caminé hacia una ventana, la abrí y respiré profundamente varias veces. Booster se levantó, caminó hacia la ventana y se acostó sobre mis pies.

Los días pasaron rápidamente y, llegó el momento de reunirnos con nuestra nueva amiga Claudia en Ciudad de México. Mi amigo Chris optó una vez más por ser nuestro chófer y nos llevó al aeropuerto de Nueva Orleans. Presenté mi pasaporte y la documentación de Booster a la persona del mostrador de la aerolínea. Pronto estuvimos sentados en la primera fila del avión rumbo a Ciudad de México. *Era un pequeño paso para el hombre, ¡un gran salto para mi Booster!* A nuestra llegada, esperamos a ser los últimos en bajar, como de costumbre. La azafata empezó a elogiar a Booster. Las azafatas solían decir que Booster se portaba mejor que muchos niños. Antes de desembarcar, Booster insistió en tomarse una foto con la azafata, quien accedió encantada.

Entramos en el aeropuerto de Ciudad de México con los papeles en la mano, listos para presentarlos a los funcionarios de inmigración mexicanos. Llevé a Booster al departamento oficial de inspección de animales. La amable señora selló su documentación. Luego pasé por inmigración. Había organizado quedarme en un hotel que aceptaba mascotas. Conseguir un taxi fue fácil y, al llegar al hotel, nos recibió el amable gerente. Una vez instalados, di de comer y paseé a Booster. A la vuelta de la esquina del hotel había un maravilloso bulevar con muchas plantas "preutilizadas" con olores caninos que Booster saboreó. Su sistema olfativo (procesamiento de olores) trabajaba vigorosamente. Estaba muy contento. Fue una delicia verlo.

Después de comer algo y tomar una margarita, volvimos a la habitación. Llamé a la Dra. Edwards, quien respondió entusiasmada. "Señor Davis, les doy la bienvenida a usted y a Booster a México, bienvenido. ¿Cómo estuvo su vuelo?" Le expliqué que todo fue genial. Mi Booster y yo estábamos muy contentos de estar allí. La Dra. Edwards me explicó entonces que, además de dar conferencias en la UNAM, había concertado muchas entrevistas. Yo estaba simplemente extasiado. Abracé a Booster, me senté en el suelo y le acaricié el estómago durante lo que me pareció una eternidad.

Al día siguiente, la Dra. Edwards me presentó a Anton, quien amablemente se ofreció a traducir mi presentación. También la puso en una memoria USB, que luego entregó al encargado de la proyección de la UNAM. La Dra. Edwards me explicó que había organizado una visita a organizaciones dedicadas a ayudar a niños con diversas discapacidades.

A la mañana siguiente, nos recibió a Booster y a mí con una enorme sonrisa y un abrazo muy fuerte. Subimos a su automóvil y nos dirigimos a conocer a los representantes de dos organizaciones. La primera, la Fundación un Ángel te Cuida, se creó para ayudar a niños con enfermedades crónicas y degenerativas. La segunda, la Fundación Casa Alianza México, atendía a niños de doce a dieciocho años víctimas de violencia, abusos, explotación sexual o trata de seres humanos.

Cuando llegamos al primer centro, varias personas sonrientes nos recibieron y nos hicieron señas para que entráramos. Booster cogió a su perro de peluche Clifford y entró como si fuera el dueño del lugar; de hecho, en cuestión de minutos, ¡lo era! Todos los niños y adultos miraban al labrador tuerto pasearse y saludar a los jóvenes de todas las edades. Al instante me sentí abrumado, pero por los niños debía mantener la compostura.

Booster hizo una demostración de cómo abrir la puerta de un refrigerador. Luego le pedí a un joven que por favor se quitara los zapatos. Entonces le dije a Booster, "Los zapatos, por favor", y él corrió por la habitación y me trajo uno de los zapatos del chico. A continuación, le dije a Booster, "El otro zapato, por favor", y al instante corrió y me trajo el otro zapato sin dudarlo. Los niños se volvieron locos al ver a Booster hacer lo que mejor sabe . . . llegar a lo más profundo del alma humana. Los niños se sentían identificados con Booster.

Entonces decidí animar un poco las cosas. Había aprendido en el Campamento Gone to the Dogs años antes cómo adiestrar a un perro para que se diera la vuelta y se hiciera el muerto después de decir *BANG* mientras le apuntabas con el dedo como si fuera una pistola. Se empieza colocando al perro boca arriba y luego retrocedes. Miré a Booster y le pregunté con entusiasmo, "¿Listo? ¿Listo?" Eso siempre sincronizaba su nivel de energía con el mío. Entonces apunté mi pistola y dije, "*¡BANG!*"

¡Booster actuó mejor que John Wayne! Los niños se volvieron locos y yo tomé el control de mi público. Los niños y sus padres ya no estaban concentrados en los retos de sus vidas, aunque solo fuera por un momento.

Me fijé en un joven ciego al fondo de la sala. Su madre estaba a su lado, explicándole lo que hacía Booster. Miré a Booster y le dije, "Siéntate, por favor". Su órdenes siempre iban seguidas por la palabra *"por favor"*, como si hablara con otra persona. Luego pregunté a la madre del niño si su hijo quería acariciar a Booster. Ella repitió mi petición a su hijo, que parecía muy indeciso. Con el aliento de su madre y de sus compañeros, se acercó cautelosamente. Mis palabras de aliento en inglés fueron traducidas tranquilamente al español.

Cuando el chico se acercó, su mano se alzó en el aire de la oscuridad, buscando valientemente acariciar a mi Booster. Tras varios intentos fallidos, Booster levantó la cabeza para encontrarse con la mano del chico. El chico retiró rápidamente la mano. Booster mantuvo la calma, y la mano del chico volvió con menos reticencia la segunda vez. Este proceso se repitió varias veces hasta que las dos almas conectaron y prevalecieron la unidad y la confianza.

De repente, vi a otro joven preguntando ansiosamente a su madre si él también podía acariciar a Booster. Pronto, el chico estaba sentado en el suelo, dándole a Booster un abrazo de oso. Lo apretó tan fuerte que pensé que Booster estallaría como una piñata. Su madre se inclinó hacia mí y me susurró al oído, "Señor, mi hijo acaba de perder la vista del ojo derecho debido a un cáncer, igual que su perro. Está creando lazos afectivos con su perro". Estaban viéndose a los ojos.

Estuve a punto de perder el control, ya que no estaba preparado de ninguna manera para manejar la emoción del momento. Me senté en el suelo con el valiente niño y ambos abrazamos a Booster. Nadie sabía que yo también necesitaba consuelo y tranquilidad. Realmente creía que Booster no tenía límites cuando se trataba de elevar las emociones de innumerables personas al mismo tiempo. Además, él disfrutaba con la oportunidad de hacerlo. Tenía un cariño especial por los niños y una habilidad extraordinaria para relacionarse con ellos.

Al concluir la presentación, les dije a los niños que Booster era un perro adiestrado profesionalmente. Les expliqué que la mayoría de los perros son muy cariñosos, pero algunos no. A algunos les han enseñado a pelear y pueden morder. Les pedí que, por favor, tuvieran cuidado con los perros que no conocieran. Una vez terminada la presentación, mis anfitriones me ofrecieron amablemente algo de beber y me mostraron unos aperitivos que estaban colocados sobre una mesa. Había estado tan ocupado y había hablado tanto que no me había fijado en la mesa. Tomé con gratitud un poco de ponche y cogí una patata frita.

Cuando me llevé la patata frita a la boca, me quedé paralizado. No podía moverme, no podía procesar el momento. Había empezado a balancearme un poco cuando una mano empática me tocó el hombro. Las lágrimas brotaron. Levanté la patata frita con mano temblorosa para que todos en la sala fueran testigos. Tenía forma de corazón. *¿Coincidencia?* De ninguna manera. Mi Poder Superior había trabajado tanto como yo. Pronto, los adultos de la sala se acurrucaron

a mi lado, igual que los niños habían hecho con Booster momentos antes. El amor engendra amor, especialmente el amor canino incondicional. Después de intercambiar abrazos, salimos de la sala, quizás un poco transformados de por vida. Las almas jóvenes y valientes de aquel día nos enseñaron lo que era el valor, y Booster le enseñó a un joven a confiar. Todos experimentamos el amor. Un amor ejemplificado por una patata frita proporcionada por un poder superior a nosotros mismos.

Un par de días después, aparecieron dos artículos en la prensa sobre nuestra visita. "Los perros de terapia deberían ser permitidos en todas partes: Activista", decía una noticia. La otra historia decía: "Davis Hawn con su perro Booster insta a no cerrar las puertas a los animales de servicio". Me sentí muy agradecido por la cobertura y el interés expresados. Fue un homenaje maravilloso para Booster, que parecía capaz de encantar a los periodistas con su singularidad. Ojalá él me hubiera enseñado a ser tan encantador. Para Booster, era algo natural. *En mi caso, quizás nunca se manifestaría,* pensé melancólicamente. A decir verdad, creo que estaba celoso.

Al día siguiente visitamos la Fundación Mosaico Down, un centro para niños autistas. Mientras esperaba a que me admitieran, reflexioné sobre cómo había estudiado el autismo en la BUCS. Había aprendido que algunos niños autistas revisaban el perímetro de un entorno, buscando la manera de salir. Algunos escapaban de su casa y acababan en la casa o el patio de un vecino. Muchos perros de servicio están adiestrados para alertar a la familia cuando el niño abandona una zona determinada. Algunos están adiestrados para alejar suavemente al niño de una salida, o agarrarlo por las nalgas, impidiéndole salir.

Un cortés "Hola, señor Davis" interrumpió de repente mis pensamientos. Booster, la Dra. Edwards y yo entramos con el director del centro en una enorme sala llena de niños autistas. Algunos de los niños estaban tranquilamente sentados, pero otros correteaban sin rumbo. Cuando Booster entró con su peluche, fue como si hubiera aterrizado un OVNI. En retrospectiva, mi Booster *era* un como un OVNI para estos niños que nunca habían recibido la visita de un perro de 45 kilos. Ninguno de los niños corrió a saludar al extraterrestre. Cuando Booster movía la cola, salían corriendo. Sorprendentemente, Booster no sincronizó su nivel de energía con la de ellos, no corrió a jugar con los niños, no se les unió. Lo vi sentarse, acostarse y permanecer imperturbable. Era un juego de esperar, observar y ver.

Al cabo de un rato, los niños se aventuraron a acercarse un poco más al tranquilo perro. Finalmente, la mayoría de los niños se sentaron en el suelo alrededor de Booster, quien disfrutó del merecido afecto. El perro que había saludado proactivamente a todos los pacientes de la residencia de ancianos de Ajo, Arizona, hizo lo contrario este día. ¿Cómo sabía que debía atender a un grupo y no acercarse a otro, independientemente del nivel de energía de la sala? Me maravillé de las asombrosas habilidades de Booster. Aún no había aprendido todos los entresijos de mi Booster. Mientras que a mí me frenaba mi incapacidad para comunicarme debido a la barrera del idioma, Booster no encontraba tal impedimento.

Pocos días después, apareció una noticia en un periódico local. En él se hacía alusión a nuestra visita a los niños a los que yo me refería como "especiales"... porque, en efecto, lo eran. Mientras leía el artículo, me sorprendió que el periodista "lo entendiera". Creo que hace falta ser una persona extraordinaria para transmitir sensibilidad de una manera tan especial.

Más tarde, la Dra. Edwards y yo comentamos los acontecimientos de los últimos días. Ambos estábamos muy orgullosos de que los caninos fueran parte integral del mundo humano. Ella estaba segura de que la sociedad mexicana tenía un gran aprecio por los caninos. Le dije que había venido a dar una conferencia para ayudar a educar a la sociedad mexicana sobre el verdadero potencial canino. Al instante me dijo, "Sí, lo sé. Y tendrás la oportunidad de hacerlo en la televisión mexicana mañana, Davis".

Mi cabeza se inclinó en un ángulo de 45 grados como un cachorro desconcertado. Ella sonrió, pues sabía que estaría muy feliz, y desde luego así fue. ¡Esta dama era realmente increíble! Trabajaba para la UNAM y la HSUS y aun así tenía tiempo para organizar cosas increíbles y acompañarme. Me quedé boquiabierto, simplemente boquiabierto. Salimos a cenar y después la Dra. Edwards me llevó de vuelta al hotel. Booster estaba en el asiento trasero, durmiendo y roncando.

La tarde siguiente, conseguí permiso del director del hotel para filmar la entrevista de Booster en el vestíbulo. Le expresé mi gratitud, a lo que respondió, "De nada". En cuestión de horas llegó un equipo de televisión de aspecto muy profesional. Pronto me encontré sentado bajo un micrófono que colgaba de lo alto y empecé a explicar la historia de mi vida y cómo Booster me salvó y cambió mi vida. No estaba seguro de si el equipo había entendido mis palabras, pero se quedaron asombrados cuando Booster empezó a actuar!

Le pedí a Booster que abriera un cajón y sacara un objeto, que buscara mis zapatos, me quitara los calcetines, etc. El camarógrafo no podía creer que un perro pudiera abrir la puerta de un automóvil y sacar un botiquín, así que salimos. Contraté un taxi en la entrada. Para asombro de todos, mi tuerto Booster corrió hacia el taxi en el momento justo, abrió la puerta, cogió un kit de afeitar/bolsa médica y me lo trajo. Después nos pidieron que camináramos por el bulevar de la ciudad mientras nos filmaban. ¡El final de la entrevista fue un despliegue de sonrisas y palmaditas en la cabeza para mi Booster!

Al día siguiente se emitió el reportaje. Era una historia bastante larga con música de fondo. Si hubiera pagado por una producción así, habría costado miles de dólares. Fue todo un honor y un homenaje para Booster, que una vez más había demostrado cómo los caninos pueden ayudar a sus compañeros humanos. Era otro país, otro idioma, pero Booster nunca dejó

de transmitir su mensaje. Me sentí muy honrado de que la cadena de televisión encontrara mérito en nuestro viaje y dedicara sus valiosos recursos para compartirlo con los telespectadores. Era un buen augurio de la posibilidad de que el concepto de perro de servicio fuera aceptado a nivel nacional. ¡En Ciudad de México parecían "entenderlo"!

Esa noche, busqué en Internet un bar de karaoke y encontré uno cerca de nuestro hotel. Entré en el bar con Booster y rápidamente encontré una mesa. Estaba un poco nervioso porque entré con un perro de 45 kilos, que llamaba mucho la atención. A los pocos minutos, el camarero me hizo señas, ¿cerveza, señor? mientras dos atractivas mujeres mexicanas preguntaban si podían acariciar a Booster. Fueron muy amables, al igual que los demás clientes. Nos lo pasamos muy bien esa noche, ¡aunque Booster fue el único

que recibió caricias en la barriga!

Al día siguiente, practiqué mi conferencia. No sabía qué esperar, ya que nunca había dado una conferencia ante una audiencia universitaria. El público era realmente especial, ya que estaba compuesto por estudiantes de veterinaria, profesionales y personas cultas que habían expresado su interés por el bienestar animal. Tenía que dar lo mejor de mí, concentrado y sereno. Fue una hazaña que nunca habría conseguido años atrás. Fueron necesarios años de aprendizaje bajo la tutela de Booster para adquirir esa habilidad.

Aquella noche no dormí bien, a pesar de que Booster estaba a mi lado con la cabeza apoyada en mi pecho. De repente, sonó el teléfono. Era la llamada del despertador, indicándome que el día empezaba. Me vestí, di de comer a Booster y bajamos en el ascensor al vestíbulo para comer algo. Cuando terminé, nos acercamos al ascensor para volver a la habitación. Se me cayó la correa de Booster. Antes de que pudiera recogerla, se abrió la puerta del ascensor y le dije a Booster que entrara. Al entrar en el ascensor, la puerta se cerró y la mitad de la correa quedó atrapada en la puerta. *No pasa nada,* pensé. *La recogeré cuando se abra la puerta del ascensor.*

De repente, mientras el ascensor subía, la correa estaba siendo tirada hacia la puerta con Booster siendo arrastrado por el cuello. *Casualmente*, la correa de cuero que había utilizado estaba bastante vieja y seca. Cuando la cabeza de Booster estaba en la puerta, la correa se rompió. Si no se hubiera roto, el cuello de Booster habría sufrido un corte profundo, en el mejor de los casos, o muy probablemente se habría roto. Se me paró el corazón. Cuando se abrió la puerta, luché por recuperar la compostura lo mejor que pude y salí tambaleándome del ascensor. Después nos dirigimos a la recepción y explicamos lo sucedido.

A la mañana siguiente, el hombre que estaba detrás del mostrador me llamó y me entregó la mitad de una correa encontrada en el hueco del ascensor, debajo de éste. Mi cuerpo empezó a temblar. Me esforcé por beber zumo de naranja y no pude comer, aunque sabía que nos esperaba un largo día. Tuve la tentación de buscar un poco de vodka para prepararme un cóctel destornillador, pero aquellos días habían quedado atrás. Todo lo que necesitaba era un poco de descanso con Booster para calmar mis nervios y controlar mi cuerpo. Al cabo de unos minutos, entró la Dra. Edwards, sonriente como el sol de la mañana.

Tenía una personalidad agradable que te tranquilizaba al instante. Con Booster y la Dra. Edwards a mi lado, sabía que todo estaría bien.

Cuando llegamos a la UNAM, vi innumerables carteles de "Booster" adornando las paredes. Cuando entré en el auditorio, miré a un público que había hecho un espacio en su agenda para venir a escuchar lo que teníamos que decir. Fue reconfortante y recibí una inyección de confianza. Poco tiempo después, la Dra. Edwards me hizo señas para que subiera al escenario. Me acerqué y le di las gracias, miré a Booster y le dije de manera muy concisa, "Y gracias a ti también". Entonces empecé mi presentación de setenta y ocho diapositivas en PowerPoint. Como hablaba un español imperfecto, al que me refería en broma como *spanglish*, mis palabras estaban escritas en español en las diapositivas para asegurarme de que el público entendía lo que decía.

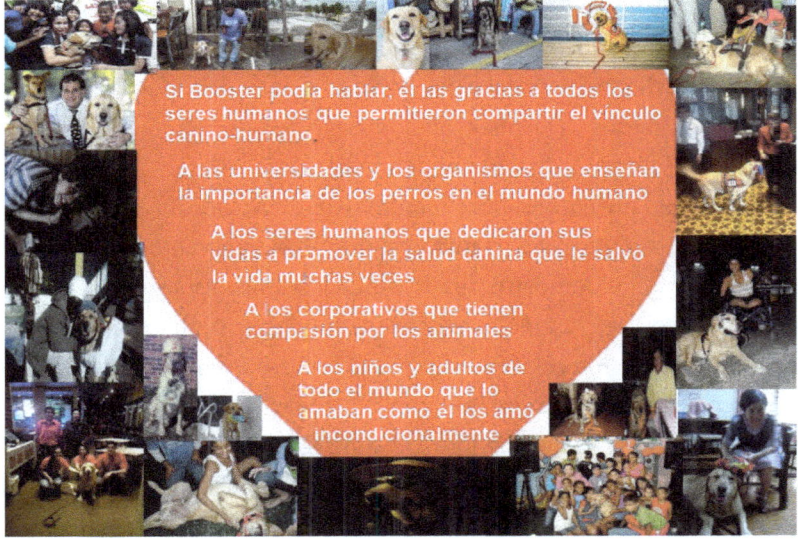

Compartí detalles íntimos sobre mi vida y luego expliqué que los perros ayudan a los humanos de muchas maneras, tanto física como psicológicamente. Me referí a ello como medicina canina holística y no adictiva, y expliqué además que mueren más soldados estadounidenses por suicidio que en combate. Cuando presenté una diapositiva que demostraba cómo los caninos ayudan a los soldados con los miembros o la psique dañados, las fotos hablaban por sí solas. Mi penúltima diapositiva mostraba fotos de los viajes de Booster, tanto nacionales como internacionales. Era todo un testimonio de la ética de trabajo de un perro que viajó por el mundo intentando hacer de él un lugar mejor. Miré a mi Booster y le dije suavemente, "¡Ves, te dije que te compartiría con el mundo!"

Entonces dije, "Si Booster pudiera hablar, daría las gracias:

A todos los seres humanos que nos permitieron compartir el vínculo canino-humano. . .

A todas las universidades y organizaciones que enseñan la importancia de los perros en el mundo . . .

A todas las personas que dedicaron su vida a promover la salud canina que le salvó la vida . . .

A todas las empresas que sienten compasión por los animales . . .

A todos los niños y adultos de todo el mundo que le manifestaron amor, ya que él les mostró amor incondicional".

Mi última diapositiva daba las gracias a los individuos que estudian para ser veterinarios. Después de todo, yo estaba en la mejor escuela veterinaria de México y ¡había que felicitarlos!

En general, mi conferencia mantuvo la atención del público durante una hora. Booster, mientras tanto, estaba profundamente dormido a mis pies. Lo desperté y demostró sus habilidades, para asombro de todos. Al terminar, se nos acercaron asistentes de todas las clases sociales. Fue conmovedor ver el interés genuino que expresaron. Una señora de aspecto particularmente aristocrático se me acercó y, en poco tiempo, nos enfrascamos en una conversación sobre perros. Enriqueta (Queta) era una experta en adiestramiento canino y humano. Era profesora jubilada de psicología de la UNAM.

Por un momento, recordé aquel día en la clase de la BUCS cuando escuchábamos al psicólogo infantil mientras nos enseñaba a utilizar su metodología para trabajar con los perros. Supe al instante que esta señora se convertiría en una buena amiga. Antes de despedirnos, me presentó a su esposo, Antonio, un caballero de aspecto distinguido y abogado.

Intercambiamos información de contacto e hicimos la promesa mutua de reunirnos para comer en algún momento de los próximos días.

Al día siguiente, la Dra. Edwards me presentó al director de los equipos caninos K9 de Búsqueda y Rescate (SAR) de la UNAM. Él tuvo la amabilidad de enseñarme sus instalaciones de adiestramiento, situadas en los terrenos de la universidad. Conocí a algunos de sus adiestradores y supe que todos eran voluntarios. El director era la única persona a la que le pagaba por entrenar y trabajar con perros SAR. México había sufrido terremotos devastadores en el pasado y era probable que sufriera más. Los equipos de perros SAR de la UNAM practicaban sin descanso, sin saber si se les necesitaría. La devoción del equipo a sus perros y al trabajo SAR era asombrosa.

Antes de abandonar las instalaciones, pregunté al director si su equipo estaría interesado en aprender a adiestrar perros de servicio para discapacitados. Parecía interesado y reunía todos los requisitos, incluido un equipo dedicado y unas instalaciones maravillosas. En mi mente estaba la posibilidad de establecer una colaboración entre la BUCS y la UNAM. Pensé que podría ser fructífero que uno de los miembros del equipo asistiera al seminario de formación de verano de seis semanas de la BUCS.

Después de lo que me pareció una eternidad, casi era hora de volver a casa, a Estados Unidos. Decidí patrocinar una cena en un restaurante local e invité a la Dra. Edwards y a su esposo, a Paco, al director canino del SAR, a Enriqueta y a su esposo Antonio, y a los miembros de la prensa que habían escrito historias maravillosas sobre mi Booster. Elegí un restaurante de lujo especializado en mariscos y, como quería concluir mi aventura con otra aventura más, invité a Booster a acompañarme. En la mayoría de los países no se admiten perros en los restaurantes de lujo. Demonios, ¡en Estados Unidos, suele ser difícil que entren como perros de servicio en los restaurantes! Iba a ser interesante.

Llegué al restaurante media hora antes. Entré con Booster a mi lado. Su chaleco naranja brillante tenía un parche que decía "Perro de Servicio". El recepcionista de la puerta se quedó atónito y me dijo, "Un momento por favor".

Pensé que *eso era mucho mejor que "¡lárguese de aquí con ese perro, señor!"*

A los pocos minutos, el encargado me saludó y me explicó que no permitían perros dentro.

Le expliqué que era discapacitado y que Booster era un perro adiestrado profesionalmente con una educación de 50.000 dólares. Luego le dije que se comportaría mejor que yo, ¡sobre todo si me bebía unos cuantos margaritas especiales de la casa!

El gerente se rio y dijo, "Sígame, señor". Así lo hicimos, y nos sentaron en una bonita mesa en la terraza.

Cuando llegaron mis invitados, me pidieron que explicara cómo había logrado que Booster entrara. Expliqué que fue una combinación de confianza y hospitalidad mexicana; el gerente confió en mí y fue muy hospitalario. También expliqué que en la BUCS nos habían enseñado a entrar siempre en un local público como si fuéramos los dueños, mostrando un lenguaje corporal que irradiara seguridad. Si pareces inseguro, es más probable que te cuestionen. Así me ocurrió en mis viajes con Booster a todas partes. El camarero se ofreció a traer agua a Booster y yo bromeé, "No, gracias, él preferiría una cerveza". ¡Nos reímos todos! Que conste que nunca damos de comer ni de beber a un perro de servicio en un restaurante.

El camarero compartió la historia con los demás empleados, que se acercaron a saludarnos. Fue una gran oportunidad para explicarles que eran afortunados de tener dos ojos, dos piernas, etc. Además, les recordé que no todo el mundo tenía esa suerte. Les expliqué el concepto de perro de servicio y luego miré a mi alrededor. Había pocos clientes, así que me levanté despreocupadamente, crucé el salón, me quité los zapatos, volví a la mesa y me senté. El personal debió pensar que las cervezas habían ganado la batalla. Miré a Booster y le dije tranquilamente, "Los zapatos, por favor". Sin dudarlo ni un momento, Booster se levantó, tomó un zapato y me lo trajo. Le dije, "El otro zapato, por favor". En cuestión de segundos, tenía el otro zapato en la mano, aunque con algo de saliva. En ese momento supe que nunca me olvidarían en ese restaurante. También supe que si alguna vez regresaba a Ciudad de México, éste sería mi restaurante preferido, aunque me gustaría entrar también en otros restaurantes para difundir el concepto de perro de servicio y perfeccionar mis habilidades de entrada!

Me quedé muy impresionado con México, al menos con Ciudad de México. Tenía sus problemas, como cualquier otra gran ciudad, pero era la sede de la prestigiosa UNAM. Con frecuencia me preguntaba cómo se mantenían motivados los voluntarios del equipo SAR de la UNAM. Habían pasado unos treinta años desde el famoso terremoto de magnitud 8,0 de 1985, que mató e hirió a decenas de miles de ciudadanos mexicanos. Debido al catastrófico suceso, el gobierno contrató a una persona para establecer una fundación de perros SAR. Con el paso de los años, la fundación mexicana de perros SAR creció bajo el liderazgo del director. Se dispuso de un terreno en el campus de la UNAM y se construyó un edificio. Durante los siguientes treinta años, los dedicados adiestradores voluntarios vivían en casa con sus perros y los adiestraban en las instalaciones. Nunca recibieron una llamada de socorro, pero no se desmoralizaron. ¡Felicitaciones!

Cuando regresé a casa, me enteré de que el alcalde de Ciudad de México, el Dr. Mancera, había firmado una propuesta de enmienda a una ley existente que obligaba a los perros a llevar bozal en lugares públicos. Eso anulaba gran parte del valor de un perro de servicio, adiestrado para llevar objetos a una persona discapacitada en un lugar público. No creí que la enmienda tuviera efecto, pero sin duda fue un paso en la dirección correcta. Previamente había conseguido que el ayudante del alcalde le llevara una copia de una carta, en la que le pedía que considerara la posibilidad de proponer una ley de acceso para perros de asistencia. Aunque dudo que la carta, o mis apariciones, tuvieran algo que ver con la propuesta del alcalde, ¡el momento fue muy oportuno!

Al enterarme de la noticia, escribí inmediatamente una carta de agradecimiento al Dr. Mancera. Había leído que se había educado en Europa y, por tanto, suponía que era un visionario. Me habría encantado conocerlo, pero nunca tuve la oportunidad. Más adelante en un viaje, asistí a un acto al aire libre relacionado con la discapacidad y lo vi en el escenario, así que me acerqué y entregué mi carta de agradecimiento a su ayudante.

Meses después de volver a casa, me puse en contacto con el director de perros SAR y con Enriqueta. Tenía una idea que creía que sería beneficiosa para México, sus ciudadanos y también para la población canina. Imaginaba a los miembros del equipo canino SAR de la UNAM entrenando perros de servicio. Los miembros del equipo estarían motivados de trabajar con la comunidad de discapacitados. Ya tenían un edificio y un terreno en el campus de la UNAM, con un número potencialmente ilimitado de estudiantes universitarios voluntarios. El escenario parecía realmente perfecto. Le di a un miembro del equipo de perros SAR de la UNAM una beca para asistir al seminario de verano de entrenamiento de perros de servicio de la BUCS. El director de perros SAR sugirió a un miembro del equipo que también era adiestrador privado de perros. Entonces organizó un encuentro entre nosotros.

Decidí volar de vuelta a Ciudad de México unos seis meses después para reunirme con el miembro del equipo y el director del SAR y discutir mi idea con la Dra. Edwards, Enriqueta, su esposo y otras personas. También tenía un motivo oculto, el Departamento de Transporte de Estados Unidos había impuesto dos sanciones a Aeromar Airlines y yo quería comprobar si la compañía había aprendido la lección. Hice una reserva con el mismo itinerario que antes y, una vez más, planeé visitar a mi amiga Peggy en McAllen, Texas. Notifiqué al agente de reservas de Aeromar que volaría con mi perro de asistencia y tenía todos los papeles en regla. Decidí llevar a Savior para recrear exactamente la misma situación con un "perro de servicio labrador grande".

Cuando llegué al aeropuerto de McAllen y me acerqué al mostrador de venta de tiquetes, esta vez la situación fue muy diferente. La señora que estaba detrás del mostrador era la misma que me había denegado el abordaje con Savior el año anterior. Me reconoció al instante y se disculpó por la indiscreción anterior. Le dije que no era su culpa y le expliqué que la compañía aérea había sido sancionada por infringir la ley. En quince minutos subimos al avión y nos trataron como reyes.

Quedé de verme con todos en el restaurante donde antes nos habíamos reunido. La Dra. Edwards hizo que un miembro de la prensa nos acompañara. Pasé mucho tiempo en la mesa discutiendo el valor de los perros de servicio en la sociedad. Aunque los perros SAR y los perros guía eran conocidos en la sociedad mexicana, el concepto de perro de servicio era relativamente nuevo. Hablé de la posibilidad de conceder a un miembro del equipo de perros SAR una beca financiada para asistir al seminario de formación de verano de la BUCS. Pensé que era una oportunidad única para que un adiestrador de perros mexicano asistiera a la BUCS y trabajara junto a la Dra. Bergin. El miembro del equipo dijo que estaba interesado. Decidí dejar que la oferta se asimilara y esperar a ver si se podía seguir adelante.

La Dra. Edwards mencionó entonces que había una organización dirigida por un par de mujeres mexicanas que entrenaban perros de servicio. Me dijo que me daría más información para que pudiera visitarlas si quería. También mencionó la existencia de una escuela de perros guía en Ciudad de México. Sabía que tendría que visitar ambos lugares para hacerme una idea de cómo se entrenaba a los perros de trabajo en México. Antes de que terminara la semana, visité al grupo de perros de servicio dirigido por las dos mujeres. Era más como un centro con muchos animales rescatados o maltratados, algunos de los cuales eran perros con un pasado desconocido que eran entrenados. Fue interesante. Las mujeres eran maravillosas, pero se hacía necesario un centro de formación profesional. Es todo lo que puedo decir. Las mujeres hacían todo lo posible por adiestrar a perros callejeros utilizando una metodología introducida por una organización española llamada Bocalan Madrid.

Después de la cena, Savior hizo su debut en el bar de karaoke que Booster y yo habíamos frecuentado el año anterior. Entramos, nos sentamos y la historia se repitió. Recuerdo que pensé que era más fácil llevar a un perro de servicio a un lugar público en Ciudad de México, donde no existían leyes de acceso, que ingresar en lugares similares en Estados Unidos a pesar de que existían leyes de acceso. Esas leyes existían, en gran parte, porque la Dra. Bergin luchó ante el Congreso para que se aprobaran. Cuando me tocó cantar, subí al escenario y expliqué que Savior "era mi perro de servicio y me ayudaba a vivir mejor". Luego, intenté entonar una bonita canción en español titulada "Tu Primera Vez", escrita por el famoso cantante mexicano José José, que principalmente componía canciones sobre el amor y la soledad. *Casualmente*, él solía hablar de su lucha con las relaciones y el alcoholismo. Era una hermosa canción sobre un joven a punto de hacer el amor con su novia, que era virgen; por lo tanto, era su *primera vez*.

Al día siguiente, me desperté renovado. Había disfrutado mucho de la cena de la noche anterior y de la compañía de los mexicanos del bar, que me aceptaron como extranjero y, lo que es más importante, a mi Savior. Aunque me entristecía irme, extrañaba a mi manada en casa. Tenía mucho en qué pensar y me preguntaba, *¿Podré recrear en México lo que había hecho en las Bahamas?* Quería ayudar a los mexicanos a que se aprobara una ley de acceso para discapacitados. El potencial estaba ahí. Sólo tenía que reunir la energía y la convicción necesarias para hacerlo realidad. En el avión de regreso, me preguntaba si el director de perros SAR ayudaría realmente a poner en marcha un programa mexicano de adiestramiento de perros de servicio. Visualizaba una alianza entre el Booster Center y la BUCS. Ese era mi nuevo sueño.

Muchas historias aparecieron en los periódicos mexicanos. Los reporteros habían hecho su trabajo y yo apreciaba su consideración y minuciosidad. Estaba muy orgulloso, no de mí, sino de mi Booster y, a su vez, de su hijo, Savior. Me quedó muy claro que los caninos tienen una ética de trabajo muy arraigada. Disfrutan del trabajo.

No hace falta mucho esfuerzo para obtener grandes resultados con una aportación mínima. Basta con una palmadita en la cabeza y un contacto visual de elogio. ¡Por supuesto, una o dos golosinas ayudan a aumentar la dedicación!

Una vez en casa, me mantuve en contacto con mi siempre creciente grupo de amigos mexicanos amantes de los perros. Más tarde, recibí un correo electrónico de Enriqueta, notificándome de una próxima conferencia sobre perros de asistencia que se llevaría a cabo en Ciudad de México. Escribí al comité de la conferencia y les pedí que me permitieran compartir la historia de Booster e invitar a la mundialmente famosa Dra. Bergin para dar una conferencia. Recibí rápidamente una invitación para que los dos asistiéramos. Aunque la conferencia ya estaba programada, los organizadores les quitaron quince minutos a otros presentadores para acomodarnos en su horario.

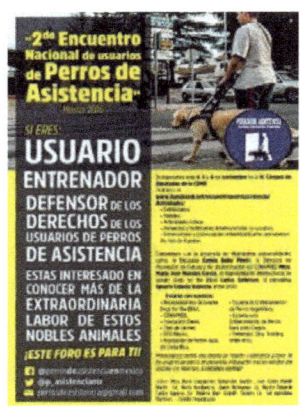

¡Yo estaba emocionado! Miré a Boosted y Busted y les dije, "Ahora les toca a ustedes continuar el legado de su padre". Se me empañaron los ojos. Echaba de menos a mi Booster. Habían pasado dos turbulentos años desde su fallecimiento. No sé si lo habría logrado sin "Boo y Bus" a mi lado. Pronto sería su oportunidad de brillar. Yo sabía que podían hacerlo, ya que tenían su herencia.

Llamé a Bonnie y ella aceptó amablemente la invitación para dar una conferencia. También llamé a mi buena amiga Sharon, que me había acompañado a las Bahamas, y se mostró interesada en asistir. Queríamos darle una sorpresa a Bonnie. Hacía años que no nos veíamos. Sabía que Bonnie estaría encantada de ponerse al día con los viejos tiempos. También invité a mi hermano mayor y me sorprendió que expresara su interés en ir. Sentado en el sofá con Boosted a un lado y Busted al otro, los apreté y abracé, los miré a los ojos y sonreí. Tenían sus bocas abiertas y las lenguas afuera, como si ellos también sonrieran. Antropomorfismo o no, ¡sabía muy bien que sonreían!

Unos días después, Enriqueta me envió una copia del cartel que anunciaba el "Segundo Encuentro Nacional de Usuarios de Perros de Asistencia". Me quedé impresionado y emocionado cuando leí que asistirían personas de muchos otros países. Iba a ser genial para la BUCS tener presencia en México. Me sentí orgulloso de que Bonnie estuviera dispuesta a asistir, ¡especialmente porque no le gustaba volar! Inmediatamente empecé a trabajar en una nueva conferencia en PowerPoint. Esta vez me dirigiría a profesionales del campo de los perros de asistencia. Quería impartir lo que había aprendido en el aula de la

BUCS, junto con los conocimientos adquiridos a través de experiencias del mundo real. También quería que mi hermano supiera un poco más sobre mi vida personal y lo que había estado haciendo con la educación que él había considerado un "desperdicio de dinero".

Con el paso del tiempo, continué en comunicación con el director de perros SAR y con el miembro del equipo sobre la posibilidad de poner en marcha un centro de adiestramiento de perros de servicio en la UNAM utilizando sus instalaciones de adiestramiento. El director se mostraba escéptico respecto a contar con estudiantes voluntarios, mientras que yo valoraba mucho el voluntariado. Cualquiera puede trabajar para cobrar un cheque, pero querer trabajar gratis demuestra dedicación. Creo que el director había sido agraviado por un voluntario en el pasado, pero eso no debería haber impedido el voluntariado. Entrenar perros de servicio es agotador, física y económicamente. Se trata de ayudar a los discapacitados, no de obtener beneficios. La mayoría de los centros de adiestramiento de perros de asistencia son sin ánimo de lucro. Algunos adiestradores trabajan gratis y donan su tiempo. Algunos adiestradores, muchos con títulos universitarios, ganan un promedio de 40.000 dólares al año. Algunos adiestradores de perros guía ganan más de 100.000 dólares al año. Teniendo esto en cuenta, sigue costando más de 50.000 dólares adiestrar a un perro de servicio y 100.000 a un perro guía. Tener al lado, a una universidad conformada por estudiantes brillantes era un recurso muy valioso.

Mis conversaciones con el miembro del equipo eran con frecuencia difíciles, pero no por la barrera del idioma. Él estaba muy dedicado al trabajo SAR pero expresó su deseo de aprender a adiestrar perros para ayudar a los discapacitados. Había pasado mucho tiempo desde el famoso terremoto de Ciudad de México y los miembros del equipo de perros SAR seguían yendo fielmente día a día para trabajar con sus perros de una manera muy devota. Fue muy inspirador. Pensé, *si puedo aprovechar esa misma dedicación para adiestrar perros de servicio, los miembros del equipo obtendrán una gratificación instantánea que los inspirará, a ellos y a otros, a seguir trabajando con los perros.* Para mí era obvio.

El tiempo pasó muy rápido y no tardé en encontrarme sentado junto a mi hermano en la primera fila de un avión que se dirigía a Ciudad de México. Boosted y Busted yacían dormidos a nuestros pies, ganándose la admiración de las azafatas. Les dije: "Se puede distinguir un perro de servicio falso de uno de verdad en cuestión de segundos, ¿cierto?"

"Por supuesto", fue la respuesta.

Al cabo de una hora, entramos en el aeropuerto de Ciudad de México. Nos dirigieron a la Oficina de Inspección de Sanidad Animal (OISA). Una vez más, Boosted y Busted cautivaron al público, ¡esta vez a los inspectores de animales!

Una hora más tarde, mi hermano y yo nos registramos en nuestras habitaciones del Hotel del Principado, un lugar pintoresco y de precio razonable que había encontrado en un viaje anterior a la ciudad. El gerente era amante de los perros, y el personal del hotel también era muy complaciente. Tenía un bar y un restaurante pequeños y encantadores. Más tarde, me reuní con Sharon en el vestíbulo y le expliqué que Bonnie llegaría pronto. Sharon no había visto a Bonnie desde su graduación, casi una década antes. Sharon había puesto en práctica su título trabajando en una prisión del estado de Florida, enseñando a los reclusos a adiestrar perros de servicio. Estaba impaciente por sorprender a Bonnie, que no tenía ni idea de que una de sus graduadas también iba a estar presente.

Hice que Sharon esperara entre bastidores la llegada de Bonnie. Con buen ánimo, le presenté a Bonnie a mi hermano, también a Boosted y Busted, y luego le expliqué que había una persona muy importante que quería que conociera. Dicho esto, Sharon entró y dos sonrisas radiantes chocaron en una euforia sin límites. Fue el calentamiento global en su máxima expresión, ya que todos compartimos el momento. Pronto acordamos reunirnos para cenar en el pequeño restaurante del hotel en lugar de salir a celebrarlo. Nos esperaba un gran día y necesitábamos dormir.

A la mañana siguiente, tomamos un desayuno rápido. El director del hotel organizó un taxi para que nos recogiera y nos llevara al lugar de la conferencia. Cuando llegamos, Enriqueta nos esperaba pacientemente afuera. Después de presentarnos, entramo y tomamos asiento. La persona encargada del proyector salió a nuestro encuentro y recogió las memorias USB que se utilizarían para nuestras presentaciones en la pantalla grande. Bonnie fue la primera en exponer la historia del perro de servicio y la evolución de este concepto desde su creación. La traductora era una dulce joven de Venezuela a la que había conocido en la última conferencia. Se había casado con un mexicano y se había trasladado a México para formar una familia. La contraté para que nos tradujera e hizo un gran trabajo.

Cuando me llegó el turno de hablar, Boosted y yo subimos al escenario. Lloraba por dentro al pensar en Booster, que por derecho debería haber estado a mi lado. Pero no dejé que mis pensamientos me abrumaran mientras acariciaba con decisión a Boosted, quien me brindaba apoyo con su sola presencia. Hablé de mi historia y de cómo Booster cambió mi vida y la de otras personas en todo el mundo. Luego expliqué que los perros de servicio son una prolongación del propio cuerpo y un medio de independencia para las personas con deficiencias físicas. Expliqué además que es imperativo que a los discapacitados, acompañados de todo tipo de perros de asistencia, se les permita el acceso público con sus perros. "¿Por qué una persona ciega, que depende de un perro guía para ver, debe afrontar la dificultad de dormir en la calle?"

Hablé de mis viajes al extranjero con Booster y de la necesidad de educar a más personas sobre la importancia de los perros de asistencia. Además, conté que en Ciudad de México me permitieron el acceso público con mis perros de asistencia, a pesar de que ninguna ley lo garantizaba. Expresé mi más sincero agradecimiento e insinué que me esforzaría por ayudar a la comunidad de discapacitados a conseguir la aprobación de una ley de acceso. A continuación, hice una demostración de cómo Boosted abría la nevera y me traía agua, me quitaba los calcetines, ladraba para pedir ayuda y todas las demás tareas habituales. A Boosted no se le escapó ni una... por así decirlo. Desbordaba confianza, como siempre había hecho Booster. Una vez más, me tambaleé emocionalmente, pero el orgullo y el asombro me salvaron. Estaba muy orgulloso de Boosted y Busted, de quienes obtenía mi fortaleza emocional.

Cuando bajé del escenario, miré al público. Bonnie estaba sentada al lado de mi hermano, y ambos sonreían como diciendo "lo hiciste muy bien". En ese momento, me sentí muy agradecido de que Bonnie hubiera sacado tiempo de su apretada agenda para acompañarme. Mi hermano, que antes consideraba que mis estudios eran un gasto frívolo, igualmente me apoyó. Cuando Boosted y yo llegamos a nuestro asiento, Sharon se inclinó y me dijo, "Buen trabajo, Davis". Me había ganado la trifecta del apoyo. Luego me volví hacia Boosted y Busted y los abracé con fuerza.

Después de un almuerzo rápido, Enriqueta y yo asistimos juntos a las reuniones de la conferencia. Me senté en una fila con otros ponentes y compartimos ideas y conceptos. No pude evitar fijarme en que muchos de los ponentes que iban acompañados de sus perros de asistencia llevaban collares de púas que aprisionaban a sus perros. En otras partes del mundo, este tipo de control mediante el dolor era mal visto.

Un famoso adiestrador canino mexicano ensalzaba universalmente los méritos de ser dominante y obligar a los perros a someterse. Esa mentalidad está pasada de moda. Sus técnicas incluían supuestamente la dominación física de los perros mediante pellizcos, patadas en el estómago, puñetazos, descargas eléctricas, collares de púas, collares de pellizco y otras acciones aversivas. Ya no pateamos a los perros para que se sometan, ni los ponemos boca arriba para demostrarles quién manda, ni les clavamos tortuosas espigas en el cuello. Francamente, quedé horrorizado. Asistí a la conferencia para ayudar a los discapacitados y concienciar sobre el valor de los perros en la sociedad. No tenía ninguna posibilidad de cambiar la mentalidad de los adiestradores que seguían las viejas metodologías.

Forzar a un perro a someterse crea miedo y pánico, es perjudicial para el perro. Inculcar miedo a un perro adiestrado para el acceso público, que ayuda a una persona con capacidades físicas limitadas, es un error. Los padres (espero) no golpean a sus hijos contra el suelo ni utilizan cadenas de estrangulamiento para provocar un comportamiento apropiado. Creo que lo mismo ocurre con los dueños de mascotas y sus perros. Fue duro ver lo que yo percibía como un comportamiento sin escrúpulos. Conseguir que una persona *desaprenda* lo que le han enseñado, incluso por décadas, es casi imposible. Me recordó al veterinario de edad avanzada que vacunó a Booster en la cadera, provocándole una hinchazón, simplemente porque se negaba a adoptar prácticas más modernas y aceptadas de administrar las vacunas por debajo del cuello, en el hombro del perro. En ese momento, elegí conscientemente cuál sería mi batalla.

En la BUCS, había leído estudios que demostraban que los perros adiestrados con collares de choque realizaban la tarea pero rara vez ofrecían algo más porque temían recibir una descarga. Es posible que trajeran un zapato, pero no él otro por miedo al castigo. Hoy en día, la mayoría de los adiestradores emplean el refuerzo positivo, muchas veces en forma de golosinas. Yo *trato* a mis hijos caninos con golosinas en forma de abrazos y elogios emocionales. Con frecuencia les doy golosinas, pero la inspiración emocional es mi método preferido. De niño, mi madre me elogiaba, acompañada de otras personas, cuando construía algo o hacía algo creativo. Nunca olvidé lo motivado que esto me hacía sentir. Me dieron algunos azotes, pero nunca nada excesivo. Incluso ahora, me siguen sorprendiendo los padres que alaban su metodología de dar palizas a sus hijos cuando han hecho algo que se percibe como malo. Peor aún, me pregunto cómo los humanos más enfermos apoyan las descargas eléctricas, la terapia de conversión gay, para "curar" la homosexualidad. ¡SORPRENDENTE!

La tarde siguiente, mi comitiva (Boosted, Busted, Sharon y mi hermano) nos acompañó a Enriqueta y a mí a la UNAM para reunirnos con algunos jefes de departamento. Enriqueta había concertado la reunión con mucha antelación. Quería hablar de la oportunidad de que los estudiantes, especialmente los de psicología y sociología, participaran en el adiestramiento de perros de servicio. Pensé que sería una gran oportunidad para que los estudiantes aprendieran de motivación canina junto con el voluntariado. Los estudiantes podrían adiestrar perros en el campus, en las instalaciones caninas de SAR. Sería un acto altruista en beneficio de la comunidad mexicana de discapacitados. No veía ningún inconveniente en la propuesta. Los jefes de departamento y los profesores asistentes parecían muy interesados. Al final de la reunión, la sala estaba bien iluminada con cálidas sonrisas.

Esa noche, organicé una cena en *mi* restaurante mexicano. Mi hermano y yo estábamos sentados con Boosted y Busted a nuestros pies. La Dra. Edwards y su esposo Paco, fueron los primeros invitados en llegar y trajeron un perro pequeño. Curiosamente, el personal del restaurante intervino y dijo que entendían lo de mis perros de servicio adiestrados, pero que los perros en general no estaban permitidos en el restaurante. Me dio un poco de vergüenza que se cuestionara a la Dra. Edwards, pero el personal tenía razón 100% en su apreciación. Cedieron en su decisión y permitieron que el perro de la Dra. Edward se quedara solo por esta vez. Recuerdo que pensé que ojalá más establecimientos de Estados Unidos desafiaran a quienes tienen perros de servicio falsos.

Al poco rato, Enriqueta y su esposo Antonio llegaron y se unieron a la alegría que ya había comenzado. Al cabo de unos minutos, entraron el director y un miembro del equipo de perros SAR. Les conté lo que había ocurrido en la UNAM ese mismo día y les dije que me encantaría ayudar a poner en marcha un centro de adiestramiento. Dije además que el personal de la universidad parecía interesado y que había un gran potencial. Luego mencioné que me gustaría ayudar a que se aprobara una ley de acceso público a los perros de asistencia en México porque, sin acceso público, los perros y sus compañeros humanos son discapacitados. Esto reflejaba mis sentimientos expresados en las Bahamas cuando escribí una carta al Primer Ministro explicando que la falta de una ley de acceso para los discapacitados era una desventaja.

Nunca olvidaré lo que ocurrió a continuación. El miembro del equipo se inclinó hacia delante y dijo resueltamente en voz alta, "En México, nada sucede rápidamente". La connotación era extremadamente negativa, pero quizás esa era la realidad en México.

Yo no había vivido en ese país, así que no lo sabía. Instintiva e instantáneamente, repliqué, "Bueno, si *crees* que no puede pasar nada, ¡entonces nada sucederá!" Entonces compartí que había escuchado esa misma tesis en Cuba y, sin embargo, las cosas sucedieron demasiado rápido a mi modo de ver, en ese país. También hablé de mi experiencia en las Bahamas ayudando a que se aprobara allí una ley de acceso.

El miembro del equipo me miró como diciendo, "Ya verás, tú no entiendes como son las cosas en mi país".

Pensé, "*Tiene toda la razón. La ignorancia es una bendición.* **No entendía que algo no se pudiera lograr.** Me encantaban los buenos retos.

Cuando era niño, mis padres se fueron de viaje, así que me quedé con una de sus mejores amigas. Por aquel entonces yo trabajaba diligentemente en un kart y necesitaba un motor. Localicé uno usado y le pregunté a la señora si me acompañaría a traerlo. Le expliqué que tenía dinero para comprarlo. Ella no quería ser cómplice por si mis padres no aprobaban que me gastara el dinero de esa manera. Al día siguiente, la señora llegó a casa y me vio lavando el motor que había comprado ese mismo día. Me preguntó cómo lo había conseguido y le expliqué que había tomado un autobús y lo había cargado por toda la ciudad. Ella me recordó que me había dicho que esperara y que había hecho algo que no estaba bien. Así que me puso el apodo de Stinky (Apestoso), que me quedó durante años. Yo a eso lo llamé determinación. Hice que sucediera.

Hubo muchas ocasiones en las que me empeñaba en hacer algo cuando me decían que no se podía. Decirme que algo era imposible me motivaba aún más. Contra todo pronóstico, había entrado en Cuba como estadounidense, con un perro, y había aparecido en televisión en directo. Había contribuido decisivamente a que se aprobara una ley sobre discapacidad y acceso en las Bahamas. Volví a la universidad a una edad avanzada, obtuve un máster y lo utilicé más allá de lo que podía imaginar. También había conseguido clonar a Booster cuando el precio era prohibitivo. Mi alma, en antaño vencida, consideraba que hablar en público era la perdición de mi existencia. Con el paso del tiempo, mi Booster cambió todo eso exponencialmente. En el fondo, yo sabía que estaba a la altura *del reto de ser miembro del equipo*. Estaba dispuesto a hacer lo que fuera necesario para perfeccionar el cambio en México. ¡y rápidamente! El hecho de que amara tanto al pueblo mexicano era un buen augurio para mi éxito potencial.

El último día de la conferencia me reuní con todos los asistentes en la Plaza de la República, Monumento a la Revolución. También hubo una gran afluencia de público. Tenía programada una demostración en vivo de perros de servicio en un lugar público del centro de la ciudad. Había hecho muchos amigos mexicanos maravillosos, amantes de los perros. Varios de ellos se presentaron para ayudarme a organizar la demostración de las

habilidades de los perros de servicio. Un amigo compró una pequeña nevera, la llevó en un camión y la devolvió inmediatamente después, a cambio de un crédito. Otro preparó un taxi con la condición de que un perro abriría la puerta y saltaría al interior para buscar una botella de agua.

Otro amigo trajo una silla y una mesa. Resulta reconfortante que personas de tanta calidad se unan para promover la labor de los perros de asistencia.

Busted era mi perro del día simplemente porque Boosted se había presentado en la conferencia días antes. Cuando llegó el momento de la demostración, me volví hacia Busted y le pregunté, "¿Estás listo?" Era una pregunta tonta, ya que Boosted y Busted siempre estaban dispuestos a demostrar su talento, como Booster había hecho una década antes. Mientras que mis habilidades como adiestrador de perros podían ser cuestionables, las de los clones no lo eran. Confiaba en ellos al 100%, igual que en Booster.

Le dije, "Busted, siéntate, por favor", y se sentó educadamente. Caminé despreocupadamente por el cemento y me quité los zapatos. Luego volví a sentarme en la silla y le pedí con calma, "Zapato, por favor". Sin dudarlo, Busted corrió y me trajo el zapato izquierdo. Entonces le pregunté con toda naturalidad, "¿Dónde está mi otro zapato?" Levanté ambas palmas al
cielo, con los hombros encogidos, de manera cómica, y añadí, ¿Donde? De nuevo, el confiado can corrió, cogió mi zapato derecho y me lo entregó. Entonces me senté tranquilamente en una silla y le dije, "El calcetín, por favor", y Busted se llevó el calcetín a la boca y me lo quitó del pie. A continuación dije, "El otro calcetín, por favor", y Busted me quitó el otro calcetín y me lo dio. Meneó la cola, elogiando su logro. Empecé a llorar al recordar cuando Booster había hecho exactamente lo mismo en Cuba años atrás. Mi público mexicano respondió con sonrisas e instantáneamente estuvo más atento.

Después de elogiar a Busted, seguí con "Estoy sediento". "¡Tráeme agua por favor! ¡NEVERA!!!" Busted corrió hacia la mini nevera, abrió la puerta de un tirón y cogió la botella de agua. Sin dudarlo, corrió y me la puso en la mano. Entonces le pedí al público, que se había multiplicado exponencialmente, que por favor esperara un segundo porque necesitaba una bolsa de medicamentos de mi automóvil. Señalé hacia el taxi y le dije a Busted, "Necesito mi bolsa, por favor. . . TIRA". Como un caballero de brillante armadura, se acercó al taxi, abrió la puerta, saltó dentro, encontró mi bolsa de medicamentos y me la trajo.

En ese momento, el nivel de energía del público era igual al de Busted. Recordé que los perros responden a los niveles de energía y a la intensidad

de los sonidos. Busted estaba entusiasmado, y se habría lucido todo el día si hubiera tenido la oportunidad. Le hice una última petición, "Un ABRAZO, por favor", y el jadeante Busted saltó y me dio el abrazo de su vida. Era como un padre con su hijo exitoso. Una síntesis de orgullo y amor encapsulada en un abrazo canino-humano.

También conocimos a muchos mexicanos discapacitados que observaron atentamente nuestra demostración. Fue una experiencia muy cálida y amistosa. Muchos expresaron su deseo de tener perros entrenados en sus vidas. Les presenté a todos a Busted, y estoy seguro de que vi cómo su cabeza se inflaba más y más a medida que avanzaba el día. Pensaba en silencio en cómo mi vida se había convertido en tal bendición con el apoyo de Booster, mi educación en la BUCS y la magnánima ayuda del profesor coreano Hwang. Sin el don de la clonación del profesor, este día y muchos otros no habrían sido posibles. Cuando el día llegó a su fin, estaba agotado. Miré a Busted, y él me miró a mí, ¡listo para seguir! ¡Cómo deseaba tener el nivel de energía que él poseía! Tomamos un taxi y nos fuimos al hotel. Después de un par de copas con mi hermano y Sharon, volvimos a nuestra habitación para descansar.

Por la mañana, desayunamos apresuradamente y tomamos un taxi hasta el aeropuerto que ya conocía muy bien. México y su gente estaban ahora arraigados en mi alma, como los bahameños, tailandeses, cubanos y coreanos. Booster había cambiado la esencia de mi ser, y sus hijos de alta tecnología, Boosted y Busted, estaban haciendo lo mismo. Aquella noche reflexioné sobre ello durante horas. A pesar de lo agotado que estaba, el resorte principal de mi mente analítica estaba muy tenso. Tardé horas en relajarme mientras mis hijos caninos roncaban con la satisfacción de un día cumplido.

A la mañana siguiente, me reuní con mi hermano y mis hijos caninos para desayunar. No tardamos en despedirnos de Bonnie y Sharon y nos fuimos al aeropuerto. El viaje de vuelta a casa fue tranquilo. Boosted, Busted y yo recibimos un saludo real de la manada canina cuando llegamos a casa. Pasé los días siguientes enviando correos electrónicos de agradecimiento. También envié al miembro del equipo de perros SAR una oferta para asistir al seminario de adiestramiento de perros de servicio de la BUCS el verano siguiente. Ese fue el primero de muchos intercambios de correo electrónico que tuve con el miembro del equipo de perros SAR y su supervisor.

A medida que pasaban los meses, recibí muchos correos electrónicos y mensajes de texto de la Dra. Edwards y de Enriqueta. Ambas eran unas educadoras divinas y talentosas. Era como si Dios las hubiera puesto en la tierra para enseñar y generar sonrisas y comprensión. Me considero muy afortunado de haberlas conocido e incorporado a mi clan de amantes de los perros. Enriqueta enviaba muchas fotografías y videos mios, cada vez que hacía presentaciones en diversos lugares de

México. Fue muy reconfortante. Puede que mi memoria se desvanezca, pero las fotos y los videos orquestados con tanto esmero perdurarán. De hecho, he utilizado muchos de ellos en este mismo libro. Ojalá pudiera incluir los videos, porque son un montaje de actuaciones acompañadas de música y subtítulos maravillosos. La buena noticia es que se pueden encontrar en mi página web de autor. Puedes ver la evolución de Booster y los clones en videos, clips de televisión, noticias de periódicos y mucho más ¡Te animo a que los veas! Por favor, visita www.boosterelperrodeservicio.com para más información.

Una mañana, me desperté con otro correo electrónico de Enriqueta. Me preguntaba si me gustaría participar en la reunión de la Federación Mexicana de Canofilia que se celebraría en Ciudad de México dentro de unos meses. ¡Inmediatamente le contesté que por supuesto! Lo organizó todo y recibí una invitación formal la semana siguiente. Me alegré de tener la oportunidad de contribuir al progreso de la comprensión canina, en un país al que visitaba con tanta frecuencia. Estaba decidido a contribuir al acceso público de los perros de asistencia. Esta era otra oportunidad para hacerlo. También teníamos preparada otra presentación en la UNAM.

Cuando se acercaba la fecha de la conferencia, llamé a mi amigo Rocky y le pregunté si quería ir a México. Tras obtener el permiso de su esposa, aceptó acompañarme. Necesitaba un par de manos adicional, ya que estaba decidido a llevar a Boosted y a Busted. También había estado en contacto con un entrenador y criador de perros mexicano, que estaba inscrito en el programa de grado asociado de la BUCS. Isaac era una década más joven que yo, pero igualmente dedicado al avance de los caninos en la sociedad. Se ofreció a ayudarme a traducir y a coordinar las cosas en México.

Organicé un vuelo para que Rocky e Isaac se reunieran conmigo en la cercana Nueva Orleans. En grupo, humanos y perros de servicio abordamos el vuelo a Ciudad de México. Me hice amigo de la tripulación de cabina y les presenté a los "mundialmente famosos perros de servicio clonados". Durante el vuelo, como de costumbre, entregué a las azafatas mi dossier de logros caninos para que lo leyeran. ¡Siempre ayuda tener amigos en las altas esferas! Boosted y Busted se comportaron como siempre, ganándose los cumplidos de la tripulación de cabina y de los pasajeros sentados cerca. Era reconfortante tenerlos a los dos conmigo, comportándose con tanto profesionalismo. Recordé los meses que pasé en Corea, adiestrándolos, cuando eran cachorros y solo tenían unas semanas.

Cuando el avión aterrizó, organizamos el transporte al hotel. Me subí en la parte trasera del taxi con Boosted, Busted y Rocky. Isaac se sentó adelante. Esta vez me acompañaban Boosted, Busted, Rocky e Isaac. ¡Los cinco éramos una mano de póquer ganadora si alguna vez existió una! Llegamos al Hotel Principado, saltamos jubilosos del taxi y nos registramos en nuestras habitaciones. Poco después, dimos un paseo por el amplio bulevar adyacente al hotel. Nos detuvimos en la cantina de la esquina y celebramos nuestra llegada. Boosted y Busted disfrutaron de los tacos tanto como nosotros. Bebimos muchas margaritas.

Como Boosted y Busted no tenían edad para beber, saciaron su sed con agua embotellada. ¡No iba a darles agua del grifo para que tuvieran problemas estomacales y no pudieran asistir a la conferencia!

Enriqueta nos había organizado una visita a la Escuela para Entrenamiento de Perros Guía para Ciegos IAP. Al instante recordé una excursión de la BUCS para visitar el campus de Guide Dogs for the Blind en San Rafael, California. Algo que me impresionó mucho fue la forma en que se utilizaban diferentes tipos de música en el campus para que los ciegos supieran exactamente dónde estaban. Mientras yo estaba allí, estaban adiestrando a su último grupo de pastores alemanes. Nuestro guía nos explicó que hoy en día, gracias a la medicina moderna, la gente no se quedaba ciega a una edad tan temprana. Los veteranos de guerra de antaño solían quedarse ciegos en combate. Los veteranos de hoy tienen más probabilidades de sufrir una lesión cerebral traumática (LCT). La población mayor es la que sufre problemas de ceguera. A veces, una persona mayor no puede soportar la musculatura del pastor alemán. Nuestro guía nos explicó que el can preferido actualmente era el Labrador o el Golden Retriever. Aquella noche fue tranquila. Salimos todos a cenar y disfrutamos del ambiente mexicano y de los turistas que paseaban por el bulevar. Muchos vendedores ambulantes, jóvenes y mayores, vendían sus productos para deleite de los transeúntes. Me alegré de que mis amigos estuvieran contentos y de que Boosted y Busted fueran felices.

A la mañana siguiente, íbamos a visitar la escuela de perros guía. Boosted y Busted subieron al taxi dispuestos a emprender un nuevo viaje. Cuando llegamos a la escuela, nos recibieron el director y el adiestrador jefe. La directora era una mujer ciega con una sonrisa radiante y una gran personalidad. El entrenador llevó a Boosted y Busted a sus habitaciones de hotel. En lugar de estar en el centro del escenario, estaban confinados en cuartos, encerrados en una celda extranjera. Me sentí un poco culpable, pero las instalaciones estaban excepcionalmente limpias y eran hospitalarias.

Nos acompañaron al interior y nos invitaron a reunirnos con los demás en la mesa del desayuno. Una vez sentados, nuestra amable anfitriona nos entregó vendas para los ojos y nos pidió amablemente que nos las pusiéramos. Una vez puestas, nosotros también éramos ciegos. Al instante me sentí indefenso y muy claustrofóbico. Nos dieron la bienvenida y nos dijeron que comiéramos. Yo estaba hipnotizado, por no decir otra cosa. *¿Cómo diablos voy a comer si no puedo ver la maldita comida? ¿Dónde está mi tenedor, mi plato, mi vaso? Extendí la mano para coger el vaso de zumo de naranja y lo volteé. Tal vez pueda empaparlo en una servilleta y metérmelo en la boca... ¡si pudiera encontrar la servilleta! Esto apesta. No estoy preparado para esto"*. Mi mente estaba en una sobrecarga sensorial. Al instante, me sumí en profundos pensamientos. La mayoría de la gente no está preparada para quedarse ciega, y sin embargo ocurre.

Que conste que aquella experiencia fue como arrojar a un río turbulento a alguien que no sabe nadar. Fue horripilante y a la vez educativo como ninguna otra cosa. En lugar de una mirada de reproche, coseché un aura de satisfacción por la experiencia educativa única. Nunca la he olvidado ni la olvidaré. Más tarde pensé que tenía que agradecerles a Booster, Boosted y Busted por otra experiencia enriquecedora. Mi hermano alguna vez me preguntó, "¿Qué vas a hacer con ese perro?" En retrospectiva, la pregunta pertinente debería haber sido, "¿Qué va a hacer ese perro *contigo*?"

Cuando por fin me dijeron que me quitara la venda, miré al otro lado de la mesa para ver las reacciones de Rocky e Isaac. Sus expresiones faciales eran como una sola, expresando un innegable "wow". Aprendimos una lección de vida en una hora... una "visión" inestimable, aunque solo fuera por un momento, de los retos que enfrentan los ciegos. El simple hecho de comer era una tarea a tener en cuenta. De repente me acordé de mi amigo Ed Eames, que tenía problemas para llamar un taxi en Nueva York simplemente porque utilizaba un perro guía para abrirse paso por el peligroso laberinto de las calles de la ciudad. Mi experiencia de aquel día en la escuela reforzó mi decisión de seguir  ayudando a los discapacitados a utilizar perros para mejorar sus vidas.

A la mañana siguiente, Rocky e Isaac se reunieron conmigo, junto con Boosted y Busted, para desayunar en el restaurante del hotel. Hablamos de la visita del día anterior a la escuela y yo esperaba con impaciencia mi conferencia de ese mismo día. Aunque estaba un poco nervioso, hablar en público me resultó más fácil con los años, ya que siempre encontré aceptación, sin importar si era en un país cuyos ciudadanos eran de otro color, hablaban otra lengua o tenían otra forma de gobierno. Siempre había sacado fuerzas de Booster y su progenie, Boosted y Busted. Esa mañana decidimos dar un largo paseo juntos para estirar nuestras piernas y las de nuestros acompañantes caninos. Caminamos por las calles de Ciudad de México admirando la cultura. Se respiraba un ambiente cálido y acogedor. Me sentí más seguro allí que paseando por muchas ciudades de Estados Unidos. Curiosamente, los mexicanos no parecían tenerles miedo a los dos perros grandes. Reflexioné sobre la gran cantidad de perros que paseaban los domingos por la calle principal.

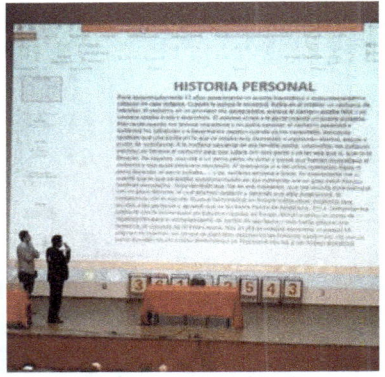

Pronto, llegó la hora de salir. Cogimos un taxi y los perros no supusieron ningún problema. Siempre me aseguraba de decir "gracias por ayudar" a los taxistas y solía explicarles que yo ayudaba a adiestrar "perros de asistencia para personas discapacitadas". Enriqueta nos recibió en la puerta del recinto, entramos juntos y tomamos asiento.

Observamos las demostraciones y escuchamos las conferencias que eran muy interesantes. No tardó mucho en llegar mi turno, y subí al escenario acompañado por Isaac, que hizo un gran trabajo de traducción. Estaba totalmente en sintonía con el público y me sentía totalmente cómodo. Estaba donde debía estar.

Cuando terminé mi presentación de PowerPoint, llevé a Boosted al escenario. Su actuación fue impecable, igual que la de Booster en años anteriores, y la de Busted recientemente. Es muy gratificante ver el duro trabajo que supone adiestrar a un perro para que realice tareas de perro de servicio de forma impecable una y otra vez.

Cuando la conferencia terminó, me entregaron un certificado de agradecimiento. Para mí era más que un certificado. Era una confirmación de los años de estudio en conjunción con una asimilación cultural inculcada por Booster. Me sentí aceptado y apreciado, y eso resonó muy dentro de mí. Entonces me presentaron a un periodista que quería hacer un reportaje. Salimos al exterior, hablamos y yo hice una demostración de las tareas de un perro de servicio, como abrir la puerta de un automóvil para traer una botella de agua o un botiquín. Un amable caballero me ofreció su automóvil para la demostración de Boosted y Busted. Me hice amigo suyo y le invité a unirse a nosotros en una gran cena que patrociné la noche siguiente. El ayudante del periodista no paró de tomar fotos.

A los pocos días, el gran reportaje apareció en los periódicos para que todos lo leyeran. También estaba en Internet. Me sentí orgulloso y agradecido de que el periódico hiciera eco de la noticia. Me sentí aún más orgulloso de Boosted y Busted que volvieron a ganarse sus alas. Me acordé del arte canino de Stephen Huneck con labradores que posaban como ángeles alados.

Al día siguiente, paseamos por las calles de Ciudad de México, entablando amistad con todo tipo de personas que representaban el denominador común de la amistad y el amor. Boosted y Busted atrajeron a personas de todos los ámbitos que anhelaban saludarlos. Era reconfortante ver a la humanidad exhibir tal cantidad de amor.

Concluí mi visita la noche siguiente patrocinando una cena formal para todos aquellos que me habían ayudado a unirme a la lucha por el reconocimiento y los derechos de los perros de asistencia en México. Fue una cena maravillosa y el ambiente se llenó de entusiasmo. Mis amigos mexicanos procedían de todos los ámbitos de la vida, desde profesores universitarios hasta ejecutivos de empresas, pasando por periodistas y amantes de los perros. La hija de uno de ellos lo acompañó y más tarde asistió a la BUCS. ¿No es genial?

Aunque el miembro del equipo mexicano de perros SAR me aseguró que no pasaría nada en México, yo sabía en mi corazón que iba a pasar. Había sido testigo del mucho amor, devoción y dedicación que había en los ciudadanos mexicanos. Las asociaciones de ciegos llevaban años luchando por el acceso. Me sentí orgulloso de haber apoyado sus esfuerzos.

Una mañana, mientras revisaba mis correos electrónicos, leí lo siguiente:

> Hola, ¡una muy buena noticia! hoy se aprobó una nueva Ley de Derechos de los Usuarios de Perros Guía y Animales de Servicio. Es sólo el principio de una ardua lucha. Bonnie y tú contribuyeron con su participación a hacer visibles los problemas que enfrentan las personas

con discapacidad al intentar acceder a los servicios a los que todos tenemos derecho. Les envío el video de este hecho histórico.

12 de abril de 2018

Es un día lleno de emoción, agradezco a los diputados de la LXIII legislatura por su confianza al aprobar por unanimidad la Ley de los Derechos de los Usuarios de Perros Guía y Animales de Servicio. # EstamosContigo

En 2016 aprobaron exitosamente una ley de acceso público para los perros guía en la Ciudad de México. Esa fue la primera vez que visité y promoví la defensa de los perros de servicio. En 2018, la ley de acceso se modificó para incluir a los perros de servicio. Independientemente de eso, esperaba que mi labor hubiera ayudado de alguna manera. Aún más emocionante fue una propuesta de 2019, para una ley de acceso para perros guía y perros de servicio para toda la República Mexicana. El proyecto de ley estaba en revisión en el Senado en 2020. Maldición, ¡otra vez tenía H_20 en los ojos!

Basta decir que tenía más fe en los ciudadanos mexicanos que en el miembro del equipo de perros SAR. Desafortunadamente, las cosas nunca progresaron en México. Yo estaba molesto por la actitud del miembro del equipo de perros SAR al regresar a su hermoso país. Decidió que no quería entrenar perros de servicio y me preguntó cuánto le pagaría por hacerlo. La verdad es que debí habérmelo imaginado, debido a su mentalidad. Me culpé a mí mismo, como siempre. Tampoco recibí ayuda de mis amigos al sur de la frontera. El director de perros SAR parecía reacio a coger el toro (perro) por los cuernos y hacer que las cosas sucedieran. Nunca sabré si estaba demasiado ocupado o simplemente era reacio a emprender otra aventura de adiestramiento canino. Poco después, mi salud empeoró repentinamente y el COVID-19 hizo su aparición. Mi mundo, y el mundo mismo, se transformaron. No podía viajar, y el acceso público ya no era una opción. La calidad de mi vida y la de los demás en todo el mundo era pésima. La gente adoptaba perros de refugio como nunca antes. Los seres humanos necesitaban el consuelo que les proporcionaba el vínculo canino-humano. Millones de personas murieron a causa de la pandemia, y muchas familias recibieron el consuelo de sus adoradas mascotas. No me cabe duda de que muchos humanos experimentaron la compañía canina por primera vez y la tendrían en alta estima durante el resto de sus vidas, sin volver a ignorar su valor en la sociedad. Es como la virginidad, una vez perdida, nunca vuelve.

Aunque no podía viajar, me entrevistó un periodista de una revista mexicana de amantes de los perros. El reportaje apareció meses después. Me asombró el contenido de la revista, desde temas médicos como los tumores de lipoma hasta la reproducción y los perros de asistencia. Los artículos estaban muy bien escritos y eran muy completos. Yo aporté fotos y hable de infinidad de temas. El autor sintetizó milagrosamente el material que yo le había proporcionado.

Meses después, me pidieron que hiciera una entrevista en video para una presentación que se colocaría en un monitor, en un museo de Ciudad de México. El entrevistador planteó preguntas maravillosas basadas en la información que yo había proporcionado previamente. Respondí a gran cantidad de preguntas y esperé que fuera esclarecedor y canino-positivo. Debido al COVID-19, la entrevista se publicó en Facebook y no en el monitor de video del museo. Mientras que antes me preocupaba por mi salud, agradecido de estar vivo, ahora veía el video avergonzado por las ojeras. ¡Así es la vida! Todas mis respuestas estaban en el contexto canino-humano. Pueden parecer obvias para muchos, pero no lo son. Esto es especialmente cierto en los países extranjeros, cuyos ciudadanos quizá nunca hayan pensado en entrar en edificios públicos con un perro... ¿A menos que se trate de un anfiteatro con perros de pelea?

CAPÍTULO 20
EL AMOR CORRESPONDIDO

Tras un par de años devastadores, mi salud mejoró y el COVID-19 se volvió menos problemático. Echaba de menos viajar y me quedé extasiado cuando recibí una invitación para dar una conferencia en un congreso de perros de asistencia en Guadalajara, México en diciembre de 2022. Los perros no abandonan a los humanos que aman, ¡y yo tampoco! Mi Booster me enseñó lo que es el amor, a respetarlo y a compartirlo tan a menudo como sea posible. ¡Y vaya si lo hizo! Esas mismas cualidades se manifestaron en sus clones, Boosted y Busted, ellos las tenían profundamente arraigadas. Confiaba en que demostrarían sus habilidades, y que estas se mantendrían intactas con el paso del tiempo.

Yo, en cambio, era un poco mayor y un poco más débil. Así que le pedí a mi vecina, mi querida amiga Ilene, que me acompañara y me ayudara. Ella aceptó amablemente mi invitación y, a su vez, invitó a su amiga Becky. El grupo de cinco, volamos a Guadalajara. Mi amigo mexicano Isaac se unió a nosotros y nos convertimos en un grupo de seis. Recorrimos el terreno y llevamos a los niños caninos con nosotros. Estábamos muy alegres.

El día de la conferencia, entregué mi corazón, y mi alma e hice la presentación en PowerPoint. Había lágrimas en los rostros del público cuando concluí mi charla. Era una afirmación absoluta del viaje de mi vida, en compañía de la espiritualidad canina, lo que había provocado la reacción emocional. Me reafirmó que podía utilizar con éxito las palabras para transmitir emociones insondables que emanaban de lo más profundo de mi psique.

Durante una pausa para comer, dos dulces señoras se me acercaron y me explicaron que trabajaban para el Sistema Nacional para el Desarrollo Integral de la Familia (SNDIF), conocido simplemente como DIF. Se trata de un organismo gubernamental que promueve el bienestar social de las familias mexicanas. Eran de una pequeña ciudad llamada Tepic. Me preguntaron si estaría dispuesto a asistir a su conferencia sobre discapacidad dentro de dos semanas. Por supuesto, dije que sí, y se hicieron los planes para ello. Estaba muy agradecido de estar lo suficientemente saludable como para seguir ayudando a los demás.

Volamos a casa un par de días después, llenos de buenos recuerdos. Para Ilene y Becky, que nunca habían salido del país, fue todo un aprendizaje. Isaac se aseguró de que las chicas estuvieran cómodas y las acompañó a todas partes, traduciendo cuando era necesario. Los miembros del grupo también aprendieron técnicas para viajar con miembros de la familia canina, desde la etiqueta adecuada en el avión hasta el acceso al público. Una vez en casa, tenía unos diez días antes de participar en la siguiente conferencia.

Antes de volar a la conferencia de Tepic, Busted orinaba mucho porque estaba tomando un antibiótico fuerte debido a una pata infectada. Entonces, opté por llevar a Boosted a la conferencia. El vuelo de United Airlines a Ciudad de México fue tranquilo, pero la inquietud surgió cuando United volvió a ponerme en un vuelo de Aeromar Airlines de Ciudad de México a Tepic. Era la única opción. Tenía que ir al mostrador de Aeromar con dos horas de antelación porque volaba con un perro de servicio. ¿Había aprendido Aeromar la lección de no denegar el abordaje a un perro de servicio? En México, no tenía la ley de apoyo estadounidense a la cual recurrir.

Pasé la noche en Ciudad de México y llegué al mostrador a las 4 de la mañana, listo para la batalla. Afortunadamente, había allí un caballero que sabía de perros de servicio. Tardó un poco, pero la aerolínea emitió el boleto mientras Boosted se relajaba delante del mostrador a la vista de todos. ¡Boosted y yo le debíamos gratitud a Savior, que había abierto el camino años antes!

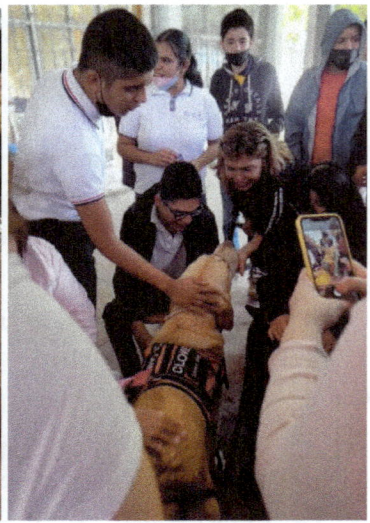

Cuando llegué al aeropuerto de Tepic, me recibieron las damas del DIF que originalmente me habían invitado. Todo eran sonrisas. Me llevaron a mi Airbnb. La esposa del anfitrión me recibió en la puerta de la unidad y me dijo que su hija estaba casualmente en la escuela de veterinaria. Fue un intercambio muy cálido y emotivo. Poco después, las señoras me llevaron a una escuela para niños discapacitados. La escuela era impresionante y era evidente que el personal disfrutaba de su vocación. Mi corazón explotó y mi alma se expandió.

Boosted actuó como el mago que era. Al final de la visita, señalé espontáneamente con el dedo a Boosted y dije, "¡Bang!" Me sorprendió su destreza. Se dio la vuelta inmediatamente y permaneció en esa posición hasta que le dije, "OK, todo está bien". Mis lágrimas de aquel día fueron de doble naturaleza. Me alegré de que los niños estuvieran contentos y de que Boosted estuviera feliz demostrando sus habilidades. Al mismo tiempo estaba triste, porque pensaba en Booster todo el tiempo, cada segundo, minuto y hora. Recordé cómo mi Booster había hecho el mismo truco para niños discapacitados mexicanos años antes.

Ese mismo día realizamos dos entrevistas de radio. Uno de los

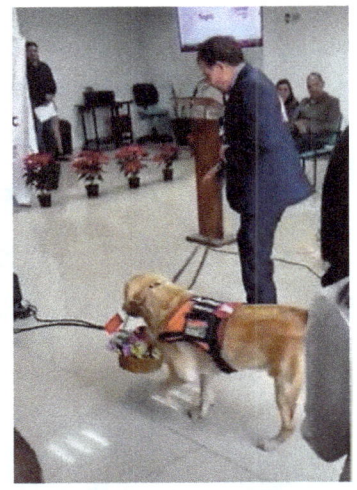

locutores era un hombre y el otro una mujer. Ambos se emocionaron, sus ojos brillaban y se humedecieron cuando compartí el viaje de mi vida, hecho posible gracias al amor canino incondicional. Al día siguiente, la alcaldesa de Tepic celebraba una pequeña rueda de prensa para hablar sobre un proyecto de repavimentación de una carretera. Los empleados del DIF nos llevaron a Boosted y a mí a la rueda de prensa con la esperanza de que conociéramos a la primera alcaldesa elegida

en ese estado. Ella nos saludó con entusiasmo; resultó que tenía cinco perros.

Al día siguiente, la alcaldesa celebró una gran rueda de prensa. Me invitó, con antelación, para que hablara con los lugareños mientras los miembros de la prensa escuchaban atentamente. Ese mismo día había pedido a los empleados del DIF que me llevaran a una floristería. Compré una cesta de mimbre con flores y le puse una pequeña estatua de perro. En la rueda de prensa, coloqué la cesta de flores en una

esquina del escenario, detrás de la cortina. Mientras la cámara del noticiero grababa, expliqué que "Una persona que ama a los animales tiene un gran corazón, es digna de confianza y probablemente ayuda a los demás. Me enteré que eligieron a la primera alcaldesa de su Estado. También sé que tiene cinco perros. Probablemente han elegido a la mejor alcaldesa, la más empática de la historia de la ciudad... ¡y no me han pagado ni un peso por decirlo!"

Como de costumbre, inyecté humor como mecanismo de defensa, ya que estaba un poco nervioso. Luego hice que Boosted recogiera la cesta de flores, cruzara el escenario y se la entregara a la alcalde. (Puede verlo en mi página web de autor). Después de la conferencia, volvimos al edificio del DIF, donde Boosted y yo fuimos entrevistados por un reportero y un equipo de filmación enviados por la mayor cadena de televisión de ese estado.

Salió al aire unos días después. El equipo de rodaje y el editor hicieron un trabajo increíble. La entrevista duró más de cuatro minutos en el noticiero nocturno. La gente que la vio, llamó a la emisora y les pidió que la repitieran en la emisión de la noche siguiente. Efectivamente, emitieron el reportaje la noche siguiente. Me explicaron que la emisora rara vez repite una noticia porque es muy caro hacerlo. Estaba muy orgulloso de Boosted y de toda mi conexión canina.

Más tarde, llevé a comer a dos empleados. Les expliqué que quería ir a un restaurante elegante. Cuanto más lujoso es un restaurante, más probabilidades hay de que surjan problemas de acceso al entrar con un perro de asistencia. Quería que los empleados que trabajan con discapacitados fueran testigos de primera mano de lo que ocurriría. Efectivamente, cuando nos dispusimos a entrar en el restaurante, no me dejaron pasar porque no se admitían *mascotas*. Miré al encargado, asentí y le dije con naturalidad, "Bien, porque esta no es una mascota. Es un perro de servicio". Entré y me senté en una mesa en el centro del restaurante. Sucedió tan rápido que el

personal no sabía cómo manejar la situación. Era territorio conquistado; ¡la batalla había terminado antes de empezar!

Cuando terminamos de comer, llamé al chef. Le expliqué que habíamos disfrutado mucho de la comida y le di las gracias por compartir su talento con nosotros. También le expliqué al encargado que supervisaba la conversación, que el joven que colocó la vajilla en la mesa había agarrado el extremo de cada tenedor con el pulgar y el índice... el extremo con las puntas... que va a tu boca. Me levanté, me rasqué el trasero y luego dije, "¡El pelo de perro es mucho más limpio que la mano que se limpia el trasero y agarra el tenedor!" Antes de irnos, el gerente nos explicó que

nunca habían tenido un perro de asistencia o un perro guía en el restaurante. Fue cordial, y tanto él como los empleados del DIF recibieron una lección ese día.

Al día siguiente fuimos a un estudio de televisión y participamos en un programa de entrevistas. El presentador me hizo preguntas y yo respondí lo mejor que pude. Conté lo emocionado que me sentía de visitar a los niños a los que ayuda el DIF. En un momento dado, rompí a llorar mientras explicaba cómo los caninos pueden ayudar a los niños que han sufrido malos tratos; los niños maltratados a veces hablan con un animal, pero no con una persona. Al fin y al cabo, fue un humano quien les hizo daño. ¡Mi bomba de emociones estaba al tope!

Había ido a Tepic para dar una conferencia sobre discapacidades, siendo mi especialidad los perros de asistencia. Yo iba a ser uno de los dos ponentes; sin embargo, la otra persona canceló. La Presidenta Estatal del DIF nos presentó a mí y a Boosted. La conferencia se celebró en un edificio tipo museo de estilo romano con un enorme anfiteatro de dos plantas, que estaba abarrotado, arriba y abajo. Aunque un poco abrumado, hice mi presentación, que había sido completamente revisada por mis anfitriones del DIF. Contenía efectos, GIFs, caricaturas, fotos, etc. Cuando

Boosted y yo terminamos, se produjo un terremoto. Todo el público se puso en pie y nos bendijo con una gran ovación.

Una vez más, se abrieron las compuertas emocionales, las lágrimas de agradecimiento estaban siempre presentes. De repente, se formó una larga cola. La gente preguntaba tímidamente si podían tomarse una foto con Boosted y conmigo. Mi anfitriona de Airbnb y su hija, estudiante de veterinaria, aparecieron de la nada y me dieron un fuerte abrazo. Habían organizado sus agendas para poder asistir a la conferencia. Yo sabía que mi Booster me miraba desde el cielo y me decía, "¡Ves, te dije que los humanos no son todos tan malos!

Esa noche, estaba decidido a celebrar y agradecer a los empleados del DIF su excelente trabajo. Invité a media docena de dedicados empleados a cenar en un buen restaurante de mariscos. En grupo, nos acercamos a la puerta doble del restaurante. Una cadena amarilla brillante cruzaba la entrada para asegurar que los comensales esperaran a ser acomodados.

Como si fuera una señal, el encargado dijo tajantemente, "¡No se admiten perros, señor!" Mi explicación sobre los perros de servicio cayó en saco roto. Me volví hacia mis invitados del DIF y les dije que entraran y disfrutaran de su comida. Luego me senté en la acera sucia, con mi vestido elegante, y le dije al gerente del restaurante que por favor me trajera el sushi donde estaba sentado. "Si es aquí donde sirven a los ciegos o discapacitados, ¡que así sea!" A los pocos minutos, me hicieron señas para que entrara y Boosted y yo nos unimos a mis invitados en la mesa.

Al día siguiente por la tarde, las damas del DIF me llevaron al autobús turístico de la ciudad. Boosted y yo lo encontramos divertido y muy relajante. El último día, una de las empleadas del DIF y su esposo insistieron en llevarme a la playa, a unas 35 millas de distancia. Hacía un día precioso y todos pudimos relajarnos.

Por si fuera poco, la noche siguiente recibí una llamada de mi anfitriona de Airbnb. Me dijo que ella y su hija tenían un regalo que querían darme por la mañana. Le expliqué que mi taxi salía puntualmente a las 6 a.m., así que no estaba seguro de que fuera posible. Me dijo que estaría allí antes de que me fuera. Efectivamente, a la mañana siguiente, a las 5:45, llamaron a la puerta. Me saludaron con un "buenos días". La hija me tomó la mano y la levantó con cuidado. A continuación, me colocó una preciosa pulsera en la muñeca. Era de un precioso tono azul oscuro con la palabra BOOSTER escrita en amarillo. Una vez más, mis emociones superaron cualquier sentido de normalidad que pudiera haber tenido en ese momento. "Hemos hecho esta pulsera para ti. Las cuentas de cristal fueron cosidas por los nativos mexicanos", me explicó. Había hecho bordados una vez en mi vida, así que tenía una idea del talento que se necesitaba para hacer una pulsera así. Cada cuenta tenía que estar alineada, igual que las cariñosas personas mexicanas que me habían honrado pidiéndome tomarme fotos con ellos el día anterior. Cuando llegué a casa tenía MUCHO en qué pensar.

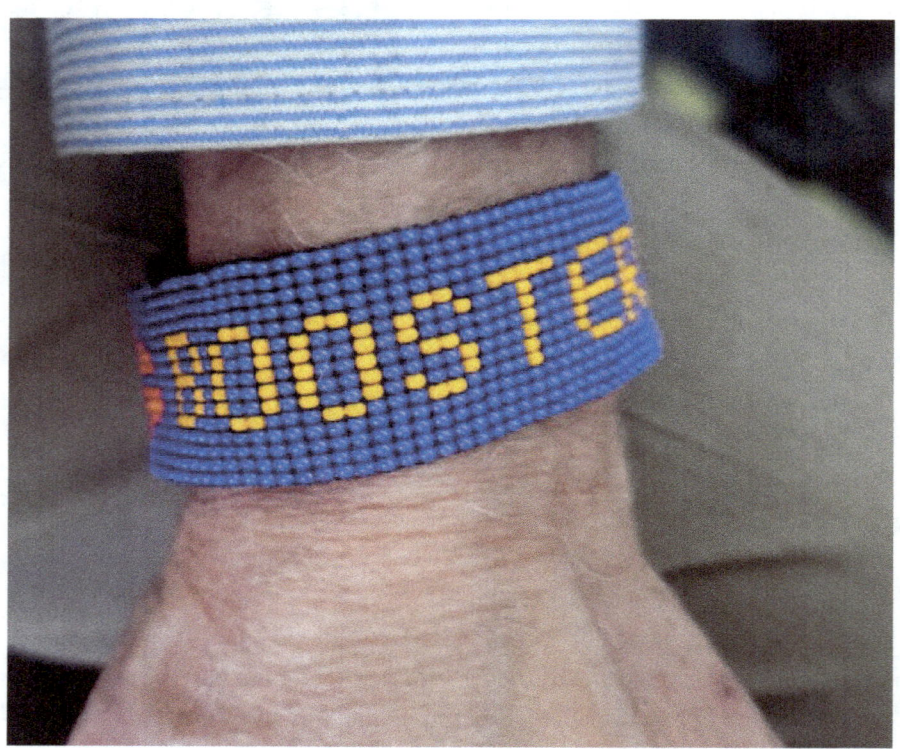

CONCLUSIÓN

"¿Qué vas a hacer con ese perro? Sabes que no puedes cuidar de un perro", me dijo mi hermano hace más de una década. A decir verdad, ¡ese perro cuidó de *mí*! De hecho, fue el mejor maestro que he conocido (lo siento, Bonnie... pero sé que estarías de acuerdo). Mi Booster me devolvió la vida que casi había desperdiciado. Tocó mi alma, algo que no sabía que tenía, y me motivó a regresar a la universidad en mis últimos años y obtener una maestría en Ciencias de la Vida Canina, con énfasis en la educación de perros de servicio, en la milagrosa y única BUCS. Esa educación verdaderamente impulsó mi vida a tal ritmo que compensó todo lo que me había perdido. Con Booster a mi lado, aprendí lo que es el amor genuino. Aprendí a amar a las personas, y a evitar el resentimiento. Cuando Warren Buffet dio una conferencia en la Escuela de Negocios de la Universidad de Florida, habló de vivir una vida feliz y afirmó:

> *La forma de hacerlo es jugar y hacer algo que disfrutes toda la vida. Asóciate con personas que te agraden. Yo sólo trabajo con gente que me gusta. Si pudiera ganar 100 millones de dólares con alguien que me hace sentir malestar, diría que no. Tu felicidad general en la vida se reduce realmente a cuatro simples palabras... haz lo que amas.*[6]

Esto resonó profundamente en mi psique. Pasé más de dos décadas de mi existencia haciendo aquello para lo que estaba programado, rescatar al pájaro herido. Sólo más tarde, en la hoja árida y amarilla de la vida, descubrí aquello a lo que hacía referencia Buffet. Me rodeé de perros y de personas amantes de los caninos que me caen bien. Invertí en mí mismo

---

[6] Warren Buffett, "Warren Buffett dice que tu felicidad general en la vida se reduce realmente a 4 simples palabras," *Inc.* (Sept 16, 2022). https://www.inc.com/ marcel-schwantes/warren-buffett-says-your-overall-happiness-in-life-really-comes-down-to-4-simple-words.html

capacitándome en la BUCS para poder hacer lo que amo. A medida que el tipo de interés subía, también lo hacía mi bienestar. Cuanto más invertía, más ROI recibía... ROI canino.

CRISIS DE LOS MISILES EN CUBA: La bomba atómica explotó en los Estados Unidos y los cubanos se consuelan con sus perros. Les quedan momentos de vida antes de las represalias. Conozca al Fat Man y al Little Boy de un Proyecto Manhattan que visitó Hiroshima y Nagasaki. (derecha)

CAMBOYA: El famoso personaje de cómic europeo Tintín visitó Camboya con su perro y pisó una mina terrestre abandonada por la guerra. Su perro nos enseña que los humanos no pueden ir de picnic con sus perros sin miedo a pisar artefactos explosivos no detonados. (derecha)

Viajé por el mundo, a menudo con Booster, y compartí el amor. Sin importar si mis congéneres eran negros, blancos, amarillos, gays, heterosexuales, hombres, mujeres, comunistas, capitalistas, cristianos o musulmanes, encontré aceptación universal en todo el mundo, emulando a mi Booster. Con pocas excepciones, él aceptaba a todos los que se le acercaban. Seguí sus enseñanzas y aprendí a confiar y amar incondicionalmente. Mi vida tomó otro rumbo como resultado directo de la milagrosa intervención canina. Lo que antes era un callejón sin salida se convirtió en una autopista de iluminación y enriquecimiento. Mi vida se convirtió en la Octava Maravilla del Mundo cuando empecé a viajar con Booster a mi lado. La casa de madera de tres plantas que construí en Pyatt, Arkansas, en 120 acres cerca de Branson, Missouri, se convirtió en el Retiro Canino. Adorné las paredes con obras de arte canino de todo el mundo: Cuba, Nepal, Tailandia, Colombia, Argentina, Vietnam, las Bahamas y otros países. En las escaleras hay labradores tallados a modo de postes. En la parte superior de los muebles de madera hay cabezas de perro talladas, y la tapicería presenta un collage de labradores. Todas las plantas tienen bebederos automáticos para los sedientos huéspedes caninos.

Decidí compartir esta casa única con otros amantes de los perros, así que la anuncié en Airbnb y VRBO. Era un homenaje a Booster; no se trataba de dinero. El resultado fue una cascada de familias amantes de los perros compitiendo por alquilarla. Todos los comentarios mencionaban que a sus perros les encantaba la propiedad. El Retiro Canino ofrece a los perros y a las personas la oportunidad de caminar por los senderos, nadar en los arroyos y observar a los ciervos. Para los perros, el Puente del Arco Iris empieza en el Retiro Canino de Arkansas y termina en Dog Mountain, en Vermont. Me conecté con nuevas almas caninas y humanas que compartían un espíritu afín. Fue una asombrosa confirmación de años de aprendizaje basados en mi educación con Booster y la BUCS.

A mi pesar, lamento haber otorgado mi confianza a quienes no la merecían. Hay un dicho que dice, "Más vale haber amado y perdido que no haber amado nunca". En mi caso, es "Mejor haber confiado y ser decepcionado que nunca haber confiado". Me decepcionaron las acciones de algunas personas en las que confié. El cubano al que apadriné y en el que gasté mis ahorros simplemente me utilizó para entrar en Estados Unidos. El miembro del equipo canino SAR aceptó la costosa educación y la asignación, regresó a México y nunca miró atrás. Ambos individuos no sólo me defraudaron a mí, sino también a sus compatriotas.

Con frecuencia reflexionaba sobre el hecho de que ambos decían que nada sucede rápidamente en sus respectivos países. Ambos estaban equivocados, víctimas de su negatividad. Quizá esa convicción fue precursora de su fracaso para alcanzar su potencial. Yo creo que son solo humanos que no han ascendido a la categoría canina para manifeestar un positivismo abrumador, una sed inquebrantable de aprendizaje y un amor incondicional. Quizá ellos también necesitaban un *Booster* en sus vidas.

Mi Booster burló a la muerte en innumerables ocasiones. Creo que tanto él como su poder superior sabían que tenía un destino que cumplir. Aunque falleció sigue siendo una parte muy importante de mí. Tengo su progenie, a Boosted y Busted, para continuar dejando huella. No sé si alguna vez ha existido una relación más simbiótica entre un can y su humano. Con ese pensamiento en mente, comparto una última historia.

En enero de 2020, fui a visitar a unos amigos que Booster me presentó en Tailandia. Estuve allí alrededor de un mes y me puse bastante enfermo. Iba a ir a un hospital de Bangkok, pero decidí aguantar y volver a casa lo antes posible. Al regresar, me autoaislé para asegurarme de que no hubiera contraído el coronavirus (COVID19). Después de padecer un dolor insoportable, fui al hospital de Gulfport, Mississippi, mi ciudad natal. Tenía la bacteria *E. coli* (intoxicación alimentaria), *giardia* (enfermedad transmitida por el agua) y algún tipo de virus mexicano. Permanecí en el hospital durante una semana, recibiendo bolsas de antibióticos de alta potencia.

Antes de darme el alta, los médicos me hicieron pruebas del tracto gastrointestinal superior e inferior y determinaron que tenía varios tumores en el cuerpo, incluido uno de 5 cm que me obstruía parcialmente el colon. Se presumía que tenía cáncer de colon y de estómago. El informe patológico tardó 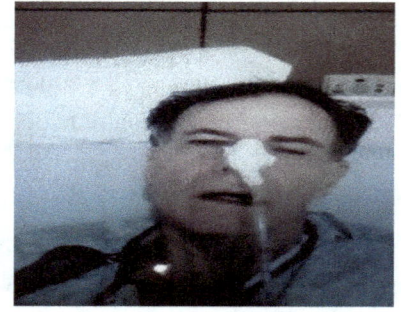 cinco días en llegar. Resultó que tenía un linfoma no Hodgkin. Estuve a 48 horas de la muerte. Me subieron a una camilla y me hicieron una punción lumbar para inyectarme quimio en la columna vertebral por si las células cancerosas habían traspasado la barrera cerebral. Fue una medida preventiva tomada por mi brillante oncóloga, la Dra. Tuli. Me tomaron una muestra de líquido cefalorraquídeo. La patología reveló que las células cancerosas habían invadido mi cerebro. Pocos días después, un neurocirujano me hizo un agujero en el cráneo, me introdujo un tubo por el cerebro y me implantó un puerto en el cráneo. Poco después, me administraron cinco bolsas de quimio al día, cinco días a la semana, alternadas durante seis semanas, a través de un puerto implantado en el pecho. Recibí dos inyecciones semanales de quimioterapia en la cabeza cada semana durante tres meses, y una vez al mes durante los tres meses siguientes. Me dijeron que había un 75% de probabilidades de que sucumbiera a la sepsis la primera semana, cuando la quimioterapia redujera el tumor en el estómago y los intestinos. Si sobrevivía la primera semana, las probabilidades eran del 25% de que ocurriera en la segunda. Me introdujeron una cámara por la nariz hasta el corazón en busca de tumores. Se me infectó el puerto torácico. La historia continuó.

Mi cáncer se atribuyó a un herbicida utilizado en mi propiedad. Su venta está prohibida en muchos países del mundo. Envié una carta a todos los congresistas y senadores de Estados Unidos explicándoles mi situación. Sentí que me correspondía a mí intentar hacer algo para evitar que otros se vieran sometidos a un posible carcinógeno vendido para obtener beneficios a costa del bienestar de las pesonas. Creo que recibí una o dos respuestas. Cuando pensé en rendirme, pensé instantáneamente en Booster. ¡Él nunca se rindió! Luchó todas y cada una de las veces que se enfrentó a experiencias cercanas a la muerte. Me concentré en la idea de que "¡Lo que es bueno para Booster es bueno para Davis!" Decidí que lucharía por mi vida y le dije a mi oncóloga, la Dra. Tuli, que quería vivir lo suficiente para terminar de escribir mi libro. Obviamente, ella consiguió sacarme del abismo, pero yo también doy crédito a mi Booster y a mi Poder Superior. Booster me dio la fuerza para someterme a los rigores de la quimioterapia extensiva y para que me hicieran un agujero en el cráneo para implantarme un puerto de quimioterapia. Él no tuvo elección cuando yo lo sometí al mismo régimen de tratamiento. Si hubiera optado por no someterme al tratamiento, habría sido un absoluto hipócrita. En otras palabras, él me salvó la vida por segunda vez. ¿Cómo no voy a llorar mientras escribo estas palabras?

Mi amigo de toda la vida Robert Bodenheimer me apoyó en mis horas más oscuras. Insistió en conducir una gran distancia para llevarme a que me realizaran la operación y me implantaran el puerto en el cerebro. Posteriormente se entrevistó con el cirujano y me aseguró que todo había salido bien, luego me miró a los ojos y me dijo, "Dave, *T E A M O*". Las lágrimas caían en cascada por sus mejillas, testimonio del amor más puro que jamás haya existido. Él gozaba de perfecta salud cuando mi vida se balanceaba precariamente en el precipicio. Él y su hijo solían visitarme cuando estaba recibiendo el tratamiento. Un año después, a mi amigo que fue mi apoyo, le diagnosticaron un tumor cerebral. Aunque lo animé a someterse al tratamiento, decidió no hacerlo. Murió, junto con una parte de mí, meses después. Yo también podría haber optado por rendirme, de no haber sido por MI BOOSTER.

Cuando terminé el tratamiento, Puffy, la novia de Booster, falleció. Sentí mucho dolor y remordimiento. Siendo bombardeado por una plétora de emociones y tras un largo examen de conciencia, decidí clonarla. La empresa que había enviado las células de mi Booster a Corea para su clonación, ahora clonaba perros en Estados Unidos. Me monté en una montaña rusa emocional. ¿Viviría para mantener al cachorro que había decidido traer al mundo? ¿Era racional añadir un sexto perro a mi clan canino? Oía a mi Booster ladrar, "Hazlo... ¡confía en mí!"

Cuando Puffy fue clonada, nacieron dos cachorros. Tenían una sobremordida importante que les hacía difícil, si no imposible, succionar la leche de la teta de la madre de alquiler. Uno de ellos falleció, pero el otro sobrevivió. La empresa se ofreció amablemente a volver a clonar a Puffy. Pregunté si podía quedarme con el cachorro defectuoso y la empresa dijo amablemente "claro". La clonación se hizo por segunda vez y, como ocurre a veces, la madre de alquiler no quedó embarazada. La empresa accedió a intentarlo de nuevo, y nació un cachorro con el mismo problema de sobremordida. No sobrevivió. En ese momento acordamos mutuamente dejarlo y no luchar contra lo que parecía ser un gen dominante y defectuoso. Me alegré de haberme quedado con el cachorro defectuoso. La generosa empresa se encargó de que el cachorro se sometiera a una cirugía oral correctiva y, posteriormente, lo entregó al Canine Retreat de Pyatt.

Una vez más, utilicé el humor para navegar por los campos de minas emocionales de la vida. Meses después, envié a la Dra. Tuli una tarjeta en la que le explicaba, "Me devolviste la vida; empezó de nuevo gracias a tu intervención". Ella conocía mi historia con Booster. Además, le decía, "Booster tenía una novia llamada Puffy que falleció recientemente. Su vida también empezó de nuevo, ya que la cloné. Era muy cariñosa, atenta, inteligente y especial... como TÚ, Dra. Tuli... así que en tu honor le puse por nombre... ¡Puffers Tuli Hawn! Lo único es que es una *auténtica perra*, ¡y ahí acaba el parecido!" Me habría encantado ver la expresión de su cara al leerlo, pero ¡ay!

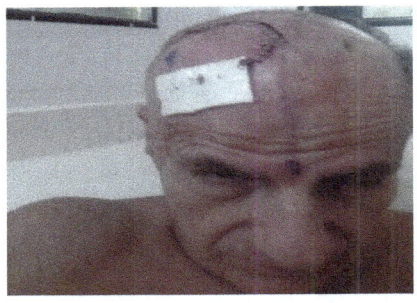

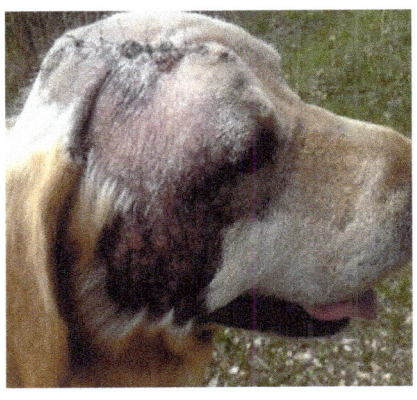

Me llevaba muy bien con todos los médicos y el personal. Muchos eran de países que yo había visitado, a menudo acompañado de Booster. Esa camaradería internacional fue el resultado directo de la presencia de Booster en mi vida. Me ayudó a sobrevivir cuando se cuestionaba mi capacidad de supervivencia. Gracias a mis médicos del pequeño hospital de Gulfport, Mississippi, mi ciudad natal, pude terminar mi libro y mi vida siguió adelante con el enriquecimiento canino.

Con Booster tenía una relación simbiótica de proporciones asombrosas. Ambos tuvimos tumores cancerígenos, perdimos el cabello, nos hicieron agujeros en el cráneo y superamos obstáculos aparentemente insalvables. Dicen que una imagen vale más que mil palabras, pero dejaré que el lector decida por sí mismo. A día de hoy, es difícil entender la enormidad de los acontecimientos que cambiaron mi vida como resultado del poderoso vínculo humano y canino. No cabe duda de que la profundidad de los acontecimientos que dieron sentido a mi vida fue una renuncia a la fragilidad humana en favor del amor canino omnipresente e incondicional y de una devoción sin igual.

Siento un gran remordimiento al pensar que pasé décadas de mi vida en un entorno engañoso de amor y propósito. El antiguo y mal concebido entrelazamiento de vidas fue suplantado por una transformación integral provocada por mi Booster. No cabe duda de que fue el resultado de una intervención divina, aunque yo no sea tan devoto. Es muy sencillo, no hay otra explicación. Booster me enseñó que las coincidencias no existen. En el tribunal de mi vida, era obvio, basado en una prevalencia abrumadora de pruebas.

En retrospectiva, una vez lamenté haber sido engañado en lo que la vida debía ser. Mi codependencia autoimpuesta casi me lleva a la muerte. Había visto comedias de televisión y escuchado canciones que ensalzaban vidas idílicas. Esa no es la realidad. Todos los seres humanos enfrentan adversidades o dificultades, unos más que otros. Aprendí a vivir la vida en sus términos bastante tarde. Aprendí a amar a Booster como él me amó... incondicionalmente. Aún no estoy seguro de ser digno de tal amor. Por la presente hago una nueva promesa a mi querido Booster, esforzarme por lograr la autoaceptación, y ayudar a otros a lograr lo que Booster me ayudó a lograr a mí, la independencia a través de la asistencia canina, espiritualmente entregada en forma de perro de servicio/perro de asistencia.

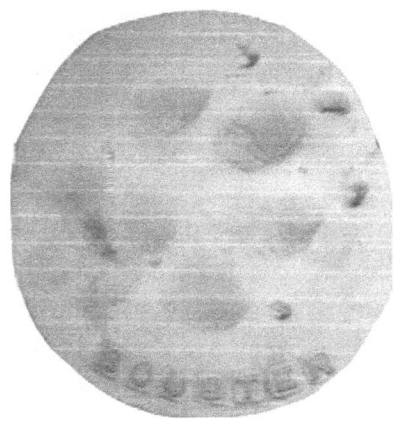

Para terminar, le pido que acaricie a su perro en la cabeza, lo mire a los ojos y le diga que lo ama. Luego, dele un abrazo prolongado y envolvente Tal vez oirá el latido melódico y simultáneo de su corazón y su cola, y recibirá un beso húmedo en la cara. Esa es la expresión pura del amor sin reproche.

MI BOOSTER DEJÓ SU HUELLA DIVINA
E INDELEBLE EN EL MUNDO

EPÍLOGO

Mi Booster es la culminación de diez años de escritura, que con frecuencia tuvo lugar en un avión a 30.000 pies de altura, viajando por el mundo con mi mejor amigo Booster, en una labor de apoyo, con su cabeza descansando sobre mis pies. Mi ardiente deseo de cumplir mi promesa, de compartirlo con el mundo, me motivó a llamar a innumerables periódicos y cadenas de televisión para inmortalizar sus logros caninos. Esa promesa dio lugar a una presencia involuntaria en Internet que resultó útil cuando decidí escribir *su* libro, *¿otra **coincidencia**?*

Me puse en contacto con la prestigiosa editorial FriesenPress para que me ayudara a hacer realidad la promesa que le hice a mi querido Booster. Presenté mi manuscrito para que lo revisaran y no estaba preparado para lo que vino después... lágrimas y ***coincidencias*** en forma de respuesta:

> *Voy a empezar diciendo que soy una amante de los perros, una firme creyente del valor que ofrecen los perros de servicio, y madre de un hijo autista (ahora de 16 años) que en estos momentos tiene su segundo perro de servicio. Estoy increíblemente agradecida por todo el trabajo que usted y Booster, junto con muchos otros, han hecho para abrir puertas (literalmente) y proporcionar acceso a estos compañeros integrales en la vida de las personas con discapacidades. ¡Sinceramente, no sé dónde estaría mi familia hoy si no fuera por nuestros perros de servicio, por lo que leer su historia y tener la oportunidad de ayudar a que se publique es un gran honor!*

Aunque alguna vez me había dado por vencido conmigo mismo, mi Poder Superior nunca lo hizo, nunca lo ha hecho. Mi Booster me enseñó lo qué es la espiritualidad, cómo reconocerla y cómo incorporarla a mi vida. Comparto con ustedes esta afirmación de la devoción de Mi Poder Superior por mejorar mi vida en combinación con las enseñanzas de Mi Booster. Afirmo resueltamente una vez más, ¡que no existen las *coincidencias*!

Mi amado clon Puffers acaba de presentarme una prueba más de que no existen las *coincidencias*. Ella es muy cariñosa pero rechaza las insinuaciones amorosas de Boosted y Busted. La inseminé artificialmente con todo lo que Busted *parecía* ofrecer. (Para que conste, sigo poniendo humor en mis diálogos, pero ya no digo palabrotas.) Fue una reproducción clon a clon. Más tarde se le hicieron radiografías y se determinó que probablemente tenía 7 cachorros que nacerían el 12 de septiembre. Entró en trabajo de parto la noche anterior y dio a luz a 6 preciosos cachorros. Los cachorros de clon a clon nacieron el 11 de septiembre, igual que Boosted y Busted. Sí, ¡otro 11 de septiembre en mi vida! Me preguntaba cómo era posible.

Milagrosamente, al día siguiente, fui a limpiar la caja de parto, ¡y conté 7 cachorros! Pensé que estaba soñando. Miré las fotos que había tomado el día anterior y, efectivamente, sólo había 6 cachorros. Fue como si mi Poder Superior me hubiera dicho, "Los cachorros debían nacer el 12 de septiembre, pero adelanté el parto al 11 de septiembre porque sabía que era otro acontecimiento del 11 de septiembre en tu vida. Sin embargo, ¡hice que uno naciera el 9/12 sólo para recordarte lo que debería haber sido de no ser por la intervención divina." ¿Coincidencia?

Había dos cachorros machos. Uno era blanco y el otro amarillo oscuro como mi Booster. Él será mi perro de servicio sucesor. Obtuve a Busted en Corea, y tardé 8 años, pero al fin recibí a Bail. ¡Mi nuevo cachorro se llama Bail! El abogado a quien entregué un cachorro grande, y blanco años atrás, cuando sus hijos estaban de luto, se mantuvo en contacto a lo largo de los años y no dejaba de preguntarme si tenía cachorros. Estaba eufórico cuando se enteró del cachorro blanco y más tarde lo recibió con los brazos y el corazón abiertos. ¡Esto habla de un encargo personalizado entregado desde el cielo! *¿Coincidencia?*

Me esforcé por encontrar hogares especiales para los otros 5 cachorros. Encontré sin duda los mejores hogares, pero quizás puedas juzgarlo tú mismo. Un día, unos padres trajeron a sus 3 hijos a ver a los cachorros. A los niños les encantaron. El papá quería el más pequeño, pero algunos de los niños querían uno de los otros. La mamá sugirió llevarse los 2, pero el papá no estaba seguro. Acepté quedarme con los cachorros hasta que tomaran una decisión. Un par de días después, el padre me llamó y me dijo que quería los dos cachorros. Vinieron a recogerlos después de las vacaciones de Acción de Gracias... *qué apropiado, ¿verdad?*

Cogí un cachorro y se lo puse en las manos a la adorable niña. Los niños se volvieron locos. Tomé el segundo cachorro y los niños me miraron perplejos. El padre se dirigió a los niños y les dijo, "Chicos, se van a quedar con los dos". Resulta que los padres no se lo habían dicho a los niños, ¡prefirieron darles la sorpresa! Los niños estaban entusiasmados. Entonces les pregunté a los niños, "¿Quiénes tienen los mejores padres del mundo?" Al unísono gritaron con alegría, "¡NOSOTROS!" "¡NOSOTROS!"

Al día siguiente, un orgulloso abuelo, acompañado de su hija y su nieto, vino a ver a los cachorros. ¡Era un regalo de Navidad

en proceso! El niño era tímido y un poco reacio a establecer un vínculo con el cachorro cuando se conocieron. A la mañana siguiente, recibí dos hermosas fotografías del niño encantado con su nuevo cachorro, Riley. Cuando le pregunté por qué el cachorro se llamaba Riley, el abuelo dijo, "Ni idea, ¡se le ocurrió al nieto!" El hermano pequeño del niño es autista y comparten el amor canino incondicional de Riley.

El amor engendra amor. La genética de mi Booster, auspiciada por mi Poder Superior, ¡estaba en acción nuevamente! ¡No es *coincidencia*!

OMPS, Oh Dios mío, oh... Declaro resueltamente una vez más, ¡no existe tal cosa llamada *coincidencia*! Simplemente no existe. Mi Bocster me lo enseñó una y otra y otra vez.

MI BOOSTER CAMBIÓ EL MUNDO DE
UNA MANERA POSITIVA.

SUS CLONES, BOOSTED Y BUSTED
ESTÁN HACIENDO LO MISMO

SOBRE EL AUTOR

Davis Hawn le prometió a Booster que lo compartiría con el mundo. Al hacerlo, Davis se convirtió en un promotor, divulgando el gran impacto que tienen los perros, en general, y los perros de servicio, en particular, en la sociedad. Él cree que nuestros compañeros caninos tienen un gran potencial para hacer aún más y le cuenta a cualquier persona, dispuesta a escuchar, que el amor incondicional de los perros puede cambiar y salvar vidas, y de hecho lo hace.

Davis tiene un máster en Ciencias de la Vida Canina con énfasis en Educación de Perros de Servicio por la aclamada Universidad Bergin de Estudios Caninos, y se capacitó bajo la tutela de la Dra. Bonita Bergin, EdD, fundadora del concepto de perro de servicio. Él viajó internacionalmente durante más de una década, compartiendo sus conocimientos, dando conferencias, haciendo reportajes en prensa y apareciendo en televisión, y ocasionalmente creando "problemas" al defender los derechos de los perros de servicio y sus humanos. Juntos, Davis y Booster ayudaron a que se aprobaran leyes sobre discapacidad en todo el mundo.

Miembro de Al-Anon y de la Asociación Internacional de Perros de Asistencia, Davis vive en tierras rurales de Mississippi y Arkansas con su familia de labradores entrenados.

www.ingramcontent.com/pod-product-compliance
Lightning Source LLC
Chambersburg PA
CBHW070901120626
46546CB00001B/96